School to Career

J.J. Littrell, Ed. D.
Arizona State University
Tempe, Arizona

James H. Lorenz, Ed. D.
Middle Tennessee State University
Murfreesboro, Tennessee

Harry T. Smith, Ed. D.
Tennessee Technological University
Cookeville, Tennessee

Publisher
The Goodheart-Willcox Company, Inc.
Tinley Park, Illinois
www.g-w.com

The Goodheart-Willcox Company, Inc. Brand Disclaimer: Brand names, company names, and illustrations for products and services included in this text are provided for educational purposes only and do not represent or imply endorsement or recommendation by the author or the publisher.

The Goodheart-Willcox Company, Inc. Safety Notice: The reader is expressly advised to carefully read, understand, and apply all safety precautions and warnings described in this book or that might also be indicated in undertaking the activities and exercises described herein to minimize risk of personal injury or injury to others. Common sense and good judgment should also be exercised and applied to help avoid all potential hazards. The reader should always refer to the appropriate manufacturer's technical information, directions, and recommendations; then proceed with care to follow specific equipment operating instructions. The reader should understand these notices and cautions are not exhaustive.

The publisher makes no warranty or representation whatsoever, either expressed or implied, including, but not limited to, equipment, procedures, and applications described or referred to herein, their quality, performance, merchantability, or fitness for a particular purpose. The publisher assumes no responsibility for any changes, errors, or omissions in this book. The publisher specifically disclaims any liability whatsoever, including any direct, indirect, incidental, consequential, special, or exemplary damages resulting, in whole or in part, from the reader's use or reliance upon the information, instructions, procedures, warnings, cautions, applications, or other matter contained in this book. The publisher assumes no responsibility for the activities of the reader.

Library of Congress Cataloging-in-Publication Data
Littrell, Joseph J. (Joseph Junior), 1920-
  School to career / by J.J. Littrell, Ed. D., Arizona State University,
Tempe, Arizona, James H. Lorenz, Ed. D., Middle Tennessee State University,
Murfreesboro, Tennessee, Harry T. Smith, Ed. D., Tennessee Technological
University, Cookeville, Tennessee. -- Tenth edition.
    pages cm

  Includes index.
  ISBN 978-1-61960-304-2
  1. Education, Cooperative--United States. 2. Students--Employment--United
States. 3. Career education--United States. 4. School-to-work transition--
United States. I. Title.
  LC1049.5.L58 2014
  370.1′3--dc23
                    2012046003

Introduction

As a young adult, an important key to your success will be preparing for the transition from high school to your first career. To help you make this transition, **School to Career** will guide you through important twenty-first century life and career skills that you will need as you graduate from high school.

By studying this text, you will learn personal skills, decision-making skills, and employability skills that will help create a foundation as you prepare to be on your own. Skills for success such as teamwork and problem solving, communicating on the job, and leadership are also covered. You will have an opportunity to research and learn about careers using the States' Career Clusters to help you define your future goals. As part of the learning process, you will assess your skills and abilities to help make decisions about a career that is a good fit for you. Included in your exploration will be learning about college and other postsecondary programs that might help you reach your goals.

School to Career is the first step for preparing for the challenges you will face after graduation. By studying this text, you will be able to make the most of your study time and learn how to prepare for your future.

About the Authors

Joseph J. Littrell, the original author of this text, taught industrial and vocational education to teachers in training at Arizona State University. Littrell began his career teaching industrial education in Nebraska and Oregon public schools. Later he taught engineering at the University of Missouri. He earned degrees from Peru State College in Nebraska, the University of Minnesota, and the University of Missouri.

James H. Lorenz is professor emeritus and chair of the department of engineering technology at Middle Tennessee State University. He has taught graduate and undergraduate teacher certification courses and undergraduate drafting courses for over 25 years. Lorenz conducts numerous in-service training programs for teachers and has directed SkillsUSA activities at district and state levels. He began his career teaching drafting, cooperative education, and graphic arts at the secondary level. Lorenz holds degrees from the University of Wisconsin-Stout, the University of Minnesota, and the University of Georgia.

Harry T. Smith served as a professor emeritus of curriculum and instruction at Tennessee Technological University where he was the program supervisor of industrial education from 1975 to 2002. Smith's primary responsibility was teaching instructional media technology and occupational education licensure courses to undergraduate and graduate students in the college of education. Earlier, Smith taught industrial education at the secondary level in Missouri and the postsecondary level in Missouri and Michigan. Smith holds degrees from Northeast Missouri State, Central Missouri State, and Michigan State Universities.

Reviewers

The authors and publisher are grateful to the following reviewers who provided valuable input to this edition.

Terry Aunchman
Supervisor, Career and Technical Education
District School Board of Pasco County
Land O'Lakes, FL

Cheryl Berryman-Burkett
Department Chair, School to Career Transition
Hereford High School
Baltimore, MD

Rula Bilbeisi
Marketing/Business Teacher
Hamtramck High School
Hamtramck, MI

Tammy Brinkley
Career, Technical, and Agriculture Education
    Teacher
Dawson County Hightower Academy
Dawsonville, GA

Sharon Burleson Ray, Ed. S.
Teacher and Technology Coordinator
Holly Pond High School
Holly Pond, AL

Margie Coates
Career Readiness Teacher
Aztec High School
Aztec, New Mexico

William Ellis
President
EduCon, Educational Consultants
Four Oaks, NC

Kelli Harris
Family & Consumer Sciences Teacher
John Horn High School
Mesquite, TX

Ronita Jacobsen
Family & Consumer Sciences Teacher
Plainview High School
Plainview, NE

Molly D. Kyler
Organizational and Leadership Development
    Director
Pioneer Technology Center
Ponca City, OK

Rick Larsen
President, Retired
Flexial Corporation
Cookeville, TN

Barney McClure
Executive Director
Agriculture Teacher's Association
Austin, TX

Sharon S. Murphy
Career and Technical Education Teacher
Carmel Middle School/Charlotte Mecklenburg
    Schools
Charlotte, NC

Christy Norris
Work-Based Learning Coordinator
Jeff Davis High School
Hazlehurst, GA

Robin Painovich
Executive Director
Career and Technology Association of Texas
Austin, TX

Carrie Anne Smith
Marketing and Entrepreneurship Instructor
Lapeer County Ed-Tech Center
Attica, MI

Avil Snow
Career and Technical Education Teacher
Heber Springs High School
Heber Springs, AK

Shirley R. Voran
Family & Consumer Science Instructor
Dodge City High School
Dodge City, KS

Claire Zevnik-Cline
Instructional Development Specialist
Oklahoma Department of Career and
    Technology Education
Stillwater, OK

Contents in Brief

Unit 1 Career Exploration 2

Chapter 1   Making the Transition from School to Career 4
Chapter 2   Understanding Work-Based Learning. 22
Chapter 3   What Your Employer Expects 46

Unit 2 The Job Hunt 70

Chapter 4   Finding and Applying for a Job. 72
Chapter 5   Taking Preemployment Tests 108
Chapter 6   Interviewing for Jobs. 126

Unit 3 Skills for Success 150

Chapter 7   Teamwork and Problem-Solving Skills 152
Chapter 8   Communicating on the Job. 178
Chapter 9   Math in the Workplace 210
Chapter 10   Using Technology in Your Career 236
Chapter 11   Looking Good on the Job 262
Chapter 12   Safety on the Job 284
Chapter 13   Leadership and Group Dynamics 312
Chapter 14   Participating in Meetings 334

Unit 4 Career Planning 354

Chapter 15   Learning about Yourself 356
Chapter 16   Learning About Careers 378
Chapter 17   Making Career Decisions 406

Unit 5 Job Satisfaction 424

Chapter 18   Succeeding on the Job. 426
Chapter 19   Diversity and Workplace Rights 454
Chapter 20   Succeeding in Our Economic System 474
Chapter 21   Entrepreneurship: A Business of Your Own 494

Unit 6 Managing Your Income 524

Chapter 22   Understanding Income Taxes. 526
Chapter 23   Managing Spending 554
Chapter 24   Using Credit 584
Chapter 25   Banking, Saving, and Investing 616
Chapter 26   Insurance 650
Chapter 27   Managing Family, Work, and Citizenship Roles 674

Career Cluster Handbook 702

Glossary 718

Index 727

Table of Contents

Unit 1 Career Exploration 2

Chapter 1   Making the Transition from School to Career .4
- Section 1.1 Importance of Work 6
- Section 1.2 Preparing for Career Success 14

Special Features
- Career Snapshot: Fish and Game Warden. 5
- Lifespan Plan 2
- Picture Success 3
- Go Green. 6
- Ethical Leadership 9
- Case 16
- Event Prep 17

Chapter Review and Assessment
- Chapter Summary 18
- Review Your Knowledge 18
- Apply Your Knowledge 19
- Teamwork. 20
- Common Core 20
- College and Career Readiness Portfolio 21

Chapter 2   Understanding Work-Based Learning 22
- Section 2.1 Work-Based Learning Programs 24
- Section 2.2 Work-Based Learning. 29
- Section 2.3 Importance of Study 37

Special Features
- Career Snapshot: Computer-Aided Drafter 23
- Ethical Leadership 26
- Go Green. 31
- Case. 32

Chapter Review and Assessment
- Chapter Summary 42
- Review Your Knowledge 43
- Apply Your Knowledge 43
- Teamwork. 44
- Common Core 45
- College and Career Readiness Portfolio 45

Chapter 3   What Your Employer Expects 46
- Section 3.1 Being an Effective Employee 48
- Section 3.2 Behaving in an Ethical Manner 60

Special Features

Career Snapshot: Web Page Designer 47
Ethical Leadership 56
Go Green... 50
Event Prep 62
Case.. 53

Chapter Review and Assessment

Chapter Summary 66
Review Your Knowledge 66
Apply Your Knowledge 67
Teamwork.. 68
Common Core 68
College and Career Readiness Portfolio 69

Unit 2 The Job Hunt   70

Chapter 4   Finding and Applying for a Job 72

Section 4.1 Searching for a Job 74
Section 4.2 Applying for a Job 85

Special Features

Lifespan Plan... 70
Picture Success.. 72
Career Snapshot: Tractor-Trailer Truck Driver............. 73
Go Green... 76
Ethical Leadership 79

Chapter Review and Assessment

Chapter Summary 104
Review Your Knowledge 105
Apply Your Knowledge 105
Teamwork.. 106
Common Core 106
College and Career Readiness Portfolio 107

Chapter 5   Taking Preemployment Tests 108

Section 5.1 Preemployment Assessments 110
Section 5.2 Predicting On-the-Job Performance.......... 115

Special Features

Career Snapshot: Heating and Air-Conditioning Technician.... 109
Ethical Leadership 118
Go Green... 113
Event Prep 112
Case.. 117

Chapter Review and Assessment

Chapter Summary 122
Review Your Knowledge 123
Apply Your Knowledge 123
Teamwork.. 124
Common Core 124
College and Career Readiness Portfolio 125

Chapter 6   Interviewing for Jobs 126
        Section 6.1 Preparing for the Interview 128
        Section 6.2 Completing the Interview Process 136

Special Features
        Career Snapshot: Portrait Photographer 127
        Ethical Leadership 129
        Go Green 135
        Case 138

Chapter Review and Assessment
        Chapter Summary 146
        Review Your Knowledge 146
        Apply Your Knowledge 147
        Teamwork 148
        Common Core 148
        College and Career Readiness Portfolio 149

Unit 3 Skills for Success   150

Chapter 7   Teamwork and Problem-Solving Skills 152
        Section 7.1 Teamwork 154
        Section 7.2 Problem Solving 164

Special Features
        Lifespan Plan 150
        Picture Success 151
        Career Snapshot: Administrative Assistant 153
        Ethical Leadership 160
        Go Green 158
        Event Prep 156
        Case 168

Chapter Review and Assessment
        Chapter Summary 174
        Review Your Knowledge 174
        Apply Your Knowledge 175
        Teamwork 176
        Common Core 176
        College and Career Readiness Portfolio 177

Chapter 8   Communicating on the Job 178
        Section 8.1 Effective Communication 180
        Section 8.2 Communication Channels 190
        Section 8.3 Written Business Communication 194

Special Features
        Career Snapshot: Exercise Physiologist 179
        Ethical Leadership 186
        Go Green 181
        Case 195

Chapter Review and Assessment

Chapter Summary 206
Review Your Knowledge 207
Apply Your Knowledge 207
Teamwork. 208
Common Core 208
College and Career Readiness Portfolio 209

Chapter 9   Math in the Workplace 210

Section 9.1 Practical Math. 212
Section 9.2 Metric System 222
Section 9.3 Analyzing Data 227

Special Features

Career Snapshot: Cashier 211
Ethical Leadership 217
Go Green. 224
Event Prep 226
Case 230

Chapter Review and Assessment

Chapter Summary 232
Review Your Knowledge 233
Apply Your Knowledge 233
Teamwork. 234
Common Core 234
College and Career Readiness Portfolio 235

Chapter 10   Using Technology in Your Career 236

Section 10.1 Technology Overview 238
Section 10.2 Tools and Devices. 243
Section 10.3 Impact of Technology 253

Special Features

Career Snapshot: Call Center Employee. 127
Ethical Leadership 243
Go Green. 241
Case 255

Chapter Review and Assessment

Chapter Summary 258
Review Your Knowledge 259
Apply Your Knowledge 259
Teamwork. 260
Common Core 260
College and Career Readiness Portfolio 261

Chapter 11   Looking Good on the Job 262

Section 11.1 Staying Healthy 264
Section 11.2 Make a Good Impression 272

Special Features

Career Snapshot: Chef 263
Ethical Leadership 267
Go Green. 266
Event Prep 274
Case 273

Chapter Review and Assessment

Chapter Summary 280
Review Your Knowledge 281
Apply Your Knowledge 281
Teamwork. 282
Common Core 282
College and Career Readiness Portfolio 283

Chapter 12   Safety on the Job .284
Section 12.1 Accidents. 286
Section 12.2 Accident Procedures. 296

Special Features

Career Snapshot: Travel Agent 285
Ethical Leadership 293
Go Green. 288
Case 304

Chapter Review and Assessment

Chapter Summary 308
Review Your Knowledge 309
Apply Your Knowledge 309
Teamwork. 310
Common Core 310
College and Career Readiness Portfolio 311

Chapter 13   Leadership and Group Dynamics 312
Section 13.1 Leadership in the Workplace 314
Section 13.2 Leadership at School. 318

Special Features

Career Snapshot: Childcare Worker 313
Ethical Leadership 320
Go Green. 322
Event Prep 327
Case 328

Chapter Review and Assessment

Chapter Summary 330
Review Your Knowledge 331
Apply Your Knowledge 331
Teamwork. 332
Common Core 332
College and Career Readiness Portfolio 333

Chapter 14   Participating in Meetings. 334
Section 14.1 Types of Meetings 336
Section 14.2 Parliamentary Procedure 341

Special Features

Career Snapshot: Emergency Dispatcher 335
Ethical Leadership 340
Go Green. 339
Case 344

Chapter Review and Assessment

Chapter Summary 350
Review Your Knowledge 350
Apply Your Knowledge 351
Teamwork. 352
Common Core 352
College and Career Readiness Portfolio 353

Unit 4 Career Planning   354

Chapter 15   Learning about Yourself 356

Section 15.1 Assessing Yourself 358
Section 15.2 Exploring Who You Are. 365

Special Features

Lifespan Plan 354
Picture Success. 355
Career Snapshot: President of the United States 357
Ethical Leadership 361
Go Green. 365
Event Prep 369
Case. 373

Chapter Review and Assessment

Chapter Summary 374
Review Your Knowledge 374
Apply Your Knowledge 375
Teamwork. 376
Common Core 376
College and Career Readiness Portfolio 377

Chapter 16   Learning about Careers. 378

Section 16.1 Research Potential Careers. 380
Section 16.2 Prepare for Career Success 386

Special Features

Career Snapshot: Dental Hygienist 379
Ethical Leadership 382
Go Green. 383
Case. 398

Chapter Review and Assessment

Chapter Summary 402
Review Your Knowledge 402
Apply Your Knowledge 403
Teamwork. 404
Common Core 404
College and Career Readiness Portfolio 405

Chapter 17   Making Career Decisions 406

Section 17.1 Career Decisions 408
Section 17.2 Your Career Plan. 413

Special Features

Career Snapshot: Marine Biologist. 407
Ethical Leadership 413
Go Green. 409
Event Prep 415
Case. 417

Chapter Review and Assessment

Chapter Summary 420
Review Your Knowledge 420
Apply Your Knowledge 421
Teamwork. 422
Common Core 422
College and Career Readiness Portfolio 423

Unit 5 Job Satisfaction   424

Chapter 18   Succeeding on the Job 426

Section 18.1 Your First Job 428
Section 18.2 Changing Jobs. 440
Section 18.3 Labor Unions 446

Special Features

Lifespan Plan 424
Picture Success. 425
Career Snapshot: Security System Installer. 427
Ethical Leadership 430
Go Green. 433
Case. 438

Chapter Review and Assessment

Chapter Summary 450
Review Your Knowledge 451
Apply Your Knowledge 451
Teamwork. 452
Common Core 453
College and Career Readiness Portfolio 453

Chapter 19   Diversity and Workplace Rights 454

Section 19.1 Understanding Workplace Diversity. 456
Section 19.2 Equality and Rights in the Workplace 461

Special Features

Career Snapshot: Special Education Teacher. 455
Ethical Leadership 463
Go Green. 461
Event Prep 460
Case. 468

Chapter Review and Assessment

Chapter Summary 470
Review Your Knowledge 470
Apply Your Knowledge 471
Teamwork. 472
Common Core 472
College and Career Readiness Portfolio 473

Chapter 20   Succeeding in Our Economic System 474

Section 20.1 Our Economic System 476
Section 20.2 Business Organization 483

Special Features

Career Snapshot: Cosmetologist 475
Ethical Leadership 478
Go Green. 480
Case. 488

Chapter Review and Assessment

Chapter Summary 490
Review Your Knowledge 490
Apply Your Knowledge 491
Teamwork. 492
Common Core 492
College and Career Readiness Portfolio 493

Chapter 21   Entrepreneurship: A Business of Your Own . . 494

Section 21.1 Entrepreneurship 496
Section 21.2 Starting Your Own Business .511

Special Features

Career Snapshot: Entrepreneur 495
Ethical Leadership 499
Go Green. 503
Event Prep 504
Case. 516

Chapter Review and Assessment

Chapter Summary 520
Review Your Knowledge 520
Apply Your Knowledge 521
Teamwork. 522
Common Core 522
College and Career Readiness Portfolio 523

Unit 6 Managing Your Income   524

Chapter 22   Understanding Income Taxes 526

Section 22.1 Understanding Income 528
Section 22.2 Paying Taxes 540

Special Features

Lifespan Plan 524
Picture Success. 525
Career Snapshot: Child, Family, and School Social Worker 527
Ethical Leadership 530
Go Green. 529
Case. 532

Chapter Review and Assessment

Chapter Summary 550
Review Your Knowledge 550
Apply Your Knowledge 551
Teamwork 552
Common Core 552
College and Career Readiness Portfolio 553

Chapter 23   Managing Spending 554

Section 23.1 Managing a Budget 556
Section 23.2 Spending Wisely 562

Special Features

Career Snapshot: Industrial Engineer 555
Ethical Leadership 559
Go Green 564
Event Prep 567
Case 571

Chapter Review and Assessment

Chapter Summary 580
Review Your Knowledge 580
Apply Your Knowledge 581
Teamwork 582
Common Core 582
College and Career Readiness Portfolio 583

Chapter 24   Using Credit 584

Section 24.1 Credit Overview 586
Section 24.2 How to Use Credit 605

Special Features

Career Snapshot: Hazardous Waste Technician 585
Ethical Leadership 595
Go Green 593
Case 600

Chapter Review and Assessment

Chapter Summary 612
Review Your Knowledge 613
Apply Your Knowledge 613
Teamwork 614
Common Core 614
College and Career Readiness Portfolio 615

Chapter 25   Banking, Saving, and Investing 616

Section 25.1 Banking 618
Section 25.2 Saving and Investing 636

Special Features

Career Snapshot: Air Traffic Controller 617
Ethical Leadership 626
Go Green 620
Event Prep 633
Case 638

Chapter Review and Assessment

Chapter Summary 646
Review Your Knowledge 647
Apply Your Knowledge 647
Teamwork. 648
Common Core 648
College and Career Readiness Portfolio 649

Chapter 26   Insurance 650

Section 26.1 Managing Risk. 652
Section 26.2 Types of Insurance 658

Special Features

Career Snapshot: Criminal Investigator. 651
Ethical Leadership 659
Go Green. 654
Case. 668

Chapter Review and Assessment

Chapter Summary 670
Review Your Knowledge 671
Apply Your Knowledge 671
Teamwork. 672
Common Core 672
College and Career Readiness Portfolio 673

Chapter 27   Managing Family, Work, and Citizenship Roles .674

Section 27.1 Family 676
Section 27.2 Citizenship 689

Special Features

Career Snapshot: Computer Programmer 675
Ethical Leadership 679
Go Green. 677
Event Prep 683
Case. 692

Chapter Review and Assessment

Chapter Summary 698
Review Your Knowledge 698
Apply Your Knowledge 699
Teamwork. 700
Common Core 700
College and Career Readiness Portfolio 701

Career Cluster Handbook .702

Glossary 718

Index 727

Student Focused

The future is now. **School to Career** will help you succeed in school and in your future career.

School to Career was designed with you, the student, in mind. Current issues and a fresh presentation of concepts invite you to connect with this text.

Exploring the many career options available will help you find the career path that is just right. To help you investigate career opportunities, a **Career Snapshot** opens each chapter with information about the 16 Career Clusters. This feature gives specifics about each career, including what someone who has that career does day-to-day, what the work itself is like, and what education and skills are needed for that career.

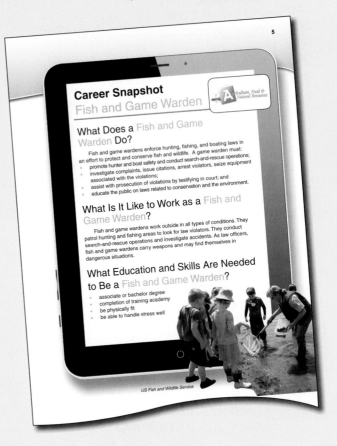

Career Snapshot
Fish and Game Warden

What Does a Fish and Game Warden Do?

Fish and game wardens enforce hunting, fishing, and boating laws in an effort to protect and conserve fish and wildlife. A game warden must:
- promote hunter and boat safety and conduct search-and-rescue operations;
- investigate complaints, issue citations, arrest violators, seize equipment associated with the violations;
- assist with prosecution of violations by testifying in court; and
- educate the public on laws related to conservation and the environment.

What Is It Like to Work as a Fish and Game Warden?

Fish and game wardens work outside in all types of conditions. They patrol hunting and fishing areas to look for law violators. They conduct search-and-rescue operations and investigate accidents. As law officers, fish and game wardens carry weapons and may find themselves in dangerous situations.

What Education and Skills Are Needed to Be a Fish and Game Warden?

- associate or bachelor degree
- completion of training academy
- be physically fit
- be able to handle stress well

US Fish and Wildlife Service

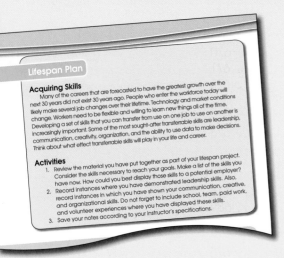

Lifespan Plan

Acquiring Skills

Many of the careers that are forecasted to have the greatest growth over the next 30 years did not exist 30 years ago. People who enter the workforce today will likely make several job changes over their lifetime. Technology and market conditions change. Workers need to be flexible and willing to learn new things all of the time. Developing a set of skills that you can transfer from use on one job to use on another is increasingly important. Some of the most sought-after transferrable skills are leadership, communication, creativity, organization, and the ability to use data to make decisions. Think about what effect transferrable skills will play in your life and career.

Activities

1. Review the material you have put together as part of your lifespan project. Consider the skills necessary to reach your goals. Make a list of the skills you have now. How could you best display those skills to a potential employer? Also, record instances where you have demonstrated leadership skills.
2. Record instances in which you have shown your communication, creative, and organizational skills. Do not forget to include school, team, paid work, and volunteer experiences where you have displayed these skills.
3. Save your notes according to your instructor's specifications.

What's next? That's a question that is probably at the front of your mind right now. The best way to be prepared for the challenges and opportunities ahead is to have a plan. The on-going **Lifespan Plan** activity provides a project-based, hands-on learning experience with real-world applications. By completing a Lifespan Plan, you will develop a route to achieve your life goals. You will explore career selection, education and training opportunities, lifestyle goals, and uncover financial resources necessary to reach those goals.

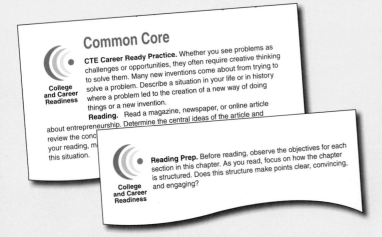

College and Career Readiness

Common Core

CTE Career Ready Practice. Whether you see problems as challenges or opportunities, they often require creative thinking to solve them. Many new inventions come about from trying to solve a problem. Describe a situation in your life or in history where a problem led to the creation of a new way of doing things or a new invention.

Reading. Read a magazine, newspaper, or online article about entrepreneurship. Determine the central ideas of the article and review the conc... your reading, m... this situation.

College and Career Readiness

Reading Prep. Before reading, observe the objectives for each section in this chapter. As you read, focus on how the chapter is structured. Does this structure make points clear, convincing, and engaging?

It is all about getting ready for college and your future career. College and Career Readiness activities address literacy skills to help prepare you for the real world. The Common Core State Standards for English Language Arts for reading, writing, speaking, and listening are incorporated in a **Reading Prep** activity as well as end-of-chapter **Common Core** activities. Common Career Technical Core **Career Ready Practices** are also addressed.

Content Connected

Authoritative content is presented in an easy-to-comprehend and relevant format. The material focuses on the acquisition of research, problem-solving, and academic skills required for those taking the next step on the path to college and career readiness.

- **Picture Success** features open each unit with a real-life student who was a member of his or her high school Career and Technical Student Organization.
- **Cases** simulate real-world scenarios to give context to issues that arise in the workplace.
- **College and Career Readiness Portfolio** activities allow you to create a personal portfolio for use when exploring volunteer, education and training, or career opportunities.

It is important to assess what you learn as you progress through the text. Multiple opportunities are provided to confirm learning as you explore the content. **Formative assessment** includes the following.

- The **Lifespan Plan** is an ongoing project-based activity that guides you through setting personal and professional short- and long-term goals.
- **Checkpoint** activities at the end of each main section of the chapter provide you with an opportunity to review what you have learned before moving on to the additional content.
- **Review Your Knowledge** covers basic concepts presented in the chapter so you can evaluate your understanding of the material.
- **Apply Your Knowledge** challenges you to combine what you learned in the chapter with your own experiences and goals.
- **Teamwork** encourages a collaborative experience to help you learn to interact with others in a productive manner.
- **College and Career Readiness** activities provide ways for you to demonstrate the literacy and career readiness skills you have mastered.

Features Spotlighted

Practical information helps you prepare for your future. Special features add realism and interest to enhance learning.

Ethical Leadership offers insight on ethical issues with which you will be confronted as you prepare for your future.

Ethical Leadership

Integrity

"In looking for people to hire, you look for three qualities: integrity, intelligence, and energy. And if they don't have the first, the other two will kill you."–Warren Buffet

People who act with integrity are honest and have strong moral principles. A popular expression is "I don't care who gets the credit as long as the job gets done." However, the opposite approach, taking credit for work you didn't do, shows a lack of integrity. It will hurt your reputation and ability to work with others.

Go Green

When you go to the store to shop, be sure to bring your own reusable bag. We can save thousands of pounds of landfill waste every year just by using reusable bags to carry products home from the store. While there are different schools of thought on this topic, it is generally accepted that plastic bags take almost 1,000 years to degrade. Additionally, discarded plastic bags can pose threats to wildlife and the soil. Did you know that store owners have to purchase the plastic or paper bags, and they pass on the cost to the consumer through higher product prices?

Go Green gives tips and other helpful information about how to use natural resources wisely.

Role Playing and Interviews

Role playing and interviews are competitive events you might enter with your Career and Technical Student Organization (CTSO). Those who participate in a role-play event will be provided information about a company or situation and given time to practice. A judge or panel of judges will review the presentations.

To prepare for the role-play or interview event, complete the following activities.

1. Read the guidelines provided by your organization. Make certain that you ask any questions about points you do not understand. It is important you follow each specific item that is outlined in the competition rules.
2. Visit the organization's website and look for role-play and interview events that were used in previous years. Many organizations post these tests for students to use as practice for future competitions. Also, look for the evaluation criteria or rubric for the event. This will help you determine what the judge will be looking for in your presentation.
3. Using previous events, write your response to the situation or questions. Time yourself to see if you are within the allotted time frame. Repeat this several times, so that you are comfortable with preparing the presentation.
4. Practice in front of a mirror. Are you comfortable speaking without reading directly from your notes?
5. Ask a friend or teacher to listen to your presentation. Give special attention to your posture and how you present yourself.
6. Concentrate on your tone of voice. Be pleasant and loud enough to hear without shouting.
7. Make eye contact with the listener. Do not stare, but engage the person's attention.
8. After you have made your presentation, ask for constructive feedback.

Event Prep presents information to use when preparing for Career and Technical Student Organization competitions.

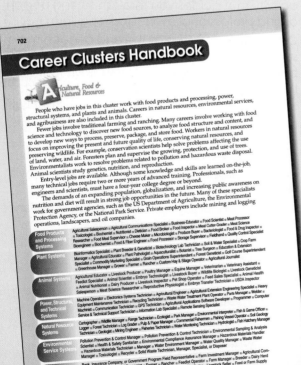

Career Clusters Handbook contains a description of each of the 16 career clusters and a partial list of possible occupations within each cluster.

Technology Applied

Technology is an important part of your world. So, it should be part of your everyday learning experiences. In this text you will find the following:

- **Pretest** and **posttests** are available for each chapter on the student companion website as well as the G-W Learning mobile site. Taking the pretest will help activate your prior knowledge of the content. Taking the posttest will help evaluate what you have learned about the chapter content.
- **Data files** are downloadable activities relating to each chapter that allow you to meaningly engage with technology and the text material.
- Creating the **Lifespan Plan** project is a valuable experience for your personal success. To make the experience more meaningful, the capstone document is available on the companion website as a downloadable file.

G-W Learning Companion Website

G-W Learning companion website for **School to Career** is a study reference that contains e-flash cards and vocabulary exercises. Also included are data files that will help you practice what you learned in the chapter as well as complete the Lifespan Plan project.

G-W Learning companion website: www.g-wlearning.com

G-W Learning Mobile Site

The G-W Learning mobile site* is a study reference to use when you are on the go. The mobile site is easy to read, easy to use, and fine-tuned for quick access.

For **School to Career**, the G-W Learning mobile site contains chapter pretests and posttests as well as e-flash cards and vocabulary practice. These features can be accessed by a smartphone or other handheld device with Internet access. These features can also be accessed using an Internet browser to visit the G-W Learning companion website.

G-W Learning mobile site: www.m.g-wlearning.com

Scan now!

Goodheart-Willcox QR Codes

This Goodheart-Willcox product contains QR codes*, or quick response codes. These codes can be scanned with smartphone bar code reader to access information or online features. For more information on using QR codes and a recommended QR reader, visit the G-W Learning companion website at www.g-wlearning.com.

*An Internet connection is required to access the QR code destinations. Data-transfer rates may apply. Check with your Internet service provider for information on your data-transfer rates.

Scan now!

Unit 1 Career Exploration

Lifespan Plan

Getting Started

It is often easier to imagine where you want to be than to see the steps needed to get there. To help you more clearly see the steps necessary to reach your goals, you will create a lifespan plan as part of an ongoing project for this course. The time between birth and death is called a *life span*. The lifespan plan you develop will have five elements that directly relate to achieving your life goals. The elements are career selection, education and training, skills, and lifestyle goals and financial resources.

Activity

1. The first step in creating your plan is to set goals. Create a list of 10 goals you would like to accomplish over your lifetime. Include both short-term and long-term goals. A short-term goal is a goal you want to reach tomorrow, next week, or over the next few months. A long-term goal is a goal that might take several months or years to achieve. These goals will be the basis of your lifespan plan.
2. Review both your short-term and long-term goals after you read each chapter in this unit. You may want to revise them as you progress through the text.
3. Save your list of goals according to your instructor's specifications.

Unit Overview

As you progress through this text, you will explore the many options open to you after high school. In Unit 1, you will see how important work is for your well-being and self-image. You will also see how work-based learning programs provide valuable insight into the world of work. The unit wraps up with an exploration of what employers expect. Being prepared to meet those expectations is the key to landing a job and having a successful career.

Chapter 1 Making the Transition from School to Career
Chapter 2 Understanding Work-Based Learning
Chapter 3 What Your Employer Expects

Picture Success

Darlene Uren
BPA

A Career and Technical Student Organization (CTSO) can have a positive impact on its members and sponsors. Read about Darlene's experience with Business Professionals of America (BPA) in her own words.

"'Work for the job you want, not the job you have.' I first heard this advice at a BPA leadership workshop. I made a decision then to apply this idea to every job that I would ever have.

Darlene Uren

I remember starting my professional career as a personal assistant. This was an entry-level position. However, there was opportunity for growth within the company. As a personal assistant, I slowly learned how my department worked and how the company functioned. While completing my work assignments and observing others, I recognized ways to be more efficient. When possible, I would share these ideas with my managers and team members. It took a while, but eventually the human resources manager noticed me. Over time, I received promotions, and I am now the plant manager.

BPA has had such a positive impact on my life and career. I now volunteer as a judge at BPA state and national competitions. It is such a joy to see the competitors' skills and confidence grow."

Making the Transition from School to Career

Section 1.1
Importance of Work

Section 1.2
Preparing for Career Success

College and Career Readiness

Reading Prep. Review the table of contents for this text. Trace the development of the content that is being presented from simple to complex ideas.

Introduction

Deciding what to do to earn a living is one of the most important decisions you will ever make. Like any important decision, having all the information you need improves your chance of making a good one.

Before making a career decision, you will need to become familiar with the workplace and the requirements of different occupations. Basic information about the world of work can be obtained in many ways. Information can be obtained from school counselors, the Internet, the library, as well as many other sources. It is very important, however, to confirm what you learn about the work world through actual exposure to the workplace.

Check Your Career IQ

Before you begin the chapter, see what you already know about careers by taking the chapter pretest. Use the related QR code to view the pretest on the mobile site. If you do not have a smartphone, visit the G-W Learning companion website to access the pretest.

www.m.g-wlearning.com
www.g-wlearning.com

G-W Mobile

Career Snapshot
Fish and Game Warden

Agriculture, Food & Natural Resources

What Does a Fish and Game Warden Do?

Fish and game wardens enforce hunting, fishing, and boating laws in an effort to protect and conserve fish and wildlife. A game warden must:

- promote hunter and boat safety and conduct search-and-rescue operations;
- investigate complaints, issue citations, arrest violators, seize equipment associated with the violations;
- assist with prosecution of violations by testifying in court; and
- educate the public on laws related to conservation and the environment.

What Is It Like to Work as a Fish and Game Warden?

Fish and game wardens work outside in all types of conditions. They patrol hunting and fishing areas to look for law violators. They conduct search-and-rescue operations and investigate accidents. As law officers, fish and game wardens carry weapons and may find themselves in dangerous situations.

What Education and Skills Are Needed to Be a Fish and Game Warden?

- associate or bachelor degree
- completion of training academy
- be physically fit
- be able to handle stress well

US Fish and Wildlife Service

1.1 | Importance of Work

Terms

job
occupation
career
associate degree
bachelor degree
occupational trend
career clusters
career pathway
job shadowing

Objectives

After completing this section, you will be able to:
* **Describe** the reasons most people work.
* **Explain** how the career clusters can help you prepare for college and career success.

Why Do People Work?

Have you ever wondered why people work? Most people might say it is to earn money. It has to be much more than that. Chances are you will spend more time working than doing any other activity in your lifetime. If your primary goal in working is to earn money, there is a good chance you will spend many hours doing something you really do not want to do.

Work is very important in our lives. Often, one of the first things people ask when introduced is "What do you do for a living?" Work helps to define who we are. It also gives meaning to our lives. Work can help you feel good about yourself and have a positive attitude about life. It is a way to make lifelong friends. Work will help you continue to learn and grow. Many of the things you learn at work will help you in your personal life. For example, taking more responsibility at work may give you the confidence to assume more responsibility at home.

Work can be either drudgery or a joy. Do you know people who love work so much they say they will never retire? On the other hand, how many people do you know who hate going to work each day and cannot wait for the weekend? If you take time now to fully explore your career options, you will be able to find something that pays you a good wage. You will also be able to find something that you will love to do and that you do well. It is a wonderful feeling to wake up each morning and look forward to going to work.

Go Green

Aggressive driving, such as accelerating quickly, speeding, and stomping on the brakes, can be very dangerous. It can also reduce your gas mileage by as much as 5 percent in town and 33 percent on the highway. Driving aggressively also increases the wear and tear on vehicles. For example, brakes may need to be replaced more often. This is not only more costly but adds more trash to landfills.

If you take time to fully explore your career options, you will be more likely to enjoy the job you ultimately earn.

GW Images/Shutterstock.com

Exploring the World of Work

A key concern of people entering the workforce is finding a job they enjoy. A **job** is a task performed by a worker, usually to earn money. It is rare for a person to stay at the same job for a lifetime and not want increased variety, responsibility, and pay. Such rewards are provided by a series of more challenging jobs. When work requires the use of related skills and experience, that work is called an **occupation**. However, an occupation is not a career. A **career** is a progression of related occupations that results in employment and personal growth.

Each person is unique, so your idea of the ideal career will not match someone else's. Making a good career decision requires knowing yourself, your strengths, and your interests. It also involves knowing about the different types of jobs that make up the world of work.

Education and Training Requirements

Some people are not aware of the educational requirements for various occupations. Having the education necessary to enter a profession of choice is very important. Jobs that do not require a degree or technical training after high school usually provide on-the-job training. Often, these are lower-paying positions that people use as stepping-stones to better jobs. See Figure 1-1 for a list of jobs open to workers without a degree or technical training.

Top Jobs through 2016 Not Requiring a Degree	
Occupations	**Total Job Openings**
Retail salespersons	5,034,000
Office clerks, general	3,604,000
Cashiers (except gaming)	3,382,000
Combined food preparation and serving workers (including fast food)	2,955,000
Customer service representatives	2,747,000
Janitors and cleaners (except maids and housekeeping cleaners)	2,732,000

Goodheart-Willcox Publisher

Figure 1-1.
This table shows the projected number of job openings available to those without additional training beyond high school.

Top Jobs through 2016 Requiring an Associate Degree	
Occupations	**Total Job Openings**
Registered nurses	3,092,000
Computer support specialists	624,000
Legal secretaries	308,000
Paralegals and legal assistants	291,000
Radiologic technologists and technicians	226,000
Dental hygienists	217,000

Goodheart-Willcox Publisher

Figure 1-2.
This table shows the projected number of job openings available to those with two-year degrees.

Top Jobs through 2016 Requiring a Bachelor Degree	
Occupations	**Total Job Openings**
Elementary school teachers (except special education)	1,749,000
Accountants and auditors	1,500,000
All other business operations specialists	1,261,000
Secondary school teachers (except special and career/technical education)	1,096,000
All other teachers (primary, secondary, and adult)	805,000
Computer software engineers, applications	733,000

Goodheart-Willcox Publisher

Figure 1-3.
This table shows the projected number of job openings available to those with four-year degrees.

Many jobs require at least an associate degree. An **associate degree** is a two-year college degree. Sometimes students take a two-year program to jump-start a career. Once working, they seek additional education and training. See Figure 1-2 for a list of jobs open to workers with an associate degree.

About 20 percent of jobs may require at least a four-year college degree, known as a **bachelor degree.** These jobs are usually higher paying than those requiring less education. See Figure 1-3 for a list of the most available jobs through 2016 for individuals with a bachelor degree.

Future Occupational Trends

What are the jobs of the future? No one knows for sure, but researchers continue to study occupational trends. **Occupational trends** are research-based forecasts about which jobs will most likely be needed in the future.

One such trend is the ever-growing number of service-related jobs. These jobs are expected to account for most of the new jobs generated by 2020. The majority of new service positions will be in business, health, social services, and technology.

Advances in technology and changes in society shape occupational trends. Some important societal changes that are shaping US occupations include:

- an aging population;
- an increased concern for health and fitness;
- a high interest in recreation and entertainment; and
- new ways of communicating based on new technologies.

You will see many of these changes reflected in Figure 1-4, which shows projected growth by major occupation groups.

Ethical Leadership

Truthful Communication

"If you tell the truth, you don't have to remember anything."—Mark Twain

The ability to communicate effectively is an important leadership quality in both business and personal life. Effective communication involves the ability to clearly state your ideas and to do so honestly. Facts should be given without distortion. If the information is an opinion, label it as such. Do not take credit for ideas that belong to someone else; always credit your sources.

Figure 1-4.   *Source: US Bureau of Labor Statistics, 2012*

Occupational groups projected to experience the greatest growth are those that require education or training beyond high school.

You and your peers will likely work in 10 or more jobs for 5 or more employers before retirement. Some of the occupations you will hold may not exist today. This means it is your responsibility to manage your own career and watch for new opportunities.

Keep career flexibility in mind as you explore various occupations and careers. Success in the workplace requires self-reliance, adaptability, transferable skills, and the willingness and ability to learn new skills.

Career Clusters

One of the best ways to learn about careers is by studying the **career clusters**, the groups of occupational and career specialties as shown in Figure 1-5. The clusters and career pathways were developed by educators, employers, and professional groups. These experts carefully examined what students must know to explore educational opportunities and be better prepared for college and career success.

The 16 Career Clusters

Careers involving the production, processing, marketing, distribution, financing, and development of agricultural commodities and resources. 	Careers involving management, marketing, and operations of foodservice, lodging, and recreational businesses. 
Careers involving the design, planning, managing, building, and maintaining of buildings and structures. 	Careers involving family and human needs. 
Careers involving the design, production, exhibition, performance, writing, and publishing of visual and performing arts. 	Careers involving the design, development, support, and management of software, hardware, and other technology-related materials. 
Careers involving the planning, organizing, directing, and evaluation of functions essential to business operations. 	Careers involving the planning, management, and providing of legal services, public safety, protective services, and homeland security. 
Careers involving the planning, management, and providing of training services. 	Careers involving the planning, management, and processing of materials to create completed products. 
Careers involving the planning and providing of banking, insurance, and other financial-business services. 	Careers involving the planning, management, and performance of marketing and sales activities. 
Careers involving governance, national security, foreign service, revenue and taxation, regulation, and management and administration.	Careers involving the planning, management, and providing of scientific research and technical services. 
Careers involving planning, managing, and providing health services, health information, and research and development. 	Careers involving the planning, management, and movement of people, materials, and goods. 

Figure 1-5.

States' Career Clusters Initiative 2008

Each of the 16 career clusters contains several career pathways.

Reading the titles of the career clusters is the simplest way to begin thinking about career opportunities. Each cluster shows a grouping of occupations and industries and the skills that are required for each. Each cluster includes several career directions, called **career pathways.** Within each pathway are various occupations ranging from entry-level to very challenging. All the career choices within a given pathway require a set of common knowledge and skills. This means the related careers require very similar programs of study. Being prepared for more than one career in a related field allows more flexibility when you are ready to look for a job.

Students usually begin thinking about their future in the workforce by trying to imagine themselves in different work settings. They consider how well different occupations match their talents, abilities, and interests. Eventually, they narrow down the many choices to two or three careers that seem most interesting.

The career clusters are important because they are part of a broad plan that links school preparation to college and career success. You will be able to see exactly what it takes to identify and prepare for a career that will build on your talents and interests. You will know if the career path you have chosen will require a college degree or if you will be able to go straight to work after high school.

With the help of teachers and counselors, you will develop a *personal program of study* matched to your career goals. Compatible activities and learning experiences will be added as you refine your career choice. If you follow your plan, you will be prepared to enter a community college, university, or the workplace.

Career Exploration

Making a career decision is not always easy because there are hundreds of choices to consider and many strategies you can use. Remember, this decision can affect how happy and successful you will be for the rest of your life. It is a very personal process. What your friends decide should not affect your decision. Your final choice must result in a career that takes full advantage of your interests and abilities. So take time to do it right. Use as many different resources as you possibly can. There are a number of career-guidance tests that students can take. The results of these tests can be used as a step in the career-exploration process.

Attending career events at school and listening to guest speakers are activities that can help make the right career choice for you. These speakers can provide practical information on what it takes to get into their fields. Another way to explore the workplace is by participating in field trips to different employers in your community. You can help arrange field trips as part of a class project. Most employers are happy to conduct group tours during slow business periods. You can also try contacting a company that interests you and planning a visit on your own.

Another way to learn more about the world of work is through job shadowing. **Job shadowing** is following a worker on the job and observing what that job involves. If you know someone who has a job that sounds interesting, ask if it is possible to spend some time with him or her at work. The experience may last a few hours or a couple days. Permission from the employer is always required.

Volunteering is another way to learn about work. Animal shelters, recycling centers, and many other nonprofit operations rely on volunteer help. By volunteering, you can observe different types of work while contributing to activities that benefit your community.

Checkpoint 1.1

1. Why is work important?
2. Explain the difference between an associate degree and a bachelor degree.
3. What do occupational trends tell us about jobs?
4. Why are career clusters important?
5. List two ways to explore career opportunities.

Build Your Vocabulary

As you progress through this text, develop a personal glossary of career-related terms and add it to your portfolio. This will help build your vocabulary and prepare you for your career of choice. Write a definition for each of the following terms, and add it to your personal career glossary.

job
occupation
career
associate degree
bachelor degree
occupational trend
career clusters
career pathway
job shadowing

1.2 | Preparing for Career Success

Objectives

After completing this section you will be able to:
- **Describe** the difference between possessing knowledge and having skills.
- **Explain** the importance of transferable skills as you consider college and career opportunities.

Career Knowledge and Skills

Different jobs require different skills and knowledge. However, different jobs also require certain similar abilities in all workers, no matter what jobs they hold. Companies try to hire workers who possess the knowledge and skills needed for success. **Skills** are the things that you do well. Employers tend to prefer employees with skills that can transfer from one job to another.

Preparation for the world of work begins long before you actually have a job or career. Workplace readiness involves the knowledge and skills you are learning now. Employers have identified what learners

Having or acquiring the skills employers want is one element you will use to determine a career that is right for you.

cihanhizal/Shutterstock.com

and employees should know and be able to do to be successful in their work. Their recommendations were condensed into a list of 10 essential knowledge and skills. This list is used to identify the specific requirements of a given career as shown in Figure 1-6.

For example, thinking logically, reading, and writing are skills you strengthen through class participation and homework. They are the same skills used by a worker when communicating with coworkers. In the workplace, being able to write instructions for coworkers can mean the difference between getting the job done well and having it done poorly or not at all.

Possessing the required knowledge and skills makes employees more valuable to their employers. When you focus on a career goal, you will recognize the link between the knowledge and skills and the career requirements shown in Figure 1-6. You will have many opportunities to develop the necessary knowledge and skills long before you join the workforce. Taking advantage of these opportunities will help you develop your full potential.

Career Knowledge and Skills	
Basic Knowledge or Skill	**Expression of a Career Requirement**
Academic foundations	Knowing how to read, write, make presentations, and listen well, and use math and science principles
Communications	Using illustrations to convey complex concepts
Problem solving and critical thinking	Analyzing, synthesizing, and evaluating data
Information technology applications	Using Internet searches, presentation software, and writing/publishing applications
Systems	Understanding roles within the team, work unit, department, and organization
Safety, health, and environment	Knowing and following procedures required by health and safety codes
Leadership and teamwork	Demonstrating integrity, perseverance, self-discipline, and responsibility
Ethics and legal responsibilities	Behaving in ways that are appropriate for the workplace
Employability and career development	Recognizing what needs to be learned or accomplished to gain a promotion
Technical skills	Correctly using technological systems and equipment common to a chosen career

Figure 1-6.   *Goodheart-Willcox Publisher*
Acquiring basic career knowledge and skills are the foundation for career success.

Case

Stephanie Wants to Be an Architect

Stephanie was just finishing junior high school and very excited about entering high school the following fall. The high school counselor, Mrs. Walsh, visited Stephanie's school one day to meet with her and other students. Mrs. Walsh met individually with students to help them decide which courses they would take during their freshman year at North High School.

The counselor suggested Stephanie take some exploratory classes to help her decide which careers fit her interests. Stephanie said, "Oh, I don't need that. I already know that I want to be an architect. I've loved to draw and design houses since I was a little girl. My dad even built me a dollhouse from drawings I made."

The counselor tried to convince her to at least consider some other areas, but Stephanie stood firm. Mrs. Walsh reluctantly agreed to set up a program of study based on Stephanie's wishes. We will enroll you in the college-preparatory track with a heavy emphasis on math and science," said Mrs. Walsh. "Oh, no!" cried Stephanie, "I hate math, and I'm not very good in science. I don't want to go to college. I just want to get through high school and go to work as soon as possible."

Critical Thinking

1. Do you think Stephanie had a realistic picture of what an architect does?
2. Why would an architect need math and science?
3. Are there occupations in the "Architecture and Construction Cluster" that might not require a lot of math and science?
4. Do you think Stephanie might learn to like math and science if she knew how an architect used those skills?

Transferable Skills

Transferable skills are skills used in one job that can also be used in another job. A specialized skill, such as speaking a second language, is an example. People who possess transferable skills can easily use them in other jobs if required.

Specialized skills are not the only skills that qualify as transferable skills. Broader skills (such as good writing, problem solving, and leadership) are transferable skills, too. Your future success will depend on developing skills that can be used now and applied to future work opportunities. This means using the skills you develop as a student and transferring them to the workplace. There you will polish your skills and learn other skills, all of which can be transferred later to another job.

Continue developing transferable skills. They are very important. Transferable skills make you a more capable person and help expand the knowledge and skills you will need in the workplace.

Introduction to Student Organizations

Professional student organizations are a valuable asset to any educational program. These organizations support student learning and the application of skills learned in real-world situations. Also, participation in Career and Technology Education Student Organizations can promote lifelong interest in community service and professional development.

There are a variety of organizations from which to select, depending on the goals of your educational programs.

To prepare for any competitive event, complete the following activities.

1. Contact the organization well in advance of the next competition. This will give you time to review and decide which competitive events are correct for you or your team.
2. Read all the guidelines closely. These rules and regulations must be strictly adhered to or disqualification can occur.
3. Competitive events may be written, oral, or a combination of both.
4. Communication plays a role in all the competitive events, so read which communication skills are covered for the event you select. Research and preparation are important for a successful competition.
5. Go to the website of your organization for specific information for the events. Visit the site often as information changes quickly.
6. Select one or two events that are of interest to you. Print the information for the events and discuss your interest with your instructor.

Checkpoint 1.2

1. What does workplace readiness involve?
2. Identify skills you strengthen through class participation.
3. Identify one specialized, transferable skill.
4. List three broad, transferable skills learned in school.
5. Why should you continue to develop transferable skills?

Build Your Vocabulary

As you progress through this text, develop a personal glossary of career-related terms and add it to your portfolio. This will help build your vocabulary and prepare you for your career of choice. Write a definition for each of the following terms, and add it to your personal career glossary.

skill
transferable skill

Chapter Summary

Section 1.1 Importance of Work

- People work for many reasons. Work helps provide meaning to life.
- Making a good career decision involves studying the career clusters and knowing about the many career choices available. Your career choice will affect your future happiness.

Section 1.2 Preparing for Career Success

- Career decisions require knowing one's abilities and interests. Take advantage of opportunities that allow you to develop knowledge and skills.
- Transferable skills enable you to work in a variety of workplaces. Employers tend to prefer employees with transferable skills.

Check Your Career IQ

Now that you have finished the chapter, see what you learned about careers by taking the chapter posttest. The test can be accessed on the mobile site by using a smartphone or on the G-W Learning companion website.

www.m.g-wlearning.com
www.g-wlearning.com

Review Your Knowledge

1. Explain why most people work.
2. Compare and contrast the terms *job, occupation,* and *career.*
3. What is required in order to make a good career decision?
4. Why should a person study the career clusters?
5. How does a career cluster differ from a career pathway?
6. List two ways students can gain actual exposure to the workplace other than holding a job.
7. Identify the volunteer opportunities suggested to help you learn about work.
8. When does job preparation begin?
9. Why are transferable skills important?
10. Give examples of transferable skills.

Apply Your Knowledge

1. Interview at least five people in different occupations to determine why they work. Try to identify specific reasons. Then, ask them if they enjoy their work. Decide if there is a relationship between work satisfaction and why people work. Is there a relationship between the type of work they do and how much they enjoy it? Summarize your findings in a one-page paper.

2. Investigate volunteer opportunities in your community. Report on one that appeals to you. Identify how the volunteer activity contributes to preparing individuals for a future job.

3. Which do you see more often—people treating work as a problem or as an opportunity? Discuss what may inspire workers to view work as fun and exciting.

4. Examine two career clusters that include careers you may decide to pursue. What new facts did you learn during the search? Did your research help you move closer to making a career decision?

5. Think of a job in which you might be interested. Arrange to spend a few hours visiting a company and observing a person who does that type of work. You may want to ask your teacher to help you arrange the visit. Prepare a list of questions you want answered or things you want to see before you visit. Share your experience in a written or oral report to your class.

6. Select a career cluster that is of interest to you. Do an Internet search on that cluster and analyze the future employment outlook for the careers in that cluster. Create a chart that summarizes your findings.

7. Carefully consider the figures in Section 1.1 of this chapter. From the data provided, what can you conclude about the jobs that will be in demand and those that will not? What do you think accounts for this?

8. Choose an occupation from Figure 1-2. Conduct research to identify the area of study and degree requirements for the occupation you selected. Visit the website of a college or university to view classes and any additional requirements needed to complete the specific college degree. Compare this information to that of another college or university. Compile your information in a chart. Share your findings within a small group.

9. Consider career options for your future. List three jobs you might want to have as an adult. Using a three-column chart, make a list of five things that you must do in the next two years to prepare yourself for each job.

10. Think about your knowledge, skills, and interests. Next, review the career clusters. Select a field that is of interest to you. Write a one-page essay explaining why you would pursue a career in the field you selected.

Teamwork

Work with a small group of classmates to create a list of adjustments students may encounter as they make the transition from being full-time students to being full-time employees. Share your findings with the class.

G-W Learning Mobile Site

Visit the G-W Learning mobile site to complete the chapter pretest and posttest and to practice vocabulary using e-flash cards. If you do not have a smartphone, visit the G-W Learning companion website to access these features.

G-W Learning mobile site: www.m.g-wlearning.com

G-W Learning companion website: www.g-wlearning.com

Common Core

College and Career Readiness

CTE Career Ready Practices. Exceeding expectations is a way to be successful at school and in your career. Make a list of five things that you expect of yourself on a daily basis, such as, being on time, completing tasks as assigned, and being courteous.

For each of the things you expect from yourself, record what you could do to exceed those expectations. What effect do you think exceeding expectations has on your success?

Reading. Take a look at how the authors have structured this chapter. How do the numbered sections of the text relate to the chapter title? How is the information presented? Why do you think this chapter is the first in the textbook?

Apply Your Technology Skills

Access the G-W Learning companion website for this text at www.g-wlearning.com. Download each data file for this chapter. Follow the instructions to complete activities to practice what you have learned.

Data File 1–1—**Creating a Personal Program of Study**

Data File 1–2—**Researching Post High School Programs**

College and Career Readiness Portfolio

College and Career Readiness

When you apply for a paid or volunteer job or for admission to a college, you may need to tell others about why you are qualified for the position. A portfolio is a selection of related materials that you collect and organize. These materials show your qualifications, skills, and talents. For example, a certificate that shows you have completed lifeguard and first-aid training could help you get a job at a local pool as a lifeguard. An essay you wrote about protecting native plants could show that you are serious about eco-friendly efforts and may help you get a volunteer position at a park. A transcript of your school grades could help show that you are qualified for college.

Two types of portfolios are commonly used: *print portfolios* and *electronic portfolios* (e-portfolios). An e-portfolio is also known as a *digital portfolio.*

1. Use the Internet to search for "print portfolio" and "e-portfolio." Read articles about each type of portfolio. Create a chart that gives the characteristics of each type.
2. You will be creating a portfolio in this class. Which portfolio type would you prefer to create? Write a paragraph describing the type of portfolio you would prefer and why.

Chapter 2

Understanding Work-Based Learning

Section 2.1
Work-Based Learning Programs

Section 2.2
Work-Based Learning

Section 2.3
Importance of Study

College and Career Readiness

Reading Prep. Before reading, observe the objectives for each section in this chapter. Keep these in mind as you read. Focus on the structure of the writing. Was the information presented in a way that was clear and engaging?

Introduction

As a student in a work-based program, your daily schedule may be different from those of other students. Your behavior will be governed by certain state and federal laws that did not affect you before. Schedule adjustments will need to be made to allow for new school and work hours. Be prepared to meet new people and accept new responsibilities. You will spend more time on your own, which means you will have more freedom. Remember, your success in a work-based learning program depends a great deal on how well you handle your freedom and responsibilities.

Check Your Career IQ

Before you begin the chapter, see what you already know about careers by taking the chapter pretest. Use the related QR code to view the pretest on the mobile site. If you do not have a smartphone, visit the G-W Learning companion website to access the pretest.

www.m.g-wlearning.com
www.g-wlearning.com

G-W Mobile

Career Snapshot
Computer-Aided Drafter

What Does a Computer-Aided Drafter Do?

Computer-aided drafters prepare technical drawings used by construction workers to build commercial and residential buildings. Most drafters use computer-aided design and drafting (CAD) software to prepare their drawings. Computer-aided drafters are often referred to as *CAD operators.* A computer-aided drafter must:

- make detailed drawings such as floor plans, wall sections and exterior views, and may be involved in the design process;
- be able to communicate effectively both orally and in writing; and
- have strong math and engineering skills.

What Is It Like to Work as a Computer-Aided Drafter?

Computer-aided drafters work closely with architects to help transform their ideas into reality. They may also interact with clients. Drafters spend many hours at the computer and are subject to eye and back strain as well as hand and wrist problems.

What Education and Skills Are Needed to Be a Computer-Aided Drafter?

- high school diploma or GED
- post-secondary training in drafting is preferred
- coursework in math, science, engineering, and CAD
- strong critical thinking and interpersonal skills
- time-management skills

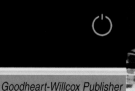

Goodheart-Willcox Publisher

2.1 | Work-Based Learning Programs

Objectives

After completing this section, you will be able to:
- **Explain** how a work-based training program is organized.
- **List** the benefits of work-based training programs.

Opportunities to Learn on the Job

Work-based learning programs are types of school programs designed to prepare students for work. These programs provide students with job training.

Work-based learning programs bridge the gap between school and work. They help students make the adjustment from being full-time students to being full-time employees. Students attend classes and work part-time alongside full-time employees in business and industry. These programs give students an opportunity to learn in two places—school and work. The programs are especially valuable to students who want to succeed in a full-time occupation immediately after high school. For students planning to attend a technical school or college, these programs can help them decide which study plan to pursue.

Work-based learning opportunities do not just happen. They are developed by contacting businesses and convincing them to work as partners with high schools for the benefit of students. Finding business partners and handling the details of creating and operating a work-based learning program can be a full-time job.

Students in work-based learning programs have a special teacher or counselor assigned to them called a **program coordinator.** The program coordinator works on the student's behalf to help make the work-based learning experience successful. He or she consults with everyone who must be informed about the student's progress. This person also provides the information, support, and help needed to solve problems and make decisions.

Your contact with your future employer is through the program coordinator. He or she is responsible for reviewing your application for work-based experience. An effort is then made to match your occupational goals with an available work-based experience.

©Vadym Drobot/Shutterstock.com

Work-based learning programs provide opportunities to learn valuable on-the-job skills.

The coordinator carefully discusses your qualifications for a work-based experience with one or more potential employers before you are assigned to a training station. A **training station** is a job site where a student works to learn job skills. A training station may be a manufacturing company, hospital, hair salon, bank, construction site, auto service center, or some other workplace. The training stations available to you depend on the type of work-based learning program you follow and the cooperating employers in your area. Usually, you are responsible for providing your own transportation to the job.

When you report to the job on your first day of work, you will be introduced to your supervisor. The **supervisor** is your manager in the workplace. He or she explains what is expected on the job and evaluates how well you do your work. The supervisor is responsible for the training station and your job training.

The supervisor explains the job and the company as much as possible, but often assigns a work-based mentor to help the student worker. A **work-based mentor** is an assistant who helps with day-to-day questions. Another common term for this worker is *training sponsor*. A work-based mentor is an employee who knows how to do the job and teaches you to do it well. Students tend to form friendships with their mentors and feel more relaxed when they are around.

Remember, the work-based learning experience is a three-way relationship. It involves you, your program coordinator, and the employer. You have the most to gain from this relationship. It will help you build self-confidence and develop marketable skills through on-the-job experiences. You will also be able to explore your career interests while learning to work with others and earning money. Two common types of work-based learning programs are *cooperative education programs* and *internships*.

Ethical Leadership

Honesty

"Whoever is careless with the truth in small matters cannot be trusted with important matters."—Albert Einstein

Honesty involves acting truthfully and sincerely. It is always the best policy. However, some students believe cheating on homework or a test at school is not really being dishonest. It is just school, and everybody does it. Cheating is dishonest no matter where it occurs. Habits are hard to break. Once cheating is justified at school, it becomes easier to justify it in other aspects of life.

Cooperative Education

Cooperative education is a school program that prepares students for an occupation through a paid job experience. Cooperative education programs are also called *co-op programs.* They team a school with a local employer who agrees to hire a student part-time and pay an hourly wage. The employer provides job training to help a student prepare for a career goal.

At school, the student takes classes for approximately a half-day to meet requirements for graduation. The student also takes a cooperative education class. The class is taught by the coordinator and focuses on learning how to set career goals, apply for jobs, and manage finances. The student earns credit toward graduation for both the cooperative education class and the work experience.

Internship

An **internship** is a school program providing paid or unpaid work experience for a specified period as a way to learn about a job or an industry. Students participate in this supervised work experience by enrolling as they would for a class. Instead of attending a formal class, however, the student works or volunteers at a temporary position during or after school hours and earns credit toward graduation.

Internships are available, providing many different learning opportunities. An internship may involve routine duties as well as specially designed projects. As a rule, students must work for a specific number of hours and prepare a formal report that records their experiences. The school offering the internship establishes the requirements.

Benefits of Learning on the Job

Participating in a work-based learning experience has many benefits. Such school-to-career programs can help students in the following ways:

- build self-confidence;
- gain on-the-job experience;
- acquire marketable skills;
- explore career goals;
- learn to work with others; and
- earn money.

A good way to improve self-confidence is to try new things. Work-based learning is a great way to bring you out of your comfort zone. As you become competent on your job, you will feel better about yourself and be more willing to try new experiences in the future. Every occupation requires certain skills and knowledge as basic job requirements. However, on-the-job experience helps develop these requirements. It also helps students make the personal transition from school to work.

By working in a real job under real working conditions, you develop useful skills needed to perform the job now. These skills will also help you get other jobs in the future. Work-based learning gives you a chance to test some of your career interests. You can discover what you like to do and are able to do. In addition, you can discuss your career goals with others at work as well as in school.

Many students start their first jobs through work-based learning programs.

imageegami/Shutterstock.com

You will learn to communicate with a variety of people as you learn to work with others, including supervisors, coworkers, and customers. In addition, you learn how to conduct yourself in a work situation.

Many work-based learning programs provide opportunities to earn an income. The expression *earn while you learn* applies to work-based learning.

Employers benefit from work-based learning programs, too. They earn recognition in the community for their willingness to help young people. They receive interested part-time workers who are eager to learn and do a good job. In addition, employers have access to a supply of short-term labor they can pair with short-term projects. However, employers often are so pleased with the job performance of students that they offer them full-time employment after they graduate.

Checkpoint 2.1

1. What is a work-based learning program?
2. Who is usually responsible for providing transportation for the student from school to work?
3. Who is in charge of a training station?
4. Which work-based learning program(s) may consist of an unpaid work experience?
5. Name four benefits of a work-based learning program.

Build Your Vocabulary

As you progress through this text, develop a personal glossary of career-related terms and add it to your portfolio. This will help build your vocabulary and prepare you for your career of choice. Write a definition for each of the following terms, and add it to your personal career glossary.

work-based learning program
program coordinator
training station
supervisor
work-based mentor
cooperative education
internship

Your Training Station

You will receive on-the-job training at a school-approved training station. The training station is the place where you will work. The training station may also be referred to as the *worksite* or the *employer*.

Your program coordinator will help you arrange an interview with a potential employer. An **interview** is a planned meeting between a job applicant and an employer. During or after your interview, the employer will show you where you will work if you are selected for the job.

The employer may interview several other students for the same job. After the interviews, the employer will decide whether to hire you or another student. Once an employer has agreed to hire you, you are ready to prepare for your work experience.

Get a Social Security Number and a Work Permit

A Social Security card is a requirement for work. **Social Security** is the federal government's program for providing income when earnings are reduced or stopped by retirement, disability, or death. Employers use Social Security numbers for reporting earnings to the federal government for income tax purposes. Social Security numbers are also used for enrollment in health insurance or retirement programs offered by the employer, among other reasons.

A Social Security number is required to perform everyday activities. For example, you need a Social Security card, like the one in Figure 2-1, to open a savings account. You may even need one to enroll in school or get a driver's license.

Figure 2-1.   *Goodheart-Willcox Publisher*
A Social Security card is required when opening a bank account or applying for a federal student loan among other things.

Identity theft occurs when someone uses your name and pretends to be you. Stealing a Social Security number is one of the fastest-growing crimes in the country. Your Social Security number should be kept private and given only to people who need to know it. The Social Security Administration suggests you ask the following questions before giving out your Social Security number:

- Why is my number needed?
- How will my number be used?
- What happens if I refuse?
- What law requires me to give my number?

If you have lost your Social Security card, you must apply for a replacement card at a Social Security office. You should also apply for a replacement card if you change your name. You must show evidence of your age, identity, and US citizenship or immigrant status when you apply. You can learn more about the proper use of Social Security numbers and the application process through the Social Security Administration.

If you are under age 16 (under age 18 in some states), you will also need a work permit before you begin work. A **work permit** makes it legal for otherwise underage students to work for an employer. A work permit limits the number of hours a student can work each school day and the types of jobs a student can do. Work permits may be issued by schools. Check with your school to see if you will need a permit.

Abide by the Training Agreement

You will be expected to assume the responsibilities outlined in a training agreement during your work experience. A **training agreement** is an agreement between you, your school, and your employer. The obligations of each party are outlined. The training agreement may have different names or formats depending on your specific work-based learning program. Such an agreement is similar to a contract. It outlines the purposes of the work-based

Go Green

Computers left on for several hours consume a lot of energy. To remedy this situation, software companies are creating new applications for computers. These applications monitor how much energy and money can be saved when you take advantage of a computer's sleep and shutdown schedules. Taking advantage of these applications can save energy and extend the life of your equipment.

program and defines the responsibilities of everyone involved. The agreement requires signatures from the student, student's parent(s) or guardian, school coordinator, the employer, and sometimes a school administrator. Although the wording varies from school to school, all training agreements serve the same general purposes. To assure the:

- employer that the student is committed to the work experience;
- student that the employer is committed to training him or her to do the job;
- parent(s) or guardian that the student is involved in a well-planned educational experience; and
- program coordinator that all parties understand their responsibilities and are committed to the student having a successful work experience.

Follow the Training Plan

In addition to the training agreement, there is the training plan. A **training plan** consists of a list of attitudes, skills, and knowledge that the student plans to learn during the work experience. The plan is usually developed by student, program coordinator, and employer. The purpose of the plan is to help the student progress on the job toward his or her career goals. Like training agreements, training plans vary in form. Some are detailed plans, while others consist of a few general statements describing what you will learn.

Another purpose of the training plan is to formally identify your training supervisor on the job. The supervisor is responsible for the training station and your on-the-job training. This is the person your program coordinator contacts about your progress.

To help everyone evaluate progress, most schools require students to keep a **training record**, which includes a weekly or monthly job record of duties performed and skills learned. Each week or month, you will write down the functions you performed as well as the attitudes, skills, and knowledge you learned at work. Periodically, you and your program coordinator will check your accomplishments to see if you are progressing toward the goals listed in your training plan. During these evaluation checks, you will learn how much you have accomplished and what you still want to achieve. Your supervisor will also do a formal evaluation of the tasks on the training plan during each grading period.

Case

New Outlook for Tony

At 7:30 on a February morning in northern Texas, it's very cold! It seemed even colder to Tony when his car didn't start. The engine coughed once, then twice, and finally started. Tony muttered to himself, "Eleven more car payments to make, and it needs a new battery."

As Tony drove to school, he thought about quitting and looking for a job. During his three years in high school, he experienced nothing but discouragement. Freshman year was okay, but school had become a drag since then.

Tony didn't fail any of his classes, but he didn't study much either. Three reasons accounted for Tony's lack of enthusiasm. First, he had no goals for his future. His study habits were very poor. Finally, he had recently burdened himself with monthly car payments.

Tony was considering dropping out of high school when a friend suggested applying for the cooperative education program. The friend said, "You go to school for half the day and work part-time. You get paid for your work and school credit for the job."

"Oh, I've heard about that," Tony said. "But how do I get into the program?"

"See Mr. Lamas, the program coordinator. You had two courses in auto mechanics and enjoy working on cars. Maybe you can get a job at an auto repair shop. Then you won't need to quit school."

Tony met with Mr. Lamas and applied for the cooperative education program. The day Tony was accepted, his outlook on life seemed to change. All summer Tony looked forward to his senior year and his cooperative work experience.

During his senior year, Tony worked for an auto service center. He learned how to tune car engines and repair brakes, transmissions, and other car parts. He also learned something about running a business. It was hard work, but Tony enjoyed it. Not only did Tony pay for his car and learn new skills, but he also made the B honor roll in his last semester.

Critical Thinking

1. Why do you think Tony's outlook on life changed when he was accepted into the cooperative education program?
2. Why do you suppose Tony's grades improved in his senior year?
3. How did the cooperative education experience benefit Tony?
4. What do you think would have happened to Tony if he had quit high school?

Guidelines set by the federal government help make sure workers are paid fair wages for the work they are employed to do.

JohnKwan/Shutterstock.com

Know the Law

There always are school rules and regulations to follow. Now that you will be working away from school as part of your school assignment, there will be new rules governing your actions. Some of these are covered in your training plan and agreement. Others may involve state or federal laws.

Fair Labor Practices

The **Fair Labor Standards Act (FLSA)** protects workers from unfair treatment by their employers. Passed in 1938, the law deals with relationships between employees and employers.

All employees who work for employers involved in interstate or international commerce are covered by this act. Therefore, any business producing, handling, or selling a product or service outside the state must comply with this law. Employees who work in education and health care are also covered. In fact, there are few workers who are not covered by the FLSA.

If an employee believes that rights protected by fair labor laws have been violated, he or she may complain. Complaints should be directed to the Employment Standards Administration or the Wage and Hour Division of the US Department of Labor. Complaints are investigated by government officers. If an employer is found in violation of the law, the business may be prosecuted in court and fined.

Minimum Wage

An FLSA amendment established the creation of a minimum wage. **Minimum wage** is the lowest hourly rate of pay that most employees must receive. Employers, of course, may pay more than minimum wage, but they cannot pay employees less. The minimum hourly rate is set by the federal government. It is changed periodically to meet the needs of inflation and recession.

Some employees are excluded from the minimum wage law by specific employer exemptions. For instance, food service workers who earn tips can lawfully be paid less than minimum wage. It is also lawful to pay employees less during a training period when they first start a new job. There are special rules for full-time students and students enrolled in school-based training programs such as cooperative education.

Overtime Pay

Another FLSA amendment sets guidelines for overtime pay to employees. **Overtime pay** must be paid at a rate of at least 1 1/2 times the employee's regular pay rate. Overtime is paid for each hour worked in excess of the maximum hours allowed. For example, suppose an employee who earns $8 an hour works 44 hours in a workweek. The employee is entitled to at least 1 1/2 times $8, or $12, for each hour over 40. That person's pay for the week is $320 for the first 40 hours plus $48 for four hours of overtime—a total of $368.

regular earnings = $8 × 40 = $320
hours worked overtime = 44 (total hours worked) – 40 (regular hours
    per week) = 4
overtime pay per hour = 1.5 × $8 = $12
overtime earnings = $12 × 4 (hours worked overtime) = $48
total weekly pay = $320 (regular pay) + $48 = $368

Saturdays, Sundays, and holidays are treated like any other day of the week. Employers are not required to pay overtime on weekends and holidays unless the hours worked exceed the maximum allowable. Like minimum wage, some employees are exempt from receiving overtime pay.

Students working in school-based training programs are considered *trainees,* not employees. Consequently, this law will not apply to you during your work-based learning experience. However, some employers may pay overtime voluntarily.

Equal Pay

An amendment to the FLSA resulted in the Equal Pay Act of 1963. The **Equal Pay Act** requires equal pay be given to employees of both sexes for doing equal jobs. Jobs performed under similar working conditions that require the same level of skill, effort, and responsibility are considered equal. Pay exceptions may occur for differences in seniority, skill, productivity, services performed, or shift time. Any violation of equal-pay requirements encountered by employees should be reported to the Equal Employment Opportunity Commission (EEOC). The **Equal Employment Opportunity Commission (EEOC)** is a federal agency that oversees equal employment opportunities for all Americans.

As a trainee, you will not be entitled to the same pay level as an employee. However, your pay as a trainee should match the pay that other trainees receive for doing the same work.

Child Labor Standards

The FLSA child-labor provision is designed to serve two functions. It protects the educational opportunities of children. It also prohibits the employment of children in jobs that may be hazardous to their health or well-being. Your state may have laws that are stricter than these provisions, particularly as they apply to full-time students. See Figure 2-2 for an overview of child-labor standards.

A special provision applies to 14- and 15-year-olds enrolled in an approved work program through school. They may be employed for up to 23 hours per school week and three hours per school day even during school hours.

The minimum age for most nonfarm work is 14. However, young people of any age may deliver newspapers or work for parents in a nonfarm business. They may also perform in radio, television, movie, or other theatrical productions.

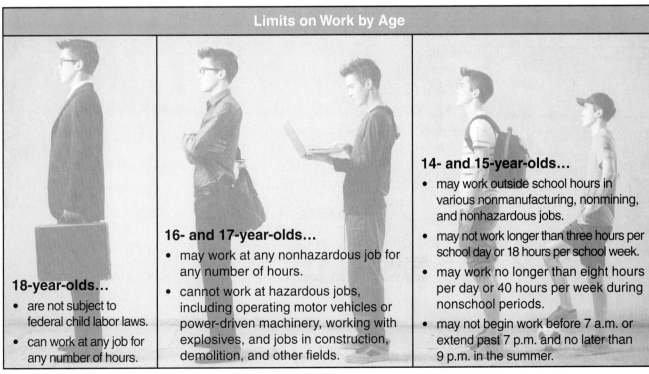

Limits on Work by Age

18-year-olds...
- are not subject to federal child labor laws.
- can work at any job for any number of hours.

16- and 17-year-olds...
- may work at any nonhazardous job for any number of hours.
- cannot work at hazardous jobs, including operating motor vehicles or power-driven machinery, working with explosives, and jobs in construction, demolition, and other fields.

14- and 15-year-olds...
- may work outside school hours in various nonmanufacturing, nonmining, and nonhazardous jobs.
- may not work longer than three hours per school day or 18 hours per school week.
- may work no longer than eight hours per day or 40 hours per week during nonschool periods.
- may not begin work before 7 a.m. or extend past 7 p.m. and no later than 9 p.m. in the summer.

Figure 2-2.   *Goodheart-Willcox Publisher*
Federal and state laws place restrictions on the type and duration of work a young person can perform.

Safe Labor Practices

Safety in the workplace is so important that it is the sole focus of one government agency. The **Occupational Safety and Health Administration (OSHA)** sets and enforces safety and health standards for workers. The agency's goal is to prevent accidents and injuries in the workplace. Employers must provide a safe workplace, and workers are required to follow all safety rules. Before you begin working, your supervisor will review the specific safety rules that apply to your training station.

Checkpoint 2.2

1. Who will assist the student in finding a suitable training station?
2. Why does an employer need a worker's Social Security number?
3. What questions should you ask before giving out your Social Security number?
4. What are the purposes of a training agreement?
5. What are the purposes of a training plan?

Build Your Vocabulary

As you progress through this text, develop a personal glossary of
career-related terms and add it to your portfolio. This will help build your vocabulary and prepare you for your career of choice. Write a definition for each of the following terms, and add it to your personal career glossary.

    interview
    Social Security
    work permit
    training agreement
    training plan
    training record
    Fair Labor Standards Act (FLSA)
    minimum wage
    overtime pay
    Equal Pay Act
    Equal Employment Opportunity Commission (EEOC)
    Occupational Safety and Health Administration (OSHA)

Objectives

After completing this section, you will be able to:
- **Describe** study skills that will help you become prepared for college and career.
- **List** steps to take to improve study habits.

Terms

priority
summarize

Study and Learn

Students in work-based learning programs sometimes say, "I want to work, not study." You will need to do both to be successful in your work-based learning experience and your future career. Part of your success in the program may depend on your desire to study and learn. The study skills you use in the classroom are just as important as the job skills you will learn. As you move into your future career, you will be able to use many of the same skills.

Develop Organization Skills

As a student working part-time, learning to organize your schedule is an important skill. You may want to develop a daily schedule to help balance your time for work, study, and recreation. This is very important. Providing time for rest and relaxation will help make you more productive when you study and work.

You can balance your schedule by making a list of all the important tasks you must do each day. Then you can arrange your list in order of priority. A **priority** is the first ranking in a "to do" list. When items are ranked by priority, they are listed by importance from first to last.

A list of things to do helps you decide which tasks are most important and which must be done ahead of others. Because both school and work are important to you in this program, tasks for both should be done well and on time. Getting organized helps you use time wisely each day.

Improve Reading Skills

The skill that is basic to all studying and schoolwork is reading. The better you read, the more effective studying will be and the more you will learn. Some readers may take more time to read and complete their assignments. However, a person's reading skills can be improved. The more a person reads, the easier and faster reading becomes. A way to improve your reading skills is by setting aside more time for studying and reading. You may also want to ask your teachers or counselor if you could join a reading improvement program at school.

To understand the written material better, think about what you are reading before you begin. Observe the chapter title, subheadings, photos, and charts. What are the main ideas the writer is trying to express? When you know the main ideas, reading becomes easier.

Do not just focus on single words. Read sentences and paragraphs to understand the details of an idea. It takes many words together to express a thought, idea, or fact. Read the assignment more than once, and reread sections you do not understand. The first reading will help you understand the main idea. Additional readings will help you understand details.

Develop Participation Skills

Pay close attention to the teachers in all your classes, even in the classes you dislike. Be a good listener. Focus on the teacher or speaker and think about what is being said. Also, be sure to sit where you can see and hear well.

If you do your assignments regularly, it is easier to make contributions during class. State facts as you know them. Ask questions about ideas or concepts that you do not completely understand. Even lessons that seem uninteresting take on new meaning when you get involved in the discussion and participate in class.

Take Notes

You can improve your learning skills by taking notes during or after reading an assignment. Summarize information to help you understand the text. When you **summarize**, you write down the main ideas of an assignment to express key thoughts. To summarize, go back to each page, section, or paragraph, and write down the main ideas in a study notebook. This process helps you remember what you have read. It also helps you review the information for a test.

When taking notes, organize the information by chapter or date, whichever is best for you. Write the notes in your own words, and be brief. Do not try to copy the idea word for word from the book.

You may want to consider using a computer to take notes. Keyed notes are more legible and easier to edit. You will find it easy to search for specific terms or assignments. A laptop or tablet will enable you to take notes in class. However, it is important to resist the temptation to play games or search the Internet during learning or study time.

Reading both nonfiction and fiction books helps build your skills as a reader.

OLJ Studio/Shutterstock.com

Practice Good Study Habits

To complete your assignments, you need to study to the best of your ability. Sometimes this means making an extra effort to improve your study skills. Your efforts will reap benefits now and in the future. You can use your attitudes, skills, and knowledge to complete your education and finish school. For most people, learning to study is not difficult. The key to success starts with improving your study habits. To develop good study habits, practice the following study suggestions.

- **Commit to your education.** Having success in school begins with doing your best on every school assignment and each learning activity.
- **Keep a separate notebook for each class.** A spiral notebook can help you organize your notes and assignments.

- **Make sure you clearly understand the assignment.** When you do not understand what to do, ask the teacher.
- **Complete your class assignments every day.** Completing assignments is especially important during the classroom portion of your experience.
- **Set aside a time and place to study.** If possible, study at the same time every day, and make sure the atmosphere is appropriate for the way you learn best.
- **When it is time to study, begin immediately.** Go to your study place with an attitude that studying is the only thing you want to accomplish.
- **Study in small segments of time.** Two separate 30-minute study periods may be better for you than an hour-long study period.
- **Do the more difficult assignments first.** Studying only the easy subjects may leave little time for harder assignments.
- **Use your time wisely.** Effective use of time will give you more time for yourself and the activities you particularly enjoy doing.
- **Use your computer.** Using your computer is a great way to take notes as well as improve your writing skills; for example, spreadsheets can help you organize and prioritize your assignments.

Your teacher will give you assignments related to your job experiences and personal life. By completing these assignments, you will gain knowledge and skills that will help you succeed in both school and work. You will also find that the more success you have the more you will enjoy school.

Taking part in a study group can be an effective way to study for big tests.

Checkpoint 2.3

1. What can you do to help balance your time for work, study, and recreation?

2. Can you improve your reading skills? If so, explain how?

3. What are some ways you can improve your class participation skills?

4. Why is it important to summarize information?

5. List four ways a student can develop good study habits.

Build Your Vocabulary

As you progress through this text, develop a personal glossary of career-related terms and add it to your portfolio. This will help build your vocabulary and prepare you for your career of choice. Write a definition for each of the following terms, and add it to your personal career glossary.

priority
summarize

Chapter Summary

Section 2.1 Work-Based Learning Programs

- Work-based learning programs help students build skills through on-the-job training. These school programs are designed to prepare students for work.
- Participation in a work-based experience offers a variety of benefits. Students are able to learn important skills on the job.

Section 2.2 Work-Based Learning

- On-the-job training takes place at the assigned training station. This is the worksite or location of the employer.
- A Social Security card is required for work. A Social Security number is needed for employment and income tax purposes.
- The obligations of each party involved in a work-based program are explained in a training agreement. A training agreement outlines the purposes of the work-based program.
- With a training plan, the student worker is able to evaluate his or her progress. A training plan helps the student-worker and employer set work-related goals.
- Labor laws establish state and federal regulations. These laws ensure the safety and fair treatment of employees.

Section 2.3 Importance of Study

- As you move into the future, you will continue to use skills in the areas of reading, organization, and participation. Study skills developed in the classroom are also used daily in the workplace.
- Practicing good study habits is essential. Good study habits lead to success in the classroom and beyond.

Check Your Career IQ

Now that you have finished the chapter, see what you learned about careers by taking the chapter posttest. The test can be accessed on the mobile site by using a smartphone or on the G-W Learning companion website.

www.m.g-wlearning.com
www.g-wlearning.com

Review Your Knowledge

1. Briefly explain how a work-based learning program is organized.
2. Compare and contrast a cooperative education program and an internship.
3. Explain how employers benefit from work-based learning programs.
4. What is the purpose of a work permit?
5. What is the purpose of a training agreement?
6. Why is a training station report necessary in a work-based program?
7. What is the Fair Labor Standards Act (FLSA)? When was it passed?
8. Explain the function of the Equal Employment Opportunity Commission (EEOC).
9. What two things can you do each day to help balance your schedule?
10. List three skills you can develop to help you study and learn.

Apply Your Knowledge

1. Identify at least six instances where you may be required to provide your Social Security number. Use the Internet and personal interviews to answer the following questions for each instance. Why is my number needed? How will my number be used? What happens if I refuse? What law requires me to give my number?
2. Take a close look at the training agreement related to a work-based learning experience at your school. Make a list of the responsibilities of the student as outlined in the agreement. Rank the responsibilities in their order of importance. Which responsibility do you consider most important? Why?
3. Research the work conditions and labor practices that were common before the Fair Labor Standards Act was passed. Write a paper to report your findings. Document your sources.
4. Write a half-page summary explaining why a student should consider enrolling in a work-based learning program. Explain what he or she might expect to gain from the experience.
5. Determine the current federal minimum wage and when the rate was last changed. Based on a 40-hour workweek, what would be the annual salary before taxes for a person making the minimum wage?
6. New job responsibilities added to your school and leisure activities will place new demands on your time. Develop a two-column spreadsheet for each day of the week to help you allocate your time wisely. Record the times of day in one column and scheduled activities in the other. Keep a detailed daily journal for your first week of work. Afterward, consider if changes are needed. In a brief report to the class, explain what you learned through this exercise.
7. Gather information on the history of OSHA from their website. Develop an outline of the points that you learned. Give an oral report on your findings to the class using a presentation software program.

8. Use a software program to diagram a comparison of the two types of work-based learning programs described in this chapter: cooperative education versus an internship. Use the diagram to show commonalities shared by both programs as well as characteristics unique to each.

9. Do an Internet search to identify different types of work-based learning programs offered to high school students throughout the United States. Write a brief description of each program and prepare a spreadsheet or chart to summarize your findings. How do these programs compare to the one at your school?

10. Imagine you are a student in a work-based learning program. Consider the activities and responsibilities you have daily. Next, create a schedule for the week, including time slots for school, work, homework, extracurricular activities, family time, and any other activities that are important to you. Share your schedule with your class. Discuss which activities take up the most time during your week and the least time? List ways to make your schedule more manageable.

Teamwork

 Working with a small group of classmates, interview a former student from your school who participated in a work-based learning program. The person you interview can be someone you know or a person whose name is provided to you by the school-to-work coordinator. Create a list of questions to ask before the interview. Determine how the former student's work experience helped him or her develop the knowledge and skills needed in the workforce. Show your findings in a chart and briefly report them to the class.

G-W Learning Mobile Site

 Visit the G-W Learning mobile site to complete the chapter pretest and posttest and to practice vocabulary using e-flash cards. If you do not have a smartphone, visit the G-W Learning companion website to access these features.
G-W Learning mobile site: www.m.g-wlearning.com
G-W Learning companion website: www.g-wlearning.com

Common Core

College and Career Readiness

Speaking. Working in small groups, develop a list of rules that you would like to have in your classroom and your reasoning for each one. Develop a presentation in which you attempt to persuade your classmates to adopt your regulations. Then, develop a separate presentation in which you attempt to persuade your teacher, acting as a member of the school board, to adopt your regulations. How will you alter your presentations for the two different audiences?

Listening. Research the positives and negatives of taking part in work-based learning. Using the Internet, find video footage that discusses work-based learning. Compare and contrast the speakers' information, points of view, and opinions. How are they similar and different? Using the information presented, create a list of positives and negatives that you might encounter when taking part in a work-based learning program.

Apply Your Technology Skills

Access the G-W Learning companion website for this text at www.g-wlearning.com. Download the data file for this chapter. Follow the instructions to complete activities to practice what you have learned in this chapter.

Data File 2–1—**Managing Your Time**

College and Career Readiness Portfolio

College and Career Readiness

A portfolio can contain different items, depending on the purpose for the portfolio. The same or similar items could be included in a portfolio that you use in applying to a college or for a job. For example, you could include school transcripts, diplomas, and awards. If you are applying for a community service position, you may want to include a variety of items. For example, you might want to include letters from teachers or youth group leaders explaining how you are qualified for a position.

A checklist can be helpful as you complete work on your portfolio. Do research and then create your own checklist.

1. Search the Internet for articles that discuss items to include in a portfolio.
2. Create a checklist to use as an ongoing reference as you create your portfolio. Note items that will be helpful when applying for a job, to a college, or for a community service position.

Chapter 3

What Your Employer Expects

Section 3.1
Being an Effective Employee

Section 2.2
Behaving in an Ethical Manner

College and Career Readiness

Reading Prep. Before reading the chapter, skim the photos and their captions. As you are reading, determine how these concepts contribute to the ideas presented in the text.

Introduction

Your employer will make a major investment in time and money to help you become an effective employee. As a result, he or she will have certain expectations of you. Many of these expectations will not be unique to your employer. All employers appreciate good work habits, honesty, willingness to learn new skills, and the ability to get along well with others.

As soon after you are hired as possible, determine what level of performance your employer expects. Those who are successful and advance in their careers continually look to exceed their own and their employer's expectations.

Check Your Career IQ

Before you begin the chapter, see what you already know about careers by taking the chapter pretest. Use the related QR code to view the pretest on the mobile site. If you do not have a smartphone, visit the G-W Learning companion website to access the pretest.

www.m.g-wlearning.com
www.g-wlearning.com

G-W Mobile

Career Snapshot
Web Page Designer

Arts, A/V Technology & Communications

What Does a Web Page Designer Do?

Web page designers are responsible for creating and maintaining a client's website. They use a variety of software and programming languages to create web pages. They must:
- communicate effectively with the client to determine the site's users, the information that will be contained on the site, and how the site will be displayed; and
- have a strong background in graphic design in addition to computer skills.

What Is It Like to Work as a Web Page Designer?

Web page designers spend long hours at the computer and often work under tight deadlines. They frequently meet with clients in creating and maintaining web pages. They often spend time researching and learning new and emerging web technologies.

What Education and Skills Are Needed to Be a Web Page Designer?

- associate or bachelor degree or certification in web page design
- willingness to continually update technologic skills
- creativity and attention to detail
- strong analytical and problem-solving skills

AngelaWay/Shutterstock.com

3.1 | Being an Effective Employee

Terms

attitude
self-esteem
dependability
punctuality
individual responsibility
initiative
self-management skill
sociability
supervisor
courteous

Objectives

After completing this section, you will be able to:

- **Explain** the importance of positive personal qualities in an employee.
- **Describe** how a good employee works as part of a team.

Personal Qualities Needed on the Job

As an employee, there are certain guidelines your employer will expect you to follow. Your employer will expect you to have a positive attitude, be dependable, attend work regularly, be on time for work, and perform well on the job. Your company or business will also expect you to be honest, show initiative, be loyal, and be cooperative. You are expected to be courteous and well-groomed. Your ability to meet these expectations will depend partly on your health and fitness.

You have many responsibilities to meet as an employee. When you work for someone else, you will need to follow his or her rules. Employers expect the people they hire to use their attitudes, skills, and knowledge to help the business operate and make a profit. Your employer will expect you to do the same and to work to the best of your ability.

Positive Attitude

Your attitude will play a big part in your success on the job. An **attitude** is an outlook on life. It reflects how you feel and think about other people and situations.

What types of employee and employer attitudes have you observed on the job? If people have positive attitudes, they usually get along well with other people and enjoy sharing ideas. They tend to be friendly, cheerful, and treat others with respect. People with negative attitudes do not get along well with other people. They may complain, argue, or get angry easily. Some are unhappy and withdraw from others.

A positive attitude is beneficial to your employer and to you. Your employer expects you to have a good attitude while you are working. When you take a positive approach to your work, you tend to be more productive. Your work performance improves. This makes you a more valuable employee and helps you get along well with other people.

How you feel about yourself
is projected in your attitude.

David Gilder/Shutterstock.com

To a great extent, your self-esteem determines your attitude. **Self-esteem** is having confidence and satisfaction in yourself. It is a measure of how you see yourself. People who think they will fail have low self-esteem. People who think they will succeed have a positive outlook on life and high self-esteem.

Dependability

Dependability is one of the most important characteristics of a good worker. **Dependability** demonstrates a person's ability to be reliable and trustworthy. Being dependable means someone can count on you to do something. Going to work each day and being on time are signs that you are dependable. However, being dependable is much more than that. Others know they can rely on a dependable

Go Green

It is estimated that the United States uses more than 25 percent of the world's petroleum. Automobiles are a major source of this usage, and they add a great deal of pollution to the atmosphere. Car pooling, riding the bus, and driving less can greatly reduce this consumption. An even better approach is riding a bike or walking. Both will have the added benefit of improving your physical fitness.

person to do what he or she said would be done. Dependable people keep their word, are honest, and carry their share of the load. Being dependable also means being reliable. A reliable person does not need to be watched closely because he or she always does what is expected. The important jobs in a company go to dependable workers.

A dependable person can be counted on to do the right thing every day. We all have days when we are tired or do not feel well. There are times when other workers' comments or actions may be very irritating. On days like these, it is tempting to do less than your best. However, a dependable person can be counted on to put his or her feelings aside and perform with the same energy and good humor as they would on their best day.

Attendance

Both the employer and the school will expect you to be at work every working day. When a person is absent, it causes extra work for others. Poor attendance also reduces the effectiveness of the work experience.

Because absenteeism is a major concern of employers and teachers, many schools require students and parents to read and sign an absenteeism policy. This type of policy stresses the importance of regular attendance at school and at work. By signing the policy, students are saying they will attend school, work regularly, and notify their employer and coordinator if they must be absent. Violating this policy may cause the student to be dismissed from work as well as from the work-based learning program.

Students with good attendance records avoid asking for time off from work to do personal errands. Scheduling doctor appointments, car repairs, and other personal needs outside work hours is best. In case of illness, a death in the family, or an emergency, you should contact your employer and your coordinator to explain your absence from work. This should be done prior to missing work whenever possible.

Be sure to ask your teachers what work you will miss or have missed. Make up assignments promptly. However, completing make-up work does not fully compensate for lost class time. Teacher presentations, learning activities, and discussions are impossible to make up. Ask your employer, too, if there is anything you can do to compensate for the lost hours. It may be that your employer was counting on you to get an important job out on time.

Being on time and showing up to work when scheduled is an important factor in workplace success.

STILLFIX/Shutterstock.com

Punctuality

Punctuality means being on time. Being late may make your employer think you are not interested in your job. Frequent lateness indicates an *I don't care* attitude. Being late is inconsiderate and is not tolerated in the working world. You cannot make up being late one day by going in early the next day. You must be on time every day.

Do not make the mistake of thinking that being a few minutes late will make little difference. It makes a big difference, and you will be noticed. It is your responsibility to be at your job at starting time or earlier, never later. Plan your schedule so you will always be on time. If you take a bus to work and arrive late, you will need to catch an earlier one. If you drive, bicycle, or walk, allow plenty of time for delays caused by bad weather or heavy traffic. In other words, you should make it a policy to be five minutes early, not one minute late. Being late is a bad habit that can be costly to you and the company. Develop the good habit of being prompt.

Some companies require workers to check in and out by punching a time clock or starting a computer. These methods clearly show when employees arrive late or leave early. If you do not follow your work schedule, the company may subtract a percentage of your pay.

Punctuality is a habit that can be developed. School is a good place to start. You should be in your seat and ready to work when the class bell rings each and every day. Once you decide to commit to being on time, you will find that punctuality will be an important part of your daily routine.

Performance

Although you will be learning new skills on the job, your employer will expect you to have some basic attitudes, knowledge, and skills in your area of employment. If you will be employed as an office assistant, you will need to have keyboarding skills. You cannot expect your employer to teach you the basics of a skill you should already possess.

You will be expected to possess **individual responsibility**, which is a willingness to answer for your conduct and decisions. People without individual responsibility try to blame a mistake on others rather than answer for their own failures. Even competent workers make mistakes, but they admit them and work to correct them.

Your employer will also expect you to put forth your best effort while on the job. As a beginner, you probably will not be expected to do as much as an experienced worker. However, you will be expected to have the same work standards. If you are an administrative assistant, you will not be expected to create a spreadsheet, for example, as fast as an employee with five years of experience. You will, however, be expected to complete a letter correctly and accurately. As you gain more experience, you will be expected to increase your speed. Working quickly and efficiently should be one of your goals at work.

Organization

The ability to organize your time and work assignments is another important skill. The difference between average and excellent workers is often not how hard they work, but how well they prioritize assignments. "Work smarter, not harder" is a phrase frequently quoted in business and industry.

Put forth your best effort in all that you do.

Gorilla/Shutterstock.com

Case

Michael Shares a Secret

Michael arrived at work early one morning for his job at a furniture distribution warehouse. When he entered the building, he saw his supervisor, Doug, in his office. The office door was open, so Michael stepped inside to say good morning. It was then that he noticed that Doug was checking out a dating website.

Doug looked startled when Michael entered and quickly shut down the computer. Doug laughed nervously and said that he had reached the site in error as he searched for the website of Love's Furniture Company. Michael said he could see how that could happen and left the office. He felt a little embarrassed since he knew Doug was married.

However, later that morning Michael decided to share what he had seen with a group of coworkers during their morning break. He embellished the story and made it seem like his supervisor was actively searching for a date. He conveniently left out how Doug said he had reached the site in error. All his coworkers had a good laugh. As Michael walked away, he saw Doug standing within earshot.

Critical Thinking

1. How do you think Michael's supervisor felt?
2. How do you think Michael felt when he knew his supervisor had overheard his conversation?
3. What should Michael do next?
4. What should Doug do next?
5. How could Michael have avoided the situation?

Your work assignment may include a variety of tasks. In many cases, you will need to work on several tasks at the same time. You will be expected to learn to determine the order in which the tasks need to be completed. For example, while you are sorting the mail, your supervisor may ask you to run some copies needed for an important meeting. Before you get to the copier, the telephone rings with an urgent request to deliver an important message. How do you decide what needs to be done first?

Many factors can affect your decision. These may include important deadlines, your supervisor's priorities, the importance of the assignments, and the time you have available. It is also important to develop time-management skills. However, if you are uncertain as to what is most important, it is always best to consult your supervisors or mentor.

Initiative

When at work, your supervisor and work-based mentor will tell you what your job is. When one project is complete, you are expected to immediately start working on the next without someone reminding you. This quality is called initiative. **Initiative** means making oneself do what is necessary.

Another term for initiative is self-management. **Self-management skills** are the abilities to manage your own activities to get the job done. Employers want employees with self-management for the obvious reason: they cannot afford employees who work only when reminded. They need independent thinkers who can recognize what needs to be done next.

Looking for new skills to learn on the job is another way to show initiative. Once you have gained some job experience, your employer will expect you to find tasks to do without being told. Use common sense, however, and do not try to do work that you are not qualified to do.

Cooperation

To be effective at your job, it is important for you to get along with your supervisor and coworkers. This is a sign of sociability. **Sociability** means interacting easily with people. On the job, you will need to be sociable with employees, customers, and everyone you meet. Being sociable will make it easier for you to do your job well and get ahead.

To be cooperative, accept your share of the work and perform your job to the best of your ability. Make sure you follow directions carefully. Always ask questions when you do not understand how to do a certain task.

Be friendly, respectful, and considerate of other workers' feelings. A smile and a few minutes of friendly conversation are good ways to promote good working relationships. Also, be enthusiastic about your job. Expressing enthusiasm will help you become a part of the working team.

Being Part of a Team

Many employers consider teamwork to be the key to competing successfully in the workplace. You may be asked to work as a member of a team to meet the demands of your employer. Being a team member of a company work group is similar to playing on a basketball or soccer team. Success is measured in terms of the team's success, not the individual's.

A company will ask you to join its team based on what you can contribute to its success. These characteristics become even more important as you work closely with coworkers. Failure to come to work, for example, not only affects your performance but also that of the team. If you are absent, your coworkers must do their jobs plus yours to keep the team on target.

Every individual has certain strengths and weaknesses. Often the difference between a good team and a championship team is finding the right people to play the right positions. In the workplace, you need to be honest about your strengths and weaknesses. You must be willing to play the position that helps the team most. As a beginning worker, your role may often be one of a support. Play the role effectively, and be someone on whom your team can rely.

A key to working successfully on a team is getting to know and trust your fellow team members. It is also important that your fellow workers be able to trust you. When team members trust each other, they work more effectively. Trust in your coworkers helps when you have problems or make a mistake because you know your team members are there to support you. You feel freer to share your feelings and ideas with others.

Finally, you must be willing to put the team's goals ahead of your personal goals. Ask questions concerning the purpose of the group. Be sure you can state the team's long-term and short-term goals. Understand why the team's goals are important and how they fit in the company's overall plan.

Working productively as part of a team is a highly desirable skill.

Golden Pixels LLC/Shutterstock.com

Ethical Leadership

Leading by Example

"Example is not the main thing in influencing others; it is the only thing."--Albert Schweitzer

Ethical leaders not only help to establish rules, they obey rules already in place. For example, your school may limit computer usage to school activities. If so, it is unethical to use the computer, without permission, for personal means such as playing games, shopping, and other activities that are outside of your assignments. Doing so is unethical and sets a poor example for others to follow.

Working with Your Supervisor

A **supervisor** is the team leader of a work group. He or she has the role of seeing that work is completed. The supervisor is also responsible for the quantity and quality of the product or service your department produces. When one or both is lacking, the supervisor must take the necessary steps to correct the problem. The supervisor may suggest a new way of getting the job done. The supervisor may also ask employees to work faster or change roles within the team.

You need to realize that your supervisor probably has a supervisor to whom he or she must report. Therefore, your performance on the job directly influences your supervisor's job performance. This, in turn, affects the progress of your employer.

At times, you may be assigned tasks that you would rather not do. You may even be asked to do things that are not part of your job description. Very few workers enjoy taking time from their assigned duties to sweep the floor or help clean up after someone else. However, these are jobs that must be completed, and you may be the only person available to do them. You must remember that you are a beginner. Beginners start with basic tasks and work their way up. Accept the tasks you are given with a pleasant attitude, and perform them as well as you would any others.

Sometimes you may not mind the tasks you are assigned but dislike the way you are told to do them. Different supervisors have different ways of supervising. You may have the type of supervisor that shouts orders and gives no explanation. These people tend to be impersonal and strictly business-focused. This type of manager is likely to say, "Bob, clean up the storeroom before you leave work today, and make sure you do a good job."

Other types of managers make requests rather than give orders. They usually explain what they want done and why. This type of manager might say, "Bob, there will be an inspection at the plant tomorrow, and everything needs to look as nice and clean as possible. I would like you to be in charge of cleaning the storeroom today. I am sure you will do a good job."

Most of us prefer the second type of manager, but sometimes we get the type that shouts orders. No matter what type of manager you have, work with your supervisor, not against him or her. Try to adapt to his or her style of management. You will find all types of people in the work world. Prepare yourself to get along with them all.

Courtesy

Being **courteous** means showing concern for other people and being mannerly with them. Courtesy can help you get along with your supervisor, coworkers, and customers. Showing respect for your employer is a form of courtesy. Being polite and considerate to your coworkers is another form of courtesy. Being polite instead of rude will also make your job more pleasant. Figure 3-1 gives examples of courteous and professional employee behavior versus discourteous or unprofessional behavior when dealing with a customer.

Personal Appearance

In many jobs, a worker's personal appearance has a great deal to do with his or her success. Your appearance is a reflection of you. While on the job, you should try to look your best. A neat, clean appearance starts with good grooming. Clean, neatly combed hair, clean hands, and trimmed nails show cleanliness.

Your clothes are also important to your personal appearance. Wearing clean, neat clothes that are appropriate for your job shows that you take pride in yourself. Before you go to work, think about your appearance. How do you look to your employer, coworkers, or customers?

It is important to avoid extremes in your appearance. Multiple skin piercings and tattoos, for example, may impress your friends but could turn off customers and fellow workers. Some employers may not hire you if they feel your appearance could cause a distraction in the workplace.

Good Health and Fitness

Your employer expects you to be alert when you arrive on the job and remain so for the entire workday, no matter how long or short the workday may be. Your alertness and job performance will depend on your health and fitness. To stay healthy and physically fit, you need to follow these basic guidelines.

- Eat well-balanced, nutritious meals.
- Get adequate sleep and rest.
- Stay physically active and exercise regularly.

Looking and feeling your best is nearly impossible if you get five hours of sleep nightly, never exercise, skip breakfasts, and have soda and chips for lunch.

The customer...	Courteous and Professional	Discourteous or Unprofessional
	The employee...	The employee...
asks a question the employee does not know the answer to.	says, "I will find out."	says, "I don't know."
behaves rudely to the employee.	remains courteous and businesslike.	is rude in return, or refuses to deal with the customer.
disagrees with information provided.	tries to defuse the situation while remaining courteous.	argues with the customer.
asks that the employee take an additional step.	follows through with the promise.	does not follow through because he or she will probably never see that person again.
is waiting.	tries not to keep the customer waiting and acknowledges the wait when the customer is next.	takes his or her time getting to the customer.
is in front of the employee or on the telephone.	focuses on the current customer.	is distracted by another customer, coworker, or something else going on.
sees an employee doing something incorrectly.	waits until later to point out the problem or brings it to the attention of a supervisor.	corrects the coworker publicly.
does not complain about the service he or she has received.	asks if the customer's needs have been met and if there is anything further the employee can do.	assumes the customer must be satisfied.
is present when a problem arises.	takes responsibility and fixes the problem.	blames the customer, a coworker, or the company's processes for the problem.
complains.	tells the customer that the employee will follow up on the complaint and fix the issue—and does just that.	ignores it.

Figure 3-1.   *Goodheart-Willcox Publisher*
Focusing on the customer in person or on the phone is not only courteous, it is also good business.

In addition to good physical health, you need to stay healthy and fit mentally. You may be in perfect physical health but appear pale and ill if you are unhappy. To keep mentally fit, remember to make time for play as well as work. Set aside time to spend with friends and to participate in new activities. Exercising your brain is just as important as exercising your body.

Eating fruits and vegetables as part of a balanced diet is essential for good health.

Tyler Olson/Shutterstock.com

Checkpoint 3.1

1. List five personal qualities needed on the job.
2. How might your absenteeism affect your coworkers?
3. What should a student worker do if unable to attend work?
4. What can you do to demonstrate cooperation in the workplace?
5. What is the responsibility of a supervisor?

Build Your Vocabulary

As you progress through this text, develop a personal glossary of career-related terms and add it to your portfolio. This will help build your vocabulary and prepare you for your career of choice. Write a definition for each of the following terms, and add it to your personal career glossary.

attitude	initiative
self-esteem	self-management skill
dependability	sociability
punctuality	supervisor
individual responsibility	courteous

3.2 | Behaving in an Ethical Manner

Terms

ethics
moral values
work ethic
integrity
confidential
loyalty
constructive criticism
job evaluation

Objective

After completing this section, you will be able to:

- **Discuss** the importance of ethics in the workplace.
- **Explain** the importance of constructive criticism.

Ethics

A very important personal quality in one's personal life and in the workplace involves ethics. **Ethics** is a guiding set of moral values. Good **moral values** are a code of behavior that is considered acceptable in society. Long-term success for a business is due in a large part to the ethics practiced by its employees. People with ethical behavior use moral values to guide their actions. They do what society considers right and fair.

Closely related to personal ethical behavior is a person's work ethic. **Work ethic** is how you feel about your job and how much effort you put into it. People with a strong work ethic view their work as a vital part of their lives. They arrive at work early, take pride in their work, and always do their very best. How dedicated a person is to a job reflects the strength of his or her work ethic.

Unethical behavior demonstrates a poor work ethic. Lying, cheating, and stealing are clear examples of unethical behavior in the workplace, but some examples are not so obvious. Consider the employee who uses the company phone to make personal phone calls. This is unethical in two ways. The employee is wasting the company's money on a non-business call and using work time for personal matters instead of doing the job.

Computers provide another tempting source for unethical behavior. Most people like to use the computer to search the Internet and play games. However, using the company computer for personal business or entertainment is unethical.

Employers know that workers who disregard moral values will disregard company values, too. Consequently, they look for workers whose behavior reflects moral values. People who firmly follow moral values have integrity. The fact that employers consider this quality necessary for effective workers indicates how highly they value integrity in the workplace. **Integrity** is the quality of firmly following one's moral values.

Using software for which you do not have a license is not only unethical, it is illegal as well.

Juniah Mosen/Shutterstock.com

Behaving ethically is often a step above behaving legally. For example, it may not be against the law for you to speak badly about your boss behind her back, but it is unethical to do so. Ethical behavior involves such qualities as honesty, confidentiality, and loyalty. These personal qualities play a part in shaping a person's work ethic.

Honesty

Your employer expects you to do an honest day's work for an honest day's pay. That means doing the job you are assigned and not wasting time. An employee who loafs on the job is actually stealing time away from his or her employer. Employers cannot afford to pay employees for services not performed.

Being honest on the job also includes not taking your employer's supplies for personal use. If you work in a grocery store, you should not take groceries without paying for them. Likewise, working in an office does not mean you are entitled to take home paper, pens, tape, or other supplies. Companies have been known to go out of business due to the dishonesty of their employees.

Anyone caught stealing company supplies or property from coworkers can expect to be fired. Once a person has a reputation for being dishonest, it is difficult for that person to be hired anywhere else.

Honesty not only involves what you do; it may also involve what you do not do, but should. Knowing that someone is stealing from the company and failing to report it is another form of dishonesty. When you learn that a coworker is doing something illegal or against company policy, you have an obligation to report it to your supervisor. If the activity involves your supervisor, then report the matter to your

Ethics

There are many competitive events that participants may enter as a member of various student organizations. Review the events offered by your organization and the rules and regulations that apply to each activity. The ethics event is a competition in which teams participate to defend an ethical dilemma or topic.

To prepare for the ethics event, complete the following activities.
1. Review the ethics section in this chapter.
2. Read each of the special Ethical Leadership features that appear throughout this book.
3. Put a team together of others also interested in this event.
4. Work collaboratively with your team to review and discuss each Ethical Leadership feature in this text.
5. Use the Internet to find more information about ethics. Print this information for future study material.

program coordinator who will help decide what steps to take. Always keep your program coordinator informed of any unethical behavior you report or observe at work.

Confidentiality

Sometimes employees have the opportunity to hear or see things that should be kept private. Perhaps you will learn of new products the company will make, new employees it will hire, or locations it will close. Such company matters are **confidential**, or private, and should not be shared with those who do not need to know. Discussing these matters with outsiders could harm the company's future and give its competition an unfair advantage.

Just as you keep company matters private, you should also keep personal matters about coworkers private. You would not want someone to reveal private facts about you, and you should never do this to others. Discussing the private matters of others may make you popular with those who spread office gossip, but your reputation with your supervisor will suffer. You will not be viewed as a person who can be trusted for important jobs.

Loyalty

Loyalty means being faithful to your coworkers and to your employer. Workers who are loyal to their employers are proud of their company and the products or services it provides. These workers speak well of their companies inside and outside the workplace. Therefore, you need to always display a positive attitude about your work and your employer.

If you disagree with policies or decisions your employer or supervisor makes, talk with your program coordinator about them. Do not criticize the decision of your supervisor. Most likely your coordinator will be able to help you understand why such policies and decisions were made. He or she can also help you decide how to deal with problem situations.

Accepting Criticism

One more responsibility your supervisor has is giving constructive criticism. **Constructive criticism** is pointing out a weakness to analyze it and bring about improvement. The goal of constructive criticism is not to embarrass an employee, but to help that person do a better job. The term *constructive* indicates that a positive motive prompts this type of criticism. Graciously accepting constructive criticism is a mark of a person who wants to improve.

The only way you will know how to work better is by being told how or shown a better way. For example, being ordered to work faster is not very helpful. Hearing tips on how to gain speed is helpful.

Constructive criticism helps workers improve their skills so they can work more efficiently. This, too, is the purpose of a job evaluation. A **job evaluation** is a written review of your work performance by your supervisor. During your work-based learning experience, your supervisor will be asked to evaluate your job performance and provide constructive criticism. A sample student job evaluation form is shown in Figure 3-2. Your supervisor's evaluation should help you and your program coordinator identify your strengths and weaknesses at work.

As an employee, it is your responsibility to accept criticism and improve your performance. Listen to what your supervisor says and follow his or her suggestions.

Student Job Evaluation Form

Student: _____   Training Station: _____

Evaluation Period: _____   Evaluator: _____

Instructions: Please place a check mark on the line preceding the statement that most accurately describes your student-learner's attitude or performance. Evaluate each category without regard to the student's rating in any other category.

1. Cooperation ————————————————————————————————— **Comments** ——
_____ A Gets along well with others; is friendly with others.
_____ B Cooperates willingly; gets along with others.
_____ C Usually gets along with others.
_____ D Does not work well with others.
_____ E Is antagonistic; pulls against rather than works with others.

2. Initiative ————
_____ A Is resourceful; looks for tasks to learn and do.
_____ B Is fairly resourceful; does well by himself/herself.
_____ C Does routine work acceptably.
_____ D Takes very little initiative; requires urging.
_____ E Takes no initiative; has to be instructed repeatedly.

3. Courtesy ————
_____ A Is very courteous and very co
_____ B Is considerate and courteous.
_____ C Usually is polite and considera
_____ D Is not particularly courteous in
_____ E Has been discourteous to the

4. Attitude Toward Constructive Crit
_____ A Accepts criticism and improve
_____ B Accepts criticism and improve
_____ C Accepts criticism and tries to
_____ D Doesn't pay much attention to
_____ E Doesn't profit by criticism; rese

5. Knowledge of Job ————
_____ A Knows job well and shows des
_____ B Understands work; needs little
_____ C Has learned necessary routine
_____ D Pays little attention to learning
_____ E Has not tried to learn.

6. Accuracy of Work ————
_____ A Very seldom makes errors; do
_____ B Makes few errors; is careful, th
_____ C Makes errors; shows average c
_____ D Is frequently inaccurate and ca
_____ E Is extremely careless.

7. Work Accomplished ————
_____ A Is fast and efficient; production
_____ B Works rapidly; output is above
_____ C Works with ordinary speed; wo
_____ D Is slower than average.
_____ E Is very slow; output is unsatisf

8. Work Habits ————————————————————————— **Comments** ——
_____ A Is industrious; concentrates very well.
_____ B Seldom wastes time; is reliable.
_____ C Wastes time occasionally; is usually reliable.
_____ D Frequently wastes time; needs close supervision.
_____ E Habitually wastes time; has to be watched and reminded of work.

9. Adaptability ————
_____ A Learns quickly; is adept at meeting changing conditions.
_____ B Adjusts readily.
_____ C Makes necessary adjustments after considerable instruction.
_____ D Is slow in grasping ideas; has difficulty adapting to new situations.
_____ E Can't adjust to changing situations.

10. Personal Appearance ————
_____ A Is excellent in appearance; always looks neat.
_____ B Is very good in appearance; looks neat most of the time.
_____ C Is passable in appearance; but should make effort to improve.
_____ D Often neglects appearance.
_____ E Is extremely careless in appearance.

11. Punctuality ————
_____ A Never tardy except for unavoidable emergencies.
_____ B Seldom tardy.
_____ C Punctuality could be improved.
_____ D Very often tardy.
_____ E Too frequently tardy.

12. Dependability ————
_____ A Never absent except for an unavoidable emergency.
_____ B Dependable.
_____ C Usually dependable.
_____ D Not regular enough in attendance.
_____ E Too frequently absent.

13. Identify major strengths of this student-learner.

14. Identify any major weakness in the attitude or performance of this student-learner.

15. Is improvement needed in any particular skills related to the student's job?

16. List the dates the student-learner was absent from work during this grading period.

Did the student-learner call in to report his or her absence?

_____ Yes   _____ No

Were the reasons for absence justifiable?

_____ Yes   _____ No

Student Comments _____

_____

Student Signature _____ Date _____

Evaluator's Signature _____ Date _____

Figure 3-2.   *Goodheart-Willcox Publisher*
Many factors are considered as part of a job evaluation.

Checkpoint 3.2

1. What are some examples of unethical behavior in the workplace?
2. Why is loafing on the job a form of dishonesty?
3. Identify personal qualities that play a part in shaping a person's work ethic.
4. What should be done when a student worker finds it difficult to be loyal to the employer because of a disagreement with policies and decisions?
5. What is the goal of constructive criticism?

Build Your Vocabulary

As you progress through this text, develop a personal glossary of career-related terms and add it to your portfolio. This will help build your vocabulary and prepare you for your career of choice. Write a definition for each of the following terms, and add it to your personal career glossary.

ethics
moral values
work ethic
integrity
confidential
loyalty
constructive criticism
job evaluation

Chapter Summary

Section 3.1 Being an Effective Employee

- Meeting your employer's expectations will help you be successful on the job. Your employer expects you to keep a good attitude, attend work regularly, be on time, perform well on the job, and show initiative.
- Teamwork is essential in the workplace. To be successful, a worker must be able to demonstrate teamwork.

Section 3.2 Behaving in an Ethical Manner

- Ethics is a guiding set of moral values. Displaying high ethical standards such as honesty, confidentiality, loyalty, and a strong work ethic is essential.
- Learning to accept criticism will help you continue to improve your job performance. Constructive criticism is provided to help a worker become better.

Check Your Career IQ

Now that you have finished the chapter, see what you learned about careers by taking the chapter posttest. The test can be accessed on the mobile site by using a smartphone or on the G-W Learning companion website.

www.m.g-wlearning.com
www.g-wlearning.com

Review Your Knowledge

1. Describe the behavior of a person who has a positive attitude on the job.
2. How can a worker demonstrate that he or she is dependable?
3. What is an absenteeism policy?
4. What might an employer do when a worker arrives late or leaves early?
5. Explain the difference between initiative and self-management skills.
6. Why do employers seek workers with self-management skills?
7. Why is it important to be honest about your strengths and weaknesses when working with a team?
8. Why is it unethical to make personal phone calls on the job?
9. How should a worker deal with confidential matters regarding an employer and coworkers?
10. Explain how a student worker should respond to constructive criticism.

Apply Your Knowledge

1. Describe a positive example of how an employee might handle a sensitive situation with a customer. Analyze what factors contributed to the outcome. Repeat the activity for a negative example.

2. List actions that might cause a student to be fired from his or her work experience. Discuss in class why each behavior might deserve this action.

3. In two paragraphs, describe your idea of a good supervisor. Use information from the chapter to support your description. Share your answers with classmates in a small group. Identify how your idea of a good supervisor differs from your classmates.

4. Over the next few days, make an effort to practice good attendance and punctuality. For each day, keep a journal to track your attendance. Identify when you are on time and late for school, work, and special activities. At the end of the week, note what you could do in the future to maintain good attendance and punctuality.

5. With a partner, role play one of the following events: finding private, company files; taking initiative to complete a task; or receiving a job evaluation. One student should act as the employee, while the other student acts as the supervisor. Demonstrate how a responsible employee would behave in each case. With your partner, take turns playing each role.

6. Outline your current career plans. Where do you see yourself in five years? What could you do now to help you meet your goals?

7. Write a one-page essay on the importance of having a positive attitude in the workplace. In your essay, be sure to explain the meaning of the word *attitude*. Discuss the benefits of having a positive attitude. Also, discuss effects of having a negative attitude.

8. If you were a supervisor, which personal qualities would you look for in a candidate during an interview? Explain why. Discuss with your classmates.

9. Create a two-column chart. In the first column, list ten traits that you think make a strong leader. Next, identify a businessperson in your community whom you consider to be a strong leader, and interview that person. Ask him or her to list ten traits that make a strong leader. Write those traits in the second column of your chart. Compare your list with that of the person you interviewed. What did you learn from the interview?

10. Review the personal qualities needed on the job. Create a document that lists the personality traits you feel you already have and those that you need to develop in the next two years. How do you plan to develop them?

Teamwork

Together with your team, prepare a short video on personal qualities needed for success on the job. Demonstrate both good and bad examples. Discuss why each is important. Also, address how developing skills and good habits now will affect your career later in life. Share your video with the class.

G-W Learning Mobile Site

Visit the G-W Learning mobile site to complete the chapter pretest and posttest and to practice vocabulary using e-flash cards. If you do not have a smartphone, visit the G-W Learning companion website to access these features.
G-W Learning mobile site: www.m.g-wlearning.com
G-W Learning companion website: www.g-wlearning.com

Common Core

College and Career Readiness

Reading. Read a magazine, newspaper, or online article about a recent unethical work situation. Determine the central issues and conclusions of the article. Provide an accurate summary of the article, making sure to incorporate *who, what, when*, and *how* the unethical situation happened.

Writing. Go to the Bureau of Labor Statistics (BLS) website. What kinds of data does the BLS gather on the labor market in the United States and why? Write an informative report consisting of several paragraphs to describe your findings.

Apply Your Technology Skills

Access the G-W Learning companion website for this text at www.g-wlearning.com. Download the data file for this chapter. Follow the instructions to complete activities to practice what you have learned in this chapter.

Data File 3–1—Evaluating a Case Study

College and Career Readiness Portfolio

College and Career Readiness

Before you begin collecting information for your portfolio, you should write an objective related to this task. An objective should be a complete sentence or two that states what you want to accomplish. The language should be clear and specific. The objective should contain enough details so that you can easily judge when the objective has been accomplished.

Consider this objective: "I will try to get better grades." Such an objective is too general. A better, more detailed objective might read: "I will work with a tutor and spend at least three hours per week on math homework until my math grade has improved to a B." Creating a clear objective is a good starting point for beginning work on your portfolio.

1. Do research on the Internet to find articles about writing objectives. Also, look for articles that contain sample objectives for creating a portfolio.
2. Write an objective for creating a portfolio that will be used in applying for a job or to a college. Include statements for both a print portfolio and an e-portfolio.

Unit 2 The Job Hunt

Lifespan Plan

Selecting a Career

Having a lot of choices can be a good thing or a not so good thing. Too many choices may make it difficult to choose or even understand the differences between the choices. You may feel overwhelmed by the array of career choices available to you. You might feel like you would prefer if someone chose a career for you or that it would be easier to pursue the same path on which you see others travelling. However, only you can find the career that is right for you because you know yourself best. Find the place where your interests and skills intersect with the features of a specific career, and you will know in what direction you should go.

Activities

1. Take a close look at the Career Clusters Handbook that appears at the back of this text. It contains a description of each of the 16 career clusters and a partial list of possible occupations within each cluster.
2. From that list, select a career in which you are interested. Forecast a job profile 10 years from now by using information in the *Occupational Outlook Handbook* (located on the Bureau of Labor statistics website at www.bls.gov). Include information about how economic, technological, and societal trends may impact your career.
3. Save your job profile according to your instructor's specifications.

Unit Overview

In Unit 2, you will explore how to use networking and other strategies to find job openings as well as how to put your best foot forward when applying for a job. If your application materials get you noticed, the next step will be the interview. This is the time to convince a potential employer that you are the right person for the job. In addition to the interview, an employer may require applicants to take preemployment tests. These tests are used to determine whether or not an applicant is offered the position. After working through this unit, you will be better prepared for a successful job hunt.

Chapter 4 Finding and Applying for Jobs
Chapter 5 Taking Preemployment Tests
Chapter 6 Interviewing for Jobs

Picture Success

Luke Christie
DECA

©Luke Christie

A Career and Technical Student Organization (CTSO) can have a positive impact on its members and sponsors. Read about Luke's experience with DECA in his own words.

"For more than four years, I have represented the Muscular Dystrophy Association at fundraising events and sponsor conferences as its National Youth Chairman, a role amounting to more than just a title. My position is one of an active 'junior executive.'

I work one-on-one with sponsors, helping conceptualize and launch fundraising campaigns, awareness initiatives, and professional communication materials. Through the instruction I received in technical education classes, I developed a set of word processing and basic desktop publishing skills that I utilize daily.

Attending DECA conferences helped me develop an understanding of how the business world works. This also gave me opportunities to showcase and improve on my public speaking and networking abilities. DECA also helped foster my passion for nonprofit work. The skill set and experience I gained through my career and technical education has enabled me to be a young professional in a field I love."

Finding and Applying for a Job

Section 4.1
Searching for a Job

Section 4.2
Applying for a Job

College and Career Readiness

Reading Prep. As you read this chapter, determine the point of view or purpose of the author. What aspects of the text help to establish this purpose or point of view?

Introduction

Once you know what kind of job you want, the exploration can begin. Half the battle of job hunting is finding openings. The other half is getting interviews with employers.

To be successful, have a plan. First, list all the companies where you would like to work. Second, prepare a résumé summarizing your education, work experience, and other qualifications for the position you want. Finally, contact the person in each company who has the responsibility for hiring.

Check Your Career IQ

Before you begin the chapter, see what you already know about careers by taking the chapter pretest. Use the related QR code to view the pretest on the mobile site. If you do not have a smartphone, visit the G-W Learning companion website to access the pretest.

www.m.g-wlearning.com
www.g-wlearning.com

G-W Mobile

Career Snapshot
Tractor-Trailer Truck Driver

Transportation, Distribution & Logistics

What Does a Tractor-Trailer Truck Driver Do?

Tractor-trailer drivers operate trucks with a capacity of at least 26,001 pounds gross vehicle weight. Most are long-haul drivers. Their truck has a cab, which is also called a *tractor*, and a trailer. Tractor-trailer drivers must:
- transport materials over long distances often crossing state lines; and
- follow rules and regulations set by the US Department of Transportation in doing so.

What Is It Like to Work as a Tractor-Trailer Truck Driver?

Many drivers are given a destination and a deadline. They must plan their own routes. In addition to spending long hours alone behind the wheel, they may also assist in loading and unloading their cargo. Long-haul drivers may spend days or even weeks on the road at a time. They often work nights, weekends, and holidays.

What Education and Skills Are Needed to Be a Tractor-Trailer Truck Driver?

- high school diploma or GED
- training at a vocational or technical school to obtain a commercial driver's license (CDL)
- be physically fit
- be at least 21 years of age
- meet state and federal standards
- able to stay focused and concentrate on the task at hand

R Carne/Shutterstock.com

4.1 | Searching for a Job

Terms

networking
résumé
human resources
  department
blind ad
job-search website
identity theft

Objectives

After completing this section, you will be able to:
- **Explain** how to find job openings.
- **Use** the Internet to find job openings.

Finding Leads

Job hunting takes work. Job openings will not wait for you; you must find them. To find available jobs, locate employers who are looking for a worker with your qualifications.

How do you find these employers? You can find them through a variety of sources. Some excellent sources of job leads include friends, relatives, and networking. **Networking** is talking with people and establishing relationships that can lead to more information or business opportunities. Other sources of job leads include school placement services, direct employer contact, want ads, trade and professional journals, as well as state and private employment services. Try using most or all of these sources in your job hunt. The more sources you use, the more job openings you will likely find. Then, you will have a better chance of finding a job you really like instead of taking the first job that becomes available.

Friends and Relatives

Friends and relatives can be excellent sources of job leads. They may know employers who need a person with your skills. They may also know people who do the kind of work that interests you and the places where these job openings exist.

When you mention your job search to friends and relatives, be sure to explain the type of job you want. Also, give them copies of your résumé. A **résumé** is a brief history of a person's education, work experience, and other qualifications for employment. (Résumés are discussed later in this chapter.) The more your friends and relatives know about you, the more they are able to talk about your skills and abilities to potential employers.

You should not be bashful about asking friends and relatives for job leads, but do not expect them to find a job for you. It is your responsibility to check job leads, arrange interviews, and "sell" yourself to a future employer.

Your network of family, friends, and acquaintances may know of an open position that is just right for you.

©Luba V Nel/Shutterstock.com

Involving friends and relatives in your job search does have a downside. If you accept a job as a result of their recommendation, you may be under added pressure to do well. This is especially true if the friend or relative has contacted the employer on your behalf. If you do poorly, it could affect your relationship with the person who recommended you. It could also affect the reputation of the person who made the recommendation. He or she may feel disappointed, and future relationships with these individuals may be strained. On the positive side, getting a job on a friend or relative's recommendation may make you want to work harder to prove that person right to have believed in you.

Networking

Networking can begin long before you look for that first job. Networking involves developing contacts with people who are interested in you and are willing to help your search. These people make up your network. As you develop your network of contacts, you may eventually be in a position to help others. A good network of contacts should benefit all who are involved.

Both social and professional networks can help you find a job. A strong professional network, however, may be more important. This type of network includes people who are in a position to help you make job contacts. You can develop strong networks by taking part in a variety of activities. For example, you will meet local employers serving as guest speakers and judges when you participate in career and technical student organization activities. If you impress these employers, they may offer you a job months or even years after the competition. The more contacts you make and the more you demonstrate your ability to work hard and effectively, the stronger your network will become.

School Placement Services

Many schools have a placement office or a school or vocational counselor to help students find jobs in the community. Students are usually asked to register with the placement office. When a job becomes available, the placement office then contacts qualified students for job interviews.

Your school placement office can be a good source for job leads, but competition is often stiff. Keep in mind that you may be only one of many selected to interview. Investigate and use the many other sources available to you.

Direct Employer Contact

One of the best ways to find job openings is to contact employers directly. Many of the people who use this method of job hunting are successful in finding a job. To help you make a list of possible employers, conduct an Internet search or look through the Yellow Pages in your phone book. Visit your chamber of commerce and public library. Ask your friends and relatives for contacts. Be sure to record the names, addresses, and phone numbers of all employers that may have the job you want. Also, do not overlook the job possibilities where you work now or have worked in the past.

Go Green

The next time your home printer needs ink or toner cartridges, take the empty cartridge to a local office supply and see if they will refill or recycle it. Some retailers give credit toward future purchases for recycled cartridges. These are important ways to decrease the amount of materials that go into landfills while saving you money.

Once you have a list of employers, begin contacting the person in each company who is responsible for hiring. A good place to find this person is the company's human resources department. The **human resources department** handles various responsibilities in an organization related to employment. These include screening potential job candidates, interviewing applicants, filing the necessary employee paperwork, and overseeing company benefits, such as health insurance and paid vacation time. The person responsible for hiring is often the department director or manager. He or she will know the available jobs and the procedure to follow when applying for them.

In companies without a human resources department, the person to contact may be the manager of the specific department or even the president. If you know someone working for the company, ask him or her who to contact. You may also request permission to mention this person's name when inquiring about an opening. It is always helpful to know an employee of the company who can speak positively about you.

When you know who to contact at the organization, write an e-mail or make a phone call to express interest in working there. The interview process may be very formal or informal, depending on the employer. Companies that employ only a few people may invite job seekers to visit and fill out an application form. After a short interview, the job seeker may be hired within an hour. Larger companies and government agencies often require a screening process that usually takes much longer, sometimes weeks or even months.

By looking closely at newspaper want ads, you will be able to see what skills and experience real-world employers require for positions in your area.

©pistolseven/Shutterstock.com

Want Ads

Newspaper advertisements are another source of job leads. These advertisements are listed in newspapers under a section called *classified ads* or *want ads*. You may also find them in the newspaper's online edition. Online editions often have the advantage of allowing you to search by key words. They may also provide a link that will allow you to apply for the position online. Such ads provide much information about the job market, while furnishing job leads. You can learn which types of jobs are most available, what skills are needed for certain jobs, and what salaries are common. This basic information about the job market is helpful to all job seekers.

The best day to find want ads is Sunday. The Sunday edition of newspapers tends to have more ads than papers published any other day. Look through all the jobs listed. Sometimes an interesting job appears under the most unlikely heading. As you read, you may see unfamiliar abbreviations. Figure 4-1 lists the most commonly used abbreviations in want ads and the words they represent.

Circle the ads that match your job interests and abilities. Then, answer them as soon as possible. The longer you wait to apply,

Abbreviations in Want Ads	
Abbreviations	**Words**
appt	appointment
ass't	assistant
avail	available
ben or bene	benefits
co	company
EOE	Equal Opportunity Employer
exc	excellent
exp	experience
hrs	hours
hs grad	high school graduate
med	medical
mfg	manufacturing
morn/aft/eve	morning/afternoon/evening
nego	negotiable
ofc	office
p/t or PT	part-time
pos	position
pref	preferred
ref	references
req	required
sal	salary
temp	temporary
w/	with
wpm	words per minute

Figure 4-1. *Goodheart-Willcox Publisher*
To understand the information in want ads, become familiar with common abbreviations.

Ethical Leadership

Imagination

"Imagination will often carry us to worlds that never were, but without it we go nowhere."— Carl Sagan

Imaginative leaders are creative. They use their imagination in positive ways to inspire and solve problems. However, your imagination can also be used unethically. For example, when writing a résumé you will want to make yourself look as good as possible. However, do not let your imagination take you away from the truth. It would be unethical to state that you coordinated your previous employer's advertising campaigns if you only proofread advertising flyers.

the more likely the jobs will become filled by other applicants. Unfortunately, most job openings are not advertised. The want ads represent only a fraction of the total number of jobs available. Consequently, you should not rely solely on want ads to find a job.

As you job hunt, you may find blind ads. A **blind ad** is a job advertisement that does not include the name of a company or contact person for the position. Instead, you may be asked to respond to a post office box, fax number, or e-mail address. Blind ads are used by employers for many reasons. They may want to avoid the time and expense of responding to a large number of applicants. A company with a poor public image may use blind ads to attract people who would not otherwise apply. In some cases, a company may want to keep the job opening a secret from their current employees. In any case, your chance of receiving a response to a blind ad is very slim. Blind ads are difficult to respond to since you know little about the position or the company. If you do decide to respond, address your cover letter to a specific position title, such as *Human Resources Manager,* and include a copy of your résumé.

Trade and Professional Journals

Many trades and professions publish their own magazines or journals. These journals can be in print or available as an online publication. These publications sometimes include advertisements for job openings.

Most of the ads seek experienced workers. In national publications, the jobs may be located anywhere in the United States or abroad. Journals published by state and local chapters are usually more helpful in providing local job leads.

Trade and professional journals contain up-to-date information about the latest developments and trends in a given field. Reading them will help know your occupational area better and become more informed for job interviews.

Government Employment Services

State employment offices are located in most large cities and towns. These offices are available to help job seekers find job openings within and outside government. To locate your nearest state employment office, go online or look in your local telephone directory under the name of your state. For example, the state employment office in *Chicago* is listed under *Illinois (State of), Employment Service.*

To use this free job service, you may need to fill out an application at a state employment office. Sometimes, an employment counselor will interview you to determine your skills and interests. If a job becomes available for which you qualify, the office will arrange an interview for you. Keep in mind, however, that only a small percentage of job seekers find a job through state employment services. Therefore, register for work at a state office, but use other job sources to find job leads.

The US Department of Labor's Employment and Training Administration sponsors a variety of websites. These are designed to assist workers in career development. The sites include information about specific jobs, such as their education requirements, predicted job-market growth, and salary ranges. Some sites also include tools to help the user assess personal skills and abilities. On the USA Jobs website, you can search for federal jobs at all levels. See Figure 4-2.

Many of the websites may be accessed through CareerOneStop (www.careeronestop.org). These include:

- O*NET Online (www.online.onetcenter.org)
- America's Career InfoNet (www.acinet.org)
- America's Service Locator (www.servicelocator.org)

Figure 4-2.   *USAJobs.gov*
The appearance and search features of job-search sites will vary.

Private Employment Agencies

Private employment agencies are in the business of helping employers locate workers and job seekers locate jobs. To stay in business, agencies must charge fees for their services. They charge either the job seeker or the employer. For most entry-level jobs, the job seeker can expect to pay the fee. For most high-paying professional jobs, the fee is usually paid by the employer. When employment agencies advertise job openings, they usually state "fee paid" if the employer is paying the fee.

If you apply to a private agency, you may be asked to sign a contract concerning the payment of fees. Be sure to read and understand all conditions of any contract before signing it. Make sure you know exactly what you are agreeing to pay if you take a job the agency locates for you.

Before registering with a private agency, ask your school coordinator or counselor if any particular agency is recommended. Some agencies specialize in placing people in certain jobs, such as office, technical, or sales jobs.

Only a small percentage of job hunters find jobs through private agencies, so you should not spend a great deal of time with them. Concentrate your efforts on other job-finding methods.

Using the Internet

Technology is linked to everything people do, including searching for employment. An Internet-based job search may allow you to find job openings that you are unable to locate any other way.

Searching Websites

Job-search websites are sites designed to find job openings posted at a variety of locations. These locations include websites for companies, trade associations, and newspapers. Job-search sites allow users to search for jobs by type, title, and location. For example, you could look for jobs in automotive sales in the Los Angeles area. These sites may also list educational requirements for various careers, allow you to post your résumé, and provide direct links to companies with openings. Four of the more popular websites are Monster.com, LinkUp.com, SimplyHired.com, and Indeed.com. See Figure 4-3. The governmental websites discussed earlier are also good places to search for jobs.

Job Site	Available Search Categories				Includes Career Tools
	Keyword or Skill	**Company**	**Location**	**Category or Industry**	
Monster.com	X	X	X	X	X
LinkUp.com	X		X	X	
Simply Hired	X	X	X	X	X
Indeed	X	X	X	X	X

Figure 4-3.   *Goodheart-Willcox Publisher*
Bring your personal fact sheet with you when filling out applications at a potential employer's location.

Specialized job-search websites are more specific. They return results for jobs by the type of industry, career field, or position. For example, AGcareers.com focuses on careers in the agriculture, food, natural resources, and biotechnology industries. You can find specialized job-search websites by conducting an Internet search for that term.

Social networks, such as Facebook, can also be used in your search. For example, you can receive regular updates on a company if you select the *Like* button on its website or Facebook page.

Figure 4-4.   vichie81/Shutterstock.com
Today, there are more options than ever when searching for a job.

In addition, you can learn about job openings on company websites. There might be a link at the bottom of the home page that says *Careers* or on the *About* page. In addition to employment opportunities, you can find out about the company, its business, and its products and services.

By frequently checking the company's website, for example, you can learn what is new with the company. The information will help you determine if a job with some branch of the company seems right for you. With the new information, you can develop a letter of application that demonstrates your knowledge of the company and be better prepared for an interview. Interviewers expect applicants to take the time to become familiar with their company and be able to ask intelligent questions about it.

Job-search websites are usually free to the person seeking employment, but check for possible costs before using the service. Also, research the credibility of the job search site as well as the company that posted the job before providing personal information. Remember, whatever information you provide is potentially available to everyone on the Internet. Never post your Social Security number or other personal information that could lead to identity theft. **Identity theft** is the illegal use of another's name and personal information to impersonate him or her. *Identity fraud* occurs when such information is used to open credit accounts, withdraw money from bank accounts, or make purchases using stolen credit card numbers.

Social Media

Social media networking sites can be very effective in finding job leads. Twitter and Facebook are examples of free social media tools that can be used to get the word out that you are looking for a job. These tools can also be used as a way of showcasing a special talent or skill of yours. LinkedIn is a social media site for professionals. In addition to the networking opportunities the site provides, job seekers can search and apply for jobs through the site.

If you use social media as part of your job search, make sure your profile on each site is up-to-date. Do not include information you do not want an employer to see. Only include information and photos you are comfortable with anyone viewing.

Using all of the resources available to you, as illustrated by Figure 4-4, increases your chances of finding the best job most quickly.

Checkpoint 4.1

1. What three steps should be taken to be successful in a job hunt?
2. Who in a company should be contacted about a job?
3. What can be learned about the job market by reading want ads?
4. Why might a company use a blind ad?
5. How can the Internet assist in your job search?

Build Your Vocabulary

As you progress through this text, develop a personal glossary of career-related terms and add it to your portfolio. This will help build your vocabulary and prepare you for your career of choice. Write a definition for each of the following terms, and add it to your personal career glossary.

networking

résumé

human resources department

blind ad

job-search website

identity theft

Personal Fact Sheet

You may want to contact a long list of employers. However, before you begin applying for jobs, it is important to record key information about yourself in one place. You can use a personal fact sheet for this purpose. A **personal fact sheet** is a brief written summary of key facts that helps a person write letters of application, prepare job résumés, and fill out application forms. A personal fact sheet is shown in Figure 4-5.

Begin your personal fact sheet with your name, address, and phone number. Do not include your Social Security number. If you should lose or misplace your fact sheet, someone else could use this number to access important personal financial information. However, you will need to memorize your number so you have it available when needed. If you have an e-mail address to use, include it here.

Next, summarize your education. Include the names of your high school and any other school such as college or technical school. List enrollment and graduation dates by month and year. Also record your grade average with a letter such as "A average" or "B average" or with a grade point such as "3.0 on a 4.0 scale." All job application forms do not request all this information, but you will be prepared for those that do.

Next, list all your work experiences. For each employer, write the name, address, telephone number, and employment dates. Be sure to list part-time jobs, such as babysitting, delivering papers, mowing lawns, and volunteer jobs such as helping at a hospital.

Other types of information to record are your skills, honors, activities, hobbies, and interests. Under *Skills*, list what you do well that relates to the jobs you seek. For example, if you apply for administrative assistant jobs and you are a fast, accurate typist, list keyboarding as a skill. Under the heading *Honors and Activities,* list the

Personal Fact Sheet

Name _____

Address _____

Telephone _____

E-mail _____ Date of birth _____

Education	Name	Location	Date Attended	Date Graduated	Grade Average
Junior high school	_____	_____	_____	_____	_____
High school	_____	_____	_____	_____	_____
College	_____	_____	_____	_____	_____
Technical school	_____	_____	_____	_____	_____
Other	_____	_____	_____	_____	_____

Work Experience

Name of employer _____

Address _____
            (street address)   (city)   (state)   (zip)

Telephone _____ Employed from _____ to _____
                                                                (mo./yr.)   (mo./yr.)

Job title _____ Supervisor _____

Starting salary _____ Final salary _____

Job duties _____
_____

Name of employer _____

Address _____
            (street address)   (city)   (state)   (zip)

Telephone _____ Employed from _____ to _____
                                                                (mo./yr.)   (mo./yr.)

Job title _____ Supervisor _____

Starting salary _____ Final salary _____

Job duties _____
_____

Skills _____

Honors and Activities _____
_____

Hobbies and Interests _____
_____

References

Name/Title _____

Address _____

Telephone (daytime) _____ E-mail _____

Name/Title _____

Address _____

Telephone (daytime) _____ E-mail _____

Name/Title _____

Address _____

Telephone (daytime) _____ E-mail _____

Figure 4-5.   *Goodheart-Willcox Publisher*

Having a personal fact sheet can help you fill out job application forms thoroughly and accurately.

school and community organizations in which you have participated. Also, list awards received, club offices held, and other important accomplishments. Under the heading *Hobbies and Interests,* list the activities you enjoy, especially those that relate to your job interests.

You will also need a list of three or four references. A **reference** is a person who knows you well and is willing to discuss your personal and job qualifications with employers. Current and former teachers, employers, and club advisors make good references. Be sure to ask permission before listing someone as a reference. Accurately record each person's name, title, address, and daytime telephone number. Most application forms require this information. If the reference uses an e-mail address, also record it. Both personal and professional references may be listed, but do not use relatives.

Résumés

A résumé summarizes a person's educational background, work experiences, and other qualifications for employment. A résumé is usually sent to a potential employer with a letter of application or given to an employer with a completed application form. Reading a résumé is a quick and easy way for an employer to learn about an applicant.

You will need to write more than one résumé. Each résumé should be tailored to fit a specific position. Carefully review the information in the description of the job you are seeking, and focus your résumé on the skills required for that position. Include keywords or phrases mentioned in the description in your résumé. Employers often just check résumés during the initial screening process for these words.

A well-prepared résumé can help draw an employer's attention to your qualifications. It can help you get a job interview. It can also help give the employer a starting point for conducting the interview. On the other hand, a poorly written résumé may result in your not even being considered for the job.

Résumé Information

An example of a well-written résumé is shown in Figure 4-6. It includes all the information that is important for an employer to know about the applicant. Your résumé should be concise. One page is best early in your career. Going beyond a single page is not a problem if you have meaningful information to include. However, avoid having just a few lines on the second page. Do not use words such as *I* or *me*. Résumé writing follows trends. Use the Internet and other resources to determine what is current.

At the top of the résumé is the information an employer needs to know first: your name, address, telephone number, and e-mail address. Be sure to include your zip code and telephone area code. You want to make sure the employer can quickly contact you if he or she wants to interview you. Telephone numbers should be identified as home or cell. If you include your cell number, make sure your outgoing message is not one that might be offensive to a prospective employer. You will also want to be alert that an employer may contact you on your cell, and always answer in a professional manner. Do not use an e-mail address that sounds unprofessional. For example, GoofySam@server.net may cause prospective employers to take

JENNIFER S. FITZPATRICK
204 West Pickford Road
Jefferson City, MO 65001
Home: 573-555-1234
Cell: 573-555-4321
E-mail: jfitzpatrick@e-mail.com

OBJECTIVE
To obtain an administrative position as an executive assistant to a senior-level executive in an institution of higher education, private industry, or large government agency.

EXPERIENCE
August, 2009–present
Administrative Assistant to the Director of Education, College of San Mateo, Redwood City, CA
Develop Correspondence
- Screen the director's correspondence and assist with preparation of responses
- Prepare e-mails, memorandums, and letters to ensure accuracy and timely response
- Assist with research, editing, and final preparation of reports

Assist with Staff Management
- Manage the calendars of five staff members and the director
- Write meeting notifications, agendas, and minutes
- Schedule meetings and make special arrangements, such as catering and A/V equipment
- Maintain up-to-date personnel data for staff members
- Supervise two student clerks

June, 2008–August, 2009
Receptionist and Administrative Assistant, Principal's Office, Jefferson High School
- Scheduled appointments for student, faculty, and parents
- Answered telephones, screened, and directed calls
- Greeted visitors, faculty, and students and provided assistance as needed
- Prepared letters and documents
- Scheduled appointments and maintained the calendars of the principal and vice principals

EDUCATION
Associate Degree, June, 2008, Essex Community College, Baltimore, MD
Major: Office Administration

SPECIAL SKILLS
Computer: Microsoft Office Suite, Adobe InDesign, HTML
General: Excellent speaking and written-communication skills, highly organized, and able to prioritize organizing and planning of multiple projects.

Figure 4-6.   *Goodheart-Willcox Publisher*
A well-written résumé impresses potential emplyers and encourages them to learn more about you.

you less seriously. An e-mail address containing your last name is preferred.

Experiment first to develop a résumé that will work best for you. You may want to use résumé-writing software. There are excellent programs that will help you organize and format your résumé, giving it a professional appearance.

Use keywords to call a prospective employer's attention to skills and experience. Keywords are particularly important in electronic résumés because employers may perform a computer search for these terms. They may only look at résumés that contain them.

Beneath the block of contact information, the résumé is organized into sections using headings. This makes it easy to read. You may want to have the same headings used in Figure 4-6 or something similar when preparing your own résumé. The order in which you list the headings may also vary. If you think your work experience will be more important to your employer than your education, list work experiences before education. The headings most often used in résumés are described as follows.

Job Objective

The first heading on a résumé is usually *Job Objective*. Sometimes this heading is called *Objective, Career Goal,* or *Career Objective*. The purpose of stating a job objective is to give the employer some idea of the type of job you seek. This is the most important part of your résumé. It is the first thing the employer reads. He or she may not read any further if the job objective is poorly written or does not match the job opening.

When composing your résumé, consider writing a more general job objective. Sometimes it is better to list the area in which you want to work instead of a specific job. For example, suppose you want to be a company sales representative. However, you would be interested in other jobs in sales. Therefore, it might be best to state your job objective as *a challenging position in sales* instead of *a position as a sales representative*. This makes your job objective flexible enough to encourage employers to consider you for related jobs instead of one specific job.

The job objective should be customized to align with the position for which you are applying. For example, if you are applying for jobs as an office assistant and an airline reservations assistant, you will need to write a different job objective for each job and, therefore, create separate résumés.

Case

Roberta Applies for a Job

Roberta stopped at Roger's Dairy on her way home from school to check possible job openings. All parking spaces for visitors were used, so she parked in a space marked "Reserved for David Parks." The security guard asked her to move, but Roberta insisted she wouldn't be gone too long. Not until the guard threatened to have her car towed did Roberta finally leave the reserved parking space.

Roberta entered the building and said to the receptionist, "You don't have any job openings, do you?" The receptionist asked Roberta what type of position she wanted. "It doesn't matter 'cause I can do anything," Roberta said. The receptionist was tempted to say all jobs were filled, but knew the shipping department desperately needed help.

She reluctantly gave Roberta an application and asked her to fill it out in the lobby. Roberta promised to fill it out later and bring it back. The receptionist explained that all applicants had to fill out their applications in her presence. "But I have to meet my boyfriend at the mall at 3:00," Roberta complained. The receptionist quietly replied, "Anyone who wants a job with us must fill out the application here."

As Roberta began filling out the form, she noticed several questions she couldn't answer. She didn't know the address of her former employer or the exact dates she was employed. She could only think of one person to list as a reference. She was in such a hurry to meet her boyfriend that her writing became unreadable and full of mistakes. She scribbled over her errors, wrote corrections in the margins, and used arrows to indicate where the new information belonged. She dropped the pen and application, unsigned, on the receptionist's desk as she raced out the door.

The receptionist looked at the application, took a deep breath, and sighed. Then, she dropped the application in the wastebasket when Roberta's car pulled away.

Critical Thinking

1. Why was the receptionist tempted to tell Roberta there were no openings?
2. What mistakes did Roberta make? What should she have done or said in each case?
3. Why did the receptionist insist the application be filled out immediately in her presence?
4. Why didn't the receptionist give Roberta's application to the human resources manager?

Education

Under *Education,* list the names of all schools attended from high school onward. Primary and junior high schools should not be listed. The last school you attended should appear first on the list. For example, suppose you attended a community college for two years after high school. Your résumé would list the community college first and your high school second. Omit your high school education if you have completed a college program unless there is something you want to call to an employer's attention.

For each school, include the name, location, and dates attended. Note when you graduated (or expect to), the diploma or degree you earned (or will earn), and what program you studied. Also, mention any skills acquired, such as *keyboarding* or *carpentry.* If you received good grades, you may want to mention your grade point average.

Work Experience

In this section, list the jobs you held and dates of employment, starting with your most recent job first. Include work-based learning courses, part-time jobs, summer jobs, and other significant work experience. Seeing that you have some work background is very important to employers because it shows that you can assume responsibility.

If you have never held a paying job, list any volunteer work done. Specifically mention work that directly relates to the job you seek. For example, any volunteer babysitting is important to list when looking for a job with a child care center. Even if you have held a job for pay, list volunteer work you have done. This shows you have an interest in your community.

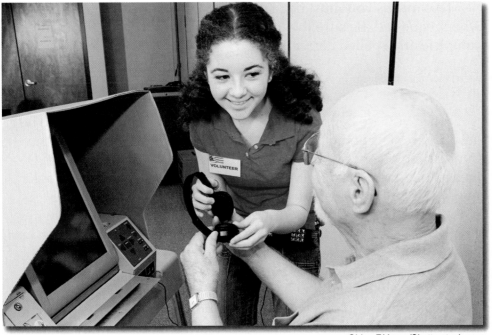

Including your volunteer activities on a résumé will show potential employers that you are a responsible person.

For each job you have held, include the title of the job, the employer's name, and the location. Also, include a brief description of the work you did and any special contributions or accomplishments.

Honors and Activities

Other names for the *Honors and Activities* head are *Honors and Organizations,* or just *Activities* or just *Organizations.* In this section, list the school and community organizations and activities in which you participated. These experiences will help the employer get a better picture of your interests and abilities. Include any offices held and honors received. If your volunteer work is not worth mentioning as work experience, you should list it here.

Personal

Personal information, such as your interest in certain hobbies, is optional and normally not listed in a résumé. By law, employers cannot ask about personal matters. However, if you have a personal qualification that demonstrates a job-related skill or ability, you can list it here.

References

Instead of including details about your references in the résumé, most people simply say that the information is available. They do so by including the following near the bottom of the page: *References available on request.* It is a common practice for employers to express interest in your references only when they are interested in you. Consequently, many believe that information about their references should be kept private and shared with only those who need it. Maintaining a separate list also helps prevent the information from being used dishonestly.

This means you must be prepared to provide the list of references when requested. Be sure the information about your references is complete and spelled correctly.

Preparing a Résumé

When you are happy with the content, the résumé is ready to be keyed. Except as noted earlier, you should be able to include all the information on one sheet of standard white bond paper, 8 1/2 by 11 inches. Use a standard font for text and boldface type for headings. Avoid using unusual or colored fonts that may detract from the presentation. The information should appear neatly organized with evenly spaced margins. Be sure to review it carefully for spelling, punctuation, and grammar errors.

After completing your résumé, set it aside for a day or two. Then read it again. Did you include all the important facts about yourself? Did you organize the information well? Is it easy to read and understand? Ask your coordinator, counselor, or teacher to read it. They may be able to offer some constructive comments.

After the résumé is prepared, you will need to make copies. A printed copy is usually mailed, but may be hand delivered instead. Print your résumé using the highest-quality option supported by the printer. Print on good-quality paper, not standard bulk printer paper. The paper should be white or off-white. Colored and patterned paper should not be used.

If you are mailing your résumé, do not fold it. If it has been folded, it may not feed properly through a scanner. Instead, mail your résumé and cover letter in an envelope large enough to accommodate the unfolded letter.

Many employers expect résumés to be submitted in an electronic format. Do not use any special characters or fonts as they may not be read correctly when transmitted. Likewise, do not use a font in a color other than black in an electronic résumé. Employers may offer instructions for submitting electronic résumés. See Figure 4-7.

If you are responding to a job posting on a job search site, you may be able to upload your résumé directly from the search site. If applying by e-mail, include a cover message addressed to the recipient with the electronic version of the résumé.

A **video résumé** is a short one- to three-minute video presentation used to reinforce the material presented on your résumé. It can be posted on your personal website or on networking sites. Not everyone needs a video résumé, and not all employers will take the time to review one. However, it can be very useful to individuals applying for positions in which communication skills are particularly important.

If you decide to develop a video, make sure to take the time to do it correctly. A poorly created video could end up hurting you more than it helps. Begin by checking the Internet for video résumé tips and examples. Be creative and do not just recite the information included in your résumé. Talk about why you want the job and what skills you have to offer. Stick to content related to employment, not your personal life. Be sure to dress appropriately. Speak clearly and directly to the camera.

When you are finished with your video, share it with your teacher, family, and friends. Get feedback on whether or not the image and content you are presenting truly reflects who you are. If you post your traditional résumé online, you will want to include a link to your video.

JENNIFER S. FITZPATRICK
204 West Pickford Road
Jefferson City, MO 65001
Home: 573-555-1234
Cell: 573-555-4321
E-mail: jfitzpatrick@e-mail.com

OBJECTIVE
To obtain an administrative position as an executive assistant to a senior-level executive in an institution of higher education, private industry, or large government agency.

EXPERIENCE
August, 2009–present
Administrative Assistant to the Director of Education, College of San Mateo, Redwood City, CA
Develop Correspondence
Screen the director's correspondence and assist with preparation of responses
Prepare e-mails, memorandums, and letters to ensure accuracy and timely response
Assist with research, editing, and final preparation of reports
Assist with staff management
Manage the calendars of five staff members and the director
Write meeting notifications, agendas, and minutes
Schedule meetings and make special arrangements, such as catering and A/V equipment
Maintain up-to-date personnel data for staff members
Supervise two student clerks

June, 2008–August, 2009
Receptionist and Administrative Assistant, Principal's Office, Jefferson High School
Scheduled appointments for student, faculty, and parents
Answered telephones, screened, and directed calls
Greeted visitors, faculty, and students and provided assistance as needed
Prepared letters and documents
Scheduled appointments and maintained the calendars of the principal and vice principals

EDUCATION
Associate Degree, June, 2008, Essex Community College, Baltimore, MD
Major: Office Administration

SPECIAL SKILLS
Computer: Microsoft Office Suite, Adobe InDesign, HTML
General: Excellent speaking and written-communication skills, highly organized, and able to prioritize organizing and planning of multiple projects.

Figure 4-7.   *Goodheart-Willcox Publisher*
Keep the design and layout of a résumé that will be uploaded simple to avoid any technical glitches.

Job Portfolio

A **portfolio** is a well-organized collection of materials that provides solid evidence of your qualifications. It can be used during an interview to show examples of your talents and capabilities.

Your portfolio should include a cover sheet, a letter of application, and a copy of your latest résumé. The cover sheet should list the contents of the portfolio in outline form. You may also want to include a list of job-related skills you have mastered. The heart of your portfolio, however, should be a collection of actual samples of your best work specifically related to the job you seek. For example, an excellent paper you wrote for an English language arts class would show that you can effectively organize and express your ideas in writing. It could support your application for a position as an office assistant. A drawing made in drafting class or a part made in machine tool technology class shows the technical skills you have mastered for related occupations. Certificates of completion and awards should also be included.

Do not limit your portfolio to items from school activities. You could include photographs and a written description of a community service project accomplished by you working with others. Cleaning a park would demonstrate your ability to help a group plan and carry out a worthwhile project. These skills are valuable in many different occupations.

You should take special care to make sure your portfolio is well organized and neatly presented. Choose a strategy that works best for your material. For example, if you use photographs and written documents, a three-ring binder is appropriate. Photographs are an excellent way to record items you cannot take to an interview, such as a special dish made in foods class. On the other hand, a large 18- by 24-inch artists' envelope is best for displaying drawings from art or drafting classes. An electronic, or *e-portfolio,* may be right for your needs. Use a method that allows you to easily add and remove materials.

The order of the materials in your portfolio is also important. You may want them organized according to their completion dates, or you may prefer groupings of similar projects or themes. Choose a strategy that shows your work to its best advantage. Temporarily remove items that should be reserved for some other job interview. For example, photos showing cooking skills are perfect for a foodservice job interview, but English papers may not be.

Portfolios are essential for those trying to get a job in a creative industry, such as photography.

©iofoto/Shutterstock.com

It may take months or even years to assemble a good portfolio. Start today by working hard in each class and keeping samples of your best work. Update your portfolio on a regular basis by adding new items and replacing others as your work improves. The College and Career Readiness Portfolio feature at the end of each chapter of this text provides a step-by-step explanation of how to build a portfolio you can use when applying for jobs or admission to training and post-high school education programs.

Developing an Online Presence

Your online presence is what an Internet search reveals about you. By using social networks, blogging, and personal websites you can positively affect the impression prospective employers will have of you.

Social Networks

Social networks can provide an excellent opportunity to share information about your job-related skills and interests. If you already have a personal profile on a social network, like Facebook, take a close look at it before beginning your job search. Remove photos and comments that might give prospective employers a negative impression of you. Most employers will perform an Internet search on potential employees. Therefore, carefully consider what information to include when developing your social networking profiles. Remember that once a comment or photo is shared online, it may be accessed years later. A photograph you thought was cute as a teenager might be very embarrassing to you as an adult. As a rule, you should never post anything on the Internet that might be embarrassing or harmful if read by friends, relatives, or potential employers.

Do not post your home address or telephone number. Using your e-mail address as a method of contact is safer and more private.

Blogging

You may want to start a blog as part of your career search. A weblog, or *blog,* is an online journal that contains comments and reflections. Using Twitter, which limits individual posts to 140 characters, to send messages is a form of blogging. A blog can let people know that you are looking for a job. It also allows you to share information about your job-related skills and interests. In the same way that you would not want to use an unprofessional e-mail address, you would not want to blog using an unprofessional user name, like *TuffENuff* or *QueenBee.*

It is important to remember that once you start a blog, you must keep it up-to-date. Try to make entries on a daily basis. Also, keep blog posts positive. Do not post negative comments about present and former employers and coworkers. Make a special effort to keep your blogs interesting and free of grammatical and spelling errors.

Hiring managers will often review your online presence before offering a position or even an interview.

auremar/Shutterstock.com

Personal Website

You may want to create your own website to display employment-related information. The site can include samples of your work in the form of an *ePortfolio*. It may also include testimonials, references, and links to the websites of schools you have attended or organizations for which you have volunteered or are a member. It is a good idea to keep a personal website related to job searches separate from a personal website you might use for recreational purposes.

Contacting an Employer by Telephone

Your first contact with an employer may be by telephone. You may have a job lead from a friend, relative, newspaper want ad, or the Internet. Or, you may have just a company representative's name and telephone number to contact for more information. A call will help you learn more about the job available and how to apply.

Plan ahead and be prepared when you call the company representative. Choose a quiet room for making the call. Background noise from loud music or people talking can be distracting. Make a list of the questions you want to ask. Also be prepared to briefly list your background and qualifications for the job opening. You may wish to refer to your personal fact sheet.

Place a pencil and paper by the phone so you can take notes. Use good telephone manners when you make the call. In your best conversational voice, introduce yourself and state your purpose for calling. If there is a job opening and you are interested in applying, ask for a personal interview. Be sure to note the correct date, time, and location for the interview. You may also need to ask directions to the interview.

Letter of Application

A **letter of application**, or cover letter, is to get an employer interested in your qualifications so he or she will ask you for an interview. A letter of application is needed in the following situations:

- answering a newspaper ad or posting on a job board;
- mailing a résumé to a prospective employer; and
- responding to an employer's request for an application letter.

A letter of application should be written to the person in the organization who has the ability to hire you. This may be the human resources manager, department manager, or president of the company. Visit the organization's website, and click on the *Contact Us* or *Staff* tab to locate the name of the appropriate individual. If this information is not available on the website, call the company and ask the receptionist for the name and title you need. Ask the receptionist to spell the name so you can write it down correctly. Some smaller companies may not have an employee with the title of human resources director. In that case, ask the receptionist for the name and title of the person to whom a letter of application should be written. All employers have someone in charge of employment.

When writing the letter, keep it short and to the point. You want to attract the employer's attention but not overload him or her with too many facts. Three or four carefully worded paragraphs should be all you need to write a convincing letter of application.

In the opening paragraph, tell why you are writing. Mention the job or type of work you seek. If you know a position is open, explain how you learned this. For example, if you learned about the job through a want ad or one of your teachers, mention this to the employer. Include a brief statement about the company to show you have taken the time to do research.

In the second paragraph, tell why you think you are right for the job. Briefly explain how your qualifications have prepared you for this type of work. If you are enclosing a résumé, mention it here. Encourage the employer to refer to it for further information about your qualifications.

In the last paragraph, ask the employer for an interview and thank the employer for considering your application. Make sure to mention where and when you can be reached by telephone.

The content of a letter of application is very important and so is its appearance. A letter of application should be printed on standard 8 1/2- by 11-inch white bond paper. Use a standard type size and font. A handwritten letter is not recommended. Remember, your letter of application is a business letter that should follow a standard business style. Your letter should include a return address, date, inside address, salutation, body, and complimentary close. A sample letter of application is shown in Figure 4-8.

Jennifer S. Fitzpatrick
204 West Pickford Road
Jefferson City, MO 65001
(Home) 573-555-1234
(Cell) 573-555-4321

June 5, 20--

Ms. Cheryl Lynn Sebastian
Director of Administration
Office of the Secretary of State
100 E. High Street
Jefferson City, MO 65101

Dear Ms. Sebastian:

The position you advertised in the *Missouri State Journal* on March 14 for an executive assistant is exactly the kind of job I am seeking. According to your ad, this position requires good business communication and organization skills. As you can see by my résumé, my educational background and experience working as a receptionist and administrative assistant prepared me for this position.

For the past four years, I worked as the Administrative Assistant to the Director of Education at the College of San Mateo. While working there, I gained experience preparing e-mails, memorandums, and letters, as well as assisting with research, editing, and final preparation of reports. In addition, I assisted with staff scheduling by managing the calendars of five staff members and the director and scheduling meetings for the department. I also had the opportunity to develop my managerial skills by scheduling and supervising two student clerks.

As the enclosed résumé shows, I have an Associate Degree in Office Administration from Essex Community College. While in college, I took many business communication and administration courses. In addition to my education and work experience, I can offer your organization a strong work ethic and the ability to successfully plan and manage multiple projects.

I would like very much to meet you and hope that you will contact me by phone or e-mail to schedule an interview for the position.

Sincerely yours,

Jennifer S. Fitzpatrick

Enclosure

Figure 4-8.   *Goodheart-Willcox Publisher*
A good letter of application attracts attention to the sender's qualifications.

After preparing the letter, read it carefully one more time. Make sure you have complete sentences and that all words are spelled correctly. The spell checker in your software can help you check spelling and grammar, but it may not catch all errors. By preparing a good first letter of application, you can use it to help prepare others.

Job Application Forms

When applying for a job, most employers ask you to fill out an application form. You may be asked to complete it in person or online. An employer uses the application form to screen job applicants. It provides the employer with a uniform way to compare candidate qualifications and employment history. Therefore, the information you give on a form is very important. An application that is incomplete, difficult to read, or smudged with dirt may not make it beyond the first screening. Use a black pen to increase legibility. Do not risk being eliminated from consideration for a job just because your application form is incorrect or sloppy. Figure 4-9 provides an example of a properly completed form.

Completing an Application

Now is the time to rely on the personal fact sheet you prepared earlier in the chapter. With this information, all personal facts are at your fingertips.

If the application asks for references and their phone numbers, there is no need to fumble through a telephone book. You will have the information in front of you. The personal fact sheet will help you fill out application forms accurately and completely. Always remember to carry this sheet and a pen with you when applying for jobs.

When filling out an application form, follow these tips.

- **Read the entire application before you begin writing any information.** Make sure you understand all the questions.
- **Carefully follow the instructions for filling out the form.** If you are asked to print, type, or use black ink, be sure to do so. Be careful not to write in the sections marked *for employer use only.*
- **Complete every question on both sides of the form.** If some questions do not apply to you, draw a dash through the space or write "does not apply," letting the employer know you read the question and did not overlook it.
- **You may wish to omit your Social Security number and write "will provide if hired."** This may help protect your identity if the application is left on someone's desk or disposed of improperly.

APPLICATION FOR EMPLOYMENT

PERSONAL INFORMATION

Date _May 14, 20—_   Social Security Number _Will provide if hired_

Name _Park_ Last   _Mary_ First   _Rachel_ Middle

Present Address _1036 Spring Street_ Street   _Milwaukee,_ City   _WI_ State   _53172_ Zip

Permanent Address _1036 Spring Street_ Street   _Milwaukee,_ City   _WI_ State   _53172_ Zip

Phone No. _(414) 555-3214_

If related to anyone in our employ, state name and department

Referred by _Mr. James Mitchell_ _Career Counselor_

EMPLOYMENT DESIRED

Position _Office Assistant_   Date you can start _June 10, 20—_   Salary desired _Open_

Are you employed now? _yes_   If so may we inquire of your present employer? _yes_

Ever applied to this company before? _no_   Where _____   When _____

EDUCATION

Name and L

Grammar School _Spring Gro_ _Brookfield,_

High School _Washingto_ _Milwaukee,_

College _____

Technical, Business or other School _____

Subject of special study or research work _____

What foreign languages do you fluently speak? _____   Read? _____   Write? _____

U.S. Military or Naval service _____   Rank _____   Present membership in National Guard or Reserves _____

Activities other than religious (civic, athletic, fraternal, etc.) _Office Education Association, Student Council,_ _Washington Marching Band, 4-H Club_

Exclude organizations the name or character of which indicates the race, creed, color or national origin of its members

FORMER EMPLOYERS List employers starting with last one first

Date Month and Year	Name and Address of Employer	Salary	Position	Reason for Leaving
From _9/—_ To _6/—_	_Watkins Insurance Agency_ _1122 Market Street_ _Milwaukee, WI 53177_	_$8.50/Hour_	_Office Assistant_	_Seeking full-time job after graduation_
From _9/—_ To _6/—_	_McDonald's Restaurant_ _1301 Main Street_ _Milwaukee, WI 53177_	_$8.00/Hour_	_Grill Crewperson_	_Summer job_
From To				
From To				

REFERENCES List below at least two persons not related to you whom you have known at least one year

	Name	Address	Job Title	Years Acquainted
1	_Mr. James Mitchell_	_Washington High School_ _3300 W. Glendale Ave._ _Milwaukee, WI 53180_	_Career Counselor_	_3_
2	_Ms. Angelica Ortiz_	_Watkins Insurance Agency_ _1122 Market Street_ _Milwaukee, WI 53177_	_Office Manager_	_1_
3				

I authorize investigation of all statements contained in this application. I understand that misrepresentation or omission of facts called for is cause for dismissal.

Date _May 14, 20—_   Signature _Mary R. Poston_

Figure 4-9.
Application forms must be filled out accurately and neatly.

- **Write "open" or "negotiable" for any question regarding salary requirements.** You do not want to commit yourself to a figure too high or too low.
- **In the section marked** *employment history,* **remember part-time jobs.** Include babysitting and mowing lawns.
- **For each job, there may be a question asking your reason for leaving the job.** Avoid writing any negative comments about yourself or a former employer.
- **Be as neat as possible.** If you must change any information you wrote, neatly draw a line through the wrong words and do not get the form dirty or stained.

As soon as you finish the form, hand it to the correct person. You may also want to offer a copy of your résumé for their files. However, do not expect your résumé to substitute for a completed application form. A résumé is not necessary for getting a job, but a completed application form usually is.

Illegal Questions on Job Applications

When you apply for a job, you have certain legal rights protected by law. These federal laws state what questions employers can and cannot ask on application forms. This prevents discrimination in job hiring related to race, color, religion, national origin, sex, age, and disability.

Legally, you are not required to answer any question unrelated to your ability to do the job. The following questions are not job-focused and, therefore, are illegal: Do you live in an apartment or house? Do you have any serious debts? Do you own a car? Do you have a disability?

A disability can be addressed, however, if it may affect job performance. For example, if you are applying for a sales position, it may be legal to discuss if you have a hearing or speech problem that may affect your job performance.

There are other jobs that require special questions. For example, if you apply for a job delivering flowers, the job description may say, "Must provide transportation." In this case, it is legal to ask if you own a car and have a good driving record. Otherwise, the employer can only ask if you have a dependable way to get to work.

Sometimes employers interpret these laws differently and may innocently ask you a discriminatory question. If you suspect a discriminatory question on a form, write "willing to discuss" or "not clear." During the interview you can ask how the question and job are related. At the same time, emphasize your desire to provide accurate answers to all job-related questions.

Checkpoint 4.2

1. List the headings most often used in résumés.
2. For each job listed under *Work Experience* on a résumé, what information should be included?
3. How does an electronic résumé differ from a print version?
4. If a question on an application form does not apply to you, what should you do?
5. What is the best way to respond to questions about wages or salary expectations on an application?

Build Your Vocabulary

As you progress through this text, develop a personal glossary of career-related terms and add it to your portfolio. This will help build your vocabulary and prepare you for a career as an entrepreneur. Write a definition for each of the following terms, and add it to your personal career glossary.

personal fact sheet
reference
video résumé
portfolio
letter of application

Chapter Summary

Section 4.1 Searching for a Job

- Using a variety of sources can improve your chances of finding a job. The more sources you use, the more likely you are to find a job opening to which you would like to apply.
- The Internet is commonly used when conducting a job search. Many people locate jobs via online sources, including company and job-search websites.

Section 4.2 Applying for a Job

- A personal fact sheet includes personal and work-related information. It can be used to prepare a résumé, letter, or application for employment.
- Résumés summarize a person's work experience, education, and qualifications. A well-prepared résumé includes information the employer needs to know about the applicant.
- To learn more about the employer or job opening, a person may need to contact an employer by telephone. The job seeker should be well prepared prior to calling.
- Job seekers are able to create online profiles using the Internet. Social networks, blogging, and personal websites allow job seekers to display personal and employment-related information.
- Portfolio items show examples of your talent and previous work. It may take years to assemble a good portfolio.
- A job seeker may write a letter of application to inquire about a position. Content and appearance should be considered carefully.
- A completed job application is required by most employers. The job seeker should read the form carefully and fill it out completely.

Check Your Career IQ

Now that you have finished the chapter, see what you learned about careers by taking the chapter posttest. The test can be accessed on the mobile site by using a smartphone or on the G-W Learning companion website.

www.m.g-wlearning.com
www.g-wlearning.com

Review Your Knowledge

1. Why might friends and relatives be excellent sources of job leads?
2. What are some traditional methods used to find jobs?
3. Which office is a good source for job leads at many schools?
4. Why do employers have a human resources department?
5. What might be included in your portfolio?
6. Why should you carefully consider what you post online?
7. List three things you should do before contacting an employer by phone.
8. What is the purpose of a letter of application?
9. What main points should be covered in a letter of application?
10. Recall two questions that you are not required to answer on a job application.

Apply Your Knowledge

1. Visit your school or public library. Inform the librarian of the career area that interests you. Ask to see the related trade or professional journal(s). Note the latest developments or trends in the trade or profession, and check for job ads.
2. Visit the state employment office nearest you. Learn how to register with their employment service. Also learn the procedure for applying and qualifying for state and federal government jobs.
3. Prepare a résumé. Ask a teacher, counselor, mentor, or supervisor to review it and offer suggestions.
4. Prepare a portfolio following the suggestions in this chapter as well as the College and Career Readiness Portfolio activity presented at the end of each chapter. Ask a potential employer to review it with you.
5. Write a sample letter of application for a job you want. Follow the guidelines in the chapter. Save the letter electronically and use it to write future application letters.
6. Collect several different application forms. Display them for classmates to see. Choose one and complete it neatly and correctly.
7. List any extracurricular activities you are involved in at school and in your community. For each activity, note any special talents, abilities, or skills you have gained through your involvement. Evaluate which activities would be best suited to list on your résumé. Share your information with a partner.
8. Using a video camera or smartphone, create a video résumé approximately two minutes long. Reinforce your education, honors, and any work or volunteer experience you have. Be sure to identify the job for which you are applying. Discuss why you would be the best person for the position and point out your job skills. Remember to speak clearly and look directly into the camera.
9. Review want ads in your local newspaper. Note the style and format for these ads. Next, imagine you are a hiring manager for a major business. Create a want ad for an opening in your department. Be sure to include the necessary information. Study the abbreviations in Figure 4-1 and use a few of them to create your ad.

10. Ask a family member or friend to assist you with the following activity. You will act as the job seeker, while he or she acts as the employer. Using a telephone, call "the employer" to inquire about a job opening. Ask questions to learn more about the job and the company. Review the tips provided in this chapter before calling. With your class, discuss what you did well and what you might need to improve. What are the advantages of being able to call instead of visit the office?

Teamwork

Working with two classmates, imagine your group is assigned the task of finding the right person to hire for a job as restaurant assistant. You want a high school graduate who will check in and put away shipments of food and supplies, operate the cash register, and greet customers. What type of information should the right person's résumé contain? Prepare an ideal résumé for the position.

G-W Learning Mobile Site

Visit the G-W Learning mobile site to complete the chapter pretest and posttest and to practice vocabulary using e-flash cards. If you do not have a smartphone, visit the G-W Learning companion website to access these features.
G-W Learning mobile site: www.m.g-wlearning.com
G-W Learning companion website: www.g-wlearning.com

Common Core

College and Career Readiness

CTE Career Ready Practices. You will have a number of options to consider when thinking about your future plans. Approaching the different options available to you in a logical way helps in the decision-making process. One simple way is to create a pros and cons chart. Create such a chart showing the pros and cons of pursuing a career that requires additional schooling after high school. Place all of the good or positive things about it on the left on the "pro" side and all the negative things on the right on the "con" side. Circle the items on your list that you consider the most important when considered rationally. Put a star or asterisk by all those you consider important emotionally. Reflect on the items on the list. Has the list helped you come to a decision? Why or why not?
Writing. Conduct research online or in the library on the history, purpose, and examples of civil service tests. Write a three paragraph essay discussing how the tests help place workers in jobs in the state and federal government. Give examples of different government jobs and discuss the qualifications necessary for each job.

Apply Your Technology Skills

Access the G-W Learning companion website for this text at www.g-wlearning.com. Download the data file for this chapter. Follow the instructions to complete activities to practice what you have learned.

Data File 4–1—Learning More about Résumés

College and Career Readiness Portfolio

College and Career Readiness

As you collect items for your portfolio, you will need a method to keep the items clean, safe, and organized for assembly at the appropriate time. A large manila envelope works well to keep hard copies of your documents, photos, awards, and other items. Three-ring binders with sleeves are another good way to store your information. If you have a box large enough for full-size documents, it will work also. Plan to keep like items together and label the categories. For example, store sample documents that illustrate your writing or computer skills together. Use notes clipped to the documents to identify each item and state why it is included in the portfolio. For example, a note might say, "Newsletter that illustrates desktop publishing skills."

1. Select a method for storing hard copy items you will be collecting for your portfolio. (You will decide where to keep electronic copies in a later activity.)
2. Write a paragraph that describes your plan for storing and labeling the items. Refer to this plan each time you add items to the portfolio.

Chapter 5

Taking Preemployment Tests

Section 5.1
Preemployment
Assessments

Section 5.2
Predicting On-the-Job
Performance

College and Career Readiness

Reading Prep. Before reading this chapter, look at the chapter title. What does this title tell you about what you will be learning? Compare and contrast the information to be presented with information you already know about the subject matter from sources such as videos and online media.

Introduction

Why do employers give tests as part of the employment process? Many employers give preemployment tests to screen, or examine, prospective employees. The results of these tests help a company select the best people for the jobs.

To streamline the screening process, some companies offer preemployment testing online when the job seeker completes the application. Applicants may or may not be given immediate results of their tests. The only indication of passing the test might be the invitation to interview.

Preemployment tests can help *you* as well as the employer. Taking a preemployment test may reinforce your interest in your chosen career. On the other hand, test results may show that you are seeking a job for which you are not suited. You may find more training is needed to meet an employer's requirements. Or, you may learn that your skills and interests are better matched to another career field.

Check Your Career IQ

Before you begin the chapter, see what you already know about careers by taking the chapter pretest. Use the related QR code to view the pretest on the mobile site. If you do not have a smartphone, visit the G-W Learning companion website to access the pretest.

www.m.g-wlearning.com
www.g-wlearning.com

G-W Mobile

Career Snapshot
Heating and Air-Conditioning Technician

Architecture & Construction

What Does a Heating and Air-Conditioning Technician Do?

Heating and air-conditioning technicians install and service heating, ventilation, air-conditioning, and refrigeration (HVACR) systems. They must:
- work on mechanical, electrical, and electronic HVACR components; and
- possess a broad technical understanding to be able to diagnose and correct problems related to these systems.

What Is It Like to Work as a Heating and Air-Conditioning Technician?

Often called *HVACR technicians*, heating and air-conditioning technicians work on a variety of components such as motors, compressors, pumps, fans, ducts, pipes, thermostats, and switches. They use tools including wrenches, pipe cutters and benders, and acetylene torches. Some technicians specialize in either installation or repair.

HVACR technicians are subject to a variety of work-related environmental hazards including burns, electrical shock, and contamination from handling refrigerants. They work both inside and outdoors, in cramped spaces and at great heights.

What Education and Skills Are Needed to Be a Heating and Air-Conditioning Technician?

- high school diploma or GED
- complete a technical school or community college program or a formal apprenticeship
- be licensed by state or local agencies
- have strong math, science, and reading skills

5.1 | Preemployment Assessments

Terms

psychological test
polygraph test
Employee Polygraph
  Protection Act (EPPA)
honesty test
Americans with
  Disabilities Act (ADA)

Objectives

After completing this section, you will be able to:

- **Explain** the purpose of a psychological test when given to a prospective employee.
- **Identify** cases when an employer is permitted to use a polygraph test.
- **Recognize** the difference between a polygraph test and an honesty test.
- **Explain** why an employer might require a medical examination prior to employment.

Psychological Tests

A **psychological test** is a test that examines a person's personality, character, and interests. These tests do not measure a person's knowledge or aptitudes. Instead, they measure factors such as cooperation, assertiveness, adaptability, loyalty, honesty, as well as personal likes and dislikes. Some employers give these tests to determine how well an applicant will adjust to the job and get along with coworkers.

If you are asked to take a psychological test, do not be concerned. There are no *right* or *wrong* answers for these tests; so, you should not feel stressed. Most psychological tests involve written answers, multiple-choice questions, or short essays. A common essay instruction is: "Write a paragraph that describes you." Oral psychological tests are given by a psychologist. The questions may be about you or your opinions on certain issues.

Simply answer the questions as well as you can. The best approach is to be positive and truthful.

Polygraph Tests

A **polygraph test**, also called a *lie-detector test*, is given with a polygraph machine. The machine measures and records the changes in the subject's blood pressure, perspiration, and pulse rate when an examiner asks questions. To conduct a polygraph test, an examiner places an inflated blood-pressure cuff around the subject's arm, a rubber tube around the chest, and small electrodes on one hand. Then, the examiner asks the subject questions.

A specific series of questions are asked in a specific sequence. The questions usually fall into two broad categories: *relevant* and *control*. A relevant question is very specific. For example, "Did you steal from your last employer?" A control question is less precise, such as, "In the last 10 years, have you ever stolen anything?" Examiners say that a person who is lying will usually react more strongly to the relevant questions.

After a polygraph test, the examiner analyzes the graph and decides whether the subject is lying or telling the truth. The machine by itself cannot do this. It only measures levels of stress. The examiner studies the stress levels and determines if the stress was caused by lying or an emotion, such as anger or fear.

The **Employee Polygraph Protection Act (EPPA)** of 1988 prohibits most private employers from using lie-detector tests for preemployment screening or during the course of employment. The EPPA does not apply to federal, state, and local governments.

The law does, however, permit the use of polygraph tests by private employers in certain cases. For example, lie-detector tests may be given to employees suspected of theft, embezzlement, or other activities resulting in economic loss or injury to the employer. The test may also be used in certain firms that deal with security issues, armored cars, or alarms. The polygraph test may also be used by pharmaceutical manufacturers, distributors, and dispensers.

Polygraph tests are subject to strict standards under the law. These standards control the administration of the test and the certification of the examiner. The EPPA strictly limits the disclosure of information obtained during a test. For more information about polygraph tests, contact the Employment Standards Administration's Wage and Hour Division of the US Department of Labor.

Preemployment testing is widely used to narrow a field of job candidates to only those who will likely do the job well.

Lisa F. Young/Shutterstock.com

Role Playing and Interviews

Role playing and interviews are competitive events you might enter with your Career and Technical Student Organization (CTSO). Those who participate in a role-play event will be provided information about a company or situation and given time to practice. A judge or panel of judges will review the presentations.

To prepare for the role-play or interview event, complete the following activities.

1. Read the guidelines provided by your organization. Make certain that you ask any questions about points you do not understand. It is important you follow each specific item that is outlined in the competition rules.

2. Visit the organization's website and look for role-play and interview events that were used in previous years. Many organizations post these tests for students to use as practice for future competitions. Also, look for the evaluation criteria or rubric for the event. This will help you determine what the judge will be looking for in your presentation.

3. Using previous events, write your response to the situation or questions. Time yourself to see if you are within the allotted time frame. Repeat this several times, so that you are comfortable with preparing the presentation.

4. Practice in front of a mirror. Are you comfortable speaking without reading directly from your notes?

5. Ask a friend or teacher to listen to your presentation. Give special attention to your posture and how you present yourself.

6. Concentrate on your tone of voice. Be pleasant and loud enough to hear without shouting.

7. Make eye contact with the listener. Do not stare, but engage the person's attention.

8. After you have made your presentation, ask for constructive feedback.

Honesty Tests

An **honesty test** is a type of test designed to measure a person's honesty in the workplace. Another term for these tests is an *integrity test*. These tests are intended to help employers identify job applicants who are likely to be dishonest employees. They are often used where people handle cash or merchandise. They may also be used where individuals must work with little supervision. However, the results of the test may not always be accurate. The test should be used as a part of the total job-screening process. It should never be used as the sole reason for hiring someone. Unlike polygraph tests, honesty tests can be given in most states. However, some states have laws restricting their use.

Go Green

Water is one of our most important natural resources and the supply is limited. Water conservation also conserves energy and reduces your electric bill. Some very simple steps can help conserve water. For example, turning the water off while you are brushing your teeth saves up to 2.5 gallons per minute. A three-minute shower instead of a bath can save as much as 15 gallons of water.

Two types of questions are commonly asked on honesty tests. There are overt questions, such as "Have you ever stolen anything from an employer?" A second type of question is more subtle. Examples of subtle questions include: "Do you think a person should be arrested for downloading songs from the Internet without paying?" or "Do all people steal at some point in their lives?" These types of questions are often designed in a way that makes it difficult for a person to cheat. More than one question may be included to identify the same type of dishonest behavior. This makes it hard to know the "right answer."

You should not be afraid to take an honesty test. Just answer all questions truthfully.

Medical Examinations

Do not be surprised if you are asked to take a medical or physical examination before you are hired for a job. Some large companies even have their own clinics and doctors. One purpose of a medical exam is to identify health problems that might prevent a person from performing his or her job safely and successfully.

Certain jobs, such as flying passenger airplanes or playing professional sports, require top physical condition. Some hospitals, medical clinics, and restaurants require workers to have medical exams for health reasons. It is also a common practice for workers in management or stress-related jobs to have a complete medical exam prior to employment and periodically thereafter.

Physical Disabilities and the Screening Process

The **Americans with Disabilities Act (ADA)** has caused major changes in the employment of individuals with disabilities. The employment section of the act prohibits discrimination against individuals with disabilities who otherwise are qualified for a given job or position.

The act requires employers to make reasonable accommodations for a person with disabilities who can perform the essential functions of the job. Employers must eliminate all attempts, intentional or otherwise, to screen out individuals with disabilities during the interview process.

Drug Testing

In addition to medical exams, many employers require drug testing as part of the screening process. Drug use in the workplace has become a major concern to employers. Workplace accidents, high absenteeism, reduced productivity, and high health costs are linked to drug use by workers. Since drug use can affect future job performance, applicants who test positive for drugs are usually not hired. Laws governing the use of drug tests vary from state to state.

Drug abusers endanger themselves and coworkers. They have more accidents due to carelessness and poor judgment. Coworkers are endangered when drug users take risks and ignore safety rules. These problems cost employers billions of dollars every year.

To help fight the growing drug problem, many employers have started drug prevention programs for employees. The main purpose of the programs is to provide workers with a safer work environment. These programs usually include some form of drug testing. Employees may be tested periodically without prior notification of the specific time and date of the test. Company policies for employees who test positive may vary, but may include suspension or dismissal.

Drug testing is a controversial issue for both employers and employees. Workers most likely to be tested are those in jobs involving workplace or public safety, such as public transportation workers and police officers. Employees have concerns, too, such as the right to privacy and test accuracy.

Checkpoint 5.1

1. Why do some employers give psychological tests to job applicants?
2. What stress changes in the body do polygraph tests measure?
3. Who determines if a person taking a polygraph test is lying or telling the truth?
4. What types of workplaces most often use honesty tests?
5. What are the two main reasons for giving medical examinations to prospective employees before hiring them?

Build Your Vocabulary

As you progress through this text, develop a personal glossary of career-related terms and add it to your portfolio. This will help build your vocabulary and prepare you for your career of choice. Write a definition for each of the following terms, and add it to your personal career glossary.

psychological test
polygraph test
Employee Polygraph Protection Act (EPPA)
honesty test
Americans with Disabilities Act (ADA)

Skill Tests

A **skill test** is a test used to determine the physical or mental abilities of a job applicant. An employer uses one or more of these tests to determine if an applicant has the skills to do a job. Skill tests may be performance, written, or oral. *Performance tests* check an individual's ability to operate tools and machines. Written and oral tests examine understanding of the practices or facts needed to perform in the workplace.

A word processing test is a good example of a performance test. When a person applies for a job that involves keyboarding, he or she may be asked to prepare a one-page sample or letter. From the sample, the employer will rate the person's speed, accuracy, and the ability to use a given software application. The applicant who keys in material

The test you take to get your driver's license is a type of a skill test.

Lisa F. Young/Shutterstock.com

the fastest with the fewest errors will probably be the person offered the job. A performance test may also be required for CAD operators, welders, truck drivers, machine operators, and instrument technicians.

If you apply for a job as a bank teller, clerk, or cashier, you may be asked to take a math test. A math test is an example of a written test that checks your ability to perform needed work skills. A basic math test examines your ability to add, subtract, multiply, divide, find percentages, and work with fractions.

Clerical skill tests are examples of combined written and performance tests. These tests are often given to applicants seeking employment as office assistants. They are given to measure such abilities as performing simple math operations, copying numbers and names correctly, and placing files in alphabetical order as shown in Figure 5-1.

Do not be afraid to take a skill test. If you have the skills to perform the job for which you are being tested, you will not have problems. If you do poorly on a skills test, it is not the end of the world. Instead, it is an opportunity to find out how you can improve your skills. If you express a sincere interest in the job, the employer may offer to teach you the skills you need.

Whatever you do, never tell an employer you possess skills that you do not have. Eventually, the employer will discover the truth. You could then be fired for being dishonest, not being able to perform the duties of the job, or both.

Filing Speed and Accuracy Tasks

This task measures your ability to quickly and correctly file records alphabetically. Below are two lists of files identified by names—last names followed by first and middle initials. **List A** consists of files to put away. **List B** represents a drawer of files already in alphabetical order. Determine where the **List A** files correctly belong in the file drawer. You will do this by placing the numbers corresponding to the **List A** files in the appropriate spaces in **List B**. For example:

LIST A (To be filed)   LIST B (Already filed)

Lockport, H.A.
Logan, K.L.

Lober, D.F.	Logan, J.G.
(1)	(2)
Lockwood, R.E.	Long, C.F.
( )	( )
Lodge, H.A.	Lopez, J.M.
( )	( )
Loffredo, S.A.	Loren, L.P.
( )	( )

Figure 5-1.   *Mountain Bell*
A filing speed and accuracy test provides an applicant with the opportunity to demonstrate whether he or she is able to perform a job-related task.

Case

Alan and Hal

Alan and Hal recently graduated from different high schools. They don't know each other, but they are alike in many ways. Both studied vocational electronics in high school and had similar work-based learning programs. Both also applied for the following job.

Electronics
Ground floor opportunities with growing national computer firm. Must be HS grad exp'd in electronics, microcomputer assembly & repair, digital electronics, data communications. Will be trained to work for a team of experts. Contact: P.O. Box 1354, Chicago, IL 60606

After completing their application forms, Alan and Hal were scheduled for interviews on the same day—Alan in the morning and Hal in the afternoon. When Alan and Hal arrived, each was asked to take a written test. It wasn't an electronics test, but a psychological test. Here are some of the questions asked and their responses.

1. Why do you want to work in electronics?
    - Alan: I like electronics and feel it has good future opportunities.
    - Hal: I like to work in electronics, and I want to make a lot of money.
2. Would you enter a nine-month training program at a lower salary?
    - Alan: Yes, if it meant I would learn the business.
    - Hal: No. I'm prepared to go to work right now. I don't need much more training.
3. Do you prefer to work alone or with a group?
    - Alan: Either. At times I like to work alone, but I also like to work with others.
    - Hal: In a group. I like to be with people.
4. Answer yes or no to this: I always control my temper.
    - Alan: No. I try, but sometimes I get mad and raise my voice.
    - Hal: Yes. No matter how unreasonable others are, I control my temper and never get angry.

The company wanted young people with knowledge and experience in electronics who were willing to be trained according to the company's system. Who do you think was hired—Alan, Hal, or both?

Alan was offered a position, but Hal was not. The main reason for Hal not being hired was his answer to the last question about controlling his temper. Very few people, if any, never get angry. Hal's reply sounded unrealistic. His answer also gave the impression that he thinks he's always right and incapable of making mistakes. The interviewer concluded that Hal's attitude would probably lead to problems in getting along with others and accepting constructive criticism.

Critical Thinking

1. Do you think the test questions were fair?
2. Do you agree with the interviewer's interpretation of Hal's answer? Why?
3. Whom would you hire? Why?
4. Would you feel uncomfortable taking a similar psychological test? Explain.

Ethical Leadership

Originality

"There is much difference between imitating a man and counterfeiting him."—Benjamin Franklin Originality is the ability to think independently and creatively. It is a very valuable leadership trait. However, there may be times when you are unable to think creatively. You may be tempted to plagiarize. Plagiarism is a form of theft that occurs when one person used somebody else's material without permission. Just about everything you see in print, the music you listen to, and almost all information on the Internet is copyrighted. If you use material without the permission of the copyright holder, you have committed theft.

Aptitude Tests

An aptitude test does not measure an individual's ability to do a job. Instead, an **aptitude test** measures a person's potential to perform the job after training. These tests may be written, oral, or performance. They often measure reasoning ability, written and verbal skills, and manual dexterity. The test may be specific to the job you are applying for or measure general aptitudes. An IQ test is an example of a general aptitude test. The SAT and ACT are also types of aptitude tests that are meant to predict how an individual will perform as a college student.

Situational Tests

Many employers find that traditional performance, written, and oral tests do not reveal how well a worker will actually perform on the job. Consequently, they use a **situational test** to examine the ability of job applicants in a work setting similar to that of the job. These tests examine the skills, knowledge, and attitudes required by the job. For example, for a job involving frequent teamwork, applicants may be grouped with four or five other applicants. The group is then given a problem to solve. A trained observer judges how successfully each team member works with others, solves problems, and demonstrates leadership skills.

In another case, potential assembly-line workers may be placed on a test assembly line. They may be judged for their dexterity and patience in performing simple routine tasks for long periods. These tests can be very helpful to both the employer and the potential employee. Often it is the applicant who decides not to take the job after getting a chance to experience the work involved.

Government Tests

The US government is the nation's largest employer. It hires many people for civilian jobs as well as military jobs. In addition, a variety of jobs are filled by people working for state and local agencies. Two types of tests you may encounter if you apply for a federal or state government job or pursue a military career are discussed here.

Civil Service Test

A **civil service test** is an examination a person may be required to take as part of the application process for a government job. The *Civil Service Commission* is the federal agency that administers the civil service tests and hires employees for federal government jobs. The employment service of each state administers tests and hires workers for state jobs. Both federal and state governments test job applicants to select the best qualified person for the job without regard to sex, race, religion, or political influence. The testing system attempts to give all US citizens a fair chance at government jobs.

To learn about these job openings and the testing required, call your nearest state employment service. You can find the phone number by looking under your state's name in a telephone directory. For example, in *Illinois,* look under *Illinois, State of.* Then, look for jobs or employment. The exact title will vary from state to state. You can also find information on your state's website.

The ASVAB test is useful for those considering a career in the military.

Shutterstock.com

Armed Services Vocational Aptitude Battery

The **Armed Services Vocational Aptitude Battery (ASVAB)** is an aptitude test designed to measure strengths, weaknesses, and potential for future success. There are three versions of the test. Two versions are designed for use by military recruiters. The third version is the student ASVAB, which is part of the *ASVAB Career Exploration Program.*

The student ASVAB is for juniors and seniors in high school and postsecondary students. It is given in high schools, colleges, and vocational schools. The test provides three overall scores in verbal, math, and science and technical skills. In addition, eight sub scores in areas, such as auto and shop information, arithmetic reasoning, paragraph comprehension, and electronics comprehension are included.

The ASVAB Career Exploration Program is designed to help you learn more about yourself and explore various occupations. It can help you determine if you are ready for more training in different career areas. A program will provide you with a variety of career planning tools. For example, the *Find Your Interests (FYI)* inventory will help you identify your work-related interests. It will help you explore occupations in relation to the scores you received on the ASVAB and FYI.

How to Take Preemployment Tests

Unlike most tests, there are few preemployment tests for which you can study. However, there are several steps you can take to prepare yourself for any test. Follow these suggestions to help you feel calm and composed at test time. Remember that tests are only part of the hiring process:

- Try to find out in advance what type of tests you must take. If it is a skill test, such as welding, you should practice. However, do not practice so much that you tire yourself just before test time.
- Get plenty of rest the night before the test, so you will feel refreshed and alert.
- **Do not test on an empty stomach.**
- If you are taking a written test, bring an extra pencil just in case you need it.
- Arrive at the test site early. If possible, make a trial run to the test site a day or two before the test. Select a seat where you can see and hear the examiner well.
- While instructions are being given, be sure to ask questions about anything you do not understand. Follow directions exactly. Know how and where your answers are to be made.
- When taking a written test, read the questions carefully. Try not to stay too long on one question. Answer the easiest questions first. Then, go back and try to answer the harder questions.
- Have confidence in your ability.

Checkpoint 5.2

1. Why do employers use skill tests?
2. Who administers civil service tests?
3. Why do state and federal governments test job applicants?
4. Why may someone with no plans for a military career want to take the ASVAB?
5. What are three things you should do before taking a preemployment test?

Build Your Vocabulary

As you progress through this text, develop a personal glossary of career-related terms and add it to your portfolio. This will help build your vocabulary and prepare you for your career of choice. Write a definition for each of the following terms, and add it to your personal career glossary.

skill test
aptitude test
situational test
civil service test
Armed Services Vocational Aptitude Battery (ASVAB)

Chapter Summary

Section 5.1 Preemployment Assessments

- Psychological tests are often used to find out more about an applicant's personality, character, and interests. Some employers give psychological tests to determine how well a person might adjust to the work environment.
- Polygraph tests help employers judge an applicant's honesty. Polygraph tests are subject to strict standards under the law.
- Medical exams are required by some employers to determine an applicant's physical condition. Increasing concerns about drug abuse on the job have led some employers to start drug-testing programs for job applicants.

Section 5.2 Predicting On-the-Job Performance

- Several types of preemployment tests may be given to prospective employees. Skill tests evaluate physical abilities or knowledge.
- Aptitude tests help assess a person's potential for learning how to do the job well. These tests may be written, verbal, or performance-based.
- Situational tests give the employer a better idea of how a person will perform under actual job conditions. These tests examine skills, knowledge, and attitudes required by the job.
- Civil service tests are designed to place people fairly in state and federal government jobs. The Armed Services Vocational Aptitude Battery test is used to assess those interested in joining the military.

Check Your Career IQ

Now that you have finished the chapter, see what you learned about careers by taking the chapter posttest. The test can be accessed on the mobile site by using a smartphone or on the G-W Learning companion website.

www.m.g-wlearning.com
www.g-wlearning.com

Review Your Knowledge

1. What are some things an applicant can learn from taking a preemployment test?
2. How does a polygraph test work?
3. Which government agency should you contact to learn more about polygraph tests and the Employee Polygraph Protection Act (EPPA)?
4. Why are private employers unable to use a lie detector during an interview?
5. What is the purpose of a medical examination in the workplace?
6. What does the American with Disabilities Act (ADA) require employers to do?
7. How is the workplace affected by employees who use drugs?
8. Explain why someone might be given a clerical skill test.
9. Give examples of two government employment tests.
10. What should you do during a preemployment test to help you complete the test successfully?

Apply Your Knowledge

1. Use the Internet to learn more about the Americans with Disabilities Act (ADA). Write a one-page summary of your findings.
2. Practice taking a standard keyboarding test. Rate yourself for speed and accuracy. Evaluate your results and determine areas that need more work.
3. Should private employers be allowed to give polygraph tests for preemployment screening? Write a one-page paper to support or argue against the use of polygraph tests at work. Be sure to state your position and include at least two points to support your claim. Use facts and solid reasons to support your position. Share your ideas with your class.
4. Assume the role of an employer. Make a list of the skills a job applicant needs to qualify for a specific job in your company. Then, describe a performance, written, or oral test you could give applicants to evaluate their skill levels.
5. Video record yourself answering questions commonly asked in an oral psychological test. View the video and critique your test. Did any of the questions make you appear visibly nervous?
6. Determine the types of preemployment tests you may be asked to take when applying for jobs in your career area. Write a brief summary of each test and discuss how relevant each one is.
7. How much do you know about the Civil Service Commission? Visit your school library to research the subject. Prepare a one-page report or brief presentation.
8. In a small group, discuss the preemployment tests covered in this chapter. Review the purpose of each test and talk about the advantages of each.

9. Present a speech in class. Discuss the subject of integrity in the workplace. Talk about why integrity and honesty are important on the job. Use information from this chapter and provide examples to support the key points in your speech.

10. Research the requirements to become a police officer, firefighter, and paramedic in your area. Identify the educational requirements and any physical or written examinations necessary for each job. Compile your information in a chart.

Teamwork

Working with two or three classmates, design a written honesty test for an entry-level position for one of the following employers: a child care center, a restaurant, or an auto repair shop. Talk with someone employed in the chosen career field to get a better understanding of the job. Present your written honesty test to the class. Explain why honest employees are important to the employer you selected. Also explain how your test will help identify people that may not be honest.

G-W Learning Mobile Site

Visit the G-W Learning mobile site to complete the chapter pretest and posttest and to practice vocabulary using e-flash cards. If you do not have a smartphone, visit the G-W Learning companion website to access these features.
G-W Learning mobile site: www.m.g-wlearning.com
G-W Learning companion website: www.g-wlearning.com

Common Core

College and Career Readiness

CTE Career Ready Practices. Read the Ethical Leadership features presented throughout this text. What role do you think that ethics and integrity have in decision making? Think of a time when you used your ideals and principles to make a decision. What process did you use to make the decision? In retrospect, do you think you made the correct decision? Did your decision have any consequences?

Reading. Locate different articles related to preemployment integrity and personality tests. Read the articles closely. List three facts you were able to learn from the articles. List three inferences you were able to draw from the text. What evidence in the text supports your inferences?

Apply Your Technology Skills

Access the G-W Learning companion website for this text at www.g-wlearning.com. Download the data file for this chapter. Follow the instructions to complete activities to practice what you have learned in this chapter.

Data File 5–1—**Preparing to Take a Skill Test**

College and Career Readiness Portfolio

College and Career Readiness

You will create both a print portfolio and an e-portfolio in this class. You have already decided how to store hard copy items for your print portfolio. Now you need to create a plan for storing and organizing materials for your e-portfolio. Ask your instructor where to save your documents. This could be on the school's network or a flash drive of your own. Think about how to organize related files into categories. For example, school transcripts and diplomas might be one category. Awards and certificates might be another category, and so on. Next, consider how you will name the files. The names for folders and files should be descriptive but not too long. This naming system will be for your use. You will decide in a later activity how to present your electronic files for viewers.

1. Create a folder on the network drive or flash drive in which you will save your files.
2. Write a few sentences to describe how you will name the subfolders and files for your portfolio.
3. Create the subfolders to organize the files, using the naming system you have created.

Section 6.1
Preparing for the Interview

Section 6.2
Completing the Interview Process

College and Career Readiness

Reading Prep. As you read the text, try to determine the authors' point of view. What can you infer about their point of view from reading the chapter? What evidence in the chapter shows their point of view?

Introduction

The interview is usually the most important step in getting a job. Your application form, résumé, letter of application, or telephone call may have caught the employer's attention. However, it is the interview that will determine if you are offered the job.

For the employer, the purpose of an interview is to evaluate the job seeker in person. The interviewer wants to find out if you have the skills to do the job and if you will work well with the other employees.

For you, the job seeker, the purpose of the interview is to convince the employer that you are the right person to hire for the job. The interview also gives you a chance to learn more about the job and the company. It may also convince you that the job is not right for you.

Check Your Career IQ

Before you begin the chapter, see what you already know about careers by taking the chapter pretest. Use the related QR code to view the pretest on the mobile site. If you do not have a smartphone, visit the G-W Learning companion website to access the pretest.

www.m.g-wlearning.com
www.g-wlearning.com

G-W Mobile

Career Snapshot
Portrait Photographer

Arts, A/V Technology & Communications

What Does a Portrait Photographer Do?

Portrait photographers take pictures of individuals or groups of people. They must be able to:

- digital as well as film cameras; and
- use light sources, different lenses, and camera angles to enhance their subject's appearance.

What Is It Like to Work as a Portrait Photographer?

Portrait photographers spend most of their day interacting with customers. They must be upbeat and conversational to help their clients relax and look their best. Some photographers are self-employed and often have their own studios. Other photographers work for large companies with studios in shopping malls and discount stores. Portrait photographers may have a specialty such as school photos or weddings and, as a result, often work on location.

What Education and Skills Are Needed to Be a Portrait Photographer?

- high school diploma or GED
- some formal coursework through universities, colleges, or technical schools or experience
- pleasing, outgoing personality to get the best out of the client
- good eyesight and a creative nature
- strong computer skills
- business and entrepreneurial skills if self-employed

Danie Nel/Shutterstock.com

6.1 | Preparing for the Interview

Objectives

After completing this section, you will be able to:
- **Explain** how to prepare for an interview.
- **Demonstrate** appropriate attire and demeanor for interviewing.

Learn about the Employer and the Position

An interview is a conversation between a job applicant and an employer. It can be a very important 20 or 30 minutes in your life. You should never expect to just walk into an interview without preparing yourself ahead of time. The better prepared you are for an interview, the better the impression you will make on the interviewer. To prepare for an interview, follow the tips listed in Figure 6-1.

Learn about the Employer and the Job

Become familiar with the employer before you go on your interview. Find out about the company's products or services, size, reputation, and the possibilities for growth and expansion. Some companies publish annual reports that include this information. Having some knowledge of the company will help you talk intelligently with the interviewer. You may also want to check out the company's competition. Being able to discuss the industry the company is involved in may impress the interviewer. It also shows the interviewer that you are interested enough in the company to do outside research.

Tips for Preparing for an Interview
• Learn about the employer and the job.
• Make a list of questions to ask.
• List the materials to take with you.
• Polish your appearance.
• Be prepared for questions.
• Practice for the interview.
• Know where to go for the interview.

Figure 6-1.   *Goodheart-Willcox Publisher*
Being prepared will show the interviewer that you take things seriously.

A good place to start is to check the company's website. There you will often find information on the company's history, products, and employment needs. Companies cite their Internet addresses in television commercials and magazine ads. You can also do an Internet search to locate their websites.

Another place to look for information about potential employers is at your local or school library. Descriptions of most corporations appear in business and industrial directories and library references. Ask the librarian to help you locate sources and obtain the information you need.

Your program coordinator and guidance counselor may be able to provide information about the company. Talking with someone who works for the company will help you learn about the employer. Check with your chamber of commerce for information on companies in your area.

Find out as much as you can about the job. Get information on specific duties and responsibilities, physical requirements, qualifications, hours, and opportunities for advancement. You can do this by requesting a copy of the job description. Job descriptions and other information may be available from the company's human resources department. Save questions to which you cannot find answers for the interview.

Make a List of Questions to Ask

As you prepare for the interview, write down a few questions you would like to ask the interviewer about the job and the company. Asking questions, like researching the company, shows the employer that you have a serious interest in the organization. The questions you ask can also help you decide if you really want to work for the company.

You may want to ask the following questions:
- Would I receive training for this job?
- What hours would I work?
- Are there opportunities for advancement?
- May I see the work site?
- Is there anything I should read or study to get a head start on learning this job?

Ethical Leadership

Trustworthiness

"The only way to make a man trustworthy is to trust him."—Henry L. Stimson

A leader or any person who is trustworthy can be relied on to be honest and truthful. You expect your boss to be trustworthy, and he or she expects the same of you. If your employer gives you a 15-minute break, you are expected to return to work as soon as your break is over. It may be tempting to take an extra five minutes since no one is watching. Take an extra five minutes each day and you will soon have cheated your employers out of hours of work time.

Do not ask questions that can be readily found on a company's website. It shows that you have not done your research in advance. Wait until the end of the interview to ask about the job's salary range and benefits. Sometimes these topics are covered more fully in a second interview.

List the Materials to Take with You

When you go to an interview, there are a few items you will need to take with you. You will need a pen and your personal fact sheet for filling out an application. You will also need your résumé and the list of questions you plan to ask the interviewer. To keep your papers neat and clean, carry them in a file folder or large envelope.

If you apply for a job as a photographer, writer, or artist, you should also take samples of your work. This is the time to display your portfolio. Take only your best samples to the interview. Your three best samples will have more impact than ten average samples. Do not bring your cell phone or MP3 player.

Polish Your Appearance

Think carefully about the impression you want to present to the interviewer several days in advance. Your appearance will influence the employer's impression of you. **Appearance** is the outward impression you give to people. It involves your facial expressions, posture, the clothes you wear, and personal grooming. To make a good impression, you should strive to look your very best.

Your facial expressions should be natural and not forced. You will want to smile frequently and give the overall impression you are enjoying the interview process. Stand and sit up straight. Poor posture may give the impression you lack confidence.

Let the type of position determine your choice of clothing. A guideline you may want to follow when making your selection is: *Dress one step above what is worn on the job.* For example, if you are interviewing for a job as an auto technician, casual clothes or business dress would be appropriate to wear. Avoid wearing work clothes, jeans, T-shirts, and tennis shoes. These clothes would probably appear too casual. It is always best to lean toward conservative in either professional or business attire. If you are still in doubt about what to wear, ask your instructor or counselor for advice. Figure 6-2 shows guidelines for appropriate attire.

Clothes should be clean, neat, and in good condition. Do not wear a torn shirt, a wrinkled coat, or muddy shoes. Have the shirt mended or choose something different. Get your coat pressed ahead of time, and clean and polish your shoes.

Remember, however, that neat, clean clothes will not leave a positive impression if you are not neat and clean. Hair should be well styled. A beard should be neatly shaven or trimmed. Makeup and perfume should be applied sparingly. While tattoos are becoming more acceptable in society, it may still be best to keep tattoos covered if possible.

Appropriate Interview Attire		
	Professional	**Casual Business**
Men Minerva Studio/Shutterstock.com	Two-piece suit—dark colors	Sport coat or blazer—not required, but avoid loud colors and patterns Pants—no jeans, avoid baggy pants
	Long-sleeved shirt coordinated with suit—white, blue or conservative stripe, no bright colors	Shirt—button-down or polo shirt—wear collar open if not wearing a tie
	Tie—coordinated with suit and shirt, conservative colors and patterns, no character ties	Tie—not required but appropriate
	Socks—calf-length coordinated with suit (usually black or brown)	Socks—conservative, mid-calf length
	Belt and shoes—leather, black or brown to match suit; no boots	Shoes—leather loafers or dress; no sandals, athletic shoes, or boots
	Jewelry—very little; conservative watch, no body piercings or chains	Jewelry—very little; no chains or body piercings
	Cologne—very little	Cologne—very little
Women stockyimage/Shutterstock.com	Two-piece dress or pants suit—conservative color (navy, dark gray, black, or brown); avoid short or tight skirts; no revealing slits	Skirt or pants—casual, solid conservative colors, avoid short or tight skirts, no revealing slits
	Blouse—tailored, cotton or silk, small collar, sleeves; no cleavage	Shirt or blouse—conservative, tailored, no cleavage
	Scarves—if worn, should be conservative colors that complement suit and blouse	Sweater—tailored knit or sweater set
	Shoes—pumps with low heel; color should match suit; toes should be covered	Shoes—leather or fabric loafers; dark colors to coordinate with wardrobe
	Hosiery—light color to match wardrobe, no patterns	Hosiery—light color to match wardrobe, no patterns
	Purse—small and simple	Purse—small and simple
	Jewelry—small, conservative; no body piercings except earrings	Jewelry—small, conservative; no body piercings except earrings
	Cosmetics—conservative, less is better	Cosmetics—conservative, less is better
	Perfume—very little	Perfume—very little

Figure 6-2.   *Goodheart-Willcox Publisher*
If in doubt as to what to wear to an interview, lean more toward professional rather than casual business dress.

Be Prepared for Questions

During an interview, you will be asked many questions to determine if you are the right person for the job. There are some questions that almost every job seeker can expect during an interview, as shown in Figure 6-3. You need to become familiar with these questions and think about how to answer them. In fact, it is a good idea to write your answers on paper. Then, you can read them over and decide if you phrased your thoughts clearly and positively. You

Interview Questions	
Possible Questions	**Shaping Your Responses**
What can you tell me about yourself?	Succinctly summarize your abilities as they relate to the job qualifications or your career goals. Do not provide a general life history.
Why do you want to work for this company?	Tell what you know about the company. Explain how your abilities match the company's needs.
Why do you think you would like this kind of work?	Relate the job requirements to your successful past experiences.
What were your best subjects in school?	Name two or three subjects and relate them to job qualifications.
What were your poorest subjects in school?	Explain what you have done to try to improve.
What other jobs have you held?	Focus on jobs with skills that relate to the jobs you are seeking.
Why did you leave your last job?	Be honest. However, avoid saying anything negative about your previous employer.
Have you ever been fired from a job? If so, why?	Answer honestly. If you have been fired, try to turn it into a positive by sharing what you learned from the experience. Avoid trying to blame others.
What is your major strength?	Select one of your strengths that relates to the job qualifications.
What is your major weakness?	Be honest but explain what you have done to improve. Give an example.
Have you ever had a conflict with a coworker? How did you handle it?	Briefly describe the situation and how you handled it. Avoid placing all the blame on the other person. Explain what you learned from the experience.
What do you expect to be paid?	If possible, determine the salary range before the interview. Say that you are willing to discuss the salary or state a range you feel comfortable with.
Are you willing to work evenings and weekends?	Ask how much evening and weekend work would be required and then answer honestly.
What are your future plans?	Describe how the need to learn and grow is important to you. Confine your answer to the company with which you are interviewing.
Why should I hire you?	Be specific. Explain how your qualifications match the job requirements.

Figure 6-3.   *Goodheart-Willcox Publisher*
Be prepared with answers to these questions before going on your first interview.

may also want to try an Internet search using the term "interview question answers" and practice formulating answers to the questions you find.

Early in the meeting, the interviewer is likely to say, "Tell me about yourself." What do you suppose the interviewer wants to learn? He or she is exploring your educational background and job skills. At the same time, the interviewer is checking how well you express yourself. Provide the interviewer with responses that highlight your qualifications for the job.

Also, be prepared for questions about postings on your social media accounts. Some employers may ask questions about things they have seen on sites, such as Facebook.

An interviewer may even ask permission to perform a credit check on you. Explain why your credit score may be low if you have a poor credit history. If you have legitimate reasons for failing to make a loan payment, it may not be held against you.

Keep in mind the subjects that interviewers cannot explore and the questions they cannot ask. These questions involve a job candidate's race, religion, national origin, sex, age, or disability.

Although laws to prevent discrimination make certain questions illegal, that does not mean they will not be asked. Prepare yourself now and you will not be taken off guard if you hear an improper question. For example, you might respond by saying, "Please explain how that relates to the job," or "I would rather not answer personal questions." You could also respond to the intent of the question without answering it directly. For example, if the employer asks how old you are, you could respond by saying, "My age won't be a factor in performing the duties of this job."

If the interviewer innocently asked a borderline question, he or she will restate the question and keep the interview on a professional course. If questions or comments of a questionable nature continue, you should become suspicious of the interviewer. Remember, you are not obliged to answer illegal questions. When you suspect an interviewer of violating your legal rights, simply end the interview. Politely say that you are no longer interested in the job.

Practice for the Interview

Take some time to rehearse your interview. Ask a friend, family member, or other adult with business experience to interview you. This practice interview is known as a **mock interview.** Practice answering questions in front of a mirror. However, do not memorize your answers. Try to make them sound natural and positive. It is important to let your personality show through.

Most people feel nervous when interviewed. That is why practicing ahead of time is important. Practicing builds your self-confidence and helps you feel more relaxed during the actual interview.

Know Where to Go for the Interview

What a waste of time and energy it is to prepare for an interview and miss it by going to the wrong place. This has happened. One job seeker, for example, assumed his interview would be at the company's manufacturing plant. When he arrived at the scheduled time, he learned that all interviews were held at the company's headquarters across town. Another job seeker missed her interview because she wrote down the wrong time and did not double-check. For these reasons, it is important to keep an accurate record of the company's name, time, date, and location of each interview you schedule.

It is a good idea to visit the company before the interview to be sure you know how to get there and where to go. The trip will help you estimate the travel time. Be sure to allow extra time on the day of the interview so you arrive early.

One easy way to keep your interviews organized is by preparing an index card for each as shown in Figure 6-4. Write the date and time of the interview, the employer's name, and the exact location. Also, note the name of the person to contact and the title of the job for which you are applying. Be sure to double-check all information to make sure you have recorded it correctly.

On the bottom and back of the card, leave space for comments. After each interview, make notes about what questions were asked and how well you answered them. Evaluating yourself can help you have a more successful interview next time.

Job Interview

Date of interview __May 14, 20--__

Time of interview __8:30__

Employer __Whitaker Publishing Company__   Contact __Robert Drake__

Location __1822 W. Meridian St.__

_____ __Milwaukee, WI 53172__   Phone no. __(414) 555–2323__

Job title __Office assistant__

Comments __I interviewed with Mr. Robert Drake, Human Resources Manager.__
__He was very interested in my business education background and keyboarding skills.__
__He plans on making a decision about the position by next Friday.__

Figure 6-4.   *Goodheart-Willcox Publisher*

Use a separate note card to keep track of the important facts about the employer and the result of each interview you.

Go Green

Turning the power off to equipment at the end of the day can save up to 25 percent on energy costs. Whenever you leave a room or if there is enough natural light to brighten the room, turn off the lights. Use a power strip for all of your equipment so one flip of the switch turns off all of your devices. Power-down your computer, and turn off the printer to save energy each evening.

Checkpoint 6.1

1. What is the purpose of the interview for the employer? For the job seeker?
2. List four ways to prepare for an interview.
3. Why is it important to prepare a list of questions to ask the interviewer?
4. What items should be taken to an interview?
5. What information should be included in your record of each interview?

Build Your Vocabulary

As you progress through this text, develop a personal glossary of career-related terms and add it to your portfolio. This will help build your vocabulary and prepare you for your career of choice. Write a definition for each of the following terms, and add it to your personal career glossary.

mock interview
appearance

6.2 Completing the Interview Process

Objectives

After completing this section you will be able to:
- **Explain** how to make a good impression in an interview.
- **Describe** the factors to consider before accepting or rejecting a job offer.

Interview

Once you have prepared for an interview, you are ready to meet your interviewer face to face. However, there are a few other details you need to consider. For example, how is your attitude? What time should you arrive at the interviewer's office? How should you greet him or her? How should you behave during the interview? How should you end the interview? Knowing the answers to these questions will help you handle yourself with confidence and make a good impression on the interviewer.

The attitude you display during the interview may be critical in determining whether or not you will land the job. **Attitude** is the way you feel about someone or something and is often reflected in your behavior. Your attitude will tell the interviewer a lot about you. For example, a "know-it-all" attitude may indicate you are insecure in your ability to perform the job and are trying to cover it up. Give yourself a pep talk prior to stepping into the building or office, and try to maintain a positive attitude throughout the interview process.

Arrive five to ten minutes early for the interview. Relax, and be yourself. Tell the receptionist or person in charge who you are and who you are scheduled to see. Do not take someone with you to the interview. Taking a friend or family member may give the impression that you will not be comfortable working alone. You certainly do not want to give that impression. Be sure to turn off your cell phone.

The interview begins with a formal introduction. This may be one of the most important parts of the interview. It is the first impression your prospective employer will have of you. It is important that you make eye contact when you are introduced to someone and maintain it throughout the entire conversation.

Chances are that you will first introduce yourself to a receptionist. Smile and offer a friendly greeting such as "good morning." Clearly state your name and the purpose of your visit. You will probably be asked to take a seat to wait for your appointment. It is important that you conduct yourself professionally at this time. Sit up straight. Use

Konstantin Chagin/Shutterstock.com

Greet each interviewer with a smile and a handshake.

this time to review your résumé and notes or look over any brochures or professional magazines in the reception area. Of course, be prepared to carry on a conversation with the receptionist if prompted.

When the interviewer arrives, the receptionist may introduce you. If so, stand and wait for him or her to complete the introduction. If not, stand and introduce yourself. In either case, be sure to include a friendly greeting and restate the interviewer's name. This will help you remember it. Ask the individual to repeat his or her name if you did not hear it clearly or are unsure of the pronunciation. It is very important to smile and act relaxed.

When you are offered a seat, sit in a comfortable position, but do not slouch. Sit straight and look alert. Your body language often tells the employer as much about you as what you say. Avoid doing anything distracting, such as chewing gum or cracking your knuckles. It is natural to be nervous, but do your best to appear relaxed.

As the interviewer asks you questions, listen very carefully. Then, respond positively and honestly about yourself and your experiences. Keep your answers brief and to the point. Do not brag about your qualifications. Do not be bashful about telling the interviewer about your accomplishments either. A question frequently asked is "What is your greatest weakness?" Do not give a standard answer, such as "I work too hard." Instead share a real weakness that will not harm your chances of getting the job. Then, explain the steps you are taking to help overcome the weakness.

Throughout the interview, show interest in what the interviewer is saying. Do not look out the window, around the room, or at the floor. Look pleasantly at the interviewer and maintain eye contact. Show you are enthusiastic about the job and the company.

Case

The Perfect Interview

Nia was very pleased when she received an offer to interview for a job as a receptionist in the emergency room at the local hospital. It was a very good job, and she knew there were many applicants. In fact, more than half of her classmates in health occupations applied for the job.

Nia prepared herself well for the interview by finding out as much as she could about the hospital and the position. On the day of the interview, she dressed appropriately and followed all the interview tips she had learned in class. The interview went extremely well. As the interview closed, Nia felt certain she would be offered the position.

The last step in the interview process was a tour of the emergency room. As they were about to leave, the ambulance arrived with an accident victim. The patient was in very serious condition with deep cuts to the face and neck. When Nia saw the victim, she almost panicked. She felt faint and sick to her stomach. She quickly looked away and managed to hide her reaction from the human resources director and head nurse who were conducting the tour. She knew immediately that she would never be able to work in an emergency room.

They left the emergency room and returned to the human resources office. The director asked Nia if she had any questions and whether she still wanted the job. Nia said all her questions had been answered and that she knew she would be perfect for the job.

A few days later, Nia received a telephone call from the human resources director. The job was hers if she wanted it. Nia told the director she was very excited and flattered by the offer and was pleased to accept. The director told her to report to the emergency room in two weeks to begin her orientation training.

The next week was very difficult for Nia. She knew she didn't want the job and would take another as soon as possible. She couldn't think about anything else and began to lose sleep agonizing over her decision. She finally called the director the day before she was scheduled to start training and declined the offer. When asked why, Nia said she had too much schoolwork and couldn't handle both the job and school.

Critical Thinking

1. What might be some reasons Nia accepted the job? What should she have done differently?
2. Do you think Nia should have at least tried to do the job?
3. Were her actions fair to the hospital?
4. Why do you suppose she lied to the human resources director? Do you think Nia's behavior affected the director's opinion of her classmates who also applied for the job?

When the interviewer asks if you have any questions, this is usually a signal that he or she has all the information needed about you. It is your turn to find out more about the job to help you decide if it is really for you. It is important to have your questions ready. You will want to ask the questions about the job and the company that you have not been able to answer from your research. For example, you might ask about the opportunity to learn and grow on the job. What are the opportunities for advancement? You might also ask about a typical workday or what the interviewer likes about working for the company. However, these types of questions should have a low priority. After your questions are answered, the interview is just about over. At this time, thank the interviewer for seeing you and again express your interest in the job.

Seldom will you be offered a job at an interview. Most likely, the interviewer will want time to consider your qualifications and those of the other job candidates. The interviewer may promise to contact you on a certain date to let you know if you have the job. Sometimes the interviewer may ask you to call him or her at a later date. If you do not get the job, the interviewer is not likely to call you at all.

If no mention is made at the end of the interview about what happens next, it is appropriate to ask when a hiring decision will be made. You should leave an interview with a clear idea of when the newly hired person will be notified.

It is possible that you may be asked to interview for a job over dinner or lunch. You may also be asked to attend a dinner meeting as part of your job. In these situations, it is important to follow etiquette. Observing proper table manners is an example of etiquette. Your behavior while dining can influence whether you are offered the position or have a successful meeting.

Table etiquette begins as you approach the dining table and does not end until you have left the dining area. Be sure to say "please" and "thank you" to both your server and host. Begin by removing the napkin and placing it in your lap. If you are dining in a formal situation, you will notice that the dinnerware and eating utensils are placed in a specific order as shown in Figure 6-5. The forks will be on your left and the knife and spoons on your right. If the utensils are wrapped in a napkin, you should place them in their proper place. As you begin eating, always use the utensils on the outside of your place setting first. For example, the fork farthest away from your plate will be the salad fork. The spoon on the far right will be the soup spoon. When in doubt, follow the lead of your host.

As you begin eating, it is important to note that you will be expected to engage in conversation. Of course, you should not chew or talk with your mouth full. Therefore, you will need to control the amount of food you place in your mouth at one time. Take small bites so you can chew, swallow, and still converse in a timely manner. You will want to order foods that allow you to do this easily. Avoid ordering messy foods, such as pasta or ribs. Bread and rolls should be broken into small pieces as you eat them. Cut meat as you eat each piece. Certain foods such as olives and corn on the cob are considered finger foods. Finger foods may be picked up by hand, but other foods may not. You may place your elbows on the table between courses, but not while eating.

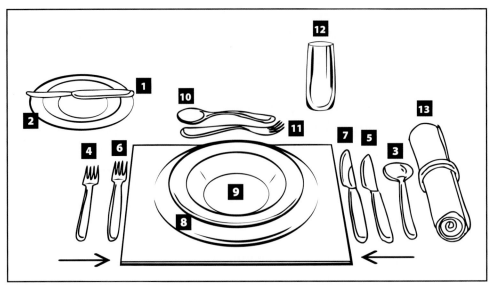

Figure 6-5.   *Liza Dmitrieva/Shutterstock.com*

Being aware of how a place setting might look, will help you to concentrate on what is being said and what you want to say during a dinner interview, rather than on what fork to use.

1.) bread and butter knife   2.) bread or roll plate   3.) soup spoon   4.) salad fork
5.) dinner knife   6.) dinner fork   7.) dinner knife or meat knife   8.) dinner plate
9.) soup or salad bowl   10.) dessert spoon   11.) dessert fork   12.) water glass

Try to pace your eating so you do not finish too soon or too late. Wait for your host to conclude the meal. Place used utensils back on your plate when you are finished eating.

If you have been invited to dinner for a job interview, your host will pick up the check. Avoid ordering the most expensive items from the menu if others are paying. Be sure to thank your host at the conclusion of the meal.

After the Interview

After an interview, do not just sit back and hope you will get the job. At your first opportunity, immediately send a **follow-up message** written in business form to thank the interviewer for his or her time. Send it as an e-mail message to everyone you met as soon as possible after you leave the interview. If you send written letters, they should be postmarked within two days of the interview.

A follow-up letter reminds the interviewer of your interest in the job. You may want to include a brief comment on how your qualifications match the job requirements. Figure 6-6 shows an example of a follow-up letter.

If the interviewer promised to contact you by a certain date and does not, also follow up with a telephone call. Be as pleasant and positive as you were during the interview. You may want to say something like this: "Mr. Roberts, this is Terry Brooks. I interviewed two weeks ago for the auto mechanic position. You mentioned that a decision about the job would probably be made by now. I am still interested in the job and wonder if you have made your decision." You may learn the job has been filled. On the other hand, you may learn that you are still in the running, and a final decision will be made in two weeks. Whatever the response, you will know where you stand.

Do not be discouraged if you do not get a job offer right away. Very few job seekers land a job after just one or two interviews. You may need to interview with a number of employers to find the best job for you. However, if you have missed out on several jobs, try to figure out why. Check the comments you have written down on your interview cards. Have you had any problems on your interviews? You

---

204 West Pickford Road
Jefferson City, MO 65001
July 3, 20--

Ms. Cheryl Lynn Sebastian
Director of Administration
Office of the Secretary of State
100 E. High Street
Jefferson City, MO 65101

Dear Ms. Sebastian:

Thank you for taking time yesterday to interview me for the executive assistant position.

After talking with you, I am very excited about the possibility of joining your company. I am confident I have the ability to help your office become more efficient and organized, which you indicated was of high priority.

I look forward to hearing your decision and hope it will be a favorable one.

Sincerely,

Jennifer S. Fitzpatrick

Jennifer S. Fitzpatrick

Figure 6-6.   *Goodheart-Willcox Publisher*
Sending a follow-up letter after an interview is a courtesy the interviewer will appreciate.

may discover there is a specific reason why you are not getting job offers. To help you evaluate yourself on the job hunt, ask yourself the questions found in Figure 6-7.

One way to improve your job-seeking skills is to conduct an informational interview. An **informational interview** is a planned meeting in which a job applicant learns more about an occupation from a person employed in that job area. Informational interviews can take place whether or not an actual position is open. Locate someone who is employed in a job area in which you are interested. Call the company and arrange for an interview with that individual. Tell the individual you are trying to learn more about an occupation and that you will not take more than 15 or 20 minutes of his or her time. Use the interview to learn more about the occupation and yourself.

Because you will not be under the pressure of applying for a job, you should be more relaxed and able to work on the interview skills discussed earlier. You may even want to ask what the interviewer seeks in a job candidate. Near the end of the interview, ask the interviewer to recommend how you might improve your interview skills. Be sure to express sincere thanks at the close of the interview, and send a follow-up e-mail or letter, just as you would for an actual interview. This effort could even result in a future job offer.

Accepting a Job Offer

Before accepting a job offer, consider all the factors about the job. This will help you evaluate the job and the company. An important factor to consider is whether you will be happy in the position. Excellent working conditions and good pay will not mean much if

Assessing Your Job Search	
Are you qualified for the jobs for which you are applying?	• Perhaps you are applying for jobs that require more training and experience than you have. • Be willing to start in an entry-level position if necessary.
Are you applying to the wrong businesses?	Apply where there are likely to be job openings.
Are you filling out job application forms properly?	• Being careless when filling out applications may lead employers to think you will not be able to perform a job properly. • Read the directions carefully on all applications and answer all the questions completely.
Do you lack interest and energy?	Not asking questions about the job or seeming uninterested could convince the interviewer you do not really want to be hired.
Do you lack confidence?	Appearing very nervous and uneasy may make it difficult for the interviewer to talk with you.
Are you being discourteous?	Arriving late for the interview or not thanking the interviewer for seeing you may result in a negative impression.

Figure 6-7.   *Goodheart-Willcox Publisher*
Ask yourself these questions as a way of keeping your job search on track.

you hate to go to work each day. Now is also the time to ask questions about the job's responsibilities, pay, and benefits.

The salary for a job should be in line with the salaries paid for similar jobs at other companies. If the salary is a lot lower, you should probably consider a job with an employer that pays a more reasonable salary. However, a lower salary is sometimes balanced with excellent opportunities for advancement or very good fringe benefits. Check to see if your employer provides any of the following fringe benefits.

Insurance

Does the company offer group health, dental, or life insurance? If so, how much coverage do the policies provide? Does the employer pay all or much of the cost?

Paid Vacation

Will you receive paid vacation time? If so, how many days? Will you receive more paid vacation days after working for a certain number of years?

Sick Pay

Will the company pay for any days you are sick and unable to come to work? How many paid sick days are available per year? After being hired, be sure to ask what is considered an appropriate *sick day* and the preferred way of reporting or requesting a sick day.

Retirement or Profit-Sharing Plans

Does the company contribute a set amount of money to a retirement plan or a percentage of its profits to a profit-sharing plan for you? Will a portion of your income also be contributed to one of these plans? If so, how much? Must you work for a certain number of years before you are eligible to participate in plans offered by the employer?

Bonuses

Does the company give yearly or holiday bonuses? How are the amounts of bonuses determined? As discussed earlier, pay and fringe benefits are just two factors to consider about a job. Also consider the location of the job, working conditions, work hours, and opportunities for advancement before you make a final decision about a job.

If you do decide to accept a job offer, let the interviewer know. Tell him or her you are glad to accept the offer. Then, find out everything you need to know to start your first day of work. Remember to ask when, where, and to whom you should report for work. Also ask whether you need to bring anything with you.

Following acceptance of a position, you will be required to complete an I-9 Form. An **I-9 Form** is used to verify an employee's identity and that he or she is authorized to work in the United States, as shown in Figure 6-8. Both citizens and non-citizens must complete this form. You will be required to present one of many documents the government will accept as proof of employability. The employer may not specify which document you must present. Common documents would be a valid driver's license or photo ID. It must include a photo or information such as name, date of birth, gender, height, eye color, and address.

The employer must keep this form on file for three years or one year after the employee is terminated. It must be made available for inspection by authorized US government officials, such as representatives of the Department of Homeland Security, Department of Labor, or Department of Justice.

Department of Homeland Security
U.S. Citizenship and Immigration Services

Form I-9, Employment Eligibility Verification

Read instructions carefully before completing this form. The instructions must be available during completion of this form.

ANTI-DISCRIMINATION NOTICE: It is illegal to discriminate against work-authorized individuals. Employers CANNOT specify which document(s) they will accept from an employee. The refusal to hire an individual because the documents have a future expiration date may also constitute illegal discrimination.

Section 1. Employee Information and Verification *(To be completed and signed by employee at the time employment begins.)*

Print Name: Last	First	Middle Initial	Maiden Name

Address *(Street Name and Number)*	Apt. #	Date of Birth *(month/day/year)*

City	State	Zip Code	Social Security #

I am aware that federal law provides for imprisonment and/or fines for false statements or use of false documents in connection with the completion of this form.

I attest, under penalty of perjury, that I am (check one of the following):

☐ A citizen of the United States
☐ A noncitizen national of the United States (see instructions)
☐ A lawful permanent resident (Alien #) _____
☐ An alien authorized to work (Alien # or Admission #) _____
until (expiration date, if applicable - *month/day/year*)

Employee's Signature   Date *(month/day/year)*

Preparer and/or Translator Certification *(To be completed and signed if Section 1 is prepared by a person other than the employee.)* I attest, under penalty of perjury, that I have assisted in the completion of this form and that to the best of my knowledge the information is true and correct.

Preparer's/Translator's Signature   Print Name

Address *(Street Name and Number, City, State, Zip Code)*   Date *(month/day/year)*

Section 2. Employer Review and Verification *(To be completed and signed by employer. Examine one document from List A OR examine one document from List B and one from List C, as listed on the reverse of this form, and record the title, number, and expiration date, if any, of the document(s).)*

	List A	OR	List B	AND	List C
Document title:					
Issuing authority:					
Document #:					
Expiration Date *(if any)*:					
Document #:					
Expiration Date *(if any)*:					

CERTIFICATION: I attest, under penalty of perjury, that I have examined the document(s) presented by the above-named employee, that the above-listed document(s) appear to be genuine and to relate to the employee named, that the employee began employment on *(month/day/year)* _____ and that to the best of my knowledge the employee is authorized to work in the United States. (State employment agencies may omit the date the employee began employment.)

Signature of Employer or Authorized Representative	Print Name	Title

Business or Organization Name and Address *(Street Name and Number, City, State, Zip Code)*	Date *(month/day/year)*

Section 3. Updating and Reverification *(To be completed and signed by employer.)*

A. New Name *(if applicable)*	B. Date of Rehire *(month/day/year) (if applicable)*

C. If employee's previous grant of work authorization has expired, provide the information below for the document that establishes current employment authorization.

Document Title: _____   Document #: _____   Expiration Date *(if any)*: _____

I attest, under penalty of perjury, that to the best of my knowledge, this employee is authorized to work in the United States, and if the employee presented document(s), the document(s) I have examined appear to be genuine and to relate to the individual.

Signature of Employer or Authorized Representative	Date *(month/day/year)*

Form I-9

Figure 6-8.   *US Department of Homeland Security*
Form I-9: Employment Eligibility Verification

Rejecting a Job Offer

On rare occasions, an employer may make a job offer at the conclusion of your interview. If you need more time to evaluate the job, you may want to ask the interviewer for a few days to think about it. Most employers will usually agree.

On the other hand, you may be asked to decide immediately whether to accept the offer. If you have evaluated the job and decided it is not what you really want, you will probably choose not to accept the offer. At this point, politely thank the interviewer. Explain briefly why you feel you are not the right person for the job. However, do not say anything negative about the company or its employees. The interviewer will appreciate your direct, honest answer.

Most jobs are not offered at the end of the interview. You may receive a job offer later, either by telephone, mail, or e-mail. If you do not want to accept the job offer, let the employer know right away via phone that you will not accept the offer. Do not reject a job offer by e-mail. Thank the employer and give a brief explanation for your decision. It is a good idea to follow up the telephone call with a short letter thanking the interviewer for the offer.

Checkpoint 6.2

1. Why should a job seeker go to an interview alone?
2. If an interviewer does not mention when a hiring decision will be made, what can a job applicant do?
3. Why is it important to send a follow-up letter immediately after an interview?
4. What can a job seeker do to improve his or her job-seeking skills?
5. What is the purpose of an I-9 Form?

Build Your Vocabulary

As you progress through this text, develop a personal glossary of career-related terms and add it to your portfolio. This will help build your vocabulary and prepare you for the career of your choice. Write a definition for each of the following terms, and add it to your personal career glossary.

attitude
follow-up message
informational interview
I-9 Form

Chapter Summary

Section 6.1 Preparing for the Interview

- A personal interview with an employer is an important step in getting a job. The applicant should be prepared for the interview.
- Making a good impression is necessary when interviewing for a job. Appearance, including style of dress and cleanliness, should be considered carefully.

Section 6.2 Completing the Interview Process

- It is important to make a good impression during the interview. For example, the applicant should be on time, listen carefully, and speak positively and honestly.
- Evaluate the job and the company before accepting or rejecting a job offer. Consider salary and other fringe benefits.

Check Your Career IQ

Now that you have finished the chapter, see what you learned about careers by taking the chapter posttest. The test can be accessed on the mobile site by using a smartphone or on the G-W Learning companion website.

www.m.g-wlearning.com
www.g-wlearning.com

Review Your Knowledge

1. Before the interview, what information should a job seeker learn about the employer?
2. Where can a student job seeker find information about a company?
3. Why is it important to have some knowledge about a company before the interview?
4. How should you respond if you suspect a violation of your legal rights occurs during an interview?
5. Why is it important to practice for an interview?
6. Explain why you should keep a record of each interview.
7. What guideline should a person follow when dressing for an interview?
8. Briefly describe appropriate attire for a woman dressed for a professional event.
9. Why is a formal introduction one of the most important parts of the interview?
10. What should you do if you decide to reject a job offer?

Apply Your Knowledge

1. Review Figure 6-1. Explain the benefits of each tip for preparing for an interview. Compile your opinions in a chart.
2. Select a position for which you would be interested in applying. Create a list of ten questions to ask during the interview.
3. Assume you are going to interview for the position you selected in question number 2. Come to class dressed for an interview for that position. Explain why your appearance would be considered appropriate for the interview. What impression might your attire have on the interviewer?
4. Assume that you actually interviewed for a position. Write a follow-up letter thanking the interviewer.
5. Research proper dinner etiquette. Share your findings in a class presentation.
6. Ask your guidance counselor for help arranging an informational interview with a local company. Actually take part in the interview in person or on the telephone. Share your experience with the class.
7. Select three or four companies that interest you as a potential employer. Research each company. Develop a list of the strengths and weaknesses of each employer as they relate to your interests and abilities. Then, rank the companies in terms of how well they suit you. Justify your rankings.
8. Select a company where you might apply for a position. Enter the name and address in a GPS, smartphone, or map on the Internet for directions. Perform a simulated trip to each company. Considering traffic and construction delays, has the electronic device provided the best possible route? Discuss why using a GPS or smartphone to provide directions to an interview may or may not be a good idea.
9. With a teammate, discuss factors that would influence your decision to accept a job. Rank these factors in the order of importance. Identify those factors you might consider negotiable or unimportant to your decision.
10. Review the interview questions in Figure 6-3. Identify three questions that you lack confidence in answering. Prepare a written response for these three questions. Practice responding to each question in the mirror to test your ability to answer with confidence.

Teamwork

Role-play and video record a mock interview for the job of your dreams. One person on the team serves as the potential employer, and one person serves as the person being interviewed. Before the interview, record important information on note cards. List three questions to ask the interviewer. List five questions that the interviewer is likely to ask the person being interviewed. Next, decide what is appropriate to wear for the interview. After the interview is complete, switch roles. View and discuss the interviews in class.

G-W Learning Mobile Site

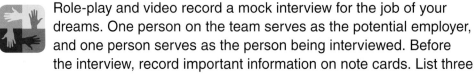

Visit the G-W Learning mobile site to complete the chapter pretest and posttest and to practice vocabulary using e-flash cards. If you do not have a smartphone, visit the G-W Learning companion website to access these features.
G-W Learning mobile site: www.m.g-wlearning.com
G-W Learning companion website: www.g-wlearning.com

Common Core

College and Career Readiness

Speaking. The way you communicate with friends and family is different than the way you should communicate in a business setting. Take turns with the person next to you, relating three things you each think you do well. Consider if the three things you shared would be the same three things you would share with a prospective employer. Explain why they would be the same and why they might be different.

Listening. Do an Internet search for interview tips, videos, or webcasts. Select one of the videos and watch it in its entirety. Present your findings and supporting evidence of the line of reasoning, organization, development, and style the speaker used to prepare his or her information. Identify the target audience and the purpose of the video.

Apply Your Technology Skills

Access the G-W Learning companion website for this text at www.g-wlearning.com. Download the data file for this chapter. Follow the instructions to complete activities to practice what you have learned in this chapter.

Data File 6–1—Evaluating Interview Scenarios

College and Career Readiness Portfolio

College and Career Readiness

Your e-portfolio may contain documents you have created. Scanned images of items, such as awards and certificates, may also be included. You need to decide which file formats you will use for electronic documents. You could use the default format to save the documents. For example, you could use Microsoft Word format for letters and essays. You could use Microsoft Excel format for worksheets. Someone reviewing your e-portfolio would need programs that open these formats to view your files. Another option would be to save or scan documents to PDF (portable document format) files. These files can be viewed with Adobe Reader and some other programs. Having all the files in the same format can make viewing the files easier for someone who wants to review your portfolio.

1. Search the Internet and read articles to learn more about PDF documents. Download a free program, such as Adobe Reader, that opens these files.
2. Practice saving a Microsoft Word document in different file formats. (Use the Save As command. Refer to the program Help if needed.)
3. Create a list of the format(s) you will use to store your electronic files.

Unit 3 Skills for Success

Becoming Aware of Education and Training Requirements

Today's actions dictate tomorrow's outcomes. The career you choose to pursue requires that you make certain decisions and take targeted actions as you move through the stages of your life. Most careers require training and preparation beyond a high school diploma. In addition, admission to some training and education programs require specific course work to be taken while still in high school. Stay focused on your ultimate career goal by becoming aware of the education and training requirements associated with your career choice.

Activities

1. Review the list of goals you created earlier along with the job profile for your preferred career. Carefully consider how the goals do and do not work with the career you choose. What training and education is required before you will be able to fulfill your goals or find a position in the field that interests you?
2. You can find the answer to that question by doing some research. Use the term *career cluster + personal program of study* to search the Internet. How does the course work for your future career align with the courses you have taken so far in high school? What additional training and education is needed before you will be qualified for an entry-level position? Does your high school have a partnership with another school where you can get training or course credit while still in high school? Record your answers to these questions.
3. Save your research findings according to your instructor's specifications.

As you proceed through Unit 3, you will see how important certain skills, such as teamwork and communication, are essential for success in life and on the job. Math is another essential skill for success. Knowledge of fractions, decimals, and percentages are necessary on the job and can help you in your daily life as well. In this unit, you will see what skills employers expect their employees to have when they hire them. Practicing these skills and knowing what employers expect will help prepare you for transition from high school to your future career.

Chapter 7   Teamwork and Problem-Solving Skills
Chapter 8   Communicating on the Job
Chapter 9   Math in the Workplace
Chapter 10 Using Technology in Your Career
Chapter 11 Looking Good on the Job
Chapter 12 Safety on the Job
Chapter 13 Leadership and Group Dynamics

Picture Success

Jennifer Freeman
Future Educators of America

A Career and Technical Student Organization (CTSO) can have a positive impact on its members and sponsors. Read about Jennifer's experience with Future Educators of America in her own words.

Jennifer Freeman

"While traveling, most people rely on a road map or a GPS to reach a destination. Future Educators of America (FEA) was my road map to reach my goal of becoming a teacher. My involvement in this Career and Technical Student Organization gave me my first exposure to college campuses and community service. It fostered my academic achievement and showed me the power of giving.

Through FEA, I became a tutor, which provided me with invaluable hands-on experience. Conferences and competitions allowed me to put into practice what I had learned. I am able to apply this knowledge to real-life career situations. I love teaching, but sponsoring a successful FEA chapter at Southern High School is my greatest joy because it allows me to promote the benefits of a CTSO.

FEA, like other CTSOs, serves as a road map to reach a certain career goal. CTSOs provide the basic skills, financial assistance, and real-world experience needed to be successful. Participation in CTSOs is an exciting way to have networking opportunities as well as develop and maintain a support system. Most importantly, you build lasting friendships with people that share your passion."

Chapter 7

Teamwork and Problem-Solving Skills

Section 7.1
Teamwork

Section 7.2
Problem Solving

College and Career Readiness

Reading Prep. Before reading this chapter, look at the chapter title. What does this title tell you about what you will be learning? Compare and contrast the information to be presented with information you already know about the subject matter from sources such as videos and online media.

Introduction

Working well with others is an important skill for future success at work. People who work together need to communicate well and know how to listen. These skills are important in solving problems, working on teams, and dealing with customers.

Working with others can be fun and rewarding. It can also be frustrating and irritating. This chapter explains the importance of working as a team member in the workplace and ways to promote team harmony.

Check Your Career IQ

Before you begin the chapter, see what you already know about careers by taking the chapter pretest. Use the related QR code to view the pretest on the mobile site. If you do not have a smartphone, visit the G-W Learning companion website to access the pretest.

www.m.g-wlearning.com
www.g-wlearning.com

G-W Mobile

Career Snapshot
Administrative Assistant

Business Management & Administration

What Does an Administrative Assistant Do?

Administrative assistants perform a variety of clerical tasks on behalf of an individual, team, or department. They work in many fields, including law, medicine, and education. They must:

- compose routine correspondence;
- answer the telephone;
- read and route incoming correspondence;
- schedule meetings and appointments;
- file and retrieve correspondence; and
- create spreadsheets, documents, and presentations.

What Is It Like to Work as an Administrative Assistant?

Administrative assistants usually work in an office environment where they likely spend many hours sitting at a desk. They must frequently stop what they are doing to interact with their supervisor, fellow staff members, and visitors. As a result, they often find themselves trying to juggle a number of different tasks at the same time. Some administrative assistants serve as virtual assistants performing their duties from home.

What Education and Skills Are Needed to Be an Administrative Assistant?

- high school diploma
- certificate or degree from a technical school may be required
- well-developed interpersonal skills
- communication, writing, computer, and organizational skills

7.1 | Teamwork

Terms

globalization
quality
team
interpersonal skills
virtual team
functional team
cross-functional team
self-directed team
multifunctional team
norm
Gantt chart
goal

Objectives

After completing this section, you will be able to:
- **Describe** how the workplace has changed.
- **Discuss** teams and their role in the workplace.
- **Identify** the stages of team development.
- **Recall** the characteristics of an effective team.

The Need for Teams

Not too long ago, managers made the decisions, and workers followed their orders. Workers spent long hours doing repetitive tasks that often required little or no formal training or creative thinking. These jobs paid a good wage and provided good benefits. Workers could count on holding a lifelong job with one company that provided their families with a high standard of living.

Over time, trade agreements, as well as advancements in technology and transportation, led to globalization. **Globalization** is the process of international businesses and financial markets becoming more interconnected. Globalization increases both competition and opportunities for companies and workers. This effect has changed the role of the typical worker. Workers are now expected to help solve problems and make decisions about procedures, quality, and finances. Successful companies use teams of workers to solve problems once handled by top managers. All of this has created a need for a more highly educated American workforce.

This need for a highly trained workforce is even more apparent today. Foreign companies with low labor costs are able to produce and sell their products very cheaply. In an effort to be more competitive, many American companies have moved their manufacturing and assembly operations overseas where labor costs are much lower. This is particularly true of jobs that require little or no education. As a result, low-skill jobs that pay a reasonable wage and require little or no education are quickly disappearing from the American scene.

Employers want well-educated workers who are comfortable working in teams and sharing ideas with others. They expect workers to stay knowledgeable about their work and continually make improvements. Employers want workers who can work with others, solve problems, and manage conflict. **Quality** is a commitment by everyone in an organization to exceed customer expectations.

Effective teams have team members with strong interpersonal skills.

Golden Pixel LLC/Shutterstock.com

Teams in the Workplace

A **team** is a group of people working together for a common purpose. Depending on its purpose, the typical number of members on a team ranges from 3 to 15 people.

Many companies use teams to help solve problems and increase productivity in the workplace. Teams are an effective way to promote ownership and commitment to accomplish a purpose or objective.

For a team to be successful, good communication skills must be demonstrated by each team member. Working as a part of a team requires good interpersonal skills. **Interpersonal skills** are the skills people use to positively interact with one another. Having the skills to get along with others to solve problems or accomplish a task is expected in today's workplace.

Types of Teams

Teams may be formal or informal. Some teams are set up to serve an ongoing need, while others operate on a temporary basis. Teams set up to meet a workplace need are usually formal teams.

Formal Teams

Formal teams are organized for a specific purpose and have an appointed leader. The sales team in an organization is an example of a formal team. There is a manager appointed to run the group.

It is often difficult to get formal team members together in one place. People who work together may be in different parts of the country or different parts of the world. A **virtual team** is a team that is made up of people of members from different locations. Through the use of

Team Presentation

Team presentation is a competitive event you might enter with your Career and Technical Student Organization (CTSO). This activity is a case study for which your team will provide a solution. You may be asked to interact with the judges as they ask you questions about the case or role play the scenario. This event will demonstrate your team's ability to make a persuasive oral presentation.

To prepare for a team presentation event, complete the following activities.

1. Read the guidelines provided by your organization. Make certain that you ask any questions about points you do not understand. It is important you follow each specific item that is outlined in the competition rules.

2. Do an Internet search for *case studies* that relate to your organization's area of focus. Your team should select a case that seems appropriate to use as a practice activity. Look for a case that is no more than one page long.

3. Read the case and discuss with your team members. What are the important points of the case?

4. To practice your note-writing techniques, each team member should have two index cards. Make important notes on the card that will help with a presentation.

5. Team members should exchange note cards so that each can evaluate the other person's notes. Are your cards accurate enough to help as you are presenting?

6. Assign each team member a role for the presentation. Ask your teacher to play the role of competition judge as your team reviews the case.

7. Ask a fellow student to be the timekeeper as the presentation is made.

8. Each team member should introduce him- or herself, review the case, make suggestions for the case, and conclude with a final summary.

9. After the presentation is complete, ask for feedback from your teacher. You may consider having a student audience to listen and give feedback.

technology, virtual teams can function successfully. Team members use technologies such as e-mail, video conferencing, telephone, and local- and wide-area networks to communicate with one another. Virtual teams are sometimes called *geographically dispersed teams.* Virtual teams are a popular solution and enable companies to save money and time in travel.

Virtual teams, however, may present challenges that teams in the same location may not face. Without face-to-face contact, communication may be difficult. Body language, facial expressions, and eye contact are a very important part of face-to-face communications. When members cannot see each other, important details may be lost. When participating in remote meetings, members must conduct themselves in a manner as if the meeting was taking place in the same room.

Informal Teams

Informal teams are teams that are created usually for a social purpose. A softball team is an example. The leader may be voted on by the members of the team rather than appointed.

Functions of Teams

Teams in the workplace are formed for different functions or purposes. Functional, cross-functional, and multifunctional teams are characterized by who serves on the team and the role each member plays. Figure 7-1 provides an overview of how members function within different teams.

Teams and Their Members	
Team Type	**Characteristics of Team Members**
Functional Team	• may work in the same department but meet as a team only some times • work on different problems over time • have similar skills and expertise but unable to perform each others' jobs • may develop strong allegiance to one another
Cross-Functional Team	• come from different departments within a company • work on a specific problem • are selected based on their expertise in a given area • can solve problems quickly • cease working together when problem is solved
Multifunctional Team	• are cross trained to perform each others' jobs • are assigned to specific tasks

Figure 7-1.   *Goodheart-Willcox Publisher*
This chart shows the relationship between a team's members and how a team functions.

Go Green

When you go to the store to shop, be sure to bring your own reusable bag. We can save thousands of pounds of landfill waste every year just by using reusable bags to carry products home from the store. While there are different schools of thought on this topic, it is generally accepted that plastic bags take almost 1,000 years to degrade. Additionally, discarded plastic bags can pose threats to wildlife and the soil. Did you know that store owners have to purchase the plastic or paper bags, and they pass on the cost to the consumer through higher product prices?

Functional Teams

A **functional team** is a team that has similar skills and expertise. Although members would not be able to perform one another's jobs, they can easily share technical expertise. Team members usually work in the same department. Functional teams solve problems based on their understanding of the work to be done and each team member's unique contribution. For example, a functional team for plant maintenance might be composed of a variety of workers such as electricians, plumbers, and air-conditioning specialists. They would have a common understanding of the department's role in keeping a plant running and could help solve maintenance-related problems.

Cross-Functional Teams

A **cross-functional team** is a team that consists of individuals from different areas within a company who are assigned to work on a specific project. Members are selected based on their expertise and ability to make a unique and meaningful contribution. For example, a team whose purpose is to create a new car design might consist of representatives of the company's design, manufacturing, marketing, and financial departments. The marketing representative could share information on special features that help the car sell better. The manufacturing representative would comment on the company's ability to build the new design. Working together, their goal would be to produce a well-designed car that is relatively easy to build and can be profitably sold at a reasonable price. These teams can be very effective and quick to solve problems.

Cross-functional teams may be self directed. A **self-directed team** has been given full responsibility for carrying out its assignment. The traditional supervisor is replaced by a team leader who leads rather than supervises. Although someone serves as team leader, the team's members set work-related goals and objectives. They identify priorities, set budgets, develop work plans, and solve problems. Self-directed teams evaluate their own progress and often hire, train, and evaluate their team members. For example, if a worker becomes seriously ill, the team decides whether to hire a temporary replacement or to have the other team members work overtime.

Multifunctional Teams

A multifunctional team is a team that consists of members who have been cross-trained to do another worker's job. Each person is able to perform the duties of all the other team members. An example might be a team of workers who assemble automobile air conditioners. Each member of the team would be able to perform all the jobs on the assembly line. When a worker is ill or takes a break, another team member can step in and do the job without additional instruction.

Stages of Team Development

You cannot group strangers together and expect them to perform well right away. Because teams are composed of people, they go through stages of development just as people do. It takes time for team members to learn to work together.

Team development evolves in stages. See Figure 7-2. One way to identify these stages is by the terms that follow:

- forming,
- storming,
- norming, and
- performing.

These stages were developed by group dynamics expert Dr. Bruce Tuckman. Generally, team members do not begin to work well together until the last two stages. However, not all teams make it to stage four. Some teams may not make it past stages one or two.

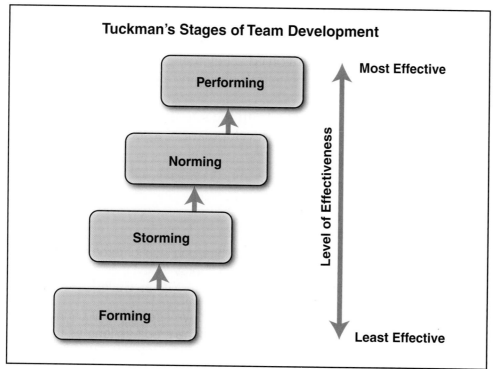

Figure 7-2.   *Goodheart-Willcox Publisher*

Teams progress through the stages of development at different rates.

Stage 1: Forming

Teams go through the forming stage when they first come together. At this stage, the team members may feel good about what the team can do. Individuals may be excited about being chosen for the team.

In many cases, members of the team do not know each other very well. They may feel uncomfortable, afraid to speak, and full of doubts. They may not understand why the team was formed or what is expected of them. During this stage, team members become acquainted. They also discuss the purpose of the team. There may be no leadership, or someone may step up and take charge.

Stage 2: Storming

Disagreements are likely to occur as team members get to know each other. Team members may distrust or not understand one another. They may even question why the team was formed.

There may be disagreements over how the team operates, who is in charge, or when and where the team meets. Sometimes these conflicts are discussed openly during meetings. In other cases, there may be personality clashes and arguments. As a result, team members may find it hard to work together and make decisions. However, this is also the stage when members begin to trust each other and share their feelings more openly.

Stage 3: Norming

At this stage, team members begin to work together, and leaders emerge. Teams resolve the disagreements that began during the second stage. The members openly discuss issues, listen to one another, and become more involved. They feel good about themselves and the team. They accept the team's decisions and are willing to work hard to carry them out.

The title of this stage comes from the scientific term *norm*. A **norm** is a pattern that is typical in the development of a social group.

Ethical Leadership

Integrity

"In looking for people to hire, you look for three qualities: integrity, intelligence, and energy. And if they don't have the first, the other two will kill you."–Warren Buffet

People who act with integrity are honest and have strong moral principles. A popular expression is "I don't care who gets the credit as long as the job gets done." However, the opposite approach, taking credit for work you didn't do, shows a lack of integrity. It will hurt your reputation and ability to work with others.

Stage 4: Performing

This is the highest level of team performance. The positive feelings that developed during the norming stage continue to grow. Members are committed to the team and the organization. They take responsibility for making improvements and examine the best way for the team to function. Different team members may take charge, depending on the task at hand. The team is most effective in this stage.

Characteristics of an Effective Team

When a team becomes effective, it is a sign the team has reached the highest level of development, the performing stage. The members of a team in the performing stage assume leadership and other team roles as needed. They stay focused and work for the common good.

Shares Leadership

Leadership on effective teams is shared among the members. Often the person who knows the most about a given problem serves as team leader until the problem is resolved. When a new problem is faced, the most expert person on that issue becomes the next team leader.

When leadership is shared, everyone feels responsible for the success or failure of the team. All members of the group are more willing to make decisions and take responsibility for them. Leadership does not mean telling others what to do. Instead, it involves helping the team move forward. A leader listens and encourages the team members. People who like to control others are not very effective team leaders.

Rotates Team Roles

A good team keeps everyone involved. One way to accomplish this is to assign roles to members. Besides rotating the role of leader, other roles are assigned to different members, too. This is particularly true in team meetings. The roles that rotate among members are shown in Figure 7-3.

Team Roles

- **Leader**—sets the team's agenda and helps the group make progress
- **Encourager**—inspires everyone to participate and makes certain that everyone's opinions are heard
- **Taskmaster**—keeps the group focused on achieving its goal(s)
- **Critic**—questions the assumptions expressed and decisions made
- **Recorder**—keeps detailed notes

Figure 7-3.   *Goodheart-Willcox Publisher*
For a team to work effectively, all the roles must be filled.

These roles may vary, depending on the needs of the team. Interest increases when team members take turns performing roles. The team leader one week may be the recorder the next week.

Stays Focused

An effective team consists of members who are aware of their mission. There are several ways to keep the team focused on its mission, including using humor effectively, taking a break, and listing goals.

One tool used to help a team maintain focus is a Gantt chart. A **Gantt chart** is a graph that shows the steps of a task divided across a timetable. See Figure 7-4. Team members can tell at a glance what phase of the goal should be in progress and what steps have been completed.

Uses Humor Effectively

Humor relaxes team members and helps them focus on the issues. There are times when groups become frustrated or tense. A humorous comment helps to release the tension. However, make sure humor is never used to "put down" or embarrass another team member.

Takes a Break

A break can also relieve pressure, reduce tension, and get a team back on track. A break can be a few minutes or a few days long, depending on the situation. Team members often return with fresh ideas and more positive attitudes, even after a ten-minute break.

Lists Goals

Making a list of goals helps team members continually move forward. A **goal** is something you want to attain. For example, a team may work toward the goal of reducing department injuries in June by 50 percent. Concentrating on the steps everyone must take to achieve that goal keeps the team focused.

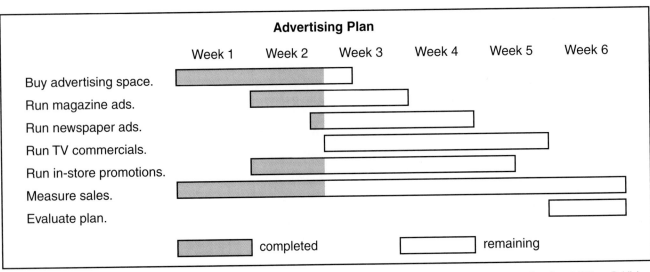

Goodheart-Willcox Publisher

Figure 7-4.
This Advertising Plan is an example of a Gantt Chart.

Works for the Common Good

Members of effective teams agree on what they are trying to do. The team members are able to set and meet deadlines. They encourage each other and celebrate both team and individual accomplishments. Effective teams make sure everyone understands the plan and helps carry it out. The team checks on the way it operates to see if it can work better.

Checkpoint 7.1

1. What part did globalization play in changing the role of the worker?
2. How do formal and informal teams differ?
3. What three common types of teams are used in the workplace?
4. Briefly describe the four stages of team development.
5. What are the four characteristics of an effective team?

Build Your Vocabulary

As you progress through this text, develop a personal glossary of career-related terms and add it to your portfolio. This will help build your vocabulary and prepare you for your career of choice. Write a definition for each of the following terms, and add it to your personal career glossary.

globalization
quality
team
interpersonal skills
virtual team
functional team
cross-functional team
self-directed team
multifunctional team
norm
Gantt chart
goal

7.2 | Problem Solving

Terms

problem
problem solving
criteria
constraint
Pareto Principle
brainstorming
compromise
consensus
conflict

Objectives

After completing this section, you will be able to:
- **Discuss** how teams work together to solve problems in the workplace.
- **Explain** how conflict can be managed when working as a team.

Problem Solving as a Team

A **problem** is a difference between reality (what you have) and expectation (what you want). **Problem solving** is the process of making an expectation a reality. The methods used to solve problems are the same for teams and individuals.

Employers benefit when workers are given more responsibility for solving work problems. Workers take greater pride in their work, and employee morale increases. Employees also tend to support an action plan they helped develop and complete successfully. Employers expect their workers to be able to solve problems.

Solving problems as a team will involve the same basic steps as solving them as an individual. The important difference is that everyone should be involved as much as possible to keep the team functioning effectively. Problem-solving skills can be developed, if you learn and follow several basic steps.

Steps in Problem Solving

Knowing the steps involved in solving problems will increase your chances of success. Although the steps in Figure 7-5 are listed in a recommended order, it is not simply a matter of doing one step at a time. Very often, information you obtain at one step may send you back to a previous step. As you gather data in Step 2, for example, you may find that you did not fully do Step 1. When this occurs, simply go back to the beginning and through the steps again.

Step 1: Identify and Analyze the Problem

Unsuccessful problem-solvers tend to jump right in and start trying to find solutions. Successful problem-solvers take time to identify and analyze the problem. It is very important to learn as much as you can about the problem before taking any action.

Problem-Solving Steps

1. *Identify and Analyze the Problem*

2. *Collect and Analyze Data*

3. *Consider Possible Solutions*

4. *Choose the Best Plan*

5. *Implement the Plan*

6. *Observe, Evaluate, and Adjust*

Figure 7-5.   *Goodheart-Willcox Publisher*
These steps can be used by teams or individuals to solve problems in a systematic way.

Do you understand what the problem is? Can you state it accurately? For example, you may not be getting along well with your employer. A major cause for this friction is your frequent tardiness to work. The reason why you are often tardy is because your friends pick you up late when giving you a ride to work. The problem is your late arrival to work, which is caused by riding with your late friends. The friction with your boss is only a result of the problem not the problem itself.

The first step in solving a problem is to state it accurately. As you try to determine the basic problem, you will identify factors related to the problem. These factors will be useful when you consider possible solutions in Step 3. The factors to consider are criteria and constraints.

Criteria are standards you use to find the best solution. Without the criteria to help make an evaluation, it is difficult to know if the problem is really solved. For this example, you may need a solution that incorporates the following criteria: arriving five minutes early to work and arriving dressed in your work uniform. Evaluation criteria will have an important influence on which solution you choose.

Constraints are factors that may restrict or hinder your ability to solve the problem. One hindrance to arriving on time to work may be a lack of transportation, or not having your own car. Another constraint may be having just 50 minutes between your last class and the time work starts. At this point, your identification and analysis of the problem would resemble the chart in Figure 7-6.

Identifying the "Late Arrival" Problem

Problem

- Late arrival at work caused by riding with friends who are usually late

Criteria

- Arriving five minutes early to work
- Arriving dressed in uniform

Constraints

- No car
- Just 50 minutes between the last class and the time work starts

Figure 7-6.   *Goodheart-Willcox Publisher*
Careful examination of the problem helps identify all the relevant factors.

Step 2: Collect and Analyze Data

In this step, you collect and analyze data related to the problem and ask yourself certain questions. What do you need to know about the problem that you do not already know? What information is available to help you solve the problem? Do you have everything you will need? If not, can you obtain what you need or must you make adjustments?

As you go through this process, other questions may arise. These questions will vary depending on the type of problem being solved. For example, what type of public transportation is available? Can you get a ride to work from more reliable friends, relatives, or coworkers?

You can gather data at the same time you develop your questions. This information should help you better understand the problem and provide ideas for possible solutions to it. If it does not, you may need to go back and reconsider how you identified and analyzed the problem.

One of the problems in collecting data is organizing it in a form that team members can easily understand and apply. Pareto analysis is one strategy for accomplishing this. The **Pareto Principle** states that as a general rule, 20 percent of causes produce 80 percent of the effects, or 20 percent of the effort produces 80 percent of the results. If you can discover which areas to concentrate on, you will be much more productive in solving problems and accomplishing goals. For example, imagine that 100 students were surveyed to determine the type of fund-raiser in which they would be willing to participate. Forty-four percent would prefer a car wash, while 30 percent prefer a spirit wear sale. The remaining 26 percent of responses are divided among four other activities. The students conclude that if they concentrate on just the car wash and spirit wear sale, they will have the largest percent of student participation. See Figure 7-7.

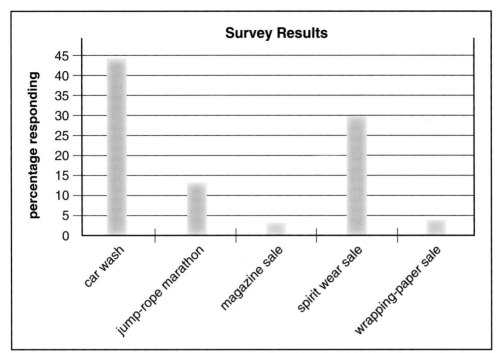

Figure 7-7.
Goodheart-Willcox Publisher
Collecting and analyzing data is an important part of the problem-solving process.

Once you are satisfied that you have accurately defined the problem and collected all-important data, you can focus on possible solutions.

Step 3: Consider Possible Solutions

Considering possible solutions is the first step in actually solving the problem. Your first concern is the quantity of ideas you develop, not their quality. Try to think creatively. Even wild ideas may have some value. Keep your ideas simple and brief at first. Do not worry about details.

Some possible solutions to the problem of tardiness may be to take a cab, ride the bus, or buy a car. Once you list various ideas, you can begin to narrow the list. Now is the time to think about the quality of your ideas. If you do not have enough money to buy a car or take a taxi, these are not practical solutions to your problem. Keep your evaluation criteria in mind, but do not be overly concerned about that at this point. Add more details to the ideas that seem workable. You may even consider combining several ideas. This process should result in a few workable solutions.

Step 4: Choose the Best Plan

When you have two or three good ideas, it is time to select the best one. Evaluate each in terms of the problem, the evaluation criteria, and the constraints that you identified in Step 1. After considering all options, you may decide that the solution to your late-arrival problem is to take the city bus.

Case

Pit Crew Members Are Team Players

Pit crews are critical to the success of professional racecar drivers. The crew may include a chief mechanic, general manager, driver assistant, "fuel person," "tire crew," transportation personnel, and others. Pit crews must set up the pit hours before a race. They make sure gasoline, tires, and anything else they may need is available in the pit.

Before the race, the pit crews wheel pit buggies and huge toolboxes into the pit area. The equipment and supplies include jacks, spare chassis, a drink holder with extended handle for the driver, a brush with extended handle to clean the car's grill, and spare shocks. Three gas cans, each containing 11 gallons of fuel, are placed in the pit. There is also a broom in the pit for cleanup and a gas catch-can to trap excess fuel during a fill-up. There are various lubricants, mufflers, lug nuts, sets of spare tires, and sometimes even a spare steering wheel. The list of items needed during a race is quite lengthy. If something is needed in a race and is not in the pit, a crew member must run to the garage to get it. That takes valuable racing time.

Around the pit buggy, five air wrenches are carefully placed. Hoses connecting them with nitrogen tanks are coiled and secured, so the crew will not trip over them. The nitrogen tanks provide the pressure needed to operate the wrenches.

Probably one of the most important tools used during pit stops is a two-way radio. Before the driver comes down pit road, he or she can tell the crew about any problems the car has. The driver can talk with the crew for instructions, such as when to make a pit stop and how many tires will be changed.

Only seven crew members are allowed over the pit wall at any time to work on the car; so, special tricks are used to perform the work at lightning speed. Pit crews can change four tires and add 22 gallons of fuel to the car in less than 20 seconds. The actual fueling process on a stock car only takes 10 or 11 seconds.

For the driver to win the race, the team has to function like clockwork. Each member has to know his or her job well and be highly skilled. The successful team not only helps the driver win a race but also assures a safe race without injuries.

Critical Thinking

1. What characteristics of an effective team are evident in a pit crew at a professional car race?
2. To what stage of team development has a racecar pit crew evolved?
3. How does teamwork solve the problems associated with driving racecars in competition?

Step 5: Implement the Plan

You should now be confident that you have a workable answer to your problem. You know which bus to catch and where to catch it. It is time to carry out your plan.

Step 6: Observe, Evaluate, and Adjust

This is one of the most important steps in the problem-solving process. Even the best plans may not go smoothly at first. Therefore, the plan must be carefully evaluated. Perhaps adjustments are needed. It is also important to allow flexibility in your plan.

Again, consider the evaluation criteria you developed when you identified the problem. The success or failure of your plan will depend largely on how well your plan meets the evaluation criteria. If the plan fails this test, it may need to be abandoned. If that happens, return to Step 1 to reexamine the problem.

To continue with our example, it is now time to check how well taking the bus solves the problem. Is it a dependable solution? Do you arrive at work five minutes early each day? Do you have enough time to dress into your work uniform before catching the bus? If this solution does not meet your evaluation criteria, discover why. Perhaps there is a better way to solve your problem.

Tools for Problem Solving

For a team to solve problems well, all members should be involved in each step of the process. Brainstorming, compromise, and consensus are tools that help teams through the problem-solving process.

Brainstorming

Brainstorming is a group technique used to list many ideas in a relatively short time. It can be used during a number of different steps in the problem-solving process. It is a very good way to identify answers to a problem. The quality of the ideas is not a major concern during brainstorming. The purpose is to identify as many ideas as possible. No idea is considered too ridiculous. See the chart in Figure 7-8 for a common way to hold a brainstorming session.

Compromise

One way to solve a problem is through compromise. **Compromise** occurs when each opposing side gives up something of value to help solve a problem. All sides accept the idea, but no one may feel it is the best one. This is because they gave up something that was important to them to reach the compromise.

Voting is often used to reach a compromise. However, the people who vote for an issue may feel more positively about carrying it out than those who vote against it.

Brainstorming Strategy
• Have the team sit in a semicircle to encourage discussion.
• Present the topic to the group.
• Have one member of the group offer his or her idea.
• Have someone record the ideas on a board or flip chart, so all can see. Do not criticize or discuss the merits of the ideas.
• Continue around the circle as each person states one idea. (It is permissible to build on someone else's ideas.) A person with nothing to contribute may pass.
• Continue around the circle as many times as necessary to identify all ideas.
• Discuss and evaluate the ideas.

Figure 7-8.   *Goodheart-Willcox Publisher*
This organized approach will help improve the results of a brainstorming session.

Consensus

Another way to solve a problem is through consensus. A **consensus** occurs when all members of a group fully accept and support a decision. Consensus is much more difficult to reach than compromise. When all members agree with a decision, they are more likely to be excited about carrying it out. Ideas must be thoroughly discussed and understood by all team members before a consensus can be reached. As a result, the process often leads to new and more creative ideas that neither side considered in the beginning. There is no need to vote, since everyone supports a decision reached by consensus.

A major problem with achieving consensus is that it is very time consuming. Therefore, you may not want to try to reach a consensus for all decisions.

Managing Conflict

As you work with others, as an individual or in teams, disagreements are bound to occur. More serious disagreements are called *conflict*. **Conflict** is a situation resulting from two or more opposing views. It is important that you know how to handle conflict so it does not become a destructive force in the workplace.

In a traditional work setting, a permanent manager supervises a group of employees. That manager is responsible for resolving conflict. In teamwork arrangements, however, the individuals have the responsibility to prevent conflict among team members from negatively affecting productivity. The person temporarily assigned to lead the team has a special responsibility. The steps to managing conflict are shown in Figure 7-9.

Steps in Managing Conflict
• Know when to intervene.
• Address the conflict.
• Identify the source and the importance of the conflict.
• Identify possible solutions.
• Develop an acceptable solution.
• Implement and evaluate.

Figure 7-9.   *Goodheart-Willcox Publisher*
Knowing how to manage conflicts when they occur is part of being an effective team player.

Know When to Intervene

Disagreements are not always bad. Constructive disagreements often lead to improvements in the workplace. One of the first decisions you must make when they arise is whether to become involved. Sometimes it is best not to act. What seems terribly important at the moment may later seem unimportant or even trivial. Premature actions may even make a difficult situation worse.

Often avoiding or ignoring a serious disagreement only postpones the time when conflict will result and action will be required. As a rule, it is time to consider action when the team or individual's happiness or productivity is affected.

Address the Conflict

When you have decided to take action, there are some rules you should follow. The first consideration, and perhaps most important, is to take a positive approach. Accept disagreement as a natural part of the group process. Then, try to follow the golden rule as you address the situation. *Treat others as you would want to be treated.* Try to understand the issue from the other person's point of view. Try to protect the person's self-esteem. Do not ever try to embarrass someone.

Whenever possible, try to avoid addressing the problem in front of others. Find a quiet place to resolve the conflict so you will not be distracted. Talk directly to the person or persons involved. Demonstrate control by speaking in a calm, firm, constructive way. Use "I" messages as you discuss the problem. For example, you might say: "I really felt embarrassed when you shouted at me" rather than "You should know better than to shout at other people." "You" messages tend to put people on the defensive.

Identify the Source and Importance of the Conflict

The next step in resolving conflict is to state the problem openly. Encourage each person to describe the problem as he or she sees it. Be sure there is a real problem, not simply a misunderstanding. Be specific in the discussion rather than general. Try to get people to focus directly on the problem. Imagine someone is continually late for team meetings. Is that the problem, or is tardiness a sign of a larger problem? What is the real problem?

Keep an open mind as the problem is discussed. Focus on getting all the facts expressed. Avoid making snap judgments and jumping to conclusions.

Identify Possible Solutions

Be sure everyone involved understands that each individual is responsible for both the problem and the solution. Anyone who is not involved in the matter should not be included in the discussion. Ask for comments and possible solutions from all sides and discuss the pros and cons.

Develop an Acceptable Solution

Focus on behavior that can be changed, not something a person cannot control. At the end of the discussion, summarize what has been decided and what action will be taken. Make sure everyone understands his or her role in solving the problem.

Implement and Evaluate

Once an agreeable solution has been reached, it is time to try it. Be willing to become involved in carrying out the plan. Avoid thinking it is not your problem. Check periodically to make sure teamwork has improved to a satisfactory extent. If not, it may be time to bring the concerned parties back together and try again to resolve the conflict. You could address the conflict from the beginning or return to the point where the breakdown occurred.

Checkpoint 7.2

1. What are the benefits when workers are given more responsibility for solving problems?

2. Explain the Pareto Principle.

3. Identify tools that help teams through the problem-solving process.

4. List the steps in managing conflict.

5. Why should a worker avoid "You" messages when attempting to resolve conflicts?

Build Your Vocabulary

As you progress through this text, develop a personal glossary of career-related terms and add it to your portfolio. This will help build your vocabulary and prepare you for your career of choice. Write a definition for each of the following terms, and add it to your personal career glossary.

problem
problem solving
criteria
constraint
Pareto Principle
brainstorming
compromise
consensus
conflict

Chapter Summary

Section 7.1 Teamwork

- Over the past century, the workplace has changed. Globalization has affected the role of the typical worker.
- Many companies use the team approach to solve problems and increase productivity. These teams are formed for different purposes.
- Team development evolves in stages. It takes considerable time to develop into an effective and smooth running team.
- An effective team shares leadership and team roles. Members are able to stay focused and work together.

Section 7.2 Problem Solving

- Employers expect workers to be able to solve problems. The first step in problem solving is to identify and analyze the problem.
- Disagreements are likely to occur in the workplace. To be successful, it is important for team members to learn how to manage conflict.

Check Your Career IQ

Now that you have finished the chapter, see what you learned about careers by taking the chapter posttest. The test can be accessed on the mobile site by using a smartphone or on the G-W Learning companion website.

www.m.g-wlearning.com
www.g-wlearning.com

Review Your Knowledge

1. Identify the effects of globalization mentioned in this chapter.
2. How are the members of a functional team different from the members of a multifunctional team?
3. Discuss why technology is so important to a virtual team.
4. What happens during the first stage of team development?
5. What happens during the second stage of team development?
6. What does a Gantt chart show?
7. Why should teams make a list of goals?
8. What is the purpose of brainstorming?
9. Explain what happens when two sides compromise.
10. In a traditional work setting, who is responsible for managing conflict?

Apply Your Knowledge

1. Think of a time when you worked with a team on a task or project. List three advantages of working with the team. Do you think the experience would have been different if you worked alone? Explain your answer.

2. Research the subject of globalization to answer the following questions: What is globalization? How does technology affect globalization? How does globalization impact me? Write a one-paragraph answer for each question.

3. Review the teams in Figure 7-1. Which team would you prefer to work with the most? Which team would you prefer to work with the least? Explain why.

4. List the times you function as part of a team throughout the week. Consider school projects, work, and extracurricular activities. How important is teamwork to you and the activities in your life?

5. Note what you learned about problem solving. Then, prepare a brief presentation to share with your class. Discuss how you might use this information in the future when working with others.

6. Do an Internet search to gather information about the purpose and use of a Gantt chart. Develop an outline of the points you learned. Share your information with the class.

7. Review articles in your local newspaper. Find an article that presents a problem between two or more parties. Which of the problem-solving tools would work best to help the parties settle their problem? Explain why.

8. Identify a problem in your community. Then, make a list of possible solutions to solve the problem.

9. Do an Internet search to gather information about the Pareto Principle. Develop an outline of the points you learned. Share your information with the class.

10. Imagine you and your team of coworkers have been assigned the task of writing an article for a magazine. Create a Gantt chart for your team to help you stay focused. Consider the following: What are the team goals? Who are the people involved? What are their responsibilities or tasks? Are there any important dates or deadlines to consider? See Figure 7-3 to help you create your team's Gantt chart.

Teamwork

Form a team of four to six members. Identify a problem for the team to solve, and role-play the four stages of team development: forming, storming, norming, and performing. End the role-play with a discussion of how members felt during each of the stages.

G-W Learning Mobile Site

Visit the G-W Learning mobile site to complete the chapter pretest and posttest and to practice vocabulary using e-flash cards. If you do not have a smartphone, visit the G-W Learning companion website to access these features.
G-W Learning mobile site: www.m.g-wlearning.com
G-W Learning companion website: www.g-wlearning.com

Common Core

College and Career Readiness

Reading. Read a magazine, newspaper, or online article about how technology plays a role in job searching. Determine the central ideas of the article and review the conclusions made by the author. Provide an accurate summary of your reading, making sure to incorporate the *who, what, when,* and *how* of this situation.

Writing. Conduct research on the techniques businesses use to increase productivity through improved teamwork. Write an informative report consisting of several paragraphs to describe your findings of the implications for the business.

Apply Your Technology Skills

Access the G-W Learning companion website for this text at www.g-wlearning.com. Download each data file for this chapter. Follow the instructions to complete activities to practice what you have learned in this chapter.

Data File 7–1—**Being a Team Player**

College and Career Readiness Portfolio

College and Career Readiness

You have identified the types of items you might place in your portfolio. You will begin adding items in this activity and add other items as you continue this class. Locate certificates you have received. For example, a certificate might show that you have completed a training class. Another certificate might show that you can keyboard at a certain speed. You might have a certificate that you received for taking part in a community project. Any certificates you have that show tasks completed or skills or talents that you have should be included. Create a document that lists each certificate and tells when you received it. Briefly describe your activities, skills, or talents related to the certificate.

1. Scan these documents to include in your e-portfolio. Use the file format you selected earlier.
2. Give each document an appropriate name, using the naming system you created earlier. Place each certificate and the list in an appropriate subfolder for your e-portfolio.
3. Place the certificates and list in the container for your print portfolio.

Section 8.1
Effective Communication

Section 8.2
Communication Channels

Section 8.3
Written Business
Communications

**College
and Career
Readiness**

Reading Prep. Review the table of contents for this text. Trace the development of the content from simple to complex ideas.

Introduction

Communication skills are very important to secure a job. Through good communication skills, people can successfully share feelings, ideas, facts, and opinions while performing day-to-day tasks the job requires.

Employers expect workers to listen, read, write, and speak accurately. If you are unsure of any required communication expectations, your supervisor will guide you. Employees with up-to-date communication skills will have no difficulty succeeding and advancing in a job. Poor communication skills, on the other hand, may result in being dismissed from your job.

Check Your Career IQ

Before you begin the chapter, see what you already know about careers by taking the chapter pretest. Use the related QR code to view the pretest on the mobile site. If you do not have a smartphone, visit the G-W Learning companion website to access the pretest.

www.m.g-wlearning.com
www.g-wlearning.com

G-W Mobile

Career Snapshot
Exercise Physiologist

ealth Science

What Does an Exercise Physiologist Do?

An exercise physiologist is trained to assess, plan, or implement fitness programs that include exercise or physical activities. An exercise physiologist is NOT a personal trainer. An exercise physiologist must:

- administer exercise stress tests in healthy and unhealthy populations;
- evaluate a person's overall health, with special attention to cardiovascular function and metabolism;
- develop individualized exercise prescriptions to increase physical fitness, strength, endurance, and flexibility; and
- design customized exercise programs to meet health care needs and athletic performance goals.

What Is It Like to Work as an Exercise Physiologist?

An exercise physiologist may be employed in a variety of settings, such as community organization venues, or in commercial and industrial facilities, health clubs, recreation centers, and educational institutions. They may also work in clinical settings prescribing exercise for cardiac, pulmonary, or other types of patients referred by a physician.

What Education and Skills Are Needed to Be an Exercise Physiologist?

- bachelor degree in physical education, exercise physiology, health science, or nutrition
- certification by the American Society of Exercise Physiologists (ASEP)
- problem-solving, analysis, and communication skills
- good interpersonal and customer-service skills

8.1 | Effective Communication

Terms

communication
sender
encoder
message
channel
receiver
decoder
feedback
noise
hearing
listening
comprehension
etiquette
nonverbal
    communication

Objectives

After completing this section, you will be able to:
- **Describe** the communication process.
- **Explain** why listening skills are important for job success
- **List** four ways to improve reading and comprehension skills.
- **Explain** why writing is an important work skill.
- **Describe** the importance of speaking skills.
- **Explain** the importance of nonverbal communication.

The Communication Process

Communication is the process of conveying a message, thought, or idea so it is accurately received and understood. Communication in the workplace is effective when the message received matches the one sent. This sounds much easier to do than it actually is. Perhaps the intended receiver of your message does not understand it. Maybe something prevents your message from reaching the intended receiver. In both cases, your communication is not effective. Ineffective communications occur more often than you might guess.

A model of the complete communication process is shown in Figure 8-1. The process includes the following parts:

- **sender**—the person (possibly you) who starts the communication process and has a mental image of what he or she wants to communicate;

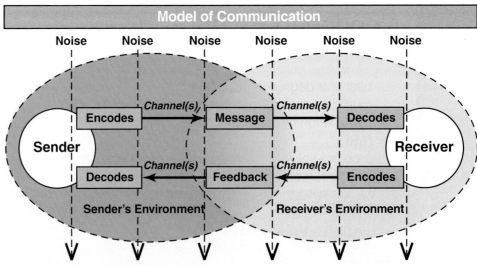

Figure 8-1.   *Goodheart-Willcox Publisher*
Understanding a communication model may help you to become a better communicator.

- **encoder**—the sender's mind, which forms a mental image of the message being sent;
- **message**—something that is understood by the senses (usually something spoken, written, or printed);
- **channel** —how the message is delivered during communication (by voice, a printed document, an image, or another means);
- **receiver**—the person who gets the message;
- **decoder**—the receiver's mind, which forms a mental image of the message received;
- **feedback**—a clue that reveals the message was received; and
- **noise**—anything that interrupts the message.

As you can see, the communication process is more complex than just speaking or writing to another person. The minds of both the sender and the receiver of the message are actively involved. The receiver's reaction signals what he or she understood. If the reaction is unusual or unexpected, it can mean that the receiver got the wrong message.

If you ask a coworker, for example, where office supplies are located, you expect an answer. If he continues staring at the computer screen, the feedback may indicate that he did not hear you. When the coworker answers with directions to the office supplies, you know your message is understood. In some cases, feedback is not necessary because you know the message was correctly communicated. However, the only way to be certain a message is understood is by the feedback provided to the sender.

Noise is any interference that distorts the meaning of the message. Noise can be a mechanical sound, such as a ringing phone, loud conversation, or squeaky machines. Noise can also be a psychological factor that takes many forms. An example of *psychological noise* is when a customer does not hear you because of anger over experience with a defective product. Psychological noise can also result from personality conflict between the sender and receiver. Psychological noise is very common.

Practically every communication in the workplace is an opportunity for a breakdown to occur. By recognizing this possibility, you are more likely to make the effort necessary to communicate accurately.

Go Green

A lot of communication today takes place electronically. People send text messages and e-mail as part of their business and personal communications every day. Sending messages electronically *can* save paper as well as the energy needed to deliver a message that would have otherwise been sent by mail. However, if you routinely print out e-mails you receive, a lot of paper is wasted. Make a practice of only printing out e-mail messages that require filing a hard copy. Create subfolders within your e-mail's inbox in which you can keep important messages to which you can later refer rather than printing a hard copy.

The workplace simply cannot function without all the workers having effective communication skills. A lack of such skills may result in a poor quality product or service, insufficient quantities of the product being produced, an uncomfortable atmosphere in the building, unsafe working conditions, or disgruntled managers and workers. It is very important to develop and use effective communicating skills in a variety of ways.

Listening Skills

Some people never seem to listen. They become so involved in what they will say that they do not bother to listen to others. Have you ever encountered people who seem to be thinking about something else when you are talking to them? Do you ever do the same to others?

Sometimes listening is considered the same as hearing, but it is not. Hearing is recognizing sound. Listening involves understanding what you hear. For communication to occur, a message must be sent, received, and understood. Therefore, if a person is not listening when a message is sent, communication does not take place.

People often fail to listen when they are in the following situations.

- **They are interrupted.** A person's ability to listen is affected when someone walks into the room, a telephone rings, or other people are talking nearby.
- **They think they know what will be said.** Sometimes people only listen to part of a conversation because they think "I've heard this before."
- **They do not agree with what is said.** When people do not agree with what is said, they often block the information from entering their minds, refusing to listen to the speaker.
- **They are having difficulty hearing.** A person may stop listening when someone is speaking so softly that what is being said cannot be understood, or that person may have a hearing impairment.
- **They are distracted by the speaker.** Sometimes the speaker has distracting mannerisms, speaks in a monotone, or does not make eye contact with the audience, which discourages listening.
- **They do not understand the words.** Not knowing the meanings of words used by the speaker hinders the listener.
- **They start thinking about something else.** When people allow their minds to wander, they fail to concentrate on what is being said.

To be a good listener, you concentrate on what is said. You do not let yourself become distracted. You block out everything except the voice of the speaker. Do not interrupt the speaker unless you do not understand what is being said. Then, ask the speaker to explain in more detail what he or she said. Being a good listener will help you be a better worker. Listening is a skill you can improve with practice.

Reading and Comprehension Skills

Reading and comprehension skills are important in the workplace. In almost every work situation, you will be expected to read many types of printed job-related materials. Reading skills involve more than just being able to say the words aloud. Comprehension is needed. Comprehension is the ability to understand information. To be an effective employee, you will need to understand the memos, reports, books, directions, and other documents associated with your job.

In Derrick's case, for example, comprehension is important. He will be operating new technical equipment. He knows he must read the instruction manuals and carefully follow directions to operate the machines safely. As a result, he will avoid an accident and prevent damage to the machines. His skill in reading and understanding what he reads will benefit him and his employer. He will gain some new skills. This could help him advance on the job. His skills will save his employer time and money.

Being able to read the printed materials at your training station will help you do the job well. Good reading and comprehension skills can help you find information quickly and save time. You can also gain knowledge and skills through reading that can help you advance to a better job.

Even good readers can improve their reading skills. Sharpening these skills will help you read faster and remember more of what you read. The following guidelines may help you become a better reader.

Read With a Purpose

Before you start to read, you should know why you are reading something. Then you can focus on reading the information you really need. For example, Derrick will read the instruction manuals so he can operate the machines safely. Your purpose might be to learn something new or to find answers.

Look Over the Material You Are Reading First

Read over the table of contents for the material or chapter. Pay attention to how the material is organized by looking at the chapter title and headings. Derrick will follow these guidelines as he reads through the manuals.

Read for Meaning

The best way to remember what you read is to concentrate. Do not let your mind wander. After you finish reading a section of material, think about the main ideas. Picture these ideas in your mind. This will help you understand what you read. Another way to understand the meaning of what you read is to organize and outline the main ideas in your mind or on paper. This can help you understand the writer's message.

Improve Your Vocabulary

Improving your vocabulary is very important to improving comprehension. As you read, you will find one or more words you do not know. Sometimes you can determine the meaning by the way the word is used in the sentence or paragraph. If the meaning still is not clear, use a dictionary to check the word's meaning. You may even come across certain words or terms that relate to the type of work you do. Many businesses have their own special vocabulary. These special words are used to describe products or operations for that specific business. Company- or process-specific terminology makes communication among employees more efficient. Learning these words or terms can help you read and understand job-related materials.

As Derrick reads his manual, he will find several new technical terms. He can ask his coworkers what the terms mean or check a dictionary. Either method will help him do his job well.

Writing Skills

Many employers consider written communication skills one of the most important job skills an employee can have. Why? Few people possess this skill. Poor communication causes employers to lose business and money. Therefore, the ability to write a message clearly and accurately is an important skill to have in the working world.

Reading and writing skills are important for students as well as employees.

Solaria/Shutterstock.com

Good writing skills involve composing written or printed communications. It requires the presentation of clear, logical thoughts. Writing skills become especially important as you advance on the job.

Today, few written communications in the workplace are handwritten. The vast majority of written and printed communications are prepared electronically.

Speaking Skills

You routinely use thousands of words. However, good speaking skills involve more than knowledge of words. You must also be able to use words effectively.

Employers consider speaking skills so important that they cite them as one of the basic skills needed to be an effective worker. How good are your speaking skills? If they need improvement, you can accomplish that with practice. Follow these guidelines when you speak to others.

Speak Clearly and Distinctly

Avoid running words together such as "whydoncha" for "why don't you." If necessary, talk more slowly. If you have a tendency to mumble, try opening your mouth a little wider when talking. Always be sure not to talk with food or anything else in your mouth.

Speak Directly to the Listener

Whether you speak to one person or more, establish eye contact. This will help hold each listener's attention and show that you are interested in the conversation. When you speak, use words the listener will understand.

Speak with a Friendly and Courteous Tone

Try to phrase what you want to say in a positive way. When you find it necessary to use criticism, be ready to offer a constructive idea. Avoid arguing and complaining.

Use Standard English

Using Standard English means you should use correct grammar and pronunciation when speaking. "Bob came here yesterday" is Standard English. "Came Bob yesterday here" is not. The person who uses Standard English on the job appears more competent and better educated.

Talk "with" the Listener, Not "to" the Listener

Keep messages short and understandable. Make sure your messages are received correctly. You may want to ask questions such as "What do you think?" or "What are your feelings about this?" This gives the listener a chance to provide feedback. From the listener's comments, you will know if your messages have been understood.

Use Proper Form When Speaking on the Phone

Using the telephone in the workplace is one of the quickest ways to communicate. A one-minute telephone call, if handled properly, can save hours or even days in communication time. If you have a job that involves a telephone, it is important to use good telephone manners. The way you communicate over the telephone can help or hurt your employer.

Etiquette is the art of using good manners in any situation. *Telephone etiquette* is using good manners when handling telephone calls. When you make and receive telephone calls on the job, good telephone etiquette is important.

When the telephone rings, answer it immediately. Greet the caller pleasantly and give the name of your company, your department, or your own name. Your supervisor will probably tell you what greeting to use. You may say something like, "Good morning, the Acme Company, may I help you?"

When talking, hold the phone about one inch from your lips and speak directly into the mouthpiece. Speak clearly and say each word distinctly. Do not eat, drink, or chew gum while speaking on the phone. Always be courteous to the caller even if it is a wrong number.

Be sure to keep a message pad or paper and pen close to the telephone to write down messages. When taking a message, record the following:

- date;
- time of the call;
- name of the caller;
- name of the person who should receive the message; and
- the message itself.

Ethical Leadership

Intellectual Property and Honesty

"The Internet has been the place where intellectual property has been least respected. You know, facts don't get in the way of this ideology."—Lawrence Lessig

An ethical leader respects the physical and intellectual property of others. Did you know you must cite any information you use that was written by someone else? Intellectual property is anything that has been created by someone else—copyrighted material, trademarks, music, etc. If you quote material for a blog, website, or even a presentation, you must give the owner credit for that material. It is unethical to present information as your own when it is not. Doing so can be illegal. Search the Internet for the proper use of intellectual material.

After writing the message, read it back to the caller to make sure you recorded the information correctly. If you are not sure how to spell a person's name or a company's name, ask the caller to spell it for you. It is important for you to copy down the message exactly.

Plan your call in advance. For example, if you are placing an order for company supplies, be sure you have all the facts you need in front of you. Know what you want to say and how you want to say it.

When any business call comes to a close, end the conversation pleasantly. If you made the call, thank the person for his or her assistance or cooperation. If you received the call, you may want to thank the person for calling. Remember, the impressions you make on others will influence the impressions they will have of you and your company.

Know Your Subject Matter When Speaking to a Group

At school, you have probably spoken in front of a group. You have likely given oral reports in some of your classes. Perhaps you have spoken in front of a club or participated in a public-speaking contest.

Practically all occupations require some form of public speaking. As an employee, you may be asked to guide a tour group through your department. You may be asked to make a sales pitch to a group of buyers or speak at a meeting. You will probably be asked on many occasions to explain your ideas to a group of coworkers. Regardless of the type of work you do, having the ability to speak in front of a group will help you be a better communicator on and off the job.

Most people are afraid to speak in front of a group because they they fear they might say or do something foolish. That becomes less of a problem when you speak on a familiar topic. You may think you do not know much, but you do. You are an expert on yourself. You could talk confidently about where you live, where you go to school, where you work, and what your interests and hobbies are. You are the expert on what you do at your training station—the tasks you perform and the skills you learn. Knowing your subject is half the work in public speaking. The other half is preparing your presentation.

When preparing your speech, outline the main thoughts you want to convey to your audience. Try to limit yourself to five main points or less. Then, organize your points in a logical order. For example, suppose you will speak about refinishing furniture, a hobby of yours. You decide there are three main points to include:
- different types of finishes;
- step-by-step explanation of how to refinish furniture; and
- materials and equipment needed for refinishing.

After reviewing these, you decide the most logical point to mention first is a step-by-step explanation. Next, you decide you want to describe the material and equipment needed. This leaves the discussion of finishes last. Therefore, you decide to organize the points as follows:

1. step-by-step explanation of how to refinish furniture;
2. materials and equipment needed for refinishing; and
3. different types of finishes.

Now you have a speech, but how do you deliver it? Here is one easy rule to follow—*tell them what you plan to tell them; tell them; then tell them what you told them*. This simply means identify your main points; discuss them; then summarize them.

When you begin your speech, catching the audience's attention is important. You may want to tell a funny story related to your subject or one that will lead into your subject. Telling a personal experience related to the subject is another idea. Next, go through your points one by one. Finally, summarize those points.

Practice before giving your speech. This will help you know what you want to say and when. You will also want to practice timing to make sure your speech is not too long or short. If you are not given a time limit, then limit yourself. It is best not to speak longer than twenty minutes. This will allow some time for answering questions from the audience.

When delivering your speech, avoid reading from your speech word-for-word. Use note cards instead. You should speak to your audience, not read to them. As you speak, project your voice so everyone can hear you clearly. It is also important to look at the people to whom you are talking. Making eye contact will help you hold the attention of your audience.

Your appearance when making a presentation is also important. Dress appropriately for the occasion and the audience. If speaking to classmates in your English class at school, dress as you would for school. If speaking to a group of employers about your cooperative work experience, dress more formally. Always make sure you look clean and neat.

Remember, when you give a speech, you are simply sharing a message with others. Give it with confidence and enthusiasm. Also, before giving your speech, look back at the communication process outlined in Figure 8-1 and be sure you are sending and encoding exactly what you want the audience to receive.

Nonverbal Communication

Nonverbal communication can affect the content of what people try to communicate more than what is said or heard. **Nonverbal communication** is any message that does not use written or spoken words. People alter the meaning of what they say with facial expressions, gestures, and the way in which they sit and stand. Even silence is a form of nonverbal communication.

Nonverbal communication is also an important workplace skill. It is important to be aware of what messages your actions as well as your words convey. Make an effort to match your nonverbal communications with your feelings and the messages you are trying to send. For example, when you sit tall in a chair and make direct eye contact, you appear interested. When you lean back, slouch, or look away from a speaker, you appear disinterested.

Greeting someone with a smile and firm handshake makes you appear happy to meet them. Using a limp handshake and staring at the floor may make you appear unconfident or disinterested. Sitting beside an individual may indicate a willingness to discuss differences and reach a solution. Standing directly in front of someone's face, practically nose to nose, may show a readiness to fight. Just staring at someone with no expression on your face communicates something to the other person. That "something" may be interpreted either negatively or positively. For this reason, it is best to give whomever you are speaking with something other than a blank stare.

Checkpoint 8.1

1. What part does the channel play in the communication process?
2. Describe an example of psychological noise.
3. What is the difference between hearing and listening?
4. Identify four guidelines that can help a person become a better reader?
5. What are some examples of nonverbal communication?

Build Your Vocabulary

As you progress through this text, develop a personal glossary of career-related terms and add it to your portfolio. This will help build your vocabulary and prepare for your career of choice. Write a definition for each of the following terms, and add it to your personal career glossary.

communication
sender
encoder
message
channel
receiver
decoder
feedback
noise
hearing
listening
comprehension
etiquette
nonverbal communication

8.2 | Communication Channels

Terms

formal communication
informal communication
communication barrier

Objectives

After completing this section you will be able to:
- **Explain** how formal communication is used in the workplace.
- **Describe** how informal communication takes place on the job.
- **List** how communication barriers can be overcome.

Formal Communication

Formal Communication is the sharing of information in which specific rules of etiquette must be followed. These rules in the workplace dictate how employees at different levels interact with each other. For example, an assistant in a marketing department would not bypass the manager and go directly to the president of the company about an issue.

Sometimes, formal communication is known as the *chain of command* as shown in the organizational chart in Figure 8-2. Each level of employee must communicate up to his or her immediate supervisor rather than bypass a manager. Understanding how to conduct formal communication is an important skill to have in the workplace.

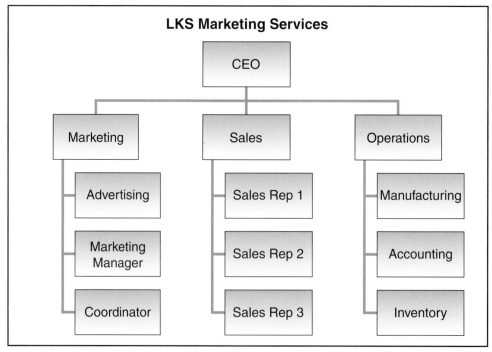

Figure 8-2.   *Goodheart-Willcox Publisher*
An organizational chart shows the structure of a company or organization.

Formal communication typically flows in three directions: upward, laterally, and downward as shown in Figure 8-3.

- **Upward communication** takes place with your supervisors, managers, and company executives.
- **Lateral communication** takes place between you and those at your same level or position.
- **Downward communication** takes place when company executives and those to whom you report communicate with you.

Formal communication typically takes place in a letter, e-mail, or other communication that is planned rather than spontaneous.

Informal Communication

Informal communication is unscheduled communication with coworkers that occurs by chance inside and outside the workplace. Informal communications may relate to your job, coworkers, or employer. Sometimes it may relate to your employer's reputation in the industry or the local community. Informal communications are common during travel between home and work, shift changes, or breaks.

Informal communication is sometimes more informative than formal communication in the workplace. On the other hand, these communications are sometimes merely gossip. It will be up to you to distinguish the *useful* from the *useless* information.

During informal communications, it is important to keep in mind you are still "on the clock" and responsible to your employer. At times it is tempting to discuss other employees, your superiors, and topics related to both work and social situations. Remember, some people do not keep confidences, and anything you say may be passed on to

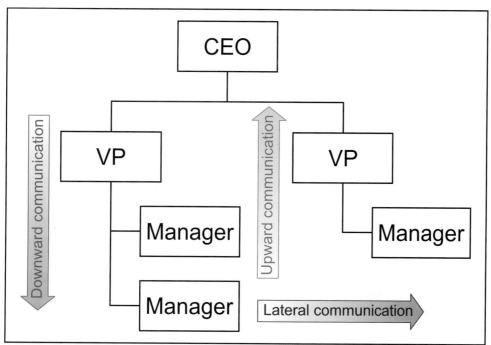

Figure 8-3.   *Goodheart-Willcox Publisher*
There are three basic directions of communication flow within a business.

anyone else. It is best to confine your discussions to subjects that relate to your employment and are harmless social conversations.

Barriers to Communications

Communication barriers are anything that prevents clear, effective communication. Ineffective communications are a result of some type of communication barrier. Unfortunately the workplace may contain many types of communication barriers. These barriers may be of a physical, cultural, or emotional nature.

Physical Communication Barriers

Physical barriers may be a closed door, a restricted area, a very noisy place, or a very large open area where hearing another person is very difficult. Even a very small work area may present a physical barrier if walls and dividers give the impression coworkers are not available or not willing to speak.

Cultural Communication Barriers

Cultural barriers may be a result of a worker being of a different culture, speaking a different language, or using different body language when conversing. Any one of these differences in

Connecting with coworkers on a personal level can help minimize potential barriers to communication.

Stephen Coburn/Shutterstock.com

communicating may present a barrier. It is important everyone works to recognize these barriers, if they exist, and work to overcome them.

Emotional Communication Barriers

Emotional barriers may cause major disruptions in communications. Emotions in the workplace may lead to fear, mistrust, and suspicion. This may cause workers to hold back their thoughts and feelings from others. It is important to determine what is causing any emotional barrier. Some people are just shy, and others wish to avoid conflict. One's personality may also lead to an emotional barrier. This is especially true if a worker is easily distracted, plays power games, is a poor listener, or avoids eye contact.

Checkpoint 8.2

1. Identify the three directions of communication that typically take place at work.
2. Explain the difference between formal communication and informal communication.
3. What types of subjects are safe to discuss during work breaks?
4. List three kinds of communication barriers that may exist among workers.
5. How can emotions negatively affect the workplace?

Build Your Vocabulary

As you progress through this text, develop a personal glossary of career-related terms and add it to your portfolio. This will help build your vocabulary and prepare you for your career of choice. Write a definition for each of the following terms, and add it to your personal career glossary.

formal communication
informal communication
communication barrier

8.3 | Written Business Communications

Terms

template
white space
block style letter
modified block style letter
memo

Objectives

After completing this section you will be able to:
- **List** important elements of a business letter.
- **Describe** the purpose and design of a memo.
- **Discuss** the purpose of a business report.

Business Letters

Writing a business letter is different from a personal letter to a friend or relative. When writing a personal letter, you can use your own style of writing. You can write just as you would talk to the person face-to-face. You can write on bright red stationery or yellow paper with polka dots. You also do not have to keep a copy of every personal letter you write.

Letters written in the workplace, however, are more formal. There are specific parts that should be included in every business letter and certain styles that should be followed. To make keying a letter easy, you can use a template. A **template** is a preformatted form available in word processing software.

Record keeping is important, so always maintain a copy of every business letter you write. You may keep an electronic copy as well as a hard copy in your files.

Parts of a Business Letter

Most business letters have eight standard parts—the return address, date, inside address, salutation, body, complimentary close, signature and name, and enclosure notation. Each part is described here as shown in Figure 8-4.
- **Return address**—tells the reader from where the letter came. Most companies have their return addresses printed on their stationery, which is called *letterhead*.
- **Date**—tells the reader when the letter was written.
- **Inside address**—includes the name, business title, and address of the person to whom the letter is written. It is the same address as that on the envelope.

- **Salutation**—is the greeting that precedes the body of the letter. The most widely used salutation is Dear Mr. (Mrs., Ms., or Miss) Jones. If you are writing to a group of men and women, you can use *Gentlemen* or *Ladies*. If you know the person on a first-name basis, you can write *Dear Terry*. A colon (:) always follows the salutation.
- **Body**—contains the message.
- **Complimentary close**—formally ends the message. Most business letters have one of the following closings: *Sincerely, Yours truly,* or *Cordially.* A comma follows the closing.
- **Signature, printed name, and business title**—follow the complimentary close. You should sign your name in ink above your printed name. Usually, you sign both your first and last name. If you are on a first-name basis with the person to whom you are writing, simply sign your first name. Your business title appears directly below your name.
- **Enclosure notation**—alerts the reader that materials are included with the letter. Spell out the word *enclosure.*

Case

Are You Listening, Quentin?

At a department meeting, Quentin's supervisor introduced a new process that the company will begin using in the manufacture of their products. He explained that the new process would require a large, new machine. In order to make room for the new machine, all the other machines in the department would need to be relocated. He said, "This new laser scanner will be placed along the east wall. All other machines will be placed along the north and west walls."

The supervisor began to explain how the heavy equipment should be moved. Suddenly Quentin said, "Why don't we put the new machine along the east wall?"

The room became silent. The supervisor replied that the idea was a good one, but had already been discussed.

Embarrassed, Quentin said, "I'm sorry. I didn't hear you."

The supervisor had spoken loud enough for everyone to hear him easily. Quentin had perfect hearing, but he wasn't paying attention. Most of his coworkers laughed at him, shaking their heads.

Critical Thinking

1. On a scale of 1 (poor) to 10 (excellent), what rating do Quentin's listening skills deserve?
2. Do you think Quentin's coworkers were rude to him? What might this incident do to Quentin's reputation?
3. What can you learn from Quentin that would make you a better listener?

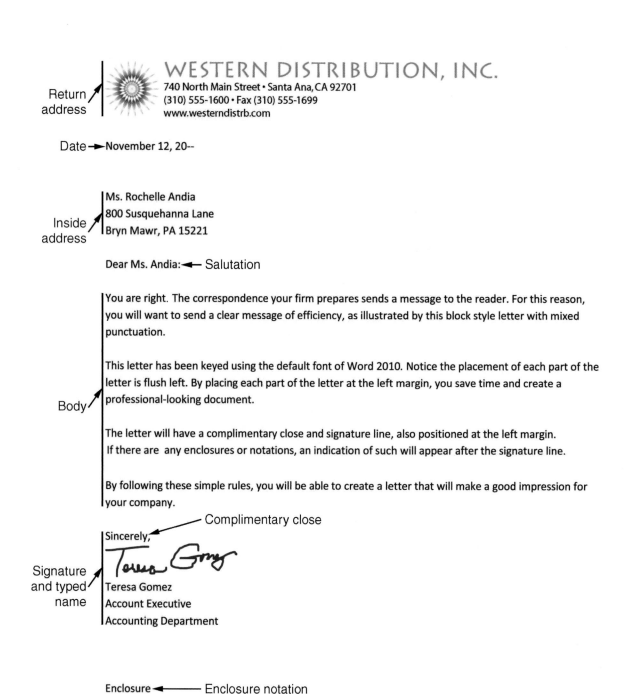

Figure 8-4.
This is an example of a properly formatted business letter.

Types of Business Letters

A business letter is usually written for one of three reasons:
1. to request information, merchandise, or service;
2. to send a positive or neutral message; or
3. to deliver bad news.

To address these different reasons, there are three main types of business letters: request letters, good news and neutral-message letters, and bad-news letters. The type of message you communicate will determine which type of letter to write and what information to include. The following are guidelines for writing each type of letter.

Request Letters

When the main purpose of your message is to ask the reader to do something, you are writing a request letter. In this case, it is important to cover three points.
1. Introduce your request, and state why you are making the request.
2. Include any details necessary for the reader to respond to your request correctly.
3. State clearly what action you want the reader to take and when.

For example, if you are ordering merchandise, it is important that you include the name of the merchandise, quantity wanted, order or catalog number, size, color, and any other required information. Also, give the reader the name and address to which the merchandise should be sent. Tell the reader when the order is needed and how it will be paid.

In the closing paragraph, you should also include a statement of appreciation as shown in Figure 8-5. You might write this: "I would appreciate a phone call at your earliest convenience."

Good-News and Neutral-Message Letters

Letters that answer requests; grant favors; express thanks; or make announcements about events, policies, and procedures can be written by using the good-news and neutral-message letter plan. These types of letters are usually easy to write because you tell the reader something pleasant or not controversial.

In a good-news and neutral-message letter, there are three important points to tell the reader.
1. State the news or the main idea.
2. Explain any details, facts, or reasons that relate to it.
3. End the letter on a positive and friendly note.

For example, suppose your job is to fill a mail order for a customer. If the customer ordered four items and you only have three items in stock, explain when the other item will be sent. Thank the customer for doing business with your company. Let the person know you will be glad to fill future orders. If your company is also sending information about a new product or service, provide complete information about it and how to obtain it. See Figure 8-6.

Basserette Industries

3370 St. Charles Avenue
New Desert, NV 89772
702.555.6612 Fax 702.555.7157
www.Basserette.com

July 17, 20--

Mr. Elmer Lipscomb
Lipscomb Advanced Laboratories
2732 Trabajo Nuevo Road
Miami, FL 33003

Dear Mr. Lipscomb:

I am the Office Manager for our company and have been given the task to research ways in which we can expand and modernize our laboratory. Our lab was organized many years ago when we were a very small company. Over the years, we have been fortunate to expand our business and greatly increase the number of staff we employ. Our engineers, chemists, scientists, and executives need a modern space with new technology at their fingertips.

I am inquiring to see if you have sample model layouts and recommendations for equipment and materials to create a new lab. We are very interested in reviewing any resources that you may have to share with us.

Also, I visited your website and noticed that you have a virtual tour of labs you have helped create for other customers. If you could give me a password to log into the demo site, I would appreciate it.

If your department is not the correct contact for new lab purchases, I would appreciate it if you could direct me to the appropriate division of your company.

Thank you very much, Mr. Lipscomb. If we are successful in our lab redesign, we would be happy to serve as a reviewer of your services.

Cordially,

Kenneth Rodriguez
Office Manager

Figure 8-5.
The main purpose of a request letter is to get the reader to do something for you.

Goodheart-Willcox Publisher

1257 Reedson Road
Worcester, MA 01601
617-555-4400/Fax 617-555-4432
www.ameriplastics.com

May 29, 20--

Ms. Constance Kennedy
Max Products Corporation
3224 Pautuset Avenue
Providence, RI 02933

Dear Ms. Kennedy:

Thank you for your letter of May 23 requesting information on our shrink-wrap, multiple-packaging equipment.

The enclosed fact sheets list the technical data and the price information you requested. In addition to packaging equipment, our company also manufactures other products that would be beneficial to your operations, particularly your canned foods division. Fact sheets for those products are also enclosed.

I would be pleased to visit your location and make a formal presentation of our product line at a time that works for you. Just let me know when you wish to schedule a meeting.

Thank you for the opportunity to introduce our company line of products to you. You may call me at 617-555-4400 if you have further questions or if you wish additional information.

Sincerely yours,

Deanna Priazai
Product Manager

Enclosures

Figure 8-6. *Goodheart-Willcox Publisher*
A good-news or a neutral request letter should follow the same format as any other business correspondence.

Bad-News Letters

Acknowledging orders you cannot fill, turning down requests, and announcing news about price increases or discontinued services are examples of bad-news messages. The wording of a bad-news letter is very important. You want to tell the reader the bad news without the reader forming a negative impression of your company.

Usually, there are four important points to tell the reader.

1. Say something positive that interests the reader, yet relates to the bad news.
2. Explain why the request cannot be granted or why the situation must be different from the way the reader wants it.
3. Offer a constructive suggestion or an alternative.
4. End the letter on a friendly, positive note.

Thank the reader sincerely for making the request, but indicate that it cannot be filled and explain why. For example, maybe your company does not carry the exact item requested, but a very similar product that may interest the reader is available. Perhaps you can direct the reader to a company that does carry the item. Finally, express continued interest in the reader, and invite him or her to contact you in the future.

Appearance of a Business Letter

The appearance of a letter is important. By adding white space on the page, the letter will be more visually attractive. **White space** includes margins, space between paragraphs, and any other blank space on the page. Writing is most readable when it is presented in small segments with adequate white space.

Businesses generally use one of two standardized letter formats: block or modified block. The **block style letter** is formatted so all lines are flush with the left-hand margin. No indentions are used. Appropriate guidelines for spacing between the date, inside address, greeting, letter body, and signature block need to be followed. The letter in Figure 8-6 is block-style on stationery.

The **modified block style letter** places the date, complimentary close, and signature to the right of the center point of the letter. All other elements of the letter are flush with the left margin. The decision to indent the paragraphs needs to be considered, depending on the guidelines of the workplace. The letter in Figure 8-7 is modified block-style.

Appearance of a Business Envelope

If you are physically mailing a letter, it is necessary to address an envelope. Most businesses generally use a standard size 10 envelope, which is 4 1/8 inches by 9 1/2 inches. The US Postal Service recommends the address be in all capital letters with no punctuation as shown in Figure 8-8.

Max Products Corporation
3224 Pautuset Avenue
Providence, RI 02933
401.555.2200
www.maxproducts.com

May 23, 20--

Ms. Deanna Priazai
American Plastics
1257 Reedson Road
Worcester, MA 01601

Dear Ms. Priazai:

I appreciate your request for me to speak at the opening ceremony of your company's annual sales meeting on June 25. It is nice to know that you value my experience and believe that it would be beneficial to your company.

Unfortunately, I will be attending a conference the week of June 25, and therefore will not be able to attend the meeting.

Thank you for considering me, and I hope that you will keep me in mind for future conferences.

Sincerely,

Constance Kennedy

Constance Kennedy
Sales Manager

Figure 8-7.   *Goodheart-Willcox Publisher*
A modified block style letter places the date, complimentary close, and signature to the right of the center point of the letter.

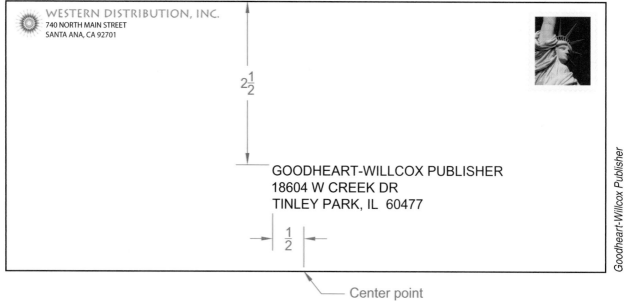

Figure 8-8.
When addressing a standard size 10 envelope, use the spacing shown here.

Memos

When you want to send a written message to someone at work, you do not send a business letter—you send a memorandum. A memorandum, or **memo**, is an informal written message from one person or department to another person, persons, or department(s) in the same company. Memos are similar to e-mails, but are more appropriate when the material is very detailed.

Memos may be created and printed on forms with the company name and logo at the top. The word *Memorandum,* or *Memo,* is in large letters at the top and the guide words *To, From, Date,* and *Subject* appear directly beneath. These words often appear in all capital letters. You may also create memos using a template.

Parts of a Memo

The standard parts of a memo are described here and shown in Figure 8-9.

To

Key the name of the recipient(s) on the *to* line. Omit courtesy titles (Mr., Ms.). Names may be in list format or on a single line separated with commas. If a memo is being sent to a group of employees, use the name of the group instead of listing all the individual names.

MEMORANDUM

Guide words {
TO: Patricia Lorenzo

FROM: Jeremy Ornstein

DATE: May 22, 20--

SUBJECT: New Catalog
}

We are preparing the fall catalog and I would like to get your opinion on the attached cover designs. Will you please look over these designs and share them with your staff?

Figure 8-9.   *Goodheart-Willcox Publisher*
This sample memo is properly formatted.

From

On this *from* line, key your full name or the name of the person for whom you are keying the memo. It is optional for the sender to initial the typed name before the memo is sent.

Date

The *date* line contains the date that the memo is being sent. Spell out the name of the month. Include the full year in numbers.

Subject

In the *subject* line, indicate the subject in language that clearly states the topic. Be concise. Also, capitalize the main words in the subject line.

Body

When keying a memo, begin the message below the *subject* line. The paragraphs are positioned flush left. Key the message in a single-spaced format with a double space between paragraphs.

Appearance of a Memo

Some businesses may have a special type of stationery to use for memos. This stationery may have *Memorandum* and the company's name at the top of the page. If your company does not have memo stationery, regular high-quality paper can be used.

In most cases, a memo format is available on your computer at work. You simply key in the information after each heading. Although there are no set guidelines for typing memos, here are some tips for memo placement. The words *To, From, Date,* and *Subject* should be followed by colons at the left margin. There should be one line of white space between each heading. The body of the memo should begin under the subject line after one or two lines of white space, regardless of the length of the message. The message is usually single-spaced.

Business Reports

Business reports are written to present a new idea, explain a problem that needs action, or summarize work done to date. They are usually written to help the receivers understand a significant business situation, solve a business problem, or make a decision. Business reports are either formal or informal.

Formal reports are usually long and about complex problems. They usually include a cover, title page, table of contents, introduction, body, summary, and bibliography. They often include graphs, tables, and illustrations to explain specific points. The parts of the report may vary depending on the purpose and the audience.

Informal reports are generally short and usually include just the body of the message, like the body of a letter or memo. Weekly reports on sales, number of phone calls received, and department accomplishments are examples of informal reports. Often, the information appears on company reporting forms.

As with letters and memos, you will need to plan what you want to include in a report before you begin writing.

- **Define the purpose.** Why are you writing the report? What do you need to tell the receiver?
- **Consider who will receive the report.** Who wants or needs the report? How much detail do they need or prefer?
- **Determine what ideas to include.** What points will you need to cover to accomplish the report's purpose?

When preparing any report, write clearly, concisely, and accurately. Present the facts objectively. This means you should make sure you do not let your personal feelings about the subject influence what you report.

Checkpoint 8.3

1. What are the three important steps in writing a request letter?

2. Name three examples of letters expressing good-news or neutral messages.

3. Why is it important to word bad-news letters carefully?

4. When would a person use a memo instead of an e-mail?

5. Why are business reports used in the workplace?

Build Your Vocabulary

As you progress through this text, develop a personal glossary of career-related terms and add it to your portfolio. This will help build your vocabulary and prepare you for your career of choice. Write a definition for each of the following terms, and add it to your personal career glossary.

template
white space
block style letter
modified block style letter
memo

Chapter Summary

Section 8.1 Effective Communication

- The communication process requires someone to send a message and some to receive it. Good communication is needed in the workplace. Communication is effective when a message is successfully sent and received.
- It is important to develop listening skills. The workplace cannot function properly unless these skills are used effectively.
- Reading and comprehension skills can be improved. Read with a purpose for the reading in mind. Look over the material before beginning to read. Seek the meaning the author is trying to convey. Improve your vocabulary.
- Few people are good writers. However, the ability to convey a message or direction in writing is an important skill for most jobs.
- Whether speaking with someone in person or over the phone, be sure to be courteous and use proper etiquette. Although speaking in groups can be intimidating, with practice and understanding of the topic, most people can become effective public speakers.
- Nonverbal communication does not involve written or spoken words. Facial expressions, gestures, and other body language sends messages to others about what you think or how you feel.

Section 8.2 Communication Channels

- Formal communication follows a set of rules and etiquette. Sometimes, formal communication is referred to as *following the chain of command*.
- Informal communication may relate to the job or coworkers. Workers often share informal communications while commuting, during shift changes, or during work breaks.
- Sometimes physical, cultural, and emotional factors can prevent effective communication. Recognizing potential communication barriers may help to overcome them.

Section 8.3 Written Business Communications

- A business letter is written to convey information in a formal way. Business letters follow a specific style.
- Memos are written messages exchanged within a company. A memo has a format of its own different from that of a letter or e-mail.
- Companies use business reports to share important information or new ideas. A business report can be formal or informal.

Check Your Career IQ

Now that you have finished the chapter, see what you learned about careers by taking the chapter posttest. The test can be accessed on the mobile site by using a smartphone or on the G-W Learning companion website.

www.m.g-wlearning.com

www.g-wlearning.com

Review Your Knowledge

1. Name the four communication skills needed in the workplace.
2. Provide examples of appropriate telephone etiquette used in the workplace.
3. Explain nonverbal communication and why it is important.
4. When are informal communications most common?
5. Describe how a personal letter is different from a business letter.
6. What is the salutation in a business letter? Provide an example.
7. Name and describe the two common formats used for business letters.
8. List the three types of business letters often used in the workplace.
9. Explain when it is appropriate to use a memo rather than a business letter.
10. What is the purpose of a business report?

Apply Your Knowledge

1. Describe a communication barrier that you have encountered recently. How did the communication barrier affect you, others, or the situation? What could be done in the future to avoid such problems?
2. What are some "safe" topics while commuting with coworkers? List five topics of conversation that would be appropriate during your commuting time after work.
3. Imagine you are in the break area at work. A coworker greets you with some interesting gossip about another employee's annual review. According to company policy, annual reviews are to be kept confidential between the employee and upper-level managers. What should you do? How can you turn this "dangerous" conversation into a "safe" conversation? Discuss with your classmates.
4. Write a business letter to request information about a product. Use the modified block style format to write your letter.
5. Create eight flashcards. On one side of each index card, write the word used to identify a part of the communication process (sender, encoder, message, channel, receiver, decoder, feedback, and noise). On the opposite side, write the definition of the word as provided in Section 8.1. Work with a partner to learn each part of the communication process and its function.
6. Imagine your local office will host the company's annual sales meeting. Write a memo to the manager in the sales department. Your memo should remind her of the date, time, and location of the meeting. Include any additional information that you think would be helpful. Include the parts of a memo as mentioned in Section 8.3.
7. Make a list of five emotions or feelings. Draw a picture for each emotion that depicts a person using nonverbal communication to express it.

8. List three activities you could do to improve your vocabulary. Explain how you think each activity will help. Choose one of the activities to practice every day for the rest of the week.

9. Write a business letter to inform a customer that you are unable to satisfy his or her order. Review the tips on writing bad-news letters. Use a block style format to write your letter.

10. Create two short plays—one that illustrates appropriate telephone etiquette and one that illustrates inappropriate telephone etiquette.

Teamwork

Together with your team, prepare a short video on personal qualities needed for success on the job. Demonstrate both good and bad examples. Discuss why each is important. Also address how developing skills and good habits now will affect your career later in life. Share your video with the class.

G-W Learning Mobile Site

Visit the G-W Learning mobile site to complete the chapter pretest and posttest and to practice vocabulary using e-flash cards. If you do not have a smartphone, visit the G-W Learning companion website to access these features.
G-W Learning mobile site: www.m.g-wlearning.com
G-W Learning companion website: www.g-wlearning.com

Common Core

College and Career Readiness

CTE Career Ready Practices. Create a one-act play for two persons that depicts a positive interaction between two students or coworkers. Be sure to include notes to the actors about body language and facial expressions. Do the same to illustrate a negative interaction on the same topic. What is the essential difference between the two interactions? How does the way you say something influence whether it will be received negatively or positively?

Writing. Conduct interviews with at least two employers to determine the importance of dependability, promptness, honesty, and getting along with others. Report your findings to the class.

Apply Your Technology Skills

Access the G-W Learning companion website for this text at www.g-wlearning.com. Download each data file for this chapter. Follow the instructions to complete activities to practice what you have learned in this chapter.

Data File 8–1—Communicating Effectively

College and Career Readiness Portfolio

College and Career Readiness

Many opportunities are available for young people to serve the community. You might volunteer for a community clean-up project. Perhaps you would enjoy reading to residents in a nursing facility. Maybe raising money for a shelter for homeless pets appeals to you. Whatever your interests, there is sure to be a related service project in which you can take part.

Interviewers for jobs or colleges look for your service activities on applications. Volunteering helps show social awareness and commitment to others or to a cause. In this activity, you will create a list of your service activities. Remember that this is an ongoing project. You will update this list when you have activities to add.

1. List the service projects or volunteer activities in which you have taken part. Give the organization or person's name, the dates, and the activities that you performed. If you received a certificate or award related to this service, mention it here.
2. Give the document an appropriate name, using the naming system you created earlier. Place the file in your e-portfolio.
3. Place a copy of the list in the container for your print portfolio.

Chapter 9

Math in the Workplace

Section 9.1
Practical Math

Section 9.2
Metric System

Section 9.3
Analyzing Data

College and Career Readiness

Reading Prep. In preparation for reading this chapter, read over the terms listed for each section. What terms are already familiar to you? Which ones are not familiar at all? As you read, think about how your understanding of the meaning of a given term agrees with the text or is different.

Introduction

Math skills are essential for workplace effectiveness and for making personal financial decisions. Companies expect their employees to have the minimal math skills required for whatever position they are seeking. It is assumed that addition, subtraction, multiplication, and division are mastered before entering high school. If job applicants lack required math skills, it will be their responsibility in most cases to acquire them.

Whether your job is working as a department manager in a clothing store, a restaurant chef, a nurse's aide, or a bank teller, some math will be essential. As you consider your career choice, you should also acquire the math skills associated with that job. Having higher-level math skills will result in having greater access to job opportunities that have room for advancement.

Check Your Career IQ

Before you begin the chapter, see what you already know about careers by taking the chapter pretest. Use the related QR code to view the pretest on the mobile site. If you do not have a smartphone, visit the G-W Learning companion website to access the pretest.

www.m.g-wlearning.com
www.g-wlearning.com

G-W Mobile

Career Snapshot
Cashier

What Does a Cashier Do?

A cashier has a very important job in an organization. If a cashier is rude, slow, or unable to provide assistance, a customer may decide to purchase that item elsewhere. A cashier has to:

- count money and ensure the accuracy of transactions;
- use point-of-sale equipment, such as cash registers, scales, as well as credit- and debit-card scanners;
- maintain an orderly checkout area;
- work quickly and accurately;
- make correct change; and
- promote positive interactions with customers.

What Is It Like to Work as a Cashier?

A cashier must be able to stand on his or her feet for hours and maintain a pleasant attitude at all times. It is important to understand customers may not always be in the best mood. No matter how the customer behaves, the cashier must always be pleasant and professional.

What Education and Skills Are Needed to Be a Cashier?

- GED or high school diploma
- efficient math skills; communication skills
- ethical standards; friendly personality

Blend Images/Shutterstock.com

9.1 | Practical Math

Terms

financial literacy
common fraction
numerator
denominator
decimal fraction
percent
linear measurement
area measurement
digital measuring
    instrument
laser measuring
    instrument

Objectives

After completing this section, you will be able to:
- **Explain** how to count change correctly.
- **Describe** the necessary steps to properly use a calculator.
- **Perform** basic mathematical computations using fractions, decimals, and percentages.
- **Read** linear measurements and determine area measurements.

Making Change

Making change for customers is a necessary skill for success in many places of employment. The skill of making change is required of salespeople in fast-food establishments, retail stores, and taxi companies as well as in many other businesses. Knowing how to make change correctly is important for providing customer satisfaction and avoiding embarrassment to you. Making correct change is also important for your personal financial well-being. It is part of being financially literate. **Financial literacy** is the ability to understand and manage one's personal finances.

When a customer makes a purchase, the change the cashier returns is determined by the amount of money the customer gave the cashier. Suppose the customer buys a video game that costs a total of $57.31, including tax. The customer gives the cashier $60. Most cash registers automatically calculate the change due, which in this case is $2.69. The cashier would give the customer the following as change:
- 4 pennies (4¢)
- 1 nickel (5¢ + 4¢ = 9¢)
- 1 dime (10¢ + 9¢ = 19¢)
- 2 quarters (50¢ + 19¢ = 69¢)
- 2 one-dollar bills ($2 + 69¢ = $2.69 total)

The cashier should count out the change as it is being handed to the customer. For example, you would say:

$17.31 and 4 (the pennies) equals $17.35… and 5 (the nickel) equals $17.40… and 10 (the dime) equals $17.50… and 50 (the quarters) equals $18… and two dollars (the bills) equals $20.

By counting the change in this manner, the cashier is helping make sure the customer receives the correct change. He or she is also making sure the cash register will balance at the end of the shift. Being able to determine whether or not you received the correct change from a purchase is part of being a responsible consumer.

Being able to handle money is an important job and financial literacy skill.

Christy Thompson/Shutterstock.com

It is important to be aware that many times a customer will pay with coins and paper currency to cover the cost of the purchase. Sometimes this can be confusing. What the customer may be doing is trying to get rid of some pocket change. For example, the total bill may be $59.37. As a cashier, you may be handed three 20-dollar bills and 37¢ in change. Therefore, the change back to the customer will be $1.

Using a Calculator

A calculator can help you solve math problems quickly. It can add, subtract, multiply, and divide as well as perform other math operations. A pocket calculator is inexpensive and easy to use. Many smartphones even have a calculator feature. However, it is very important not to be totally dependent on a calculator. You should practice your math skills without a calculator, and then use the calculator to double-check your work.

To operate a calculator properly, you need to enter information and instructions correctly. Entries are made by pressing certain numbers and symbols on the keypad. The information you enter appears in the display area. Check the display area after you have entered a number to be sure the number is correct.

The most common symbols you will find on a calculator and the function each performs are shown in Figure 9-1. Practice operating a calculator to make sure you understand each function. Press the "on" or "power" key, and follow these steps to add, subtract, multiply, and divide 63 and 21.

Using a Calculator	
Key	**Function**
C	Clears all entries.
CE	Clears last entry.
.	Enters the decimal point.
+	Adds.
−	Subtracts.
×	Multiplies.
÷	Divides.
%	Figures the percentage.
=	Figures the answer.

Figure 9-1.   *Goodheart-Willcox Publisher*
The location of the keys on a calculator may vary from model to model.

Addition

To add 63 and 21:
1. Enter 63 by pressing 6 and then 3. (63 should then appear on the display.)
2. Press the + key.
3. Enter 21 by pressing 2 and 1. (21 should appear on the display.)
4. Press the = key. (Look for the sum, 84, on the display.)

Subtraction

To subtract 21 from 63:
1. Enter 63.
2. Press the − key.
3. Enter 21.
4. Press the = key. (The answer is 42.)

Multiplication

To multiply 63 by 21:
1. Enter 63.
2. Press the × key.
3. Enter 21.
4. Press the = key. (The answer is 1,323.)

Division

To divide 63 by 21:
1. Enter 63.
2. Press the ÷ key.
3. Enter 21.
4. Press the = key. (The answer is 3.)

Using Fractions, Decimals, and Percentages

Many people have difficulty understanding fractions, decimals, and percentages. These concepts are necessary for many everyday uses, such as calculating credit card charges, payroll deductions, taxes, and sales markdowns. Knowledge of these concepts is basic to any specialized math skills your future job may require.

Fractions

A **common fraction** is one or more parts of a whole number as shown in Figure 9-2. Common fractions are written with one number over or beside the other as follows: or 1/3 or 13/15 or 5/9.

The number written above or before the line in a fraction is the **numerator**. The numerator is the number of parts present in the fraction. The number below, or after the line in a fraction, is called the **denominator**. The denominator is the number of parts into which the fraction is divided.

When reading a common fraction, you always read the numerator first, then the denominator. The fraction 3/5 is read *three-fifths*.

Decimals

You will frequently work with decimals, which are a special type of fraction. A **decimal fraction** is a fraction with a denominator (or multiple) of 10, such as 100, 1000, and 10,000. When writing a decimal fraction, you omit the denominator and place a dot, called a decimal point, in front of the numerator. Therefore, the fraction 1/10 becomes .1 as a decimal fraction. Both are read the same: *one-tenth*.

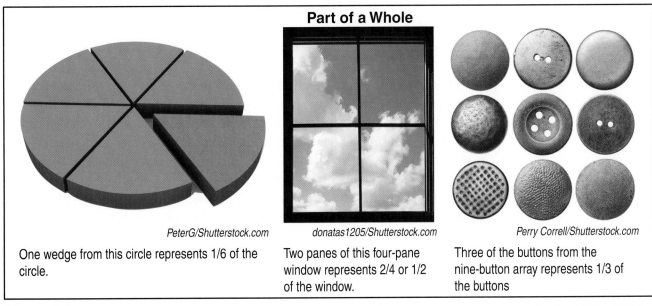

Part of a Whole

PeterG/Shutterstock.com

One wedge from this circle represents 1/6 of the circle.

donatas1205/Shutterstock.com

Two panes of this four-pane window represents 2/4 or 1/2 of the window.

Perry Correll/Shutterstock.com

Three of the buttons from the nine-button array represents 1/3 of the buttons

Figure 9-2.   *Goodheart-Willcox Publisher*
Fractions and ratios are ways to describe the relationship between parts to the whole.

The quantity of numbers to the right of the decimal point lets you know what multiple of 10 the denominator is. When there is one number to the right of the decimal point, the decimal is read as tenths. Two numbers to the right of the decimal point are read as hundredths. Three numbers to the right of the decimal point are thousandths; four numbers are ten-thousandths.

.1   = 1/10 = one-tenth
.01   = 1/100 = one-hundredth
.001   = 1/1000 = one-thousandth
.0001   = 1/10,000 = one ten-thousandths

Decimals are usually easier to work with than common fractions, and they are used in many ways. For example, decimals are used to calculate sales tax and calculate the number of miles you travel. Decimals are also used in our money system to separate dollars from cents.

Because decimals are easier to write and calculate than fractions, fractions are often changed into decimals to calculate math problems. To change a fraction into a decimal, you divide the denominator into the numerator. For example, to change 5/8 into a decimal, you divide 5 by 8 as follows:

$$
\begin{array}{r}
.625 \\
8\overline{)5.000} \\
\underline{48} \\
20 \\
\underline{16} \\
40 \\
\underline{40} \\
\end{array}
$$

The answer in a division problem is the quotient. When changing a fraction to a decimal, the number of decimal places in the quotient must be the same as the number of zeros you add to the numerator. If the division does not come out evenly, you carry it out as many decimal places as needed for the answer. Carrying the division to four or five decimal places is usually the most you would ever need.

Percentages

A very common mathematical term is **percent,** which means one part per hundred. By using percentages, you examine a number by dividing it into one hundred parts. The simplest example is a dollar, which divided into 100 parts, equals 100 pennies. One penny—just one of the dollar's 100 parts—is 1/100th of the whole. The use of a percentage sign (%) is an easier way to show this relationship. One penny is 1% of the dollar, 10 pennies is 10%, and 100 pennies is 100%, or one whole dollar. A percent can easily be converted back to decimal form with the use of a decimal point in the right place, as follows:

100% = 1
10%   = .1
1%   = .01
.1%   = .001
.01% = .0001

Ethical Leadership

Character

Character is doing the right thing when nobody's looking.
—J.C. Watts

Your character is what determines the kind of person you are, how you react to situations, and how you live your life. Your ethics are a reflection of you to your relatives, friends, and people in general. Leaders are confronted daily with the need to make decisions. The decisions they make reflects on their values and ethics. It is important to behave ethically on the job but also in the decisions you make every day. For example, you are checking out of a store. As you pay for your purchase, you hand the clerk a 10-dollar bill. You notice that as the clerk counts out your change, you are receiving change for a one-hundred-dollar bill instead. The clerk thanks you and turns to the next customer. Being ethical demands that you immediately tell the clerk you received too much in change. This is true whether it is a hundred dollar mistake or a one cent mistake.

Whole numbers need no decimal point since a fraction is not present. Consequently, 100% is expressed simply as 1. However, 150% converted to decimal form is the fraction 1.5 because there is a whole number with a fraction.

The following examples show several uses of percentages in the workplace:

- If the unemployment rate in your state is 7%, it means 7 of every hundred employable people are not employed, or 7 per 100 people.
- If the profit on a pair of water skis priced at $300 is 30%, the seller will make $90.
- The new company opening in your hometown will hire 51% of its employees locally. The business estimates it will need 780 employees. Consequently, at least 398 local residents will have jobs with the new company.

Check each of these examples to be sure you understand how percentages were used.

Taking Measurements

Being able to measure accurately is one of the basic skills employers expect of their employees. Regardless of your career, basic measurement skills are essential.

Linear Measurement

A **linear measurement** is the length of a straight or curved line taken with a ruler, yardstick, or tape measure. Some examples include the length of a proposed sidewalk, the distance around a pool, the height of a doorway, or the depth of a computer desk.

Linear measuring tools are commonly divided into equal parts called inches. Each inch is divided into equal fractional units consisting of halves (1/2), quarters (1/4), eighths (1/8), and sixteenths (1/16). Linear measuring skills require accurate measuring to at least 1/16 of an inch. More precise rulers also have the smaller divisions of thirty-seconds (1/32) and sixty-fourths (1/64).

The drawing in Figure 9-3 shows an inch divided into sixteenths. Note that the one-inch line is the longest. The 1/2-inch line is next in length, followed by the 1/4-inch line and the 1/8-inch line. The 1/16-inch line is the shortest.

When measuring, it is usually best to measure to the smallest fraction marked on your ruler. Most rulers are divided into sixteenths. Unless you need greater precision, measuring to within 1/16 inch is acceptable.

Remember, too, fractional measurements are always reduced to their lowest terms. For example, a measurement of 12/16 is expressed as 3/4; 4/16, as 1/4; and 2/4, as 1/2.

Area Measurement

An **area measurement** is the calculation of the amount of space within the borders of a geometric shape. The area may be a simple shape, such as square, rectangle, parallelogram, triangle, or circle. See Figure 9-4. You need to take linear measurements well to figure area measurements accurately.

Four-Sided Shapes

A square has four sides, all the same length. A rectangle and a parallelogram have two pairs of sides of different lengths. All three of these shapes use the same formula for measuring area:

$$\text{area} = \text{base} \times \text{height}$$

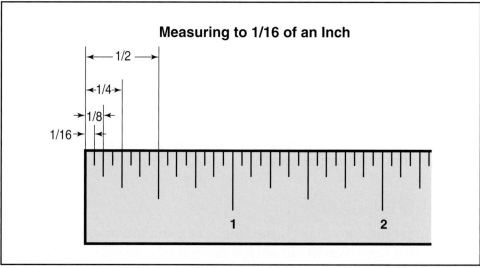

Figure 9-3.   *Goodheart-Willcox Publisher*
Most rulers have inches divided into halves, fourths, eighths, and sixteenths.

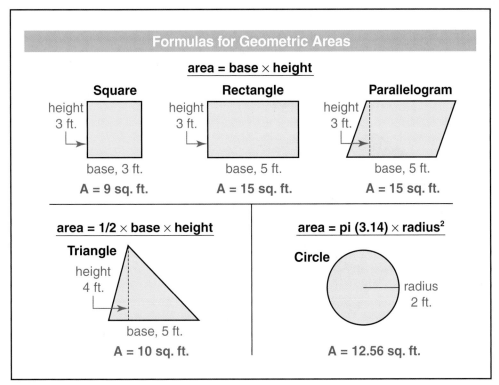

Figure 9-4.   *Goodheart-Willcox Publisher*
These formulas are used to measure the space inside a geometric feature.

If your employer wants you to measure a wall for new wallpaper, you will need to know the total wall area. If the windowless wall is 18-feet wide and 7-feet 6-inches high, the equation is written as follows:

area = 18 feet × 7.5 feet = 135 square feet

Note: the linear measurement 7-feet 6-inches was converted to the decimal 7.5 to make multiplication easier. Area is always expressed in squared units. This is true no matter what measuring unit is used—feet, inches, meters, yards, miles, or some other linear measure.

Triangles

For figuring the area of a triangle, the formula is:

area = 1/2 × base × height

If you are asked to make a triangular sail for a customer's boat, you must first calculate the area of the sail. If the height of the sail measures 24 feet and the base measures 20 feet, you have the basic facts needed to calculate the answer:

area = 1/2 × 20 feet × 24 feet = 240 square feet

The total area of the finished sail is 240 square feet, but extra fabric will probably be needed for sewing seams.

Circles

The formula for calculating the area of a circle is:

area = *pi* × radius^2

Suppose you work for a landscaping company that is installing a circular fishpond. You must calculate the area of the pond to determine how much waterproof fabric will be needed to line the

This laser measuring device has a digital readout.

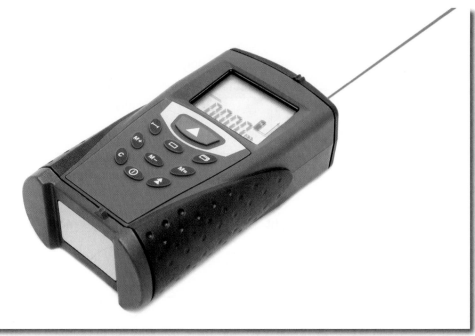

Blaz Kure/Shutterstock.com

surface. The pond has a 3-feet radius and sides 2 feet high. Therefore, the waterproofing fabric must have a radius of 5 feet to cover the bottom and sides of the pond. You would multiply *pi* (3.14) times the radius squared (5^2). *Pi* is often written with the Greek symbol π. The formula will then appear as:

$$\text{area} = 3.14 \times 25 \text{ square feet} = 78.5 \text{ square feet}$$

Again, as in the example of the boat sail, extra fabric may be needed for sewing seams.

Digital and Laser Measuring

Digital and laser measuring is the process of using instruments to directly read distance, size, temperature, and other unknowns. **Digital measuring instruments** are tools used to find distance, temperature, weights, volume of liquids, airflow, and liquid flow and pressure into numbers on a digital display. This type of measuring is more accurate than the traditional ruler, mercury thermometer, and rain gauge. The use of digital instruments usually leads to more accurate readings and better job performance.

Laser measuring instruments are used to determine a distance simply by projecting a light beam. You can also use a laser to measure for windows, tiling a room, painting, laying carpet, and many other measuring tasks. They may also be used for addition, subtraction, calculating area, and determining volume.

Checkpoint 9.1

1. What math skills will most employers expect of you?

2. How does your ability to correctly count change affect the impression the customer has of you?

3. How do you change a fraction into a decimal?

4. What is 10% of 40? What is 30% of 40?

5. When calculating the area, what shape requires the formula 1/2 x base x height?

Build Your Vocabulary

As you progress through this text, develop a personal glossary of career-related terms and add it to your portfolio. This will help build your vocabulary and prepare you for your career of choice. Write a definition for each of the following terms, and add it to your personal career glossary.

financial literacy
common fraction
numerator
denominator
decimal fraction
percent
linear measurement
area measurement
digital measuring instrument
laser measuring instrument

9.2 Metric System

Objectives

After completing this section you will be able to:
- **Explain** differences between the metric system and the US system of measurement.
- **Demonstrate** how to measure in metrics.
- **Explain** how to make conversions to and from metric measurements.

Using the Metric System

To measure distance, weight, volume, and temperature, most countries use the International System of Units, or the metric system. The **metric system** is a decimal system of weights and measures, like the US money system. The metric system uses the meter to measure distance, the gram to calculate weight, the liter to measure volume, and the degree Celsius to determine temperature.

Although the United States may eventually convert to the metric system, it still uses the US Customary Units. Inches, feet, yards, and miles are used to measure distance. Ounces and pounds are used to calculate weights. Pints, quarts, and gallons are used to measure volume, and Fahrenheit degrees are used to determine temperature.

Many US manufacturers use the metric system to compete in the world market. Speedometers on US cars show kilometers-per-hour as well as miles-per-hour. Many businesses also use the metric system to repair and service foreign products.

Since metrics is a widely used system of measurement, you may work with it on the job. Therefore, you need to learn how to measure in metrics and make metric conversions.

How the Metric System Works

Metric units increase and decrease in size by 10s. To increase the amount, you move the decimal point one place to the right or multiply by 10. To decrease the amount, you move the decimal point one place to the left or divide by 10.

Think about how you write one dollar ($1). If you move the decimal point one place to the right, you increase the amount 10 times and make it ten dollars ($10). Move the decimal point one more place to the right, and you have one hundred dollars ($100). This is ten times more than $10.00. Any metric unit works the same way. In Figure 9-5, you can see how dollars and meters are similar because they are both based on a decimal system.

Our Money System Compared to the Metric System			
Dollars		**Meters**	
$1,000.00	1,000	1,000 m	1 kilometer—km
100.00	100	100.0 m	1 hectometer—hm
10.00	10	10.00 m	1 dekameter—dam
1.00	1	1.000 m	1 meter—m
.10	1/10	.1000 m	1 decimeter—dm
.01	1/100	.0100 m	1 centimeter—cm
.001	1/1,000	.0010 m	1 millimeter—mm

Figure 9-5.   *Goodheart-Willcox Publisher*
Here dollars are compared to meters.

In the metric system, one of six prefixes can be added to *meter, gram,* or *liter* to show its level of value as shown in Figure 9-6. *Deci, centi,* and *milli* can be added to identify smaller measurements. *Deka, hecto,* and *kilo* can be added to identify larger measurements. The most commonly used prefixes are *centi, milli,* and *kilo.*

Meter

A **meter (m)** is the metric measure for length or distance. One meter is a little longer than one yard. A meter is often used to measure the dimensions of a room, the length of a racetrack, and fabric lengths among other things. A kilometer (km) is just over a half mile, or 5/8 of a mile. It is used to measure the distance between cities and the altitude of a plane in flight. A centimeter (cm) is about the length of

Units of Measure in the Metric System				
Prefix	**Number**	**Distance**	**Weight**	**Volume**
kilo	1,000	kilometer (km)	kilogram (kg)	kiloliter (kl)
hecto	100	hectometer (hm)	hectogram (hg)	hectoliter (hl)
deka	10	dekameter (dam)	dekagram (dag)	dekaliter (dal)
	1	meter	gram	liter
deci	.1	decimeter (dm)	decigram (dg)	deciliter (dl)
centi	.01	centimeter (cm)	centigram (cg)	centiliter (cl)
milli	.001	millimeter (mm)	milligram (mg)	milliliter (ml)

Figure 9-6.   *Goodheart-Willcox Publisher*
The prefixes shown here are those most commonly used to modify metric units.

Go Green

Have you noticed the Energy Star label that appears on products such as lightbulbs, computers, and other electronic devices? The EPA and the Department of Energy have created the Energy Star program to rate products. The Energy Star label guarantees the product meets a certain level of energy efficiency. When using something that is energy efficient, follow the directions provided by the manufacturer for how to get the most out of your product.

one-half inch. The length of this textbook and the width of a computer screen are among the things that can be measured in centimeters. One millimeter (mm) is about the thickness of a dime. It is used to measure short lengths such as the size of an insect or the thickness of wire.

Gram

A **gram (g)** is the metric measure for weight. One gram is a very small weight, much less than one ounce. A US dollar bill weighs about one gram. The gram is used to measure other lightweight items, such as spices. A kilogram (kg) is about 2.2 pounds, or 35 ounces. Body weights and freight weights are calculated in kilograms. A grain of sand and items too small to see without a microscope are measured in centigrams (cm) or milligrams (mg).

Liter

Often used to measure liquids, a **liter (l)** is the metric measure for volume. A liter equals a little more than one quart. Gasoline and motor oil can be sold by the liter and so can bottles of water and cartons of milk. Large tanks of liquids are measured in kiloliters (kl). Volumes less than a liter, such as recipe ingredients, are usually measured in milliliters (ml).

Degree Celsius

Degree Celsius (°C) is the metric measure for temperature. One degree Celsius (°C) is a little more than two degrees Fahrenheit (F). Water freezes at 0°C, or 32°F, and water boils at 100°C, or 212°F. A comfortable room temperature is 20°C, and a warm sunny day is about 25°C. Normal body temperature is 37°C, or 98.6°F.

Making Conversions

The best way to learn the metric system is to "think metric." This means measuring in metric instead of measuring with the US Customary Units and changing the number to metric. However, there may be times when you need to change a US unit to a metric unit or vice versa. This is called *making conversions*. Figure 9-7 shows how to make conversions to and from the metric system. To use the chart, look up the unit you know in the left column and multiply it by the known quantity in the middle column to find your conversion.

Suppose you need to learn how many meters are in 15 yards of fabric. According to the chart, you multiply 15 by 0.91 to find the length of a 15-yard piece of fabric in meters. The answer is 13.65 meters.

Making Conversions (approximate)					
Converting to Metric			Converting from Metric		
When You Know	Multiply By	To Find	When You Know	Multiply By	To Find
Distance			Distance		
inches	25.4	millimeters	millimeters	0.04	inches
inches	2.54	centimeters	centimeters	0.39	inches
feet	0.3	meters	meters	3.28	feet
yards	0.91	meters	meters	1.09	yards
miles	1.61	kilometers	kilometers	0.62	miles
Weight			Weight		
ounces	28.35	grams	grams	0.04	ounces
pounds	454	grams	grams	0.002	pounds
pounds	0.45	kilograms	kilograms	2.2	pounds
Volume			Volume		
fluid ounces	29.57	milliliters	milliliters	0.03	fluid ounces
pints	0.47	liters	liters	2.11	pints
quarts	0.95	liters	liters	1.06	quarts
gallons	3.79	liters	liters	0.26	gallons
Temperature			Temperature		
Fahrenheit	0.56 (after subtracting 32)	Celsius	Celsius	1.80 (then add 32)	Fahrenheit

Figure 9-7.   *Goodheart-Willcox Publisher*
Use this chart to convert values to and from metric units.

 **Job Interviewing**

Job interviewing is a competitive event you might enter with your Career and Technical Student Organization (CTSO). By participating in the job interview, you will be able to showcase your presentation skills, communication talents, and ability to actively listen to the questions asked by the interviewers. For this event, you will be expected to write a letter of application, create a résumé, and complete an application. You will also be interviewed by an individual judge or panel of judges.

To prepare for a job interviewing event, complete the following activities:

1. Visit the CTSO website for event rules and guidelines. You will have time to research, prepare, and practice before going to the competition.
2. Review the interviewing techniques presented in Chapter 6 of this text.
3. Write your letter of application, create your résumé, and complete the application (if provided for this event).
4. Solicit feedback from your peers, teacher, and parents.
5. Make certain that each document is complete and free of errors.

Checkpoint 9.2

1. Why do US manufacturers use the metric system?
2. Which four units of the metric system are most commonly used?
3. What is the kilometer often used to measure?
4. If using the metric system, which unit of measurement should be used to calculate body weight?
5. What does it mean to make conversions during measurements?

Build Your Vocabulary

As you progress through this text, develop a personal glossary of career-related terms and add it to your portfolio. This will help build your vocabulary and prepare you for your career of choice. Write a definition for each of the following terms, and add it to your personal career glossary.

metric system
meter (m)
gram (g)
liter (l)
degree Celsius (°C)

Analyzing Data | 9.3

Terms
- mean
- median
- mode
- table
- line graph
- bar graph
- pictograph
- circle graph
- probability

Data Analysis

In the workplace, it is a very common practice to analyze data in a variety of ways to fully understand the subject. The ability to collect and analyze data has become increasingly important.

Understanding Mean, Median, and Mode

Mean, median, and mode are three different ways to analyze data. The **mean** is the mathematical average of the data. You find it by totaling all the numbers and dividing by the quantity of numbers you have. The **median** is the number exactly in the middle when the data is listed in ascending or descending order. The **mode** is the number(s) that occurs most frequently.

Each method of examining data has its own advantages and disadvantages. When most people use the word *average,* they generally refer to the *mean.* However, some may refer to the *median* or the *mode.* It is possible for all three to be identical, but this rarely occurs.

For example, suppose you want to know if a salary offer from a certain company is good or should be better. You need to know how the offer compares to the salaries of others with that job. Using the salaries in Figure 9-8, do you think the mean, median, or mode would be quoted to you as the average salary of similar employees? Suppose the employer offers you $28,000. The offer might sound quite fair. However, your salary offer is $4,000 below the lowest mode, $8,500 below the median, and $20,500 below the mean.

What the numbers in Figure 9-8 do not show are the factors that explain the salary differences. These may include years of experience, educational levels, special abilities, and other factors important to the employer. It would be far more helpful to know how your salary offer compares to those recently offered to employees of similar ability and experience. Knowing the mean, median, and mode of that data would be far more helpful in considering yours.

Analyzing Data			
Eleven employees with various levels of experience and years of service hold the same job title within a company at the following salary levels. Examine the mean, median, and mode for this data.			
Employee Salaries			
$28,500	$31,000	$32,000	$32,000
$32,000	$36,000	$37,500	$37,500
$62,500	$91,500	$124,000	

Mean = $49,500
Median = $36,000
Mode = $32,000 (occurs three times) and $37,500 (occurs twice)

Figure 9-8.   *Goodheart-Willcox Publisher*
Mean, median, and mode are commonly used as a way to compare and analyze data such as salaries.

Again referring to Figure 9-8, suppose the employee earning $28,500 wants a pay raise. To justify a raise in pay, what figure should she or he quote as the "average" company salary—the median, mean, or mode? Why?

sum of employee salaries = 28,500 + 31,000 + 32,000 + 32,000 + 32,000 + 36,000 + 32,000 + 36,000 + 37,500 + 37,500 + 62,500 + 91,500 + 124,000 = 544,500

mean = 544,500 (sum of employee salaries) ÷ 11 (number of employees)

mean or average salary = $49,500

Using Charts and Graphs

Charts and graphs are used to display information quickly and clearly. They are commonly used in books, magazines, newspapers, on TV, and the Internet. When done well, charts and graphs make data easier to comprehend, compare, and use.

Often, the terms *chart* and *graph* are used interchangeably. Charts and graphs may take many forms. Figure 9-9 shows how four different types of graphs can be used to display the same data. A simple **table** is a visual aid that arranges data in rows and columns. A **line graph** shows the relationship of two or more variables. It can also show trends across periods of time. A **bar graph** shows comparisons between categories. Sometimes multiple lines or bars are used. A **pictograph** presents information with the use of eye-catching images.

A **circle graph** shows the relationship of parts to the whole. Figure 9-10 is an example of a circle graph that shows what proportions of a given budget are taken up by expenses in several categories.

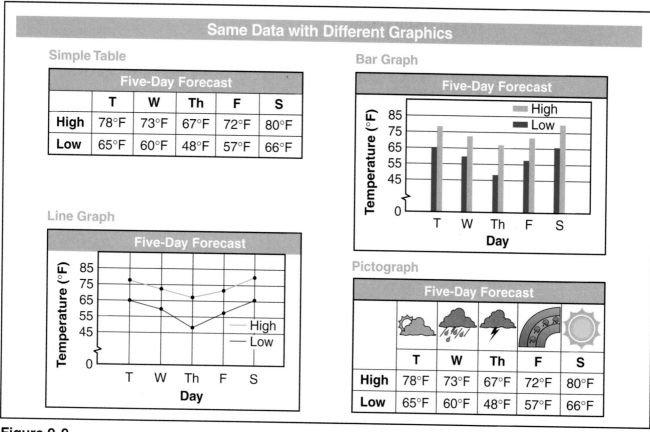

Figure 9-9.

Which chart presents information in a way that is easiest to understand?

Goodheart-Willcox Publisher

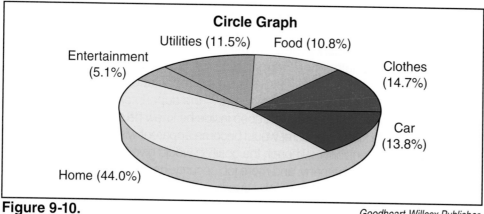

Figure 9-10.

Which is the greatest expense according to the circle graph?

Goodheart-Willcox Publisher

When a graph presents mathematical data, special care must be taken to make sure the data is presented accurately. The elements of the visual must be drawn to correct mathematical scale. A computer with the appropriate software can do the job easily.

Graphs should be planned carefully in advance so wrong proportions do not confuse the facts. It is important to know exactly what information you want to deliver. That is the first step to determining the best way to convey data visually.

Probability

Probability is the chance that something will happen or how likely it is that some event will occur. Using the mean, median, and mode, data may be used to predict events. Likewise, charts and graphs can visually illustrate the probability of an event taking place.

Probability may be stated as being *high* or *low*. For example, the chances of human beings flying unassisted are very low, while the chances, or probability, of the sun setting is very high. Employers are very concerned about the probability of workplace injuries as well as how likely it is a competitor will capture their market.

Case

Justin's Secret

Justin was very excited about his new job working on a housing construction crew. He enjoyed working outdoors. The variety of jobs gave him a chance to learn many skills. He learned to frame a complete house as well as install a roof and attach siding. Justin learned almost every job associated with carpentry and building a house. His skills with tools did not go unnoticed among his fellow crew members and his superintendent.

As time passed, Justin became the lead member on the crew. He began to fill in for crew members that were absent. His superintendent began depending on him to take full responsibility for the work done by his crew. Justin was well-liked by his crew members. He never suspected what would happen in the next few weeks.

Justin's superintendent pulled him aside late one afternoon and explained that he would take another position in the company next month. "Would you like to follow me around for a few weeks to learn the ropes and become the next superintendent of the residential work crews?" the superintendent asked.

Justin pretended to be happy, but deep inside he knew he could never be superintendent. He knew his secret would become apparent within the first few days he took on that responsibility. Although the position would give him a better salary, more status within the company, and more job security, he could not accept it.

"I am happy with my present job," Justin said to his superintendent. "I want to keep this job and stay where I am." Justin then walked away with his secret.

What was Justin's secret? As superintendent he would be responsible for all aspects of the construction. This included reading blueprints and checking the accuracy of the construction. To do that, Justin would have to read measurements, use fractions and decimals, and know simple geometry.

Justin had no math skills. In fact, he always asked his crew members to do the necessary math anytime it was needed. He even hid his lack of math skills from them.

Critical Thinking

1. Do you know anyone who hides his or her lack of math knowledge?
2. Do you know anyone that thinks math is too difficult to learn?
3. What could Justin have done to enable himself to take advantage of this opportunity for promotion?

Checkpoint 9.3

1. What are three different ways to analyze data?
2. Explain how to calculate the mean of data.
3. In data calculations, how does the median differ from the mode?
4. What are two benefits of using charts and graphs during a presentation?
5. What is the first step to determining the best way to convey data visually?

Build Your Vocabulary

As you progress through this text, develop a personal glossary of career-related terms and add it to your portfolio. This will help build your vocabulary and prepare you for your career of choice. Write a definition for each of the following terms, and add it to your personal career glossary.

mean
median
mode
table
line graph
bar graph
pictograph
circle graph
probability

Chapter Summary

Section 9.1 Practical Math

- Making change is a skill required in a variety of jobs. When handling money, workers have a special responsibility to count change accurately for customers.
- To operate a calculator properly, information and instructions must be entered correctly. Learning and using basic math to solve problems are important skills for all students to have.
- The basic math operations of addition, subtraction, multiplication, and division should be learned prior to entering high school. However, knowing how to use fractions, decimals, and percentages are necessary math skills often used at work, school, and home.
- Some jobs require the need to calculate area measurements and linear measurements. Digital measuring instruments are now very common in the workplace, too.

Section 9.2 Metric System

- The metric system is a widely used system of measurement. Most countries use the metric system to measure distance, weight, volume, and temperature.
- Metric units increase and decrease by 10s and require the correct placement of the decimal point. Four common units of the metric system are meter, gram, liter, and degree Celsius.
- Workers sometimes need to change a US system of measurement to a metric measurement or vice versa. Converting to and from metric measures is simplified by using conversion charts.

Section 9.3 Analyzing Data

- Employers use many ways to analyze data. One common way is to compare the mean average, median, and mode.
- Charts and graphs can visually illustrate the probability of an event. Probability is stated as being high or low.

Check Your Career IQ

Now that you have finished the chapter, see what you learned about careers by taking the chapter posttest. The test can be accessed on the mobile site by using a smartphone or on the G-W Learning companion website.

www.m.g-wlearning.com

www.g-wlearning.com

Review Your Knowledge

1. What does it mean to be financially literate?
2. How are common fractions written?
3. What are two ways in which decimal fractions are commonly used?
4. Explain how to change a fraction into a decimal.
5. Describe a linear measurement.
6. Describe an area measurement.
7. What is a digital measuring instrument? Give an example.
8. List five prefixes added to meter or gram to show its level of value.
9. What is a liter? How is this unit of measurement used?
10. Name and explain three common charts or graphs used to analyze data.

Applying Your Knowledge

1. If you are given a $50 bill for a $21.15 purchase, how much change would you hand back to the customer? How would you count the change to the customer?
2. At the beginning of next month, Bob will receive a 10% raise. If his hourly wage is now $8.00, how much will his new hourly wage be? How much more money will he earn per eight-hour day? How much more money will he earn per 40-hour week?
3. Estimate the length and width of your classroom in yards and in meters. Then measure the two distances with a yardstick and meter stick. What were your estimates for each unit? What were the actual measurements? Did you do better at estimating in US Customary Units or in metric units? Explain.
4. Using the Internet, research workplace accident statistics. Using spreadsheet software, prepare several types of graphs for these statistics. Present your completed graphs in class.
5. Using Internet or print sources, research the origins of the prefixes *kilo, hecto, centi,* and *milli.* Give examples of other words that begin with these prefixes. Explain how knowledge of these prefixes can make using the metric system easier.
6. Using a calculator, change each of the following fractions into decimals: 1/2, 3/4, 1/16, 6/8, 3/5, 7/8. Provide your answer in decimal form.
7. Interview three people who work in different industries. Ask each person to discuss how he or she uses math to do work on the job. Inquire about job duties that involve making calculations, taking measurement, or using basic math skills. Write a one-page summary of your findings. In your conclusion, explain the importance of math skills on the job.

8. Calculate the area of measurement for each of the following items: a box of cereal, a shoe box, and a box of bandages. Next, calculate the areas of a triangle and circle. Use a ruler to draw your triangle. To draw a perfect circle, trace around the base of a cup or can with a pencil. Apply the formulas in Figure 9-4 to find the correct area of measurement for each.

9. Conduct research to learn more about kinds of digital and laser measuring instruments. Compile your findings in a two-column table. In Column A, list the names of five digital measuring instruments. In Column B, list the names of five laser measuring instruments. Explain the purpose of each instrument or device.

10. Should the United States switch to using only the metric system? List reasons, facts, and examples to support your point of view.

Teamwork

Working with a partner, find the high and low temperatures for each day last week in your county or city. Use a calculator to determine the mean, median, and mode for the daily high temperatures. Do the same for the daily lows. To present your information, use spreadsheet software to create a line or bar graph. Present your graph to the class. Reflect on what you learned through this exercise and what difficulties you had, if any, creating the graph.

G-W Learning Mobile Site

Visit the G-W Learning mobile site to complete the chapter pretest and posttest and to practice vocabulary using e-flash cards. If you do not have a smartphone, visit the G-W Learning companion website to access these features.
G-W Learning mobile site: www.m.g-wlearning.com
G-W Learning companion website: www.g-wlearning.com

Common Core

College and Career Readiness

CTE Career Ready Practices. Go online and search for "desirable workplace skills." Identify five of these workplace skills. Beside each of the five you selected, indicate an academic skill that directly relates to that workplace skill.
Reading. Read a magazine, newspaper, or online article about a current news item related to the need for high-level math skills in the workplace. Determine the central ideas and conclusions of the article. Provide an accurate summary of your reading, making sure to incorporate the *who, what, when,* and *how* of the material.

Apply Your Technology Skills

Access the G-W Learning companion website for this text at www.g-wlearning.com. Download each data file for this chapter. Follow the instructions to complete activities to practice what you have learned in this chapter.

Data File 9–1—**Calculating Wages**

College and Career Readiness Portfolio

College and Career Readiness

Your portfolio should contain samples of your work that show your skills or talents. Now is the time to start collecting items. You can decide which documents to include later when you prepare your final portfolio. Look at past school or work assignments you have completed. Select a book report, essay, poem, or other work that demonstrates your writing talents. Include a research paper, letter, electronic slide show, or other items that illustrate your business communication skills. Look for projects that show your skills related to critical thinking and problem solving. Have you completed a long or complicated project? Write a description of the project and tell how you managed various parts of the assignment to complete it on time. Include samples from the completed project. What career area interests you most? Select completed work from classes that will help prepare you for jobs or internships in that area.

1. Save the documents that show your skills and talents in your e-portfolio. Remember to place the documents in an appropriate subfolder.
2. Place hard copies in the container for your print portfolio.

Section 10.1
Technology Overview

Section 10.2
Tools and Devices

Section 10.3
Impact of Technology

College and Career Readiness

Reading Prep. Recall all the things you know about technology. As you read, think of how the new information presented in the text matches or challenges your prior understanding of the topic. Think of direct connections you can make between the old material and the new material.

Introduction

Advances in information technology and the automation of most manufacturing processes have significantly transformed the workplace. How and where people work have changed. People are now more likely to change jobs several times over the course of their careers than to remain with one company. In addition, people are more likely to work remotely.

As a result, the types of skills in demand today are different than those that were needed in the previous century. Having the capacity to learn and use technology in new ways is highly prized. Learning new things and adapting to new situations is essential. Developing the interpersonal and technical skills employers expect will help you succeed even as the workplace changes.

Check Your Career IQ

Before you begin the chapter, see what you already know about careers by taking the chapter pretest. Use the related QR code to view the pretest on the mobile site. If you do not have a smartphone, visit the G-W Learning companion website to access the pretest.

www.m.g-wlearning.com
www.g-wlearning.com

G-W Mobile

Career Snapshot
Call Center Employee

Information Technology

What Does a Call Center Employee Do?

The purpose of a call center is to provide a central location where customers may speak directly to a company representative regarding most any aspect of an order. This may include a customer's concerns about a delay in shipping, incorrect product being received, or damage to a product. A call center employee must:

- satisfy customers and maintain a good image for the company;
- have effective questioning and listening skills;
- be able to handle special phone tasks, such as transferring calls, taking messages, call backs, holds, interruptions, and unintentional disconnects; and
- be able to quickly and accurately record the results of the telephone conversation.

What Is It Like to Work as a Call Center Employee?

A call center employee usually has a comfortable work environment where the temperature is controlled and the surroundings are pleasant. Professional dress is expected as well as a professional attitude when communicating with customers and fellow employees.

One has to be able to effectively deal with job stress, angry callers, and upset customers. The ability to build positive rapport with different personalities and satisfy various customer situations is critical. A good employee will be able to effectively control a phone call. Flexibility is also important as many call centers are open 24/7.

What Education and Skills Are Needed to Work as a Call Center Employee?

- high school diploma; college degree preferred
- on-the-job training
- communication skills
- customer-service oriented

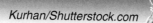

10.1 Technology Overview

Terms

World Wide Web
browser
copyright
license
software piracy
freeware
shareware
identity theft
malware
antivirus software
virus
hacking

Objectives

After completing this section, you will be able to:
- **Describe** basic steps in using the Internet.
- **Explain** how to use the Internet responsibly in the workplace.
- **Describe** ethical use of the Internet material and software.
- **List** security problems users face while exploring the Internet.

Internet

The Internet consists of thousands of computer networks around the world joined together. It is the largest computer system in existence. This network allows connected computers to exchange information and access resources at speeds and volumes once considered impossible.

When you access the Internet, you are online. To get online, you first need a computer with the appropriate software and an Internet connection. That connection is usually provided by a phone line, cable line, digital subscriber line (DSL), satellite technology or cellular technology. Wireless connections are also very popular.

In addition, you need an Internet service provider. This may be your local phone company, cable or satellite television service provider, or a commercial service provider. Usually for a monthly fee, you receive the software and the ability to go online 24 hours a day. Various other fees may also apply.

The World Wide Web is the most popular way to access the Internet. It contains huge collections of text- and multimedia-based documents on websites. These websites are maintained by various educational institutions, companies, organizations, governmental agencies, and individuals. To view material on the World Wide Web, you will need a browser. A browser is a type of program that allows you to access and view websites.

A website that can be used to search the Internet for information is called a *search engine.* You can find information faster and more accurately by searching for keywords or an exact phrase. This will help limit the search results to the most relevant website links.

Responsible Internet Use

If you use the Internet at home, you must conduct self-censorship. When you go online at work and school, your employer and your school administration have the responsibility to limit the time you can spend online and the websites you can visit. It is important to follow the Internet-usage guidelines established by your employer or school.

When using computers and the Internet on the job, workers should follow employee guidelines.

PixAchi/Shutterstock.com

If your employer gives you access to the Internet, there are responsibilities that go with that privilege. Company officials responsible for Internet policies may monitor the following:

- Internet sites visited;
- type and quantity of data downloaded; and
- amount of time spent on the Internet.

Many employers state in their employee handbook that "all communication is the property of the employer." Employees should not expect personal privacy while working at a company-owned computer or when accessing the Internet through a company-owned server.

Ethical Internet Use

Who owns the information available on the Internet? Any individual who creates an original creative work owns its copyright, or legal right. This is true whether the item has a copyright notice or not. A **copyright** is the exclusive right to copy, license, sell, and distribute material. In the United States, an original work is copyrighted as soon as it is in tangible form. For example, if you write a story, as soon as the story is transferred from your mind to the paper or computer file, it is copyrighted. Almost everything found on the Internet is copyrighted, including images, music, videos, and textual information. A copyright statement is *not* required, and lack of a copyright statement does not mean the work has no copyright.

The *fair use doctrine* allows exceptions to copyright under certain limited situations. It allows for use of copyrighted material in teaching, news reporting, editorial commentary, and other similar situations. However, the copyrighted work cannot be claimed as your own.

When you buy software, you are buying a license. A **license** is the legal permission to use a software program. All software has terms of use that outline the purpose and acceptable use of the license.

If you buy software, you have the license and you can use it on your computer. If a business buys software, the business has the license for the software. A software license allows you to use the software, just like a driver's license allows you to drive a car. **Software piracy** is the illegal copying or downloading of software. Never engage in software piracy.

When browsing the web, you may find software programs that are available for you to download. Some software may only be lawfully used if it is purchased. This is known as *for-purchase software*. Demo software may be used without buying it, but demos are either limited in functionality or time. Other software, known as **freeware**, is fully functional and can be used forever without purchasing it. To be considered freeware, the software cannot be a demo or restricted version of software meant for purchase. **Shareware** is software that can be installed and used, then purchased if you decide to keep using it. Shareware usually has a notice screen, time-delayed startup, or reduced features. Purchasing the software removes these restrictions. Figure 10-1 identifies the differences between software types.

The difference between a demo of for-purchase software and shareware is subtle. Typically, shareware software is not time limited. This means that the software remains functional forever with restrictions. Shareware is based on the honor system. Those who continue to use the software are expected to purchase it. A demo of for-purchase software, however, typically stops working after a period of time. In the case of a limited-feature demo, the best features are either not functional or are functional only for a limited time.

Public-domain software is similar to freeware in that it is free. However, freeware is copyrighted, while *public-domain software* either has no copyright, or the copyright has expired. Some photographs, music, videos, and textual information are in the public domain.

Characteristics	Software Type		
	For-Purchase	**Freeware**	**Shareware**
Cost	• Must be purchased to use • Demo may be available	Never have to pay for it	• Free to try • Pay to upgrade to full functionality
Features	Full functionality	Full functionality	Limited functionality without upgrade

Figure 10-1.   *Goodheart-Willcox Publisher*
This table identifies the differences between software types.

Security Issues

Computer security is a major concern for individuals, schools, and businesses. It is important to be aware of theft over the Internet just as you would be with theft of your personal items in your home.

Identity theft is when someone steals your identity and pretends to be you. Never give personal information over the Internet unless you know who the person is. Thieves can use personal information, such as Social Security numbers, signatures, names, addresses, phone numbers, and even banking and credit card information to commit fraud.

Identity theft is becoming another very common threat, partially as a result of people spending more time on the Internet. As you become more familiar with using websites, you will learn when you can, and when you should not, provide personal information. Only give information on a secured website. Secure websites have a URL that starts with *https.* The *s* indicates that the site is secured.

Firewalls should be set up to create a barrier to keep others from invading your computer and stealing your information. The system administrator may install a firewall to block access to the site from those seeking to cause harm. One way someone can cause harm to a computer system is through malware. **Malware** is computer software that interferes with normal computer operations and may send your personal data to unauthorized parties. **Antivirus software** is used to prevent infections as well as to detect and remove computer viruses. A computer **virus** is a type of malware used to infect computers. Do not open attachments or browse to websites unless you know they are safe. Your virus-protection software will indicate if the file is questionable before you open it.

Passwords are another way to protect your computer. Using a strong password helps to keep others from opening your files. A *strong password* is one that is at least eight characters long and includes numbers, letters, and symbols. Frequently resetting your password is another way to help prevent unauthorized access.

Hacking is another type of threat. **Hacking** is breaching security measures to access a computer or network system. A hacker breaks through the security on a computer or network to gain access to the data it contains. The purpose may be a prank, such as vandalizing a company's website. It may be gaining electronic access to a company's or individual's financial information for fraudulent purposes. Usually, a company will

Go Green

Each year hundreds of thousands of computers and peripherals are discarded. Some equipment no longer works. Other equipment, even though still working, becomes outdated and no longer useful to that person, business, or industry. Used consumer electronics that are subject to recycling are called *e-waste*. E-waste has generated new opportunities for businesses and employment. Many companies offer electronic recycling services. Many social organizations will accept some e-waste for recycling.

Protect your computer by using antivirus software and passwords. Remember never to give personal information on an unsecured website.

gualtiero boffi/Shutterstock.com

have protection to help prevent hacking. This may include a firewall or encryption on the security system. It is also important for employees to keep their passwords private. Hacking and creating or purposely sending viruses are unethical practices. Participating in either of these Internet threats on the job would most likely result in your dismissal. These acts are also considered crimes that can have legal consequences.

Checkpoint 10.1

1. What is a search engine?
2. Describe the difference between shareware and freeware.
3. Do you need a copyright notice to own the rights to an online article you wrote? Explain.
4. Identify security problems that may exist when using the Internet.
5. What is the purpose of antivirus software?

Build Your Vocabulary

As you progress through this text, develop a personal glossary of career-related terms and add it to your portfolio. This will help build your vocabulary and prepare you for your career of choice. Write a definition for each of the following terms, and add it to your personal career glossary.

World Wide Web
browser
copyright
license
software piracy
freeware

shareware
identity theft
malware
antivirus software
virus
hacking

Terms

assistive technology device
central processing unit (CPU)
mobile app
cloud computing
troubleshooting
e-mail
text messaging
social media
blog
webcast
teleconferencing
videoconferencing
web seminar

Computers

Computers come in various shapes and sizes. They have made many things easier and allowed workers to increase their productivity. The computer has made communicating easier than ever. Word processing, database, and presentation software are used routinely in business. Templates provide help formatting documents, while online dictionaries and spelling-correction tools help identify misspelled words. However, the software is not human. While a spell checker can see that the word *to* is spelled correctly, it takes a human to determine whether *to* or *too* was meant and appropriate.

Computers have made things easier for everyone, including those living with disabling conditions. **Assistive technology devices** help people with disabilities access education and other training opportunities that would otherwise be unattainable. In addition, these devices allow for persons with disabilities to more fully participate in the workforce. Voice-recognition software and specially designed keyboards are examples of commonly used assistive technology devices.

Ethical Leadership

Using Social Networking Media

"Don't say anything online that you wouldn't want plastered on a billboard with your face on it."—Erin Bury

Individual maturity is important even when you use social networking sites for personal use. Remember that a potential employer may search the Internet and see information you thought only your friends would see. When posting photos and other information to Facebook, or any other website, think about what you are posting. Only post items that are in good taste and would not embarrass you. Do an Internet search for "social networking media protocol" to find guidelines for posting personal information.

Technology is used routinely for business and personal use.

Hardware

The physical equipment in computer systems is the *hardware.* The hardware includes the computer itself and all of the items needed to use it except software.

A computer's power depends on the speed of its processor and the amount of memory it has. The **central processing unit (CPU)**, also called the processor, controls what is done with the data received. This is the component that performs the computer's functions. Processor speeds are measured in frequencies of megahertz (MHz) and gigahertz (GHz).

Computers vary in the amount of memory they have. The amount of memory is measured in megabytes (MB) and gigabytes (GB). Generally, it is a good idea to buy a computer with as much memory and as fast a processor as you can afford. Even if you do not require much power when you purchase the computer, you may need it later for software upgrades.

Printers, scanners, monitors, and mice are among the types of computer hardware called *peripherals.* Peripherals are the input and output devices, such as a mouse and printer, used to perform activities.

Software

Computers cannot operate without being told what to do. Hardware is the equipment; *software* provides the program instructions that tell a computer how to perform. A computer can be instructed to do a variety of tasks, depending on the software used. There are two basic types of computer software: operating system software and application software.

Operating System Software

Operating system software directs the use of the computer's hardware. In the case of personal computers, either the Windows operating system or the Mac operating system is typically used. Operating system software makes it possible for the computer to use compatible application software.

Application Software

Application software gives a computer, a smartphone, or other electronic device directions to perform specific tasks. Some tasks include word processing, data formatting, or Internet connectivity. Many of these programs are already installed on new devices. These programs may be purchased at computer stores or purchased and downloaded online.

Mobile apps, which is short for *mobile applications,* are relatively small, specialized programs used on wireless devices, such as tablets and smartphones. These apps are used for gaming, education, personal banking, connecting on social media, as well as serving many other functions.

Word processing software is used to enter, edit, store, and print words using a computer. Word processing software can be used to create documents, add charts, pictures, and other graphics. Most word processing programs have features for checking spelling and grammar. Proficiency with major word processing programs is something employers expect from employees.

Desktop publishing software is used to create documents that may be more professional looking than documents that have been created with word processing software. Publishers and other professionals use this software to create newsletters and other documents. Desktop

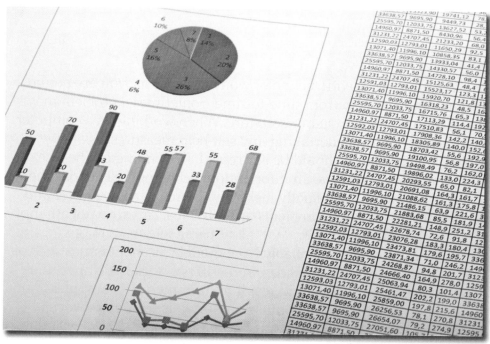

A variety of software products allow users to create charts, spreadsheets, and other visuals.

S.Dashkevych/Shutterstock.com

publishing software allows for flexibility when formatting text, the use of fonts, images, and page layouts.

Spreadsheet software is used to organize data into specific formats and perform mathematical computations. Formulas can be applied to a section so figures automatically adjust in that section when new data are entered.

Spreadsheets are used extensively in all areas of financial accounting. They provide an organized way to view numerous figures about business performance. For example, store managers may use spreadsheets to track the effect of various weekly promotions and marketing strategies on sales.

A database is a collection of related information. *Database software* is used to organize, store, and retrieve data. Most businesses use database software to track customers and their buying habits. For example, suppose your sales force wants to keep track of the action to take with each customer after a sales call. By inputting data about the visits into a database, lists can be generated to help the sales department learn which customers need more information or which customer just made a purchase.

Presentation software is an application that allows the user to create electronic slide shows. Text and images can be inserted on each slide, as well as notes for the speaker. Then, as the speaker gives the presentation, he or she moves the slide show forward by clicking the mouse or a remote.

The presentation can incorporate video and sounds if desired. The speaker can also prepare informative handouts for the audience by printing the presentation in different formats.

Cloud computing is using software applications and files stored on the Internet. This allows users to share or rent storage and computing capacity on an as-needed basis and to access files from remote locations.

Troubleshooting

When working with technology on a daily basis, you are bound to run into a problem from time-to-time. Sometimes a problem may occur with your computer or software. When working on a computer at work and before undertaking any self-help measures, ask how technology problems should be addressed. Depending on the size of the company, it may have an information technology (IT) department. An IT team member is usually tasked with providing computer and technical support when problems arise. In most cases, do not attempt to fix problems by yourself.

Your employer will probably have guidelines about issues such as downloading software upgrades. You will not want to do anything without permission that could result in harming your computer. Remember, the equipment you use on the job is your employer's property.

If you are working on your own computer and run into a problem, you may want to try to troubleshoot the problem on your own before calling for tech support. **Troubleshooting** is locating the source of a problem then fixing it. Take a few moments to see if you can solve the problem yourself. If the problem seems to be with hardware, check power and connection cables. Also try *rebooting*, which is shutting down and restarting the computer. This may help clear up some software problems as well. Keep in mind you will want to save, if possible, any files you are working on as any unsaved changes will be lost when you reboot.

Wireless Technology

Wireless technology was first used as radio transmissions. Smartphones, tablet computers, and other devices also receive and transmit data over radio waves. Wireless technology is used in business every day, allowing workers to stay connected and informed.

Cell Phones and Smartphones

You may be issued a cell phone or smartphone in your job. Remember that the phone belongs to your employer, so record a professional voice message for those times when you cannot take a call. Be respectful when communicating with others on your phone. Try to talk in a private location so that you do not disturb those around you.

Some employers will allow personal calls on a company phone, but others will not. Some employers will allow personal calls only if you pay for those calls.

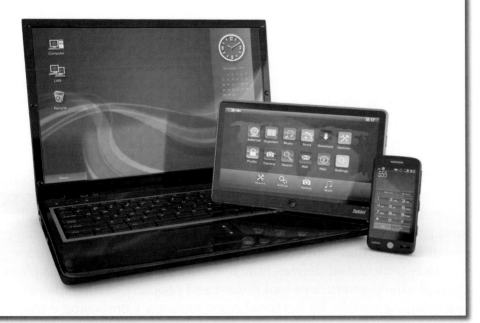

Wireless products, such as laptops, cell phones, and digital notepads, make it easier for users to stay connected to others.

Make sure you understand the policy on text messaging on your company phone. Some businesses may consider this unprofessional, while others may approve of business messages.

If your phone has a camera, do not use it for personal use. If you have e-mail access on your company phone, do not use it for personal use unless your employer approves.

Tablets and Digital Notepads

Digital notepads, also called *digital notebooks,* and tablet computers are handheld multimedia computing devices. They are designed for consumers wanting an electronic multimedia device that is larger than a smartphone, but smaller than a laptop. Digital notepads are capable of surfing the web, handling e-mail, taking photos, scanning barcodes, running office software, and a variety of other tasks previously only done on larger computers and smartphones. Digital notepads have found a wide use in business and industry as well as by individuals for personal use. More and more schools are using digital notepads in classrooms.

Electronic Communication

Few employers can afford to let their employees take extra time to prepare handwritten letters, memos, directions, and instructions. All forms of communication have become electronic in nature because of the speed provided and time saved. Manufacturing, construction, service, entertainment, and all other types of businesses depend on a variety of communication tools. Employees use electronic communication on a daily and hourly basis.

E-mail

E-mail is a system for sending messages from one device to another over an electronic network. E-mail is short for *electronic mail.* It is now a standard communication tool in business, government, and education. Much faster than mail sent through the postal service, e-mail can travel to people around the world in seconds.

E-mail messages resemble memos and are usually very brief as shown in Figure 10-2. However, like all forms of business communication, e-mail has a set of basic guidelines for proper and accepted use. Any e-mail you send from work should follow correct grammar, spelling, and punctuation rules. Using e-mail effectively and professionally may be essential to your employment success.

It is likely that your company will have an e-mail policy that restricts content and defines how it should be used in the workplace. E-mail can be an efficient tool if it is used properly, but avoid substituting e-mails for personal conversations. Composing e-mails takes up more time than talking.

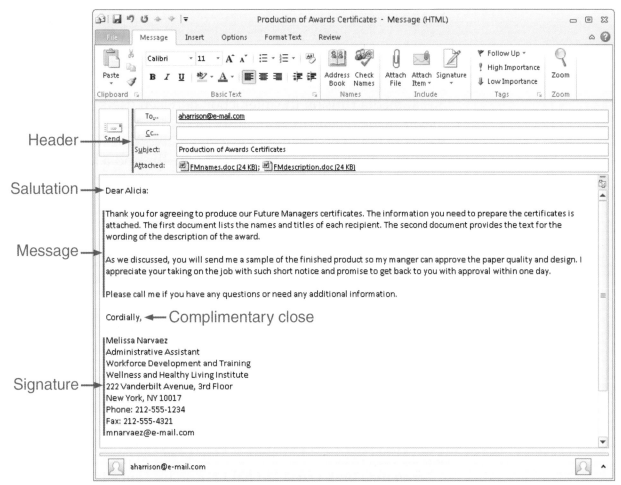

Figure 10-2.   *Goodheart-Willcox Publisher*
This figure shows an image of an e-mail with its elements labelled.

Do not use e-mail to spread gossip or rumors. Avoid opening chain mail or spam. *Spam* is unsolicited e-mail and may contain viruses or unsafe links. Never forward chain mail or spam to others. Never use work e-mail to forward jokes or any other inappropriate messages. Beware of unsolicited e-mails asking for personal information. This is called *phishing*.

E-mail blasts are often used by businesses to quickly and efficiently reach a large number of customers. These are targeted only to users who have expressed an interest in receiving information and are not considered spam.

Messaging

Text messaging, or *texting,* is the process of exchanging brief written messages between electronic devices over a network. Text messages may be either social or professional. Texting may be used as a substitute for voice calls when it is impossible or undesirable to use voice communication. As with other electronic communication, texting can be very helpful but also is subject to potential abuse. *Never* use texting language in a business situation.

Social Media

The Internet allows users to access vast amounts of data and connect with others. **Social media** are tools used to publish and share information between individuals or groups of individuals. Social media runs on the interaction between users and the content they provide. There are several social media websites. Some of the more popular sites used for social networking are Facebook, YouTube, Twitter, MySpace, Flickr, LinkedIn, and a large variety of entertainment and gaming sites. Social media sites may serve a single or a variety of purposes:

- expressing yourself to others;
- networking with others;
- sharing with others;
- gaming by and with others; and
- socializing with others.

While the adjective *social* is used, social media is also used for business purposes. Businesses use social, as well as professional, media sites to professionally share ideas, thoughts, and interests. Social media sites may be used for networking. *Networking* is building a pool of professional and personal contacts. LinkedIn is a very popular business networking site. Over 120 million professionals use this website to exchange information, ideas and opportunities. LinkedIn is also used by human resources departments to recruit skilled employees.

You may find a professional need to use some type of social media in your career. Only post or provide information as required or approved by your employer. Remember that when at work, social media is to be used for only work-related tasks.

Blogs and Webcasts

Another type of social media website is the web log, or blog. A **blog** is a website where an individual usually posts topics and opinions about subjects the owner of that website wishes to discuss. Blogs may be used for social or business purposes. Business blogs are normally used to share information with potential customers or actual customers. Blogs that use video rather than text-based posts are called *video blogs.*

An individual or organization can release a series of digital files, either audio or video, on a particular topic or topics as a webcast. A **webcast** is an event, either live or prerecorded, that is broadcast on the Internet. These files can be downloaded by a single viewer or groups of viewers. The files usually can also be downloaded and saved on the viewers' computers for later use or review.

Twitter

Twitter is a web-based messaging service. A *tweet* is a post or message sent. Tweets are a type of *microblog,* a blog posting limited to 140 characters or less. Many businesses use Twitter to quickly share

Videoconferencing allows people in different locations to conduct a meeting in a way that is both efficient and cost-effective.

imagesolutions/Shutterstock.com

information with people interested in their products and services. Twitter may also be used to gather real-time market information and feedback. Tweeting may also be used to build relationships with customers, partners, and influential people.

Connecting Remotely

Flying people to meetings in other cities can be very costly for an organization. However, technology can link people in various locations to hold a productive meeting or learn from a seminar. Participants can be as near as the next office or as far as another country.

Teleconferencing is using a phone to conduct a meeting with participants in different locations. Through the use of speakerphones in each location, everyone can contribute comments while hearing what the others are saying. During a teleconference, or *conference call,* it is important to speak loudly and clearly. Also, it is helpful for people to identify themselves each time they speak so everyone knows who is saying what. Teleconferencing is a widely used business tool.

Videoconferencing involves two or more people communicating through a video and voice linkup. Web cams are used to transmit video over the Internet. They are usually plugged into or built into computers and can provide a continuous feed. They are often used for videoconferences or video chatting. Skype can be used as means for videoconferencing.

Web seminars, also referred to as *webinars,* are a means of delivering instruction to a group located at one or more locations other than where the material is being presented. The presenter or presenters are in one location delivering the seminar while the other participants are in other locations. Web seminars allow for two-way communication between those delivering the information and those receiving it. A web seminar is similar to a videoconference except that the shared video is typically the presenter's computer screen, not a video of the presenter.

Checkpoint 10.2

1. Name four common peripherals used with a computer.
2. What is the function of the information technology (IT) department at many workplaces?
3. For what purpose are business blogs used?
4. Why is it beneficial for some companies to use teleconferencing?
5. Explain the difference between teleconferencing and videoconferencing.

Build Your Vocabulary

As you progress through this text, develop a personal glossary of career-related terms and add it to your portfolio. This will help build your vocabulary and prepare you for your career of choice. Write a definition for each of the following terms, and add it to your personal career glossary.

assistive technology device
central processing unit (CPU)
mobile app
cloud computing
troubleshooting
e-mail
text messaging
social media
blog
webcast
teleconferencing
videoconferencing
web seminar

Technology on the Job

Within the past few decades, business and industry have become entirely dependent on computers and computer software. Without computer technology, companies could not survive in today's marketplace. Whether an organization produces goods or provides a service, computer technology is used extensively in successful organizations. Many of the computer applications used in the workplace are also used in schools and homes.

Practically every business now maintains a website to promote itself in the same way it may use television and magazine advertising. The website may be used as to advertise and sell company products or services. Customers may also be able to place orders directly on a website.

Employees also use computers and the Internet in the workplace to conduct online research and gather information they need for their work. The Internet allows employees in many locations to view real-time events. *Real time* refers to something that is experienced occurring as it happens.

Many people are able to use the Internet to work outside of the office. This is convenient for salespeople or other employees who must spend significant time at other locations. The Internet also allows people to work from their homes, yet stay connected to the office.

One of the effects of technology in the workplace is globalization. With globalization, interrelations among nations of the world are strengthened through a global network of political ideas on communication, transportation, and trade. With the help of the Internet and other technology, information can travel from one side of the globe to the other in the blink of an eye. The result is that nations are more likely to engage in trade, as well as share labor, goods, and services.

A **global positioning system (GPS)** is a highly accurate satellite-based navigation system. It provides continuous worldwide coverage. Signals from four or more satellites are used to display the user's position anywhere in the world. The highly accurate data are collected and saved on memory cards.

GPS is a communication system that can be applied to many businesses. It is used for surveying, tracking people and objects, operating vehicles and robots, the precision approach and landing of aircraft, and many emergency services. GPS may be used to direct vehicle drivers and fishermen to their destinations.

More specifically, in the field of agriculture, GPS has numerous applications. It is helpful in controlling the application of agricultural chemicals and locating insect or weed problems. GPS is also used in field preparation, controlling planters, watershed mapping, controlling pesticide runoff, and mapping the proximity of agriculture to endangered species.

Technology and Your Future

From one year to the next, advances in computer technology are impossible to predict. Computers become more powerful and, at the same time, more affordable. They play major roles in entertainment, information, communication, and research functions.

It is very important to accept the changes and the challenges they present. It is equally important to continue learning about computers after high school so your skills meet the computer literacy level expected by employers. It does not matter what career area you choose. Knowing how to use computer technology will certainly improve your chances of finding a good job.

Understanding how to use technology and various software programs will increase your chances of finding a job.

Konstantin Chagin/Shutterstock.com

Case

E-Mail in the Workplace

Jodie was thrilled to have an internship with a large bank as an office assistant. The job required excellent computer skills, and she took great pride in meeting the bank's high standards. She was especially happy to be working with a family friend, Mrs. Collins, who managed the bank's office.

Several times this week, she overhead Mrs. Collins say, "It's such a pleasure to work with someone who is so capable." Jodie wanted Mrs. Collins to think she could handle any assignment.

"Please e-mail Mr. Raja in the loans department and tell him his monthly report is ready," Mrs. Collins told Jodie. Jodie often sent e-mail from home to friends, so she followed that pattern and sent this message:

Your monthly report is ready :-). Please pick it up. *S*

Jodie realized after sending the message that Mr. Raja had no way of knowing who she was or what report she meant, so she quickly sent another message.

BTW your monthly report from Mrs. Collins' office is ready to pick up :-D.

Jodie expected to see Mr. Raja step off the elevator within minutes. After several hours passed, she began to question if she sent the message to the correct e-mail address. She decided to send a message that would definitely get his attention:

FYI YOUR MONTHLY REPORT FROM MRS. COLLINS' OFFICE HAS BEEN WAITING FOR YOU SINCE NOON :-(.

A few days later, Mrs. Collins asked Jodie to explain what she e-mailed to Mr. Raja. He had called to complain about "the confusing messages and rude behavior of someone named Jodie."

Critical Thinking

1. Do you think Jodie sent confusing messages?
2. Was Jodie's behavior to Mr. Raja rude?
3. How should business e-mail look compared to e-mail sent to friends from home?
4. In business e-mail, do you recommend using shorthand and emoticons, such as *S*, :-), BTW, :-D, FYI, :-(, and others? Do you know what they mean?

Lifelong Learning

Most jobs involve the use of computers or technology in some form. Computers greatly increase productivity and reduce labor costs. Technology is continually changing. When employers add or upgrade technology systems, employees will need to adjust to the new systems and procedures. Employees may need to take classes to become acquainted with, and proficient at, using new technologies.

Lifelong learning is the continuous building of skills and knowledge throughout the life of an individual. The adjustments may be difficult and may require new ways of working. More than ever, employers expect employees to be flexible and adjust to changes in the workplace. Expect to continue to learn new technologies and processes throughout your career. An employee who is open to keeping up with developing technologies is expected in the workplace. On the other hand, those who cannot adjust may find themselves left behind to handle lower-skilled, lower-paying jobs.

Job seekers who have computer skills will have a definite advantage when interviewing for most positions. Try to take advantage of every opportunity you have to gain experience in using computers while you are still in school. Take a general computer class. Become familiar with word processing and other software programs by taking specific classes in these subjects.

Specialized Education

The type of technology you use on the job will depend on where you work and what you do. Based on your career objective, you may take specialized courses that acquaint you with specific types of technology and applications. Computer technology has created many new career opportunities. If you enjoy working frequently with computers, you might consider a career described in Figure 10-3.

A *programmer* is a person who writes computer programs. Sometimes no application software is available to perform a specific task. In such a case, a new program needs to be written. Programmers usually know several different computer languages that are used to write the new programs.

Demand is high for talented people who can design digital media. Multimedia uses digital media, such as audio, video, still images, and text. As the shift toward greater use of technology continues, more digital media designers will be needed.

Computer Careers
• Computer operators—set the computer's controls, load the software, and monitor operations and/or output devices
• Computer programmers or software developers—write the instructions for computer applications
• Data entry personnel—use keyboards to enter data into computer systems
• Service technicians—repair computers, printers, and related hardware when they break down
• Support specialists—train users of new computer programs and networks; provide technical assistance to users
• Systems analysts—resolve computer user and computer program problems; analyze existing systems to make improvements
• Systems engineers—manage servers; develop and manage computer networks; plan ways to automate business tasks
• Tool programmers—write coded instructions that operate machine tools (such as drill presses, lathes, and milling machines) used in manufacturing precision-machined metal parts
• Web programmers, web managers, or web masters—create, maintain, and update organizations' websites

Figure 10-3.   *Goodheart-Willcox Publisher*
A variety of careers exist for people interested in the computer technology.

Checkpoint 10.3

1. What are three Internet applications you may anticipate finding in the workplace?
2. How have the Internet and other technology contributed to globalization?
3. What are some ways in which a business might use the global positioning system (GPS)?
4. What are the job duties of a systems engineer?
5. How will digital media designers be affected in the future? Explain why.

Build Your Vocabulary

As you progress through this text, develop a personal glossary of career-related terms and add it to your portfolio. This will help build your vocabulary and prepare you for your career of choice. Write a definition for each of the following terms, and add it to your personal career glossary.

global positioning system (GPS)
lifelong learning

Chapter Summary

Section 10.1 Technology Overview

- The Internet is the largest computer system in existence. The World Wide Web is the part of the Internet that carries messages having pictures, color, or sound.
- The Internet is used at home and in the workplace. If allowed to access the Internet during work hours, an employee must act responsibly.
- Ethical Internet use involves respectful and legal utilization of information and software. Copyright and licenses protect the rights of the owner.
- Computer security is a major concern for users. Anti-virus software protects against hacking, computer viruses, and identity theft.

Section 10.2 Tools and Devices

- Computers, peripherals, and software are integral components in the work environment. To be effective, most employees must be able to productively use computers.
- Wireless technology is commonly used in business. Cell phones, smart-phones, tablets, and digital notepads keep workers connected and informed.
- Electronic communication allows employees to save time and money. Teleconferencing, videoconferencing, and webcasts are frequently used across long distances.

Section 10.3 Impact of Technology

- Businesses rely heavily upon computers and software. As a result of technology, companies are more likely to engage in opportunities around the world.
- Workers should continuously increase their knowledge of computers. Technology is not static and will continue to change.

Check Your Career IQ

Now that you have finished the chapter, see what you learned about careers by taking the chapter posttest. The test can be accessed on the mobile site by using a smartphone or on the G-W Learning companion website.

www.m.g-wlearning.com

www.g-wlearning.com

Review Your Knowledge

1. How are browsers and the World Wide Web related?
2. What can you do to avoid identity theft when using the Internet?
3. What are the traits of a strong password?
4. How can you protect your computer and files?
5. Identify the two types of computer software.
6. How does the global positioning system (GPS) work?
7. Explain how word processing software is used.
8. What are some uses for desktop publishing software.
9. What are common purposes for using social media sites?
10. What are the job duties of a web manager?

Apply Your Knowledge

1. Research a career of your choice to discover what computer skills you would need for that job. List the necessary skills in a report. Indicate which skills you already possess. Describe where and how you might acquire the skills you do not possess.
2. What are the advantages of using various social media? What are the disadvantages? Discuss the subject with a small group. Take notes during your discussion. Then, share your ideas with the rest of the class.
3. Using the Internet, research e-learning courses available. Name three schools that offer online courses. What is the cost to take one of these courses? What type of technology is used for the online courses at each of those schools? Summarize your findings in a written report.
4. As the president of a large company, imagine you have offices in Chicago and Miami. How can your employees use technology to stay connected during the work day? Discuss your answers with a partner. Compile your information in a chart, and present it to the class.
5. Describe how using e-mail, voice mail, and texting differs when communicating with a friend and with a business associate. Which forms of communication do you prefer and why? Record your answers on paper. Then, share them with a partner.
6. Think about how you use technology at home, work, school, and among friends. Use a three- or four-column chart to record the ways in which you use technology.
7. Research the technology that makes computer processors work. How has this technology changed over time? How have these changes affected the size, cost, and availability of computers?
8. How would your life change if you were unable to use any computer technology for a week? Write a one-page paper to explain how your life might be affected. What do you think you would learn from the experience?

9. Use the Internet to learn more about how technology is used as a tool to help students learn. Create a list of five forms of technology or tools used to teach and learn. For each example, explain how it works and the benefits it provided.

10. Develop a class presentation on technology in the workplace. Discuss specific technology and devices. Explain the impact or benefits of the technology you present. Be creative in your presentation. For example, you may use technology to create visual aids, or use a presentation program to display information. Limit your presentation to three minutes.

Teamwork

Assume you are working in a business that has daily contact with customers who buy pet food and supplies. Working with two classmates, create a list of ways the business could communicate with its customers. Include ways the business could reach out to customers as well as ways customers can contact the business. Of the methods of communication you listed, which do you think would be the most effective? Explain why.

G-W Learning Mobile Site

Visit the G-W Learning mobile site to complete the chapter pretest and posttest and to practice vocabulary using e-flash cards. If you do not have a smartphone, visit the G-W Learning companion website to access these features.
G-W Learning mobile site: www.m.g-wlearning.com
G-W Learning companion website: www.g-wlearning.com

Common Core

College and Career Readiness

Speaking. Using the Internet, research information on *software piracy*. Present your findings to the class using visuals to convey examples to your audience.

Listening. Listening combines hearing with evaluating. While your teacher is presenting a lesson, take notes and evaluate his or her point of view about the material that is being presented. What did you learn about listening?

Apply Your Technology Skills

Access the G-W Learning companion website for this text at www.g-wlearning.com. Download the data file for this chapter. Follow the instructions to complete activities to practice what you have learned in this chapter.

Data File 10–1—**Avoiding E-mail Pitfalls**

College and Career Readiness

College and Career Readiness Portfolio

Your portfolio should contain samples of your work that show your skills or talents. Now is the time to start collecting items. You can decide which documents to include later when you prepare your final portfolio. Look at past school or work assignments you have completed. Select a book report, essay, poem, or other work that demonstrates your writing talents. Include a research paper, letter, electronic slide show, or other items that illustrate your business communication skills. Look for projects that show your skills related to critical thinking and problem solving. Have you completed a long or complicated project? Write a description of the project and tell how you managed various parts of the assignment to complete it on time. Include samples from the completed project. What career area interests you most? Select completed work from classes that will help prepare you for jobs or internships in that area.

1. Save the documents that show your skills and talents in your e-portfolio. Remember to place the documents in an appropriate subfolder.
2. Place hard copies in the container for your print portfolio.

Chapter
11 Looking Good on the Job

Section 11.1
Stay Healthy

Section 11.2
Make a Good
Impression

College and Career Readiness

Reading Prep. Scan this chapter and look for the facts. As you read, try to determine which topics are facts and which are the author's opinions. After reading, research the topics and verify the facts and opinions presented in the chapter.

Introduction

When you meet someone for the first time, what do you notice right away? Most people notice a person's appearance. In fact, people tend to form first impressions about others based on appearance. Many employers assume that people who take pride in their appearance are likely to take pride in their work as well.

Looking good on the job involves more than wearing the "right clothes." Your health and grooming habits as well as your clothes influence your appearance. What impressions do you think others form of your appearance? "I want to succeed at this job" is the impression you should want to make at work. You can do this by keeping yourself in good physical condition, being neat and clean, and dressing appropriately.

Check Your Career IQ

Before you begin the chapter, see what you already know about careers by taking the chapter pretest. Use the related QR code to view the pretest on the mobile site. If you do not have a smartphone, visit the G-W Learning companion website to access the pretest.

www.m.g-wlearning.com
www.g-wlearning.com

G-W Mobile

Career Snapshot
Chef

Hospitality & Tourism

What Does a Chef Do?

Chefs prepare food, hire, train, and supervise staff for food and supplies, prepare cost estimates, set work schedules, order supplies, and ensure that the food service establishment runs efficiently and profitably. A chef must:

- ensure that sanitation and safety standards are observed and comply with local regulations;
- check that fresh food is stored and cooked properly, work surfaces and dishes are clean and sanitary; and
- protect staff and customers from food-borne illness.

What Is It Like to Work as a Chef?

All chefs may have a role in preparing the food, developing recipes, determining serving sizes, planning menus, ordering food supplies, and overseeing kitchen operations to ensure uniform quality and presentation of meals. Different types of chefs may have unique roles to perform or specialize in certain aspects of the job.

Executive chefs, head cooks, and *chefs de cuisine* are primarily responsible for coordinating the work of the cooks and directing the preparation of meals. Executive chefs are in charge of all food service operations and also may supervise several kitchens of a hotel, restaurant or corporate dining operation. A *sous chef,* or *sub chef,* is the second-in-command and runs the kitchen in the absence of the chef.

Many chefs earn fame both for themselves and for their kitchens because of the quality and distinctive nature of the food they serve.

What Education and Skills Are Needed to Be a Chef?

- 2-year or 4-year college with a degree in hospitality
- creativity
- leadership and organizational skills

11.1 Stay Healthy

Objectives

After completing this section, you will be able to:
- **Explain** how your health and eating habits influence your appearance and the way other people see you.
- **Learn** how to select and build a healthy plate.
- **Apply** the principles of being physically active.
- **Describe** the effect sleep as on overall well-being.
- **Recall** ways to manage stress.

Maintain Good Health

Looking good on the job begins with a healthy you. Good grooming and nice clothes will make very little difference if you are in poor physical health. Your health affects everything about you. It affects the way you look and feel.

To develop a healthy lifestyle, there are three basic steps to follow. You need to eat well-balanced meals, stay active, and get adequate sleep. Following these steps will make you look more attractive and help you to be more alert and productive on the job.

What you eat affects your overall health, energy, and appearance, so a good diet is important. Eating balanced meals will help you look good and feel well. One way to maintain good health is to eat the right foods. You start by building a healthy plate. For example, cut back on foods high in solid fats, added sugars, and salt. Eat the right amount of calories for your own body. Also, use food labels to select healthy foods.

Build a Healthy Plate

Before you eat, think about what goes on your plate or in your cup or bowl. What really makes your plate a "healthy plate"? As shown in Figure 11-1, foods like whole grains, lean protein, fruits, vegetables, and dairy foods contain the nutrients you need without too many calories. When you prepare a meal, include a balance of these nutritional foods.

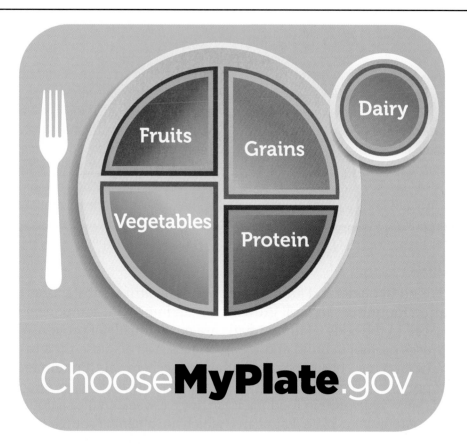

Balancing calories
- Enjoy your food, but eat less.
- Avoid oversized portions.

Foods to increase
- Make half your plate fruits and vegetables.
- Make at least half your grains whole grains.
- Switch to fat-free or low-fat (1%) milk.

Foods to reduce
- Compare sodium in foods like soup, bread, and frozen meals— and choose the foods with lower numbers.
- Drink water instead of sugary drinks.

Figure 11-1.   *Goodheart-Willcox Publisher*
This figure provides tips for building a well-balanced meal.

Grains

Whole grains, or foods made from them, contain all the essential parts and naturally-occurring nutrients of the entire grain seed. If the grain has been processed (such as, cracked crushed, rolled, extruded, and cooked), the food product should deliver approximately the same rich balance of nutrients that are found in the original grain seed. Whole grains should make up half of your total intake of grains. Choose 100 percent whole-grain cereals, breads, crackers, rice, and pasta. Check the ingredients list on food packages to find whole-grain foods.

Go Green

The next time you need to clean the smudge marks off of your LCD screen, TV screen, or computer monitor, remember to avoid harsh chemical cleaners. You can clean your monitor by using a very small amount of distilled water and a non-abrasive cloth. To clean the monitor or screen, dampen the cloth very lightly. Wring out any excess water. Then, gently wipe the monitor or screen. You can also use environmentally friendly cleaner wipes. Remember, chemical cleaners are hard on the equipment and some are bad for the environment.

Protein

Found in plants and animals, **protein** is a natural substance required for muscle and cell growth. It is an important component of every cell in the body. Hair and nails are mostly made of protein. Your body uses protein to build and repair tissues. You also use protein to make enzymes, hormones, and other body chemicals. Protein is an important building block of bones, muscles, cartilage, skin, and blood. Vary your protein food choices. Twice a week, make seafood the protein on your plate. Eat beans, which are a *natural* source of fiber and protein. Keep meat and poultry portions small and lean.

Vegetables

Many people do not eat sufficient amounts of vegetables. Vegetables help lower the risk of serious illness and health problems such as cancer, high blood pressure, and cardiovascular disease. Eat dark-green vegetables (broccoli, spinach, and kale), red and orange vegetables (tomatoes, sweet potatoes, carrots, and red peppers), beans and peas (black-eyed peas, soy beans, pinto beans, and lentils), starchy vegetables (corn, potatoes, and green peas), as well as other vegetables such as avocado, celery, cauliflower, and mushrooms.

Fruits

Fruits are rich in vitamins and fiber. Apricots, peaches, and other deep yellow and orange fruits contain a lot of vitamin A. Citrus fruits (oranges and grapefruit) as well as strawberries and cantaloupe provide vitamin C. By choosing whole fruits over fruit juices, you will get more fiber and nutrients.

Dairy

Dairy foods (milk, cheese, and yogurt) provide calcium as well as protein, potassium, and vitamin D. When choosing dairy foods, MyPlate recommends picking low-fat, reduced fat, or fat-free dairy products because they are lower in fat and calories than whole-milk varieties.

Calories

Most foods provide the body with a specific amount of calories. A **calorie** is a metric unit of energy. However, some foods are less healthy and offer empty calories and fewer nutrients. An **empty calorie** is energy present in high-energy foods with poor nutrition; with most of the energy coming from processed carbohydrates, and fats, or ethanol. Everyone has a personal calorie limit. Staying within yours can help you maintain a healthy weight. Following are a few suggestions to help you control your eating and calorie intake.

- Eat more often at home, where *you* are in control of what is in your food.
- Write down what you eat to keep track of how much you eat.
- Get your personal daily calorie limit at www.ChooseMyPlate.gov and keep that number in mind when deciding what to eat.
- Think before you eat—is your choice worth the calories?
- Avoid oversized portions.
- Use a smaller plate, bowl, and glass.
- Stop eating when you are satisfied, not full.

People who are successful at managing their weight have found ways to keep track of how much they eat in a day, even if they do not count every calorie. For example, when you eat out, choose lower calorie menu options. Select dishes that include vegetables, fruits, and whole grains. You can also order smaller portions. If you are eating with family or friends, consider sharing larger meals or appetizers.

Solid Fats, Sugar, and Salt

Many people eat foods with too much solid fat, added sugar, and salt (sodium). Added sugars and fats load foods with extra calories you do not need. Too much sodium may increase your blood pressure.

Switch to skim or one percent milk. They have the same amount of calcium and other essential nutrients as whole milk, but less fat and calories. You may also try calcium-fortified soy products as an alternative to dairy foods.

Ethical Leadership

Ethical versus Legal

"Law floats in a sea of ethics."— Earl Warren

A company's dress code for its workers may have both legal and ethical implications. On the legal side, a dress code mandated for employee protection is often the result of a law. Workers in certain occupations are required to wear clothing, footwear, and headgear that provide protection against a workplace hazard. Failure to wear protective gear, such as a hard hat on a construction site, may actually be against the law and can result in a fine or other action by enforcement officials.

Those who work in an office environment may be required to dress in business attire. Failure to comply with the company's dress code policy is not against the law, but instead may be considered inappropriate conduct and a breach of ethics.

It is important to eat fewer foods that are high in solid fats. Solid fats remain solid at room temperature. They slowly clog and even block the circulatory system. Make major sources of saturated fats, such as cakes, cookies, ice cream, pizza, cheese, sausages, and hot dogs, occasional choices, rather than foods you eat every day. Whenever possible, choose lean cuts of meats or poultry, and select fat-free or low-fat milk, yogurt, and cheese. These foods have a lower fat content. Using oils instead of solid fats in food preparation is another way to limit your intake of fat.

You should choose foods and drinks with little or no added sugars. Childhood obesity, often linked to consumption of sugary beverages, is a serious health hazard. Diets high in added sugar increase triglycerides and obesity, increasing risk factors for heart disease and diabetes.

Salt gives added flavor. However, health risks, such as high blood pressure, are associated with too much salt intake. Pay attention to the amount of salt (sodium) in foods you buy—it all adds up. Compare sodium in foods like soup, bread, and frozen meals and select those with the least sodium. Maintain the flavor in your food by adding spices or herbs instead of salt.

Food Labels

Most packaged foods have a nutrition facts label and an ingredients list. Use the labels and ingredients lists to make smart food choices. Choose foods with lower calories, saturated fat, *trans* fat, and sodium. Also, check the calorie count on the package. Be sure to look at the serving size and how many servings you are actually consuming. If you double the servings, you double the calories as shown in Figure 11-2.

Nutrition Facts

Serving Size   172g

Amount Per Serving	
Calories 200	Calories from Fat 8

	%Daily Value*
Total Fat 1g	1%
Saturated Fat 0g	1%
Trans Fat	
Cholesterol 0mg	0%
Sodium 7mg	0%
Total Carbohydrates 36g	12%
Dietary Fiber 11g	45%
Sugars 6g	
Protein 13g	

Vitamin A	1%	• Vitamin C	1%
Calcium	4%	• Iron	24%

*Percent Daily Values are based on a 2,000 calorie diet. Your daily values may be higher or lower depending on your calorie needs.

Figure 11-2.   *Goodheart-Willcox Publisher*

Nutrition labels inform you about the ingredients and nutritional value in a food product.

Check the ingredients list for added sugars. When a sugar is close to first on the ingredients list, the food is high in added sugars. Some names for added sugars include the words *sucrose, glucose, high fructose corn syrup, corn syrup, maple syrup,* and *fructose.*

Be Physically Active

Good health is not complete without regular physical activity. When good nutrition and physical activity work together, health and well-being improve. Also, body weight stays in a healthy range. It's easier to be physically active when you choose activities you like. Start by doing what you are able to do, at least ten minutes at a time. Every bit adds up, and the health benefits increase as you spend more time being active.

The body benefits from physical activity in many ways. Through physical activity and exercise, you can improve your blood circulation, increase your lung capacity, and improve digestion. As you exercise, you strengthen muscles, making them more flexible. Coordination and posture improve as a result. Physical activity also allows you to control your weight by burning stored calories. In addition to helping you relax, physical activity can help relieve anger, stress, and depression.

Exercise of any type can be helpful. Walking, jogging, team sports, or household chores are examples of good physical activities. If you spend most of your time going to school or work, watching TV, or using the computer, you need to get started on your fitness plan! Inactivity offers no benefits and may even lead to health problems later in life. The following guidelines will help you get started.

- Aim for a healthful weight and work to maintain it. Find ways to increase activity as a part of your daily routine. Take stairs instead of elevators. Walk or bike instead of riding.
- Add an exercise plan if you need more activity in your day. If you are happy with your plan, you will probably stick to it. Try joining a group program or exercising with a friend if you do not think you can exercise on your own.
- Increase activity gradually. This gives your body time to adjust to more physical demands.
- Include activities that improve your respiration and circulation, such as walking, jogging, or aerobic dancing. Exercises that develop your muscle strength, coordination, and flexibility, such as gymnastics, are also important for fitness.
- Accumulate at least 60 minutes of moderate physical activity most days of the week, preferably daily. Moderate activity is walking two miles in 30 minutes.

Get Enough Sleep

The amount of sleep needed by individuals varies. Sleep needs are different across ages and are impacted by lifestyle and health. The National Sleep Foundation has published some very general guidelines as shown in Figure 11-3.

| How Much Sleep Do You Really Need? ||
Age	Sleep Needs
Newborns (0–2 months)	12–18 hours
Infants (3–11 months)	14–15 hours
Toddlers (1–3 years)	12–14 hours
Preschoolers (3–5 years)	11–13 hours
School–aged children (5–10 years)	10–11 hours
Teens (10–17)	8.5–9.25 hours
Adults	7–9 hours

Figure 11-3.   *Source: National Sleep Foundation*
This table shows how much sleep is needed for specific age groups.

See how you respond to different amounts of sleep. Pay careful attention to your mood, energy, and health after a poor night's sleep versus a good one. Ask yourself, "How often do I get a good night's sleep?" If the answer is "not often", then you may need to consider changing your sleep habits or consulting a physician or sleep specialist. You need to get enough sleep every night to be alert and to perform at your best.

Manage Stress

Everyone experiences stress at sometime. **Stress** is the physical and emotional reaction to a challenge. When stress helps us meet tough situations or rise to a challenge, it can be a positive thing. However, when stress disturbs the body's internal balance, it may be very negative. Negative stress can cause physical and emotional symptoms such as headaches, high blood pressure, chest pains, panic attacks, anxiety, and even insomnia and depression.

It is important to find ways to manage stress. Learn to "go with the flow" rather than feeling you have to always be in control. If you begin to feel stressed out, you may need to take time to relax. For example, change your activities, listen to soothing music, meditate, or take a walk. The following are just a few more ways to positively manage stress and help control its affects.

- Get enough sleep.
- Learn to laugh more.
- Spend time with a pet.
- Take a nap.
- Eat healthy.
- Do something nice for someone else.
- Limit Internet or cell phone time.
- Keep things in perspective.

Checkpoint 11.1

1. What are the three basic steps to follow when developing a healthy lifestyle?
2. Why does the body need protein?
3. Explain the meaning of a "healthy plate."
4. What are two guidelines to being physically fit?
5. What are some effects of negative stress?

Build Your Vocabulary

As you progress through this text, develop a personal glossary of career-related terms and add it to your portfolio. This will help build your vocabulary and prepare you for your career of choice. Write a definition for each of the following terms, and add it to your personal career glossary.

whole grain
protein
calorie
empty calorie
stress

11.2 | Make a Good Impression

Terms

grooming
hygiene
dermatologist

Objectives

After completing this section, you will be able to:
- **Describe** the grooming habits a person should practice to stay neat and clean.
- **Explain** the importance of dressing appropriately for the job.
- **Describe** ways to properly care for clothes.

Practice Good Grooming Habits

Grooming is taking proper care of your body and appearance. When it comes to good grooming, there are two words you need to remember—cleanliness and neatness. You need to be clean and neat from your head to toe every day. Cleanliness is essential to getting and keeping a job.

Clean Body

Hygiene is the practice of staying healthy by keeping clean. To help stay clean, you need to bathe or shower and use deodorant or antiperspirant every day. Everyone perspires, even during the winter. When you perspire, bacteria grow and cause body odor. Frequent bathing with soap and water removes the bacteria and body odor. Because you usually do not have time to bathe several times a day, it is important for you to use a deodorant or antiperspirant.

Both deodorants and antiperspirants help control body odor by interfering with the growth of bacteria. Antiperspirants also help reduce the flow of perspiration. A deodorant or antiperspirant should be applied daily after you bathe. There are many different varieties to choose from. You may want to use a roll-on, solid, gel, or aerosol form, either scented or unscented. Experiment to find out which brand works best for you.

Smooth Shave

To shave or not to shave is a decision both men and women have to make. Men need to decide if they want to shave their facial hair or grow a mustache, beard, or both. Women need to decide if they want to shave their legs and underarms.

Some men want to have a mustache or beard. Many employers report preferring a clean-shaven look. These employers often think a clean-shaven man gives a better impression of their company. However, it is illegal to discriminate against an employee or job applicant whose religious beliefs require that they cannot shave.

Whatever decision you make, the general rule is to be neat and clean. If you want your face neatly shaved, do not go to work with stubble on it. For most men, this means they must shave every day. If you choose to have a beard or mustache, wash it regularly with a mild soap and keep it neatly combed and shaped. An unkempt beard or mustache will certainly give a sloppy appearance. Also be sure the style of beard or mustache you choose is suitable to your hairstyle and face shape.

Most young women in the United States choose to shave their legs and underarms because they think it gives a neater appearance. Women who do not shave may be considered less concerned about their appearance. Shaving under the arms can also help reduce perspiration odor.

The decision to shave or not to shave is yours. Remember, however, that many employers have preferences regarding how their employees appear to others.

Case

The Case of the Disappearing Coworkers

Brent works for Industrial Design Graphics as a graphic illustrator. His department always takes a midmorning break. He and his coworkers enjoy going to the lunchroom, relaxing, and chatting about a variety of topics.

Over the past few weeks, however, Brent has noticed people moving further away from him at the break table. In fact, some people have been going elsewhere during the break. Brent wondered why people were not meeting as a group in the break room anymore.

Brent asks, "Where is everyone? Why aren't we all meeting for breaks like we did before?"

You know the answer because it has been a topic of discussion behind Brent's back. Brent has an offensive body odor. You are the only other person in the room when he asks these questions.

Critical Thinking

1. How would you answer Brent's questions?
2. Do you feel a friend should have advised Brent about his need for good grooming before it became a public issue?

Healthy Complexion

Many young people often have problems with oily skin. This may contribute to skin problems such as pimples and acne. Regardless of the type of skin you have, you should keep your skin clean by caring for it properly.

All skin types should be cleansed regularly with warm soapy water or a cleanser to keep the skin free of bacteria, dirt, and oils. You should see a dermatologist if your skin is extremely oily and acne becomes a problem. A **dermatologist** is a doctor who specializes in treating skin. This type of specialist will be able to recommend the best cleansers and cosmetics for your skin.

Clean Hair

The hair has often been called a person's "crowning glory" because it can greatly enhance personal appearance. It is so important to keep your hair clean and neatly styled. Hair care involves three major steps: shampooing, conditioning, and styling.

Once hair is cleaned and conditioned, it needs to be styled. You should choose a style that will suit the texture of your hair, the shape and size of your face, and your lifestyle. You may want to consult a hairstylist to help you choose the best style for you. Hairstylists are trained to analyze hair and facial features and to cut and style hair accordingly.

Proper Attire

Some competitive events for Career and Technical Student Organizations (CTSOs) require appropriate business attire from all entrants and those attending the competition. This requirement is in keeping with the mission of CTSOs: to prepare students for their chosen careers. To make certain that the attire you have chosen to wear at the competition is in accordance with event requirements, complete the following.

1. Visit the organization's website and look for the most current dress code.
2. The dress code requirements are very detailed and gender specific. Some CTSOs may require a chapter blazer be worn when competing.
3. Do a dress rehearsal when practicing for your event. Are you comfortable in the clothes you have chosen? Do you present a professional appearance?
4. In addition to the kinds of clothes you can wear, be sure the clothes are clean and pressed. You do not want to undermine your appearance or event performance with wrinkled clothes that may distract judges.
5. Make sure your hair is neat and worn in a conservative style. If you are a male, you should be clean shaven. Again, you do not want anything about your appearance detracting from you performance.
6. As far in advance of the event as is feasible, share your clothing choice with your organization's sponsor to make sure you are dressed appropriately.

Attractive Hands

Because your hands are in sight most of the time, they are an important part of your appearance. You should keep your hands and fingernails clean and manicured.

If your hands and nails get heavily soiled on the job, you may need to use a special soap to get them clean. A nailbrush can also help you wash away dirt and oil from under and around the nails. For example, an auto technician will frequently handle oily machine parts or equipment. Throughout the day, he or she will need to take special care to remove dirt and oil from the hands and beneath the nails.

Fresh Breath

Your mouth plays an important role in your appearance. Because the mouth draws so much attention, you need to have clean teeth and fresh breath.

Workers in the medical field are required to wear uniforms that clean easily.

Kurhan/Shutterstock.com

Teeth are an important part of your mouth, your breath, and your smile. To help keep your teeth clean, your breath fresh, and your smile bright, you need to brush your teeth regularly. You should also floss your teeth often and schedule regular checkups with your dentist to keep your teeth and gums healthy. Caring properly for your teeth can also help you avoid cavities and gum disease.

In addition to brushing, some people find it helpful to gargle with a mouthwash to avoid bad breath. You may want to try a mouthwash as well. Whatever ensures good breath for you, do it daily. You do not want to be caught with bad breath on the job, especially if you work closely with others.

Dressing for the Job

Many people feel they have a right to wear whatever they want to work. However, employers also have the right to expect employees to dress appropriately for work. For example, some employers may view shorts or jeans as inappropriate dress. Therefore, most companies have established a dress code that their employees are expected to follow. If you choose not to dress appropriately for the job, your employer can always hire another worker who will. However, it is against the law for an employer to fire someone for wearing religiously-prescribed clothing and headpieces.

The first step to dressing right for the job is to wear clean clothes. You also need to make sure your clothes fit properly and are appropriate for the work you will be doing. To help you decide what is appropriate to wear to work, think about the responsibilities you will have on the job. Will you be lifting and bending? Will you be handling food? Will you be working at a desk in an office?

In many career fields, employees are expected to follow a specific dress code.

Konstantin Chagin/Shutterstock.com

If you are likely to get dirty and greasy, you will need clothes that are appropriate for those conditions. For example, an auto mechanic needs durable clothes to withstand wear, tear, grease, and oil. Similar clothing is needed for service station workers, carpenters, plumbers, factory workers, farmers, and construction workers. Many of these workers may even wear coveralls to protect their clothes.

Outside workers need clothes that will protect them from rain, snow, cold, and the sun. Other workers may need to wear safety clothing like a hard hat, safety shoes, safety glasses, or earplugs. Outdoor and safety clothing are usually needed for miners, welders, chemists, brick masons, and some construction and factory workers.

For health reasons, hospital workers, food handlers, and dental assistants must take extra care to stay clean and wear clean clothes. Many of these workers wear uniforms or lab coats that can be cleaned easily. Employees who work in laboratories or in food service may also be required to wear hairnets. These prevent their hair from falling into their work.

Clothing choices are important for office and business workers like salespeople, receptionists, office clerks, and cashiers because these workers come in contact with the public. A company wants workers who will make a good impression on customers and the general public. As a result, these workers will form a good impression of the company.

When washing your clothes, remember to follow the directions on the label to maintain proper care.

Andi Berger/Shutterstock.com

In general, female office workers should wear nice slacks with a blouse or sweater, or a skirt or dress. Male office workers should wear nice slacks; a shirt and tie, shirt and sweater, or a dressy, open-collar shirt; and possibly a sports jacket. Workers should avoid inappropriate clothes such as tight pants, unbuttoned shirts, and miniskirts. Tight, skimpy, or revealing clothes can send the wrong message to coworkers and customers.

Another good way to help you decide what to wear is to make sure you are aware of your company's dress code. You can also observe what others wear to work. If most of the workers tend to dress conservatively, you may want to dress this way also. If many of the employees wear nice jeans to work, you may feel comfortable wearing jeans as well. Some companies, due to the nature of their product or the customers they serve, do not want their employees to have excessive tattoos or body piercings. In some jobs, excessive body piercings may be an occupational hazard. If you are still in doubt about what is appropriate, ask your work supervisor or program coordinator. He or she will be able to give you some good suggestions.

Caring for Clothes

Even the best quality clothes will not look good if you do not care for them properly. Taking proper care of your clothes will help them look better and last longer. Clothes that are clean, neatly pressed, and mended will also help you have an attractive appearance.

Caring for clothes on a routine basis will keep clothes in good condition and ready to wear. For example, do not just pull off your clothes, wad them up, and throw them on the floor. Take an extra minute to remove your clothes carefully and put them away properly. Be sure to undo buttons, snaps, and zippers before removing a garment. This will help you avoid tearing or stretching the garment out of shape.

After each wearing, check clothes for stains, tears, and missing buttons. Be sure to remove stains right away. The longer a stain stays in a fabric, the harder it will be to remove. Small repairs, such as sewing on a button or mending a split seam, do not take long. Everyone can learn how to do these simple mending jobs.

If clothes do not need cleaning or mending, you may want to air them in an open room before storing. Then fold knits and sweaters neatly and store them in drawers or on shelves. Hang blouses, dresses, shirts, skirts, trousers, and jackets.

When clothes and accessories need cleaning, be sure to follow the directions on clothing care labels, laundry products, washers, and dryers. Washing clothes the correct way will keep them from fading, shrinking, and wrinkling unnecessarily.

Before buying clothing, you should always check the care label to learn how the garment should be cleaned. Should it be machine-washed in warm water, hand-washed in cold water, or dry-cleaned?

Can it be dried in a dryer, or should it drip-dry on a hanger? Should it be ironed with a cool iron or not ironed at all? Ask a salesperson to explain a garment's care label if the information is not clear.

It would be impractical for a childcare worker or telephone repair person to buy work clothes that must be dry-cleaned. Unless you are in a job where you must wear suits, buy work clothes that can be machine washed and dried. Wash-and-wear and permanent press clothes are great for work because they are easy and inexpensive to keep clean.

Checkpoint 11.2

1. List six good grooming practices you should follow for a neat, clean appearance.

2. Explain the job of a dermatologist.

3. How do you determine what clothes are best suited for a particular job?

4. What are some basic steps in caring for your clothing?

5. Why is it important to read clothing care labels?

Build Your Vocabulary

As you progress through this text, develop a personal glossary of career-related terms and add it to your portfolio. This will help build your vocabulary and prepare you for your career of choice. Write a definition for each of the following terms, and add it to your personal career glossary.

grooming
hygiene
dermatologist

Chapter Summary

Section 11.1 Stay Healthy

- Your good health is reflected in the way you look and feel. A healthy lifestyle is achieved through proper eating, sleeping, and exercise habits.
- A "healthy plate" provides a balanced meal with the nutrients your body needs. By following the dietary guidelines you can learn to develop good eating habits.
- Walking, jogging, playing team sports, or doing household chores are examples of healthy physical activities. Good nutrition and physical activity work together.
- Adequate sleep is essential to feeling well and energized. Sleep needs vary across age groups and are impacted by lifestyle and health.
- Negative stress can cause physical symptoms, such as headaches, high blood pressure, and chest pains. Exercise, meditation, and other activities can help relieve stress.

Section 11.2 Make a Good Impression

- Looking good on the job also involves a neat, clean appearance. A clean body, proper skin care, neatly groomed hair, and clean hands reflect good hygiene.
- Companies often have dress codes. Employees should wear clean clothes that are appropriate for the job.
- Caring for clothes properly will help them look better and last longer. Some clothes require dry cleaning and should not be washed in a washing machine or placed in a dryer.

Check Your Career IQ

Now that you have finished the chapter, see what you learned about careers by taking the chapter posttest. The test can be accessed on the mobile site by using a smartphone or on the G-W Learning companion website.

www.m.g-wlearning.com
www.g-wlearning.com

Review Your Knowledge

1. List foods that provide whole grains.
2. What are the effects of too much sodium?
3. In what way is skim milk unlike whole milk?
4. Explain the difference between a calorie and an empty calorie.
5. How can you use food labels to eat better?
6. What two problems often occur as a result of oily skin?
7. How should a mechanic dress for the job?
8. Why are clothing choices important for salespeople, receptionists, and cashiers?
9. What is a dress code?
10. How should you care for a suit after returning home from an interview?

Apply Your Knowledge

1. What fitness programs are offered in your community? Programs may be offered at the YMCA or local community centers. Name three programs and give a description of each. List three benefits of each program. Use a chart to organize the information you gathered.
2. Use the Internet to learn more about organic foods. What are organic foods? Where can you find them? What are the benefits of eating organic food items? Summarize your findings in three paragraphs.
3. List five prepackaged foods found in your kitchen or refrigerator. Study the labels to compare and contrast the nutritional values in a serving. What ingredients are used to make each item? How much sodium does the item contain? Evaluate the information and decide if you think the food item is a healthy choice.
4. Consider your eating habits. What did you have for lunch or dinner most recently? Did you build a healthy plate? What could you do to have a more well-balanced and healthy diet? Discuss your answers with the rest of the class.
5. Conduct research to learn more about the job duties of a nutritionist. What does a nutritionist do? Where might he or she work? What education and skills are required to be a nutritionist?
6. Determine what clothes you would need for work. Develop a spending plan that will help you get the most clothing items for your money. How much will you spend? Where should you shop for these items?
7. Prepare a presentation on grooming. Be sure to explain why grooming is important to one's health as well as appearance. Share your presentation with the class.
8. What is the dress code for your school? If you are working, what is the dress code for your job? Describe how they are similar or different.

9. Imagine you have graduated from school and will be starting your first job. Describe the job title and responsibilities. What do you think the dress code would be for that position? What items will you need to purchase to dress appropriately for work? Discuss your answers with a partner.

10. Describe two activities that help you manage stress. Then, explain why you think each activity helps.

Teamwork

Working with a classmate, list three different types of dress or items of clothing you have seen worn by people from different cultures. Identify the countries or cultures of the people who were wearing the clothing. Research each of these and learn their special use or significance to their cultures. What did you learn?

G-W Learning Mobile Site

Visit the G-W Learning mobile site to complete the chapter pretest and posttest and to practice vocabulary using e-flash cards. If you do not have a smartphone, visit the G-W Learning companion website to access these features.

G-W Learning mobile site: www.m.g-wlearning.com

G-W Learning companion website: www.g-wlearning.com

Common Core

College and Career Readiness

Reading. Analyze the structure of the relationship between one's health and one's appearance. What roles do nutrition and exercise play? What other factors affect a person's health and appearance?

Writing. Conduct a short research project to determine what occupations are projected to need the most workers in the next 5, 10, and 20 years. Are any of the occupations that interest you among those that will have the greatest need for workers by the time you are ready for a full-time job? What can you do to prepare for your future career? Write several paragraphs about your findings to demonstrate your understanding of the subject.

Apply Your Technology Skills

Access the G-W Learning companion website for this text at www.g-wlearning.com. Download the data file for this chapter. Follow the instructions to complete activities to practice what you have learned in this chapter.

Data File 11–1—Dressing for Workplace Success

College and Career Readiness Portfolio

College and Career Readiness

You have collected documents that show your skills and talents. However, some skills and talents are not shown effectively using only documents. Do you have a special talent in an area such as art, music, or design? Have you taken part in volunteer activities? Create a video to showcase your talents and activities. For example, if you are an artist, create a video that shows your completed works. If you are a musician, create a video with segments from your performances. If you have taken part in a volunteer or service activity, create a video that tells viewers about it. Suppose you volunteer with a group that helps repair homes for elderly homeowners. The video could show scenes from the worksites and comments from the residents. (Be sure you have permission to include other people in your video.)

1. Place the video file in an appropriate subfolder for your e-portfolio.
2. Print a few screen shots from the video. Create a document that describes the video. State that the video will be made available on request or tell where it can be viewed online. Place the information in the container for your print portfolio.

Section 12.1
Accidents

Section 12.2
Accident Procedures

College and Career Readiness

Reading Prep. Before reading this chapter, use the Internet to research the subject of workplace safety. Read one or two articles on the topic. As you read, consider the similarities and differences between the Internet articles and the text. Compare the different approaches the authors use to present the material.

Introduction

Accidents and injuries are not pleasant. No one wants to get hurt on the job or see anyone else get hurt. Workplace accidents can also cause damage to equipment. Injured workers and damaged equipment cost an employer time and money. Workers who are new to a job are more likely to have accidents than experienced workers.

Working safely is the responsibility of every worker and employer. Preventing an accident is much better than living with the results of a serious one. Although jobs in some occupations have high accident rates, accidents can occur anywhere. People are not perfect. However, many accidents can be prevented when people are alert, careful, and aware of the potential dangers around them.

Check Your Career IQ

Before you begin the chapter, see what you already know about careers by taking the chapter pretest. Use the related QR code to view the pretest on the mobile site. If you do not have a smartphone, visit the G-W Learning companion website to access the pretest.

www.m.g-wlearning.com
www.g-wlearning.com

G-W Mobile

Career Snapshot
Travel Agent

ospitality & Tourism

What Does a Travel Agent Do?

Travel agents work closely with clients to help them make the best possible travel arrangements. Travel agents must:
- help their clients select travel destinations;
- book travel arrangements and collect fees from their customers;
- arrange transportation, car rentals, and hotel accommodations; and
- advise customers on financial considerations.

What Is It Like to Work as a Travel Agent?

Travel agents often work for a travel agency located in a shopping mall or office park. The office generally has a very pleasing appearance, as it is decorated with travel posters from around the world. Agents greet customers and use a computer and brochures to help them select and arrange travel destinations. Assisting clients in getting the best value for their money is very important.

Agents may have a specialty such as domestic or foreign travel or serving senior citizens. Some travel agents further specialize in arranging group tours and often accompany groups on tours.

What Education and Skills Are Needed to Be a Travel Agent?

- high school diploma
- courses or associate degree in travel or tourism
- knowledge of the latest travel information and trends
- computer and Internet skills
- communication, organization, and sales skills
- detail-oriented

12.1 Accidents

Objectives

After completing this section, you will be able to:

- **Describe** the causes of accidents on the job.
- **Explain** how the costs of accidents can affect you, the employer, and the economy.

Causes of Accidents

Directly or indirectly, people cause accidents. According to researchers, accidents are most often caused by:

- lack of knowledge or skills;
- work-related hazards; and
- unsafe behavior.

Lack of Knowledge and Skills

Workers need training to do their jobs accurately and safely. Otherwise, mistakes and accidents are more likely to occur. Workers with less than one year of work experience account for a large percentage of all occupational accidents each year. A worker's knowledge and skills are especially important when working with machinery, equipment, chemicals, or hazardous materials.

Workers who operate machinery should learn as much as possible about the equipment before they begin operating it. They should know exactly what to do if the machine appears to be overheating or if something gets caught in it. Never attempt to operate a piece of machinery you are not trained to use.

Learn as much as you can about materials and chemicals before you use them on the job. What you do not know can be dangerous to you and other workers. For example, some liquids can cause fires or explosions when used improperly. Some materials that were once thought to be safe are now known to be harmful to your health and may cause cancer or even death. Common examples of these materials are asbestos, lead, and mercury. Protect yourself when handling any materials or chemicals. Use caution and follow label directions.

On the Job

Lack of knowledge and skill can cause accidents in any job—not just jobs involving machines. For example, consider what happened to Bob on his first day as a waiter at a nice restaurant. All the waiters carry their trays of orders high on their shoulders and gracefully place them on stands for serving. When Bob picked up his first order, he attempted to do the same. However, half his tray of food scattered across the floor, and the other half fell on his customers. Bob tried to perform a task before he developed the skill to do it.

You need to be aware of the things you can and cannot do. Do not pretend to know how to do something with which you are unfamiliar. Seek information about a task you do not know how to do. Make sure you have the knowledge and the skills to perform the task correctly and safely before you begin. Some companies provide employees with on-the-job training before they are expected to perform tasks on their own. Be sure you are familiar with your company's training policies so you know what is expected of you.

To learn a new skill, watch a skilled worker perform the task. Then ask the worker to show you step-by-step how to do it. Next, perform the task slowly yourself. Have the skilled worker watch you to make sure you do each step correctly. Afterward, practice doing the task under supervision until you can do it safely and accurately on your own.

On the Road

Traffic accidents are a leading cause of deaths among teens. Although many teens drive safely and responsibly, a good number of them do not. As a result, state and federal authorities are cracking down on teen driving in general. Lack of driving experience is the primary reason for teen traffic accidents. Another leading cause is a greater tendency to take risks.

When learning a new skill, ask questions to ensure you know how to perform the task safely.

Lisa F. Young/Shutterstock.com

As a work-based learning program participant, your employer will take a special interest in your driving record. In many cases, employers do not permit students who lose their drivers license to keep their jobs. If driving a car or truck on the job is a must, a record free of moving violations is usually a requirement for employment.

Federal and state laws limit how much driving teens can do as part of their jobs. No employee under 17 may drive on public roads as part of his or her job. For 17-year-olds, only occasional and incidental driving on the job is permitted, like running errands or making deliveries. However, there are specific limits on what is allowed regarding the following:

- distance traveled;
- number of passengers;
- type of material transported;
- number of trips made; and
- hours spent driving per day and per week.

In areas where a state law is stricter than the federal law, the state law must be followed. Federal and state laws are subject to change. Be alert to changes in the laws.

Work-Related Hazards

The very nature of the work environment can influence the number of accidents that are likely to occur on the job. Possible dangers or unsafe conditions in the workplace are known as **work-related hazards.** These hazards exist in every type of working environment—from jobs involving mechanical equipment to offices. However, accidents occur more often in dangerous jobs because more work-related hazards exist.

Hazards in Construction Jobs

It is not surprising, for example, that more accidents happen in construction jobs than in office jobs. Construction workers come in contact with a greater number of hazards more often. These hazards include heavy equipment, ladders, hand and power tools, electricity, heights, and many other potential dangers.

Go Green

What kind of light bulb is in the lamp on your desk at home? If you are using a compact fluorescent lamp (CFL), you are saving 80 percent of the energy used by a regular incandescent light bulb. A CFL will last up to 10 times longer than an incandescent bulb. However, these CFLs do contain mercury, so they must be disposed of properly. Conduct research on compact fluorescent lamps to learn more about their benefits.

Some jobs involve hazardous working conditions that require special protective equipment and safety guidelines.

Andrea Slatter/Shutterstock.com

Hazards in High-Risk Occupations

Work-related hazards exist in many industries other than construction. For instance, workers in logging, mining, agriculture, and meat processing are also involved in dangerous work. These are considered high-risk occupations. People employed in these types of jobs must be very safety conscious. Being safety conscious is being aware of potential job hazards and taking appropriate steps to avoid accidents.

The first step in protecting yourself against job hazards is to know how dangerous your job is. Many employers spend considerable time and money trying to reduce the number of on-the-job accidents. In an effort to provide a safe work environment, some companies offer safety programs, use safer equipment, and train workers. The government is also concerned about high-risk occupations. Federal and state governments keep statistics on workplace injuries and detect trends as new job dangers surface.

Hazards in Green Jobs

Jobs that help sustain or improve the environment are known as **green jobs**. People who have green jobs generally participate in activities that preserve or restore the environment. It might be assumed that green jobs offer safer working environments. However, this is not always true. These workers can be exposed to biological hazards, ergonomic hazards, and other risks. For example, removing asbestos from a building can expose a worker to respiratory health issues.

Hazards in the Office

Falling hazards, lifting hazards, and material-storage hazards account for most of the workplace accidents that occur in offices. **Falling hazards** are sources of potential injuries from slipping or falling. Falls are the most common workplace accident in an office setting. Falls can result in broken bones, head injuries, and muscle strains. To avoid workplace falls remember to:

- close drawers completely;
- do not stand on a chair or box to reach; and
- secure cords, rugs, and mats.

An open file drawer is an office hazard that could cause a person to stumble.

mmaxer/Shutterstock.com

Lifting hazards are sources of potential injury from improperly lifting or carrying items. Most back injuries are caused by improper lifting. To avoid injuries resulting from lifting:

- make several small trips with items rather than one trip with an overly heavy load;
- use dollies or handcarts whenever possible;
- lift with the legs, not the back; and
- never carry an item that blocks vision.

Material-storage hazards are sources of potential injury that come from the improper storage of files, books, or office equipment. A cluttered workplace is an unsafe workplace. Material stacked too high can fall on employees. Paper and files stored on the floor or in a hall are fire risks. To prevent injuries:

- do not stack boxes or papers on top of tall cabinets;
- store heavier objects on lower shelves; and
- keep aisles and hallways clear.

Repetitive-motion injuries are another common type of workplace injury. These injuries result from making the same motion over and over again. Repetitive-motion injuries result in tingling sensations and sharp shooting pains as shown in Figure 12-1. Destruction of nerve endings and loss of mobility in the limb can occur as a result.

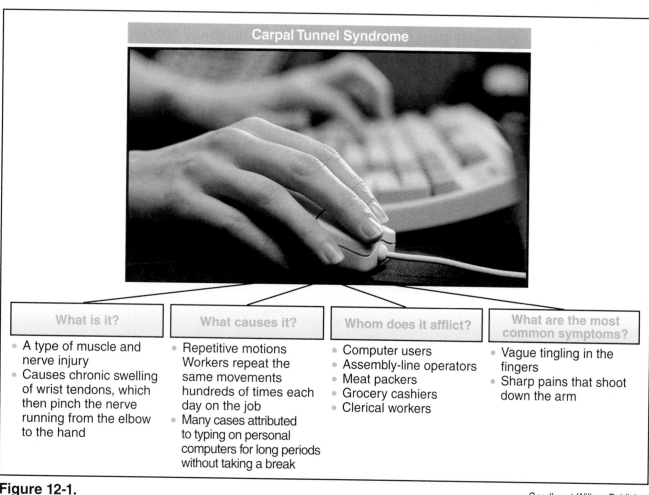

Figure 12-1.
The most familiar repetitive-motion injury is carpal tunnel syndrome.

Goodheart-Willcox Publisher

Figure 12-2 depicts the best way for a worker to sit at a computer workstation to help avoid repetitive-motion injuries. The science of examining human movement and how to lessen the chance of injury is **ergonomics**.

Unsafe Behavior

People who do not consider or practice safety on the job have poor safety attitudes. A lack of concern for safety can lead to many accidents. Unsafe behavior is a threat to everyone's safety. Try to avoid the following behaviors while you are on the job.

Recklessness

Near the end of a workday, two woodworkers start telling jokes. No one bothers to turn off the circular saw. Jokingly, one worker pushes the other, who loses her balance, falls against the circular saw, and cuts her arm. By behaving recklessly around power equipment is not only dangerous, it can be deadly.

Bad Temper

Mike works as a chef's helper in a restaurant. During the lunch rush, another worker yells at him to hurry up. While he is chopping lettuce, Mike angrily yells back. As he does, his knife slips and cuts his finger so deeply that the bleeding would not stop without stitches. Mike reacted without thinking. By losing control of his temper, he was the prime target for an accident.

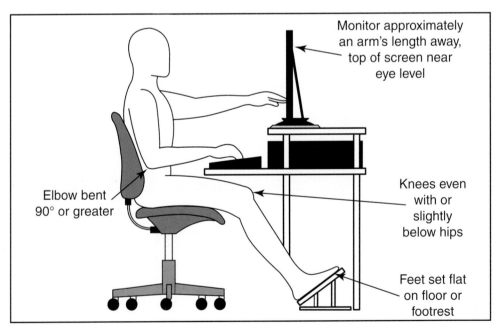

Figure 12-2.   *Goodheart-Willcox Publisher*
This image depicts an ergonomic workstation.

Lack of Consideration

An office worker takes a file from the bottom drawer of the file cabinet and does not bother to close the drawer. Another worker walks around the corner and trips over the open drawer. Not being aware of others can lead to serious injury.

Disobedience

Trisha works at a local machine shop. Because she operates machinery, she is told not to wear jewelry on the job. She refuses to take her ring off for fear of losing it. As a result, Trisha's ring gets caught on a revolving tool, and she loses her finger. Following instructions and obeying company safety rules would have saved Trisha from serious injury.

Carelessness

After mopping the hallway, Pete forgets to put up signs that warn, "Caution: Wet Floor." A customer walks in, slips on the wet floor, and injures his hip. Pete's carelessness created an unsafe condition that caused pain and injury to someone else.

Laziness

Gerry is an example of an accident waiting to happen. He will soon start working on an electrical circuit located across the room from the master lockout switch. He thinks the circuit has been properly shut off and locked out, but he is not sure. He decides it is too far to walk to check. Gerry receives an electrical shock and burn.

Fatigue

Marie works two jobs to make extra income. Sometimes she does not even have time to eat after her first job before starting the evening job. In spite of the long hours, Marie feels she can keep up the pace. One night, she fell asleep while operating her machine. The machine jams and Marie seriously injures her arm. She is unable to continue working. A lack of rest and poor diet caused her fatigue. If Marie had been alert, she might have avoided the accident. Getting plenty of rest and eating properly would have helped her operate at her best.

Ethical Leadership

Dependability

"Without dependability one's ability may be a liability instead of an asset."—Woodrow Wilson

To be dependable is to be trustworthy and reliable. Your supervisor needs to be able to depend on you to do the right thing, whether he or she is present or not. For example, wearing safety equipment, such as eye protection or gloves, is very important. However, some people do not want to be bothered and will only wear safety gear when the supervisor is nearby. This could result in a serious injury causing you pain and suffering, an increase in your employer's insurance rates, and a negative impact on your company's reputation.

Impatience

Julia is a file clerk. She decides to climb the shelves in the storage room to get a box of file folders instead of using a stepladder. She loses her footing, falls backward, and fractures her elbow.

Emotional State

The way people feel on the job can influence their attitudes about safety. Extreme emotions can make a person less concerned about personal safety. For example, some people are more likely to have an accident when they are very happy, angry, tired, or depressed. Thinking about their personal problems or not paying attention to their work can affect their job performance. To play it safe, they need to stay in full control of their emotions. Staying focused is a good way to practice safety and avoid injury.

Impairment

Many medications and other substances stay in the body hours or even days after their use. Be aware of the side effects of any prescription medication you might be taking. These substances can slow down a user's responses and reflexes, which can lead to accidents. Avoid consuming anything that may impair your physical ability or mental clarity.

Costs of Accidents

The costs of work-related accidents are high. Billions of dollars are spent each year to cover the medical costs and wage losses of people who become victims of accidents. Everyone—you, your employer, and the economy—feels the effects in some way.

Costs to You

You may not realize the importance of your health and safety until you have an accident. What is the cost to you? An accident can cost you financially and personally. It could lead to lost time on the job, possible wage loss, and even a job loss. A serious injury could cost you your career. If you cannot perform your job, you may be forced to make a career change or train for another type of work.

Dealing with an injury can be difficult. An accident resulting in a serious disability could prevent you from ever working again. A **disability** is a permanent injury. Often, there is no amount of money that could ease the suffering or personal loss that results from such an accident.

Costs to the Employer

Work injuries from accidents cost employers time and money. Production slows down when a worker cannot perform his or her duties due to an accident. Finding another experienced worker to replace the injured worker is sometimes difficult. Other workers must produce more goods and services to make up the cost of work injuries. The time required giving first aid, investigating the accident, and writing up the accident report is also part of the cost. In addition to production loss, the employer may have to deal with possible lawsuits or fines.

Most workers are covered by workers' compensation, if they are injured on the job. **Workers' compensation** is insurance against loss of income from work-related accidents. The employer rather than the employee pays the premiums for this type of insurance.

When workers are injured, they are entitled to certain benefits. Workers' compensation pays a percentage of the worker's regular wage, medical bills, and pension for a certain length of time. The program covers other benefits, too. These benefits include income for disability or death and insurance against diseases caused by working conditions.

All states in this country have workers' compensation laws although they differ slightly from state to state. Each state's Department of Labor administers this program.

Costs to the Economy

How do work-related accidents affect the nation's economy? Accidental deaths or disabling injuries affect many workers in the workforce. Billions of dollars are paid nationwide each year to injured workers covered under workers' compensation. Employers may be affected by factors such as lower production and higher insurance premiums. This means higher prices for goods and services that are passed on to the consumer. Eventually, everyone pays for the high cost of accidents and injuries.

Checkpoint 12.1

1. What are the three main causes of accidents?
2. Why is it important to learn as much as you can about materials and chemicals before using them on the job?
3. Give two examples of hazards that often contribute to workplace accidents.
4. List five unsafe behaviors that could lead to an accident on the job.
5. What are the costs to an employer if a worker is injured on the job? Provide two examples.

Build Your Vocabulary

As you progress through this text, develop a personal glossary of career-related terms and add it to your portfolio. This will help build your vocabulary and prepare you for your career of choice. Write a definition for each of the following terms, and add it to your personal career glossary.

work-related hazard
safety conscious
green job
falling hazard
lifting hazard
material-storage hazard
ergonomics
disability
workers' compensation

12.2 Accident Procedures

Terms

National Safety
    Council
flammable
first aid
universal precautions
workplace violence
Occupational Safety
    and Health Admin-
    istration (OSHA)
citation
material safety data
    sheet (MSDS)
Environmental Protec-
    tion Agency (EPA)
Centers for Disease
    Control and
    Prevention (CDC)
National Institute
    for Occupational
    Safety and Health
    (NIOSH)

Objectives

After completing this section you will be able to:
- **Identify** safety rules workers can follow to avoid and prevent accidents.
- **Identify** procedures to follow when an accident occurs.
- **Define** workplace violence and describe possible steps for prevention.
- **Explain** the role of the government in supporting a safe work environment.

Accident Prevention

Preventing accidents is everyone's responsibility. On the job, you share that responsibility with your employer. Doing what you can to prevent accidents will help make your workplace safer. This is particularly important for students who are employed part-time. For example, you may not be a part of important safety-related meetings. Perhaps changes may have been made to your work area that you are not aware of since you are only present part of the day. It is very important that you carefully examine your surroundings each day you work. Make it a point to look for changes that may have taken place during your absence, and be sure to ask questions about anything you do not understand. You will also want to keep in mind that you are a beginner, and new employees are much more likely to have an accident than experienced workers.

What can you do to prevent accidents? Learning to do your job correctly is a good way to start. Think and act safely while you are on the job. Avoid unsafe acts, and correct any unsafe working conditions. Know and follow safety rules to help prevent accidents. The tips in Figure 12-3 will also help you prevent accidents.

The **National Safety Council** is the nation's leading advocate for safety and health. Its mission states that it "saves lives by preventing injuries and deaths at work, in homes and communities, and on the roads through leadership, research, education, and advocacy."

Stay Healthy

Being alert and healthy is the best way to do your job well and safely. You can stay healthy by eating properly and getting adequate sleep. This practice cuts down on fatigue. As mentioned earlier, fatigue on the job can lead to unsafe behavior that can cause an accident. If you become ill while on the job, stop working. Your illness affects your performance and may cause you to injure yourself or someone else. Report your illness to your supervisor.

Tips to Prevent Accidents
• Stay healthy.
• Use machines and tools properly.
• Wear protective clothing and use protective safety equipment.
• Use the computer properly.
• Follow safety precautions.

Figure 12-3.   *Goodheart-Willcox Publisher*   *auremar/Shutterstock.com*
Many accidents can be prevented by following these tips.

Regular exercise will help you stay alert and physically fit. This is especially important for jobs requiring physical activity. In addition, exercise can help improve the performance of workers with jobs that are mentally demanding. In fact, something as simple as taking a short walk during a break can refresh you both mentally and physically.

Use Machines and Tools Properly

Many machines and tools can be dangerous if not handled properly. Never operate any type of machinery without receiving proper operating instructions and supervision. If you do not know, ask for help. When you use any machines or tools, work at a safe speed. Taking shortcuts, rushing, or taking chances could lead to a costly accident. Keep all work areas around machinery clean. Scraps of material or oil can cause a worker to slip or fall.

Hand tools should be used and maintained properly. Choose the right tool for the job to get it done safely. Tools should be kept clean and in working condition. Sharpen dull tools and replace broken handles. All tools should be properly stored when not in use.

Wear Protective Clothing and Equipment

Certain jobs require special protective clothing and equipment to prevent injury to the worker. Wear properly fitted clothes, especially if you work with moving machinery. Protect your feet by wearing hard-toed safety shoes on construction and industrial sites. Hard hats are required safety equipment in the construction industry. Dust masks or protective breathing devices are necessary around dust, chemical sprays, and biological agents. Protective gloves and clothing are needed when handling chemicals. Wear protective eye equipment and hearing protection when needed. Always be sure to follow company policies and procedures.

Use the Computer Properly

Today many jobs involve using a computer in one form or another. Eyestrain and repetitive-motion injuries are two problems commonly associated with extended computer use. The following tips can help you avoid many health problems.

- Use a large computer monitor, if possible, and place the top of the monitor at or slightly below eye level and 18 to 28 inches from your eyes. See Figure 12-2.
- Place your monitor in a position that avoids glare from other light sources.
- Place reference material close to you on an appropriate holder to avoid unnecessary head movements.
- Use dark lettering on a light background on your monitor display, and be sure your computer's resolution and color are properly set.
- Clean your screen regularly.
- Blink your eyes frequently to help them stay moist.
- Adjust your chair to a proper height for you.
- Maintain good posture and keep your muscles relaxed.
- Take frequent short breaks to stand up, stretch, and rest your eyes. Exercise your wrists and fingers frequently.

Follow Safety Precautions

Closely following basic safety precautions is another way for you to help prevent accidents. Practicing safety on the job includes using ladders safely, washing hands frequently, lifting properly, preventing fires, and keeping work areas neat.

Use Ladders Safely

Many jobs require the use of ladders. Ladders should be handled with care. Choose the right ladder for the job. Check the ladder to be sure it is in good condition. Do not use metal ladders near electrical equipment or high-voltage wires because metal conducts electricity. Someone standing on or touching the ladder could be seriously injured or killed if electricity comes in contact with the ladder.

Ladders should be placed firmly on level ground to prevent tipping. The base of extension ladders should be placed the proper distance from the wall or building they are leaning against. Make sure the ladder is strong enough to support you and the tools and materials you use. To avoid a fall, place the ladder within an arm's length of your work. Face the ladder when you climb up or down.

Wash Hands Frequently

Proper and frequent hand washing has proven to be a major factor in preventing the transmission of infectious diseases. Be sure to wash your hands after using the restroom and before eating or handling food. See Figure 12-4 for proper hand-washing procedure. Of course, if you work in a clinical setting or know you have been exposed to an infectious agent, stricter guidelines may apply.

Proper Hand-Washing Procedure

1.	Wet your hands with warm running water.
2.	Apply soap to all surfaces of your hands and fingers.
3.	Vigorously rub your hands together for 10 to 15 seconds.
4.	Be sure to generate friction on all surfaces of your hands and fingers, taking extra care to remove dirt from under your fingernails.
5.	Remove all soap by thoroughly rinsing your hands.
6.	Dry your hands using a paper towel or electric hand dryer if available.

Alta Oosthuizen/Shutterstock.com

Figure 12-4.   *Goodheart-Willcox Publisher*
Wash your hands thoroughly to help prevent the transmission of germs and other bacteria.

Lift Properly

Using proper lifting procedures can help prevent injury. Lifting heavy objects incorrectly or lifting too much at one time can cause strains or back injuries. To lift properly, use your leg muscles because they are stronger than your back. Keep your back straight and your knees bent when you lift a heavy object from the floor. Do not try to lift more than you can handle. Instead, ask for assistance or learn to use a mechanical aid, such as a crane or hoist, to assist you.

Prevent Fires

The best way to avoid a fire is to prevent it from starting. Faulty electrical wiring and careless smoking are the main causes of many fires. However, most workplaces prohibit smoking in the building. This decreases the risk of fire. Other causes of fire may include:
- faulty heating equipment,
- unattended open flames in labs or kitchens, and
- grease buildup in kitchen hoods.

Another cause of fire is the careless use of flammable liquid. If a material or liquid is **flammable**, it has the potential to ignite easily and burn rapidly. Gasoline is an example of a flammable liquid.

Fire needs oxygen, fuel, and heat to start. You can extinguish a fire by removing any one of those elements. Fire extinguishers are designed to help put out fires. There are four different types of fire extinguishers, each one designed to fight a specific type, or class, of fire. Using the wrong type of extinguisher could actually make the fire worse or injure the person operating it. Be sure you know if the extinguisher is designed for the type of fire you are fighting before using it as shown in Figure 12-5.

You can help prevent a fire on the job by following these other safety tips.

- Keep your work area clean.
- Do not store oily rags and paper in open containers—they could eventually ignite.
- Keep containers of flammable liquids tightly closed and store them in a cool area.
- Do not overload electrical wires because they could short-circuit and cause a fire.
- Use matches and lighters only in designated areas.

If a fire should occur in your work area, follow your company's fire plan. Review the plan periodically so you will know what to do before the need arises. Above all, stay calm.

To assist during a fire emergency, you will receive extra training in the use of fire extinguishers. If no specific fire plan exists, there are some general guidelines to follow. See Figure 12-6.

Keep Work Areas Neat

Good housekeeping helps reduce hazards in the work area. Keeping your work area neat and clean will prevent accidental

Classes of Fires	
Ordinary **Combustibles**	Class A fires involve wood, paper, cloth, rubber, many plastics, and other ordinary combustible materials. Water or solutions containing a large percentage of water stops these fires.
Flammable **Liquids**	Class B fires involve flammable liquids, gases and similar materials such as greases, oils, tars, and oil-base paints. Stopping these fires requires smothering (or exclusion of air) and the interruption of the chemical chain reaction.
Electrical **Equipment**	Class C fires involve Class A or B fires in or near live electrical equipment. A nonconductive agent must be used in the fire extinguisher to prevent injury to its operator.
Combustible **Metals**	Class D fires involve combustible metals such as magnesium, titanium or sodium. Special extinguishing agents and techniques are needed for fires of this type.

Figure 12-5.   *Goodheart-Willcox Publisher*
There are four classifications of fires, and each needs a specific type of fire extinguisher.

Being Prepared for a Fire
• Know what action you will take before the need arises.
• Know where the fire exits, alarms, and extinguishers are located.
• Find out how to use the fire alarm.
• Confine the fire by closing all windows and doors.
• Rescue persons in immediate danger if possible.
• Use the telephone to report a fire to the fire station or operator.
• Give the correct company name, address, and location of the fire.
• Participate in practice fire drills so you know how to leave the building safely.

zimmytws/Shutterstock.com

Figure 12-6.   *Goodheart-Willcox Publisher*
Review fire safety guidelines often to avoid panic in case of a fire.

tripping or being struck by falling objects. Pick up any scraps and wipe up spills immediately. Place safety cones or caution signs on freshly mopped floors so they can be seen from all directions. Store tools in a safe area after use. Do not leave any items on stairs or in walkways where someone might trip or fall.

Actions and Procedures

Every worker needs to think about safety. Rules and safety procedures are developed to protect you and others. Get into the habit of doing tasks the safe way. Wear the proper clothes and use the proper equipment. Follow all safety procedures exactly. Do not assume that a safe environment happens automatically.

No matter how careful people are, accidents *do* happen. When an accident occurs, it is very important to stay calm. The difference between staying calm and panicking is preparation. Appropriate training will teach you what to do in an emergency, and it could help save an injured person's life. In the event of an accident, be sure to report any injury that occurs on the job, no matter how small. Even a small scratch could lead to blood poisoning.

Call for Help

Call for help as soon as it is safe to do so. Who you call will depend on the extent of the accident or sudden illness. In cases of serious injury or illness, you will want to telephone for professional help. Often phoning 9-1-1 or your local emergency number accomplishes this. The Poison Control Center should be contacted immediately for accidents involving any type of poison. Review your company's emergency policy to be prepared if an accident occurs. You may also need the help of bystanders in making the 9-1-1 call, assisting the injured, or controlling traffic.

When making the telephone call, be sure to explain the nature of the accident and what type of aid has been provided. Give the precise location of the accident. Then, stay on the line until the emergency provider gets all the information needed and hangs up.

Provide First Aid

First aid is immediate, temporary treatment given to an ill or injured person before proper medical help arrives. Try to receive formal first-aid training before or while you are on the job. The Red Cross is one organization that provides training classes in first aid and CPR (cardiopulmonary resuscitation). Online first-aid training is available as well. Basic lifesaving steps are shown in Figure 12-7.

Follow Universal Precautions

Unfortunately, a workplace accident might cause a serious wound or cut. Whenever an accident occurs that involves loss of blood or vomiting, there is a danger of spreading serious viral infections like AIDS or hepatitis B. **Universal precautions** are steps designed to help prevent the spread of infection. See Figure 12-8.

One or more persons at your workplace should be trained in universal precautions. Whenever possible, rely on that person to handle accidents where a loss of blood occurs. Call him or her first.

Giving First Aid
1. Remain calm.
2. Rescue the person from the hazardous situation if possible.
3. Do not move the person unless there is an immediate threat of further injury.
4. Check to make sure nothing is in the injured person's mouth or throat that could interfere with breathing.
5. Stop any bleeding by applying pressure to the wound.
6. Help to prevent shock by keeping the person warm and flat on his or her back with the head low.
7. Call for medical help.
8. Stay with the injured person until medical help arrives.

Figure 12-7.   *Goodheart-Willcox Publisher*
This figure lists important safety tips to remember when giving first aid.

Universal Precautions
1. Use protective barriers such as appropriately designed masks, gowns, gloves, and eye protection.
2. Always wear latex gloves when handling blood.
3. Remove the first glove by touching the outside of that glove with your other gloved hand. Remove the second glove with your bare hand by touching only the inside of the second glove. To remember this procedure, think of the phrase *glove to glove-side, skin to skin-side.*
4. Dispose of gloves in a plastic bag labeled "contaminated."
5. Wash your hands after handling blood even if gloves were worn.
6. If blood has made contact with any part of your body, wash (or rinse if eyes) thoroughly and see a doctor immediately.

Figure 12-8.   *Goodheart-Willcox Publisher*
Universal precautions are especially practiced by those in the medical field.

Follow Emergency Evacuation Procedures

As in the case of some fires, there may be a time when a situation becomes so severe that it will require an evacuation of a portion or all of a facility. In other situations, such as a tornado warning, it may be more important to go to a safe place in the building rather than leave. Your employer should have specific guidelines for these situations.

It is very important that you know and understand what you are expected to do. Look for posted copies of floor plans that show emergency exits and evacuation routes. Determine their location in advance so you will be able to find them in an emergency. Many companies conduct emergency drills. Take these drills very seriously. How you behave in an actual emergency could end up saving your life and the lives of others.

Workplace Violence

Workplace violence is a very serious problem. **Workplace violence** is any violent act or threatening behavior that occurs in the workplace or at a company function. Each week thousands of individuals are victims of workplace violence. Actual numbers are hard to determine because many of these instances go unreported.

Attacks of violence in the workplace may be physical or psychological. For example, physical attacks may include shooting, hitting, pushing, or kicking. Psychological attacks may involve harassment, swearing, or verbal or written threats. The individuals involved in workplace violence may not be current or former employees. They could be customers or someone associated with an employee, such as a spouse or friend.

Case

It Is Just a Scratch?

The cleanup bell had already rung in cabinet-making class. Clarisa was running late. Her tools had not been put away, and her workbench was covered with shavings. She noticed her boyfriend waiting at the door. Just then, the floor sweeper told her to hurry because she was holding up dismissal of the entire class. So rather than take time to pick up the brush hanging on the side of the cabinet, she just used her arm to sweep the shavings to the floor. As she did so, she felt a sting on the palm of her hand and noticed a light scratch near her right thumb. She knew her teacher, Mr. Gonzales, required her to report all accidents immediately, but she just could not take the time now.

The next morning, Clarisa noticed a slight redness around the scratch. However, it was so small she had to think twice to remember how she had received it. When she entered her cabinet-making class, she decided not to report her accident. She did not want to hear another one of Mr. Gonzales' lectures on the importance of safety and how critical it was to follow all class rules.

A few days later, red streaks appeared on her hand and arm. She developed a fever and began to feel very ill. It was only then that Clarisa decided to report her illness to the school nurse. After two weeks in the hospital, she was on her way to recovery from a near fatal case of blood poisoning.

Critical Thinking

1. Would you have reported the accident when it first occurred? Why or why not?
2. What should Clarisa have done when she first noticed the scratch?
3. Do you think Mr. Gonzales' stern approach to safety contributed to Clarisa not reporting the accident?
4. Is there a way Mr. Gonzales could stress the importance of safety and not discourage students like Clarisa from reporting accidents?
5. Do you think Clarisa will think differently about Mr. Gonzales' approach to following safety rules?

There are many possible motives for workplace violence. Some may include robbery, domestic problems, or personality conflicts. It could be an employee who feels he or she has been fired or disciplined unfairly. Another cause for workplace violence could even be imagined problems by someone who is mentally unstable. Many people see workplace violence simply as an extension of the violent society in which we live.

The **Occupational Safety and Health Administration (OSHA)** is a government agency that sets and enforces job safety and health standards for workers. OSHA recommends that employees take the following steps to help prevent workplace violence. However, following them will not guarantee you will not become a victim. You can learn more about causes and prevention of workplace violence by visiting the OSHA website at www.osha.gov.

- Learn how to recognize, avoid, or diffuse potentially violent situations by attending personal safety training programs.
- Alert supervisors to any concerns about safety or security, and report all incidences immediately in writing.
- Avoid traveling alone or in unfamiliar locations or situations whenever possible.
- Carry only minimal money and required identification into community settings.

Government Agencies

The government plays an important role in promoting safe working environments. It makes and enforces laws that promote health and safety on the job. These laws led to the creation of three government agencies that carefully monitor workplace safety: The Occupational Safety and Health Administration (OSHA), the Environmental Protection Agency (EPA), and the Centers for Disease Control (CDC).

OSHA

The Occupational Safety and Health Act is a national act passed by Congress in 1970. The act calls for safe and healthful working conditions. Under this act, the Occupational Safety and Health Administration (OSHA) was formed. Most employees are covered under the act. Some who may not be covered are: self-employed persons, independent farmers, and workers covered under other legislation. Also, OSHA does not cover employees of state and local governments, unless they are in one of the states with OSHA-approved safety programs.

OSHA provides workplace inspections, training, and education programs. It also enforces the law, making sure that required health and safety standards exist in the workplace. To an employer who does not comply, OSHA gives a **citation**, which is a summons to appear in court, and may charge one or more fines.

Employers and employees both have certain responsibilities under the law. OSHA makes it mandatory for each employer to provide all its employees a safe place to work—free from safety and health hazards. The employer is also responsible for following the standards set forth by OSHA and making sure employees follow safety procedures. OSHA does not cite employees. Employees, however, are expected to adhere to OSHA health and safety standards and follow safety rules, such as the following.

- Read the OSHA poster at your job site, so that you know your rights and responsibilities.
- Follow OSHA safety standards and your employer's standards.
- Report any injury that occurs on the job.
- Wear personal protective equipment when required.
- Use safety devices properly.
- Participate in fire drills and other safety practices.
- Report unsafe working conditions and practices.

An important provision of OSHA is the Hazardous Chemical Right to Know. As an employee, you have the right to know about any hazardous chemicals in your workplace and be trained to handle and use them. This includes container labeling and other forms of warning. Your employer is also required to have a **material safety data sheet (MSDS)** for each hazardous material. These sheets provide information on the specific hazards involved and procedures for their safe use. Your employer must train you to recognize and avoid the hazards present in these materials.

EPA

Keeping the environment safe and clean is a major concern for everyone. Pollution not only damages the environment, it can cause serious health hazards and diseases. The **Environmental Protection Agency (EPA)** is a government agency formed for the purpose of protecting the environment. The EPA works to eliminate environmental hazards, such as air and water pollution. The agency works to make the United States a safer place to live. Other environmental concerns regulated by the EPA include: toxic waste disposal, pesticide standards, and radiation monitoring.

To help reduce pollution, the EPA has attacked industrial smokestack pollution, auto exhaust emissions, and contaminated rivers and lakes. As a result of the agency's work, many cities now have cleaner air. Some rivers and lakes have been reopened for fishing and swimming. Many toxic waste sites have been improved.

The EPA also conducts research on the effects of pollution and provides assistance to states and cities working to prevent pollution. You can learn more about the EPA regulations and programs by visiting their website at www.epa.gov.

CDC

The **Centers for Disease Control and Prevention (CDC)** is part of the United States Department of Health and Human Services. CDC works with worldwide, state, and local health agencies to protect the public from health threats. The agency's activities include conducting research, promoting public health policies, and providing leadership and training. Mysterious deaths or illnesses are often sent to CDC for investigation. You can find a variety of health-related information at the CDC website, www.cdc.gov.

The **National Institute for Occupational Safety and Health (NIOSH)** is an arm of the Centers for Disease Control and Prevention. It is specifically responsible for conducting research and making recommendations for the prevention of work-related injury and illness. NIOSH information related to young worker safety and health may be found on their website at www.cdc.gov/niosh/topics/youth.

Checkpoint 12.2

1. Identify four basic ways to prevent accidents in the workplace.
2. What are three ways to avoid health problems that may arise from prolonged computer use?
3. When is it particularly important to wash your hands?
4. What three requirements are needed to start a fire?
5. What are the two types of workplace violence? Give examples of each type.

Build Your Vocabulary

As you progress through this text, develop a personal glossary of career-related terms and add it to your portfolio. This will help build your vocabulary and prepare you for your career of choice. Write a definition for each of the following terms, and add it to your personal career glossary.

National Safety Council
flammable
first aid
universal precautions
workplace violence
Occupational Safety and Health Administration (OSHA)
citation
material safety data sheet (MSDS)
Environmental Protection Agency (EPA)
Centers for Disease Control and Prevention (CDC)
National Institute for Occupational Safety and Health (NIOSH)

Chapter Summary

Section 12.1 Accidents

- Safety is everyone's responsibility—especially on the job. Many accidents are caused by a lack of knowledge and skills, work-related hazards, and unsafe behavior.
- Accident costs for employers include lower production, training or hiring another worker, and dealing with possible lawsuits or fines. These costs affect the employer and employee.

Section 12.2 Accident Procedures

- Practicing safety can prevent many accidents. Using equipment properly and wearing protective clothing can prevent accidents.
- Workers should also know what to do when an accident does occur. This involves properly reporting the accident, knowing first aid steps, and following universal precautions and proper evacuation procedures.
- Workplace violence continues to be a major problem for American workers. Attacks of violence in the workplace may be physical or psychological.
- In the United States, laws have led to the creation of government agencies that monitor workplace safety. These agencies help make the work environment safer and address general health hazards and diseases.

Check Your Career IQ

Now that you have finished the chapter, see what you learned about careers by taking the chapter posttest. The test can be accessed on the mobile site by using a smartphone or on the G-W Learning companion website.

www.m.g-wlearning.com
www.g-wlearning.com

Review Your Knowledge

1. List four steps to follow when learning a new skill.
2. What is the primary reason for teen traffic accidents?
3. Explain two restrictions that apply to teens and driving on the job.
4. Describe the results of repetitive-motion injuries.
5. How might a worker's emotional state lead to an accident on the job?
6. What are two problems commonly associated with extended computer use?
7. What are the main causes of many fires?
8. Explain why a worker should be knowledgeable of the four different types of fire extinguishers?
9. When was the Occupational Safety and Health Act passed? Who is covered under the act? Who is not?
10. Describe the responsibilities of the Environmental Protection Agency (EPA).

Apply Your Knowledge

1. List two examples of accidents that have occurred in your type of work or at school. Write a paragraph about each one describing what happened. Then write another paragraph about each explaining how the accident might have been prevented.
2. Collect information about job safety, including safety tips and procedures that relate to your job. Use this information to create a poster that could be displayed at your job site. Share your poster with the class.
3. Contact two local employers. Ask them to discuss safety training or any programs they use for their employees' safety. Take notes during your interview. Share what you learned with other students in a small group.
4. Locate at least three fire extinguishers in your school or place of employment. Determine the type of extinguisher and the last date of inspection. Then write a paper summarizing your findings. State why you feel the specific type of extinguisher was used in the location you found it.
5. Identify at least three examples of workplace violence that have occurred in the last six months. Briefly describe the events and recommend changes in company policy that could help to prevent future occurrences of each event.
6. Identify a hazardous occupation that requires the wearing of personal protective equipment. Determine what the equipment is by conducting research at the library, on the Internet, and/or by visiting a worker in that occupation. Make a list and describe the purpose of each piece of equipment. Indicate the source(s) of your information.

7. Research workers' compensation laws in your state. These might be found on the Web site of your state's Department of Labor. What are the rights and responsibilities of the employer? What are the rights and responsibilities of the employee? Organize your findings in a chart.

8. Explore the OSHA website at www.osha.gov. What procedure should a worker follow if unsafe working conditions or practices exist and have not been corrected at the worker's company? Write a brief summary of your findings.

9. Visit the EPA website at www.epa.gov. Search for information about how the agency works to protect the environment and your health. Organize your findings in an outline. Use your outline to deliver a presentation to the class.

10. Investigate the CDC website at www.cdc.gov. Create a one-page paper describing a major news event in which CDC has played an important role.

Teamwork

Together with your team, create a poster that promotes safe behavior in your school. Use the behavior discussed in this chapter as well as Internet research as the basis for creating the posters.

G-W Learning Mobile Site

Visit the G-W Learning mobile site to complete the chapter pretest and posttest and to practice vocabulary using e-flash cards. If you do not have a smartphone, visit the G-W Learning companion website to access these features.
G-W Learning mobile site: www.m.g-wlearning.com
G-W Learning companion website: www.g-wlearning.com

Common Core

College and Career Readiness

CTE Career Readiness Practices. For every action, there is a reaction whether it is immediately seen or not. There are positive and negative consequences for different actions and inactions. Make a list of five things that you have done for which there were either positive or negative consequences. Put a plus sign (+) beside the positive outcomes and a minus (−) sign beside the negative outcomes. What could you have done differently that would have changed each outcome?

Writing. Conduct research online or in the library on the history, purpose, and examples of civil service tests. Write a three paragraph essay discussing how the tests help place workers in jobs in the state and federal government. Give examples of different government jobs and discuss the qualifications necessary for each job.

Apply Your Technology Skills

Access the G-W Learning companion website for this text at www.g-wlearning.com. Download each data file for this chapter. Follow the instructions to complete activities to practice what you have learned in this chapter.

Data File 12–1—Handling Aggressive Behavior

College and Career Readiness Portfolio

College and Career Readiness

An important part of any portfolio is a list of references. A reference is a person who knows your skills, talents, or personal traits and is willing to recommend you. References can be someone for whom you worked or with whom you provided community service. Someone you know from your personal life, such a youth group leader, can also be a reference. However, you should not list relatives as references. When applying for a position, consider which references can best recommend you for the position for which you are applying. Always get permission from the person before using his or her name as a reference.

1. Ask several people with whom you have worked or volunteered if they are willing to serve as a reference for you. If so, ask for their contact information.
2. Create a list with the names and contact information for your references. Save the document file in an appropriate subfolder for your e-portfolio.
3. Place a printed copy in the container for your print portfolio.

Chapter 13

Leadership and Group Dynamics

Section 13.1
Leadership in the Workplace

Section 13.2
Leadership at School

College and Career Readiness

Reading Prep. In preparation for reading this chapter, read over the terms listed for each section. What terms are already familiar to you? Which ones are not familiar at all? As you read, think about how your understanding of the meaning of a given term agrees with or differs from the text.

Introduction

Working well with coworkers, serving customers, and taking a leadership role are skills employers expect workers to possess. These interpersonal skills are considered necessary for working effectively in today's workplace. When employees do not have these skills, they may fall short of customer expectations and lose business for their employer.

Leaders are needed in every occupation at all job levels. Business and industry look for and reward workers with leadership skills. Leaders create a vision for a business or organization and motivate others to follow them. Developing your leadership skills can help you be a better worker. School groups, as well as Career and Technical Organizations, can provide that opportunity for you.

Check Your Career IQ

Before you begin the chapter, see what you already know about careers by taking the chapter pretest. Use the related QR code to view the pretest on the mobile site. If you do not have a smartphone, visit the G-W Learning companion website to access the pretest.

www.m.g-wlearning.com
www.g-wlearning.com

G-W Mobile

Career Snapshot
Childcare Worker

What Does a Childcare Worker Do?

When a child's parents or other family members are at work or otherwise unavailable, childcare workers provide for the child's basic needs for a specified period of time. Childcare workers are in some instances called *nannies* or *childcare assistants*. A childcare worker must:

- understand how to nurture, teach, and care for young children;
- be prepared to supervise older children before and after school;
- organize activities and implement curricula that stimulate children's physical, emotional, intellectual, and social growth; and
- help children explore individual interests and develop talents and independence.

What Is It Like to Work as a Childcare Worker?

A childcare worker may work in a private household and care for children at the family residence. Some childcare workers provide childcare in their residence rather than the child's residence. Other childcare workers may work at childcare centers, which include Head Start, Early Head Start, full-day and part-day preschool, and other early childhood programs.

What Education and Skills Are Needed to Be a Childcare Worker?

- high school diploma
- community college courses or a college degree in child development or early childhood education recommended
- national Child Development Associate (CDA) credential recommended
- organization and communication skills
- ability to be patient and nurturing

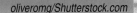

oliveromg/Shutterstock.com

13.1 Leadership in the Workplace

Objectives

After completing this section, you will be able to:
- **Describe** group dynamics and the related benefits.
- **Explain** the different types of authority leaders possess.

Group Dynamics

Dynamics are the underlying causes of change or growth. The fact that you attend high school causes change or growth within you, so the dynamics of high school impact your life. Dynamics may be one or many forces. Your personality is one such dynamic force.

Group dynamics are the interacting forces within a human group. These forces include your own personality and the personalities of all other members of the group. A spirit of cooperation fosters positive dynamics, while anger and jealousy foster the opposite. The dynamics may also include environmental factors, such as seating arrangement, room temperature, lighting, as well as the size and location of a meeting room.

Whether you work with few or many people, group dynamics are present. The dynamics of groups in the workplace affect the work environment, quality of the product, and reputation of the company in the eyes of the customers and the competition. Your understanding of basic dynamics and their effect in the workplace is important.

You have an impact on group dynamics at work, in school, and at home. When you function within a group that has positive dynamics, you benefit personally. Some of the benefits you receive as a result of positive dynamic are:
- greater self-esteem;
- increased job satisfaction;
- better understanding of others;
- improved communication and relationship skills;
- improved ability to work with people from diverse backgrounds;
- better understanding of how to work with others; and
- pride in a job well done.

When you participate in a group with positive dynamics, you develop greater self-esteem.

Mike Flippo/Shutterstock.com

In addition to the personal benefits individuals achieve, a team also benefits from positive group dynamics. Your teams will be more able to:

- understand how individuals contribute to the group's progress;
- learn how to utilize the talents of each person on the team;
- accomplish objectives;
- see a task to its completion; and
- exceed goals as a unit.

Leadership

Leadership is the capacity to direct a group. How someone leads or directs a group is his or her leadership style. There are four basic leadership styles:

- democratic,
- autocratic,
- consulting, and
- laissez-faire.

A leader with a democratic style encourages all members of the group to participate in decision making. Leaders who employ this style delegate responsibility within the group to those best able to handle it.

An autocratic leader is the opposite of a democratic leader. An autocratic leader makes all decisions him- or herself. All of the power is given to one person, the leader.

A consulting leader uses a combination of the democratic and autocratic styles. This type of leader solicits opinions from the group but ultimately makes the decision alone.

A leader who leaves decision making entirely in the hands of group members is exercising a laissez-faire leadership style. Those with this type of leadership style focus on the big picture and leave the details to others.

Skills and Qualities of a Good Leader

Different types of leadership are needed for different roles. The governor of a state may need different leadership qualities than a military leader or a business leader. There are some common qualities all leaders need. As you become involved with school clubs and work groups, think about the leadership qualities good leaders possess. A good friend or a nice person may not necessarily make a good leader.

What qualities do good leaders possess? First of all, good leaders must have vision for the future. **Vision** is an understanding of what is most important to the group and how to achieve it. Followers tend to support the leader whose vision most closely resembles their own thoughts on the group's future direction.

To carry out their vision, leaders need special skills. Many of the skills that make a good leader are shown in Figure 13-1. One of the skills is the ability to **delegate**, or assign responsibility or authority to another person or group. The only way for most work to get done is to assign some of it to others. Letting group members be responsible for certain projects makes them feel involved and more committed.

In addition to leadership skills, good leaders usually have certain personal qualities that help them lead others. These qualities include

---

Leadership Skills

Good leaders have the ability to

- motivate group members to support a vision and achieve goals.
- assume responsibility for the duties of the office or position.
- show confidence and keep a group focused.
- analyze situations clearly and take decisive action when needed.
- take risks and explore new ways of achieving goals.
- maintain enthusiasm and a positive attitude.
- encourage team spirit and cooperation among members.
- listen to others and respond to their views.
- delegate assignments and recognize the accomplishments of others.
- welcome new ideas.
- set a good example.
- work for group success, not personal success.
- do a fair share of the work.
- stay up-to-date on important issues.

Figure 13-1.   *Goodheart-Willcox Publisher*
The skills expected of a good leader can be developed.

honesty, imagination, and the desire to work hard. Not everyone has these qualities or the ability to lead others. However, many of the qualities needed to become a good leader can be learned and developed with practice.

Importance of Learning Leadership

Leadership experiences are very valuable when you apply for a job. Employers look for experiences that indicate you can take responsibility and perform well in a group. Be sure to add any leadership roles you played in school groups and student organizations to your résumé. When interviewing for a job, students who do not participate in groups or organizations are at a disadvantage. Employers know students with a record of group interaction usually make better employees.

Leadership is a very important employability skill. Understanding the necessity of both position and earned authority is key to your success in the workplace. Good leaders have certain qualities and abilities to help them carry out their leadership roles. As people work on teams, group dynamics affect the group's work and decision-making processes.

Participating in school teams, clubs, and groups can help students develop their leadership skills. Career and technical student organizations are especially useful for learning how to work with and lead a group. Through group activities, you will expand your attitudes, knowledge, and skills to contribute to the goals and objectives of the organization. Develop leadership experience while in school. As a result, you will be prepared to demonstrate leadership skills in the workplace.

Checkpoint 13.1

1. What are two benefits of positive group dynamics for the individual worker?
2. Provide an example of a force that can affect group dynamics.
3. What are the four styles of leadership?
4. List four skills a good leader should demonstrate.
5. What personal qualities should a good leader have?

Build Your Vocabulary

As you progress through this text, develop a personal glossary of career-related terms and add it to your portfolio. This will help build your vocabulary and prepare you for your career of choice. Write a definition for each of the following terms, and add it to your personal career glossary.

    dynamics
    group dynamics
    leadership
    vision
    delegate

13.2 Leadership at School

Career and Technical
  Student Organiza-
  tion (CTSO)
Business Professionals
  of America (BPA)
Workplace Skills
  Assessment
  Program (WSAP)
DECA
Family, Career and
  Community Leaders
  of America (FCCLA)
Future Business
  Leaders of America
  (FBLA)
Future Educators
  Association (FEA)
Health Occupations
  Students of
  America (HOSA)
National FFA
  Organization (FFA)
SkillsUSA
Technology Student
  Association (TSA)

Objectives

After completing this section, you will be able to:
- **Explain** ways to develop leadership skills in school.
- **Describe** the different types of Career and Technical Student Organizations (CTSOs).

Leadership in School

You have many opportunities in school to develop leadership qualities and group dynamic skills. As you work on developing these qualities, you also learn to contribute in a positive way to group dynamics. Participation in various school teams, groups, or clubs can help you develop leadership and teamwork skills you can use on the job. Under the direction of a good leader, groups are motivated to make many worthwhile accomplishments.

There are many activities and contests designed to help you develop leadership skills to your maximum. Participating in these events will help improve your understanding of group dynamics. If you are not already a member of a school group, consider joining the debate team, newspaper staff, or drama club. Band, chorus, sports, and other activity groups that interest you are also good choices. Student group activities and projects tend to center around the following types of activities:

- professional,
- civic,
- service,
- social, and
- fund-raising.

Professional activities build students' employability skills. These activities include job shadowing, field trips, and conferences. Skill contests are also professional development activities. They help students improve and expand their career-related attitudes, knowledge, and skills.

Civic activities are student group projects that serve the school and community. Projects range from helping improve the school or community to participating in fairs, trade shows, and other community events.

Service activities involve projects that emphasize the need for sharing. Making a contribution to a charity, visiting a nursing home, and making and delivering fruit baskets to shut-ins are examples of service activities.

Social activities are also an important part of student groups. These activities include parties, picnics, and socializing after meetings. The employer-employee banquet is also considered a social activity as well as a professional one.

Fund-raising activities are necessary to finance all the other activities of the group. Service projects and social functions are types of activities that may require fund-raising.

Of course, there is no limit to the types of activities an organization may sponsor. The limit is set only by the creativity of its members and officers. For a club to be successful, its members need to work willingly and enthusiastically on club activities. An active member of an organization participates in two or more of the following ways:

- attends meetings;
- learns parliamentary procedure;
- serves on a committee;
- supports or participates in organization activities; or
- holds an office, if elected or appointed.

An active organization requires all its members to work for the good of the group. Not everyone can be the president, but every member can do his or her part. Members can assume leadership roles by freely volunteering to handle their fair share of the work. Assess your own abilities and decide what you can do best for your organization. Taking an active role in an organization can help you develop as a person, leader, and team member.

Some student groupd raise money for service projects, such as for this walkathon for the March of Dimes.

National Foundation—March of Dimes

Ethical Leadership

Personal Ethics

"You're born with intelligence, but not with ethics."
—Massad Ayoob

Your ethics are what determine the kind of person you are, how you react to situations and how you live your life. Your ethics are a reflection of you to your relatives, friends, and people in general. You are confronted daily with decisions to be made. How you make those decisions also reflects on your ethics. For example, you are checking out of a store and given too much money back in change, what do you do?

Career and Technical Student Organizations

A **Career and Technical Student Organizations (CTSOs)** are national organizations that are associated with a specific occupational area, such as agriculture, marketing, and family and consumer science. CTSOs help students develop interpersonal, leadership, and teamwork skills as part of a school's career and technical education curriculum.

Your school most likely has a student organization that is related to your career interests. If there are no available CTSOs in your career interests, one can be started with your school's approval. CTSOs help reinforce and expand what students learn in the classroom and on the job. Students can participate in these organizations on the local, state, and national levels. The CTSOs commonly found in schools are described on the following pages.

Business Professionals of America

Business Professionals of America (BPA) is a cocurricular CTSO for students pursuing careers in business management, office administration, information technology, and other related career fields. BPA has more than 51,000 members in over 2,300 chapters in 23 states.

The **Workplace Skills Assessment Program (WSAP)** is the process through which BPA prepares students to assess their real-world business skills and problem-solving abilities in finance, management, information technology, and computer applications. It is a BPA showcase program that allows students to demonstrate their career skills at regional, state, and national conferences.

BPA supports business and information technology educators, offering curriculum based on national standards. Resources and materials are available online that are designed to be customized to a school's program. You can learn more about BPA by visiting their website at www.bpa.org.

Students in DECA have the opportunity to build leadership skills and compete in special team events.

DECA

DECA

DECA prepares emerging leaders and entrepreneurs in high schools and colleges around the world for careers in marketing, finance, hospitality, and management. This CTSO enhances the co-curricular education of members through a comprehensive learning program that integrates classroom instruction and meaningful interactions with businesses as well as opportunities to take part in competitive events. DECA's activities assist in the development of leaders who are academically prepared and professionally responsible. In addition, participants are encouraged to be community-oriented.

DECA has more than 5,000 chapters in all 50 states, the District of Columbia, Canada, China, Germany, Guam, Hong Kong, Korea, Mexico, and Puerto Rico, totaling a combined membership of high school and college members of more than 200,000.

DECA also offers high-quality, professional-development resources. Workshops and seminars are available to enhance the skills and performance of educators within the organization. Leaders of DECA facilitate student-centered learning, as well as foster college and career readiness.

For more information, visit www.deca.org.

Go Green

Many organizations are establishing green teams. These teams are committees comprised of members of different departments who meet (online or in person) to brainstorm ways the organization can be more environmentally responsible in its daily operations. Team leaders and team members help implement the ideas and often champion the initiatives they establish.

Family, Career and Community Leaders of America

Family, Career and Community Leaders of America (FCCLA) is a nonprofit national CTSO with an emphasis on family and consumer science. FCCLA is the only national CTSO with the family as its central focus. By addressing important personal, work, and societal issues through family and consumer science, FCCLA members make a difference in their families, careers, and communities.

Today over 205,000 members in nearly 6,500 chapters are active in a network of associations in 50 states as well as in the US Virgin Islands and Puerto Rico. Involvement in FCCLA offers members the opportunity to expand their leadership potential and develop skills for life. Planning, goal setting, problem solving, decision making, and interpersonal communication are among the skills taught and developed. Programs include Career Connection, Dynamic Leadership, and Leaders at Work.

Students who participate in FCCLA take part in conferences and leadership-development activities.

FCCLA

Career Connection is a national program that helps students discover their career interests and guide them along a career path. *Dynamic Leadership* is a program that offers project ideas, activities, and information about the lifelong benefits of developing leadership skills. Students become strong leaders for families, careers, and communities through FCCLA involvement.

Leaders at Work is a unit within Career Connection that motivates students to prepare for career success. The program recognizes FCCLA members who create projects to strengthen leadership skills on the job.

FCCLA also offers competitive events, including STAR competitions. *Students Taking Action with Recognition (STAR)* conducts national events in which members are recognized for proficiency and achievement in chapter and individual projects. Participants are also recognized for leadership skills and career preparation.

For more information about FCCLA, visit www.fcclainc.org.

Future Business Leaders of America

Future Business Leaders of America (FBLA) is a nonprofit 501(C)(3) education association, with a quarter million students preparing for careers in business and business-related fields. The association has four divisions: Future Business Leaders of America (FBLA) for high school students; FBLA-Middle Level (FBLA-ML) for junior high, middle, and intermediate school students; Phi Beta Lambda (PBL) for postsecondary students; and the Professional Division (PD) for business people, PBL alumni, and parents who support the goals of the association. The mission of FBLA is to bring business and schools together in a positive working relationship through innovative leadership and career-development programs.

FBLA offers exclusive membership and career recognition programs. These programs are designed for each division to provide additional personal and chapter development opportunities. In addition, annual competitive events are held at state leadership conferences. Winners at these events may then participate in the annual competitive events at the National Leadership Conference.

For more information, please visit www.fbla-pbl.org.

Future Educators Association

Future Educators Association (FEA) is an organization that provides activities and materials for students interested in education-related careers. FEA helps students explore the teaching profession in a variety of ways. Its mission is to foster the recruitment and development of prospective educators worldwide through the dissemination of innovative programming and relevant research.

FEA helps students develop the skills and strong leadership traits that are found in high-quality educators. FEA also contributes to the development of the next generation of great educators, emerging leaders, and entrepreneurs. FEA strives to attract dynamic and diverse students who will become tomorrow's great educators. FEA has over 11,000 members in 44 states as well as in Germany, Northern Mariana Islands, and Guam.

For more information, visit www.futureeducators.org.

Health Occupations Students of America

Health Occupations Students of America (HOSA) is a CTSO, endorsed by the US Department of Education. HOSA's mission is to promote opportunities in health care and enhance the delivery of quality health care to all people. Since its beginnings in 1976, HOSA has served nearly two million graduates. Today, HOSA serves 150,000 members and 3,500 chapters in 48 states, as well as Puerto Rico and the District of Columbia. Key national HOSA partners include the US Army, Aspen Institute, KidneyWise, US Public Health Service, US Medical Reserve Corps, HCA, Kaiser Permanente, and America's Promise. HOSA's 57 competitions give students an avenue to demonstrate their knowledge, skills, and leadership development. The areas for competition include health science professions, emergency preparedness, individual and team leadership, and recognition.

For more about HOSA, visit www.hosa.org.

HOSA is a Career and Technical Student Organization for students interested in health occupations.

HOSA

National FFA Organization

The National FFA Organization was founded in 1928 and currently has more than 523,000 members in 7,487 chapters throughout the United States, Puerto Rico and the US Virgin Islands. The **National FFA Organization (FFA)** prepares members for leadership and careers within the AFNRS Career Cluster pathways. Involvement in FFA involves:

- contextual classroom and laboratory instruction;
- experiential learning through a supervised agricultural experience (SAE) program; and
- leadership and personal development.

The combination of these activities helps students prepare for successful careers and a lifetime of informed choices in the global agriculture, food, fiber, and natural resources systems. To become an FFA member you must be enrolled in an agricultural education course (grades 7-12) that has an FFA chapter.

For more information about the National FFA Organization, visit www.ffa.org.

SkillsUSA

SkillsUSA is a national, nonprofit organization for high school and college students, as well as teachers. SkillsUSA joins students, teachers, and industry together. The purpose of the organization is to create a strong, skilled workforce for America. SkillsUSA helps students prepare for careers in technical, skilled, service, and health occupations. SkillsUSA offers

members programs that will provide education experiences. Programs focus on leadership, teamwork, character development, and citizenship.

- The Professional Development Program (PDP) teaches students 84 workplace skill competencies. This is done through a series of lessons.
- The Work Force Ready System provides assessments for career and technical education. This program is supported by industry, education, and policy leaders.
- Student2Student Mentoring allows older high school students to mentor younger students.
- The Career Skills Education Program teaches employability and life skills. This program is strictly for college students.
- CareerSafe is a 10-hour online training program. It gives students basic knowledge of safety. It also provides a credential for the job market.

Developing the student's technical, academic, and employability skills is the goal of SkillsUSA.

For more information about SkillsUSA, visit their website at www.skillsusa.org.

SkillsUSA allows students to develop skills for specific occupations, such as crime scene investigator.

SkillsUSA

Technology Student Association

Technology Student Association (TSA) is an organization that provides competitions and programs for middle and high school students with a strong interest in technology, innovation, design, and engineering. These activities prepare TSA members for the challenges of a dynamic world. TSA promotes personal growth, leadership, and problem solving skills in students. The organization reaches 150,000 members in over 1,500 chapters nationwide.

TSA hosts an annual conference that features middle school and high school competitions. Members can compete in a broad range of areas, such as robotics, CAD, engineering, film, manufacturing, and leadership. TSA's competitive events, as well as its other programs and activities, are intended to extend a student's understanding of science, technology, engineering, and mathematics (STEM). The overall focus of TSA is to promote the development, impact, and potential of technology and high-tech careers.

For more information about the Technology Student Association visit www.tsaweb.org.

Introduction to Community Service Projects

Many competitive events for Career and Technical Student Organizations (CTSOs) include a community service project. This project is usually carried out by the entire CTSO chapter and spans a number of months. The local chapter will designate several members to represent the team at the competitive event.There will be two parts of the event: written and oral.

To prepare for any competitive event, complete the following activities:

1. Read the guidelines provided by your organization. Make certain that you ask any questions about points you do not understand. It is important you follow each specific item that is outlined in the competition rules.
2. Contact the association immediately at the end of the state conference to prepare for next year's event.
3. As a team, select a theme for your chapter's community service project.
4. Decide which roles are needed for the team. There may be one person who is the captain, one person who is the secretary, and any other roles that will be necessary to create the plan. Ask your instructor for guidance in assigning roles to team members.
5. Identify your target audience, which may include business, school, and community groups.
6. Brainstorm with members of your chapters. List the benefits and opportunities of supporting a community service project.
7. This project will probably span the school year. During regular chapter meetings, create a draft of the report based on direction from the CTSO. Write and refine drafts until the final report is finished.

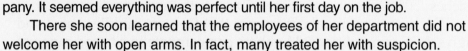

Case

Follow the Leader

Dara could not be happier. The company just announced her appointment to technical department director. She recently graduated from one of the toughest universities in her engineering field with high honors. Now she held a top job at an excellent company. It seemed everything was perfect until her first day on the job.

There she soon learned that the employees of her department did not welcome her with open arms. In fact, many treated her with suspicion.

As the weeks went by, Dara realized things were not getting done in the way she wanted. She also learned that department members were secretly discussing their assignments with Michael, the person with the most experience and longest service in the department.

Although the assignments were getting done well and on time, Dara resented Michael's interference. She especially disliked that employees were not doing things in the way she directed. However, she could not argue with the fact that their methods seemed to produce better results than hers would have. Still, she was not pleased with the way Michael was intruding on her authority.

"I'm really not happy with your inability to be a cooperative team member," Dara yelled when she saw Michael at his desk alone.

"What are you talking about?" Michael asked.

"Do you think I don't see through your plan to take my job?" Dara replied.

"I'm only trying to help," Michael explained. "Besides, there are certain ways we do things here, and your methods are different."

"If the company wanted things done according to your methods, you would be the director, but you're not. Now, start following my directions and quit telling others how to do their jobs," Dara warned.

Michael never said anything to his coworkers about the incident, but that did not matter. Several department employees were working around the corner and heard every word. They immediately told the others, and soon the entire company was gossiping about it. Ever since that day, department employees did their work precisely as Dara dictated, but silently they hoped she would transfer to another department.

Critical Thinking

1. Does this department have good leadership? Explain.
2. Who is responsible for the poor group dynamics of this department?
3. What should Dara do to improve group dynamics?
4. How should she work with Michael?

Checkpoint 13.2

1. Describe the five types of group activities that develop leadership qualities in students.
2. What are some examples of service activities?
3. What is dynamic leadership?
4. Explain the purpose of Health Occupations Students of America (HOSA).
5. Name a program offered by SkillsUSA, and explain the program's function.

Build Your Vocabulary

As you progress through this text, develop a personal glossary of career-related terms and add it to your portfolio. This will help build your vocabulary and prepare you for your career of choice. Write a definition for each of the following terms, and add it to your personal career glossary.

CTSO
Business Professionals of America (BPA)
Workplace Skills Assessment Program (WSAP)
DECA
Family, Career and Community Leaders of America (FCCLA)
Future Business Leaders of America (FBLA)
Future Educators Association (FEA)
Health Occupations Students of America (HOSA)
National FFA Organization (FFA)
SkillsUSA
Technology Student Association (TSA)

Chapter Summary

Section 13.1 Leadership in the Workplace

- As people work on teams, group dynamics affect the group's work and decision-making processes. Whether you work with few or many people, group dynamics are present.
- Good leaders have certain qualities and abilities to help them carry out their leadership roles. Understanding how leadership styles influence group dynamics is key to your success in the workplace.

Section 13.2 Leadership in School

- Leadership is a very important employability skill. Participating in school teams, clubs, and groups can help students develop their leadership skills.
- Career and technical student organizations are especially useful for learning how to work with and lead a group. Through group activities, you will expand your attitudes, knowledge, and skills to contribute to the goals and objectives of the organization.

Check Your Career IQ

Now that you have finished the chapter, see what you learned about careers by taking the chapter posttest. The test can be accessed on the mobile site by using a smartphone or on the G-W Learning companion website.

www.m.g-wlearning.com
www.g-wlearning.com

Review Your Knowledge

1. How does a person gain position authority?
2. List two examples of how a team might benefit from positive group dynamics.
3. What are the two ways a person can become a leader in the workplace?
4. Why are leadership experiences valuable when looking for a job?
5. Explain what makes professional activities different from civic activities.
6. Name three CTSOs commonly found in schools.
7. What is the purpose of the Workplace Skills Assessment Program (WSAP)?
8. Which CTSO provides opportunities for students with an interest in teaching?
9. What is Career Connection?
10. Explain the purpose of SkillsUSA.

Apply Your Knowledge

1. Using the Internet, explore the websites of the CTSOs listed in this chapter. Choose the organization in which you are most interested, and write a one-page report based on your findings.
2. Using the Internet, research famous leaders and the qualities that made them great leaders. Prepare a presentation of your findings.
3. List the aspects of your personality that would make you a productive member of a team. Next, list other traits you want to develop or improve. Explain how you lead (or would lead) a team effectively by listing the leadership traits you already possess. Then explain what you can do to develop the skills you lack. Share your responses with students in a small group. Offer ideas that might also help your group members to develop leadership traits.
4. Identify one or more groups that can help you develop the traits you lack or need to improve. Explain how these groups can help in a brief written report. Give both pages to a trusted teacher or counselor and ask for a confidential review. Can the reviewer recommend any other traits to develop or groups to explore? Record the reviewer's recommendations and refer to your lists as needed.
5. Using Internet or print sources, research how communication skills improve group dynamics. Write a report of your findings. Give an oral presentation of your report in class.
6. List at least three examples of recent civic activities conducted by student groups. Write a brief essay on how these activities benefit the community.
7. Develop a list of ways a person with position authority can make the transition to earned authority.

8. Select one of the CTSOs covered in this chapter. Create a poster ad inviting students to join. Include details about the CTSO that will inform students about its purpose and benefits.

9. With a partner, discuss the pros and cons of each of the four leadership styles described in the chapter. How would you categorize your leadership style? Under what type of leadership style would you prefer to work? Explain why.

10. Develop an idea for a new CTSO. Create a name for the organization. Write a mission statement explaining the purpose of your new CTSO. What group(s) would the organization serve? Why should people join? How will students benefit from the organization? Does the CTSO promote a specific career field? Compile your info in a chart. Share your new CTSO with the class.

Teamwork

 Working in a group, prepare a research project involving future trends in science-related careers. Elect a team leader for your group. After the project is finished, hold a group discussion about leadership in relation to the success of your project.

G-W Learning Mobile Site

 Visit the G-W Learning mobile site to complete the chapter pretest and posttest and to practice vocabulary using e-flash cards. If you do not have a smartphone, visit the G-W Learning companion website to access these features.
G-W Learning mobile site: www.m.g-wlearning.com
G-W Learning companion website: www.g-wlearning.com

Common Core

College and Career Readiness

CTE Career Ready Practices. Create an Euler diagram (a diagram with three or more intersecting circles that depicts relationships between the material contained in each circle) to show the relationship between your career interests, your preferences, your goals, and requirements of your career choice. Where do the circles overlap? What do you think this overlap signifies? What would a diagram with a lot of overlap tell you? What about one with little or no overlap?

Reading. Read a magazine, newspaper, or online article about the importance of leadership in the workplace. Determine the central ideas of the article and review the conclusions made by the author. Provide an accurate summary of your reading, making sure to incorporate the *who, what, when,* and *how* of this situation.

Apply Your Technology Skills

Access the G-W Learning companion website for this text at www.g-wlearning.com. Download the data file for this chapter. Follow the instructions to complete activities to practice what you have learned in this chapter.

Data File 13–1—Working as Part of a Team

College and Career Readiness

College and Career Readiness Portfolio

Some colleges or volunteer groups may ask you to supply one or more letters of recommendation with your application. Such a letter may also be requested in an interview. A letter of recommendation is written by someone with whom you have worked or someone who knows you personally. This letter will describe your skills, talents, work habits, or other traits.

A letter of recommendation can be written to a general audience or to a specific person or organization. For example, your high school teacher or coach might write a letter describing your skills, talents, or character. The letter could be written in a style that would be appropriate for many situations. When you apply for a job, you might ask one of your references to write a letter to the company to which you are applying. The letter can be addressed to a particular person and can discuss skills or talents directly related to the job.

1. Ask three people to write a general letter of recommendation for you.
2. Scan the letters and save them in your e-portfolio.
3. Place the original letters in the container for your print portfolio.

Chapter 14

Participating in Meetings

Section 14.1
Types of Meetings

Section 14.2
Parliamentary Procedure

College and Career Readiness

Reading Prep. Before reading this chapter, research parliamentary procedure on the Internet. Read one or two articles on the topic. As you read, consider the similarities and differences between the Internet articles and the text. Compare the different approaches the authors take to the material.

Introduction

Participating in meetings and serving on committees are very common activities, and your involvement with them will become more common as you go through life. Social and professional groups, including the workforce, are dependent on meetings. These groups rely on the work of the officers and committee members to help achieve the organization's goals. The skills in attending and actively participating in meetings, serving on committees, and leading as an officer are very desirable.

Check Your Career IQ

Before you begin the chapter, see what you already know about careers by taking the chapter pretest. Use the related QR code to view the pretest on the mobile site. If you do not have a smartphone, visit the G-W Learning companion website to access the pretest.

www.m.g-wlearning.com
www.g-wlearning.com

G-W Mobile

Career Snapshot:
Emergency Dispatcher

What Does an Emergency Dispatcher Do?

An emergency dispatcher has to determine the location, nature, and priority of an emergency call. An emergency dispatcher must do the following.

- Receive and process 911 emergency calls, maintain contact with all units on assignment, maintain status and location of police and fire units.
- Monitor direct emergency alarms, and answer nonemergency calls for assistance.
- Enter, update, and retrieve information from a variety of computer systems.
- Receive requests for information regarding vehicle registration, driving records and warrants, and provides pertinent data as needed.
- Monitor multiple complex public safety radio frequencies.
- Operate a variety of communications equipment, including radio consoles, telephones, and computer systems.

What Is It Like to Work as an Emergency Dispatcher?

An emergency dispatcher has a comfortable work environment where the temperature is controlled and the surroundings are usually pleasant. Casual dress is allowed, although some dispatch centers require a uniform. Even though the stress level on some calls may be very high, a professional attitude is expected when communicating with callers and fellow employees.

What Education and Skills Are Needed to Be an Emergency Dispatcher?

- high school diploma or GED
- minimum of two years of responsible full-time work experience
- able to key text at 35 words per minute

Diego Cervo/Shutterstock.com

14.1 Types of Meetings

Terms

informal meeting
formal meeting
bylaws
slate
remote meeting
teleconferencing

Objectives

After completing this section, you will be able to:
- **Explain** the importance of group meetings at work and school.
- **Discuss** the purpose of remote meetings.

Group Meetings

Have you ever attended a meeting for a school group or sports team? When people work together in a group or as a team, at some point, they will need to gather for meetings to share information.

Meetings of school organizations have two important purposes: to develop socialization skills and to conduct the business of the organization. Meetings in the workplace are usually held for business reasons.

There are generally two types of meetings: informal meetings and formal meetings. **Informal meetings** are meetings in the workplace where coworkers meet to brainstorm new ideas, decide how to divide the department workload, and update staff on important events. Unlike an informal meeting, a **formal meeting** is structured to be conducted in a specific way.

Regardless of the type of meeting, it costs the company money every time a meeting is held. Workers are pulled away from their jobs and not accomplishing work. As a result, everyone at a work-based meeting is expected to stay alert, make appropriate contributions, and not waste time. Use the following guidelines when you participate in meetings.

- **Be on time.** Tardiness is a sign of disrespect.
- **Be prepared.** Do any necessary homework prior to the meeting. Have any questions well-thought-out.
- **Do not monopolize the conversation.** There are times to speak and times to listen.
- **Contribute by making statements rather than always asking questions.** Only asking questions can be perceived as disrespectful and confrontational.
- **Do not allow others to intimidate you.** Give yourself "think time" before responding to any personal attacks.
- **Do not chew gum or engage in other similarly inappropriate habits.** You want people to focus on your contribution to the meeting, not be distracted by your bad habit.

Yuri Acurs/Shutterstock.com

Meetings provide teams with valuable time to share ideas and establish goals.

- **Try to read nonverbal signals accurately.** This may require taking time to get to know the other members in the room fairly well.
- **Turn your cell phone off.** You can pick up your messages after the meeting.
- **Never skip a meeting.** If you have to be absent, be sure to let the presiding person know in advance.
- **Stick to the topic.** Make notes regarding unrelated topics to be brought up at another time.

Electing Officers

Most formal groups nominate and elect new officers once a year. A group's bylaws outline how officers are nominated. **Bylaws** are written rules that spell out how formal groups operate. These rules include how officers are to be chosen, how meetings are to be conducted, and who plays what role in official meetings.

Organizations usually nominate officers by one of two methods: accepting nominations from the floor or appointing a committee to nominate a list of candidates.

Nominations from the floor are made by a member simply saying, "I nominate Li Wen for president." The chairperson waits for further nominations. After waiting a reasonable length of time, the chair asks if there are any further nominations. If there are none, he or she declares the nominations closed for the office of president and proceeds to the next office. When there is a large group participating, it is customary to have a motion to close the nominations. The motion requires a two-thirds vote.

Other groups have a nominating committee prepare a list of candidates to present to the group. On the other hand, some groups have the committee select only one person for each office, while others have at least two people nominated.

On the day of the election, the committee presents the candidates to the group. After the nominations have been presented, the president will usually ask, "Are there any further nominations from the floor?" At this point, it is still possible for members to make nominations from the floor, even if a committee has prepared a list of candidates. Usually, however, no further nominations are made because the committee was previously assigned to do the job.

Following nominations, the president will then take a vote to determine the new officers. If there is more than one candidate, a vote will be held for each office. If there is only one nomination for each office, the president can take a vote on the entire slate of officers. A **slate** is a list of candidates prepared for nomination. A majority vote will make the candidates official officers.

Forming Committees

Committees are formed by an organization or group for the purpose of carrying out a specific project or task. The work done by committees is a very important part of an organization. In fact, most groups depend on their committees to plan and initiate all the activities.

Committee chairpersons are either elected by the group or appointed by the president. The method for determining chairpersons is described in a group's bylaws.

Once elected or appointed, each chairperson asks two or more people to serve on the committee. When a committee is formed, the chairperson arranges a place and time for a meeting. At the first

Special committees may need to meet after school to plan and discuss upcoming events.

Go Green

When was the last time you looked up a phone number in a phone book? With access to business information online and via smartphones, most people don't use phone books as much as they did years ago. Just imagine how much paper is wasted in printing phone books that are never used. Encourage your school and place of employment to opt out of receiving phone books, which often end up in landfills. Instead of a printed phone book, use your computer or other electronic devices to find current phone listings.

meeting, the chairperson explains what the committee is expected to do. He or she usually asks for suggestions from the members. Every member should feel free to participate and discuss options for the committee. However, members should talk about the tasks of the committee and not stray from the subject. Part of the job of the chairperson is to guide the discussion and keep the committee focused on the business at hand.

Remote Meetings

As business becomes more global, workers are part of teams that may be in different locations. Not every team member has to be on site to participate in a meeting. Through the use of technology, remote meetings can be held any place in the world. A **remote meeting** is where people come together using a technology tool rather than meeting face-to-face. Considerable expenses may be saved by conducting remote meetings by not having to pay for airfare, hotels, meals, and rental cars for traditional face-to-face meetings.

Teleconferencing, or *conference calling,* is a meeting that takes place over the telephone between participants at two or more locations. However, with the use of a video camera, *videoconferencing* allows team members in different locations to talk as well as see each other.

Remote meetings, however, do have some disadvantages. One of the main disadvantages is the dependability of a fast, error-free Internet connection. No matter how well prepared you may be for a remote meeting, it is important to have a back-up plan in the event that the Internet connection does not work. Another disadvantage of remote meetings is the lack of personal contact with the other team members.

Ethical Leadership

Integrity

"Your reputation and integrity are everything. Follow through on what you say you're going to do. Your credibility can only be built over time, and it is built from the history of your words and actions." —Maria Razumich-Zec

When you work for a company and are asked to participate in meetings, many times you will be expected to maintain confidentiality. Your integrity is at stake! For example, you may be sitting in a committee and hear the company is considering purchasing a particular piece of property. You know a friend who is also interested in that property for her own purposes. It would be unethical for you to warn your friend that your company is looking to purchase that same property.

Remote meetings should follow the same rules of conduct as face-to-face meetings. Some basic rules of etiquette are as follows.

- Remember, manners still count.
- Be prepared to discuss and ask questions.
- Dress as you would for an in-person meeting.
- If you are in a video meeting, make eye contact with the camera.
- Avoid making excessive background noise.
- Turn off beepers, watch alarms, and cell phones.
- Use names to direct questions to specific people.

Checkpoint 14.1

1. What are two general types of meetings?
2. Why does it cost a company every time a meeting is held?
3. Name three guidelines for participating in meetings.
4. Explain the advantage of teleconferencing.
5. What is a disadvantage of conducting a remote meeting over the Internet?

Build Your Vocabulary

As you progress through this text, develop a personal glossary of career-related terms and add it to your portfolio. This will help build your vocabulary and prepare you for your career of choice. Write a definition for each of the following terms, and add it to your personal career glossary.

    informal meeting
    formal meeting
    bylaws
    slate
    remote meeting
    teleconferencing

Objectives

After completing this section you will be able to:

- **Explain** the relationship between *Robert's Rules of Order* and parliamentary procedure.
- **Describe** the role parliamentary procedure plays in conducting formal meetings.

Terms

parliamentary
  procedure
quorum
standing committees
special committees
main motion
secondary motion

Robert's Rules of Order

Many organizations follow a similar procedure for conducting meetings. This procedure, or order of business, is based on *Robert's Rules of Order*, a famous book on parliamentary procedure. **Parliamentary procedure** is a set of rules explaining how a group should gather, share information, and make decisions. During a meeting, the order of business usually follows the pattern shown in Figure 14-1, unless otherwise specified in the organization's bylaws. Many groups and organization use parliamentary procedure during important meetings. Parliamentary procedure allows groups to meet and conduct business in an orderly and effective manner.

Parts of a Formal Meeting
1. Call to order
2. Reading and approving of minutes
3. Reports of officers
4. Standing committee reports
5. Special committee reports
6. Unfinished business
7. New business
8. The program
9. Announcements
10. Adjournment

Figure 14-1.   *Goodheart-Willcox Publisher*

Learning the parts of a formal meeting can help you become a more active group member during meetings.

All members of the organization have a right to participate in each meeting. In order to understand parliamentary procedure and participate in this type of meeting, you need to be familiar with the terms as shown in Figure 14-2. When group members understand the meanings of these words, meetings can proceed much more smoothly and productively.

Terms Used in Parliamentary Procedure
Adjourn—To end a meeting
Agenda—A list of things to be done and discussed at a meeting
Amend the motion—To change the wording of a motion that has been made
Aye—The formal term for yes (pronounced eye)
Bylaws—The rules and regulations that govern the organization
Chair—The presiding officer at a meeting, such as the president or chairperson
Debate—To speak for or against a motion. Every member has a right to debate an issue
Majority—At least one more than half of the members present at the meeting
Minutes—A written record of the business covered at a meeting
Motion—A recommendation by a member that certain action be taken by the group
Nay—The formal term for no
Quorum—The number of members who must be present to legally conduct business at a meeting
Second the motion—The approval of a motion by another member
Table the motion—To delay making a decision on a motion
The floor—The right to speak in a meeting without interruption from others

Figure 14-2.   *Goodheart-Willcox Publisher*
Some of the terms used in parliamentary procedure date back to medieval England.

Conducting Meetings

The president or presiding officer of the group calls the meeting to order. He or she does this by rapping a gavel on a wooden block and saying, "The meeting will now come to order."

To proceed with the business part of the meeting, there must be a quorum present. A **quorum** is a majority of members or the number of members stated in the bylaws.

Reading and Approving Minutes

After the meeting is called to order, the president asks the secretary to read the minutes of the previous meeting. The secretary stands and reads the minutes. The president sits during the reading of the minutes. Approved minutes are a final accurate record or note of what happens at a meeting.

Taking minutes is a necessity of many organizational gatherings. If minutes are not kept, before each committee meeting is over, there should be a review or summary of the items discussed. After the meeting is adjourned, the chairperson prepares a written committee report and presents the report at the next meeting.

After the reading, the president stands and says, "You have heard the minutes of the previous meeting. Are there any corrections or additions?" At this point, any member may stand and explain corrections or additions that need to be made to the minutes. If there are no corrections, the president will say, "The minutes stand approved as read." If there are corrections, they are made, and the president will then say, "The minutes stand approved as corrected."

Reports of Officers

At this time, the president calls on the vice president, secretary, and treasurer to give any reports they may have. Often, the only officer who reports at every meeting is the treasurer. The purpose of the treasurer's report is to inform the officers and members of the group's financial status. The report should include any expenses paid since the last meeting, any income taken, and the balance in the treasury. The balance is the amount of money that exists in the group's account.

Standing Committee Reports

After the reports of officers, the president calls on each chairperson of the standing committees for a progress report. **Standing committees** are the permanent committees of a group or organization, such as the membership committee and the program committee. These committees are identified in the organization's bylaws.

Robert's Rules was first published in 1876, and is still widely-used today.

Timothy R Nichols/Shutterstock.com

Case

A Speech or a Tour?

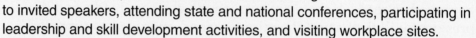

Your group has decided to organize a professional development activity for its members. Professional development activities allow members to enhance their employability skills. Some possible professional development activities include listening to invited speakers, attending state and national conferences, participating in leadership and skill development activities, and visiting workplace sites.

Gustavo Cavallaro, the president of your organization, has called for a meeting of the membership today after school. It is rumored that some members of your organization want to invite the president of Jog-a-long, Inc., a manufacturer of popular sports apparel, to speak at the next scheduled meeting. You and some other members would prefer to tour the Jog-a-long factory where the apparel is made. You see this as a better learning opportunity. Therefore, you and your friends decide to be ready with a well-thought recommendation to have a fund-raiser to cover the expenses of transportation to tour Jog-a-long's factory.

After discussing what needs to be done, your group realizes at least two transactions must take place at the meeting this afternoon. First of all, you or a fellow member must make a motion that a tour of Jog-a-long, Inc. be planned, rather than a speech from the company president. Secondly, you need to be prepared to propose an activity to raise the funds for transportation to Jog-a-long's factory.

Between classes, you check with Gustavo and find out the rumor is true. You quickly let the other members who prefer the tour know that you want to meet during lunch hour. During that time you will plan how to bring your tour idea to the floor for discussion.

Critical Thinking

1. How could you persuade a majority of members to vote favorably for the tour?
2. Why should you be prepared to list the necessary steps to secure transportation?
3. What would you recommend to raise the money needed for transportation to the Jog-a-long factory?

Special Committee Reports

While standing committees are permanent, **special committees** are established for a specific purpose or for a short period. Examples of special committees are a homecoming committee and a spring picnic committee.

A special committee has a certain job to do. After the committee completes its job and properly reports to the group, the committee disbands. During the life of the committee, however, the chairperson is asked to report on their progress at every group meeting.

Unfinished Business

Sometimes a meeting comes to an end before a topic of discussion is complete. The matter is regarded as *unfinished business,* and the topic is discussed at a specific time during the next meeting.

The president starts this part of the meeting by asking, "Are there any items of unfinished business that need to be discussed today?" Unfinished business might include topics that have been tabled, or put aside for future discussion.

Suppose at the last meeting there was a discussion to sell candy as a fund-raising project. However, there was not enough time to talk about the idea and vote on it. The idea would be tabled. Further discussion and a vote to sell candy would be considered unfinished business.

During a formal meeting, time is used carefully to ensure all necessary business matters are discussed.

Dmitriy Shironosov/Shutterstock.com

New Business

At this point in the meeting, the president says, "The next order of business is new business. Is there any new business?" New business includes such things as discussing future group activities, setting dates for activities, and presenting bills for payment. From this discussion, special committees may be formed to plan special activities. If decisions are not made on items of new business, they are usually discussed at the next meeting as unfinished business.

Program

Meetings will sometimes feature a special presentation called a *program*. At this time, the president says, "The program committee will now present the program." The president then calls on the program committee chairperson who introduces the speaker or the program presentation. At the end of the program, the program committee chairperson thanks the speaker or participants. Then, he or she returns the meeting to the president.

To prevent wasting the time of program speakers and presenters, some groups have their programs right after the call to order. Then, the business meetings follow.

Announcements

Following the program, the president should ask, "Are there any announcements?" This is the time to announce the scheduled date and time of the next meeting and to remind members of any special activities occurring before the next meeting. Any type of announcement can be made, such as a thank-you to a committee for doing a good job. Sometimes refreshments are served after the meeting. This information is included in the announcement.

Motions

Members of a group are responsible for making motions and discussing them. There are two types of motions—a main motion and a secondary motion. A **main motion** is a suggestion for the group members to consider during a meeting. It includes one item of business. The requirements for a main motion are listed below.

A main motion must be:
- made at a time when no other business is before the meeting.
- discussed in the proper order of business.
- made by a member who has the floor.
- seconded by another member.
- stated by the chair.
- handled in a manner acceptable to the group.

A **secondary motion** is one that can be made while a main motion is being considered. The purpose of a secondary motion is to amend the main motion or postpone action on the main motion. Secondary motions made while discussing the main motion must be voted on before voting on the main motion.

Making a Motion

Below is an example of the proper way to make a motion.

Amy thinks it would be a good idea for her group to have a fund-raising project to increase the amount of money available to spend on group activities. When the president asks if there is any new business, Amy stands up and says, "Madame President."

The president recognizes Amy by calling her name, "Amy."

Amy says, "I move that we have a fund-raising project to make more money available for group activities."

Kevin, another group member, agrees and says, "I second the motion."

Then, the president says, "It has been moved by Amy and seconded that we have a fund-raising project to make more money available for group activities. Is there any discussion?"

As the presenter of the motion, Amy explains why she thinks the group needs more money in its budget. Then, other members comment about the motion. Individually, they stand, address the president, are recognized, and voice their opinions.

When the comments end, the president asks, "Is there any further discussion?" If no more speakers rise, the president calls for a vote by saying, "We will now vote on the motion to have a fund-raising project. All in favor of the motion say 'aye' (or raise your hand)." The president counts the votes.

"Those opposed say 'no' (or raise your hand)." The president counts again. "The ayes have it. The motion to have a fund-raising project passes."

Amending a Motion

Suppose Randy, a member of Amy's group, is not exactly satisfied with Amy's motion. He is in favor of having a fund-raising project, but he feels all the money earned should be used toward the group's annual banquet. During the discussion of the main motion, Randy decides to amend the motion. He stands and says, "Madame President." After being recognized by the president, Randy continues, "I move to amend the motion by changing the words *group activities* to *the annual banquet*." Barbara, the secretary, seconds the motion.

The president handles this secondary motion just as she did the main motion. She says, "It has been moved by Randy and seconded that the pending motion be amended by changing the words *group activities* to *the annual banquet*. Is there any discussion?" The group can then discuss their views on this motion. After the discussion, the president calls for a vote on the amendment.

The amendment is always dealt with prior to taking action on the main motion. If the amendment passes, the issue before the group is the motion as amended. If the amendment does not pass, the issue is the original motion.

Tabling a Motion

Tabling a motion is another secondary motion that can be made. The purpose of this motion is to postpone the group from making a decision on the main motion. A member might make this motion because he or she feels the motion would have a better chance of passing at a later date. A member might also table a motion if the business meeting is running long.

The motion to table a motion is not debatable. Consequently, the president states the motion and goes straight to a vote. Again, the majority vote rules.

Adjournment

Parliamentary procedure also notes a special way to close a meeting. In order for the president to end the meeting, there must be a motion from one of the members to adjourn. The president can also ask for a motion to adjourn. After a motion and a second to the motion, the president declares the meeting adjourned.

Checkpoint 14.2

1. What is *Robert's Rules of Order*?
2. Why do many groups use parliamentary procedure during important meetings?
3. What is the difference between a standing committee and a special committee?
4. What is a *program*?
5. Explain the difference between a main motion and a secondary motion.

Build Your Vocabulary

As you progress through this text, develop a personal glossary of career-related terms and add it to your portfolio. This will help build your vocabulary and prepare you for your career of choice. Write a definition for each of the following terms, and add it to your personal career glossary.

parliamentary procedure
quorum
standing committees
special committees
main motion
secondary motion

Chapter Summary

Section 14.1 Types of Meetings

- Meetings provide opportunities for members to share information. By meeting, team members are able to conduct business and develop goals during a meeting.
- Many meetings are conducted through teleconferencing and videoconferencing. These types of meetings allow people in multiple locations to meet remotely and discuss ideas.

Section 14.2 Parliamentary Procedure

- Parliamentary procedure is a set of rules for formal meetings where official business is being conducted. The book, *Robert's Rules of Order,* contains very specific rules for how formal group should operate.
- Formal meetings should be run according to parliamentary procedure. These procedures include who will play what role in a meeting and how suggestions brought up by a member should be dealt with as part of the meeting.

Check Your Career IQ

Now that you have finished the chapter, see what you learned about careers by taking the chapter posttest. The test can be accessed on the mobile site by using a smartphone or on the G-W Learning companion website.

www.m.g-wlearning.com
www.g-wlearning.com

Review Your Knowledge

1. Provide three examples of why coworkers gather for a workplace meeting.
2. What is an *informal meeting*?
3. List three tips to remember during a web conference meeting.
4. What are the disadvantages of web conferencing?
5. How is a committee chairperson appointed?
6. What are "approved minutes"?
7. According to parliamentary procedure, who usually calls a meeting to order?
8. What is the purpose of the treasurer's report?
9. Why might a member move to table a motion?
10. Do members need to vote to adjourn a meeting? Explain.

Apply Your Knowledge

1. Review the guidelines for participating in a meeting. Identify three guidelines you think are the most important. In writing, explain why each selected guideline is most important to you.

2. Imagine you are presiding over a formal meeting. Explain how you will use the resources of time, materials, and people efficiently. Summarize your comments on one page and report the main points to the class.

3. Use the Internet to learn more about parliamentary procedure. Conduct research to answer questions that relate to *who, what, when,* and *how.* Take notes during your research. Share two interesting points you learned with the rest of the class.

4. Together with your group, create a one-act play demonstrating parliamentary procedure. Perform your play for the class.

5. Compare and contrast a video conference meeting with a face-to-face meeting. How are they alike? How are the two different? What are the pros and cons of each type of meeting? Compile your information in a chart.

6. Think of a committee on which you would like to work. What is the name of the committee? What does the committee do? Why is it of interest to you? What can you contribute to the committee? What can you do to get involved with the committee or related organization? Share your answers with a partner.

7. Approved minutes show an accurate record of what takes place during a meeting. Imagine you are the secretary for the Z Club. Last night at 7:00 p.m., your club held a one-hour meeting to discuss membership fees, a summer picnic, and an upcoming fund-raiser. Create a record of minutes noting what transpired during the meeting. What important information should be noted for future reference? Share your record of minutes with your class.

8. Choose a group or organization in your school or community. What are the offices held by the leading body? Who are the officers, and what are their responsibilities? Compile your answer in a chart. (You may speak with a person from the group or organization, or use print or online sources.)

9. Use the Internet to learn more about bylaws. What kinds of groups or organizations use bylaws? What are some common subjects covered in bylaws? Explain why bylaws are needed in an organization or group. Write a one-page paper on your findings.

10. Consider what a conversation would sound like if you and your friends used parliamentary procedure in daily conversation. With a partner, greet each other and have a conversation using parliamentary procedure. Describe your experience with the rest of the class.

Teamwork

Working in a group, practice parliamentary procedure. Take turns role-playing officers giving reports and making motions during a formal meeting. Then, consider how legislative officials would conduct business without rules. What would a legislative session without the use of parliamentary procedure look like? Why do you think most organizations use parliamentary procedure during meetings? How does parliamentary procedure make speaking out in a group easier? Share your group's answers with the rest of the class.

G-W Learning Mobile Site

Visit the G-W Learning mobile site to complete the chapter pretest and post test and to practice vocabulary using e-flash cards. If you do not have a smartphone, visit the G-W Learning companion website to access these features.
G-W Learning mobile site: www.m.g-wlearning.com
G-W Learning companion website: www.g-wlearning.com

Common Core

College and Career Readiness

Listening. Engage in a conversation with someone you rarely speak to or have never spoken to before. Ask the person what role he or she likes to play when attending a meeting—leader, active participant, active listener (someone who may ask clarifying questions and takes notes), or passive listener (someone who takes in the information without reacting to it). Actively listen to what that person is sharing. Build on his or her ideas by sharing your own. Try this again with other people you rarely speak to or have never spoken to before. How clearly were they able to articulate themselves? How do you think having a conversation with someone you do not normally speak to is different from a conversation you might have with a friend or family member you speak with every day?
Speaking. The way you communicate in the workplace will have a lot to do with the success of the professional relationships you build with others. There are different ways you communicate with different people in your life. For example, there are formal and informal ways of communicating your message. Create two short speeches introducing yourself to others. The audience for the first speech should be your friends. Design the second speech for a hiring committee or human resources director. Deliver each speech to your class. How did the words, phrases, and tone change in the different speeches?

Apply Your Technology Skills

Access the G-W Learning companion website for this text at www.g-wlearning.com. Download the data file for this chapter. Follow the instructions to complete activities to practice what you have learned in this chapter.

Data File 14–1—**Understanding Parliamentary Procedure**

College and Career Readiness Portfolio

College and Career Readiness

When you apply for a job, a volunteer position, or admission to a college, you may be asked to complete an application. An application is a form or document used to request admission, membership, or hiring. The length of an application varies, but all applications require specific information from the applicant. For example, an application will have spaces for you to write or type your name, address, phone numbers, and other contact data. Spaces for your education, skills, and work history are also typically included. Always be honest when completing an application. Do not give false information or overstate your skills or experience. You may be asked to complete the application while on site. This means you will have to fill it out by hand. Completing an application takes patience and time, so you should practice filling out several different applications.

1. Download several applications from the Internet or obtain them from other sources. Practice completing several applications by hand. Your goal is for the application to be complete and accurate. Finally, it should have a clean, neat appearance.
2. Scan the two best applications to place in your e-portfolio.
3. Place the completed applications in the container for your print portfolio.

Unit 4 Career Planning

Lifespan Plan

Acquiring Skills

Many of the careers that are forecasted to have the greatest growth over the next 30 years did not exist 30 years ago. People who enter the workforce today will likely make several job changes over their lifetime. Technology and market conditions change. Workers need to be flexible and willing to learn new things all of the time. Developing a set of skills that you can transfer from use on one job to use on another is increasingly important. Some of the most sought-after transferrable skills are leadership, communication, creativity, organization, and the ability to use data to make decisions. Think about what effect transferrable skills will play in your life and career.

Activities

1. Review the material you have put together as part of your lifespan project. Consider the skills necessary to reach your goals. Make a list of the skills you have now. How could you best display those skills to a potential employer?
2. Record instances where you have demonstrated leadership skills. Also, record instances in which you have shown your communication, creative, and organizational skills. Do not forget to include school, team, paid work, and volunteer experiences where you have displayed these skills.
3. Save your notes according to your instructor's specifications.

Unit Overview

At this point, no one expects you to make a final decision on one specific career. You still have lots of time. Some students choose a career early in their school life, and they stick with it. However, the majority will take their time and establish themselves in a career at a later date. Consider using this time in your life to develop your skills and assess your career interests. Do not let anyone rush you into a career field that is not compatible with your aptitudes. The information in this unit should help you in making decisions about future career possibilities.

Chapter 15   Learning about Yourself
Chapter 16   Learning about Careers
Chapter 17   Making Career Decisions

Picture Success

Bart Slabbekorn
TSA

A Career and Technical Student Organization (CTSO) can have a positive impact on its members and sponsors. Read about Bart's experience with TSA in his own words.

"My involvement with the TSA prepared me for the leadership challenges I have faced as a Marine officer. From the time I joined the Bearden Middle School TSA chapter in Knoxville, Tennessee, through my career in TSA at Bearden High when I became the National TSA President, I took part in many competitions. Extemporaneous Speech, Chapter Team, and Technology Problem Solving are just a few of the events in which I competed. I also attended many local, regional and national leadership training conferences and workshops. These activities helped to prepare me for my future career. I use communication and problem-solving skills every day, and I acquired many of these skills through TSA.

After college and law school, I served as a Judge Advocate, which is an attorney, in the Marine Corps for the past eight years. In that time, I tried many cases as a prosecutor and as a defense attorney. In 2008, I deployed to Iraq, where I worked with the local Iraqi people to reestablish the rule of law in their country. Now, I am an environmental law attorney. My work involves advising commanders throughout the West coast on compliance matters, from the Clean Air Act to climate change and energy."

Bart Slabbekorn

Section 15.1
Assessing Yourself

Section 15.2
Exploring Who You Are

College and Career Readiness

Reading Prep. Before reading this chapter, look at the chapter title. What does the title tell you about what you will be learning? Compare and contrast the information to be presented with information you already know about the subject matter from sources such as videos and online media.

Introduction

At this point in your life, you might think you know yourself pretty well. This might be true. However, it is also true that the better you know yourself, the better prepared you will be to make decisions about your education, career, and lifestyle.

Knowing yourself means knowing what is really important to you. If earning a lot of money is important to you, having a career that pays very well will likely be important to you too. If spending time with family and friends is important to you, choosing a career that has a set work week will be a consideration in the career you choose.

Being aware of what you do well is another piece of the career puzzle. By trying new things, you will see what you do well as well as what you enjoy doing. As you can imagine, this takes work. It requires careful self-assessment and the willingness to look inside yourself and ask questions, such as What are my lifestyle goals? What skills do I have? What do I do well? What type of work appeals to me?

Check Your Career IQ

Before you begin the chapter, see what you already know about careers by taking the chapter pretest. Use the related QR code to view the pretest on the mobile site. If you do not have a smartphone, visit the G-W Learning companion website to access the pretest.

www.m.g-wlearning.com
www.g-wlearning.com

G-W Mobile

Career Snapshot

President of the United States

Government & Public Administration

What Does the President of the United States Do?

The President of the United States is both the head of state and head of government of the United States of America. He also serves as the Commander-in-Chief of the US armed forces. The president must:

- be an inspiring example for the American people;
- serve as the "boss" for millions of government workers in the Executive Branch;
- decide what American diplomats and ambassadors will say to foreign governments;
- take charge of the US Armed Forces; and
- use the office to influence Congress during the lawmaking process.

What Is It Like to Work as President of the United States?

The President of the United States has a comfortable work environment. The office of president provides access to other top government officials all over the world. Extensive travel is required. However, the position includes flexible benefits and instant name recognition.

Some of the disadvantages are extremely long work days and a very high-pressure work environment.

What Education and Skills Are Needed to Be President of the United States?

- college degree preferred
- ability to lead and make sound decisions
- excellent problem-solving, analysis, and communication skills
- high ethical standards; strong interpersonal skills

Gary Blakeley/Shutterstock.com
Georgios Kollidas/Shutterstock.com
Christopher Halloran/Shutterstock.com

15.1 | Assessing Yourself

Terms

self-concept
self-esteem
self-assessment
soft skill
hard skill
interest
aptitude
General Aptitude Test Battery (GATB)
ability

Objectives

After completing this section, you will be able to:
- **Explain** the importance of self-concept.
- **Describe** the components of making a self-assessment.

Developing Your Self-Concept

Part of learning about yourself is thinking about your self-concept. **Self-concept** is the mental image you have of yourself. As you go through adolescence, you may feel two interacting forces pulling you. One force is the need to become increasingly independent. The other force is a need to feel good about who you are and what you do. The development of your self-concept is a lifelong process.

What you think about yourself will affect how you allow others to affect your decisions. You will be influenced in many ways. Your close friends may help you believe in your own ability to cope with pressure. On the other hand, some peer groups can have a negative influence. Classmates who believe it is okay to lie or cheat are examples of negative influences. When you have a positive, strong self-concept, you are not easily swayed by negative influences. Your personal beliefs and decision-making skills will greatly influence your self-concept.

For you to develop a strong, positive self-concept, it is important to:
- believe in your capabilities;
- believe you can control your life;
- exercise self-discipline and self-control;
- use effective communication skills; and
- demonstrate flexibility and integrity.

You will find that these skills do not develop in isolation. They are dependent on one another. For example, deciding not to experiment with illegal substances will require you to use your decision-making skills and communication skills. Self-discipline and self-control must be applied as well.

olly/Shutterstock.com

A person with a strong, positive self-concept is not easily persuaded by negative influences.

It is important to have a person in your life who exerts a strong positive influence and steers you clear of risky behavior and its pitfalls. This person may be a parent, mentor, coach, brother, sister, or friend. It is helpful to have basic positive values to rely on and someone to talk with when you are facing negative temptations. Adolescence is a time when you develop the attitudes, knowledge, and skills that will directly impact your self-concept for the rest of your life.

When you have a positive self-concept, you feel a sense of confidence and satisfaction, which leads to high self-esteem. **Self-esteem** is a feeling of self-worth and confidence. When you have high self-esteem, you recognize and value your uniqueness. You are proud of who you are and what you do.

People with high self-esteem believe they can handle life's challenges. They will often have a sense of confidence and a positive attitude. People with low self-esteem often tend to see themselves as failures and, consequently, avoid everyday challenges.

Making a Self-Assessment

Self-assessment is the process of taking stock of your skills, interests, aptitudes, and abilities. Through self-assessment you are better able to plan your future. You will find it easier to select hobbies and elective courses in school. You will also find it easier to make plans for your life. Sometimes self-assessment techniques may involve thinking exercises or written or electronic testing. Whatever method is used, take the process of self-assessment seriously.

High self-esteem leads to a sense of confidence and satisfaction.

Apollofoto/Shutterstock.com

What Are Your Skills and Interests?

To know and understand yourself, you need to analyze your skills and interests. As discussed in Chapter 1, skills are the things you do well. You will transfer many of the skills you acquire in life and school to your future career. For example, you use the skills of thinking logically, reading, writing, and speaking during class participation and homework activities. These skills will transfer to other situations, including the workplace.

Starting at birth, humans begin to develop soft skills. Influenced by one's environment, **soft skills** are personal skills that affect how an individual interacts with others. Soft skills relate to your personality traits, social interactions, communication abilities, and personal habits. Your soft skills tend to complement your **hard skills**, which are teachable skills learned as requirements of a career or other activities.

Your **interests** are the activities, events, and ideas that you like. What do you enjoy doing the most? How do you like to spend your time? What are your hobbies? What do you like most in school? What would you do if you had spare time? Your answers to these questions should help you identify careers that will be interesting to you.

Sometimes people have a hard time determining their interests. One day a person may have a strong desire to become a teacher but later have little interest in teaching. It is important for you to get involved in a variety of positive activities. Interests are learned, so unless you have tried something, you do not know for sure if you are interested in it. As you experience new activities, you are more likely to meet people and develop different interests.

Ethical Leadership

Assertiveness

"Our lives begin to end the day we become silent about things that matter." —Martin Luther King, Jr.

The workplace is where you learn   about yourself. One issue that may come up is your assertiveness, especially when your values differ from what you may see while on the job. You may observe someone stealing from the company. You may overhear other workers talking about doing something on the job you feel is unethical. You may observe someone doing something that violates your principles. What you hear or observe may put you in the difficult position of deciding whether to report it or not. You will need to carefully consider your values and your expectations as an employee to make an ethical decision.

In your work-based learning experience, you may discover new career interests. You may also realize that an earlier career interest now seems uninteresting. Learning about different careers and occupations helps you determine what careers are of interest to you. Job shadowing experiences can also be a good way to help you understand what duties are involved with a job.

If you find it hard to identify your interests, talk to others. Listen to those who know you well. Your friends and family members may be able to help you recall the activities you have enjoyed the most or the projects you have done well. Also, ask others about their careers and what they like most and least about what they do.

Another way to become more aware of your interests is to take an activities-preference inventory. Most high school guidance departments are prepared to give preference tests to students. The inventory is designed to help you determine if you prefer working with people, objects, or ideas. You are usually given several activities and asked to select the one activity that appeals to you most. After completing the inventory, you are given a key to interpret the results.

If the inventory indicates you would primarily enjoy working with people, you may want to consider a career in social work, teaching, sales, or health care services. If the inventory points to objects, you might want a job as a fashion illustrator, auto technician, baker, or machine operator. An interest in ideas would suggest careers in publishing, advertising, or marketing. These are only a few examples of the types of careers related to people, objects, and ideas.

Keep in mind that one person or test cannot tell you what to do with your life. He or she can only provide direction and help you consider possibilities of which you may not have been aware. It is up to you to make the final decisions about your career goals. The information in Figure 15-1 may help you become more aware of your interests and how they relate to choosing a career.

Career Interest Concepts	
Concepts	**Examples**
There are many interest areas in a career.	A grain farmer may have an interest in growing vegetables, working for himself, and operating machinery. The farmer might also have an interest in athletics or upholstering, but these interests are not needed in farming.
People have interest areas they do not want to pursue as a career.	An auto technician may have gardening as a hobby but may not want an occupation as a farmer or horticulturist.
Genuine interest is important for success in any career.	Working at something you like is more pleasant.
Each person has many interests.	A person may have interests in music, athletics, mechanical things, and people.
Different careers may involve the same or similar interests.	A salesperson, politician, teacher, and lawyer are interested in working with people and, in some way, influencing them.

Figure 15-1.   *Goodheart-Willcox Publisher*
As you think about your career interests, consider these basic concepts.

What Are Your Aptitudes?

To be successful in a career, you need to have more than just an interest in it. You also need to have an aptitude for it. An **aptitude** is a person's natural, physical, and mental talents for learning. If you have an aptitude for a certain skill, you will be able to learn the skill easily and perform the skill well.

If you have an aptitude for writing, for example, perhaps you could become a successful journalist or blogger. On the other hand, if you do not have this aptitude and still try to become a writer, doing well in that career may forever be a struggle for you. Be realistic about your aptitudes. Become aware of your mental and physical limitations, as well as your strengths.

To learn more about your aptitudes, ask your guidance counselor if your school gives any aptitude tests. For example, the **General Aptitude Test Battery (GATB)** is a series of tests that measure nine aptitudes. By taking these tests, you will get a better idea of the kinds of careers in which you have the best chances for success. Additional tests you may encounter in school are the SAT and ACT. The SAT assesses your readiness for college. Similarly, the ACT assesses your mastery of state and college readiness standards. Some students may also take the ACCUPLACER test, which provides information about academic skills in math, reading, and writing. The Armed Services Vocational Aptitude Battery (ASVAB) is designed to measure strengths, weaknesses, and potential for future success.

What Are Your Abilities?

Ability is a mastery of a skill or the capacity to do something. Abilities are learned through training and practice. You are born with certain aptitudes, but you must develop your abilities and skills.

Abilities are developed more easily if you have related aptitudes. For example, if you have physical aptitudes for rhythm and coordination, you will probably excel quickly in a ballroom dancing class. If you have very little aptitude for dancing, hard work and genuine interest can help you overcome low aptitudes. You can develop your aptitude through study and practice. For example, taking dancing lessons and practicing regularly will help you develop the ability to dance.

Your interests, aptitudes, and abilities all need to be considered in career planning. Most people are usually interested in the activities they do best, but sometimes that may not be the case. A person may want to become a professional basketball player but not have the physical aptitude for the sport. Sometimes a person may have the ability to play a musical instrument but not have the interest to do so. The ideal situation is to have the mental and physical aptitudes and abilities that relate to a career that interests you.

As you think about possible career choices, remember to consider your interests, abilities, and aptitudes.

Aleksandr Markin/Shutterstock.com

Checkpoint 15.1

1. Name four things you can do to develop a positive self-concept.
2. What does an activities-preference inventory help you to do?
3. What are three things you can do to help you identify your interests?
4. Explain the difference between an aptitude and ability.
5. How is it possible to overcome a lack of aptitudes for a given activity?

Build Your Vocabulary

As you progress through this text, develop a personal glossary of career-related terms and add it to your portfolio. This will help build your vocabulary and prepare you for your career of choice. Write a definition for each of the following terms, and add it to your personal career glossary.

self-concept
self-esteem
self-assessment
soft skill
hard skill
interest
aptitude
General Aptitude Test Battery (GATB)
ability

Objectives

After completing this section you will be able to:
- **Identify** how personalities may influence life choices.
- **Explain** how your values influence your behaviors.
- **Describe** the importance of creating goals.

Terms

personality
id
ego
superego
habit
learning style
values
ethics
lifestyle goal
short-term goal
long-term goal
standard
standard of living
resource

Your Personal Characteristics

Everyone has a personality. **Personality** is the unique way an individual thinks, feels, and interacts. Your personality influences the way other people feel about you.

Your personal characteristics are a combination of your personality traits and your behavioral habits. They make you distinct from everyone else. It is commonly accepted that a person's personality is influenced by the id, ego, and superego.

The **id** is the part of your mind that is driven by thrills, impulses, and desires. The drive of the id may have no awareness of reality and consequences. On the other hand, the **ego** is the part of your mind that is aware of reality and demonstrates control. The ego tries to balance the demands of the id with the constraints of reality.

The **superego** is the part of the mind that is influenced by social morals and values. Your superego serves as a counterbalance to the id by introducing morals and values during the decision-making process. As a result, the superego will help slow down the pleasure-seeking demands of the id. All three of these elements play a crucial role in the development of your personality traits and how you make decisions.

Go Green

It is important to take time to reflect and assess your current feelings about the "go green" concept. In other words: how do you feel about adopting an environmentally friendly lifestyle by recycling, buying local, reusing, minimizing driving, etc.? Are you willing to make the extra effort to sort plastics, paper, glass and metals from your household trash? Are you committed to buying local when possible, and are you really willing to walk or ride a bike when it might be a bit more convenient to drive?

Personality Traits

Different careers require different personality traits. That is why it is important to consider your personality when establishing your career goals. Suppose a person has a quiet, reserved personality and likes to spend a lot of time alone reading. This person probably would not enjoy a career in sales. Being successful in sales requires an outgoing personality and spending much time talking with others. Knowing your personality will make it easier to establish career goals that are comfortable to you. Figure 15-2 shows a list of personality traits and some career areas that complement each.

Personality and Careers	
Personality Trait	**Ideal Career Area**
helpful	food, hotel, and passenger services
artistic	decorating, creative writing, performing
detail-oriented	reporting, bookkeeping, engineering
enterprising	sales, promotions, demonstrations
questioning	inspections, research, repair services
protective	childcare, law enforcement, emergency services
social	teaching, interviewing, coaching

Figure 15-2.   *Goodheart-Willcox Publisher*
You will be happier if you select a career that suits your personality traits.

Habits

A **habit** is something you do repeatedly, in the same way. Your daily life includes many habits, such as the way you stand, sit, talk, walk, and gesture when speaking. The habits you form are a part of your personality, and they influence the way others see you.

Habits can be good or bad. For example, arriving to work and school on time every day is a good habit. Being late frequently is a bad habit. It is wise to examine your habits periodically. Do you have good grooming habits? Do you have annoying mannerisms? What new habits would you like to establish? What old habits would you like to change?

Learning Styles

Learning styles are the different ways people take in information and process it. Knowing your preferred learning style or styles can help you determine the best way for you to learn new information or skills. It can also help you identify potential career interests.

Eight common learning styles are described in Figure 15-3. While looking at the chart, keep in mind that one learning style is no better than any other. Also, notice that there is some overlap among the styles. It is common for people to use more than one learning style. However, most people have at least one preferred learning style.

Learning Style	Learning Preferences	Effective Learning Strategies
Interpersonal	work with people, talk, join groups	relating, sharing, cooperating, interviewing
Intrapersonal	work alone, pursue personal interests	setting own pace, reflecting, having private space
Kinesthetic	touch, move, balance	touching objects, moving around, understanding body movements
Logical/ Mathematical	work with numbers, perform experiments, solve problems	classifying, categorizing, identifying relationships, recognizing patterns
Musical	sing, hum, listen to music, play an instrument	listening to recordings, composing music
Naturalist	work in natural setting, explore nature, organize	working with nature, seeing patterns, connecting ideas to nature
Verbal/ Linguistic	write, read, tell stories	reading, listening to spoken works, writing, discussing
Visual/Spatial	draw, create, build, look	drawing, working with pictures, creating maps and charts, visualizing

Figure 15-3.   *Goodheart-Willcox Publisher*
Identify the learning style that best suits you.

Because of your preferred learning style, you might find it easier to learn certain kinds of information or develop specific skills. Knowing this can help you plan for college and choose a career. You will want to explore college programs and careers that complement your preferred learning style.

Your Values and Ethics

Values are the principles and beliefs that you consider important. What are your values? What principles and beliefs are important to you? To most people, friendship, honesty, good health, and compassion are important. Education, popularity, new cars, a happy family life, and money are also important to many people. Examine what is important to you and why. Identifying the ideals and objects that are important to you will help you develop your career goals.

For instance, being able to wear blue jeans and casual clothes to work may be important to you. If so, you probably would not be happy in a situation where suits or dress clothes are required. If you prefer a quiet, comfortable environment, you would probably dislike a noisy, bustling factory.

Identify your values. Then, rank them in order of importance. Your values guide your behavior and help you develop a sense of direction in your life. Being aware of them will also enable you to

Making and maintaining friendships is a value that most people consider highly important. What values are most important to you?

Edyta Pawlowska/Shutterstock.com

make lifestyle choices more easily. For example, suppose a challenging job and a well-paying job are in keeping with your values. However, you rank the challenging job near the top of your list and the well-paying job lower down. Therefore, you could probably conclude that a challenging job would be more important to you than a boring job with higher pay. The values that you have influence your decisions and actions.

Have you ever heard people say, "She is not ethical," or "He lacks basic ethics"? **Ethics** are the set of moral values that guide a person's conduct. Calling in sick to school on a sunny spring day, taking credit for another student's work, or lying to a friend are all unethical behavior.

It is important to always behave in a way that is true to your values. Your ethics should be your guide when making tough decisions. Do not let school pressures, family demands, work conditions, finances, peer pressure, or even goals keep you from acting ethically at all times.

When conflicts of ethics arise, it is helpful to carefully study all the pros and cons of different possible reactions to a situation. Take a long-term view and decide what decisions or behaviors are in keeping with your moral values. What actions will you take to resolve a problem? Will your actions conflict with your conscience? Are these actions acceptable by society's standards?

Public Speaking

Public speaking is a competitive event you might enter with your organization. This event allows you to showcase your communication skills of speaking, organizing, and making an oral presentation. This is usually a timed event you can prepare for prior to the competition. You will have time to research, prepare, and practice before going to the competition.

To prepare for the public speaking event do the following activities:

1. Read the guidelines provided by your organization. Make certain you ask any questions about points you do not understand. It is important that you follow each specific item outlined in the competition rules.

2. Ask your instructor for a list of topics you can use to practice making impromptu speeches.

3. Practice the presentation. You should introduce yourself, review the topic that is being presented, defend the topic being presented, and conclude with a summary.

4. Practice, practice, practice. Your speech will be judged by a panel of professionals. Practice your speech in front of your peers until you are comfortable.

5. Ask your teacher to play the role of Competition Judge. After the presentation is complete, ask for feedback from your teacher. You may also consider presenting your speech to your student organization or local community service organization.

Your Goals

Goals are what you want to attain. A person's goals are usually based on his or her values. For example, John likes listening to music through high quality headphones. However, John's headphones do not work very well anymore. John has set a goal to buy new headphones in six months by saving a portion of each paycheck. Have you thought about your goals? What do you want to do with your life? What do you want to accomplish?

The first step in setting and achieving life goals is to make a list of lifestyle goals. **Lifestyle goals** reflect what you want from life. Deciding where you want to live, if you want a family, and how much money you need to be comfortable are all examples of lifestyle goals. As you set goals for your life, you should also be sure to include both short-term goals and long-term goals.

A **short-term goal** is a goal to be reached tomorrow, next week, or within a few months. Getting an A on your next English assignment, becoming an officer in a school organization, and improving your tennis game are examples of short-term goals. A **long-term goal** is a goal that may take several months or years to achieve. Completing school, starting a career, and buying a car are examples of long-term goals.

Your goals will often reflect your values and your outlook on the future.

Stephen Coburn/Shutterstock.com

One important factor to remember when setting goals is to be realistic. Do you really want to reach that goal? Is it possible for you to reach it? What will it cost in terms of time, energy, and money? Is the goal in keeping with your values? Setting well-defined, realistic goals can help you develop a sense of direction and purpose in life.

Standards

A **standard** is an accepted level of achievement. There are standards for dress, cleanliness, food and drug safety, and school grades, to name a few examples. Electrical products must meet certain safety standards before they are given a seal of approval. People in professions, such as law and medicine must meet certain standards before they can practice in their fields.

Individuals also have their own personal standards, called *standards of living*. A person's **standard of living** refers to the goods and services considered essential for living. For some, an elegant residence, gourmet food, and frequent world travel are essential. For many people, their standard of living consists of a comfortable home, occasional restaurant meals, and weekend trips close to home.

Standards are closely related to values and goals. You will have high standards for whatever you consider important. For example, if you place importance on making the school honor roll, and you set aside time to study regularly, your standards for grades would be high. On the other hand, if you do not care much about clothes and pay little attention to the quality and style of clothing you wear, your standards for clothes would not be high.

Those with high standards are willing to work hard to achieve successful results.

Pete Saloutos/Shutterstock.com

What are your standards regarding work? Do you strive to do your very best on the job, or do you just put in your hours? Do you have high standards for the way you look and dress? What are your standards for education? Knowing your own standards and what you expect from life can help you understand yourself better. This can help you establish satisfying lifestyle goals.

Resources

As you pursue your goals, you should be aware of the resources you have and those available to you. **Resources** are all the things that can be used to reach a goal. For example, a Career and Technical Student Organization is a resource that can help you learn more about career opportunities. People can also be a good resource. Your academic advisor would be an excellent resource for learning more about developing an academic plan or selecting a college.

Personal resources are the resources you have within yourself, such as skills, knowledge, and experience. Personal resources are *intangible*, not concrete. To recognize your personal resources, you need to know your unique strengths and abilities. What do you do well? What are your true strengths and abilities? In addition, what personal resources do you possess? Determination, motivation, and imagination are valuable personal resources. *Tangible resources* are the material things you have or can use to achieve goals, such as money, tools, clothes, and community resources.

Identifying your resources helps you identify your strengths and weaknesses. For example, if you know you have artistic talents (a personal resource), you will probably be successful pursuing a career in art. If you want to enter college or postsecondary training but do not have enough money (a tangible resource), you may apply for a scholarship, get a loan, or work part-time. Being aware of your resources can help you set realistic goals for your life and career.

Checkpoint 15.2

1. What is the function of the superego?
2. List three things that can influence the ethics of people.
3. What is the difference between a short-term goal and a long-term goal?
4. Who determines the ethics of a group?
5. What are some examples of tangible resources?

Build Your Vocabulary

As you progress through this text, develop a personal glossary of career-related terms and add it to your portfolio. This will help build your vocabulary and prepare you for your career of choice. Write a definition for each of the following terms, and add it to your personal career glossary.

personality
id
ego
superego
habit
learning style
values
ethics
lifestyle goal
short-term goal
long-term goal
standard
standard of living
resource

Case

Reporting Expenses

Juliet is going on a business trip. This is a good opportunity for her to find new clients for her company and enjoy herself at the same time. She realizes the importance of doing a good job, but if she spends too much, she may upset her boss and get stuck with the bill. It is very important for Juliet to abide by the company's policy on travel expenses.

Juliet also has to take a mental inventory of her own values and ethics. She knows these will affect how she reports her travel expenses.

While most companies do not object to employees rounding up expenses to the nearest dollar, they consider it dishonest to turn in a receipt for an expense an employee did not have. For example, Juliet's employer says she is allowed to spend $32 on dinner. She knows it is dishonest to turn in a receipt for the entire $32 if she just grabs a hamburger and cola. In some restaurants, Juliet will be offered the temptation to cheat. Some eating establishments present the customer with the actual bill, along with a blank bill on which the customer may write any amount.

On her trip, Juliet meets an old friend from another company, and they decide to go out together to eat. After the meal, when the checks are presented, Juliet learns that her friend Cara is not required to turn in receipts for meals. Cara is simply reimbursed a certain fixed amount per day.

Cara pays for her meal, knowing that her reimbursement is automatic. Juliet considers taking Cara's receipt and turning it in with her expense account. The boss will probably think that Juliet was being a good salesperson by taking a potential client to lunch. In this way, Juliet will make some extra money.

Juliet does not tell Cara her plan, but Cara knows and simply hands her receipt to Juliet. Before heading back to their hotels, the friends promise to meet again tomorrow.

"Let's go to a real expensive place tomorrow," Juliet said. "We deserve it."

"Can you afford it?" Cara asked.

"I'll find a way," replied Juliet.

Critical Thinking

1. Is Juliet, Cara, or both guilty of unethical behavior?
2. If ethical behavior had been used, how would this story change?
3. What should Juliet do when she makes out her expense account after the trip?

Chapter Summary

Section 15.1 Assessing Yourself

- It is important to have a strong, positive self-concept. The development of your self-concept is a lifelong process.
- Through self-assessment, you are better able to plan your future. When you make a self-assessment, you should consider your skills, interests, aptitudes, and abilities.

Section 15.2 Exploring Who You Are

- Matching your personality with a suitable career will increase your chances for success and happiness on the job. You should consider your personality when choosing a career.
- Your values help guide your behavior. Once you understand your values, you can use them to help you set goals.
- When setting lifestyle goals, be sure to include both short-term goals and long-term goals. How you achieve your goals will depend on your own personal standards and the resources available to you.

Check Your Career IQ

Now that you have finished the chapter, see what you learned about careers by taking the chapter posttest. The test can be accessed on the mobile site by using a smartphone or on the G-W Learning companion website.

www.m.g-wlearning.com
www.g-wlearning.com

Review Your Knowledge

1. If you find it hard to identify your interests, why should you consider the help of family and friends?
2. What four areas should you examine when making a self-assessment?
3. Whom should you ask to learn more about aptitude tests given at your school?
4. Name the three parts of the mind known to influence a person's personality.
5. Explain the difference between the id and the ego.
6. Why is it important to understand your personality when establishing your career goals?
7. What learning strategies would be most helpful to a visual learner? Explain why.

8. In what ways does an interpersonal learner differ from an intrapersonal learner?

9. According to the authors, what is the first step in setting and achieving goals?

10. What are the two types of resources a person should use to pursue his or her goals? Give an example of each type.

Apply Your Knowledge

1. List twelve things you like to do. Next to each activity, note whether the activity involves mainly people, objects, or ideas. Evaluate your responses to see if you can form any conclusions about your interests and how they might influence your job choices.

2. Create a chart of your interests, aptitudes, and abilities. Do your interests complement your aptitudes and abilities? What might the chart indicate about your future careers? Write a brief summary of your findings.

3. Consider your values and what is important to you. Rank the following ideas in the order of importance: honesty, friendship, education, good health, compassion, and career. Which idea ranks the highest? The lowest? In the middle? Explain why.

4. Write several paragraphs that describe you. Use the following terms in your description: abilities, aptitudes, values, ethics, habits, interests, personality, resources, self-concept, self-esteem, and standards. Underline or circle the first use of each term. Then, list two or three careers that you think would be a good fit for you.

5. Make a list of your lifestyle goals. Be sure to include several short-term and long-term goals you might want to achieve.

6. Make a list of possible careers that would match your interests and aptitudes. Then write down any transferable skills that would correspond to these careers.

7. To learn more about your interests and abilities, interview two people who know you very well. Ask one friend and one family member to help you recall the activities you have enjoyed the most or the projects you have done well. List your activities in one column and your projects in a second column. Then, review the information together to choose two career clusters that might be a perfect fit for you. Below your chart, explain why these two clusters were selected. Share your findings with the class.

8. Complete the following activity with a small group. Study Figure 15-2. Select three personality traits that you think apply to you. Review the ideal career area that accompanies each personality trait you selected. How do you feel about the related career area listed in the second column? Does the chart provide an accurate match for you? Explain why the career area listed for your personality trait would or would not be of interest to you.

9. Work with a partner to demonstrate the function of the id, ego, and superego. For each situation below, what might the id, ego, and superego say during the decision-making process? You are trying to decide if you should do any of the following:
   • ride a roller coaster;
   • glance at your notes during a test;
   • go skydiving;
   • save money for a field trip;
   • help do chores on a sunny, Saturday afternoon; and
   • examine the contents of a lost wallet.
10. Write a one-page paper answering the following questions: What is self-esteem? Why is high self-esteem important? What are the effects of having high self-esteem?

Teamwork

Working with a small group, conduct Internet research on a person who is more than 50 years of age that the group admires. From the data you are able to gather, construct a career timeline that shows the person's career milestones and achievements. Review the timeline. What personality traits does this person have? How do you think these traits affected the pace and direction of his or her career? How do you think the pace of this person's career achievement compare to that of the average person?

G-W Learning Mobile Site

Visit the G-W Learning mobile site to complete the chapter pretest and posttest and to practice vocabulary using e-flash cards. If you do not have a smartphone, visit the G-W Learning companion website to access these features.
G-W Learning mobile site: www.m.g-wlearning.com
G-W Learning companion website: www.g-wlearning.com

Common Core

College and Career Readiness

Reading. Use the Internet or other resources to find articles about standardized tests. As you read, think about the author's point of view. What is the purpose of the article? What have you learned about standardized tests that you did not know before?
Writing. Using independent research and the information contained in the text, write a report in which you analyze and describe the use of aptitude tests, such as SAT, ACT, ACCUPLACER, and ASVAB. Why do these tests play such an important role in students' post-high school plans? Cite specific evidence from the text and your research to support your understanding of this issue.

Apply Your Technology Skills

Access the G-W Learning companion website for this text at www.g-wlearning.com. Download the data file for this chapter. Follow the instructions to complete activities to practice what you have learned in this chapter.

Data File 15–1—**Taking a Learning Styles Test**

College and Career Readiness Portfolio

College and Career Readiness

In an earlier activity, you completed an application by hand. However, you may need to complete an application electronically. You might do this by keying information into a form in a program, such as Microsoft Word or Adobe Acrobat. The completed form can be saved and sent by e-mail.

Another way to complete an application online is to key data in a screen on a website. *Submit* or a similar command is typically used to transmit the data. Be cautious about completing any application online in which you give personal data. Make sure the website is run by a legitimate business or organization and that the method used for sending your data is secure. You should practice filling out several online forms. If possible, review all the questions before you begin entering data.

1. Locate applications on the Internet for jobs, colleges, or volunteer service. You can also search for sample applications. Practice completing the forms, but stop there. DO NOT transmit the form. Remember, this is only a practice activity.

2. If possible, print the completed form for your print portfolio. Save or scan the form for your e-portfolio.

Section 16.1
Research Potential
Careers

Section 16.2
Prepare for Career
Success

College and Career Readiness

Reading Prep. Recall all the things you already know about choosing a career. As you read, think of how the new information presented in the text matches or challenges your prior understanding of the topic. Think of direct connections you can make between the old material and the new material.

Introduction

It is easier to consider career options for your future when you are aware of your interests and skills. Once you have that, you are ready to learn more about the career opportunities available to you. For example, do you know what careers are out there? How do you prepare for success in a chosen career? What factors might affect your career decision?

It is important to take the time to research careers that match your interests and abilities. As you begin to identify potential careers, you can more accurately determine what it takes to prepare for an occupation within a particular career cluster or pathway.

Check Your Career IQ

Before you begin the chapter, see what you already know about careers by taking the chapter pretest. Use the related QR code to view the pretest on the mobile site. If you do not have a smartphone, visit the G-W Learning companion website to access the pretest.

www.m.g-wlearning.com
www.g-wlearning.com

G-W Mobile

Career Snapshot
Dental Hygienist

Health Science

What Does a Dental Hygienist Do?

A **dental hygienist** removes soft and hard deposits from teeth, teaches patients how to practice good oral hygiene, and provides other preventive dental care. He or she examines patients' teeth and gums, recording the presence of diseases or abnormalities. A dental hygienist must:

- perform various dental procedures, which include removing tartar, stains, and plaque;
- use hand and rotary instruments and ultrasonic devices to clean and polish teeth;
- use x-ray machines to take dental pictures;
- use models of teeth to explain oral hygiene, perform periodontal therapy; and
- apply cavity-preventive agents, such as fluorides and pit and fissure sealants.

What Is It Like to Work as a Dental Hygienist?

Dental hygienists work in an environmentally controlled atmosphere, which is very comfortable and usually relatively quiet. Dental hygienists are often the first and last person to directly interact with the patient during a visit. Their demeanor in greeting patients may set the general tone for the patient's visit.

Dental hygienists may find it necessary to calm very nervous children, as well as some adults. Dental hygienists may also work beside the dentist during treatments.

What Education and Skills Are Needed to Be a Dental Hygienist?

- college degree preferred
- certification from an accredited dental hygiene school and state licensure
- excellent people skills
- detailed oriented

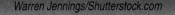

Warren Jennings/Shutterstock.com

16.1 Research Potential Careers

Objectives

After completing this section, you will be able to:
- **Identify** different types of career research sources.
- **Explain** the benefits of an informal interview.

Career Research Sources

How do you find the career that is best for you? The answer is research. To ensure you are prepared to make informed decisions, you need to research careers that match your job interests and skills. Now is a great time to learn as much as you can about opportunities available to you.

Many sources are available to help you research careers. These include local and school libraries, career information guides, the Internet, guidance counselors, and career fairs. You must take the initiative to find information about the careers that interest you. The more information you learn about careers, the more likely you will be able to select a satisfying one.

Libraries

Your local and school libraries are important sources of career information. Many books, brochures, magazines, websites, DVDs, CDs, and other resources are available on such topics as careers, occupations, job searching, and training. Once you begin your search, you will probably be amazed at the number of sources of information available.

As you begin to research careers, be sure to check your library's periodical section. The *Occupational Outlook Quarterly*, which is published by the US Department of Labor, is a good source for providing up-to-date career information. This publication can also be accessed online at www.bls.gov.

You can learn about careers by using the Internet and other resources at your local library.

BONNINSTUDIO/Shutterstock.com

Additional magazine articles can be found by searching online databases. These databases, and others like them, are available through your school library and the public library in your community. You can search for articles by subject or by specific job titles.

If you have any trouble locating information, do not hesitate to ask a librarian for help. If you know what careers you want to research, a librarian can help you locate the materials related to your interests.

Career Information Guides

The US Department of Labor provides valuable career information guides. These guides help you learn about occupations and career options. They can usually be found in local or school libraries or at your school guidance office. These guides are also available online. The **Occupational Outlook Handbook** describes the training and education needed for various occupations. It lists expected earnings, working conditions, and future job prospects.

Internet

There is a wealth of career information available on the Internet. You can go online and explore hundreds of career fields and thousands of specific jobs. Employers, as well as public and private research centers, keep their information about jobs and careers up-to-date.

Most company websites contain a link to career opportunities the company has available along with information on how to apply for a posted position. The same applies to a variety of social organizations, research companies, and educational institutions.

Ethical Leadership

Courage in a Partnership

"Courage is being afraid but going on anyhow."
—Dan Rather

At times, as a partner in a business, you may have to draw on your courage to do what is right. When faced with an ethical dilemma in a business partnership, and if you are in doubt, ask yourself these questions: Is it legal? Does it comply with the partnership's core values and beliefs? Would I want my family and friends to know about it?

If you do not feel comfortable seeking guidance from within the partnership, seek advice elsewhere. Remember to carefully consider your options. Then, make a decision that is a reflection of good ethics.

You can also locate other Internet sites for career research by using the search term *careers*. You will also find websites sponsored by professional organizations. For example, if you are interested in nursing, you can link to helpful information at the American Nurses Association website.

The following are government-sponsored sources that are a good place to begin your search.

Employment and Training Administration

The US Department of Labor's Employment and Training Administration (www.doleta.gov) is a resource for students, parents, guidance counselors, and others. It offers information and related web links for career exploration and planning. The administration offers tools for examining your interests and personality to help you identify suitable careers. Information on training and apprenticeships is also available. You can utilize the web links provided to learn more about applying to college, as well as pursuing a career in the Armed Forces.

Occupational Information Network (O*NET™)

The **Occupational Information Network (O*NET™)** (www.onetonline.org) is an Internet system that provides the latest information needed for effective training, education, counseling, and employment. The O*NET™ system offers three valuable features. The O*NET™ Database identifies and describes the key components of over 900 occupations. O*NET™ Online lets students, professionals, and job seekers explore a variety of occupations, prerequisite skills, and earning potential. The O*NET™ Career Exploration Tools are assessments that help students and job seekers identify their interests and abilities so they can search for careers that match their preferences.

CareerOneStop

CareerOneStop (www.careeronestop.org) is a website that helps students, job seekers, and career professionals explore the outlook and trends for all types of careers. You can use the library at this site to explore your career interests, assess your skills, and link to other career exploration sites.

Career Centers

Many cities have federally sponsored career centers as part of America's One-Stop Career Center System. By coordinating local, state, and national resources, **One-Stop Career Centers** can provide employment counseling, information on job trends, and assistance in filing for unemployment insurance. The centers also help individuals find job training and government funds to help pay training costs.

Different names are used for the centers in different states. Find the center nearest you by contacting your state employment office and asking for the location of the closest One-Stop Career Center. You can also visit websites such as America's Service Locator (www.servicelocator.org). An online search using the search term *One-Stop Career Centers* can also guide you to additional resources.

Guidance Counselors

Guidance counselors also play an important role in providing career information. When you want to know more about a specific occupation, a guidance counselor can direct you to the information you need. Many guidance counselors keep career files in their offices that contain up-to-date information about different occupations and their educational requirements.

If you are in the process of trying to determine a career interest, a guidance counselor can help you explore your options. A guidance counselor will help you consider career options related to your abilities and personal goals. He or she can also answer questions about admissions requirements and the costs of schools, colleges, and training programs.

Go Green

The USB flash drive is becoming a popular alternative to rewritable CDs (CD-RWs). Even though CD-RWs are reusable, they can be easily damaged and may end up in a landfill after just a few uses. USB drives, on the other hand, are more durable, reusable, and easy to carry and store.

Have you seen the new eco-friendly bamboo USB drives? Bamboo is one of the fastest growing wood plants on the planet. This renewable resource is often used in construction and design. However, manufacturers have discovered that it is also a good, eco-friendly choice for USB drive cases.

Career events and informal interviews can help you understand what qualifications and training you may need for the future.

auremar/Shutterstock.com

Career Events

Schools often have career days when representatives from various occupations, professions, and schools are available to speak to interested students. Sometimes a local community college or chamber of commerce sponsors career fairs. When you attend a career day or career fair, you have the opportunity to speak directly with people who are employees of the company they represent. An additional benefit of attending a career fair is that you can meet representatives from several companies in one day. Be sure to participate in these events and talk with representatives to learn more about your career options.

Informal Interviews and Personal Observations

Your guidance counselor can help you identify key people who can tell you more about a given career area. If you keep the interview brief and speak at a time that is convenient for them, most will be glad to meet with you. If possible, have informal interviews with workers who have jobs that interest you. An **informal interview** is a planned meeting in which a job seeker learns more about an occupation from a person employed in that job area. Having a chance to actually talk with workers will give you insight into their occupations. Informal interviews will give you a chance to seek advice and learn more about a career field.

By asking key questions, you can find out what kind of training is important and how workers got their first jobs. You can also ask workers what they like most and least about their jobs. Informal interviews will help you learn more about a specific occupation and the world of work in general. Discussions with workers will also help you practice your interview skills and make future job contacts.

You can also learn more about a career by staying alert to what is happening around you. Carefully observe people you encounter every day doing their jobs. Do any of their jobs interest you? A newspaper story or a television program might reveal facts about a certain career that is of interest to you. Perhaps your friends tell you about people they know who love their jobs.

When you learn of a career that seems promising, become your own career investigator. Gather facts and talk with people who can provide more information as you search for the right career.

Checkpoint 16.1

1. Name four sources available to help you research careers.
2. What career information is provided in the Occupational Outlook Handbook?
3. How might a guidance counselor help you research a potential career?
4. What are two benefits of attending a career fair?
5. What is the purpose of an informal interview?

Build Your Vocabulary

As you progress through this text, develop a personal glossary of career-related terms and add it to your portfolio. This will help build your vocabulary and prepare you for your career of choice. Write a definition for each of the following terms, and add it to your personal career glossary.

Occupational Outlook Handbook
Occupational Information Network (O*NET™)
CareerOneStop
One-Stop Career Center
informal interview

16.2 Prepare for Career Success

Terms

occupational training
apprenticeship
college access
529 plan
grant
scholarship
work-study program
need-based award
Free Application for
    Federal Student Aid
    (FAFSA)
fringe benefit

Objectives

After completing this section you will be able to:

- **Describe** various educational and training opportunities.
- **Evaluate** a career based on work hours, work conditions, pay, and personal goals.

Education and Training

Education is often the most important consideration when preparing for career success. The career you choose will determine the education and career you need. You may already be in the process of learning skills in your high school classes for an occupation. Most occupations, however, require further training after high school.

Do the occupations that interest you require further education? How much time, effort, and money are you willing to spend on your education? Can you receive the education you need through training? Could you learn the skills you need through an apprenticeship? Will you need a college degree? Should you consider career training through the Armed Forces? The amount of training and education you obtain will influence your earnings and your opportunities for job advancement.

Occupational Training

Occupational training prepares a person for a job in a specific field. Training can be received through occupational schools, skill centers, community colleges, company training programs, and distance learning programs, such as online and correspondence courses. Since the quality of training can vary from one source to another, it is important to investigate a training program before you enroll.

If you choose to enroll in a training program, be selective. Make sure the school has the equipment and facilities to provide you with up-to-date training. There are many fine occupational schools with excellent instructors. There are also schools that will be willing to take your money but fail to provide you with the training you need. Your guidance counselor or program coordinator can help you evaluate occupational schools so you can choose an appropriate one.

You may find distance learning courses are a good way to further your education. These courses are often offered through community colleges and universities, as well as private institutions. Through online courses, students are able to collaborate with classmates, track progress, as well as submit assignments and communicate directly with teachers online. In the case of correspondence schools, students complete the course requirements at home and mail their work to the school for evaluation and course credit. Educating yourself through distance learning usually requires a great deal of self-discipline.

Be sure to check with the US Department of Education to see if the program of study offered is accredited. You can do this by searching the database of accredited postsecondary institutions and programs on the Office of Post Secondary Education website (ope.edu.gov). If you plan to attend a college or university later but want to take a few online courses now, make sure your course work will transfer. Courses transfer when one school accepts the credit given by another. Be especially suspicious of courses that eliminate the lab work or hands-on experience that is typically required of courses taught in traditional settings.

Some companies will train employees for specific skills needed within their companies. Company trainers, through regular class instruction, may offer employees training. In some cases, trainers from outside the company may be brought in to provide instruction. Company training offers employees the chance to develop and improve their job skills on site.

Technical Certificate Programs

Technical certificate programs are offered through trade schools and community colleges. These programs offer a series of courses that provide technical knowledge and skills needed for employment. Often, full-time students can complete a program in less than a year. Examples of certificate programs appear in Figure 16-1.

Some technical certificate programs prepare graduates to enter apprenticeship programs. Graduates of technical schools often go on to participate in apprenticeship programs.

Certificate Programs	
Aviation Mechanics	Land Surveying
Bookkeeping	Landscape Design
Community Health Worker	Medical Assistant
Computer Repair	Medical Coding Specialist
Construction Safety Specialist	Office Support
Culinary Arts	Pastry Arts
Diagnostic Medical Sonography	Personal Chef
Dietary Management	Personal Fitness Trainer
Early Childhood Care and Education	Power Systems Engineering
Electronic Publishing	Production Artist
Emergency Medical Technician	Teacher Assistant
Environmental Safety and Security	Turf Grass Management
Holistic Yoga Instructor	Web Design

Figure 16-1.   *Goodheart-Willcox Publisher*
Certificate programs are offered at most community colleges and trade schools.

Apprenticeships

Employment opportunities and earnings are good for those who complete apprenticeships. If you enjoy performing technical skills and want to learn a specific trade, an apprenticeship may be right for you. An **apprenticeship** is a combination of on-the-job training and related classroom instruction in which workers learn the practical and theoretical aspects of a highly skilled occupation. Skills are mastered under the supervision of a skilled tradesperson.

Graduation from youth apprenticeships may lead to immediate employment, but several more years of training are usually required. The training is then gained through a registered apprenticeship—an advanced training program that operates under standards approved by the US Labor Department's Office of Apprenticeship.

There are approximately 29,000 apprenticeship programs registered with the Office of Apprenticeship. New programs are continually being added. Figure 16-2 provides a list of several job categories for which an apprenticeship program exists. Complete details on registered apprenticeships can be obtained by contacting the Office of Apprenticeship. For additional information, you can conduct your own Internet search using the search term *apprenticeship programs*.

A high school diploma or equivalency certificate is the general requirement for entering an apprenticeship. However, application requirements may differ in various states and from one trade to another. An applicant must be at least 16 years of age and meet the program qualifications. Generally, applicants must prove they have the ability, aptitude, and education to master the basics of the occupation and complete the related instruction required in the program. Many apprenticeship programs are difficult to enter. In some training programs, it is not unusual to have several hundred applicants for 25 new apprentice positions.

Apprenticeship Programs	
Air Transport Pilot	Graphic Designer
Automotive Technician Specialist	Hotel Associate
Boiler Operator	Machinist
Carpenter	Mechanic
Certified Nursing Assistant	Medical Transcriptionist
Crime Scene Technician	Paramedic
Computer Programmer	Pharmacist Assistant
Construction Craft Laborer	Pipefitter
Dental Assistant	Press Operator
Dispatcher	Truck Driver
Electrician	Welder
Film Editor	Veterinary Technician

Figure 16-2.   *Goodheart-Willcox Publisher*
This table shows a variety of apprenticeship programs.

Apprenticeship programs require that the apprentice learn the entire trade, not just parts of it. This is accomplished by breaking down each trade into basic skill blocks. As apprentices complete each block, their skill and understanding of the trade grows, and their pay increases. A basic math skills test is usually required for admission to most apprenticeship programs. Most apprenticeships take about four years to complete.

College Education

A high school education or occupational training is adequate for many occupations. Professional occupations in certain fields, however, require a one- or two-year technical program or a four-year college education.

Consider the examples of an architectural drafter and an architect. An architectural drafter is someone who makes drawings of buildings to be constructed, while an architect is the person who designs the buildings. Two years of training at an occupational school or a two-year college prepares an architectural drafter. However, it takes five or six years of college with two to three years of work experience to become a registered architect. Although the two occupations are in the same field, the job of an architect requires advanced training. Since an architect has more training and education than an architectural drafter, the architect has more skills to use on the job. Therefore, the architect is able to earn a higher salary.

If a four-year college is part of your career plans, be sure to choose a college or university that can help you achieve your career goals. For example, if you want to become a mechanical engineer, choose a school that has a reputable engineering department. To find out which colleges offer the programs that interest you, begin by talking with your guidance counselor. A guidance counselor can help you review college catalogs and evaluate the programs they offer. Examples of fast-growing careers for college graduates are shown in Figure 16-3.

Examples of Fast-Growing Careers for College Graduates	
Accountant	Medical Scientist
Actuary	Museum Conservator
Athletic Trainer	Occupational Therapist
Audiologist	Optometrist
Biomedical Engineer	Personal Financial Advisor
Cartographer	Physician Assistant
Computer Software Engineer	Public Relations Specialist
Employee Benefits Specialist	Social Worker
Environmental Engineer	Sports Agent
Market Research Analyst	Training Specialist

Figure 16-3.   *Goodheart-Willcox Publisher*

These are just a few examples of the exciting career possibilities for college graduates.

Compare different colleges and universities on the basis of reputation, entry requirements, cost, and convenience. Then, apply to the school or schools you would like to attend. Sometimes it is best to apply to more than one school. Because not every school admits every applicant, having a fall-back plan is a good idea. Also, applying to more than one school gives you time to consider your alternatives. A college education is an investment in your future, so make your choice carefully.

Community Colleges

Community colleges generally offer two-year associate degrees and other technical certificates. Some associate degree programs prepare students for transferring to a four-year college, while others are designed to prepare students for employment. For example, a student who successfully completes a veterinary technology program and earns an associate degree is prepared to go to work in a veterinary clinic, zoo, or humane society.

Open enrollment, small classes, and lower tuition are among the reasons students choose community colleges. Open enrollment allows all students with a high school diploma or GED to enroll. There may be additional admission requirements for specific programs.

Community colleges also offer classes for people who are not pursuing a degree. For example, a retired firefighter who enjoys going to art galleries and art museums might want to learn about art history, but she may not be interested in getting a degree in fine arts. She could enroll in an art history class at a community college.

Armed Forces

Each year the Armed Forces provide thousands of men and women educational training that can be used in both military and civilian careers. Training is available for clerical and administrative jobs, skilled construction work, electrical and electronic occupations, auto repair, and hundreds of other specialties.

Receiving educational training through a branch of the Armed Forces has a number of advantages. There is little or no cost to the student for training. The student also gets paid while being trained. In addition, the student receives many benefits, such as paid vacations, paid health care programs, free housing, and opportunities for travel and advancement.

Military life does have its disadvantages, however. It is more disciplined than civilian life. People in the military must follow orders regarding what they wear, where they go, and what they do. When a person joins a branch of the Armed Forces, he or she must serve until the end of his or her term, which could be three to six years in length. A decision to join the military should be carefully considered. Generally, military personnel cannot leave or resign before the end of their terms.

The Armed Forces offers a variety of educational opportunities and training programs.

George Fairbairn/Shutterstock.com

The Military Career Guide Online (www.todaysmilitary.com) is a good place to start your search for information about careers in the Armed Forces. The site profiles the Army, Navy, Marine Corps, Air Force, and Coast Guard. It also outlines benefits, career opportunities, and things you need to know before serving. The online guide provides additional information about entrance requirements, boot camp, officer candidate school, ROTC (Reserve Officer Training Corps), and the service academies.

Continuing Education

Many careers require you to continue your education throughout your work life. This is particularly true when your career requires a professional license or certification. For example, accountants, physicians, lawyers, and real estate agents must take classes to keep up with changes in their profession and to renew their licenses. Many companies encourage employees to take classes, attend seminars, and participate in workshops for personal growth and to learn new skills related to their jobs. Being a lifelong learner can help you improve your performance and advance your career.

College Access

Have you ever heard the term *college access*? **College access** refers to students having the following:

- awareness of college opportunities,
- guidance regarding college admissions,
- resources to complete required course work, and
- ways to pay for college.

College access includes being exposed to all kinds of postsecondary institutions, including colleges, universities, and technical schools.

Gaining access to a postsecondary institution to further your education is a critical step in your career plan and your financial future. However, preparing to go to college presents many challenges to students and families, both academically and financially. The sooner you begin planning, the better. It is never too early.

Make the Most of Your High School Education

As you plan for your education, you will want to learn as much as possible about what it takes to gain admission to the college of your choice and how to create a financial plan to pay for your education. Academic preparation includes taking the right courses and doing your best. Make the most of your remaining high school years. If you have always been a good student, do not slack off. If you have not been performing to your potential, you can demonstrate your abilities and commitment by showing improvement. Doing the very best you can and becoming involved in organizations at your high school or in your community will provide greater access to college. Most schools are looking for well-rounded individuals who participate in a variety of activities.

If you are seeking greater challenge and a way to impress college admissions departments, you might want to consider taking International Baccalaureate or Advanced Placement classes. An International Baccalaureate diploma is recognized worldwide as the culmination of rigorous course work and community service. Through the Advanced Placement (AP) Program, students can earn college credit and advanced placement in their classes. Earning college credit while still in high school is a way to spend less time in college and spend less on college tuition, making college more affordable.

Another option for earning college credit while still in high school is the dual or articulated credit approach. High school students can earn advanced credit by taking courses approved by participating colleges and universities. This opportunity is especially beneficial to those who are interested in a college or technical career requiring postsecondary education.

Use the Internet

There are many websites that provide information to help you gain access to college. Many sites offer guidance for every stage of the planning process, starting with exploring careers in grade school through applying for college. Because there are so many websites, you will need to determine which sites offer the best information for your particular situation.

You can start by searching the Internet for resources offered in your state. To get started, search using the words *college access* and the name of your state. If you have already been thinking about a specific college, make sure you check the school's official website to learn about admission requirements and financial help available to you. The US Department of Education has a website that provides information about the benefits of additional education, steps to continuing your education, and ways to manage the cost of your education. Visit www.college.gov to learn more about how to apply and how to pay for your college education.

The College Board website offers an assortment of college planning tools. Visit www.collegeboard.org and click on the link for students. One of the tools you will find is a financial calculator to help project the cost of an education. In addition, you will find information about selecting a college, the application process, and financial aid.

The National College Access Program Directory provides information about college access programs across the country. Visit www.collegeaccess.org and search for programs that might meet your individual needs.

If you have not already done so, talk to your family, friends, and your guidance counselor today for information to begin planning for college.

Have you considered how you might pay for the cost of your future education or training?

karen roach/Shutterstock.com

Funding Your Education

As you are making decisions about college, you will need to create a financial plan for paying for your education. Whether you attend a trade school, community college, or university, someone has to pay the cost of your education. Funds to pay for college come from a variety of sources. Each student's financial situation is different. You will need to figure out which sources are available to you and which ones fit your needs.

Some families can afford to pay for college with current income or savings. If your parents or other family members are able and willing to pay for your college education, by all means take advantage of their generosity. You can thank them by studying hard and earning your degree. You may be fortunate enough to have a family who established a 529 plan for you to fund your college education. A **529 plan** is a savings plan for education operated by a state or educational institution. These plans are tax-advantage savings plans that encourage families to set aside college funds for their children. These funds may be used for qualified colleges across the nation. Each state now has at least one 529 plan available. Plans vary from state to state because every state sets up its own plan. There are restrictions on how this money can be used, so make sure you understand how the plan works. Money invested in a 529 plan may only be used for college expenses.

Even if your family has a 529 plan, the amount saved might not be enough to pay for all your college expenses. Many families pay for college using savings, current income, and loans. Parents, other family members, and students often work together to cover the cost of college. For example, you might contribute money you have saved or money you earn if you work while attending school. You may even decide to finance a portion of your education using student loans, which is money you will have to repay.

There are many online calculators that can help you estimate how much money you will need to fund your education. Once you have an idea of how much it will cost to go to college, you need to figure out how you will pay for it. More than half the students attending college get some form of financial aid. Potential sources of funding for your education are shown in Figure 16-4.

Financial aid is available from the federal government, as well as nonfederal agencies. There is more than $100 billion in grants, scholarships, work-study, need-based awards, and loans available each year. If you have good grades in high school, some states also offer college money to attend a state school. Grants, scholarships, work-study programs, and need-based awards are some examples of financial aid.

- A **grant** is typically provided by a nonprofit organization, such as the government or other organization. Grants are generally need-based, do not have to be repaid, and are usually tax exempt. A federal Pell Grant is an example of a government grant.

Potential Sources of Funding a College Education		
Source	**Brief Description**	**Repayment**
529 Plan	Tax-advantage savings plan designed to encourage saving for future college costs. Plans are sponsored by states, state agencies, and educational institutions.	No repayment
Grants	Money to pay for college provided by government agencies, corporations, states, and other organizations. Most grants are based on need and some have other requirements.	No repayment
Scholarships	Money to pay for college based on specific qualifications including academics, sports, music, leadership, and service. Criteria for scholarships vary widely.	No repayment
Work-study	Paid part-time jobs for students with financial need. Work-study programs are typically backed by government agencies.	No repayment
Need-based awards	Aid for students who demonstrate financial need.	No repayment
Government education loans	Loans made to students to help pay for college. Interest rates are lower than bank loans.	Repayment required but may be postponed until you begin your career.
Private education loans	Loans made to students to help pay for college. Interest rates are higher than government education loans.	Repayment required
Internships	Internships are career-based work experience. Some internships are paid and some are not. In addition to experience, you will likely earn college credit.	No repayment
Military benefits	Education and training benefits are available to service personnel. The US military offers several ways to help pay for education. It provides education and training opportunities during service. The military also provides access to funding for veterans. The US Reserve Officers' Training Corps (ROTC) programs and the military service academies are other options to consider.	No repayment required; however a service commitment is.

Figure 16-4.   *Goodheart-Willcox Publisher*
There are many sources of funding to consider for your education.

- A **scholarship** may be based on financial need or some type of merit or accomplishment. There are scholarships based on ACT or SAT scores, grades, extracurricular activities, athletics, and music. There are also scholarships available for leadership, service, and other interests, abilities, and talents. It is surprising how many scholarships and grants go unused because no one has applied for them. Do not fail to apply for help just because you do not want to write an essay or fill out an application. Talk to your school counselor and be persistent if you think you might qualify for college money.
- **Work-study programs** provide part-time employment to undergraduate and graduate students to help with their college expenses. There are federal work-study and nonfederal work-study programs.

- **Need-based awards** are available for students and families who meet certain economic requirements. Income and other demographics determine if a student qualifies for this assistance.

The **Free Application for Federal Student Aid (FAFSA)** is the application form used to determine your eligibility for financial aid. Many institutions require the FAFSA form if you are applying for any type of financial aid. File your application online at www.fafsa.ed.gov. In addition to the financial aid application, the FAFSA website has resources to help you plan for college.

Evaluating Careers

As you continue to research careers, you will find a variety of opportunities available to you. You should consider your options carefully. Be sure to evaluate each aspect of a career that interests you. For each career you explore, you should be able to answer the following questions.

- What are the general work hours?
- Under what conditions would I be required to work?
- How much pay could I expect to earn?
- How would this career fit into my lifestyle and goals?

Finding the answers to these questions will help you choose a more satisfying and rewarding occupation.

Work Hours

In the workplace, different jobs require different work hours. A baker may start work at 4 a.m., while a night security guard may start at 7 p.m. When some people are beginning their workdays, others are ending their jobs to go home. What work hours would you prefer? Would you mind working specific workdays and times or having flexible hours? Would you prefer a seasonal occupation? It is important to consider the work hours required by a job or career. The time you spend at work can greatly impact your lifestyle, including your personal and family life.

Most employees work 40 hours per week. Office workers usually work from 9 a.m. to 5 p.m. on weekdays. Factory and service employees work in eight-hour shifts for any five days of the week. They may work the morning shift, from 7 a.m. to 3 p.m.; the afternoon shift, from 3 p.m. to 11 p.m.; or the night shift, from 11 p.m. to 7 a.m. Some employees work ten hours a day, four days a week. Other workers are allowed to set their own work schedules but must include a core period when all department employees must be present.

Many occupations require people to work irregular hours as needed. People in real estate and insurance sales often work evening hours and weekends in order to schedule appointments with their clients. Some doctors also work irregular hours occasionally. For example, an obstetrician may be called to deliver a baby any time of the day or night.

Some jobs are seasonal, such as farming field crops, playing professional sports, and operating a ski resort. Farmers usually work their longest hours when the crops must be planted, fertilized, and harvested. Athletes work many hours just before and during their playing seasons but are off the rest of the year. Winter ski resort owners only operate during cold, snowy months.

Having a balanced life is important to your happiness and well-being.

David Gilder/Shutterstock.com

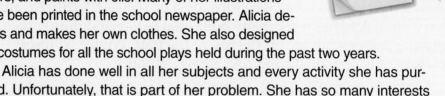

Case

What Career for Alicia?

Alicia, a senior in high school, is a very talented person, especially in art. She sketches, uses water-colors, and paints with oils. Many of her illustrations have been printed in the school newspaper. Alicia designs and makes her own clothes. She also designed the costumes for all the school plays held during the past two years.

Alicia has done well in all her subjects and every activity she has pursued. Unfortunately, that is part of her problem. She has so many interests and skills that she does not know which career to choose. Her current problem is trying to decide what type of training or educational program to take.

At the suggestion of her guidance counselor, Alicia wrote down what she hoped to accomplish over the next five to ten years. She wrote these goals:

- to work in the interior design or graphic arts industry
- to work in a career that offers possibilities for travel

Alicia began thinking about the career areas that were of interest to her. She realized that talking to people in similar careers might help her make a career decision. Her guidance counselor recommended several professionals who were willing to talk to Alicia about their careers. When it came time to actually phone them for appointments, however, Alicia always found other things to do.

After much soul-searching, Alicia believed that an interior design career suited her best. She learned that a four-year degree was required. Fortunately, a nearby university that taught the program accepted her. She spent one year there before realizing interior design was not for her.

She missed painting, sketching, and seeing her work used in publications. When a local advertising agency heard of her interest in a graphic arts career, they offered her a job on the spot. She was told about a visual arts program at the local community college that offered courses to broaden her skills. She also learned that the Armed Forces needed graphic artists and would pay the education expenses of a person who showed promise in that area. Now faced with so many options, Alicia does not know what to do.

Critical Thinking

1. Did Alicia research her career interests well? Explain.
2. How could Alicia have improved her career research?
3. What would you advise Alicia to do?
4. What have you learned from Alicia's experience that may help you make a career decision more wisely?

Work Conditions

When evaluating occupations, you should also consider the conditions in which you will be working. Are there certain environmental, physical, or mental conditions that you find uncomfortable? Would you be opposed to working in dusty, dirty, noisy, steamy, or freezing conditions? Would you dislike lifting boxes, climbing ladders, or sitting at a desk all day?

Do you prefer following a set routine over and over like an assembly line or factory worker? Would you prefer a job with constant variety, so no two days are alike? Do you want to work alone or in a team with others? Every job has desirable and undesirable working conditions. You will want to choose the job that will satisfy you most.

Pay

Although an occupation should not be selected just on the basis of earnings, pay is an important aspect to consider. How much money do you expect to earn during the first year? How much do you want to earn after two years or five years?

Learn what wages or salaries you can expect to earn in the occupations that interest you. What is the starting pay? How much do experienced workers earn? Can you support yourself on that amount of income? Could you support a family? Will additional education be necessary for significant pay increases in the future?

The amount of the paycheck is not the only financial consideration. Does the company provide any fringe benefits? **Fringe benefits** are financial extras in addition to the regular paycheck. Medical and life insurance coverage, paid vacation and sick time, bonuses, and retirement plans are examples of fringe benefits. You may be further ahead financially with a lower paying job that includes excellent benefits than with a higher paying job having few or no benefits.

Lifestyle and Goals

When you evaluate your career interests, you may also want to consider how your career will fit your lifestyle. In matching yourself to the right career, think about your personal lifestyle and goals. How would certain careers affect your lifestyle choices? When your work life and personal life are out of balance, your stress level is likely to soar. Your work-life balance is very important. Finding a suitable balance between work and daily living is a challenge that all workers face. Your career can affect many important aspects of your future— where you live, your income, your friends, and your family. What are your future goals? Do you want to complete school and start a career? Do you plan on marriage and a family? Knowing your personal goals can help you make a wiser decision about your future career.

If your goals include marriage, how will you manage a marriage and a career? Discussing both family and career goals before marriage is important. Some households include a dual-career family in which both spouses have careers outside the home. This means managing the demands of a career, as well as family responsibilities.

A dual-career family can be a beneficial arrangement for both spouses. They can experience personal growth in their careers and contribute to the family's income. Opportunities for sharing home and family tasks can help strengthen a marriage. For couples with children, relationships may improve within the family if both spouses work. Children may become more independent. When the mother works outside the home, this may give the father more time with the children. He may also share in the household tasks.

Managing a dual-career family can also lead to problems. Caring for a home and children can be challenging when a couple works. Spouses may have different working hours. For example, one spouse may work during the day while the other spouse works at night. This may affect management of personal schedules, childcare, and household tasks. One spouse may be transferred to another city, which may impact the other spouse's career plans. Home and family responsibilities may not be balanced.

Career-oriented parents need to fit childcare into their work schedules. Childcare within the home may be more convenient, but most parents take their children to a childcare center or home. Some employers recognize this concern by providing on-site facilities for their employees. Other employers may help pay part of the cost at facilities close to the worksite.

The demands of a dual-career family are unique. Family members need to work together as a team. When family members accept and share household responsibilities, they learn cooperation, self-worth, and appreciation of each other.

Making a career decision can be complex. It should be taken very seriously because it will greatly impact your future. Gain a deep understanding of yourself, and gather all the facts you can about your career interests before making a decision. Then, consider your personal lifestyle and goals. Careful thought and planning should help guide you toward your career decision.

Checkpoint 16.2

1. Where can a person go to receive occupational training?
2. What is a registered apprenticeship?
3. Name three potential sources for funding a college education.
4. What factors can help you evaluate whether a career is right for you?
5. Give examples of fringe benefits discussed in the chapter.

Build Your Vocabulary

As you progress through this text, develop a personal glossary of career-related terms, and add it to your portfolio. This will help build your vocabulary and prepare you for your career of choice. Write a definition for each of the following terms, and add it to your personal career glossary.

occupational training
apprenticeship
college access
529 plan
grant
scholarship
work-study program
need-based award
Free Application for Federal Student Aid (FAFSA)
fringe benefit

Chapter Summary

Section 16.1 Research Potential Careers

- Using the many sources available, you can research information about careers. Schools, local libraries, career information guides, and guidance counselors can help you learn more about different career options.
- Informational interviews give job seekers an opportunity to speak with a person employed in a job area. The discussion provides insight from someone who can share his or her career-related experiences.

Section 16.2 Prepare for Career Success

- Education is a significant factor to consider when preparing for a career. A variety of education and training programs are available.
- Evaluate potential careers to help you choose the best option for your future. You will need to consider work hours, work conditions, and pay levels for each career.

Check Your Career IQ

Now that you have finished the chapter, see what you learned about careers by taking the chapter posttest. The test can be accessed on the mobile site by using a smartphone or on the G-W Learning companion website.

www.m.g-wlearning.com
www.g-wlearning.com

Review Your Knowledge

1. Why should job seekers use magazines to research careers?
2. Where should you go to find career information guides?
3. What are O*NET Career Exploration Tools?
4. Why should students participate in career events?
5. What is the most important consideration when preparing for career success?
6. Explain the purpose of a technical certificate program.
7. What is the general requirement for entering an apprenticeship?
8. Why might a person take a continuing education class?
9. Describe the major difference between a student loan and a grant.
10. Why is it important to consider a job's work hours when planning a career?

Applying Your Knowledge and Skills

1. Choose three careers that interest you. Visit your school or local library to find two articles that directly relate to each career. Write a one-page report about one of the articles you selected.

2. Research a career of your choice, using one of the US Department of Labor's career information guides. Determine the following: training and education needed, expected earnings, working conditions, and job prospects for the future. Record your findings and share them with the class.

3. Consider lifestyle choices and personal goals for your future. Create a two-column chart, listing your lifestyle choices in the first column and your personal goals in the second column. Share your chart with the rest of the class. Why is it important to consider personal lifestyle and goals when evaluating a career?

4. Practice using your school or local library's technology systems, such as online card catalogs or CD indexes. Write a brief report of your experiences.

5. With a partner, discuss the importance of fringe benefits. Answer the following questions: Why should you consider fringe benefits when selecting a career? What fringe benefits might influence you to take a lower salary? What fringe benefits are most important to you? Least important? Rank your list of fringe benefits in order of importance.

6. Interview a person who has served or is serving in a branch of the US Armed Forces. Conduct an informal interview to learn about his or her personal experience in the military. Ask questions about training, general job duties, working conditions, and benefits. Summarize your findings in a written report for your personal resource file.

7. Most occupations require education and training beyond high school. Use the Internet and career guides to determine the education and training needed for four of the following jobs: elementary school teacher, college professor, police officer, FBI agent, chef, nutritionist, real estate agent, and architect. Compile your information in a chart.

8. Visit the official websites of the Armed Forces, and review the related information in Section 16.2. What are the advantages and disadvantages of receiving educational training through a branch of the Armed Forces? Would you consider joining the US military? Why or why not? Share your answers with a small group.

9. Learn about the technical certificate programs offered through your local community college. What programs are available? Identify two certificate programs. What requirements are needed prior to enrollment? How many classes are needed to complete the program? What is the cost of the program? Share your findings in a class presentation.

10. Select three sources from Figure 16-4. Conduct research to learn more about these sources of funding in your state. Summarize your findings. Share what you learned with other students in your class.

Teamwork

Work with a small group of classmates to create a plan for funding a two-year college degree at a local community college. How much will a student need to complete the program? What are the costs of tuition and other expenses? What potential sources of funding could be used? Together, create a chart displaying your plan. Share your findings with the class.

G-W Learning Mobile Site

Visit the G-W Learning mobile site to complete the chapter pretest and posttest and to practice vocabulary using e-flash cards. If you do not have a smartphone, visit the G-W Learning companion website to access these features.
G-W Learning mobile site: www.m.g-wlearning.com
G-W Learning companion website: www.g-wlearning.com

Common Core

College and Career Readiness

CTE Career Ready Practices. You may have been taught to treat others how you would like to be treated. This is often referred to as *the golden rule.* Productively working with others who have a background different from yours may require that you learn to treat others as *they* wish to be treated. Conduct research on the Internet about cultural differences related to personal space, time, gestures, body language, and relationship toward authority figures. Create a T-chart that show the differences on the left and ways you would adapt your interactions to account for that difference.

Writing. Using Internet or print sources, research the history of recruitment for one branch of the US Armed Forces. Write an informative report that summarizes your research. Include examples of current programs offered by that branch. What type of person do you think is best suited to a career in the Armed Forces? Explain your answer.

Apply Your Technology Skills

Access the G-W Learning companion website for this text at www.g-wlearning.com. Download the data file for this chapter. Follow the instructions to complete activities to practice what you have learned.

Data File 16–1—**Investigating a Career Exploration Website**

College and Career Readiness

College and Career Readiness Portfolio

Applying for a position may require you to mail or e-mail an application to a company or organization. When sending your application form, you should also include a letter of application to introduce yourself. Use a standard format for a business letter. If possible, address the letter to a specific person at the company or organization. In the first paragraph, state how you learned about the job and ask to be considered for the position. In the second paragraph, briefly discuss your skills and experience that qualify you for the job. Mention that an application is enclosed, if you have included one. In the last paragraph, restate your interest in the job and ask for an interview. Sample letters of application can be found on the Internet.

1. Find job openings by searching online or looking in a local newspaper. Select a job for which you might want to apply.
2. Create a letter of application for this position.
3. Save the document file in your e-portfolio. Place a printed copy of the letter in your print portfolio.

Section 17.1
Career Decisions

Section 17.2
Your Career Plan

College and Career Readiness

Reading Prep. Before reading the chapter, skim the photos and their captions. As you are reading, determine how these concepts contribute to the ideas presented in the text.

Introduction

As you know, there are a number of options to consider when thinking about your future plans. Choosing a career path that will suit you for a lifetime may seem like a tall order right now. However, approaching the different options available to you in a logical way helps in the decision-making process. This method may make the task seem less overwhelming.

One of the biggest decisions you will have to make is what career to pursue. Yet, the decisions you make every day will have an effect on your ability to reach your career goal. For example, you choose to take college preparatory classes. You also choose to do the work required to get good grades in those classes. Those decisions will have a positive impact on your ability to get into a good college.

You should practice making careful choices daily. Consider your options as well as the results of your final choice. As you develop your decision-making skills, you improve your ability to make wise choices for your future.

Check Your Career IQ

Before you begin the chapter, see what you already know about careers by taking the chapter pretest. Use the related QR code to view the pretest on the mobile site. If you do not have a smartphone, visit the G-W Learning companion website to access the pretest.

www.m.g-wlearning.com
www.g-wlearning.com

G-W Mobile

Career Snapshot
Marine Biologist

Science, Technology, Engineering & Mathematics

What Does a Marine Biologist Do?

A marine biologist studies living organisms and their relationship to the environment. Marine biologists are also referred to as *biological scientists.* They perform research to gain a better understanding of sea life and fundamental life processes. A marine biologist must:

- study plants and animals living in water and the environmental conditions affecting them;
- investigate salinity, temperature, acidity, light, oxygen content, and other physical conditions of water to determine their relationship to aquatic life;
- examine various types of water life, such as plankton, worms, clams, mussels, and snails; and
- specialize in the culture, breeding, and raising of aquatic life.

What Is It Like to Work as a Marine Biologist?

A marine biologist may work in offices and laboratories. They also work on boats, at sea, or in isolated coastal areas in all weather conditions. What they do during the stay depends on the animals they study. Marine biologists travel to study sites. They may also travel around the country or overseas to attend conferences or training. Marine biologists may be called on for marine-animal rescue missions after oil spills or other emergencies.

What Education and Skills Are Needed to Be a Marine Biologist?

- bachelor or master degree, usually in biology or chemistry
- doctorate degree is often necessary
- problem-solving and analytical skills
- natural curiosity about nature

Rick Carey/Shutterstock.com

17.1 Career Decisions

Objectives

After completing this section, you will be able to:
- **Recall** the difference between routine decisions and major decisions.
- **Explain** the seven steps of the decision-making process.
- **Explain** how the decision-making process can be used to make additional life choices.

Making Decisions

Making decisions is something you do every day. From the minute you get up in the morning, you begin making decisions. You decide what to wear, what to eat, and what time to leave for school. These choices are made often throughout the day. **Routine decisions** are choices most people make automatically about everyday matters. They are so minor that you probably do not even know you are making them. There are other decisions that take a little more thought, such as deciding which movie to see or what music to buy. These decisions usually require more attention but are generally very easy to make.

Then, there are the major decisions. A **major decision** is an important choice requiring careful thought because it affects a person's career and personal life. Major decisions are the toughest decisions to make because they guide your life. Deciding whether to go to college, get married, or buy a car are major decisions. These decisions are significant because they take considerable resources and tend to have long-lasting effects.

If you become a manager or supervisor on the job, you will also have major decisions to make. You may need to decide whether to hire or fire an employee. You may need to decide how to sell and market a new product. These are decisions that not only affect you but also the company and the people with whom you work.

If you make a wrong decision about something that is not very important, the decision normally will not affect your life to any great extent. For example, Bill decided to buy his father a blue shirt for his birthday, but he bought the wrong size. Although Bill made an error, he was able to take the shirt back and exchange it for the right size. A wrong decision was made, but it was corrected with little effort and time.

On the other hand, if you make a wrong decision about something important, the decision may greatly influence your life. For example, Diane decided to be a dentist just because her father was one. She went through college and dental school and later realized she had made a big mistake. Being a dentist the rest of her life was the last thing she wanted to do. In fact, she only chose dentistry because she did not take the time to investigate other careers.

Diane now realizes that teaching art is the career for her, and she wants to return to college for the required degree. Diane spent most of her college years unhappy about her career decision. She wasted thousands of dollars on an education she no longer wants to use. Now, she must work for several years as a dentist to pay for her dental school expenses before she can go back and get the education required to become an art teacher. Diane's quick career decision has affected her a great deal. It caused her much unhappiness as well as future financial problems.

Understanding the Decision-Making Process

When you have major decisions to make, you approach them carefully and logically. The decision-making process helps you do this. The **decision-making process** is a proven way to make important decisions carefully and logically. There are seven steps to follow when facing big decisions. They are summarized in Figure 17-1 and explained here.

Steps in the Decision-Making Process
1. Define the problem or question.
2. Establish goals.
3. Identify resources.
4. Consider alternatives.
5. Make a decision.
6. Implement the decision.
7. Evaluate results.

Figure 17-1.   *Goodheart-Willcox Publisher*
Following these steps will help you make careful decisions

Go Green

You may decide to choose a career that has a heavy emphasis on the *go green* concept. Jobs that focus on solar energy, wind energy, sustainable building, clean technology, skilled trades, and environmental health and safety are career areas where you may have a focus on environmental concerns.

If you have an interest in nature and preserving the environment, perhaps you might want to consider a "green job" for your future.

1. **Define the problem.** The first step is to determine what the problem, question, or concern is and its importance to your life.
2. **Establish short- and long-term goals.** Set specific goals for yourself. Identify what you want to accomplish from the decision you will make.
3. **Identify resources.** Make a list of the resources available to help you reach your goals. Include your personal resources (such as aptitudes and abilities), as well as material resources (such as a car and savings account).
4. **Consider the alternatives.** Explore all the options open to you and weigh the advantages and disadvantages of each. A good way to test alternatives is to consider the following questions: Will this decision have a negative effect on me or anyone else? Will it help me reach my goals? Is it ethical? Will I be happy with it?
5. **Make a decision.** Choose a decision that will help you reach your goals. If you have carefully thought through these steps, you will probably be happy with the decision you make.
6. **Implement the decision.** Put the plan into action.
7. **Evaluate the results.** Judge how successful your plan was. Did your decision solve the problem or address the question completely? Are your goals being met? Are you satisfied with the results of the decision? Evaluating the results of a decision will help improve your decision-making skills in the future.

Applying the Decision-Making Process

The decision-making process is something you can use throughout your life for making different kinds of decisions. Besides helping you achieve the career of your dreams, this process can help with other important considerations in life. Learning decision-making skills can positively affect your personal life, work, and your consumer decisions.

Personal Decisions

Along with career decisions, you often need to make major decisions relating to your personal life. Major decisions may involve dating, getting engaged, choosing a marriage partner, or choosing a college. Is marriage part of your future? Should you have a family before you establish a career? Should you continue your education after you choose a career? These decisions have the potential for affecting your entire life.

Some decisions involve your lifestyle and health. These decisions might involve how to fit exercise into your daily routine or whether to follow a nutritious diet plan. Relationships with your family, friends, or coworkers often involve making decisions. You may have to decide whether to confront a friend who shoplifts. Should you buy a house or live in an apartment? There are many important decisions to make in life.

Work Decisions

You will make decisions every day at work that will affect you and others. Sometimes these decisions will be simple. At other times, they will require you to gather facts and make a choice. For example, you may want to strengthen your relationships with your coworkers and improve your job performance. The decision might involve accepting a job promotion or transferring to another department. Asking for a raise, changing your work schedule, or finding a new job are other decisions you may need to make.

Using the decision-making process can be especially helpful when purchasing major consumer items.

mangostock/Shutterstock.com

Consumer Decisions

Because so many goods and services are available to you as a consumer, making choices can be difficult. Making major purchases, such as a new car or computer, require careful thinking and planning before you buy. You can use the decision-making process to help you make more satisfying choices.

Throughout your life, you will make consumer choices about food, clothing, transportation, energy, and housing. You must also make financial decisions about budgeting, saving, or investing. Buying a car is one example of a decision that may affect your life for several years. Should you buy a new car or a used one? For how many years should you make monthly payments? Can you afford the insurance and maintenance costs? The decision-making process is especially helpful when you face important decisions about major purchases.

Checkpoint 17.1

1. Provide two examples of routine decisions and two examples of major decisions.
2. What two types of resources should you consider when making important decisions?
3. During the decision-making process, what should you do to consider your alternatives?
4. What is the final step in the decision-making process?
5. Why is it often difficult to make consumer choices?

Build Your Vocabulary

As you progress through this text, develop a personal glossary of career-related terms and add it to your portfolio. This will help build your vocabulary and prepare you for your career of choice. Write a definition for each of the following terms, and add it to your personal career glossary.

routine decision
major decision
decision-making process

Objectives

After completing this section, you will be able to:

- **Recall** ways a career decision can influence your future.
- **Describe** how to create a career plan.
- **Explain** the difference between a career plan and a career ladder.

Terms

career plan
entry-level job
advanced-level job
career ladder

Making Career Decisions

Some of the hardest decisions to make are career decisions. Many people have no idea what they want to do for a living. They go from job to job and never really think about their future.

Your own career is too important for that. Career decisions are major decisions that influence your entire future. These decisions need to be made with careful thought and planning. The work you choose will largely determine the way you live, people you meet, money you earn, and satisfaction you get from life. Not only will you be affected by this decision, if you decide to have a family, they will be affected by your career decision as well.

You probably know some people who never really made a career decision. They just stayed in the first job for which they were hired. Some took any available job and hoped it would lead to a fulfilling career. Some let their parents pick a career for them. Others chose the same career their best friends selected. Do you really think you would be satisfied letting someone else make these decisions for you? You should take the time to make these decisions for yourself after careful consideration.

Ethical Leadership

Truthfulness and Persuasiveness

"To be persuasive we must be believable; to be believable we must be credible; to be credible we must be truthful." —Edward R. Murrow

When applying for a job, submitting an application to a university, or even applying for a position as a volunteer, it is important to be truthful in your application and résumé. This means always telling the truth about your skills, experience, and education. Play up your strengths without creating the illusion of being someone you are not. Present your information in a positive light, but keep it honest. Potential employers will usually discover any information that is not true.

As you make a career decision, carefully consider factors that are important to you.

iQoncept/Shutterstock.com

Developing a Career Plan

Once you know how to make important decisions using the decision-making steps, it is time to apply that skill to develop a career plan. What career will be best for you? Before that all-important question can be answered, you must first take a careful self-assessment. This means you need to know the following about yourself:

- interests,
- aptitudes,
- abilities,
- strengths,
- weaknesses,
- personality traits,
- values,
- short-term goals,
- long-term goals, and
- resources.

Earlier chapters of the text covered all these areas to prepare you for the important exercise of making a career decision. The career you choose should use your special strengths and abilities, yet challenge you to develop others.

Business Communications

A CTSO competitive event may include an objective test that covers multiple topics. One of the topics that may be covered is business communications. This portion of the event will likely touch on all aspects of effective writing, speaking, and listening skills as applied to a business environment.

To prepare for the business communications portion of the event, complete the following activities.

1. On your own, review the essential principles of business communication, such as grammar, spelling, proofreading, capitalization, and punctuation.

2. Visit your organization's website and look for business communication tests that were used in previous years. Many organizations post these tests for students to use as practice for future competitions. Up to 30 percent of the questions from tests previously used in competition will be reused. This material is an especially important resource.

3. Study all elements of business communications, taking care not to overlook digital communications, such as e-mail correspondence and netiquette.

4. Use the Internet to find additional resources that will help you prepare. Print the information you find for use as study material.

You might find that you are interested in a certain career but that your skills do not match those required to make a success of it. It is not critical that your interests and skills exactly match your career choice right now because you have not had enough time to develop all your skills.

You may also have skills that you do not want to build a career around. For example, as a result of working in a restaurant, you may be an excellent fry cook or food server. If you do not want to hold these or similar jobs for the long term, disregard the skills that relate exclusively to them. Concentrate instead on the skills necessary to pursue your desired career.

After you decide what type of career interests you most, it is important to identify what it will take to fulfill that dream. This is called a *career plan*, or *personal program of study*. A **career plan** is a list of steps required to reach a career goal. While a career plan does not assure success, it greatly improves your chances of finding jobs. For example, Chris is a junior high school student who wants to become a conservation scientist. Her career plan is shown in Figure 17-2. The purpose of a career plan is to analyze the steps a person will take to achieve the desired career goal. In Chris's case, for example, she must graduate from college first to be eligible for a job in her chosen career area.

Career Plan: Conservation Scientist			
	Extracurricular and Volunteer Activities	**Work Experience**	**Education and Training**
During Junior High School	• Help nonprofit groups and senior citizens with yard upkeep. • Select life science or environmental themes for fairs and competitive events.	Mow lawns and raise nursery plants for sale during summers.	For optional or extra credit work, select topics and do projects pertaining to environmental or life sciences.
During High School	• Help waste recycling and land-management efforts in the area. • Assist county conservation programs. • Attend public meetings on environmental matters.	Work part-time at a tree or plant nursery or in the gardening department of a local store.	Take a college preparatory program emphasizing biology and chemistry.
During College	• Help local groups identify and correct environmental problems.	Work part-time at a local conservation reserve, zoo, or botanical garden.	Take a B.S. degree program in the physical or environmental sciences in the preferred field.
After College	• Stay involved in local environmental matters and volunteer expertise as needed.	Work full-time as a conservation scientist for the state's conservation department.	Consider obtaining an advanced degree.

Figure 17-2.
This table shows a possible career path for conservation scientist.

Goodheart-Willcox Publisher

A career plan details the following within each step:
• extracurricular and volunteer activities,
• work or job experience, and
• education and training requirements.

Notice how Chris' career plan states what she will do at each step to help obtain her career goal. Notice, too, that each level of the career plan builds upon the previous one. As each step is completed, Chris gains increased knowledge and experience. Focusing on your goal will help you determine the best steps for achieving it.

Case

What Next for Vic?

Since high school, Vic worked as a welder's helper for a small company whose business was rebuilding heavy vehicle equipment. After Vic graduated, his manager offered him a full-time job, and Vic accepted. Within five years, Vic became shop supervisor, and he was practically running the place.

When the manager retired, his son became company president, and everything changed. Many employees were fired, and new work policies were posted. The manager hired a good friend who had as much experience as Vic. Now, Vic was concerned about his future with the company. He no longer felt secure about his job and wondered if he, too, would be replaced. Vic decided to use the seven steps of the decision-making process to make a sound decision about what to do next. Vic's future with the company is uncertain.

1. **Define the problem.**
2. **Establish goals.** Vic wrote down a list of the things he wants to achieve.
3. **Identify resources.** Vic also wrote down the resources he has to help him, including his skills and experience.
4. **Consider the alternatives.** Vic thought about other choices available to him. He decided to outline his options
5. **Make a decision.** After careful thought, Vic chose two alternatives. He decided to talk with his new manager about his future with the company and his interest in becoming a part owner. By doing this, he would learn what the manager's plans are for him and if there is any possibility of buying a part of the company. Vic also decided to pursue a business degree part-time and put more money into savings for a future business.
6. **Implement the decision.** The following week, Vic talked to his manager, enrolled in a business course at the community college, and began a monthly savings plan.
7. **Evaluate the results.** Talking to his manager was one of the best decisions Vic ever made. He learned that his manager was very pleased with his work and was planning to give him more responsibility. His manager even said he might sell the entire company in four or five years but would definitely pay half of Vic's school expenses for courses that would help him do a better job for the company.

Critical Thinking

1. How do you think the decision-making process helped Vic make his decisions?
2. How did Vic's goals help him make his decisions?
3. Do you think Vic made the right decisions at this point in his career? Why?
4. What can you learn from Vic's experience?

Climbing a Career Ladder

There is no single route to achieving a career goal. Your resources, abilities, and values will direct a course that is best for you. When you first begin working full-time or you join a new employer, you will most likely be assigned to an entry-level job. An **entry-level job** is work for beginners who lack experience or specialized training. With hard work and time, an employee is often promoted to an advanced-level job. An **advanced-level job** is a position that requires special skills, knowledge, and experience.

Each career is composed of a sequence of related jobs that are available at different educational levels. A **career ladder** is the job-related progression from an entry level to an advanced position along a specified career path. The Figure 17-2 shows a series of job options at different levels for a person preparing to become a conservation scientist. Chris selected some of these jobs for her career plan. Each rung of the ladder presents some job possibilities for that level of education and training. The most complex jobs at the top of the ladder require the most education and training.

Remember, a career plan can be developed for any career goal, and any number of different routes can be used to reach the goal. A career plan is simply a road map to help you get to your destination, but as the driver, you are in charge. Your career plan should be updated every time there is a change in your goals or resources.

Checkpoint 17.2

1. Name at least four categories that should be considered when taking a self-assessment.
2. What three areas of a person's life are examined at each stage of the career plan?
3. Explain the purpose of a career plan.
4. What should you do once you decide what type of career interests you most?
5. When should your career plan be updated?

Build Your Vocabulary

As you progress through this text, develop a personal glossary of career-related terms and add it to your portfolio. This will help you build your vocabulary and prepare you for a career as an entrepreneur. Write a definition for each of the following terms, and add it to your personal entrepreneurship glossary.

career plan
entry-level job
advanced-level job
career ladder

Chapter Summary

Section 17.1 Career Decisions

- You make many types of decisions every day. While some decisions are routine, the major decisions are the hardest to make because they affect your life in many ways.
- When making any major decision, you can use the decision-making process to help you evaluate your options. By following each step of the process, you can determine the best choice and work toward the results you want.
- The decision-making process can also be used when making choices about your personal life, work, and consumer purchases. Career decisions require careful thought and planning.

Section 17.2 Your Career Plan

- Your career decision will affect your future. Making a career decision takes research and planning.
- A career plan will help you decide how to achieve a chosen career. However, you must first recognize what you know about yourself, including your interests, aptitudes, strengths, and weaknesses.
- There are different ways to achieve a career goal. A career ladder offers a logical progression from one level to the next along a specific career path.

Check Your Career IQ

Now that you have finished the chapter, see what you learned about careers by taking the chapter posttest. The test can be accessed on the mobile site by using a smartphone or on the G-W Learning companion website.

www.m.g-wlearning.com
www.g-wlearning.com

Review Your Knowledge

1. Explain the difference between a routine decision and a major decision.
2. Why should a person be careful when making major career and personal decisions?
3. Besides career decisions, for what other matters can the decision-making process be used?
4. Explain what takes place during Step 6 of the decision-making process.
5. What is a consumer decision?
6. Provide two examples of minor consumer decisions. Provide two examples of major consumer decisions.
7. What is the purpose of a self-assessment?

8. What is a personal program of study?
9. Why is a career plan also called a *personal plan of study*?
10. Why are entry-level jobs good for beginners?

Apply Your Knowledge

1. Using Internet or print sources, complete a personal program of study that aligns to a career in which you are interested. Refer to the *Occupational Outlook Handbook* as one of your references. Create two career plans that begin with entry into high school. (The plan should resemble Figure 17-2.)
2. Consider the following types of decisions: personal, work, and consumer. How does your approach to decision-making change with the type of decision you need to make? What role do you think emotions play in decision-making process? Explain your answers.
3. Before you develop a career plan, you should take a self-assessment. For each of the following categories, list five examples that relate to your: interests; aptitudes; abilities; strengths; weaknesses; personality traits; values; short-term goals; long-term goals; and resources.
4. Think about a time you made an important decision. What was the important decision? Which of the steps in the decision-making process did you use to help make your decision? Explain how you applied the steps you did use. Do you feel you made the correct decision? What would you do differently if you had the opportunity to make the decision again? Record your answers on paper.
5. Review the information you learned in this chapter to write a two-page essay about the importance of making career decisions. Include vocabulary from the chapter to support your ideas.
6. Determine today's average salaries within three career areas that interest you. For each career area, research the different salary levels for four jobs with different educational requirements—for example, no high school diploma, high school diploma, postsecondary training, associate degree, bachelor's degree, or advanced degree.
7. In your opinion, what are the three most important steps in the decision-making process? Share your answer with a partner. Follow each of your answers and write three points to support your opinion.
8. Create an outline of this chapter 17. Be sure to include any major ideas and vocabulary. As you study, use the outline to help you recall important information from the chapter.
9. Interview someone who works in a career of your interest. Ask questions to learn about how he or she started in the career field. Discuss any extracurricular and volunteer activities, previous work experience, and education or training that may have taken place during high school, college, or after college. As you are considering this career for yourself, what would you do the same or differently? Share what you learned in a class presentation.
10. Record four important things you learned in Section 17.2. For each, write a paragraph about how you can use this information in planning for your future. Share your responses with the rest of the class during an open discussion.

Teamwork

With a partner, look through the career clusters and career pathways described in the appendix to this text. Choose one pathway that interests both of you. Create a career ladder like the one shown in Figure 17-2 for a career option of your choice. Next, go to the Bureau of Labor Statistics website and search for the *Occupational Outlook Handbook*. Find information about the career you chose, including median pay at each education level and growth rate (projected). Include this information on your ladder. Present your completed ladder to the class.

G-W Learning Mobile Site

Visit the G-W Learning mobile site to complete the chapter pretest and posttest and to practice vocabulary using e-flash cards. If you do not have a smartphone, visit the G-W Learning companion website to access these features.
G-W Learning mobile site: www.m.g-wlearning.com
G-W Learning companion website: www.g-wlearning.com

Common Core

College and Career Readiness

CTE Career Readiness Practices. Read the Ethical Leadership features presented throughout this book. What role do you think ethics and integrity have in decision-making? Think of a time when you used your values and principles to make a decision. What process did you use to make the decision? In retrospect, do you think you made the correct decision? Did your decision have any consequences?

Reading. Using the Internet, research the advice that experts have for choosing a career. Make sure to look at, among other sources, newspaper and magazine articles, scholarly reports, and public addresses. What suggestions were you able to find that were not covered in this chapter? Did you think the advice you found was sound? Why or why not? Consider the background and point of view of the sources that you find, as well as any bias that the source's author may bring to the issue. Write a report in which you present various approaches to choosing a career. Be sure to include accurate citations for all your sources.

Apply Your Technology Skills

Access the G-W Learning companion website for this text at www.g-wlearning.com. Download the data file for this chapter. Follow the instructions to complete activities to practice what you have learned in this chapter.

Data File 17–1—Deciding What's Next

College and Career Readiness

College and Career Readiness Portfolio

When applying for a job or to a college, you may need to submit a résumé. A résumé is a document that tells the company, organization, or college about you. It should contain data in a concise form that shows how you are qualified for a position. The résumé should begin with your contact information: name, address, and telephone numbers. You may also want to include an e-mail address. Your résumé should briefly list your education, skills, and work experience. The education section should include the names and locations of the schools you attended and the dates. Include any degrees or diplomas you received from each school. List the schools in order by the dates you attended. Also in this section, list any special skills you have that relate to the position. For example, list software programs with which you are proficient or musical instruments you can play.

1. Search for and review sample résumés on the Internet. Begin creating a résumé. Include your complete contact information. List your education and skills as described above.
2. Save the information for use in a later activity.

Unit 5 Job Satisfaction

Lifespan Plan

Understanding How Lifestyle Is Affected by Career Choice

The salary and benefits should not be the only things you consider when choosing a career, but they are important considerations. Money you earn during your career should be factored into your Lifespan Plan. The money you spend on education and training to pursue that career should be included as well. It is unrealistic to believe that you will be able to become a physician in two years without paying for or going to medical school. In addition, it is important to know what demands different careers will have on your time and the impact of that on your lifestyle. Having a realistic idea of the costs and benefits associated with careers of interest to you will help bring your goals into focus.

Activities

1. Review the goals you created in Unit 1. Consider how those goals would be affected by the work hours your career of choice requires. How would the cost in time and money needed to reach your career goal impact any of your lifestyle goals? What role would saving and living on a budget have on your goals?
2. Refer to the information you found when putting together your job profile. What yearly salary can someone expect who has the job you profiled? Estimate how much of that amount would be needed for the following: repayment of student loan debt, housing, transportation, food, entertainment, insurance, clothing, and savings. Does this rough calculation affect your goals and your career choice?
3. Save your salary and cost estimates according to your instructor's specifications.

Unit Overview

The extent to which you like your job is known as your *level of job satisfaction.* This unit details the factors that determine your level of job satisfaction. An entry-level position as your first job may be initially satisfying. Staying at that level after several years, may make the job less enjoyable. Your attitude about the position as well as whether you get along with your supervisor and coworkers affect how you feel about your job, too.

It is up to you to increase your job satisfaction by changing how you see your current position, finding a new job, or starting a business of your own. Having a job you like will help you succeed financially and personally.

Chapter 18 Succeeding on the Job
Chapter 19 Diversity and Rights in the Workplace
Chapter 20 Succeeding In Our Economic System
Chapter 21 Entrepreneurship: A Business of Your Own

Picture Success

Vanessa Sandoval
SkillsUSA

A Career and Technical Student Organization (CTSO) can have a positive impact on its members and sponsors. Read about Vanessa Sandoval's experience with SkillsUSA.

Vanessa Sandoval is a criminal justice student in Texas. She was involved in SkillsUSA throughout her high school career. Her participation in this CTSO has given her the chance to shape her leadership skills and learn more about the profession she has chosen to pursue.

Through professional development programs offered by SkillsUSA, Vanessa was able to learn essential skills she would need after high school, such as how to complete a job application and how to conduct meetings. Further, by taking part in job shadowing experiences, Vanessa was able to see what it was really like to be on the job in a criminal justice-related job. This experience helped confirm her choice of careers. Vanessa also notes that such experience can let students know early on that they will not like a particular career. As a result, they are able to save time and money by not heading too far down a career path that was not right for them.

While national president of SkillsUSA, Vanessa participated in a panel discussion in Washington, DC with a US assistant secretary of education. An experience only her involvement in a CTSO could have made possible. Vanessa believes that her participation in a CTSO helped her learn to manager her time. Not only was she able to play a leadership role in her CTSO, she was a member of the National Honor Society, played on athletic teams, and performed in area musical and theatrical productions. She loves being involved and being a member of a CTSO.

Photo: Lloyd Wolf

Chapter
18

Succeeding on the Job

Section 18.1
Your First Job

Section 18.2
Changing Jobs

Section 18.3
Labor Unions

College and Career Readiness

Reading Prep. In preparation for this chapter, use the Internet and printed materials to locate information about labor unions. Use video or audio of speeches given by union leaders as well as those opposed to unions. What role do unions play in how success on the job is defined?

Introduction

What does it mean to succeed on the job? For many people, being successful on the job means doing their jobs well and not getting fired. To others, job success is having more pay, more responsibilities, and a new title.

To succeed at any job, you must stick with it. Do not be surprised if it takes several weeks to adjust to your job and learn new responsibilities. You will need to work hard to learn all your duties, but you should not try to get too far ahead of yourself. You cannot expect to accomplish everything in only a few weeks. Success comes as you learn and acquire the skills and knowledge needed to do your job tasks effectively.

Check Your Career IQ

Before you begin the chapter, see what you already know about careers by taking the chapter pretest. Use the related QR code to view the pretest on the mobile site. If you do not have a smartphone, visit the G-W Learning companion website to access the pretest.

www.m.g-wlearning.com
www.g-wlearning.com

G-W Mobile

Career Snapshot
Security System Installer

What Does a Security System Installer Do?

An installer of security systems is responsible for installing, programming, maintaining, or repairing security or fire alarm wiring and equipment. He or she is also responsible for ensuring the work is in accordance with relevant codes. An installer must:

- examine systems to locate problems, such as loose connections or broken insulation
- test all security features to ensure proper functioning and diagnose malfunctions;
- install, maintain, or repair security systems, alarm devices, or related equipment
- determine material requirements and installation procedures; and
- demonstrate systems for customers and explain details, such as the causes and consequences of false alarms.

What Is It Like to Work as a Security System Installer?

The work environment of an installer may be varied. Some jobs may be indoors in an environmentally controlled building while other jobs may be outside in extreme temperatures of hot or cold.

What Education and Skills Are Needed to Be a Security System Installer?

- one or two years of training
- knowledge of computers and electronics
- critical thinking, complex problem solving, multi-limb coordination, and manual dexterity
- customer-relations skills

auremar/Shutterstock.com

18.1 | Your First Job

Objectives

After completing this section, you will be able to:
- **Explain** the importance of being prepared for the first day on the job.
- **Describe** how to create a positive relationship with your supervisor and coworkers.
- **Discuss** how good work habits are related to job success.
- **Identify** the effects of job stress at work.
- **Explain** the process of the performance evaluation.

Starting Your First Day

Your first step toward job success begins the first day on the job. As you learn your job duties and adjust to your job, your chances for success will increase.

Starting a new job and working with new people in a new environment may make you feel a little nervous. Most people feel this way when they start a new job. Planning ahead can help you feel more prepared for that first day. Think about how you should dress for the job and have your clothes prepared the night before. Allow yourself plenty of time to get ready. This includes getting dressed, eating a light breakfast, and preparing a lunch if necessary. Arrive a few minutes early at the job—definitely do not be late on your first day. Keeping a positive attitude will help you start your new job the right way.

What you do on the first day at work depends on your employer. A small business may want you to start working right away. Larger companies usually have an orientation for new workers. An **orientation** is a meeting at which a new employee learns the company's history, policies, rules, and safety procedures. You may also be asked to take a drug test. After the orientation, you will report to your supervisor. You may be asked to fill out payroll and other documents.

One of the first forms you will probably be asked to complete will be a W-4. A W-4 is used to determine the right amount of federal income tax to have withheld from your paycheck. Figure 18-1 is an example of a W-4 form. After you have worked for the company for a year, you may want to review your withholding amount. You can have more or less income tax withheld from your paycheck if you choose.

Cut here and give Form W-4 to your employer. Keep the top part for your records.

Form **W-4**
Department of the Treasury
Internal Revenue Service

Employee's Withholding Allowance Certificate

► **Whether you are entitled to claim a certain number of allowances or exemption from withholding is subject to review by the IRS. Your employer may be required to send a copy of this form to the IRS.**

OMB No. 1545-0074
20--

1 Type or print your first name and middle initial.	Last name	2 **Your social security number**
Home address (number and street or rural route)	3 ☐ Single ☐ Married ☐ Married, but withhold at higher Single rate. **Note.** If married, but legally separated, or spouse is a nonresident alien, check the "Single" box.	
City or town, state, and ZIP code	4 **If your last name differs from that shown on your social security card, check here. You must call 1-800-772-1213 for a replacement card.** ► ☐	

5 Total number of allowances you are claiming (from line **H** above **or** from the applicable worksheet on page 2) | 5 |

6 Additional amount, if any, you want withheld from each paycheck . . . . | 6 | $

7 I claim exemption from withholding for 20--, and I certify that I meet **both** of the following conditions for exemption.
- Last year I had a right to a refund of **all** federal income tax withheld because I had **no** tax liability **and**
- This year I expect a refund of **all** federal income tax withheld because I expect to have **no** tax liability.

If you meet both conditions, write "Exempt" here . . . . ► | 7 |

Under penalties of perjury, I declare that I have examined this certificate and to the best of my knowledge and belief, it is true, correct, and complete.

Employee's signature
(This form is not valid unless you sign it.) ► **Date ►**

8 Employer's name and address (Employer: Complete lines 8 and 10 only if sending to the IRS.)	9 Office code (optional)	10 Employer identification number (EIN)

For Privacy Act and Paperwork Reduction Act Notice, see page 2. Cat. No. 10220Q Form **W-4** (20--)

Figure 18-1. *US Department of the Treasury, Internal Revenue Service*
Employees are required to complete a W-4 form when starting a new job.

Your supervisor is responsible for your training. On your first day, he or she will show you where you work and explain your duties. You will be introduced to your coworkers. Sometimes another worker will teach you how to do the job, or you may watch an experienced worker. Depending on your job, you may attend a company training program or school. In any case, your concern at this point should be learning to do the job.

Pay close attention and show an interest in learning your job duties. Ask questions if you do not completely understand what is expected of you. Because you are new, do not try to work at full speed the first day. At this point, accuracy is much more important than speed. Try to do the job to the best of your ability, but if you make a mistake, do not worry. Inform your supervisor of your mistake and learn something from it. Making a true effort to do your best will help you succeed.

Relating to Others at Work

Learning your job duties is one of the first steps in starting a new job. To achieve success on the job, however, you also need to work well with other people. Companies function best when employees cooperate and work together as a team. Your ability to get along with your supervisor and coworkers will contribute to your success on the job.

Ethical Leadership

Dedication to Your Employer

"Dedication is not what others expect of you, it is what you can give to others."– Gail Devers

Accepting a job offer means you are dedicated and willing to work for the wages agreed to, and you are willing to abide by company policies. Most companies will have clearly defined policies regarding showing up to work every day, not taking advantage of breaks, and getting along with supervisors and coworkers. Your personal ethics will determine how dedicated you are to your employer. Being fair and honest with customers, following safety regulations, and adhering to guidelines regarding fighting, drinking, use of illegal drugs, and smoking all fall within category of ethical standards.

Working with Your Supervisor

In addition to training, your supervisor is responsible for your job performance. He or she must make sure your work is completed and done well. Your supervisor will observe your work to see how well you are doing your job and getting along with others. You may be encouraged to work faster or to try a new way of doing a job. Remember, this is constructive criticism. It can help you improve your skills and work more efficiently.

Sometimes you may be assigned tasks you do not want to do. As a beginner, you should perform these tasks as well as you would any others. Consider them learning experiences.

Supervisors have different personalities and management styles. No matter what type of supervisor you have, make the effort to learn and to cooperate with him or her. Listen and follow through on all suggestions. Most supervisors want you to succeed on the job, but you must do your part to promote a good working relationship.

Working with Coworkers

As a new employee, getting along with and being accepted by your coworkers is important. First, you will be happier and enjoy your work more in a workplace where everyone is pleasant to others. Second, you and coworkers will probably get more work done if you enjoy working together. It is important that you show an ability to work cooperatively with others. This cooperative effort could lead to future pay raises or even a better job.

Part of getting along with others depends on you. When you start your job, introduce yourself to coworkers if your supervisor has not done so. Learn their names. Try to be pleasant without overdoing it. Be friendly and most coworkers will accept you. Respect and accept them as both individuals and teammates. They have knowledge and skills to contribute to the company.

Although you may not become close friends with all of them, you should respect their positive qualities. Try to be a likable person so coworkers will enjoy working with you.

Unfortunately, there will be times you will encounter rude coworkers. Disrespectful, bad-mannered coworkers exist in most every workplace. They are usually rude because of something that is going on with them. Do not take their behavior personally. Some ways you can deal with their behavior are shown in Figure 18-2.

Bullying at Work

Bullying normally involves offensive, insulting, or threatening behavior by individuals or groups. Some tactics used by bullies are verbal, nonverbal, psychological, or physical abuse. These actions may make you feel threatened or humiliated. The bullying may come from your immediate supervisor or someone higher up, from a coworker, or even from a customer.

If you are a victim of bullying, warn the person causing the problem to stop, otherwise you will take further action. Keep a detailed diary of every incident, noting dates, times, who was

Dealing with Bullying Behavior
• **Consult a friend.** Get a second opinion about the situation.
• **Be polite.** He or she may be influenced by your positive behavior.
• **Take charge.** Stand up to the person without being disrespectful.
• **Inform HR.** Consult your human resources department as a last resort.

michaeljung/Shutterstock.com

Goodheart-Willcox Publisher

Figure 18-2.
Use these tips when confronted by rude coworkers.

involved, and what happened. If the bullying fails to stop, you may decide to make a formal complaint. If you do decide to make a formal complaint, be sure to follow the company's grievance procedure.

Remember, you are a beginner getting to know your job. Learn to accept suggestions or criticism positively as a way to improve your work. Acting like a know-it-all or being self-centered will give others a bad impression of you.

Respecting Diversity

The increasing diversity in the population of the United States is reflected in the workplace. In a workplace with workers from different backgrounds, each individual contributes something unique to the success of the business. It is important to relate to everyone you encounter at work with respect. By treating others with respect, you will be able to minimize misunderstanding and be more productive.

Developing Productive Work Habits

Your ability to develop good work habits will be a big factor in your success on the job. Good work habits start with a good attitude and the desire to be productive. Employers want workers who consistently behave properly on the job. As you progress through your career, you should work to strengthen the habits shown in Figure 18-3 and described here.

- **Follow directions.** Pay close attention and show interest in learning your job duties. Make sure you perform all your responsibilities on the job. If necessary, keep careful notes about your assignments so you do not forget any directions.

Productive Work Habits

- Follow directions.
- Upgrade your skills whenever possible.
- Find other tasks to do instead of wasting time when your work is done.
- Keep an upbeat attitude.
- Learn from your small mistakes and avoid repeating them.
- Avoid gossip and saying bad things about others.
- Try to get along with everyone.
- Assert yourself.
- Take responsibility.

Stuart Jenner/Shutterstock.com

Figure 18-3.   *©Goodheart-Willcox Publisher*
Apply these rules of good conduct to develop positive relationships with others in the workplace.

- **Upgrade your skills whenever possible.** Enjoying learning new things will make you a happier person and a better, more productive employee. Willingly try new tasks and believe in your ability to succeed.
- **Find other tasks to do instead of wasting time when your work is done.** Let your supervisor know that you need more assignments added to your workload. If something is spilled, do something about cleaning it up. This is all part of acting responsibly.
- **Keep an upbeat attitude.** Avoid letting problems at home or school interfere with your work. Peoples' attitudes are infectious. If you are enthusiastic, others might follow your lead. Graciously accept suggestions and constructive criticism about your work with a positive attitude.
- **Learn from your small mistakes and avoid repeating them.** Everyone makes mistakes. How you choose to deal with the mistakes you make will determine whether or not you will be a success. Report big mistakes to your supervisor as soon as possible and discuss how to handle them. Above all, do not cover up mistakes or deny they ever happened.
- **Avoid gossip and saying bad things about others.** In doing so, your coworkers will trust and respect you. Most office gossip is merely rumor or suspicion, neither of which is worth your time. Even if you do not spread the gossip you hear, listening to gossip can also be viewed negatively.
- **Try to get along with everyone.** Stay in full control of your emotions. At some point or another, everyone encounters a work situation that might make him or her angry. Controlling your anger at these times is very important. When events become too heated, find a way to break the tension so everyone can take time to think. Voice complaints to the proper authorities instead of complaining to coworkers.
- **Assert yourself.** Act confidently and voice your convictions in a manner that does not come across as being bossy or overly aggressive. A **conviction** is a strong belief. Defend the decisions you make and the people who support you.
- **Take responsibility.** Do assignments well, meet all deadlines, and alert your supervisor if you think you may miss a deadline. Do not make excuses for poor performance or bad decisions. Accept your errors and correct them. Do not blame problems on coworkers. Taking responsibility for your actions in your personal and professional life is a sign of maturity and trustworthiness.

Go Green

There are many on-the-job practices every employee and member of management can follow to help with the "green" philosophy. Not throwing trash on the floor or worksite is one simple example. Other examples are turning off lights as you leave a room, placing used drink containers in recycling bins, and recycling waste materials. While driving motorized vehicles, prudent driving practices will help conserve fuel. A surprising large volume of energy and materials may be conserved if everyone does a small part.

Handling Job Stress

No matter where you work or how well you get along with others, you are likely to face some sort of job stress. By understanding stress and what causes it, you can learn to handle it effectively.

People face some form of stress in their lives every day. **Stress** is a feeling of pressure, strain, or tension that results from change. Change can create different levels of stress. Major changes, such as the death of a friend or the loss of a job, are extremely stressful. Losing a homework assignment or being late for work is less stressful. Even positive changes like a pay raise or a vacation can be stressful.

Stress can have positive or negative effects on people. It can motivate them to get things done or face new challenges. On the other hand, stress can cause frustration, anger, and lower productivity. Too much stress can affect a person's body and the mind. It can eventually lead to health problems including headaches or high blood pressure.

Stress, no matter what the cause, can affect job performance. Workers react to stress in different ways. Those who feel a lot of stress are likely to be less productive and have more accidents on the job. They tend to blame and criticize others. Workers who make an effort to handle stress, however, stay in control of their emotions. They may use humor to break the tension. They may try to analyze the situation to find the problem's cause. Above all, they channel their energy to getting the problem solved and the job done.

You cannot avoid stress in your life, but you can learn how to manage it. Handling stress begins by recognizing the cause and learning to deal with it. Several ways to handle stress effectively are shown in Figure 18-4.

Handling Stress
Keep a positive attitude. Use stress in a positive way to help you set and achieve your goals.
Stay healthy. This helps you handle the causes of stress. To relieve stress, try some physical activity.
Discuss your problem. A friend, family member, or counselor may see your problem differently.
Manage your time well. List all your tasks. Do the most important first. Check off each task as you complete it.
Know your limits. Sometimes a problem may be beyond your control and cannot be changed right away. Learn to accept the situation until you can change it.
Cooperate with others. Try to give and take instead of fighting or confronting.
Find healthy ways to relieve stress. Get involved in an activity if you are lonely or sad. Try deep breaths to relieve built-up tension.
Take time to relax and have fun. Relaxing helps you slow down your pace and lessen stress. Recreation gives you a break from your everyday routine.

Jeffrey J Coleman/Shutterstock.com

Figure 18-4.   *Goodheart-Willcox Publisher*
Learning to handle stress is the key to good mental and physical health.

Evaluating Job Performance

After working at a job for several weeks, you can begin to evaluate your job performance and the job itself. To help you find out if you are succeeding on your job, ask yourself a series of questions.

Am I making progress in this job? Have I learned how to perform my job duties successfully? If you are having a problem learning how to do a task, ask your supervisor for assistance. If you are accomplishing your work with time to spare, let your supervisor know you are capable of taking on more responsibility. The more you can learn and accomplish, the faster you will succeed on the job.

Consider the example of Marla, who learned her job duties quickly and became a very productive worker in a few weeks. When she accomplished her assigned work, she asked the supervisor for other assignments to handle. Marla was a responsible and cooperative employee who was always willing to help others with tasks whenever asked. When the assistant supervisor was promoted to a new position, Marla was asked to take that position. She accepted and continued to work just as conscientiously at her new job. Marla's hard work paid off, and it helped her get better jobs in the future.

Does this job give me personal satisfaction? Do I enjoy the work I do? You cannot expect a job to be all fun and games, but it should not be all drudgery either. Job success depends on the way you feel about your job. To be successful, you must feel your job is useful and helpful to others. If you feel you are making important contributions on the job, you will probably feel pleased about your life and the work you accomplish.

Am I paid adequately for the work I do? Although salary is only one aspect of job success, it is an important one. Check to see what other people with similar jobs are making at other companies. Your wages should be in that range. However, do not expect to begin an entry-level job at a high salary. Normally, a worker can expect to start at the lower end of the wage scale and move up as he or she becomes more productive. If you do not get a salary review or pay increase after six months on the job, you should find out why.

Can I foresee opportunities for advancement? If I do well in my present job, will I be able to move to a higher-paying job with more responsibilities? If you find you are in a job that leads nowhere, it is doubtful that you will find much success in your work. Having a goal to work toward can motivate you to succeed at your present job.

Keep in mind that no job is perfect. Every job has its good and bad points. When the bad points outweigh the good, however, you may find you need to change jobs.

Job Probation

Sometimes a worker is hired on a probationary basis. A **job probation** is a trial period to test how well a worker can do the job. A probationary period can be as short as a few days or as long as a few months. During this period, a supervisor helps train the new worker and oversees his or her work. The supervisor also evaluates the worker's job skills, work habits, and ability to get along with coworkers.

Most workers complete their probationary period with very little trouble. With the help of their supervisors, they learn how to be productive at their jobs and avoid making mistakes.

If a worker does not pass probation, he or she is not hired. If this should happen to you, be sure to find out why you did not pass. You do not want to make the same mistakes again at your next job.

Students with work experience are less likely to have problems during their probationary period. This is because past work experience tends to help them adjust to new jobs more easily.

Performance Rating

Job success depends a great deal on your performance in the workplace. A **performance rating** is a supervisor's periodic evaluation of a worker's job performance. At most companies, employees are reviewed every six months or once a year, and a record is kept on file. During these reviews, employees are rated on their work and social skills as well as their attitudes on the job.

As shown in Figure 18-5, employee performance review forms are used by companies to evaluate how well an employee is doing his or her job. Employees are rated on job factors such as productivity, work quality, teamwork, dependability, and safety. The supervisor evaluates an employee's performance according to a rating scale. An overall summary may also be a part of the performance rating.

The purpose of performance ratings is to help supervisors identify the weaknesses and strengths of their employees. After a performance rating, a supervisor may decide that an employee's skills would be better used for a different job. Therefore, the supervisor may move the employee to another position or transfer him or her to another department. For example, after a performance rating, a supervisor may decide to assign a receptionist who has shown excellent keyboarding skills to an administrative assistant position. A receptionist who has been especially skilled at working with the public may be transferred to the customer service department.

If the employee is having problems with certain tasks, the supervisor can work with the employee to help improve the weaker skills. The supervisor may also assign the worker to another job.

Employee Performance Review Form

Employee Name: _____   Hire Date: _____

Job Classification: _____   Appraisal Date: _____

Supervision: _____   Last Appraisal Date: _____

Productivity. Employee's performance (is)

( ) Must Improve   ( ) Meets Expectations   ( ) Exceptional
in meeting company productivity standards.

Explain: _____

_____

Quality. Employee's performance (is)

( ) Must Improve   ( ) Meets Expectations   ( ) Exceptional
in meeting company quality standards.

Explain: _____

_____

Teamwork. Employee's performance (is)

( ) Must Improve   ( ) Meets Expectations   ( ) Exceptional
in meeting company teamwork standards.

Explain: _____

_____

Dependability. Employee's performance (is)

( ) Must Improve   ( ) Meets Expectations   ( ) Exceptional
in meeting company dependability standards.

Explain: _____

_____

Safety. Employee's performance (is)

( ) Must Improve   ( ) Meets Expectations   ( ) Exceptional
in meeting company safety standards.

Explain: _____

_____

Figure 18-5.   *Goodheart-Willcox Publisher*
Employers consider many factors when evaluating a worker's job performance.

Case

Dealing with Restaurant Customers

John worked as a server in a restaurant known for its fine food and excellent customer service. There were many restaurants in town, but this relatively new restaurant had quickly established many loyal customers. John was careful to place the table service correctly and present the menus properly. He did these tasks better than any of his coworkers.

John seemed to have a reserved manner with customers, however. He didn't smile much and his face often looked grim. When a customer complained about the food, the bill, or the service, John became irritable. He occasionally talked back to customers. This conduct was strictly forbidden in the restaurant's employee handbook. John also complained to his coworkers.

One night just before closing, a large group entered the restaurant. The people were seated in John's area. He took their orders and served them properly even though he wanted to go home early. When the group finished eating, it was after the closing hour. John noticed they left a smaller tip than he expected.

Just as the group was leaving John said, "That wasn't much of a tip for the service you got." His boss heard the comment and fired John on the spot.

Critical Thinking

1. Why was John fired?
2. What rules of proper conduct did John disobey?
3. Do you think John's boss fired him too hastily? Would you have given John another chance?

As a result of performance ratings, employees become aware of their strengths and weaknesses. Most supervisors show workers their evaluation forms or talk to them about their past performance and future with the company. In most cases, employees must sign their forms.

Performance reviews give employees a chance to learn how they can improve their work and become more productive employees. By improving their job performance, they will have an opportunity to get pay raises and take more desirable positions. It is important to examine your performance ratings and what they mean for your future employment.

Training Opportunities

The skills required for most jobs are changing rapidly. Your employer will consider how well you perform your present duties and how willing you are to upgrade skills and learn new ones. Employees who are unwilling to take advantage of training opportunities could lose their jobs.

Most companies value employees who are willing to further their training and education. These companies offer employees some type of incentive to do so. An **incentive** is something that inspires a person to act. Some of the ways employees may be inspired to pursue further training include the following:

- free in-house training;
- a pay raise; and
- complete or partial payment of tuition for approved courses taken at technical schools, community colleges, and universities.

Checkpoint 18.1

1. List three things an employee can do to prepare for the first day on the job.
2. What is a W-4 form? When should you complete one?
3. Who is responsible for your training when you start a new job?
4. What is the purpose of a performance rating?
5. What does it mean for a worker to be hired on a probationary basis?

Build Your Vocabulary

As you progress through this text, develop a personal glossary of career-related terms and add it to your portfolio. This will help you build your vocabulary and prepare you for your career of choice. Write a definition for each of the following terms, and add it to your personal career glossary.

orientation
bullying
conviction
stress
job probation
performance rating
incentive

18.2 Changing Jobs

Objectives

After completing this section you will be able to:

- **List** and describe various ways your job status could change.
- **Explain** the process of making a job change.

Changes in Job Status

Part of being successful in the workplace is being able to handle changes in your job status in a positive way. Usually, the abilities you demonstrate on the job are the reasons for a change in your job status. The ways that a person's job status can change includes promotions, lateral moves, demotions, and firing.

Promotion

A **promotion** is a transfer to a job classification with a higher pay grade. A promotion is not something an employer gives to just any employee. It is a sign your employer appreciates your job performance. A promotion is an advancement that employees earn by being productive, cooperative, dependable, and responsible on the job.

A promotion is earned as a result of being a productive and dependable employee.

bikerriderlondon/Shutterstock.com

If you are promoted, you will probably be given a new job title, an increase in pay, and more responsibility. With increased responsibility, you may be asked to supervise the work of others. This means your role would change to that of a supervisor. Not only would you be responsible for your work, but also for the work of those under your authority.

Not all promotions lead to supervisory positions. Some are simply a matter of reclassification. For example, Nadira was hired as an administrative assistant at a number three classification. After working six months and receiving a good performance rating, Nadira earned a number two classification. Although her duties stayed the same, Nadira's salary increased 10 percent. When Nadira advances to the number one classification, there is no higher level for her to achieve as a company secretary. She will continue to receive small pay increases as long as she does good work, but she will not be given any new responsibilities.

Have you ever thought of what it would be like to be the supervisor? The idea of becoming a supervisor may sound like a lot of work. In fact, you may be wondering if you can handle the responsibility. If you are asked to become a supervisor, you are capable of handling the job. Many companies have training classes to help new supervisors adjust to their new responsibilities and learn how to be successful at their jobs. If you are given the opportunity to advance to a supervisory position, consider the offer carefully. Review your occupational plans and think about how this promotion can help further your career.

The opportunity for a promotion does not come along every day. If you turn down a promotion, it may be a long time before you are offered another one.

Lateral Move

A **lateral move** is a transfer to a different department or another classification in the same pay grade. The person may receive a different title and new responsibilities, but no increase in pay. Lateral moves let workers experience different jobs or departments in a company, which makes them more valuable employees.

A lateral move may not be viewed in a positive light by some people. For example, they may consider it a demotion. To them, it signifies the boss does not consider them worthy of a promotion. However, if the company is reducing its workforce, a lateral move may be a compliment. It may mean the company wants to keep the person and is willing to find another position for him or her.

Demotion

A **demotion** is a transfer to a classification in a lower pay grade. A demotion usually indicates the company is not satisfied with the employee's work. It usually is a final warning before an employee is fired.

A demotion is never considered a positive achievement in a person's career. When it occurs, it is important for the employee to take this last opportunity to work hard and demonstrate a desire to keep his or her job. When demoted, however, the employee usually starts looking for employment elsewhere.

Termination

A *termination* occurs when a company releases a worker from a job. A person who is terminated no longer works for the company. This separation from the company is also referred to as *being fired* or *being let go*. This change in job status is the hardest to accept. Knowing the reason for being terminated sometimes helps ease the pain, but not entirely. If an employee is released because of cutbacks in the workforce, it is easier to understand.

If an employee is released because of poor work performance or other negative reasons, usually the employee is not really surprised. Employees who do not perform as expected are normally aware they may be fired.

Ninety percent of firings, however, are due to personal reasons, such as improper conduct and difficulty working with others. Often these people have good job skills. Following are the most common reasons employers give for firing employees:

- absenteeism—not showing up for work on a regular basis;
- loafing—taking long breaks, leaving workstations for no good reason, or daydreaming on the job;
- personality conflicts—not getting along with the supervisor or coworkers;
- violating company rules—primarily fighting and ignoring safety regulations; and
- incompetence—not demonstrating the knowledge, skills, experience, or attitude to perform the job responsibilities as requested.

If you should ever find yourself out of a job unexpectedly, give yourself a couple days to recover from the shock. Then try to figure out why you were fired. Did you do or say something to contribute to the situation? Was your employer fair to you? Were there financial reasons that made the action necessary?

Be honest with yourself. If you did something you were not supposed to do, admit it. Do not lie or try to blame someone else. If you care about your future and career, you will not make the same mistake again.

Changes in job status cause employees to think about how their jobs fit their plan for the future. Usually changes in job status are positive events in employment history.

Making a Job Change

Look carefully at your job status and at your performance ratings. Are you in a dead-end job? You may wonder if it is best to "stick it out" or "move on." At several points during your career, you will find yourself struggling with these questions: Should I stay with this job or find a new one? Should I leave this secure position and risk the uncertainties of another? Can I find or create my dream job right here, or must I work for someone else to achieve that goal?

Signs of a Stalled Career

In the United States, people tend to change jobs often, especially in their early years of employment. If you seem to be doing the same things over and over, then your career is not progressing and a new job may be what you need. The clues that your career may be stalled are listed in Figure 18-6 and explained here.

- **Your job responsibilities have not changed in three or more years.** If your name does not come up when a position opens, it is possible that management feels, for one or a number of reasons, you should stay in your present position.
- **Your responsibilities are reduced.** This may be a sign your job may be eliminated. Look for another way to become involved in the company, or start networking with colleagues at other companies and prepare your résumé.
- **You are not chosen for important projects or committees.** Management may feel you are a good, reliable worker, but does not consider you valuable for more challenging projects. Not participating in important committees and projects limits your exposure to the key people in the company.
- **You have been passed over for promotions or demoted.** Either situation is a definite clue your supervisor feels you should not have a job with more responsibility. It may be time to start looking for a job outside the company.

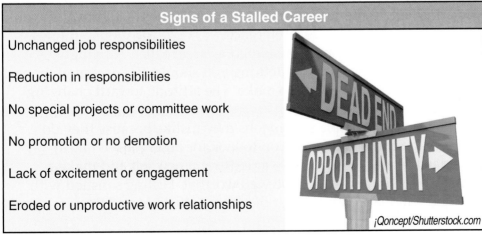

Signs of a Stalled Career
Unchanged job responsibilities
Reduction in responsibilities
No special projects or committee work
No promotion or no demotion
Lack of excitement or engagement
Eroded or unproductive work relationships

¡Qoncept/Shutterstock.com

Figure 18-6.   Goodheart-Willcox Publisher
When these signs occur repeatedly, a worker might want to consider other job opportunities.

- **You are bored, find it hard to focus, and get little enjoyment from those things that once excited you.** If this happens every day, you may be happier with other responsibilities or another job. Everyone, however, has days that are frustrating or not very exciting.
- **Your relationships with the boss or coworkers are strained or deteriorated.** Personality clashes are part of life and something experienced by everyone. If these clashes lead to extreme unhappiness for anyone, it is important to try to resolve the differences. If they cannot be resolved, work is going to suffer and a change in job status may be next.

When you decide to change jobs, plan the change carefully. Avoid making a quick decision. Think about your career and future plans. Think about the reasons you want to leave your present job and the type of job you want next. What do you plan to accomplish by making a change? You should not just walk away. Make sure you have another job lined up before leaving the one you have.

If you decide to leave a job, you should try to leave on good terms. Quitting suddenly is not fair to your employer, and it will not leave your employer with a good impression of you. As a general rule, notify your supervisor in writing at least two weeks before you plan to leave. This will give your employer a chance to find another worker to replace you. Offer to train your replacement and finish all your work. If your job involves a great deal of responsibility and training, you should try to notify your employer even earlier.

You may be expected to give your employer an exit interview. The purpose of an exit interview is to provide the employer with information to help establish and maintain good working relationships with its employees. To prepare for your exit interview, make a list of positive comments regarding your employment. You may also want to share constructive criticisms that can be helpful to the employer in the future. It is best to be as positive as possible in an exit interview.

Do not bad-mouth anyone, even the boss. In this era of networking, your negative comments may travel back to the people you criticized. In the future, you will want the boss's approval so you can use his or her name as a reference.

Job hopping was once considered a career killer. Although hopping from job to job is something you should avoid, changing jobs can be a very positive move to make. The attitude toward changing jobs has shifted.

All too often, people stay in jobs they dislike because they do not have the courage or ambition to look for other jobs. It takes considerable courage and drive to look for a new job and make a change, but the rewards can be well worth it. Feeling satisfied with your job will make you feel happier about your life and the work you accomplish.

Checkpoint 18.2

1. List the four types of changes possible in job status.

2. List the most common reasons employers give for terminating employees.

3. Name six signs that indicate your job or career may be stalled.

4. How much notice should you give your supervisor before leaving a job?

5. What is the purpose of an exit interview?

Build Your Vocabulary

As you progress through this text, develop a personal glossary of career-related terms and add it to your portfolio. This will help you build your vocabulary and prepare you for your career of choice. Write a definition for each of the following terms, and add it to your personal career glossary.

promotion
lateral move
demotion

18.3 | Labor Unions

Objectives

After completing this section you will be able to:
- **Explain** the purpose of a labor union.
- **Explain** when union membership is required.
- **Describe** the basic types of unions.
- **Explain** the process of collective bargaining.

What Are Labor Unions?

A **labor union** is a group of workers who have united to voice their opinions to their employer or the employer's representatives (management). Ideally, the purpose of a union is to help workers be successful and secure on the job by bargaining with management for better wages, working hours, working conditions, and benefits.

Labor unions developed in the early days of industry because of poor working conditions, low wages, child labor, and unfair treatment of employees. By coming together, workers found they gained strength and power to discuss these problems with management.

As a result of unions and changes in corporate attitudes, many of the problems that faced workers in the early 1900s have been solved. Workers are no longer faced with terrible working conditions. Laws have been passed to protect workers' rights and safety. Management has learned over the years that satisfied workers are more productive workers.

Some people believe unions have accomplished their original purposes and are no longer needed. They no longer want to pay union dues to support their local and national union organizations. On the other hand, others feel that unions still serve a useful purpose. They continue to campaign for improved working conditions and increased wages and benefits. Unions help retrain workers whose jobs are assumed by automation. They also influence the labor and fair trade laws legislation.

Union Membership

Must you join a union? The answer to this question depends on the state in which you work and the kind of job you have. Some occupations do not have union affiliations. However, others require union membership.

If a workplace has a *union shop agreement,* all its workers must join the union as a condition of employment. In such cases, if you were hired by a company, you would not be able to work beyond a certain initial period unless you joined the union.

If a workplace has an *open shop agreement,* its workers are free to join or not join the union. Most unions oppose this type of agreement because they represent all workers in their negotiations. Therefore, they feel every worker should be required to join the union.

To find out what type of shop agreement a company has, call the company or check with your state's labor department. If you have a choice about whether to join a union or not, do a little investigating first. To help decide if joining a union will benefit you at your job, answer these key questions.

- What has the union accomplished? What are its plans for the future?
- Are there so many workers that the help of a union is needed to negotiate terms that benefit all workers?
- What is the initial fee to join? What monthly or weekly dues are withheld from your paycheck?

Keep in mind that if you join a union, you must abide by union rules. If you have a complaint about work, you must follow a specific procedure for getting the problem solved. It is possible that you and your manager could easily solve the problem yourselves, but you must follow union rules. If the union votes to go on strike, whether you believe it should or not, you must support the decision and live with reduced pay or without a paycheck during the strike period.

Many electricians, plumbers, and carpenters are members of craft unions.

oldbunyip/Shutterstock.com

Types of Unions

Three major types of labor unions exist in the United States—craft unions, industrial unions, and public workers unions. Each of these three types of unions serves a specific group of workers.

- **Craft unions.** Craft unions are formed by workers who have the same craft or trade. There are craft unions for carpenters, painters, plumbers, electricians, and machinists. For example, the union for carpenters is called the United Brotherhood of Carpenters and Joiners. The union for electricians is the International Brotherhood of Electrical Workers (IBEW).
- **Industrial unions.** Industrial unions are formed by workers who belong to the same industry. Most industrial union members work in factories where cars, clothing, steel, and other products are made. The industrial union for autoworkers is called the United Automobile Workers (UAW).
- **Public Workers Unions.** Public workers unions may be defined as any person employed at the state, county, or municipal level of government, including governmental corporations and authorities. There are exceptions in some states. These public employees are found at all levels of government, from the federal, state, and local levels to special districts.

The basic work of unions is done in the locals. A local union has its own constitution, bylaws, and set of officers. The local union also elects shop stewards who handle members' complaints about management.

National unions consist of many local unions. For example, the UAW has local unions practically everywhere cars are manufactured in the United States. Some national unions such as the UAW have more than a million members.

Through collective bargaining, labor and management discuss how to reach an agreement that satisfies both parties.

Golden Pixels LLC/Shutterstock.com

Collective Bargaining

Collective bargaining is the process of labor and management representatives discussing what they expect from each other in the workplace. In a way, collective bargaining is like a buyer and a seller debating the price of something to be sold. Labor may first demand much more than it expects to get. Management will offer much less than it intends to give.

Through debate, discussion, and possibly arguments, a compromise is finally reached in the form of a labor contract. A **labor contract** is an agreement that spells out the conditions for wages, benefits, job security, work hours, working conditions, and grievance procedures. A *grievance procedure* is a step-by-step process for handling complaints from union members.

Bargaining for a new contract can be a long process. It usually begins weeks or months before the date an existing contract expires. Representatives from management and labor each present their positions and demands. When an agreement is reached for a new work contract, union members vote to accept or reject it. If the membership rejects the contract, union representatives go back to the bargaining table and bargain for different terms.

If no agreement can be reached and the existing contract expires, sometimes members will vote to strike. The strike will last until the company meets union demands, comes closer to meeting the demands, or the union agrees to go back to work. On the other hand, management can threaten to close down the company unless an agreement is reached. Obviously, either action can be a loss to both labor and management. This is why it is important for both labor and management to be reasonable in their expectations.

Checkpoint 18.3

1. What early concerns led to the need for unions?
2. What should a worker do to identify the type of shop agreement a company has?
3. Explain the difference between a union shop agreement and an open shop agreement.
4. What are the three types of labor unions that exist in the United States?
5. What is a grievance procedure?

Build Your Vocabulary

As you progress through this text, develop a personal glossary of career-related terms and add it to your portfolio. This will help you build your vocabulary and prepare you for your career of choice. Write a definition for each of the following terms, and add it to your personal career glossary.

 labor union
 collective bargaining
 labor contract

Chapter Summary

Section 18.1 Your First Job

- Starting a new job will require training and working with new people. An employee should prepare for the first day and be willing to learn his or her new responsibilities.
- Creating positive relationships on the job is necessary. Getting along with coworkers will encourage teamwork and make the job more enjoyable.
- Productive work habits are required in the workplace. Employers want workers who behave properly and treat others with respect.
- People face different forms of stress often. Stress can affect your body, mind, and job performance, if you are unable to control it.
- Evaluating your job performance is one way for you to judge your success on the job. A performance rating by your supervisor helps show your strengths and weaknesses.

Section 18.2 Changing Jobs

- Earning a job promotion is one step to job success. However, getting a demotion or losing a job can be an unpleasant experience.
- An employee should learn to recognize the signs of a stalled career. Prior to changing jobs, the decision should be made carefully.

Section 18.3 Labor Unions

- Unions were developed to help workers be successful and secure in their jobs. Proper working conditions, competitive wages, and good benefits are important to labor unions and their workers.
- Union membership is required if a company has a union shop agreement. If a company has an open shop agreement, a worker is free to join the union or not.
- There are three types of labor unions in the United States. These include craft unions, industrial unions, and public workers unions.
- Representatives of labor and management discuss work expectations through the process of collective bargaining. This process allows both parties to reach a compromise that is reasonable for each side.

Check Your Career IQ

Now that you have finished the chapter, see what you learned about careers by taking the chapter posttest. The test can be accessed on the mobile site by using a smartphone or on the G-W Learning companion website.

www.m.g-wlearning.com
www.g-wlearning.com

Review Your Knowledge

1. Explain how conduct is important to job success.
2. What are some of the negative effects of stress?
3. List three incentives that motivate some workers to pursue training opportunities.
4. Explain the difference between a promotion and a lateral move.
5. Identify three signs that indicate a worker lacks excitement or engagement for a job.
6. What should a worker do to prepare for an exit interview?
7. What is the purpose of a union?
8. What choice does an open shop agreement provide to workers?
9. Why do unions oppose open shop agreements?
10. Discuss why collective bargaining is beneficial.

Apply Your Knowledge

1. List five reasons why you are succeeding at your work-based learning experience. Also list five ways you can improve your job performance. Working with three classmates, share your lists. Discuss ways each person in the group can improve on his or her job performance.
2. Talk to two people who recently changed jobs. Ask why and how each person changed his or her job. Ask what he or she hopes to accomplish in the new job. Are there any similarities in the answers provided? Do you feel each person made a good decision? Be prepared to discuss your findings in class.
3. Obtain two or more employee handbooks from different companies. Take notes as you compare their policies and procedures regarding workplace behaviors and standards. Summarize your findings in writing.
4. Visit the website for the Internal Revenue Service. Print out a copy of a W-4 form. Fill out the form as best as possible. For your privacy, **do not** include your social security number. Discuss the form with your class. What are some reasons a person may want to change his or her withholding amount?
5. Use the Internet to conduct research on a labor union. When was the union founded? What is the mission or goal of the union? Who are some of the leaders or representatives? Search for additional information regarding membership, programs, and benefits. Compile your information in a chart.
6. Prepare a class presentation on the effects of stress. What are the negative effects? Are there any positive effects? What can people do to alleviate stress? Support your presentation with facts, examples, and your personal accounts.

7. Review Figure 18-2. Explain the benefits of each tip. Organize your opinions in a chart.

8. Gather information on a recent, well-publicized strike. What conditions brought about the strike? How was the strike resolved? Did the union members accomplish their goals by striking? Summarize your findings in an oral report.

9. Create a performance appraisal. Select one of the Career Snapshot features as your focus for this activity. Using a word processing program, create a performance appraisal for the job title featured in the Career Snapshot. Your appraisal should include ratings for performance areas that are significant to the job, as well as spaces for the employee's name, job title, manager's comments, and any other information you consider necessary. Refer to Figure 18-5 for guidance, but develop a form that will effectively evaluate the job you selected.

10. Complete a performance appraisal. Print out the appraisal you completed in Activity 9. Fill out the appraisal as if you are evaluating an employee from the related Career Snapshot. Write comments for each area to support your evaluation. Share your appraisal with a group of classmates. Based on this information, would you recommend a promotion for this employee? Why or why not? Discuss what you have learned about performance appraisals while completing this activity.

Teamwork

 Working with three other classmates, develop a role-play that demonstrates the rules of proper conduct in the workplace. The role-play should include examples of workers who do follow the rules and those who do not. Working with the members of your group, decide how to divide the tasks accordingly.

G-W Learning Mobile Site

 Visit the G-W Learning mobile site to complete the chapter pretest and posttest and to practice vocabulary using e-flash cards. If you do not have a smartphone, visit the G-W Learning companion website to access these features.
G-W Learning mobile site: www.m.g-wlearning.com
G-W Learning companion website: www.g-wlearning.com

College and Career Readiness

Common Core

Listening. Informative listening is the process of listening to gain specific information from a speaker. Interview a person who evaluates worker performance as part of his or her job. Ask that person to share the criteria by which employees are evaluated. Take notes. Evaluate the speaker's point of view. Do you think that a person being evaluated has a different perspective on the process than does the person doing the evaluation? Why or why not? Did you listen closely enough to accurately record the important information?

Speaking. Research the features of various job search sites. Compile information about the aspects of each type and what type of job seeker each serves. Use this information, along with what you already know to gather ideas to create the perfect search site for you. Using various elements (visual displays, written handouts, technological displays), present your site to the class. Explain why you chose the features you did.

Apply Your Technology Skills

Access the G-W Learning companion website for this text at www.g-wlearning.com. Download each data file for this chapter. Follow the instructions to complete activities to practice what you have learned in this chapter.

Data File 18–1—**Dealing with a Stressful Workplace**

College and Career Readiness Portfolio

College and Career Readiness

In an earlier activity, you learned the purpose of a résumè. You listed your education and skills to include in your résumè. Now it is time to consider your work experience and activities. In the work experience section, include the names and addresses of current and previous employers. Include your job title and the dates you worked at each job. Arrange the jobs in order by date. If you have not been employed, you can omit this section. However, you could list volunteer work instead. You may include another section on the résumè with a heading such as *Awards* or *Activities*. Here, you can list awards you received or clubs or activities in which you took part. These entries might be related directly to the position, or they might simply show your involvement with the community. At the end of the résumè, include a statement indicating that references will be provided on request.

1. Continue creating your résumè. Add a section for work experience and one for awards or activities as described above. Finish with the statement about references.
2. Save the information for use in a later activity.

Chapter 19

Diversity and Workplace Rights

Section 19.1
Understanding
Workplace Diversity

Section 19.2
Equality and Workplace
Rights

College and Career Readiness

Reading Prep. Scan this chapter and look for factual information. As you read this chapter, try to determine which topics are fact and which are the author's opinion. After you have completed the chapter, research the topics and verify which details are facts and which are opinions.

Introduction

The term *diversity* means that we are all different in our own way, coming together to share and create a dynamic workplace. Diversity involves respecting people's differences. When diversity is supported, everyone is allowed to maintain his or her individuality.

The United States is the most diverse country in the world because its population comes from every other nation. No other country in the world can make this claim. Our changing population includes a wide range of cultures, ages, and other characteristics.

Diversity brings with it communication challenges in the workplace. In order to be a productive citizen, it is necessary to learn to work and communicate with others from diverse backgrounds. Identifying and embracing diversity creates a positive workplace environment.

Check Your Career IQ

Before you begin the chapter, see what you already know about careers by taking the chapter pretest. Use the related QR code to view the pretest on the mobile site. If you do not have a smartphone, visit the G-W Learning companion website to access the pretest.

www.m.g-wlearning.com
www.g-wlearning.com

G-W Mobile

Career Snapshot
Special Education Teacher

What Does a Special Education Teacher Do?

A special education teacher works with children who have a variety of disabilities. Various types of disabilities may qualify children for special education programs, including specific learning disabilities, speech or language impairments, mental retardation, emotional disturbance, hearing and visual impairments, autism, traumatic brain injury, and other health impairments. A special education teacher must:

- use various techniques to promote learning;
- individualize instruction, problem-solving assignments, and group work;
- help students develop emotionally and interact effectively in social situations.

What Is It Like to Work as a Special Education Teacher?

Special education teachers work in a variety of settings. Some have their own classrooms and teach only special education students. Others work as special education resource teachers, offering individualized help to students in general education classrooms. Others teach with general education teachers in classes, including both general and special education students. Some teachers work with special education students for several hours a day in a resource room, separate from the student's general education classroom.

Teachers use specialized equipment such as computers with synthesized speech, interactive educational software programs, and audiotapes to assist children.

What Education and Skills Are Needed to Be a Special Education Teacher?

- bachelor degree
- certification as a special education teacher
- patience
- willingness to be patient and flexible

19.1 Understanding Workplace Diversity

Objectives

After completing this section, you will be able to:
- **Explain** the benefits of diversity in the workplace.
- **Describe** ways employers and employees can promote workplace diversity.

Benefits of Diversity in the Workplace

Being able to work with people from different backgrounds is important to employers. This requires respecting differences. It also means not allowing stereotypes to interfere with teamwork. **Stereotyping** is classifying or generalizing about a group of people. Recognizing differences without using stereotypes is a way to show respect. People from different backgrounds may have different customs and ways of looking at things. A gesture that is considered positive or respectful by some may be seen as an insult by others. Treat others with respect, and apologize if you offend someone. Your honest intention to respect others will help in building healthy, productive relationships.

Workplace **diversity** means respecting the contributions of coworkers who are unlike you. Companies have found that teaching employees to value workers' differences yields the following positive results.

- **There are fewer lawsuits.** The enormous expense of money and time devoted to defending a company against charges of unequal opportunity is reduced or eliminated.
- **Morale is high.** Employees feel more comfortable and at ease because the emphasis is on what they contribute, not who they are.
- **Creativity increases.** Since all ideas are valued, people feel greater freedom to make suggestions and present alternative views.
- **Productivity increases.** When people feel respected, they are committed to doing the best job possible.
- **Quality workers are attracted to the organization.** Most workers seek employers who respect them and value their ideas. Employers with such a reputation usually have no trouble attracting the highest quality workers.
- **The decision-making process improves.** When many different views are considered, the final plan is usually a sound one.

Improved problem-solving processes and increased creativity are among the benefits of working with diverse teams.

Yuri Arcurs/Shutterstock.com

- **Decision-making speed improves.** When frank, open discussions are common, complex issues are explored more quickly. Sensitive issues can be raised without fear of hurting coworkers' feelings. This leads to faster decisions.
- **More customers are reached.** A diverse workforce understands a wider range of customers. Consequently, market opportunities are recognized quicker and products are launched faster.
- **Goodwill and positive ties are formed with businesses and government groups.** Having a policy of accepting diversity can mean gaining public respect. For companies whose customers are organizations, it can also mean getting more business from the government and like-minded companies.

Promoting Diversity in the Workplace

Managing workplace diversity is extremely important to US organizations wanting to sell in a global environment. World markets are growing more diverse. Experts believe that enlightened management policies emphasizing diversity will help companies serve customers better everywhere. This will especially help US companies compete more effectively in worldwide markets.

What Employers Are Doing to Promote Diversity

Diversity training in the workplace is relatively new, but rapidly increasing. Large global companies have taken the lead and report that the benefits, listed earlier, far outweigh the costs. Corporate leaders agree that diversity makes good moral and economic sense. Now that diversity has been shown to make good business sense, companies without such programs are more eager to implement diversity training.

Diversity programs began as a way for companies to avoid costly legal battles and tell employees what not to do. Gradually managers with foresight recognized that a company's success hinged on its workforce. Workers preferred learning what to do instead of what not to do. Training programs were revised to emphasize positive behavior. The focus turned to understanding and accepting people's differences and viewing differences as an asset. Some of the methods that are in current use are listed in Figure 19-1.

Employer Strategies for Promoting Workplace Diversity

- Develop a diversity policy. Include the policy in the employee handbook and discuss it in company publications.
- Recruit employees for diversity task forces and advisory councils to guide the overall diversity policy.
- Reward behavior that reinforces diversity goals.
- Evaluate manager and employee performance based on diversity measures.
- Revise existing company policies and benefits so they support diverse needs.
- Place special emphasis on recruiting individuals from populations that are missing or underrepresented in the organization.
- Promote community volunteer work that encourages employees to work with diverse populations.
- Link diversity goals to business goals.
- Provide training programs that help employees examine assumptions and past attitudes.
- Provide training programs to help managers develop skills for removing communication barriers among workers.
- Keep employees informed about diversity efforts that have benefited the company.

Figure 19-1.   *Goodheart-Willcox Publisher*
Employers use one or more of these methods to encourage workers to respect their coworkers.

An increase in women's participation has contributed to a more diverse labor force in the United States.

Stephen Coburn/Shutterstock.com

What Employees Can Do to Embrace Diversity

Employees also have a role in promoting diversity. First, consider how your behavior is affected by your cultural background. Then, recognize that your value system will probably differ from that of other coworkers. All employees have a responsibility to work in harmony toward achieving company goals.

If working in a diverse environment is unfamiliar to you, you may find this quite challenging. You will want to broaden your outlook and adjust any negative viewpoints you have. Some ways to help you make that adjustment are listed in Figure 19-2. Ultimately, learning to work with diverse coworkers will build your character. You will become a more valuable team member and employee.

Employee Actions That Encourage Workplace Diversity
• Show flexibility in adapting to your coworkers and work environment.
• Examine your assumptions about people different from you.
• Explore different cultures through cultural events, movies, plays, books, and travel.
• Show patience in understanding and communicating with others when language barriers exist.
• Politely ask for clarification if a message or gesture does not make sense to you.
• Admit your unfamiliarity with diverse customs, but express a willingness to learn.
• Show respect for everyone's ideas.
• Adjust your style of humor so jokes are not made at someone's expense.
• Look beyond everyday annoyances and see the humanity in each person.
• Recognize that you are no better than your coworkers, only different.

Figure 19-2.   *Source: Bureau of Labor Statistics*
These guidelines help workers respect and appreciate their coworkers.

Ethics

There are many competitive events that participants may enter as a member of various student organizations. Review the events offered by your organization and the rules and regulations that apply to each activity. Many organizations have ethics competitions in which teams participate to defend an ethical dilemma or topic.

To prepare for the ethics event, complete the following activities.

1. Read the Ethical Leadership features that appear throughout this text.
2. Organize a team of students who are also interested in this event. Work collaboratively to review and discuss each Ethical Leadership feature.
3. Use the Internet to find additional information about ethics in the workplace. Print this information for future study material.
4. Review the Event Prep feature in Chapter 7 to help you develop an organized approach to defending your team's position.

Checkpoint 19.1

1. In what way can stereotypes negatively impact the workplace?
2. How does a diverse workforce help a company reach more customers?
3. What is the focus of current diversity training?
4. List four benefits of teaching diversity in the workplace.
5. What are two strategies an employer can use to develop diversity on the job?

Build Your Vocabulary

As you progress through this text, develop a personal glossary of career-related terms and add it to your portfolio. This will help you build your vocabulary and prepare you for your career of choice. Write a definition for each of the following terms, and add it to your personal career glossary.

    stereotyping
    diversity

The Right to Equal Treatment

Every person has the right to fair treatment. **Equity** is treating someone fairly and in the manner that gives him or her opportunities afforded to others. When a person is not treated in an equitable manner it may be due to discrimination.

The word *discrimination* has different meanings. It can mean "distinguishing one object from a similar one." It also means "using good judgment," as in deciding what to say in a letter of application to try to get the job you want.

When the word *discrimination* is used in the workplace, it usually has a negative meaning. A common understanding of **discrimination** is the negative treatment of one or more individuals compared to that of the larger group. Discrimination may also refer to excluding some people from a special treatment offered to others.

The practice of discrimination is illegal in the workplace. It is unlawful for an employer to withhold a pay raise, a promotion, or other opportunities from an employee because of age, race, ethnic background, gender, or religious association.

Discrimination can take place in many forms. An example includes the refusal to hire a woman for a management position. Another display of discrimination would include firing a person because he practices a certain religion. Discrimination may also occur when an employer does not provide reasonable assistance to employees with disabilities.

Go Green

The average worker in America spends 47 hours per year commuting. This adds up to 3.7 billion hours and 23 billion gallons of gasoline used each year in daily travel. Commuters can save energy by carpooling, taking public transit, biking, or walking. Help the environment and "go green" by going to work or school using one of these methods.

Advancing a More Equitable Workplace

Several government agencies deal with equal opportunity employment issues every day. The two federal offices that do most of the work are the Office of Federal Contract Compliance Programs (OFCCP) and the Equal Employment Opportunity Commission (EEOC).

The OFCCP actively seeks out cases of discrimination by monitoring contractors who hold federal contracts. The EEOC investigates charges of discrimination brought to it by individual workers and groups of employees. Created by the 1964 Civil Rights Act, the EEOC makes sure all laws, regulations, federal guidelines, executive orders, and collective-bargaining agreements that address discrimination are followed. Its mission is to assure equal opportunity in employment for everyone and prohibit discrimination. The EEOC's authority covers all employment practices such as interviewing, hiring, promoting, transferring, training, retiring, and firing employees. The EEOC's authority also covers membership opportunities in work-related groups.

Several important laws exist to promote fairness and fight discrimination in the workplace. These laws have been enacted over time to promote a more civil and equitable society. In addition to the work done at the federal level to maintain equal opportunity, many state and local government agencies monitor and investigate discriminatory practices locally.

Fair Labor Standards Act (FLSA)

The Fair Labor Standards Act (FLSA) of 1938 forbids unfair treatment of employees by employers. This law has been amended many times to raise the minimum wage. It also reduced the number of hours worked without overtime pay and extended coverage to many low-income workers. The law also addresses child labor standards.

The Equal Pay Act of 1963 requires that men and women receive equal pay for jobs that require the same skills and responsibilities.

iofoto/Shutterstock.com

Ethical Leadership

Being Empathetic

"So when you are listening to somebody, completely, attentively, then you are listening not only to the words, but also to the feeling of what is being conveyed, to the whole of it, not part of it."—Jiddu Kirshnamurti

As you go to school each day, you may hear others categorize people using biased words and comments. Using age, gender, race, disability, or ethnicity as a way to describe others is unethical and sometimes illegal. It is important to be empathetic to the feelings of others. Always use bias-free language to show respect for those with whom you come in contact. For more information on unbiased communication, search the Internet to find out the latest information on the topic.

Equal Pay Act

The Equal Pay Act of 1963, a FLSA amendment, forbids the practice of using different pay scales for men and women. It requires that both sexes receive equal pay for jobs in similar working conditions requiring the same level of skill, effort, and responsibility.

Civil Rights Act

The Civil Rights Act of 1964 banned employment discrimination on the basis of race, color, religion, sex, or national origin. For interfering with a person's employment rights, a 1968 amendment established criminal penalties. A **criminal penalty** is a lawful punishment involving one or more of the following: serving a jail sentence, doing community service, paying a fine, and periodically reporting to a court-ordered supervisor.

In 1991, the government strengthened the ban against discrimination of races and sexes. It also gave protection to members of groups that had a history of receiving intentional job discrimination. In cases that go to court, this law allows victims to be awarded compensatory damages (money to pay for actual losses) and punitive damages (as payment to make an example of the wrongdoer).

Age Discrimination in Employment Act

The Age Discrimination in Employment Act of 1967 banned unfair treatment of workers age 40 and older. The law was expanded by the Older Workers Benefit Protection Act of 1990, which permitted workers to sue employers over age-discrimination matters.

Immigration Reform and Control Act

The Immigration Reform and Control Act of 1986 allowed the awarding of criminal penalties to employers who discriminated against U.S. citizens born outside the country. The Immigration Act of 1990 further strengthened the law and protected these citizens by making it harder for noncitizens to obtain employment in this country.

Americans with Disabilities Act (ADA)

The Americans with Disabilities Act (ADA) of 1990 is a wide-ranging law prohibiting discrimination of individuals with disabilities in matters involving employment, government services, and transportation. The law required public transportation services to be accessible to individuals with disabilities. It also required employers to provide such employees with reasonable accommodations in physical facilities. The law gives people with disabilities a chance to be hired for their skills rather than turned away for an unrelated disability.

Persons with disabilities may use service animals to help them with their work or in everyday tasks.

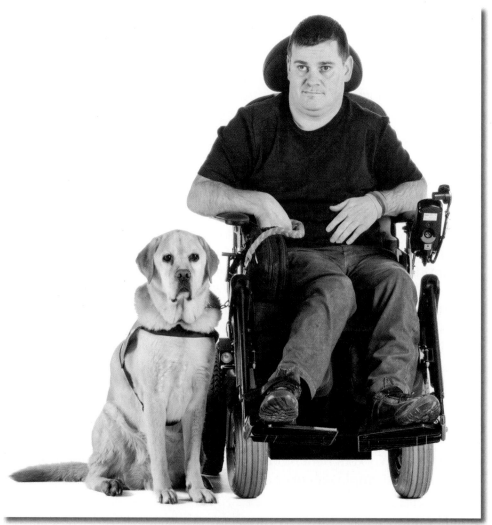

Micimakin/Shutterstock.com

Freedom from Sexual Harassment

Sexual harassment is a broad term that refers to a wide variety of behaviors. **Sexual harassment** is unwanted advances, requests for favors, or other verbal or physical conduct of a sexual nature. Women are the most common victims, but both the victim and the aggressor can be either male or female. Approximately 8 percent of the cases handled by the EEOC involve female harassers.

Sexual harassment is primarily an issue of power because the victim is usually a subordinate or less influential person in the organization. Because sexual harassment is a deliberate attempt to take advantage of a person's rights, it is prohibited by law. There are two basic types of sexual harassment defined by EEOC guidelines: quid pro quo harassment and hostile environment harassment.

Quid pro quo harassment occurs when one person makes unwelcome sexual advances toward another while promising certain benefits if the person complies. The promise of a promotion or pay raise is an example. The threat of firing or demotion if the victim refuses also is a form of quid pro quo harassment.

Hostile environment harassment is behavior that makes an atmosphere uncomfortable enough to interfere with a person's performance. Examples of unlawful behavior include inappropriate remarks or questions and unwanted staring or touching. This form of sexual harassment also includes posting pictures, playing music, using body language, or communicating a sexual message in any other way. **Body language** is a means of expressing a message through body movements, facial expressions, or hand gestures.

The effects of sexual harassment are numerous. Sexual harassment undermines employment relationships. It also affects morale and interferes with workplace productivity. Victims are likely to suffer stress, depression, and inability to focus on their work. The employer suffers, too, since both the victim and the aggressor are less effective in their jobs.

Recognizing Sexual Harassment

Obvious acts of sexual harassment, such as threats and inappropriate physical contact, are easy to identify. However, some behavior that seems fairly innocent may still leave a person unsure. In the case of sexual harassment, there are several questions to ask to help clarify any confusion. See Figure 19-3.

Identifying Sexual Harassment
Ask the following questions about the behavior being examined:
• Is it sexual in nature?
• Does it violate my employer's (or school) written sexual harassment policy?
• Is it offensive to me? Unwelcomed?
• Does it interfere with my work (or school) performance?
• Does the harasser know that I want it stopped?

Figure 19-3.   *Goodheart-Willcox Publisher*
Employers have a responsibility to promote diversity in the workplace.

A key component of sexual harassment is not considering the feelings of the person receiving the aggressive behavior. If the victim does not want certain sexual behaviors to occur and says so, yet the behaviors continue, he or she is being sexually harassed. Some aggressors may try to make the matter seem less serious by saying they were simply joking. It is important for everyone to know that the behavior is not only wrong, but also illegal. The person being harassed is not at fault for the aggressor's actions.

On the other hand, if a person is comfortable with the inappropriate behavior or encourages it, then he or she is not considered a victim. In this case, the behavior would not be considered sexual harassment.

Another factor that is considered in deciding a claim of sexual harassment is the setting. Certain behaviors that do not involve sexual contact are considered acceptable for some settings but not others. For example, gestures such as "blowing kisses" and "looks of desire" are inappropriate in the workplace. On a date, of course, these actions would not be considered sexual harassment. However, these same gestures at a restaurant dinner may be considered sexual harassment when a supervisor and his assistant are on a business trip. The reason is that the dinner is not a date, but an extension of the workplace.

Students in work-based learning experiences should immediately discuss any harassment they receive with their school coordinator. That person is most qualified to help determine the next steps to take. After graduation, however, you may find it helpful to discuss the problem and sort through the facts with a trusted friend or an adult who is not involved in the matter.

Take action and report the offense if you feel you are a victim of discrimination or sexual harassment.

Yuri Arcurs/Shutterstock.com

Most employers have programs in place to prevent sexual harassment and discrimination, but no workplace is immune to it. If you should ever believe that you are a victim of either form of unlawful behavior, prepare to take steps to stop it. Letting time go by and hoping that the aggressor will stop rarely works.

Taking Action

When a person is the victim of discrimination or sexual harassment, there is a danger of becoming too emotional to effectively do the work that must be done. The first priority is to remain professional as you handle the following steps:

- **Tell the aggressor to stop.** Let the person know you consider his or her conduct illegal. Insist that the conduct stop. If it continues, write the person explaining what you want stopped and why. Keep a copy and preserve it in your files. Send the letter by certified mail, with a return receipt requested to get signed proof the person received the letter.
- **Keep detailed records.** Maintain a journal, describing each incident and its date. Start with the event that convinced you to tell the aggressor to stop. Explain the *who*, *what*, *when*, *where*, and *how* of each incident. Be prepared to provide names of witnesses or others who can support your claim.
- **Report the offense.** If your company has a written policy, be sure to follow it. If not, your supervisor is generally the one to hear your complaint and receive your report, unless he or she is the aggressor. In that case, go to the person's supervisor or someone of higher authority.

Sometimes employees who resist harassment or discrimination fear reprisal from their supervisor or employer. **Reprisal** is the revenge-motivated act of retaliating, or "getting even" with someone. Workers have been demoted, transferred, and even fired for challenging harassment or discrimination. It is important to know that EEOC considers such acts or reprisal unlawful. Workers are protected from retaliation when they file discrimination complaints, oppose illegal practices, or participate in related investigations.

Case

Hiring Discrimination?

The XYZ Publishing Company, which prints a major city newspaper, made plans for hiring two reporters. The position required the new employees to cover local business news and events as well as report on individual company successes and failures. Extensive interviewing of company employees and executives would be a key requirement.

Andre and Heidi applied for the positions. Both were college graduates with journalism degrees and similar work experience on college and hometown newspapers. Their résumés were very similar as they both possessed the same skills and abilities.

Both were interviewed during the same afternoon for nearly 30 minutes. They were questioned intently on their interpersonal skills, communication skills, computer skills, and reporting experience. They were also questioned about their flexibility to work late or overtime as the work required. Both said their schedules were flexible.

Andre wore a dress shirt and tie, pressed trousers, and polished shoes to the interview. His hands and nails were well-groomed and his hair was neatly combed. Heidi wore jeans, a wrinkled shirt, tennis shoes, a nose ring, and a row of four pierced earrings in each ear. She wore no makeup because of her religious beliefs.

A week later, both Andre and Heidi received a letter from the employment office, but only Andre was offered a job. Heidi believed she was the most qualified person for the position. She wondered if she was a victim of sex discrimination. She also wondered if she was a victim of religious discrimination. Heidi decided to write a letter to the president, charging the company with discrimination in its hiring practices.

Critical Thinking

1. Do you believe that discrimination played a part in the hiring decision? Explain.
2. If you had to handle Heidi's complaint letter, how would you respond?
3. What advice would you give Heidi for her next interview?

Checkpoint 19.2

1. Provide an example of discrimination in the workplace.
2. Which law gives people with disabilities a chance to be hired for their skills?
3. What is the primary government agency that investigates charges of discrimination brought by individuals and groups?
4. What should a student in a work-based program do if he or she is a victim of sexual harassment?
5. What three steps are important in taking action against sexual harassment and discrimination?

Build Your Vocabulary

As you progress through this text, develop a personal glossary of career-related terms and add it to your portfolio. This will help you build your vocabulary and prepare you for your career of choice. Write a definition for each of the following terms, and add it to your personal career glossary.

equity
discrimination
criminal penalty
sexual harassment
quid pro quo harassment
hostile environment harassment
body language
reprisal

Chapter Summary

Section 19.1 Understanding Workplace Diversity

- Employers seek employees who are able to work with people from diverse backgrounds. The benefits of diversity include higher employee morale, more productivity, and more creative solutions.
- Diversity is very important to companies participating in the global market. Both employers and employees have a responsibility to promote workplace diversity.

Section 19.2 Equity and Workplace Rights

- Discrimination can take place in many forms. When a person is not treated in an equitable manner, it may be due to discrimination.
- Discrimination is unethical and prohibited by law. The government enforces labor laws to protect the rights individuals.
- Sexual harassment is another example of unlawful behavior in the workplace. Victims of sexual harassment must take action and report the incident.

Check Your Career IQ

Now that you have finished the chapter, see what you learned about careers by taking the chapter posttest. The test can be accessed on the mobile site by using a smartphone or on the G-W Learning companion website.

www.m.g-wlearning.com
www.g-wlearning.com

Review Your Knowledge

1. How can a gesture be misinterpreted?
2. What should you do if you unintentionally offend someone in the workplace?
3. Discuss why diversity is beneficial to problem-solving and developing new ideas.
4. Explain the purpose of diversity programs when they were first developed.
5. What are two things an employee can do to promote workplace diversity?
6. Provide an example of discrimination in the workplace.
7. Explain the purpose of the Fair Labor Standards Act of 1938.

8. What did the Civil Rights Act of 1964 prohibit?

9. What are the two basic types of sexual harassment defined by EEOC guidelines?

10. What information should be noted when keeping a record of sexual harassment?

Apply Your Knowledge

1. In what ways are you exposed to diversity? How can you improve upon this? What can you do to be more aware of the ideas, traditions, and experiences of others? Discuss these ideas with your classmates. Create a list of ways to add diversity to your life.

2. Explore the EEOC website including links to mediation, filing charges of employment discrimination, and current enforcement statistics. Take notes during your research. Identify four things you found most interesting. Share these ideas with your class.

3. Conduct research to learn more about laws in your state that address discrimination in the workplace. Use the Internet and other library resources for information. Take notes during your search. Write a summary of your findings.

4. Identify employers that have taken the lead to promote workplace diversity and recruit underrepresented groups? Use the Internet to learn about two of them. Summarize your findings. Discuss the information in a small group.

5. Create a poster that promotes diversity. Include an insightful motto or slogan to support your message. Be creative in your visual display. Present your poster to the class.

6. Imagine you are the manager of a software company. You work with a diverse team of 80 people. What four things can you do to promote workplace diversity? Provide a detailed example how you would carry out each of your ideas. Compile your information in a chart.

7. Research the Americans with Disabilities Act (ADA) of 1990. Summarize your findings in a two-page paper.

8. In a small group, create a schedule for a two-day conference on workplace diversity and training. Each day of the conference will have three sessions. Consider the following: What topics will be discussed during each session? Will your sessions have keynote speakers? If so, who? Write a brief description of each session, including the name of the session and time. Your team's schedule should note times for breaks and lunch. Participants will include employers and employees from companies in your state.

9. Use the library to research articles and photographs related to one of the laws discussed in the chapter. Create a bulletin board of headlines and photos depicting issues and events related to the law you selected.

10. Interview an older relative, friend, or neighbor who is currently employed. Ask the person what new technology skills have they had to learn to stay competitive as an employee. Ask whether he or she found learning these skills difficult. What changes does he or she foresee that could affect how the current job is done? Take notes during your discussion.

Teamwork

Work with three classmates to plan an employee picnic for ABC Company. Imagine the company includes employees from India, Saudi Arabia, and others who follow Jewish dietary traditions. Your team is in charge of food, activities, and scheduling the event. Decide when the event will be held; what food will be served; and what sports, games, or other activities to arrange. Your plans must be sensitive to employees' customs, traditions, and religious beliefs. Research the topics necessary for developing a plan and report it to the class. Explain the factors that prompted your decisions.

G-W Learning Mobile Site

Visit the G-W Learning mobile site to complete the chapter pretest and posttest and to practice vocabulary using e-flash cards. If you do not have a smartphone, visit the G-W Learning companion website to access these features.

G-W Learning mobile site: www.m.g-wlearning.com

G-W Learning companion website: www.g-wlearning.com

Common Core

College and Career Readiness

CTE Career Ready Practices. Read the Ethical Leadership features presented throughout this book. What role do you think ethics and integrity have in decision-making? Think of a time when you used your ideals and principles to make a decision. What process did you use to make the decision? In retrospect, do you think you made the correct decision? Did your decision have any consequences?

Writing. Research the merits of diversity. Write a persuasive essay in which you argue for greater diversity in school, the workplace, or another arena. Use valid reason and cite evidence from your research to support your argument.

Apply Your Technology Skills

Access the G-W Learning companion website for this text at www.g-wlearning.com. Download the data file for this chapter. Follow the instructions to complete activities to practice what you have learned in this chapter.

Data File 19–1—**Understanding Functional Diversity**

College and Career Readiness Portfolio

College and Career Readiness

You have learned the purpose of a resume and collected the information you need to create your resume. Now consider how to present the information effectively. The first impression you make on an employer or interviewer may be through your resume. A résumé that is attractive and error-free will help make this impression a positive one. For a paper resume, you can use special effects to make the résumé attractive and easy to read. For example, you might use bold type or a larger font size for your name at the top of the page and for headings. You might use a table to group data or bullets to highlight key points. The resume should be printed on quality paper and be clean and free of errors.

1. Search the Internet for articles and examples of print résumés. Pay special attention to the design and formatting.
2. Finish creating your resume. (Assume that this resume will be presented and viewed on paper. You will modify the resume for electronic use in a later activity.)
3. Save the resume file in your e-portfolio. Place a printed copy in the container for your print portfolio.

Succeeding in Our Economic System

Section 20.1
Our Economic System

Section 20.2
Business Organization

College and Career Readiness

Reading Prep. Think of some of your life goals. How are these goals affected by the US economy? As you read the chapter, focus on how your goals can be affected by economic conditions.

Introduction

In the United States, businesses and consumers have the freedom to buy, sell, and conduct transactions. This means that consumers are free to purchase goods and services. It also means that businesses are allowed to provide these products with the goal of making a profit. Although the government does not control business and industry, laws are passed and enforced to protect the rights of consumers.

The ways businesses are organized differs. A single owner might operate a small, local coffee shop with six other employees. On the other hand, a corporation might be the driving force behind a chain of restaurants located throughout the country. Whether big or small, a business must set goals, have a plan, and be well-managed to be successful.

Check Your Career IQ

Before you begin the chapter, see what you already know about careers by taking the chapter pretest. Use the related QR code to view the pretest on the mobile site. If you do not have a smartphone, visit the G-W Learning companion website to access the pretest.

www.m.g-wlearning.com
www.g-wlearning.com

G-W Mobile

Career Snapshot
Cosmetologist

What Does a Cosmetologist Do?

Cosmetologists are often referred to as stylists, hairdressers, beauty operators, or beauticians. They cut, style, color, and shampoo hair. Cosmetologists may also:

- advise on home hair care and offer makeup analysis;
- create, clean, and style wigs;
- recommend and sell hair-, skin- and nail-care products; and
- give manicures, pedicures, and scalp and facial treatments.

What Is It Like to Work as a Cosmetologist?

Most cosmetologists work in beauty salons and many own their own shops. Shop owners must have a strong business sense as they may manage employees and need to keep accurate business records, order supplies, and advertise. Cosmetologists usually work a forty-hour week in clean and pleasant surroundings. They may be required to work evenings and weekends.

What Education and Skills Are Needed to Be a Cosmetologist?

- high school diploma or GED may be required
- cosmetology training from a certified technical school
- state license is required in most states
- good heath and stamina
- strong customer relations skills

20.1 Our Economic System

Objectives

After completing this section, you will be able to:
- **Explain** how the patent system influenced economic growth in the United States.
- **Describe** the free enterprise system in the United States.

Development of the US Economic System

The United States is a highly industrialized nation with a strong economy. This was not always the case. In the early years of our nation, agriculture was the main industry. Land was available to farmers and ranchers who moved freely across the country. The land was developed, and thousands of communities emerged. The United States did not develop into a great producer of world goods until the 1800s.

With the advent of the Industrial Revolution, American industries were born. Machines were invented to mass-produce goods. The production of goods steadily increased, which made more goods available to more people. Manufacturers worked hard to produce more and better goods at lower prices.

Along with a good production system, the United States had great supplies of natural resources, such as lumber, coal, iron ore, and copper. Rivers were used to supply power and energy and provide easy transportation of goods.

The **patent system** is an arrangement that protects inventors from having someone else claim their ideas and inventions as his or her own. Through the US patent system, inventors can register their original invention with the federal government. The federal government then issues a patent.

Through the introduction of the US patent system, inventions of all kinds were encouraged. As a result, many inventors around the world moved to the US for this protection. With the invention of new products and processes, industries grew and everyone seemed to benefit.

Through the US patent system, inventors can register their original invention with the federal government.

Ralf Kleemann/Shutterstock.com

Craftsmen who immigrated to the United States brought their training and skills with them. What tools they could not bring, they made. With their skill and desire to succeed, these workers provided a very productive labor force that US industries needed to manufacture goods.

To pull the entire industrial system together required organization. Business leaders gave the needed direction. They built their companies and produced goods and services for the world market. As businesses continued to grow and expand, more emphasis was placed on management. The owners of many companies continued to provide **capital**, which are the material resources used to grow businesses. However, business owners eventually depended on highly trained persons to manage their businesses and keep them profitable.

Why did the United States develop into such a strong industrial nation? It became strong economically because it had natural resources, a patent system, skilled labor, good management, and capital for investments. The United States also had another very important asset—a system of government that permitted industry to operate as a free enterprise. It was the free enterprise system that allowed individuals and groups the right to start businesses and earn profits from them.

Free Enterprise System

Free enterprise is only one of many names used to describe the US economic system. This system is also referred to as a *consumer economy,* a *market economy,* a *profit system,* or *capitalism.* Although these terms have slightly different meanings, they all represent the same basic economic system. In a **free enterprise system**, people are free to make their own economic decisions. This system is based on the following factors:

- private ownership and control of productive resources;
- a free market;
- the profit motive;
- supply and demand;
- competition; and
- limited government involvement.

Private Ownership and Control of Productive Resources

The government does not own or control business and industry. Private citizens do. Individuals and businesses decide how to use their productive resources to produce and provide goods and services. **Productive resources** are resources such as labor, land, and equipment that can be used to produce and provide goods and services.

Consumer decisions about which goods and services to buy or use are affected by resources. Resources are limited, but needs and wants are unlimited. **Needs** are basic necessities a person must have to live. **Wants** are the items a person would like to have, but can live without. Having nutritious food is a need, but having dessert is a want.

Individuals and families have limited resources, such as time and money. However, their needs and wants for food, clothing, and entertainment are unlimited. Because their resources are limited, they must first take care of their needs before they decide which wants to

Ethical Leadership

Principled Leader

"A people that values its privileges above its principles soon loses both." -Dwight D. Eisenhower

A principled leader recognizes right from wrong. He or she understands that rules are made for a purpose. For example, it may be tempting to use school or work computers to access confidential information, download copyrighted material, or send personal e-mails. However, in some cases, to do so is unethical. Such practices could also expose the computer network to viruses. It is important to understand and follow the computer policies set by your school or workplace. Rules and guidelines are set for a purpose. Ethical leadership involves doing the right thing and following the rules.

satisfy. With additional money available, a person may choose to go to a play, concert, or sporting event. If money is limited, he or she may be forced to choose between saving money for college costs and taking a vacation. Some choices are more difficult than others.

Free Market

In the free enterprise system, the market is not controlled by the government. People have the right to decide how and where to earn, spend, save, and invest their money. They also have the freedom to produce whatever they think they can sell, provided they follow existing rules and laws. If there is a demand for their product, they make a profit. On the other hand, if the demand is small and they make too many products, they suffer financial losses.

When losses occur, a company will search for ways to become profitable again. It may mean reorganizing the company, laying off workers, or installing newer technology. Sometimes a company cannot produce goods as cheaply as its competition. If a company cannot turn losses into profits, they may need to take more serious action. They may reduce the number of workers they employ, or in some cases close the business.

Profit Motive

The main reason for operating a business is to make a profit. **Profit** refers to the amount of money a business makes from selling goods and services beyond the cost of producing them. Businesses, motivated by their desire to earn profits, use their resources to produce goods and services. If consumers buy enough of the product and the

If orange crops are damaged due to a winter frost, a reduction in supply will often lead to an increase in the price of oranges for consumers.

holbox/Shutterstock.com

production costs are not too high, then the business makes a profit. This reason for doing business is called the *profit motive.*

Profits motivate people to be productive. Without this opportunity to earn a profit, they would not be motivated to work or to invest their money. Business owners receive a profit in the form of income, called a *return on their investments.* Without productive people, there would be no labor or money to produce goods and services.

Supply and Demand

Our economic system is based on supply and demand. **Supply** is the amount of products and services available for sale. The amount of products and services consumers want to buy is called **demand**. Businesses decide what and how much to produce based on consumer demand. Consumers express their demand for products and services through their spending choices in the marketplace. Whatever consumers are willing to buy, there are usually businesses willing to supply the product.

Prices can change as the supply of an item increases or decreases. A product shortage can cause prices to rise. When the supply of a product is limited, it is harder for distributers to provide the expected quantities. As a result, they will often need to increase the price of an item to cover normal operating costs. This price increase is passed on to the consumer. For instance, when bad weather ruins the orange crop, the supply is low and prices are higher. When the supply increases, creating a surplus, orange prices go down.

Competition

Any individual or business has the right to enter into the same business as any other company and compete for consumer dollars. Competition encourages businesses to produce quality goods and services at low prices. If a company charges too high a price for a product or service, consumers can go to a competitor who sells a similar or better product or service and buy it for less. The company that produces the best products and services at the lowest prices will earn the most profits.

Go Green

Paper manufacturers are always looking for renewable resources and new ideas to produce environmentally-friendly paper products. One kind of eco-friendly paper is made from by-products of sugarcane with no wood involved in its production. Sugarcane products actually biodegrade faster than wood products. In addition, sugarcane paper is cleaner to make than wood-based paper. Many office supply companies are carrying sugarcane paper with more new products to come.

The US government enforces laws to protect consumers from unsafe business practices.

Frank Jr/Shutterstock.com

Jay's Shoe Store is an example of how consumers benefit from competition. Since no other shoe stores were in the area, customers paid Jay's prices for years. When a competitive shoe store opened a block away, it advertised the same quality shoes at much lower prices. As a result, Jay's sales dropped. To stay competitive, Jay's owner decided to lower prices and advertise more. To compete successfully, he knew he had to offer lower prices than his competitor.

Without competition, prices tend to be high for a couple reasons. First, businesses can charge whatever price they think consumers will pay without fear of losing business to someone selling for less. Secondly, if there is only one manufacturer and it is successful, there is little need for the company to reduce production costs. Competitors usually must work harder to get a share of the business. Consequently, they find ways to make products quicker and less expensively. They also explore consumer needs and wants, then offer products and services that address them more directly.

Limited Government Involvement

To keep the free enterprise system fair requires some government involvement. Federal, state, and local governments establish and enforce economic laws and policies to promote economic growth and stability. They also protect consumers from unsafe and unfair business practices.

To promote fair competition among businesses, the government enforces laws that prevent monopolies. A **monopoly** is a single company that controls the entire supply of a product or service. If a monopoly was allowed to exist, it could charge consumers unfair prices for goods and services and limit their production and availability. This practice prevents competition and does not allow the economy to operate on a free enterprise basis.

Checkpoint 20.1

1. What was America's main industry during the early development of the country? What major era in history moved America in a new direction of economic development?
2. What are other names used to describe free enterprise?
3. What are the six basic factors on which the US free enterprise system is based?
4. Name three things a company might do to become more profitable in a free market.
5. What are the disadvantages of a monopoly?

Build Your Vocabulary

As you progress through this text, develop a personal glossary of career-related terms and add it to your portfolio. This will help you build your vocabulary and prepare you for your career of choice. Write a definition for each of the following terms, and add it to your personal career glossary.

patent system
capital
free enterprise system
productive resources
need
want
profit
supply
demand
monopoly

How Businesses Are Organized

As a result of the free enterprise system, the United States has thousands of businesses that produce a variety of products and services. Businesses range from only one person as the owner-worker to thousands of employees in a large company. However, they all operate on the same basic principle. They must earn a profit to stay in business. This means all businesses depend on consumers to buy their goods and services, which creates a demand for more goods and services.

To understand more about the way businesses operate in our economic system, it helps to understand the three forms of business ownership—sole proprietorship, partnership, and corporation.

Sole Proprietorship

A **sole proprietorship** is a business that has only one owner. It is the simplest form of business organization because usually only one person makes the decisions and manages the business. There are no business partners or board of directors to consult. For these reasons, there are many single-owner businesses.

In a sole proprietorship, the owner or proprietor supplies all the money to start and operate the business. As a result, the owner receives all the profits that are made and assumes all the debts and losses.

Many sole proprietorships are small companies in which the owner does much of the work. Many retail and service shops, such as the corner restaurant, barbershop, hair salon, dry cleaner, and auto repair shop are sole proprietorships. However, a sole proprietorship can be a multimillion dollar business with hundreds of employees.

Partnership

A **partnership** is a form of business organization where two or more people go into business together. In a partnership, all the partners pool their money to establish and operate the business. The partners share the work responsibilities as well as the profits and debts.

One of the advantages of a partnership over a sole proprietorship is that more money may be available to finance the business. A partnership also brings together the skills and experiences of two or more people. This often makes it easier for a partnership to solve problems and make wise business decisions. It follows the adage that "two heads are better than one."

Partnerships may have their disadvantages as well. Problems can arise when partners do not agree on business decisions. There can also be problems when one partner feels he or she is assuming more of the work and responsibility than the other partner(s).

In addition to regular partnerships, there are limited partnerships. A limited partnership is an agreement between two or more parties to join together on a specific business venture. For example, an investor might form a limited partnership with a real estate developer to build 30 single-family homes in a community.

Limited partners, sometimes called *silent partners,* invest money or property into a business but do not work in the business. As the business makes a profit from the sale of its goods or services, limited partners receive a percentage of those profits. If the business fails, limited partners are only responsible for any debts of the business up to the amount of their investments.

A partnership is a form of business that is established when two or more people agree to go into business together.

Stephen Coburn/Shutterstock.com

Corporation

A **corporation** is a business owned by many people. A corporation is formed by selling portions or shares of a business that are called *stocks*. The people who buy the stocks become part owners of the business and are called *stockholders*.

A stockholder is only responsible for business debts up to the amount of his or her investment. Therefore, if a stockholder invests $500 in a corporation, the most the stockholder can lose if the business fails is $500. This is called *limited liability*. Stockholders are only liable for the amounts they have invested. If the corporation makes a profit, the stockholder receives a share of those profits according to the amount he or she has invested.

Two advantages of corporate ownership are limited liability and access to capital. Limited liability is one of the major advantages of forming a corporation. The other advantage of corporate ownership is available capital. Large amounts of money can be raised among the owners to expand a business and produce more goods or services.

Although stockholders are part owners in a corporation, they have very little input in the decision making. A board of directors, elected by stockholders, makes most of the business decisions along with the leaders hired to run the corporation. The president and vice presidents of a corporation are the top level managers. These officials give leadership and direction to the entire corporation. They work together to see that the corporation makes a profit.

Figure 20-1 shows the levels of management that exist in some corporations. The president oversees all corporate activities and hands down decisions to the vice presidents. The vice presidents delegate responsibilities to managers (in this example, plant managers). The plant managers oversee the department heads. The department heads

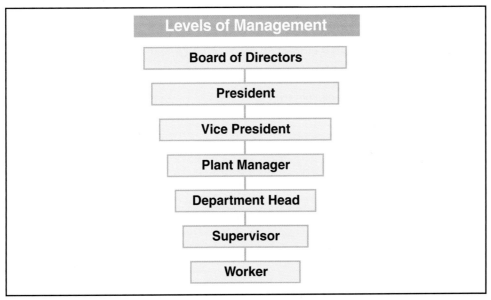

Figure 20-1.   *Goodheart-Willcox Publisher*
Many levels of management exist in some corporations. Most of the important decisions are made by the board of directors and top-level managers.

oversee the supervisors. The supervisors comprise the lowest level of management and oversee the workers. Each person reports to the person in the next highest position and, in turn, receives direction from that person. The larger the corporation, the more specialized the levels of management become.

How Businesses Are Structured

There are many different management structures within businesses. The type of management structure within a company may directly influence the responsibilities of your job. Two common types of management structures are a tall management structure, sometimes called a *vertical structure*, versus a flat management structure, sometimes called a *horizontal structure*. A chart that shows an organization's internal structure is called an **organization chart** as shown in Figure 20-2.

In the tall structure, a low-level worker is quite removed from the top managers. Jobs tend to be more specialized, requiring very specific skills. Responsibilities also tend to be narrower.

In the flat structure, a worker usually has closer contact with supervisors, vice presidents, and other personnel. Employees usually have a broader range of skills. They also tend to have greater

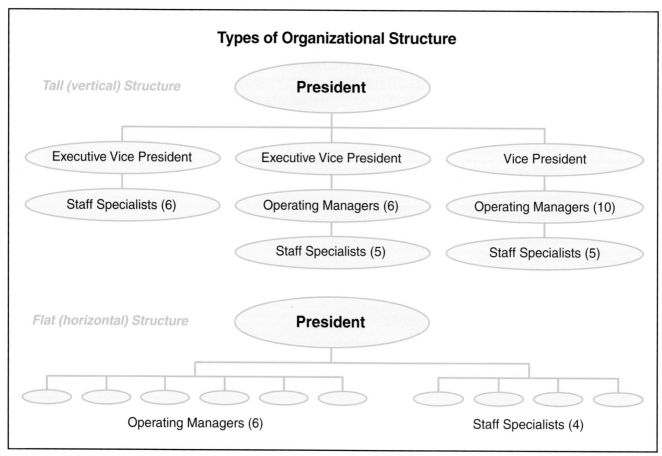

Figure 20-2.   *Goodheart-Willcox Publisher*
The type of organizational structure by which a company operates will often depend on the size of the business.

responsibility for their work. More emphasis is placed on teamwork, with each member of the team having a major role in the work being done. There may be fewer delays and mistakes with fewer layers of personnel due to improved communications.

Business Management

For a business to be successful, it must be well managed. Managing a business involves many responsibilities. It requires careful attention to the details of the specific business. It also requires planning, staffing, directing, marketing, and financing.

The purpose of planning is to set goals for the business to make it more successful and profitable. This involves deciding which goods to produce or services to provide and how to market them well. Planning includes researching the competition and turning out the products or services consumers prefer. Planning also includes organizing the business so it can operate efficiently and reach its goals.

Staffing involves hiring workers to help produce, market, and distribute goods and services. The larger the business, the larger this function is. In large corporations, the staffing and training of employees is usually handled by a human resources manager.

Directing the production of goods is another job for management. Production managers and supervisors oversee the manufacture of goods. Managers of stores, restaurants, health clubs, and other service businesses make sure they operate efficiently and provide customer satisfaction. Production and service managers are both responsible for the quality of goods and services their businesses provide.

Marketing includes the promotion, selling, and distribution of goods and services. The purpose of marketing is to persuade customers to buy the products or services and become repeat customers.

Financing involves keeping records of accounts, paying debts, collecting payments from customers, handling the payroll, and paying taxes.

As managers plan, staff, direct, market, and finance their businesses, they must constantly make decisions. A human resources manager must decide who to hire. A production manager must decide how goods will be manufactured. A marketing manager must decide how products or services will be promoted. A business manager must decide how to keep accurate financial records. Because decision making is such an important part of management, workers with the most training and experience are most often promoted to management positions. The more knowledge and experience people have, the more likely they are to make wise business decisions.

Case

Starting a Multimedia Business

Renata and Marc are close friends. Both want to start a business they can operate from a home office. They both have experience with multimedia. Coincidentally, both are considering similar business ideas.

One business idea involves creating interactive high school yearbooks. Since the majority of high school students have access to computers in their own homes, it is felt there may be high potential in this product.

The other business idea is designing Web sites for individuals and businesses. They both feel they have the background in computer language to use simple software to make Webpages come alive. They know how to use graphics, animation, and sound in Websites. They both have successfully created Websites for several local companies.

Since Renata and Marc have such similar career plans, they wonder if a partnership is a better work arrangement for them than individual sole proprietorships. Perhaps they should consider forming a corporation.

Critical Thinking

1. What type of business organization would you recommend for Renata and Marc? Explain.
2. If they asked you to invest money in their business venture(s), how would you respond?
3. Which business management responsibilities will Renata and Marc probably handle well, based on their abilities? For which business management responsibilities might they need help?

Checkpoint 20.2

1. Name and describe the three forms of business ownership.
2. Name two advantages of a partnership over a proprietorship.
3. What is a limited partnership?
4. What are the two major advantages of corporate ownership?
5. What is marketing? Explain its purpose in business.

Build Your Vocabulary

As you progress through this text, develop a personal glossary of career-related terms and add it to your portfolio. This will help you build your vocabulary and prepare you for your career of choice. Write a definition for each of the following terms, and add it to your personal career glossary.

sole proprietorship
partnership
corporation
organization chart

Chapter Summary

Section 20.1 Our Economic System

- With the advent of the Industrial Revolution, American industries were born. Business leaders developed companies and produced goods and services for the world market.
- The free enterprise system allows people the freedom to make their own economic decisions and possess property. Also referred to as a *consumer economy* or *capitalism,* free enterprise gives people control over their money and the ability to be both buyers and sellers in the marketplace.

Section 20.2 Business Organization

- The United States has thousands of businesses that produce a variety of products and services. There are three basic types of business ownership—sole proprietorship, partnership, and corporation.
- Businesses may be structured in many different ways. Two common types of management structures are a vertical structure and a horizontal structure.
- All types of business organizations must be well managed to be successful. Business management involves careful planning, staffing, directing, marketing, and financing.

Check Your Career IQ

Now that you have finished the chapter, see what you learned about careers by taking the chapter posttest. The test can be accessed on the mobile site by using a smartphone or on the G-W Learning companion website.

www.m.g-wlearning.com
www.g-wlearning.com

Review Your Knowledge

1. What is the Industrial Revolution?
2. What natural resources contributed greatly to American production during the Industrial Revolution?
3. What must an inventor do to receive a US patent?
4. In what way does a product shortage affect prices?
5. Explain the difference between wants and needs. Provide two examples of a need and two examples of a want.
6. How does a sole proprietorship differ from a partnership?
7. If a stockholder invests $2,000 in a corporation, what is the maximum amount she is liable for in the event of a business loss? Explain.

8. If a stockholder invests $2,000 in a corporation, how much does she gain if the corporation makes a profit? Explain.

9. Describe the differences between a vertical management structure and a horizontal management structure.

10. Who makes most of the business decisions in a corporation?

Apply Your Knowledge

1. Give examples of technology invented during the Industrial Revolution. Explain how these inventions changed America's economy. Summarize your findings in a two-page report.

2. Find examples of companies that were declared monopolies in the United States. What actions were taken against these companies? Share your information with others in a small group.

3. Use the Internet to learn more about patents in the United States. Conduct research to answer questions that relate to *who, what, when,* and *how.* Take notes during your research. Share two interesting points you learned with the rest of the class.

4. Create an organization chart showing the levels of management that exist in your school system. Begin with the school board and work down to the teaching and nonteaching positions.

5. Prepare a presentation on current examples of products in high demand. How has demand affected the price of the products? What is likely to happen to the prices once a surplus of the product is available? Present your findings to the class.

6. Work with two classmates to create a new business on paper. Imagine that your group's life savings will be invested into its development, so select a business venture that everyone believes will be successful. Answer the following questions on paper: What product(s) and/or service(s) will your business provide? What type of business organization will it have? Approximately how many people will it employ? Will the organization chart be tall or flat? Why will consumers patronize your business instead of your competitor's? Provide an explanation for each decision made. Be prepared to present your business idea to the class.

7. Research the differences between the United States' free enterprise system and economic systems in other countries. Discuss your findings in class.

8. Using the vocabulary words in this chapter, create a vocabulary activity that will allow you and your classmates to learn the featured words and definitions in the chapter. Bring three copies of your activity to class. One copy should be given to your teacher. During class, exchange activities with a partner. You should then complete your partner's activity. Next, have your partner evaluate your performance. Repeat this process with another student.

9. Create an outline of the information presented in Section 20.2. Be sure to include important ideas and vocabulary. Use the outline to study for a chapter quiz or test.

10. Consumer decisions are often affected by resources. Make a list of four wants that you would like to have over the next year. How do you plan to finance or obtain these wants? If money is needed, how much? What are your available resources? Can any of these items be acquired through trade? When do you plan to obtain them? Create a plan that will allow you to acquire the items on your list. Organize your information in a chart.

Teamwork

Work with a small group of classmates to locate someone in your area who operates a business as a sole proprietorship. Create a list of 10 questions you would like to ask about the business. Among your questions, be sure to ask about the advantages and disadvantages of running a small business independently. After evaluating the answers provided, create a presentation that shows the features of the business, as well as the characteristics of an individual who succeeds as a sole proprietor.

G-W Learning Mobile Site

Visit the G-W Learning mobile site to complete the chapter pretest and posttest and to practice vocabulary using e-flash cards. If you do not have a smartphone, visit the G-W Learning companion website to access these features.
G-W Learning mobile site: www.m.g-wlearning.com
G-W Learning companion website: www.g-wlearning.com

Common Core

College and Career Readiness

CTE Career Ready Practices. Whether you see problems as challenges or opportunities, they often require creative thinking to solve them. Many new inventions come about from trying to solve a problem. Describe a situation in your life or in history where a problem led to the creation of a new way of doing things or a new invention.

Writing. Conduct a short research project to learn about a planned economy? What countries today have planned economies? What is the difference between a planned economy and a free market economy? What impact does a country's economic system have on the types of careers people are able to have?

Apply Your Technology Skills

Access the G-W Learning companion website for this text at www.g-wlearning.com. Download the data file for this chapter. Follow the instructions to complete activities to practice what you have learned in this chapter.

Data File 20–1—**Learning about the US Commerce Department**

College and Career Readiness

College and Career Readiness Portfolio

You have created an effective print résumé. However, your résumé might be entered online on a company website or job board. Rather than keying the information each time, you can cut and paste from a document you have prepared earlier. This will save time and reduce the chance of keying errors. You could also be asked to submit a résumé that will be scanned into a database or other program. The database can be searched using key terms to find applicants that match open jobs. The format used for a résumé that will be entered online or scanned should be different from that used for a print résumé. For these résumés, it is best to use very simple formatting. Do not use bullets, bold type, or other font effects that may not appear correctly when scanned. Avoid using tables that may make data appear out of order when scanned. Remember to proofread carefully and correct errors before submitting the data.

1. Modify a version of your résumé to make the format appropriate for submitting online or for scanning.
2. Save the résumé file in your e-portfolio. Place a printed copy in the container for your print portfolio.

Chapter 21

Entrepreneurship: A Business of Your Own

Section 21.1
Entrepreneurship

Section 21.2
Starting Your Own
Business

College and Career Readiness

Reading Prep. Before reading, observe the objectives for each section in this chapter. As you read, focus on how the chapter is structured. Does this structure make points clear, convincing, and engaging?

Introduction

Can you name people in your community who own their own businesses? Your list may include florists, restaurant or catering company owners, and barbers who have their own shops. These people are entrepreneurs. An entrepreneur is a person who starts a new business.

Starting a business is a serious endeavor. The entrepreneur or owner must make decisions daily about how to operate and manage the business. He or she must develop a business plan and decide how to use available resources efficiently. It is the entrepreneur's responsibility to lead the business venture to success.

Check Your Career IQ

Before you begin the chapter, see what you already know about careers by taking the chapter pretest. Use the related QR code to view the pretest on the mobile site. If you do not have a smartphone, visit the G-W Learning companion website to access the pretest.

www.m.g-wlearning.com
www.g-wlearning.com

G-W Mobile

Career Snapshot
Entrepreneur

What Does an Entrepreneur Do?

An entrepreneur is a person who starts a new business and takes on the risks, responsibilities, and potential rewards of operating and building the business. An entrepreneur must:

- focus on building and growing an enterprise;
- make adjustments when a business venture lacks production or fails;
- implement financial and management decisions that will increase profitability; and
- take action to achieve goals.

What Is It Like to Be an Entrepreneur?

No one description can explain what it is like to work as an entrepreneur. Some entrepreneurs work in air conditioned offices, while some work in changing environments both inside and outside. An entrepreneur might work alone, with a partner, or with a team. Work hours vary and depend on the kind of work that is performed. Some entrepreneurs work part-time. Others may work full- and over-time hours.

What Education and Skills Are Needed to Be an Entrepreneur?

- may range from high school diploma to a doctorate degree
- ability to lead and make sound decisions
- problem-solving, analysis, and business skills
- highly motivated, goal-driven, passionate about ideas
- willingness to learn new skills and processes

StockLite/Shutterstock.com

21.1 Entrepreneurship

Objectives

After completing this section, you will be able to:
- **Explain** the importance of small businesses to the US economy.
- **Describe** the factors to consider when planning a small business.

The Importance of Entrepreneurship

An **entrepreneur** is a person who starts a new business and takes on the risks, responsibilities, and potential rewards of building and operating that business. Entrepreneurs play an important role in the economy of the United States. Since the nation was founded, Americans have been free to own businesses. They have been able to watch their business dreams become realities. Businesses owned by entrepreneurs help keep the economy strong by creating jobs.

Entrepreneurship is taking on both the risks and responsibilities of starting a new business. A culture of entrepreneurship has contributed to the high standard of living in the United States. When people are working, they have more money to spend. This creates more demand for the goods and services provided by independent businesses. Entrepreneurs then must hire more people to help meet the increased demand for their products. As more people are put to work, more money is spent, and the standard of living increases.

Entrepreneurs identify and meet consumer needs. Businesses they create can provide specialized products and services that large corporations do not. These businesses start out small, but have been known to grow into large corporations. America's 23.7 million small businesses employ the majority of workers who are not employed by the government. Often, this sector is the principal source of new jobs in the US economy. See Figure 21-1 for more facts about the impact of small businesses on the economy.

Starting a new business, significantly enlarging it, or reorganizing a failed business are challenges few can handle. However, entrepreneurs are willing to spend the time and energy needed for success.

Facts about Small Businesses
Small businesses employ
• 53 percent of the private workforce
• a larger proportion of employees who are younger workers, older workers, female workers, and people seeking part-time work
Small businesses provide
• 47 percent of all sales in the country
• initial on-the-job training in basic skills to 67 percent of beginning workers
Small businesses account for
• 28 percent of jobs in high technology
• 51 percent of private sector output
• 55 percent of innovative products and services

Figure 21-1.
Small businesses are a driving force in the US economy.

Goodheart-Willcox Publisher

Advantages of Entrepreneurship

People become entrepreneurs for many different reasons. Being an entrepreneur can be very exciting and rewarding. It gives people the sense of accomplishment that comes from doing something on their own.

Entrepreneurs are their own bosses. They have the freedom to make their own decisions. They are in charge of setting their own schedules. Entrepreneurs have the opportunity to try out new ideas that might get overlooked in a big company. If the ideas are accepted by their customers, the entrepreneurs see greater success as reflected in increased sales.

Profit is another factor that motivates many people to become entrepreneurs. **Profit** is the money remaining from business income after paying all expenses. Successful entrepreneurs may earn more money working for themselves than for someone else.

Disadvantages of Entrepreneurship

Being an entrepreneur is not all positive; it has drawbacks. Entrepreneurs must be willing to do everything connected with a new business. He or she must do the jobs of a bookkeeper, manager, salesperson, administrative assistant, often custodian, too. Doing all these jobs may require many extra hours of work. It is not unusual for a small business owner to work at least 60 hours per week.

An advantage of entre-
preneurship is having the
freedom to make your own
decisions.

PETER CLOSE/Shutterstock.com

Owning your own business also involves emotional strain.
Entrepreneurs worry about being able to make a profit. They must
bear the burden of making decisions that can affect the success of
their businesses. If they make the wrong decisions, they may not make
enough money to meet expenses. When cash flow is strained, the
entrepreneur is often the first to give up a paycheck.

Being an entrepreneur places a heavy burden on a family. The
family has to be committed to the business. In many cases, family
plans may have to be postponed until the business is stable.

Entrepreneurs feel the pressure of knowing their businesses
could fail if they make too many mistakes. Hiring may be difficult,
especially for a business requiring unique skills.

Types of Business Ventures

What kinds of businesses can entrepreneurs own? The
possibilities are almost endless. As an entrepreneur, you could start
any type of business you think would be successful. You could sell
homemade products, such as clothing, artwork, or food. You could
offer a service, such as housecleaning, childcare, or car repair. You
might even decide to build a factory and manufacture items, such as
tools, toys, or furniture.

Your company could involve an established business concept,
or you might introduce new ideas. For instance, dry cleaners and
restaurants are established concepts. These types of businesses have
existed for a long time. A social media company is an example of a
newer business idea.

Franchises

One type of entrepreneurial opportunity you might explore is a franchise. A **franchise** is the right to sell another company's product or service for profit in a certain area. Purchasing this right usually costs thousands or even tens of thousands of dollars. Restaurants, convenience stores, and dry cleaners are businesses that are often sold through franchises.

Purchasing a franchise has several advantages. It allows the entrepreneur to buy a business with a proven track record of success. Often the buyer is granted exclusivity, which means no one else can buy into the same franchise in the same area. As a franchise owner, you would also receive support from the franchiser. The company that sold you the franchise rights may help you find a good location. You may receive training and business tips the company has found successful in the past.

Buying a franchise also has some disadvantages. You need a lot of money for the initial investment. You also have to pay ongoing fees to retain the right to use the company's name. You may not be free to run the business as you wish. You may be required to follow company guidelines instead. Also, some franchises require you to purchase their equipment and products for resale.

If you ever consider investing in a franchised business, be sure to investigate it carefully. Talk to people who own the same franchise in other areas. These owners are called *franchisees.* They have purchased a franchise from the same *franchisor,* which is the one who sells a franchise. Franchisees can provide you with insight about the franchisor and the success of their franchises. This information can help you make the right decision. If the franchisor is your only source of information, you may not get the whole picture.

You are probably familiar with several franchises. Figure 21-2 is a list of some of the most successful currently in operation. Many other franchises may be successful but not as well known. The Federal Trade Commission and the International Franchise Association (IFA) can provide invaluable information on franchise and business opportunities.

Ethical Leadership

In the Entrepreneurial World

"A company will nurture an organizational culture that encourages its employees to give critical feedback on unethical practices, and even 'blow the whistle' when their voices are ignored"—David Batstone

As an entrepreneur decides to start a business, it is very important to be ethical and promote honest practices. This may be done by putting the best interests of your customers first. As an entrepreneur, it will be your responsibility to set the standards and tone of how your business will be run. Lead by setting an example for others to follow. One good approach would be to develop a code of ethics for your business and following it.

Successful Franchises	
• Big Apple Bagels	• Quiznos
• Compu-Fun	• RE/MAX International, Inc.
• Copy Club	• Resort Maps Franchise Inc.
• Curves	• 7-Eleven
• Dunkin' Donuts	• Signs By Tomorrow
• Executive Tans Inc.	• Taco Bell
• Great Clips, Inc.	• TCBY Treats
• House Doctors	• The Athlete's Foot
• Juice Stop	• The Coffee Beanery
• KFC	• The Little Gym
• Lawn Doctor	• The UPS Store
• Liberty Tax Service	• We Care Hair
• MaidPro	• Wendy's
• Mail Boxes, Etc.	• Window Works
• McDonalds	• Yogen Fruz Worldwide
• Nursefinders	• Ziebart-TidyCar

Figure 21-2.   *Goodheart-Willcox Publisher*
Some of the most well-known companies are franchises.

Buying an Existing Business

Another opportunity open to some entrepreneurs is buying a business that is already established. Business owners who want to change careers, move, or retire often put their businesses up for sale. Buying an established business can eliminate much of the work and expense of starting a business. Your location will already be decided. The business name will already be familiar in the community. If the existing business is successful, you will already have loyal customers.

As with a franchise, you must carefully investigate before buying an existing business. Be sure the business has a good reputation. Make sure the equipment is in good condition. Be aware of new laws and any competition that might affect the business. It is also very important to check for possible environmental issues as well as potential or pending lawsuits the company may be facing.

Planning Your Own Business

As a child, did you ever try to run a small business, such as a lemonade stand? Many successful entrepreneurs started their careers with similar business ventures as youngsters. If you still have thoughts of running your own business, entrepreneurship may be for you.

Making the decision to open a small business should be done only after careful study and thought. The checklist in Figure 21-3 offers helpful guidelines for those planning to become entrepreneurs. If you are going to continue planning your own business, it will be necessary to develop a business plan.

Business Planning Checklist
❏ Contact your local library, chamber of commerce, SBA office, and/or state Department of Commerce for information about starting a business.
❏ Identify the product or service your business will offer.
❏ Ask people already in the business for advice and insight about potential problems.
❏ Conduct a market survey to identify potential customers and assess their need for your business.
❏ Investigate the possibility of purchasing a franchise or an existing business.
❏ Investigate the strengths and weaknesses of your competitors.
❏ Choose a business location.
❏ Price your product or service.
❏ Contact a lawyer to help you set up your chosen business structure.
❏ Check your local government for information about local zoning laws.
❏ Contact your state commerce department for information about necessary licenses and permits.
❏ Contact an accountant to help you establish a financial record keeping system.
❏ Contact sources of financing to arrange for a loan, if necessary.
❏ Contact an insurance agent for advice about your needs for business insurance.

Figure 21-3.   *Goodheart-Willcox Publisher*
This checklist covers the most important tasks an entrepreneur must do before operating a new business.

A Business Plan

A sound business plan is fundamental and essential to a startup business. Because no two businesses are identical, you should avoid generic business plans that simply require you to fill in the blanks. Your business plan should be as personal as your business and reflect your personality as well as the structure of your business. Keep in mind your business plan is *not* a public document. Keep all discussions regarding your business plan confidential. At a minimum, your business plan should include:

- the market your business will address;
- a description of your customer base;
- your five most important vendors and what they will supply;
- information of existing business loans or government grants;
- your hiring plan;
- a plan for repayment to the bank or lender;
- the amount you will be personally investing; and
- assets required for security.

A **business plan** is a document used to help guide an entrepreneur in organizing and running a business. It should outline the type of product or service you will offer. It should state where your business will be located and when you plan to open. It should identify your competitors and why you think you will be able to compete with them. Your business description should explain who your customers will be and your promotional plan for attracting them. It should also specify your needs for space, equipment, and employees. It also provides information required by most lending institutions. A well-thought-out business plan will be a required piece of documentation if you need to borrow money to get your business started.

What Does It Take to Succeed?

Before you plan to start your own business, you need to know what it takes to succeed. Successful entrepreneurs seem to have certain skills or qualities that make them successful. One key quality for success is optimism. You must believe in yourself and in your business. This positive attitude will help you succeed.

To be an entrepreneur, you must be able to see what needs to be done and then take the initiative to do it. You cannot wait for someone else to tell you to get busy. It has to be your time, energy, and interest that make your business successful.

Many entrepreneurs are inclined to pursue a business venture alone. While this has worked for a few, the general consensus is you will need at least one or two other good people you can work with to brainstorm through problems.

Being innovative is another quality needed to run a business. This is the ability to come up with new ideas. The right idea for a new product, service, or sales technique can lead you to success.

An entrepreneur must be creative and have the ability to make firm decisions.

Yuri Arcurs/Shutterstock.com

Entrepreneurs need skill in making decisions. You must be able to make decisions about routine issues and major problems. Sometimes choices have to be made quickly. In large corporations, several people might be involved in the decision-making process. However, if you become an entrepreneur, the ultimate responsibility for making decisions is yours.

A willingness to take risks is another success factor for entrepreneurs. Starting a business involves many risks. You might risk losing the money you have invested. You may also risk losing self-esteem and community standing if your business fails. If you believe in your ability to succeed, however, you will be willing to take those risks.

Being able to set and achieve goals is another skill for success. You will be expected to identify when you expect your business to become profitable. You must also set goals for the growth of your business. After setting these goals, you will need to make and carry out plans for reaching them.

Successful entrepreneurs must be good managers. If resources are not used wisely the business will probably fail. Entrepreneurs must also make the best possible use of their human, material, and financial resources. These resources can be described as follows:

- *human resources* are employees and customers;
- *material resources* are the supplies and other items needed to run the business; and
- *financial resources,* also called *capital resources,* is the money needed to start the business and keep it going, including profits.   If financial resources are limited, it may be best to start as a side business and stay employed in your regular job as long as possible.

Using Resources

One textbook chapter cannot tell you all you need to know to become an entrepreneur. You will need to spend time doing your research before becoming too deeply involved financially in a new business. The Internet is a valuable tool to help you research starting a new business. Your local library, local chamber of commerce, and state commerce department can provide you with more information. Community college classes and retired university professors may help get you started.

Go Green

Did you know that the batteries in cell phones and iPods are composed of hazardous material that will harm the environment if thrown away? Batteries should always be properly recycled by a reputable organization and never thrown in the regular trash. To be environmentally friendly and save money, consider using rechargeable batteries. Rechargeable batteries, like those in cell phones, can be used many times over and will save you trips to the store to purchase disposable batteries.

 **Entrepreneurship Project**

Some Career and Technical Student Organizations (CTSOs) have competitive events in which the chapter develops and executes a plan for a real business. A school store would be an example of this type of activity. The store would sell products, generate revenue, and operate as a small business.

For the competition, the chapter is required to prepare a report detailing how the business contributes to the community, a business plan, and how the plan was implemented. Students must provide a written document and a presentation to the judges.

To prepare for a chapter project on entrepreneurship marketing campaigns, complete the following activities.

1. Read the guidelines provided by your organization. Make certain that you ask any questions about points you do not understand. It is important to follow each specific item that is outlined in the competition rules.

2. Contact the association immediately at the end of the state conference to prepare for next year's event. The activity may begin any time after the state conference.

3. As a team, select a project that will involve the members of the chapter.

4. Decide which roles are needed for the team. If a school store is selected, there will be an accountant, inventory person, etc. Ask your instructor for guidance in assigning roles to team members.

5. Identify your target audience, which may include business, school, and community groups.

6. Make a decision as to how the business will be set up, where it will be located, how the revenues will be distributed, and all other details on how to run a profitable business.

7. This project will span the school year. During regular chapter meetings, create a draft of the report based on direction from the CTSO. Write and refine drafts until the final report is finished.

A prime source of information for beginning entrepreneurs is the SBA. The **Small Business Administration (SBA)** is an agency that provides assistance to small business owners in a number of ways. Established in 1953, SBA provides financial, technical, and management assistance to help start, run, and enlarge a business. It offers a start-up kit that helps you determine if owning a business is for you. The kit also provides information on what you will need to get started. The SBA can help you develop the business plan that is required by lending institutions. While it does not make direct loans, the SBA can guide you through the process of applying for a business loan. The SBA also offers workshops, seminars and courses on marketing, purchasing, and planning a small business. Many SBA resources are available online (www.sbaonline.sba.gov).

Many entrepreneurs have found SCORE (Service Corps of Retired Executives) to be very helpful. SCORE is a nonprofit association dedicated to helping small businesses get established, grow, and achieve their goals through education and mentorship.

Choosing a Business

What is the best business for you? This is one of the first questions to answer if you become an entrepreneur. Answering this question takes time and study.

Your business should involve your interests and abilities. Ideally, it would relate to your work experience or a favorite hobby. You might choose to sell a product that you enjoy. You might choose to offer a service that uses your skills.

The needs and wants of consumers in your area should also be considered when choosing a business. You may need to conduct a survey to find out more about consumers' interests. Your product should be something that customers would be willing to buy. If you want to start a service business, the service should fill a consumer need.

Once you choose a business, you need to learn more about it. Research the subject of your business. Read about it. Take a class or workshop. Talk to those already in the same business. Your investigation may convince you to choose another business, but do not let that discourage you. It is better to choose another business than to open a business that will soon fail.

Avoiding Fraud

People wanting to start their own businesses have been "taken" for tens of thousands of dollars by illegal and unethical marketers of franchise and business opportunities. People who rush into these businesses are prime victims of franchise and business fraud. **Fraud** is the act of deceiving or cheating a business or person.

Some examples of fraudulent businesses are advertised as follows: "Huge Profit Opportunity: $3,000 to $4,000 weekly income possible. Zero down and instantly qualified." Certainly something this profitable would require a substantial investment. Other fraudulent schemes claim to pay big money for assembling products at home or setting up product display racks. Yet others promote big profits for processing medical claims for health care providers.

While a business opportunity may seem ideal for you, it is important to take time to check it very carefully. A call to the consumer protection agency in your state and the local Better Business Bureau, as well as the local chamber of commerce, can reveal if advertisers are the subject of an existing lawsuit or legal order. The Better Business Bureau will also tell you if there have been complaints filed against the company.

Follow these additional tips to avoid fraudulent businesses.

- Contact those who have posted online reviews regarding the business opportunity.
- Try to contact the persons submitting reviews.
- Perform online searches for comments about the business or product.
- See if required training materials are frequently resold through online auctions. This may indicate a lack of quality and effectiveness.

Choosing a Location

The importance of location depends on the kind of business you have. For instance, if you have a mail-order business, location is not very important. On the other hand, if your business is a restaurant, a good location could greatly affect your success.

Keep several factors in mind when choosing a location. Choose a site that is close to your customers and easy for your suppliers to find. Look for neighboring businesses that will help attract people to your business. Know where your competition is located. Find out if the population that would use your services is growing or shrinking in the neighborhood. Check with local authorities to be sure the location is not in a potential flood zone and that it is legal for a business to operate there.

The features of any building you use should also meet your needs. Evaluate the size and number of rooms. Look at the electricity and plumbing capacity. Check out the parking facilities. Verify the facility does not have environmental issues. The Environmental Protection Agency (EPA) can steer you to local offices. See if you can find a building that is already equipped with any special fixtures you need. If a building does not meet your specific needs, think about how costly it will be to make changes.

Using Social Media to Advertise

Various social media, such as Facebook and other similar websites, may be very helpful and inexpensive in advertising your business. Online advertising can be a very valuable marketing tool. The process is often simple and may require only a minimal cost.

If using social media to advertise, do not use your personal social media account. You do not want your friends to be saturated with your marketing messages. You also do not want to accidentally post personal messages on your business account.

Give your customers reasons to come back to your page or website. This may be done by running promotions, discounts, and even contests in which you give away a product, service, or prize. The more value people see in your posts, the more likely they will be to return to your website.

Like any other media, high-quality photos and graphics are very important. You can even use your smartphone to take the pictures and send them to your website. Social media, with a little work, may play a big role in making your business more profitable.

Working from Your Home

Many entrepreneurs start their businesses in their homes. This helps keep costs down while the business is getting established. As the business grows and profits increase, there may be a need to move to a larger location. More than 4.5 million people work at home. Close to 300,000 people working from home make over $100,000 a year.

Some types of businesses work well as home-based operations. Caterers can use their kitchens, and garment makers can use home sewing machines. Artists, photographers, architects, and graphic designers can work out of home studios. Other professions suited for a home-based business include consultants, computer programmers and repairers, engineers, marketers, and writers.

Be careful of work-at-home rip-off artists. Ads like that shown in Figure 21-4 are found every day in newspapers and magazines. While some work-at-home plans are legitimate, many are not. Be wary of schemes involving envelope-stuffing, assembly work, and craft work. Scam artists are experts at concealing the true nature and extent of the work and its cost to you.

Legitimate work-at-home program sponsors are willing to tell you, in writing and for free, what exactly is involved. Ask for a list of requirements needed for the job and an explanation of every step involved in the process. They should be able to answer the following questions, so you can make an informed decision.
- What tasks will I be required to perform?
- Will I be paid a salary or a percentage of sales?
- Who will pay me?
- When will I get my first paycheck?
- What is the total cost of the work-at-home program, including supplies, equipment, and membership fees?
- What will I get for my money?

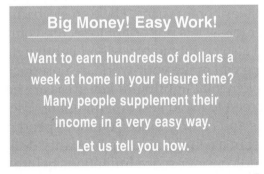

Big Money! Easy Work!

Want to earn hundreds of dollars a week at home in your leisure time? Many people supplement their income in a very easy way.

Let us tell you how.

Figure 21-4.   *Goodheart-Willcox Publisher*
Fraudulent ads are designed to advertise false promises as amazing opportunities. These business deals often produce little results.

Be sure to check out the company with the consumer protection agency in your state and the Better Business Bureau in your own area. Also check those agencies in the city and state where the company is located.

Advantages and Disadvantages of Working from Home

Working from home has several advantages. You are not committed to pay rent or a lease for office space. You do not have to spend time getting to and from work. You avoid the problem and expense of parking. You can handle home responsibilities throughout the workday. Working out of your home also has certain tax advantages.

Working from home may have some disadvantages. Family concerns may disrupt your business. Neighbors may object to having a business near their homes, especially if it draws traffic. Some clients may not take your business seriously. They may feel that your worksite is unprofessional. Also, be sure to check with your local zoning commission. **Zoning laws** regulate what types of business activities can be performed in certain areas. For instance, you may not be able to open a store in a residential area.

Setting Up a Home Office

Setting up a home office involves more than getting a desk and a chair. It involves planning carefully and making many decisions. It also involves very organized and detailed recordkeeping. A tax accountant or attorney can advise you on which records you need to save and for how long. For tax purposes, it is important to keep copies of all business-related receipts, bank statements, charge account statements, mileage logs, and cash receipts. When making cash purchases, write the date and item purchased on the receipt. Keep your personal and business finances separate with separate bank accounts. All your records should be kept in a locked, fireproof cabinet.

Under certain conditions, people who work from home can deduct a part of their utility costs and other business-related expenses from their income tax each year. However, the requirements are very specific. For example, you may not claim deductions if your office is a space used, even part-time, for purposes other than running the business. Consult knowledgeable people on what is deductible and what is not.

Safety is important in a home office. Office equipment may exceed the capacity of regular home wiring. Have an electrician check your circuits and power loads. It is important to secure your windows and doors. You should also be sure to have good lighting inside and outside.

Good planning can make your work area productive. Indirect lighting and supplemental lighting in key areas are helpful. Position your computer screen to avoid sun or lamp glare. Use light-colored paint for the walls and ceiling. Since you may spend most of your time sitting, invest in a comfortable, high-quality desk chair. Map your work area and consider space limitations before purchasing equipment and furniture. More tips on working successfully from home are shown in Figure 21-5.

Guidelines for Working Smarter from Home
Use technology to help speed up daily tasks. Invest in office equipment that meets your needs, such as a computer and software to organize your records, help with money/time management, and prepare tax records.
Keep track of your business and personal contact. File this information or use an electronic database.
Save your energy for important matters. Make a decision and go with it.
Build a reputation. Market your business by telling people who you are, what you do, and what makes your business better than the competition's. Word-of-mouth marketing really works.
Target your customer. Provide a sample of your product or service for free, if possible.
Network with others in your field. Join trade and industry associations in your area and attend social gatherings. Establish relationships that may lead to additional business or information.
Develop a mailing list. Send out regular mailings about your business. Use newsletters as another way to keep your name in the customer's mind.
Be prepared to sacrifice. You may need to lose a little sleep and do a little more work without always sending a bill. If you help a customer once or twice for no charge, you will be remembered.
Be as public as you can. Be seen and heard often.
Give your services to charities. Give as much as you can afford, and "get credit for it". This is not a time to be humble and reserved.
Get to know your local media. Get to know the writers, reporters, and photographers. If you are not strong at writing, get help.
Join your local chamber of commerce. Make yourself known within your community. Volunteer for small projects.

Figure 21-5.   *Goodheart-Willcox Publisher*

Follow these guidelines for building a successful home-based business.

Pricing Your Product or Service

Are you charging enough for your products or services? Many entrepreneurs and home-based workers are not. They are not sure what a fair rate is or do not have enough confidence in the value of their goods or services. The following tips should be kept in mind when deciding what prices to charge.

- **Survey other people working in the same area.** Determine the highest and lowest acceptable rates. You may then set a rate within that range that will allow you to be competitive.
- **If your field is not crowded with competition, you can likely charge more.** If you are an expert at what you do, do not hesitate to charge appropriately.
- **If you find yourself in a very busy season, or your product or service suddenly booms, you may want to consider raising your rates a bit.** Although you may have fewer customers, a higher profit will create less stress and make it easier for you to maintain quality.

- **How highly your customers value your product or service is another issue.** If you are providing something your clients cannot do without, you can charge more for it.

There are several factors you can keep in mind to help you figure your prices. You need to charge enough to pay for the materials and labor used to produce your product or service while making a profit. Overhead expenses are also part of your costs. *Overhead expenses* are any costs beyond materials and labor, such as rent, utilities, office supplies, postage, and advertising costs.

Checkpoint 21.1

1. What is the principal source of new jobs in the US economy?
2. Identify three advantages of being an entrepreneur.
3. What are two benefits of owning a franchise?
4. Why do some entrepreneurs start their businesses in their homes?
5. What are overhead expenses? Provide four examples of overhead expenses.

Build Your Vocabulary

As you progress through this text, develop a personal glossary of career-related terms and add it to your portfolio. This will help build your vocabulary and prepare you for your career of choice. Write a definition for each of the following terms, and add it to your personal career glossary.

entrepreneur
entrepreneurship
profit
franchise
business plan
Small Business Administration (SBA)
fraud
zoning laws

Objectives

After completing this section you will be able to:
- **Describe** legal matters an entrepreneur should know about when starting a small business.
- **Identify** sources used to finance a business and the methods used to keep financial records.

Terms

license
undercapitalization
capital expenses
fixed expenses
variable expenses
assets
liabilities
bookkeeping
accounting
receipts
profit ratio
break-even point

Legal Matters

A number of legal issues will affect you if you become an entrepreneur. You will need to choose your business structure and meet any zoning and licensing requirements. If you operate a business from your home with clients coming and going, you should find out if your homeowner's policy protects you. Find professional help to assist you with these legal matters.

Choosing Your Business Structure

As an entrepreneur, you must decide how to structure, or set up, your business organization. You learned in Chapter 21 about the three basic business structures—sole proprietorships, partnerships, and corporations. Each of these structures has advantages and disadvantages for entrepreneurs.

A sole proprietorship is the simplest type of business and the least costly structure to form. You would be the only owner of the company. This gives you the freedom to run your business any way you want. However, it also makes you entirely responsible for the business and the risks associated with it.

A partnership has the advantage of giving you someone with whom to share business responsibilities. With a partner, you may be able to borrow more money than you could by yourself. However, if you and your partner disagree, deciding who has the final say may be difficult. Getting rid of a lazy or dishonest partner may be difficult, too. If something should happen to your partner, you would be legally responsible for his or her business debts. The business could be jeopardized.

If your business is organized as a corporation, you may have an easier time raising money. You may have less risk to your personal assets. However, this form of business costs more to set up. It is also subject to more taxes. The corporate structure places limits on the head of the company.

In a partnership, owners share the responsibilities of the business.

ZINQ Stock/Shutterstock.com

Obtaining Zoning, Licensing, and Permits

A number of laws apply to businesses and how they must be run. Failing to follow these laws could put you out of business. Therefore, you need to find out what your legal responsibilities are before you begin operation.

If your business plan does not conform to local zoning laws, you may have to change your plan. You might also be able to apply for an exception to the law or have the law changed. Your municipal government can provide you with information about zoning laws. Your local newspaper can help you keep up with changes in these laws.

You must be licensed to operate certain businesses. A **license** is official permission to do something or own something. Hairstylists and barbers, for instance, must be licensed by the state. They must pass a test to show they are qualified to perform the services of a hairstylist or barber. Aside from a license, you may be required to obtain a permit to run your business. You will probably pay small fees for any licenses and permits you need.

Contact your state department of commerce before you start your business. They can tell you how to register your business. They can also help you gather information about the licenses and permits you will need.

Receiving Professional Assistance

Starting and operating a business involves a lot of details. Being sure your financial records are correct and you have met all your legal obligations can be a little unnerving. Fortunately, you can turn to a number of professionals to help you with these tasks.

Stephen Coburn/Shutterstock.com

When starting a business, an entrepreneur should receive professional advice from an attorney, accountant, and insurance agent.

A lawyer can be one of your most valuable resources when starting a business. A lawyer can help you set up your business structure. He or she can be sure you are operating within zoning laws and licensing requirements. Your lawyer can also help you with any legal problems that involve your business.

In addition to your lawyer, your accountant can be one of your best sources when going into business. An accountant can help you choose a record-keeping system that will meet your needs. He or she can help you with loan applications and tax records. Accountants can also analyze your books and give you advice about how to increase your profits.

When choosing a lawyer and an accountant, look for people who have small business experience. This will help assure you they have the background necessary to meet your needs as an entrepreneur. Other business owners or your local chamber of commerce can refer you to experienced professionals.

Discuss fees before hiring a lawyer or an accountant. Legal and accounting fees are high. The money is well spent if it can keep your business from failing.

An insurance agent is another professional whose advice you should seek before starting a business. Of course, you will need insurance to protect you in the event of fire or theft. You will also need liability coverage in case your product or service causes an injury. You may want disability coverage to provide for you in case you become unable to work. Your insurance agent can recommend the types of coverage that will best meet your needs.

Financial Matters

Starting a business costs money. The amount of money depends on the business. However, many entrepreneurs get into trouble because they fail to obtain enough money to keep their new businesses running. As an entrepreneur, you must obtain financing to start your business. You will also have to maintain accurate financial records to keep it going.

Sources of Financing

Entrepreneurs can turn to a number of sources for the money needed to get their businesses going. Your own savings account is the best place to begin looking for money to start a business. Using your savings allows you to avoid the interest costs of borrowing from someone else. It demonstrates that you are willing to take a risk with your own money. It also shows that you have confidence in your ability to succeed.

Your business may require a larger investment than your savings account can cover. In this case, you can turn to other sources for financial help. Many entrepreneurs borrow money from family and friends to get their businesses started. If you decide to do this, be sure to put your loan agreements in writing. State how much you borrowed; when you plan to pay it back, and the rate of interest you will pay. Having this information in writing will help you avoid misunderstandings.

Getting a bank loan may be an option as well. However, getting a loan for a new business is usually difficult. Banks are more likely to issue loans to existing businesses that need funds to expand. Your bank may also be able to direct you to some state-supported financing. The SBA may be able to help you get a bank loan. They can review your business plan and financial statements. They may also be able to recommend specific types of loans for which you should apply. The SBA can help entrepreneurs secure bank loans as well as other financing.

Another source of money is outside investors. Some individuals and companies are interested in investing in business ideas that have a high profit potential. These people are called *venture capitalists.* You can try to persuade such investors that you have the ability to run a successful business. If you are convincing, they may be willing to take a chance on you. Entrepreneurs tend to be deep-rooted optimists and many fail due to undercapitalization. **Undercapitalization** refers to any situation where a business cannot acquire the funds they need. An undercapitalized business may be one that is overexposed to risk or cannot afford current operational expenses due to a lack of capital. An undercapitalized business may be financially sound but does not have the funds required to expand to meet market demand.

An entrepreneur may choose to apply for a loan to help finance a business venture.

JohnKwan/Shutterstock.com

Applying for a Loan

When you apply for a loan, you must be willing to provide detailed information about your business. This is true even if you are borrowing from family or friends. Having your business plan written in detail will show that you have thought about your business seriously. It shows that you are taking a professional approach to entrepreneurship and will be required by the lender.

The loan officer will also want to see financial statements. These statements will include cost estimates for all your anticipated expenses. Your expenses may be grouped into the following categories.

- **Capital expenses** are one-time costs needed to get the business started; an example of which are machines purchased for the business.
- **Fixed expenses** are those that must be paid regularly in set amounts; examples are monthly rent payments, garbage removal fees, and insurance payments.
- **Variable expenses** are those that vary from month to month; examples are advertising costs, repairs, utility bills, and supplies needed for the business.

Do not forget to include salaries, franchise fees, and legal and accounting fees when creating your cost estimates. Your loan request should also include a cushion to cover unexpected expenses. You should not apply for just start-up money only. If possible, you may want to borrow enough to cover the cost of operation until the business becomes profitable. This usually takes at least a year.

Case

Joseph's Complete Editorial Services

After graduating from college, Joseph worked as an editor for a book publisher for four years. When his wife was transferred to another state, he quit his job. Rather than look for a new job in their new state, Joseph decided to start his own business.

He liked working as an editor. He already owned a computer with the necessary software. Therefore, Joseph decided to open an editing business.

First, he investigated the market. He found that many small business owners needed newsletters, flyers, and press releases. However, they often had trouble working with existing editorial services that handled only large orders. Joseph decided he could make his business more successful if he focused on handling small jobs for other entrepreneurs.

Next, he decided he would work from his home. He could use the spare bedroom as an office. This would save him the cost of renting office space. He would call on clients at their businesses. Therefore, having a home office would have little effect on his professional image.

Joseph joined a business organization and met other editors there. They gave him ideas about how much he should charge for his services and how to attract clients. They also told him where to buy office equipment at good prices.

Joseph consulted a lawyer about setting up his business as a sole proprietorship. The lawyer also helped him check local zoning laws. He wanted to be sure there were no restrictions against working from his home.

Although he didn't need to borrow money, Joseph did consult with an accountant for some other advice. Joseph's accountant helped him set up a system for billing his clients. The accountant also told Joseph how to keep his books to make it easier to file taxes.

An insurance agent helped Joseph evaluate his insurance needs. Joseph wanted to know if his homeowner's policy would cover his business.

Critical Thinking

1. Was Joseph's choice of business wise? Explain.
2. Do you think Joseph made the right decision by choosing to work out of his home? Explain.
3. What problems might Joseph have faced if he had not consulted a lawyer, an accountant, and an insurance agent?

The loan officer will want an idea of the future of your business. You should be prepared to discuss your plans for future growth. This will give the officer an idea of when you anticipate being able to repay the loan.

The loan officer needs information about your personal financial status. The officer will check your personal credit history to see how well you have managed past loans. Do you pay your bills on time? How much debt do you already have? A good credit rating is essential. Some people have missed out on the opportunity of a lifetime because of an unpaid debt. You should prepare a statement showing your personal assets and liabilities. Assets are items of value owned by a person or business. These may include cash, stocks, bonds, and property. Liabilities are the debts owed by a person or business, such as payments on a car or home loan.

You will also need to provide the loan officer with personal data. You must show that you have the experience and knowledge needed to run your proposed business. Your résumé should summarize this information.

All of this detailed preparation may take considerable time and effort on your part. If you are successful in getting a loan, your effort will have been well spent.

Keeping Financial Records

Over 50 percent of small businesses fail within the first five years of operation. The reasons for this high failure rate vary. However, lack of financial planning is often part of the problem. Keeping good financial records can help you plan wisely once your business is up and running.

It is not only good business practice to keep thorough records; the law requires it. There are two basic aspects to recordkeeping. One is bookkeeping, which involves the recording of income and expenses for a person or business. The other is accounting, which involves an analysis of the financial data you have recorded.

The type of record-keeping system you use will depend on the type of business you own. If you have a store, you will need to keep track of the products you have in stock. If you have employees, you will need to keep track of the number of hours each works and the many related taxes and expenses. If you have a service business, you must record how much time you spend performing different tasks. A bookkeeper can help you choose a record-keeping system that will work for your business. There are several excellent computer accounting applications to help with these tasks.

The way information is recorded will vary from one record-keeping system to another. However, all systems will help you keep track of your receipts and expenses. Your receipts, also called *revenues,* include all the money you receive from your customers for cash and credit sales. You may be able to keep track of your receipts by using a computer application or on paper sales slips. Record the date and the customer's name and contact information. You should also keep a record of what was sold, the quantity, the price per item, sales tax, and the sales total. All this information will be helpful when you review your books to make plans for the future.

Subtracting your expenses from your receipts (income) yields your profits. To evaluate the success of your business, you need to compare your profits from one year to the next. When making this comparison, the dollar amount of your profits is not as significant as your profit ratio. Your **profit ratio** is the percentage of receipts that are profit. It is calculated by dividing the total profit by the total receipts. The dollar amount of your profits may increase from one year to the next. However, if your expenses also increase, your profit ratio may drop. See Figure 21-6.

Keeping up with your records on a regular basis is important. Depending on the business, you may do your bookkeeping daily, weekly, or monthly. The more detailed your records are, the more helpful they will be when making future business decisions.

The main goal of owning a business is to make a profit. You do not want to simply break even. The **break-even point** is when income equals expenses. Figure 21-7 illustrates an example of a business with a 20 percent profit ratio in the first year, reaching the break-even point in September of the given year. The fact that this business was profitable in its first year makes it an exception, not the rule. As you learned earlier, most new businesses operate at a loss for more than a year.

Comparing Annual Profits		
	Year 1	Year 2
Income	$100,000	$120,000
Expense	−80,000	−98,000
Profit	$ 20,000	$ 22,000
Profit ratio = $\dfrac{\text{profit}}{\text{receipts}}$	$\dfrac{\$ 20,000}{\$100,000} = 20\%$	$\dfrac{\$ 22,000}{\$120,000} = 18\%$

Figure 21-6.   *Goodheart-Willcox Publisher*
Entrepreneurs compare annual profit ratios to get a better idea of the success of their business.

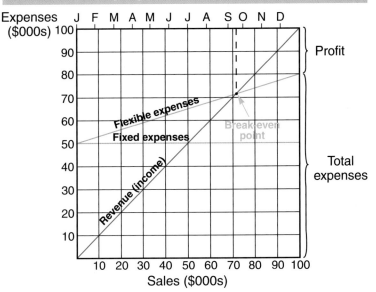

Figure 21-7.   *Goodheart-Willcox Publisher*
A break-even point shows when the total income of a business surpasses its expenses.

Checkpoint 21.2

1. List the three basic structures used to organize a business.
2. Describe three possible characteristics of an undercapitalized business.
3. Explain how capital expenses differ from fixed expenses.
4. What is the purpose of a business license? Name an occupation required to have a state license.
5. How is profit ratio calculated?

Build Your Vocabulary

As you progress through this text, develop a personal glossary of career-related terms and add it to your portfolio. This will help build your vocabulary and prepare you for your career of choice. Write a definition for each of the following terms, and add it to your personal career glossary.

license	liability
undercapitalization	bookkeeping
capital expense	accounting
fixed expense	receipt
variable expense	profit ratio
asset	break-even point

Chapter Summary

Section 21.1 Entrepreneurship

- Entrepreneurs and the businesses they run are important to the US economy. Small businesses help keep the economy strong by creating jobs.
- Making the decision to open a small business should be done only after careful study and thought. The type of business to pursue, its location, and how to price products or services should be considered.

Section 21.2 Starting Your Own Business

- Before opening a small business, a number of legal matters must be addressed. The owner must choose a business structure, adhere to zoning laws, and obtain any needed licenses and permits.
- Entrepreneurs need financial resources prior to starting a business. Sources of finances may include savings, bank loans, and outside investors.

Check Your Career IQ

Now that you have finished the chapter, see what you learned about careers by taking the chapter posttest. The test can be accessed on the mobile site by using a smartphone or on the G-W Learning companion website.

www.m.g-wlearning.com

www.g-wlearning.com

Review Your Knowledge

1. Explain the meaning of *exclusivity* as it relates to franchises?
2. What are the two types of business ventures commonly used by entrepreneurs to start a business?
3. Identify at least three things a person should investigate prior to buying an existing business.
4. What are material resources? How are they different financial resources?
5. List three advantages of working from a home office.
6. What tax benefits are available to business owners with home offices?
7. In what ways can a lawyer assist an entrepreneur when starting a business?
8. What is a statement of need? When might an entrepreneur need one?
9. Identify the two aspects of record keeping for a business.
10. Name three professionals that can assist an entrepreneur with the details of starting and operating a business.

Apply Your Knowledge

1. Search the Internet for information on a popular franchise. Consider using one from the list provided in Figure 21-2. Find information on company guidelines, business structure, training, and the investment required to open a franchise. See also the website for the Federal Trade Commission (www.ftc.gov) if needed. Compile your findings in a chart.

2. Interview a bookkeeper or an accountant to learn more about financial record keeping for a small business. Create a list of ten questions to ask about starting a small business, tips for keeping records, and any other financial questions you think are important. Discuss your interview with a small group.

3. What is ergonomics? Why is ergonomics important to companies and home-based businesses? What are some issues addressed by ergonomics? Research the subject. Write a one-page summary of your findings.

4. Create two posters to be used in the workplace. One poster should demonstrate proper posture at the computer and any additional supporting information. The second poster should provide information on carpal tunnel syndrome and tips or exercises that may help prevent the injury.

5. Use library resources to research the impact of small business on the economy in the United States. Summarize your findings in a two-page report, citing at least three sources.

6. Make a list of all of the qualities and skills you think an entrepreneur must have to succeed. Place a check beside each quality or skill that applies to you. Write a few lines explaining why you think you would or would not be a successful entrepreneur.

7. Think of one or two businesses you would consider running. Are they new businesses, established businesses, or franchises? Do you want to invent a new product or service? How does the idea of being an entrepreneur fit in with your careers plans?

8. Use one of the businesses you considered as part of question 7. Where would that business be located? Why do you think this location is right for that kind of business?

9. Research a famous entrepreneur. Give an oral report on this person's contributions to the business world. Why did the entrepreneur start the business? How did the person prepare to open the business? Why did the business succeed?

10. Visit the website for the Small Business Administration (www.sba.gov). What information are you able to find there? How might you use this information to start a business? Take notes during your review. Give an oral report on the resources available.

Teamwork

Work with three classmates to develop a business idea and present it to the class. Determine the following about the business: the product or service offered, business structure, major competitors, and potential customers. Also describe the location and appearance of your business. Present your plan to the class, using whatever props or visual aids would clarify your ideas. Decide among yourselves who will do specific parts of the project.

G-W Learning Mobile Site

Visit the G-W Learning mobile site to complete the chapter pretest and posttest and to practice vocabulary using e-flash cards. If you do not have a smartphone, visit the G-W Learning companion website to access these features.
G-W Learning mobile site: www.m.g-wlearning.com
G-W Learning companion website: www.g-wlearning.com

Common Core

College and Career Readiness

CTE Career Ready Practices. Whether you see problems as challenges or opportunities, they often require creative thinking to solve them. Many new inventions come about from trying to solve a problem. Describe a situation in your life or in history where a problem led to the creation of a new way of doing things or a new invention.

Reading. Read a magazine, newspaper, or online article about entrepreneurship. Determine the central ideas of the article and review the conclusions made by the author. Provide an accurate summary of your reading, making sure to incorporate the *who*, *what*, *when*, and *how* of this situation.

Applying Your Technology Skills

Access the G-W Learning companion website for this text at www.g-wlearning.com. Download the data file for this chapter. Follow the instructions to complete activities to practice what you have learned.

Data File 21–1—Seeing Yourself as an Entrepreneur

College and Career Readiness

College and Career Readiness Portfolio

The purpose of your portfolio is to help you get a job or volunteer position or get accepted at a college. You should build a network of contacts who can also help you in these efforts. You have probably already begun to build a network, even if you have not thought of it in those terms. People in your network include your teachers, employers, coworkers, or counselors who know about your skills and interests. People you have requested to serve as references for you are part of your network. Those who participate with you in volunteer efforts, clubs, or other organizations can also be part of your network. These people can help you learn about open positions and other opportunities.

1. Identify people who are part of your career network as described above.
2. Create a database to contain information about the people. Include each person's name, contact information, and relationship to you. For example, the person might be a coworker, employer, or fellow club member.
3. Save the file in your e-portfolio. Place a printout in the container for your print portfolio.

Unit 6 Managing Your Income

Lifespan Plan

Completing Your Lifespan Plan

It is not always easy to visualize what your life will be like years from now. Technological, economic, and societal changes make it impossible to create a perfect plan for the future. This Lifespan project will help you make better and more informed decisions about what you will pursue after high school. Apply what you have learned in this text and in this project to create your Lifespan Plan.

Activities

1   Download the data file named "Lifespan Plan" from the *School to Career* student companion website (www.g-wlearning.com).
2.   Use the information you have collected throughout this course to complete each section of the plan. The questions in the data file will guide you through the exercise. Delete the instructions and questions as you complete each section.
3.   Save your Lifespan Plan according to your instructor's specifications.
4.   You are not finished yet. Having a Lifespan Plan is just the first step. Whether or not you put your plan into action will affect what you are able to achieve in the future.

Unit Overview

As an employee, you will receive payment for the work you do. While it would be nice to be able to spend all of your earnings as you choose, a portion of your pay will be subtracted from your paycheck before you even receive it. Much of this amount will be in the form of taxes.

In the United States, all employees are taxed according to their earnings. You should understand how much income you receive and how the taxed amounts are used. Each year, workers must report their earnings to the government for tax purposes.

After receiving your paycheck, you will need to make choices about how to spend, save, and invest that money. Banks and insurance companies offer services to help people make these important financial decisions.

Learning more about income, taxes, and spending will prepare you for your future by giving you the knowledge needed to manage the money you earn.

Chapter 22 Understanding Income Taxes
Chapter 23 Managing Spending
Chapter 24 Using Credit
Chapter 25 Banking, Saving, and Investing
Chapter 26 Insurance
Chapter 27 Managing Family, Work, and Citizenship Roles

Picture Success

Brandon Graham
SkillsUSA

Photo: Lloyd Wolf

The connection between being a member of a CTSO and being a professional football player may not seem obvious. But Brandon Graham sees the connection.

Brandon attended Crockett High School in Detroit, Michigan. While at Crockett High, Brandon was an active member of the SkillsUSA chapter at his school and of the school football team. While he was helping his SkillsUSA team place among the top ten in national competitions, he was also being recognized for his accomplishments on the football field. A winning combination.

Brandon credits his participation in SkillsUSA with preparing him for life after high school. "In the three years I attended the nationals," Brandon recalled, "I learned that you must be professional at all times. I learned to develop my leadership skills by standing in front of people and talking without being too nervous. I improved my communication skills, and that helped both on and off the football field."

After high school, Brandon went on to play college football for the University of Michigan. In 2010, he was drafted in the first round by the Philadelphia Eagles franchise as a defensive lineman to play for the National Football League.

Section 22.1
Understanding Income

Section 22.2
Paying Taxes

College and Career Readiness

Reading Prep. Before reading, observe the objectives for each section in this chapter. Keep these in mind as you read. Focus on the structure of the writing. Use the organization of the text to help you understand the information presented.

Introduction

As an employee, you are paid for the work you do. There are many ways your employer can choose to pay you for your work. The employer may pay you by the hour, a yearly salary, or for a project that you complete. You may be paid in cash or by a paper check. Or, the money you earn may be deposited directly into your bank account.

Most of the money you earn is yours to spend, but do you know what happens to the money taken out of your paycheck? Most of it goes toward paying taxes. When you begin working, you are responsible for paying your fair share of taxes. You, along with all other citizens, share the benefits of taxes in the form of government protection and services.

By studying this chapter, you will get a better understanding of how employees are paid and how a paycheck works. In addition, you will learn more about your role as a taxpayer.

Check Your Career IQ

Before you begin the chapter, see what you already know about careers by taking the chapter pretest. Use the related QR code to view the pretest on the mobile site. If you do not have a smartphone, visit the G-W Learning companion website to access the pretest.

www.m.g-wlearning.com
www.g-wlearning.com

G-W Mobile

Career Snapshot
Child, Family, and School Social Worker

What Does a Social Worker Do?

The responsibilities of a social worker include monitoring the safety and well-being of children and family. Some social workers are employed by government agencies such as the Department of Children and Family Services. Others work in schools to help parents, teachers, and students deal with academic, social, and behavioral problems. The job of a social worker may require visits to the homes of assigned families. Child, family, and school social workers help people with problems that impact daily life. They work to protect the safety and care of others. A social worker may:

- assist with adoptions;
- aid abused and neglected children;
- find foster homes for children;
- work with schools or government agencies; help parents learn how to better care for their children; and
- ensure the well-being of elderly people by working with families and care facilities.

What Is It Like to Work as a Social Worker?

Social workers meet with parents, teachers, family, and children in schools, homes, or care facilities. They must constantly deal with a variety of the client's personal problems. Social work can be very rewarding, but it can also be very stressful.

What Education and Skills Are Needed to Be a Social Worker?

- bachelor degree in social work, psychology, or sociology
- master degree, state license, and certification may be required
- solid problem-solving and interpersonal skills
- strong communication skills

Golden Pixels/Shutterstock.com

22.1 Understanding Income

Terms

earned income
wage
salary
commission
piecework
tips
Internal Revenue
    Service (IRS)
bonus
profit sharing
gross pay
payroll deduction
Form W-4
FICA
Medicare
workers' compensation
unemployment
    insurance

Objectives

After completing this section, you will be able to:
- **Describe** common ways in which most employees are paid.
- **Explain** how earned pay is affected by deductions.
- **Discuss** various benefits available to a person who is disabled or unemployed.

Forms of Income

When you were hired, you probably discussed how you would be paid by your employer. **Earned income** is the money you receive for doing a job. The form of income you earn may depend on the type of job you have. If you work in an office, you may be paid an hourly wage. As a barber, you would probably receive a wage plus tips. If in the future you become a manager, you may earn an annual salary. From these examples alone, you can see there are many different forms of income. Understanding each form of income will help you learn what goes into your paycheck. The following are the most common forms of income paid to workers:

- wages,
- salary,
- commission,
- piecework,
- tips,
- bonus, and
- fringe benefits.

Wages

Many people earn wages as payment for doing their jobs. A **wage** is a set amount of pay for every hour of work. An hourly wage can vary depending on the type of job. Skilled or experienced workers usually earn a higher wage than unskilled or beginning workers. Unskilled or beginning workers may receive a minimum wage. *Minimum wage,* which is set by law, is the lowest amount of money an employer is allowed to pay a worker per hour for most jobs.

Workers who are paid by the hour receive a paycheck based on how many hours they work each week. Kristy, for instance, works in a restaurant where she earns a wage of $8 per hour. When she works 20 hours per week, she receives $160 before taxes. By working 40 hours

Go Green

More than 70 percent of those who file their income taxes use the e-file service. Even those who file paper returns often download forms from the IRS website. Using the e-file service is a more eco-friendly alternative to filing in the traditional way. Filing electronically saves on the use of paper and gas used to deliver the forms to the IRS office. The IRS also sees the benefits of "going green" to help the environment. If you get a tax refund, you may choose to have the amount deposited directly into your bank account. This reduces the use of paper, ink, and envelops used to print and deliver refund checks.

per week, she earns $320. If she works beyond a normal 40-hour work-week, she is paid overtime. Overtime pay is usually 1 1/2, or 1.5, times the worker's regular wage. Her overtime pay, therefore, is $12 per hour for each extra hour of work. Hourly wages are most common in office, manufacturing, maintenance, retail, and service jobs.

total earnings = hourly wage × hours worked
$160 = $8 × 20
$320 = $8 × 40

overtime earnings = 1.5 × hourly wage
$12 = 1.5 × $8

overtime earnings = overtime hourly wage × overtime hours
$36 = $12 × 3

total earnings = regular earnings plus overtime earnings
$356 = $320 × 36

Salary

In certain types of jobs, workers receive salaries instead of hourly wages. A **salary** is a set amount of money paid for a certain period of time. For example, an annual salary is the total amount of money for a full year of work. The salary amount is divided into equal payments. Salaried workers may be paid once a week, every two weeks, or once a month. Highly skilled or experienced workers, such as teachers, managers, and some office workers, are examples of workers who earn salaries. Salaried workers may work overtime, but they receive no extra pay. This often is the case in management or supervisory jobs, which involve more responsibilities.

Commission

Some workers in sales positions earn a **commission**, which is a percentage of the sales they make. For example, a 10 percent commission on a $100 sale is $10. The more salespeople sell, the more money they earn. The purpose of a commission is to encourage employees to sell more of a product or service for the company. Some good salespeople may prefer to be on commission because they can earn more money. Other salespeople prefer more stable incomes. They choose to receive a wage or salary, plus a smaller commission. Those who work on commission include some retail salespeople, real estate agents, and insurance agents.

Piecework

Piecework is a form of income in which an employee is paid a fixed amount of money for each piece of work that is completed. For example, Ardis works in a manufacturing plant painting faces on toys. She works along with several other workers on an assembly line. Each worker is paid a set amount for each toy painted. The more toys Ardis paints, the more money she earns. Pieceworkers who qualify for minimum wage must be paid no less than the minimum hourly wage.

Tips

Tips are small amounts of money given by customers to service workers in return for their help. Food servers, porters, and taxi drivers are examples of workers who may get tips. Tipping is one way for a customer to reward a worker for good service. It can also encourage a worker to continue providing good service. However, giving a tip is voluntary, as is the amount of money given. Service workers may not get a tip from every customer.

Usually tips are not a service worker's only source of income. In many cases, workers receive an hourly wage plus the tips they earn. Since tips are considered part of total income, workers must keep track of them for tax purposes. If you receive tips, you may need to get a copy of Form 4070A, "Employee's Daily Reporting of Tips," to report these earnings for income tax purposes. This form is contained in Publication 1244, *Employee's Daily Record of Tips and Report to Employer*. It is available online

Ethical Leadership

Decisiveness

"In any moment of decision, the best thing you can do is the right thing, the next best thing you can do is the wrong thing, and the worst thing you can do is nothing."—Theodore Roosevelt

An entrepreneur must be decisive and lead by example in regard to promoting ethics in his or her company. Attempting to cut corners in business under pressure to meet the numbers; or failure to deliver according to agreements only hurts the entrepreneur and those served. An internal set of ethics promotes greater freedom, enhances the entrepreneurial spirit, and helps the company succeed. Doing the right thing works from an internal core of self and forms an upright character.

from the IRS at www.irs.gov. The **Internal Revenue Service (IRS)** is the federal government agency that enforces federal tax laws and collects taxes. Form 4070A will help you keep track of your income from tips.

Bonus

Some employers may offer their workers a **bonus**, which is extra payment in addition to the workers' regular pay. Usually it is taken from the company's profits. Two types of bonuses are common: incentive and year-end bonuses.

The purpose of an incentive bonus is to encourage workers to increase their production. For example, a salesperson may receive a bonus if his or her sales total ranks highest in the department. Each member of a production team may receive a bonus for exceeding their scheduled production goal. Some professional athletes earn incentives for achieving specific goals. For example, a football player may earn a bonus for running for a predetermined number of yards.

A year-end bonus may be given to employees, usually at the end of the calendar year. The amount of a bonus will often depend on the company's profits and the length of time a worker has been with the company. A person with ten years of service, therefore, will receive a larger bonus than a person with one year of service. Some employers feel a year-end bonus encourages workers to stay with a company.

Some common forms of income include a salary, hourly wage, and commission.

Zagibalov Aleksandr/Shutterstock.com

Profit Sharing

Profit sharing is a form of income, usually company stock or bonuses, given periodically throughout the year. If the employees' hard work results in greater profits for the company, the company returns some of those profits to the employees. Profit sharing is an incentive to make employees more productive. Each employee's share may be based on seniority, productivity, employee evaluations, or other criteria.

Case

Gary's First Paycheck

Gary couldn't wait to get his first paycheck. He had worked hard for two weeks and had carefully calculated how much he would be paid. He had big plans for every penny of it.

First, he planned to fill his truck with gas. The gas gauge on his old pickup truck hadn't surpassed a 1/4 tank in the two years he owned it. Next, he would pay off the portable DVD player he had on layaway. Finally, he would celebrate on Saturday night. It had taken all his courage to ask Janet for a date, and she had accepted. Gary planned to take her to a rock concert down-town—a date that would surely impress her as he shared his new wealth.

When Gary opened his pay envelope, he was shocked! It was less than half of what he had expected. He would hardly have enough to pay for his gas and lunches for the next two weeks. The DVD player had to stay on layaway. He'd have to borrow money from his parents again if he wanted to keep his date with Janet.

"It's not fair!" Gary shouted as he looked at his check in disbelief. He was also surprised that the pay was for one week instead of two.

He quickly focused on the check stub to try to find errors. There were deductions titled FICA, Fed W/H, State W/H, Pension Fund, and Employee Stock Purchase Program. He could only remember agreeing to the stock purchase program and wondered what all the other deductions were.

Critical Thinking

1. Why did Gary's employer withhold one week's pay from his first paycheck?
2. What does *Fed W/H* and *State W/H* mean? Why were these deductions automatically withheld from Gary's paycheck?
3. Why was Gary required to contribute to both FICA and a private pension fund? Why should he be required to contribute to retirement funds at all?

Fringe Benefits

In addition to the types of income described, many full-time workers receive extra financial rewards called *fringe benefits*. These benefits are provided by an employer along with the worker's regular paycheck.

Tamika is working at a job where she receives fringe benefits. These benefits are provided by the company in addition to a regular paycheck. Her company provides payments for time not worked, such as vacation time, holidays, and sick leave. The company also pays for employees' health and life insurance. Both the employees and the employer contribute to the company's retirement plan. Tamika does not receive cash payments for these fringe benefits, but she knows they are a significant part of her income. The company also has a childcare facility available to employees that Tamika does not use.

Fringe benefits are an important factor for a worker to consider in deciding which job to take. Employers consider fringe benefits an incentive for their employees. Employees receiving fringe benefits tend to be more satisfied and loyal to the company. Some employee benefits even help the employer. For example, the employer may provide tuition aid to further an employee's education. As the employee learns new skills, he or she becomes a more productive worker with more knowledge to contribute.

Interpreting Your Paycheck

The amount reflected on a paycheck is less than the total amount earned. Gross pay is the total amount earned for a pay period before payroll deductions are subtracted. A payroll deduction is an amount subtracted from your gross pay. The difference between your gross pay and the total of all deductions is called *take-home pay* or *net pay*.

Form W-4

When you begin a job, your employer will ask you to fill out an *Employer's Withholding Allowance Certificate*, which is better known as a Form W-4. This form is shown in Figure 22-1. A Form W-4 is used to give your employer the information needed to determine how much tax to withhold from your paycheck. On this form, you claim a number of allowances that correspond to the number of dependents you have. A *dependent* is a child or other person for whom a taxpayer is financially responsible. If no one else claims you as a dependent, you may claim an allowance for yourself on your Form W-4. For example, Eduardo is married with two children. He may claim four allowances. The greater the number of allowances claimed on the W-4, the less will be withheld from your check for federal taxes.

------- Cut here and give Form W-4 to your employer. Keep the top part for your records. -------

Form **W-4**	**Employee's Withholding Allowance Certificate**	OMB No. 1545-0074
Department of the Treasury Internal Revenue Service	▶ Whether you are entitled to claim a certain number of allowances or exemption from withholding is subject to review by the IRS. Your employer may be required to send a copy of this form to the IRS.	20--

1 Type or print your first name and middle initial.	Last name		2 Your social security number

Home address (number and street or rural route)

3 ☐ Single ☐ Married ☐ Married, but withhold at higher Single rate.

Note. If married, but legally separated, or spouse is a nonresident alien, check the "Single" box.

City or town, state, and ZIP code

4 If your last name differs from that shown on your social security card, check here. You must call 1-800-772-1213 for a replacement card. ▶ ☐

5	Total number of allowances you are claiming (from line **H** above **or** from the applicable worksheet on page 2)	**5**	
6	Additional amount, if any, you want withheld from each paycheck	**6** $	
7	I claim exemption from withholding for 20--, and I certify that I meet **both** of the following conditions for exemption.		

• Last year I had a right to a refund of **all** federal income tax withheld because I had **no** tax liability **and**
• This year I expect a refund of **all** federal income tax withheld because I expect to have **no** tax liability.
If you meet both conditions, write "Exempt" here . . . . ▶ **7**

Under penalties of perjury, I declare that I have examined this certificate and to the best of my knowledge and belief, it is true, correct, and complete.

Employee's signature
(This form is not valid unless you sign it.) ▶   Date ▶

8 Employer's name and address (Employer: Complete lines 8 and 10 only if sending to the IRS.)	9 Office code (optional)	10 Employer identification number (EIN)

For Privacy Act and Paperwork Reduction Act Notice, see page 2.   Cat. No. 10220Q   Form **W-4** (20--)

Figure 22-1. *Goodheart-Willcox Publisher*
A W-4 form is used to provide an employer with information to determine how much tax will be taken out of a worker's paycheck.

Paycheck Stub

Your gross pay and the amount deducted from your earnings are found on the stub attached to your paycheck. The stub states the total amount of money you made for the pay period. It also lists all payroll deductions.

The paycheck stub in Figure 22-2 gives an example of earnings and deductions. Marcus worked 40 hours during a given week at a wage of $8.50 per hour. His gross pay is $340 because 40 multiplied by $8.50 is $340. His net pay is $281.75 because it is the difference between his gross pay and the total of all his payroll deductions.

Employee:	Marcus Park 225 West Second Street Frankfort, KY 40601-0225		**Date:** 6/24/--	Jake's Skateboards 82 Hudson Hollow Road Frankfort, KY 40601-0082	
Gross Pay $340.00	**Fed. Income Tax Withheld** $18.06	**State Income Tax Withheld** $13.80	**FICA Tax Withheld** $21.39	**Medicare Tax Withheld** $5.00	**Net Pay** $281.75
Gross Pay Year-to-Date $8,484.50	**Federal Year-to-Date** $444.16	**State Year-to-Date** $339.38	**FICA Year-to-Date** $526.04	**Medicare Year-to-Date** $123.03	**Net Pay Year-to-Date** $7,051.89

Figure 22-2. *Goodheart-Willcox Publisher*
This is an example of a paycheck stub, which is also known as an *earnings statement*.

deductions = fed income tax + state income tax + FICA tax + Medicare
58.25 = 18.06 + 13.80 + 21.39 + $5

net pay = gross pay – deductions
$281.75 = 340 – 58.25

After deductions were made for federal, state, FICA, and Medicare taxes, the net pay came to $281.75. What percentage of $340 was deducted for taxes? To find this answer, add the deductions together and divide the total by $340. The answer is 17 percent.

percent of taxes to net pay = total deductions/net pay
17% = $58.25/$281.75

On your paycheck, FICA is the amount withheld for both Medicare and Social Security. FICA stands for the *Federal Insurance Contributions Act*. Federal income tax and FICA are mandatory deductions. You may also choose to have money deducted from your paycheck for health insurance premiums, union dues, or as part of a savings plan.

Social Security Tax

Social Security is the federal government's program for providing income when family earnings are reduced or stopped because of retirement, disability, or death. Most workers, including those who are self-employed, pay Social Security taxes and are eligible to receive benefits. Social Security taxes help provide medical insurance to older adults and people with disabilities through the Medicare program. Together, Social Security taxes and Medicare taxes are known as FICA taxes.

Social Security provides a basic level of income that people can build on with savings, pensions, investments, or other insurance. It is not intended to replace the paycheck a person formerly earned. The amount of the retirement benefits received depends on a worker's average earnings over a period of years and the worker's age.

The employer must match the employee deduction for Social Security taxes. Whatever amount the employee pays on his or her earnings, the employer must match the amount. The employer sends the employee and employer share of Social Security taxes to the IRS under the employee's name and Social Security number. Once an employee reaches a specified income amount, no additional Social Security taxes are withheld.

Medicare Taxes

Medicare taxes are also withheld. Currently, 1.45 percent of your paycheck is deducted for Medicare taxes. Employers also pay a matching amount for employees. However, there is no cap on earnings subject to Medicare taxes.

Medicare is a national health program run by the US government. It is reserved for people 65 or older, people of any age with permanent kidney failure, and certain people with disabilities. Medicare was created to provide these groups of people with affordable health insurance. The Medicare program provides hospital and medical insurance and drug coverage.

How Deductions Are Calculated

The amount of Social Security tax withheld from your paycheck is a percentage of your gross earnings. The amount of federal income tax withheld depends on how much you earn and the number of allowances you claimed on your W-4. Tax tables, like the one shown in Figure 22-3, are used to determine the amount of federal tax that will be withheld. Using this table, you can determine the amount withheld from a weekly paycheck for a single person. For example, Joella claimed one withholding allowance on her W-4, and she earned $605 for a given week. According to the table, $66 in federal income tax will be deducted from her gross earnings.

SINGLE Persons—WEEKLY Payroll Period

(For Wages Paid through December 20--)

And the wages are–		And the number of withholding allowances claimed is—										
At least	But less than	0	1	2	3	4	5	6	7	8	9	10
		The amount of income tax to be withheld is—										
$300	$310	$32	$21	$12	$5	$0	$0	$0	$0	$0	$0	$0
310	320	33	22	13	6	0	0	0	0	0	0	0
320	330	35	24	14	7	0	0	0	0	0	0	0
330	340	36	25	15	8	1	0	0	0	0	0	0
340	350	38	27	16	9	2	0	0	0	0	0	0
350	360	39	28	18	10	3	0	0	0	0	0	0
360	370	41	30	19	11	4	0	0	0	0	0	0
370	380	42	31	21	12	5	0	0	0	0	0	0
380	390	44	33	22	13	6	0	0	0	0	0	0
390	400	45	34	24	14	7	0	0	0	0	0	0
600	610	77	66	55	45	34	23	14	7	0	0	0
610	620	78	67	57	46	35	25	15	8	1	0	0
620	630	80	69	58	48	37	26	16	9	2	0	0
630	640	81	70	60	49	38	28	17	10	3	0	0
640	650	83	72	61	51	40	29	18	11	4	0	0
650	660	84	73	63	52	41	31	20	12	5	0	0
660	670	86	75	64	54	43	32	21	13	6	0	0
670	680	87	76	66	55	44	34	23	14	7	0	0
680	690	89	78	67	57	46	35	24	15	8	0	0
690	700	90	79	69	58	47	37	26	16	9	1	0
700	710	92	81	70	60	49	38	27	17	10	2	0
710	720	94	82	72	61	50	40	29	18	11	3	0
720	730	97	84	73	63	52	41	30	20	12	4	0
730	740	99	85	75	64	53	43	32	21	13	5	0
740	750	102	87	76	66	55	44	33	23	14	6	0
900	910	142	124	106	90	79	68	57	47	36	25	15
910	920	144	126	109	91	80	70	59	48	38	27	16
920	930	147	129	111	93	82	71	60	50	39	28	18
930	940	149	131	114	96	83	73	62	51	41	30	19
940	950	152	134	116	98	85	74	63	53	42	31	21
1,050	1,060	179	161	144	126	108	91	80	69	59	48	37
1,060	1,070	182	164	146	128	110	93	81	71	60	49	39
1,070	1,080	184	166	149	131	113	95	83	72	62	51	40
1,080	1,090	187	169	151	133	115	98	84	74	63	52	42
1,090	1,100	189	171	154	136	118	100	86	75	65	54	43

Figure 22-3.   *Department of the Treasury, Internal Revenue Service*
This chart is only a portion of a tax table, which can be more than 100 lines long.

When You Cannot Work

Unfortunately, there may be times in your life when you will lose your job either temporarily or permanently through no fault of your own. Workers' compensation and unemployment insurance are there to help address the financial burdens that may result from your lack of income.

Workers' Compensation

Workers' compensation is an insurance program managed by the states to provide payments to workers after they are injured or become ill in the course of their work. Laws may differ slightly from state to state. The premiums are paid by the employer to the state.

When workers are injured on the job, they are entitled to certain benefits. A deceased worker's family is also eligible for certain benefits. Insurance in case of diseases caused by working conditions is also covered by workers' compensation. The major benefits provided by workers' compensation are the following:

- **Medical expenses.** This program covers the cost of all medical expenses, usually without any time or cost limitations. It includes hospital costs, doctors' fees, and rehabilitation services.
- **Disability income.** When workers are disabled and unable to return to work, they receive income benefits. They are paid a portion (usually 2/3) of their average weekly wage until they return to work. Permanently disabled workers receive payments for the rest of their lives.

Workers' compensation is an insurance program that provides benefits to qualified workers if they have been injured on the job.

Shellyagami-photoar/Shutterstock.com

- **Rehabilitation benefits.** Each state provides funding for retraining workers who must give up their jobs due to injuries. Medical and vocational rehabilitation, which includes training, counseling, and job placement, are available.
- **Death benefits.** The surviving spouse or children of a deceased worker receive a certain amount of income as a death benefit. The amount is usually based on the worker's average wage, but this varies from state to state.

Unemployment Insurance

Unemployment insurance provides benefits to workers who have lost their jobs. Someone who is self-employed would not be eligible for unemployment insurance benefits. Each state manages its program within guidelines provided by the federal government. In most states, benefits are provided solely through taxes on employers. In a few states, employees contribute a small amount. The federal government pays the administrative costs.

To receive benefits, unemployed workers must meet certain requirements. Each state has its rules, but some common requirements exist. Workers must have worked for a certain period of time, usually one year, before becoming unemployed. They must have lost their job through no fault of their own. For example, if business is slow, some employers may be forced to lay off workers. In this case, the workers would not be at fault. Workers should file a claim with their state's agency that deals with unemployment as soon as possible after losing their job. They must file weekly or biweekly claims thereafter and respond to questions concerning their continued eligibility. There may be additional requirements to continue receiving benefits. For example, unemployed workers may be required to register for work with their state employment service.

Unemployment benefits are temporary, not permanent. Their purpose is to provide some income security until workers find new jobs or are rehired by their employer. A maximum number of weeks for receiving benefits are set by each state. Benefits are sometimes extended in difficult economic times. The federal government may pay part or all of these extended benefits. Workers receive benefits based on length of employment and amount of earnings. Unemployment benefits are taxable as wages.

Checkpoint 22.1

1. Name four forms of income an employee may receive for doing a job.
2. Explain the difference between gross pay and net pay.
3. Who sets guidelines for the exemption amount as it applies to earnings?
4. For what purposes might a worker need to fill out a Form 4070A?
5. How long is a permanently disabled worker allowed to receive disability income?

Build Your Vocabulary

As you progress through this text, develop a personal glossary of career-related terms and add it to your portfolio. This will help you build your vocabulary and prepare you for your career of choice. Write a definition for each of the following terms, and add it to your personal career glossary.

earned income
wage
salary
commission
piecework
tips
Internal Revenue Service (IRS)
bonus
profit sharing
gross pay
payroll deduction
Form W-4
FICA
Medicare
workers' compensation
unemployment insurance

22.2 Paying Taxes

Objectives

After completing this section you will be able to:
- **Explain** the various types of taxes most people pay.
- **Describe** the forms commonly used when filing income taxes.
- **Summarize** the process of completing a tax return.

Understanding Taxes

Government plays a very important role in your life. It provides many services and benefits, such as parks, highways, public schools, and police and fire protection. It also helps people financially when they retire, become disabled, or lose their income unexpectedly. Government can provide these services and benefits because of our tax system.

Taxes are payments that citizens and businesses are required to pay to city, county, state, and federal governments. Very few people like or want to pay taxes. However, without taxes, governments would not be able to provide the variety of services and facilities they do. Figure 22-4 shows a list of services supported by taxes.

Services and Facilities Funded by Tax Dollars	
Airports	Police protection
Community colleges	Public schools
Fire protection	Public transportation
Garbage collection	Public welfare
Hospitals	Road maintenance
Libraries	Scientific research
Medicaid benefits	Social Security benefits
Medicare benefits	State universities
National defense	Unemployment insurance
Parks and recreation	Workers' compensation

Figure 22-4.   *Goodheart-Willcox Publisher*

Taxes are used to fund a number of services and facilities that are available to the public.

Types of Taxes

As you are probably aware, there are many types of taxes. The four most common taxes you will probably pay are the following:

- property tax;
- sales tax;
- excise tax; and
- payroll tax.

Property tax is a tax on the value of land and any buildings on that land. Property taxes are assessed by city, county, and/or state governments.

Sales tax is a tax on goods and services. You pay this tax at the time of purchase. Sales taxes may be charged by the state, county, city, or all three. Food and drugs may be exempt from sales tax in some states. In other states, all merchandise is subject to a sales tax.

An excise tax is a tax charged to the producer or seller of the product or service rather than the consumer. It is placed on certain products or services, such as gasoline and telephone service. City, state, and federal governments can place excise taxes on products and services.

A payroll tax is a tax an employer withholds from an employee's pay check as discussed in Section 22.1 of this chapter. It is based on the amount of money the employee earns. The amount withheld is then sent to the appropriate government entity by the employer.

Payroll taxes are taken directly from your earnings before you receive your paycheck. Because payroll taxes are taken out before you have a chance to use it, it may be a less painful and less noticeable tax than are sales taxes.

Sometimes these types of taxes may fit one or more classifications, including:

- **Direct tax.** Personal income taxes and property taxes are examples of direct taxes and are charged directly to the taxpayer.
- **Indirect tax.** Taxes are levied on goods and services rather than the individual. As part of a sales transaction, sellers collect the taxes from consumers. The sellers then pass that amount onto the appropriate taxing authority. Sales tax and excise taxes are examples of indirect taxes.
- **Progressive tax.** These are taxes levied in proportion to a person's income. Those who earn less pay less. Those who earn more pay more. For example, federal income tax is a progressive tax because taxpayers are charged different tax rates depending on the amount and type of income they earn.
- **Regressive tax.** These taxes account for a greater proportion of a poor person's income than that of a rich person as the tax rate is aligned to the good or service rather than the person's income. Sales tax is an example of a regressive tax. For example, if Jeffrey, who earns $100,000 per year, pays $100 in sales tax, that would account for 1/1000 of his income. If Simon earns $10,000 per year and pays $100 in sales tax, it would accounts for 1/100 of his income. A greater proportion of Simon's income goes to taxes than does Jeffrey's.

Filing a Tax Return

Your employer deducts taxes from every paycheck you receive. However, it is possible that too much or not enough tax is deducted at the end of a year. To declare how much income you made and how much federal tax you owe each year, you must file the required paperwork, called a *tax return*. Wage earners must file a federal tax return. If their state taxes income, a state return should be filed also. If too much tax was withheld during the year, you can receive a refund from the federal or state government. If too little tax was withheld, you must pay the amount owed.

In January of each year, you will receive a Wage and Tax Statement. This form is commonly known as Form W-2 as shown in Figure 22-5. A **Form W-2** is used for tax purposes to show the amount you were paid in the previous year. It also gives the amounts of income tax and Social Security tax (FICA) withheld during the year. Form W-2 is used to prepare your federal income tax return.

On a tax return you must list all the income you made from wages, salaries, tips, and bonuses. You must also include any money made from savings accounts, stocks, bonds, and other financial investments.

22222	**a** Employee's social security number 123-45-6789	OMB No. 1545-0008		
b Employer identification number (EIN) 75-1234567			**1** Wages, tips, other compensation $8,939.75	**2** Federal income tax withheld $1,314.00
c Employer's name, address, and ZIP code Main Street General Store 123 Main Street Franklin, IL 65432			**3** Social security wages $8,939.75	**4** Social security tax withheld $762.12
			5 Medicare wages and tips $8,939.75	**6** Medicare tax withheld $197.10
			7 Social security tips	**8** Allocated tips
d Control number 123456789			**9** Advance EIC payment	**10** Dependent care benefits
e Employee's first name and initial Last name Suff. Kristy A. James 1027 Cedar Street Franklin, IL 65432			**11** Nonqualified plans	**12a**
			13 Statutory employee ☐ Retirement plan ☐ Third-party sick pay ☐	**12b**
			14 Other	**12c**
				12d
f Employee's address and ZIP code				
15 State Employer's state ID number	**16** State wages, tips, etc.	**17** State income tax	**18** Local wages, tips, etc.	**19** Local income tax **20** Locality name

Form **W-2** Wage and Tax Statement   20--   Department of the Treasury, Internal Revenue Service
Copy 1—For State, City, or Local Tax Department

Figure 22-5.   *Department of the Treasury, Internal Revenue Service*
A W-2 form is used to show the amount an employee was paid in the previous year.

The three common forms for filing a federal tax return are the 1040EZ, 1040A, and the 1040. Form 1040EZ is called a *short form* because it is the easiest and quickest to file. This form is usually used by single people with no deductions or unearned income. Form 1040A is for taxpayers who have a specified income level and no deductions. Form 1040 is referred to as the *long form*. This form is used by taxpayers who do not qualify to use a Form 1040EZ or Form 1040A. You can obtain these forms from the IRS website.

Figure 22-6 shows a blank 1040EZ and 1040A form.

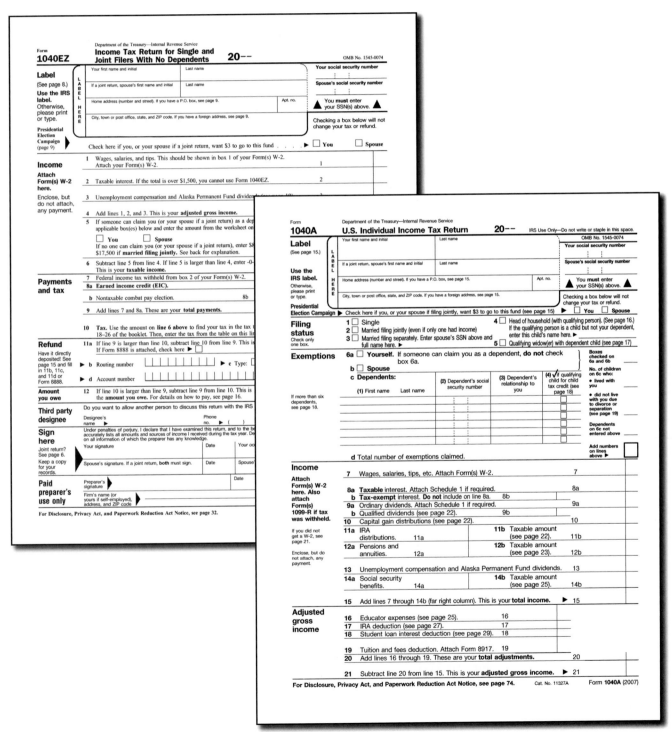

Figure 22-6.   *Department of the Treasury, Internal Revenue Service*
Many taxpayers can use Form 1040EZ or Form 1040A to file their taxes.

On a year-by-year basis, taxpayers should decide which tax form works for their needs. Since a person's financial situation may change significantly in a year, it is best to check which form is most appropriate for your situation. Failing to declare income or falsifying information is illegal and is considered tax evasion. It is a criminal offense that can involve fines and even a jail sentence.

Figure 22-7 provides suggestions for preparing your federal income tax return. In addition, the IRS offers a variety of sources to help you fill out your tax returns. You can telephone an IRS agent or listen to prerecorded messages on a variety of topics. You can use the IRS website to obtain help filing your return or to obtain the correct forms and publications.

The final date for filing tax returns is April 15 of the following year in which income was earned. If that date falls on a Saturday, Sunday, or legal holiday, returns are due on the next business day. Returns must be postmarked no later than the due date. If you file late, you may have to pay penalties and interest fees. Be sure to mail the return to the IRS center for your state or file your return electronically. As a wage earner, it is your responsibility to prepare and file a tax return on time.

Completing a Tax Form

You may want to consider filing your tax return electronically. When you file electronically, you will receive your refund quickly and be provided options on how to pay any taxes you owe.

The Internal Revenue Service offers two strategies for doing this: Free File and e-file. If your income is $58,000 or less, you can use Free File, which is available only through the IRS. You can use the electronic version of Free File or use the online fillable forms. You simply download the necessary forms, complete them, and then submit them electronically.

Suggestions for Preparing Your Federal Income Tax Return
1. Gather your financial records. You may need them to verify your deductions, adjustments, and credits. For tax purposes you may need: • records of income including wages, tips, and taxable benefits; • records of interest earned and dividends received; • canceled checks or receipts for expenses entered on tax returns as deductions; • interest payment records for a home mortgage; and • past tax returns. 2. Read all the instructions carefully before you begin. 3. Make a copy of the completed form and keep it with other important papers.

Figure 22-7.   *Goodheart-Willcox Publisher*
Use these tips when preparing federal income tax forms.

With e-file, you use tax preparation software. You can purchase a home version or use an online version. You then prepare and file your return electronically as instructed in the software. Do not use e-mail to file your return. Most professional tax preparers now offer you the advantages of filing electronically through e-file. Both Free File and e-file are available at www.irs.gov.

Form 1040EZ

The following steps will serve as a guide to help you complete a 1040EZ form manually. Of course, if you are using tax preparation software, be sure to follow the instructions provided with the software.

With the example of college student, Kristy A. James, you can see how to complete a Form 1040EZ. Kristy James worked part-time as a supermarket cashier. Income tax was withheld according to her W-4 Form. At the end of the year, Kristy received copies of Form W-2 from her employer as shown in Figure 22-8. It showed that $1,314 was withheld for income tax from Kristy's total earnings of $8,940.

Kristy can use Form 1040EZ to file her income tax return because she is single and has no dependents. In addition to her wages, Kristy's savings account earned $75 in interest. Figure 22-8 shows Kristy's completed return.

After reading all instructions carefully, you can seek help from a knowledgeable person—such as a parent or guardian—if you have any questions about the form. Teachers and counselors are also good sources of information. The IRS also provides taxpayers with assistance regardless which form they use. Simply contact the IRS at their website.

Kristy carefully read all the instructions on Form 1040EZ. She felt confident that she could complete the form without additional help. Refer back to Figure 22-7 as you follow the steps described in this section.

Kristy printed her full name, address, and Social Security number in the space provided at the top of the form. Kristy did not want to contribute to the Presidential Election Campaign Fund and left the "You" and "Spouse" boxes unchecked. Congress established this fund to help pay the campaign expenses of presidential candidates. If you pay income tax, you may contribute three tax dollars to this fund by checking the box. Kristy knew that checking this box would not affect the amount of taxes she paid or the refund she received.

Filing Status

Kristy did not complete either line under "Spouse" because she is single. If Kristy were married and filing a joint return, she would have filled in the line under her name with her spouse's name and inserted her spouse's Social Security number.

Form **1040EZ**

Department of the Treasury—Internal Revenue Service

Income Tax Return for Single and Joint Filers With No Dependents   **20--**

OMB No. 1545-0074

Label
(See page 8.)
Use the IRS label.
Otherwise, please print or type.

L A B E L H E R E

Your first name and initial: Kristy A.   Last name: James

If a joint return, spouse's first name and initial   Last name

Home address (number and street). If you have a P.O. box, see page 9.   Apt. no.
1027 Cedar Street

City, town or post office, state, and ZIP code. If you have a foreign address, see page 9.
Franklin, IL 65432

Your social security number: 000 00 0000

Spouse's social security number

▲ You **must** enter your SSN(s) above. ▲

Checking a box below will not change your tax or refund.

Presidential Election Campaign (page 9)

Check here if you, or your spouse if a joint return, want $3 to go to this fund . . . . ▶ ☐ **You**   ☐ **Spouse**

Income

Attach Form(s) W-2 here.

Enclose, but do not attach, any payment.

1 Wages, salaries, and tips. This should be shown in box 1 of your Form(s) W-2. Attach your Form(s) W-2.   1   8,940 | 00

2 Taxable interest. If the total is over $1,500, you cannot use Form 1040EZ.   2   75 | 00

3 Unemployment compensation and Alaska Permanent Fund dividends (see page 10).   3

4 Add lines 1, 2, and 3. This is your **adjusted gross income.**   4   9,015 | 00

5 If someone can claim you (or your spouse if a joint return) as a dependent, check the applicable box(es) below and enter the amount from the worksheet on back.

☐ **You**   ☐ **Spouse**

If no one can claim you (or your spouse if a joint return), enter $8,750 if **single;** $17,500 if **married filing jointly.** See back for explanation.   5   8,750 | 00

6 Subtract line 5 from line 4. If line 5 is larger than line 4, enter -0-. This is your **taxable income.**   ▶   6   265 | 00

Payments and tax

7 Federal income tax withheld from box 2 of your Form(s) W-2.   7   1,341 | 00

8a **Earned income credit (EIC).**   8a

b Nontaxable combat pay election.   8b

9 Add lines 7 and 8a. These are your **total payments.**   ▶   9   1,341 | 00

10 **Tax.** Use the amount on **line 6 above** to find your tax in the tax table on pages 18–26 of the booklet. Then, enter the tax from the table on this line.   10   25 | 00

Refund

Have it directly deposited! See page 15 and fill in 11b, 11c, and 11d or Form 8888.

11a If line 9 is larger than line 10, subtract line 10 from line 9. This is your **refund.** If Form 8888 is attached, check here ▶ ☐   11a   1,316 | 00

▶ b Routing number   ▶ c Type: ☐ Checking   ☐ Savings

▶ d Account number

Amount you owe

12 If line 10 is larger than line 9, subtract line 9 from line 10. This is the **amount you owe.** For details on how to pay, see page 16.   ▶   12

Third party designee

Do you want to allow another person to discuss this return with the IRS (see page 16)? ☐ **Yes.** Complete the following. ☑ **No**

Designee's name ▶   Phone no. ▶ (   )   Personal identification number (PIN)

Sign here

Under penalties of perjury, I declare that I have examined this return, and to the best of my knowledge and belief, it is true, correct, and accurately lists all amounts and sources of income I received during the tax year. Declaration of preparer (other than the taxpayer) is based on all information of which the preparer has any knowledge.

Joint return? See page 6.
Keep a copy for your records.

Your signature: *Kristy A. James*   Date: 2/15/20--   Your occupation: Supermarket cashier   Daytime phone number: (815) 555-5555

Spouse's signature. If a joint return, **both** must sign.   Date   Spouse's occupation

Paid preparer's use only

Preparer's signature ▶   Date   Check if self-employed ☐   Preparer's SSN or PTIN

Firm's name (or yours if self-employed), address, and ZIP code ▶   EIN   Phone no. (   )

For Disclosure, Privacy Act, and Paperwork Reduction Act Notice, see page 32.   Cat. No. 11329W   Form **1040EZ** (20--)

Figure 22-8.   *Department of the Treasury, Internal Revenue Service*

An employee must fill out Form W-4 when he or she begins working for an employer.

Reporting Income

Line 1. Kristy wrote in the total she received in wages, salaries, and tips on Line 1. (Tips include cash, merchandise, or services you receive directly from customers. It also includes amounts customers add to credit or debit card purchases and amounts shared from other employees.) The amount shown in Box 1 of her W-2 Form is $8,939.75. Kristy wrote in $8,940 because taxpayers are allowed to round off figures to the nearest dollar. If Kristy had more than one job, she would have included earnings from all of her employers.

Line 2. Kristy wrote in the rounded amount of total interest she received. In this case, she earned $75 from her savings account. (Prior to filing for your income taxes, you should receive an interest statement from your bank and any other institution that pays you interest.)

Line 3. Kristy skipped Line 3. She would have completed this line if she had been laid off and received unemployment payments. Unemployment payments must be claimed as income.

Line 4. Kristy added Lines 1 and 2—the $8,940 from wages plus the $75.00 from interest on her savings. Note that Kristy wrote $9,015 on Line 4.

Line 5. Kristy lives in her own home, and no one claims her as a dependent. Because she did not check either "You" or "Spouse" on Line 5, Kristy entered $8,750—the amount given for a single person. This amount is the total of the standard deduction and her exemption. (Note: If someone could claim Kristy as a dependent, she would have turned to the worksheet on the back of Form 1040EZ as directed. She then would have completed the steps of the worksheet. Kristy would have entered the number result on Line 5.)

Line 6. Kristy calculated the amount of income on which she had to pay tax by subtracting Line 5 from Line 4 ($9,015 – $8,750). Kristy entered the result of $265 on Line 6.

While many people complete the process of filing income taxes on their own, others prefer to use the services of an accountant or tax consultant.

Zadorozhnyi Viktor/Shutterstock.com

Identifying Payments and Taxes

Line 7. Kristy looked at the Form W-2 she received from her employer. Box 2 of that form showed that Kristy's employer withheld $1,341 of income tax. She wrote $1,341 on Line 7.

Line 8. Kristy used the Earned Income Credit (EIC) Assistant at irs.gov to determine she did not qualify for the tax credit.

Line 9. Kristy added the figures on Lines 7 and 8. She wrote $1,341 on line 9.

Line 10. Kristy is asked to look at Line 6 on her tax form. She found $265 on Line 6. This is Kristy's taxable income. She then looked in her 1040EZ instruction booklet and found the tax table and column that applied to single taxpayers. The amount of tax due on $265 was $25. She wrote $25 on Line 10.

Determining the Refund or Amount Owed

Line 11a. Because the amount on Line 9 is larger than the amount on Line 10, Kristy subtracted the amount in Line 10 from Line 9. She entered $1,316 on Line 11a. This is the amount of Kristy's refund.

Kristy can receive a refund in two ways. She can get a check from the US Department of the Treasury. The check will be mailed directly to her. As an alternative, Kristy can choose to have a direct deposit made to her bank account. If Kristy chooses direct deposit, she must complete Lines 11b, 11c, and 11d.

Line 12. If Line 10 on Kristy's form had been greater than Line 9, she would have owed tax. She would have subtracted Line 9 from Line 10. Kristy would have entered that amount on Line 12. This would be the amount of additional tax Kristy would have to pay. She would need to attach a check for that amount to her tax form. However, since Kristy was entitled to a refund, she did not write anything on this line.

Signing the Return

Kristy marked "No" in the section titled "Third party designee" because she prepared her own return. If the IRS has questions, she is the best person to contact, not someone else. Kristy simply left the rest of the section empty.

Kristy read the statement, "Under penalties of perjury, I declare that I have examined this return, and to the best of my knowledge and belief, it is true, correct, and accurately lists all amounts and sources of income I received during the tax year." She followed the instructions carefully. Kristy went back and rechecked her figures. To the best of her knowledge, Kristy had correctly completed her return. She signed her name and wrote the date on the form. She also wrote in her occupation and phone number.

As the last step, Kristy attached Copy B of her Form W-2 to her Form 1040EZ. She sent her return by mail to the Internal Revenue Service Center that serves her area.

Filing a tax return using Form 1040EZ is not difficult if you carefully follow each step. A checklist appears in the instructions for Form 1040EZ to help taxpayers avoid making common mistakes when preparing their tax returns.

Checkpoint 22.2

1. List five services or facilities funded by tax dollars.

2. Name the four most common taxes people pay during their lives.

3. Explain the difference between direct and indirect taxes. Give an example of each.

4. What is the purpose of the Social Security program?

5. List four examples of deductions often used to lower tax bills.

Build Your Vocabulary

As you progress through this text, develop a personal glossary of career-related terms and add it to your portfolio. This will help you build your vocabulary and prepare you for your career of choice. Write a definition for each of the following terms, and add it to your personal career glossary.

taxes
property tax
sales tax
excise tax
payroll tax
Form W-2

Chapter Summary

Section 22.1 Understanding Income

- As an employee, you are paid some form of income for the work performed. Wages, commissions, and tips are common types of income.
- Your paycheck contains information about earned income and deductions. It is important to carefully review each paycheck for accuracy.
- Workers' compensation and unemployment insurance are available to help people address the financial burdens that may result from a lack of income. Those receiving these benefits must meet certain qualifications.

Section 22.2 Paying Taxes

- Tax dollars paid to the government help provide a variety of services and facilities. Common taxes include property, sales, excise, and payroll taxes.
- As a wage earner, you are responsible for filing an income tax return each year. Wage earners must file a federal tax return and, if their state taxes income, a state return should be filed also.
- Common tax forms used to file federal taxes include Forms 1040EZ, 1040A or 1040. When filing taxes, a person may choose to complete the form in writing or file electronically.

Check Your Career IQ

Now that you have finished the chapter, see what you learned about careers by taking the chapter posttest. The test can be accessed on the mobile site by using a smartphone or on the G-W Learning companion website.
www.m.g-wlearning.com
www.g-wlearning.com

Review Your Knowledge

1. What is the purpose of the IRS?
2. For what purposes might a worker need to fill out a Form 4070A?
3. Explain the two most common types of bonuses.
4. Describe an example when a fringe benefit for an employee is an advantage for the employer.
5. How do exemptions affect a worker's paycheck?
6. Explain the difference between progressive and regressive taxes.
7. How does an employee earn Social Security credit?

8. Why was Medicare created?
9. What are the three common forms used for filing a federal tax return?
10. For what reason might an employee receive an income tax refund?

Apply Your Knowledge

1. Record four important things you learned about income. For each, write a paragraph about how you can use this information in planning for your future. Share your responses with the rest of the class during an open discussion.
2. Interview a family member or friend to learn more about the process of filing income taxes. Create a list of ten questions to ask prior to the interview. Take notes and summarize your findings. Share what you learned with the class.
3. Visit the website for your state's employment services. Learn more about the requirements an unemployed worker must meet to receive unemployment benefits. Compile your information in a chart.
4. Review the information you learned in this chapter to write a two-page essay about understanding income and taxes. Include vocabulary from the chapter to support your ideas.
5. Using sample pay stubs provided by your instructor, calculate what percentages of the gross pay on each pay stub were deducted for FICA, federal withholding tax, state withholding tax, insurance, union dues, or retirement plan.
6. Create an outline of this chapter. Be sure to include any major ideas and vocabulary. As you study, use the outline to help you recall important information from the chapter.
7. Investigate government services paid for by taxes. These might include police and fire department services; water and sewer; and garbage collection. How much money is spent on these services? Share your findings with a group.
8. With your partner, discuss the benefits of salary incentives. Do you think salary incentives work to produce performance? Explain why? If you owned your own company, what factors would you use to promote production and performance? Support your answers with detailed explanations. Share your responses with the class.
9. Use the Internet to research information about Social Security and Medicare. Using this information, explain in a one- or two-page written report who can receive Social Security benefits and Medicare insurance. Also, explain how a person obtains each.
10. Contact two or three companies in your area that offer profit sharing. Learn more about what kinds of rewards are offered and what the employees must do to qualify for them. Report your findings to the class.

Teamwork

Participate in a class debate to argue one of two opinions. The subject of the debate is Social Security. One team will prepare an argument for why the Social Security system should be eliminated. The other team will prepare an argument for why the Social Security system should increase benefits. Before the debate, members should research five facts to support the team's position. Conduct a live debate in class. Video record the debate to review your performance.

G-W Learning Mobile Site

Visit the G-W Learning mobile site to complete the chapter pretest and post test and to practice vocabulary using e-flash cards. If you do not have a smartphone, visit the G-W Learning companion website to access these features.
G-W Learning mobile site: www.m.g-wlearning.com
G-W Learning companion website: www.g-wlearning.com

Common Core

College and Career Readiness

Listening. Practice active listening skills while listening to a broadcast business report on the radio, television, or podcast. Pick a single story about the employment rate. Create a report in which you analyze the following aspects of the story: the speaker's audience, point of view, reasoning, word choice, tone, points of emphasis, and organization.

Speaking. Research the features of the US tax system in relation to those of other countries. Do you think the US system is fair? How would you change it if you could? Using various elements (visual displays, written handouts, technological displays), present your views to the class. Support your views with your research findings.

Apply Your Technology Skills

Access the G-W Learning companion website for this text at www.g-wlearning.com. Download each data file for this chapter. Follow the instructions to complete activities to practice what you have learned in this chapter.

Data File 22–1—**Comparing Tax Return Options**

Data File 22–2—**Comparing Tax Return Software**

College and Career Readiness Portfolio

College and Career Readiness

Before you can apply for a job, you must first find job openings or identify possible employers. You may learn about jobs from people in your career network. Newspapers typically contain job ads to which you can respond. The Internet is another good source of job information. You may find information about job openings on the website for a company. For broader information, you can access a job board, such as Monster.com. Job boards are Internet sites that allow employers to post job openings and job candidates to search for jobs. Sites vary; however, you can typically search for jobs by title, geographic location, salary range, or type of work. Some state governments and the federal government also have sites that list jobs. For example, USAJobs is the official website for federal government jobs.

1. Search the Internet to find job boards and job openings on other sites. Make a list of three companies that list job openings on their sites. Make a list of three job boards. Include the name and Internet address for each site.

2. Save the file in your e-portfolio. Place a printout in the container for your print portfolio.

Section 23.1
Managing a Budget

Section 23.2
Spending Wisely

College and Career Readiness

Reading Prep. Recall all the things you already know about managing money. As you read, think of how the new information presented in the text matches or challenges your prior understanding of the topic. Think of direct connections you can make between the old material and the new material.

Introduction

Now that you are earning an income, what are you going to do with it? Are you going to spend it or save it? What expenses do you have now? What do you want to be able to buy in the future? How will you get the best value for the money you spend?

The ability to buy wisely is just as important as planning your budget. With so many choices and temptations available in the marketplace, being a wise consumer is a challenge. Learning to spend your money wisely is a skill you can develop with practice.

In this chapter, you will learn how to create and manage a budget and to make purchases intelligently.

Check Your Career IQ

Before you begin the chapter, see what you already know about careers by taking the chapter pretest. Use the related QR code to view the pretest on the mobile site. If you do not have a smartphone, visit the G-W Learning companion website to access the pretest.

www.m.g-wlearning.com
www.g-wlearning.com

G-W Mobile

Career Snapshot
Industrial Engineer

What Does an Industrial Engineer Do?

The industrial engineer's job is to analyze and evaluate production methods and make suggestions to improve efficiency and product quality. An industrial engineer is required to perform a variety of tasks related to machines, materials, and energy. Industrial engineers:

- use mathematical methods and models to design manufacturing and information systems; and
- assist in designing the layout of plants so production runs smoothly and efficiently.

What Is It Like to Work as an Industrial Engineer?

Industrial engineers often work in factories. Their time may be divided between working in an office and on the floor of the plant. While on the plant floor, they check to see that operations are running smoothly and gather information about how systems may be improved. Industrial engineers frequently interact with factory workers, engineers, and management staff. From time-to-time, industrial engineers travel to observe operations and processes at other facilities.

What Education and Skills Are Needed to Be an Industrial Engineer?

- bachelor degree in industrial engineering
- strong math and science background
- people oriented
- good oral and written communication skills
- strong problem-solving skills

23.1 Managing a Budget

Terms

budget
emergency cash fund

Objectives

After completing this section, you will be able to:
- **Explain** the difference between a want and a need.
- **Describe** the process of creating a budget to help you manage your money wisely.

Needs versus Wants

A need is something you must have to live. Needs should be taken care of first. Housing, food, and clothing are examples of basic needs. Wants are things you would like to have but can do without. A new tablet computer or smartphone are examples of wants. However, the difference between what you want and what you need is not always so simple. Even basic needs can offer choices between what you really need and what you would like to have. Figure 23-1 is a chart that shows the difference between wants and needs. Recognizing the difference between what you need and what you want is essential when creating a budget. A **budget** is a written plan to help you make the most of the money you have. A budget will go a long way toward helping you decide if you need something or just want it. For example, as you complete your budget, you may find you can only allot $50 per week for food. While you would really like to eat out every day, your food budget may not allow it. The shopping strategies described in Section 23.2 of this chapter will also help you manage your spending. A closely managed budget will help you pay for the things you need and allow you to have money left for some of the things you want.

Needs	Wants
transportation	sports car
clothing	designer jeans
housing	upscale apartment
food	dinner at a fancy restaurant
basic medical care	unnecessary cosmetic surgery
exercise	high-end mountain bike

Figure 23-1.   *Goodheart-Willcox Publisher*
When preparing a budget, your needs should take priority over your wants.

Developing a budget will involve making a number of difficult decisions. You will soon find that your money may not go as far as you thought it would. It will be necessary to decide how to divide your income between the things you need and the things you want.

Budgeting Your Money

To make the most of the dollars you earn, you need to know how to manage your money. A budget should guide your spending and savings decisions. Once you plan your budget, you will be more aware of how and why you spend your money.

Consider the story of Tyrone and Cory. Both have worked for four years, earning the same income from their jobs. They each pay the same amount for rent, food, and transportation. Tyrone has a good used car, a versatile wardrobe, and a few nice pieces of furniture. He has also taken two out-of-state vacations since working. On the other hand, Cory has a beat-up car, an outdated wardrobe, and no savings. For four years, Cory has said he wants to take a vacation, but he never has enough money to do it. It seems he is constantly in debt or borrowing money.

Why is there such a difference between Tyrone's and Cory's finances? Tyrone has learned to manage his income, and Cory has not. Tyrone's secret to good money management is a budget. A budget helps you do the following:

- control where your money goes;
- work toward short-range and long-range goals;
- keep from overspending; and
- reduce wasteful spending.

Developing a budget involves five major steps:
1. establishing financial goals,
2. estimating your income and expenses,
3. balancing your budget,
4. keeping track of your income and expenses, and
5. evaluating the budget.

A budget worksheet is shown in Figure 23-2. This worksheet should help you organize a monthly budget of your own. You may also want to consider using one of the budget templates that are included with spreadsheet software. Free budget templates may also be found online.

Establish Financial Goals

As with any plan, the first step in developing a budget is to set goals. Decide what you need and want. Start with your short-range goals; then, write down your long-range goals. Short-range goals may include buying a smartphone, a camera, or a new pair of shoes. Long-range goals may include saving money for a college education, a car,

Sample Plan for a Monthly Budget

Goals   **Approximate cost**   Date you want to attain the goal

Short-range _____ $_____   _____

_____   _____   _____

Long-range _____   _____   _____

_____   _____   _____

Income	Budgeted	Actual	Difference	Expenses	Budgeted	Actual	Difference
				Fixed			
Salary	$_____	$_____	$_____	_____	$_____	$_____	$_____
Interest on savings	_____	_____	_____	_____	_____	_____	_____
Interest on investments	_____	_____	_____	_____	_____	_____	_____
Part-time work	_____	_____	_____	_____	_____	_____	_____
Other	_____	_____	_____	Variable	_____	_____	_____
	_____	_____	_____	_____	_____	_____	_____
	_____	_____	_____	_____	_____	_____	_____
	_____	_____	_____	_____	_____	_____	_____
	_____	_____	_____	_____	_____	_____	_____
Total Income	$_____	$_____	$_____	**Total Expenses** $_____	$_____	$_____	

Figure 23-2.   *Goodheart-Willcox Publisher*
A budget should include a list of your financial goals, income, and expenses.

or a home. Another major goal should be to establish an emergency cash fund. An **emergency cash fund** is money saved and available to cover unexpected expenses, such as a new car tire. Once you have your goals listed, estimate the cost of each as well as the date you want to attain each goal. Then, calculate how much money you would have to set aside each month to reach your goals.

Estimate Your Monthly Income and Expenses

The next step is to estimate your income. This includes your net pay and any other sources of income, such as interest on savings and investments, part-time earnings, and allowances. Be conservative in estimating your income. For example, suppose you work twenty hours a week but may be able to work extra hours occasionally. Estimate your income on the twenty hours. Do not include hours that are not in your normal work schedule. You do not want to make plans to spend money you will not have if the extra hours are not available to you.

The opposite is true of expenses. List all potential expenses, even if you are not certain they will occur. For example, you will want to budget some money for car repairs. Although you do not expect

Ethical Leadership

Virtue

"The most virtuous are those who content themselves with being virtuous without seeking to appear so."—Plato

A virtuous person has high moral standards. You have purchased an MP3 player. In your excitement to open the package, you drop the player. You don't want a damaged player, so you decide to return it and claim it was damaged before you opened it. The store has a liberal return policy and gives you a new player. Returning an item you damaged is unethical. You have failed to take responsibility for your behavior, and in doing so, you cost the store and the manufacturer money.

Ethics should be practiced at all times—even when no one else is looking.

anything will go wrong with your automobile, a minor purchase or repair might be needed. If you are aware of potential expenses, you will be more prepared to handle any that do occur.

There are certain expenses or commitments you will want to list first. A good rule of thumb is to put savings at the top of that list. This practice is known as *paying yourself first*. Be sure to set aside money for each of the financial goals you established in step one. Setting aside money for your emergency fund is also a must. As you record other potential expenses, list them under two headings: *fixed expenses* and *variable expenses*.

Fixed Expenses

Fixed expenses are the sums that must be paid regularly. They include rent or mortgage payments, car payments, and insurance premiums. Since you have agreed to pay these expenses by a certain due date, you must consider them first when listing expenses. You will want to keep fixed expenses to a minimum. For example, it would be better to purchase an older, less expensive car for cash than buy a new one on credit. Paying for something on credit locks you into paying a fixed expense over a number of months or years.

Variable Expenses

Variable expenses are all the other expenses you have for which you pay varying amounts. Food, clothing, utilities, home furnishings and equipment, transportation, health care, recreation, and education are some of the variable expenses you may have. The amount you spend on each of these items is likely to change from one month to the next.

Check your budget often, especially when your goals, income, or expenses change.

Morgan Lane Photography/Shutterstock.com

Balance Your Budget

To balance your budget, subtract the expenses you expect to have from the income you expect to get. If your monthly expenses exceed your income, you will need to either increase your income or decrease your expenses.

First, try decreasing your expenses. Carefully examine your list of expenses. Do you really need everything on the list? You may have to make some hard choices. For example, you may have to give up that new shirt or video game you have been wanting. You still may be able to purchase a shirt but not the expensive name brand you prefer.

Your expenses should equal your income when you finalize your budget. It is very important that you account for every penny on paper before you actually start spending.

Now comes the hard part—living within your budget. Keeping accurate records of your actual income and expenses will help you accomplish this task.

Keep Track of Income and Expenses

Keep a record of all income you receive. Compare it to the income you estimated for yourself by recording it on your written budget. Record the difference between the estimate and the actual amount.

Keep a written list of everything you buy and the exact amount you pay for it. Record every purchase on your budget plan. Avoid spending any money that was not on your planned list of expenses. Again, compare your real expenses to the estimated total and record the difference.

It is important to remember that income and expenses must be tracked on a daily basis. If you wait days or weeks to record your spending, you probably will not remember where the money went. A daily record also encourages you to stay focused on your budget.

Evaluate the Budget

The final step is to evaluate the budget. This step helps you see if your budget is working. Consider the following questions as you evaluate your budget: Do you have enough income to cover your expenses? Is the budget flexible enough to handle unexpected expenses and emergencies? Is your money doing what you want it to do? Is your budget helping you reach important goals on schedule?

If you answered "no" to any of these questions, you will probably need to make some changes just as you did when planning your budget. You will need to find ways to increase your income or reduce certain expenses.

Keep in mind that your goals will change. As your goals change, your budget will need to change as well.

Checkpoint 23.1

1. What are the benefits of having a budget?
2. Name the five steps involved in developing a budget.
3. What are fixed expenses? List three examples of fixed expenses.
4. When evaluating a budget, why is it important to track income and expenses on a daily basis?
5. What questions can be asked to help evaluate a budget?

Build Your Vocabulary

As you progress through this text, develop a personal glossary of career-related terms and add it to your portfolio. This will help build your vocabulary and prepare you for your career of choice. Write a definition for each of the following terms, and add it to your personal career glossary.

budget
emergency cash fund

23.2 Spending Wisely

Terms

consumer
goods
service
warranty
impulse buying
comparison shopping
recourse
Better Business
    Bureau (BBB)
Consumer Product
    Safety Commission
    (CPSC)
Food and Drug
    Administration (FDA)
Federal Trade Com-
    mission (FTC)
Federal Communica-
    tions Commission
    (FCC)
Consumer Financial
    Protection Bureau
    (CFPB)
consumer fraud
phishing

Objectives

After completing this section, you will be able to:
- **Describe** the steps for managing your spending.
- **Explain** consumer rights and responsibilities.
- **Discuss** the importance of being aware of consumer fraud.

Being an Informed Consumer

A **consumer** is a person who buys and uses goods and services. **Goods** are any type of item that can be sold, such as food or clothing. **Services** are any type of work performed for pay—hairstyling, accounting, car repair, or cleaning are examples of service.

Whenever you buy something—your lunch, a book, or a concert ticket—you are a consumer. You have been a consumer since your first purchase. As a consumer, you can choose from a wide variety of goods and services.

Doing research ahead of time will help you find the right product for your needs. You can find consumer information for almost every product and service available by searching the Internet, visiting a library, or by talking with others who have already made a purchase.

Various nonprofit consumer organizations also test, evaluate, and rate consumer products. Perhaps the best known is Consumers Union, which reports its test results in a monthly magazine called *Consumer Reports*. At the end of each year, it also publishes a buying guide with summaries of product test results.

How do you evaluate the many sources of information available? When evaluating consumer information of any kind, use the questions listed in Figure 23-3 as a guide.

Understand Advertising and Other Promotional Methods

Businesses use advertising, sales, and incentives to attract your attention and encourage you to buy. They do this to increase sales and profits.

Advertising plays an important role in our economy. Through advertising, consumers learn more about the many goods and services available to them. Consumers can use ads to compare products and prices. Businesses market their products using advertising. Advertising

Evaluating Consumer Information

Quality and Reliability of the Source
- Is the source well-known and respected in the field?
- Does the source have a reputation for being knowledgeable in the subject area?

Purpose of the Information
- Is the information designed to be factual and informative or merely entertaining?
- Is the information designed to promote one product (or service) over another?
- Does the information present all the pros and cons of buying the product (or service)?

Usefulness of the Information
- Is the information up-to-date, factual, and easy to understand?
- Does it tell you what you want to know about the features, quality, and price of the product (or service)?

Figure 23-3.   Goodheart-Willcox Publisher
Use these questions to help you evaluate consumer information.

helps introduce new or better products to the marketplace. The economy grows as consumers buy more goods and services.

Advertising, however, can be misleading. By law, businesses are banned from using false or misleading advertising to sell their goods or services. However, many ads still make exaggerated claims about goods or services. Since ads are designed to show products in positive ways, most ads tell you only the good things about the products.

As a consumer, you must carefully evaluate all the information in ads. Select only the information most helpful to you. Beware of ads that try to persuade you to buy what you do not need, do not want, or cannot afford. This approach will help you improve your buying decisions.

In addition to advertising, businesses use special sales or promotions to attract customers and increase sales. Special sales offer products or services at reduced prices. Reduced prices benefit businesses because their sales and profits increase. Promotions draw attention to a product or service through advertising or publicity. "Buy one, get one free" is an example of a promotional strategy used to attract consumers.

Businesses often offer buying incentives to consumers to help sell products. Free shipping, coupons, prizes, and in-store games are examples of buying incentives. They can be found online and in retail stores, magazines, and newspapers.

If you are interested in buying or trying certain products or services, you may benefit from using these promotional methods. When you buy something you need on sale, you are spending your money wisely. If you do not really need it or cannot use it, it is not a good buy. Also, remember that just because something is on sale does not mean that it is a good value. One store's sale price may be higher than another store's everyday price.

Go Green

Recycling is important so that landfills do not become over-loaded. Paper and cans are often recycled, but communication tools should also be recycled. Cell phones, computers, and other office equipment are considered electronic waste. Electronic waste should be properly disposed of, not just placed in the trash. Electronic equipment can be donated to charities to refurbish for use in locations that are in need of electronic equipment. However, if the equipment is beyond repair, locate a reputable electronic manufacturer, reseller, or community service center that will make sure the equipment is properly recycled.

Know Where to Shop

Once you have chosen an item to buy, you must decide where to purchase it. The marketplace available to consumers is quite large. Shopping online provides opportunities to purchase products that may not be available at a shop in your area or may be priced higher there. You can also find repair parts for items you already own. It is a great way to do comparison shopping. You can check out the features and warranties on products by visiting the website of the companies that manufacture the product. You can also buy or sell items directly from other people on websites such as eBay.

Take into account all the costs associated with online shopping, including shipping costs. Even if the seller pays to have the item shipped to you, it may not pay to ship it back should you decide you want to return it. In addition, you must factor in the time it will take to get to you.

If you purchase items on the Internet, make sure the website is secure and reliable. When you purchase an item online using a credit card, it may become available for others to see. If someone gets your credit card number, he or she could use it to make purchases. Most companies have security features built into their checkout sites. Look for features such as security icons that tell you the site is secure. Look for an "s" after *http* in the website address. The letter "s" indicates the site is secure. Take extra precautions if you are purchasing directly from another individual. Make certain the individual is reliable and the product is as advertised.

There are several things you can do if you have a problem with a product you purchase through the Internet. First, complain to the merchant who sold you the product. If that does not work and you used a credit card to make the purchase, you can contact your credit card company. Finally, you can contact the Federal Trade Commission (www.ftc.gov).

As a consumer, you have a variety of products and services from which to choose. It is important to know where to shop for the best prices available.

Monkey Business Images/Shutterstock.com

While you can buy just about everything online, in fact there are many things that you will need to purchase from a store. Location is an important factor to consider. Neighborhood stores and shops may offer more personalized service and convenient locations. However, they may have a limited selection and charge higher prices because of less competition and fewer sales. The higher prices may be offset by the savings in the time and gas it would take to drive to another store.

Purchasing products from catalogs, television advertisements, and through direct sale presentations may be wise but should be considered as carefully as when making any other kind of purchase.

Before making a catalog purchase, consider the pros and cons of this type of shopping as shown in Figure 23-4. Remember, most mail-order retailers try to provide quality items and good customer service. They depend on repeat orders to stay in business. Some mail-order retailers, however, may take advantage of customers. They may fail to deliver an item or send a poor quality item.

Entire televisions networks are devoted to home shopping. In addition, there are a number of commercials advertising products that can be ordered over the phone. Some commercials have lengthened into longer programs called *infomercials*. These are commercials that appear to be news or other programs. Infomercials provide more facts than standard television commercials do, but they have the same purpose—convincing consumers to buy.

Shopping by Mail, TV, or the Internet
Advantages
• Time savings—Busy people can avoid shopping crowds and traffic by shopping from home.
• Money savings—Some items may be purchased for cheaper prices than those at retail stores. The cost of driving to the store is eliminated.
• Wide selection—A variety of items is offered.
• Convenience—Customers can shop from home.
Disadvantages
• Possible extra charges—Some retailers charge extra handling fees or a cost to obtain their catalogs.
• Must rely on pictures—You can't see, feel, or try on the actual item before buying it. Colors, materials, and sizes may not be as they appear.
• Shipping delays—You have to wait for the item to be shipped, which may take days or weeks. It may not arrive in time for a special occasion, such as a birthday or holiday.
• Shipping charges—Sometimes shipping charges can greatly increase the cost of the item.
• Merchandise-return hassles—If the item you receive does not fit, is not the right color, is damaged, or is the wrong item, you are responsible for returning it. This often involves extra postage charges.
• Possible failure to deliver—The company may take your money but fail to deliver your merchandise. You are then responsible for taking action against them.
• Security—Providing personal information including credit card numbers over the Internet or by mail could result in identity theft.

Figure 23-4.   *Goodheart-Willcox Publisher*
An informed consumer will carefully weigh the pros and cons of shopping by mail, television, or the Internet.

Buying from a door-to-door salesperson or from an in-home party is a form of *direct selling*. Use caution when dealing with door-to-door salespeople. Most of them represent reliable companies with good products. However, it is up to you to check them out first. Ask to see their identification and selling permit or license. If you are still in doubt, call the Better Business Bureau or local chamber of commerce. Deal only with well-known sellers.

Know How to Shop

Making wise consumer decisions means choosing carefully from many goods and services. Prices, quality, and selection can vary among businesses. With practice, you can learn how to shop wisely and develop good shopping skills. When you have certain items in mind to buy, plan your shopping before you go. To get the best price and quality, practice comparison shopping.

Proper Attire

Some Career and Technical Student Organizations (CTSOs) require appropriate business attire from all entrants and those attending the competition. This requirement is in keeping with the mission of CTSOs: to prepare students for professional careers in business. To be certain that the attire you have chosen to wear at the competition is in accordance with event requirements, complete the following.

1. Visit the organization's website and look for the most current dress code.

2. The dress code requirements are very detailed and gender specific. Some CTSOs may require a chapter blazer to be worn during the competition.

3. Do a dress rehearsal when practicing for your event. Are you comfortable in the clothes you have chosen? Do you present a professional appearance?

4. In addition to the kinds of clothes you can wear, be sure the clothes are clean and pressed. You do not want to undermine your appearance or event performance with wrinkled clothes that may distract judges.

5. Make sure your hair is neat and worn in a conservative style. If you are a male, you should be clean shaven. Again, you do not want anything about your appearance detracting from your performance.

6. As far in advance of the event as is possible, share your clothing choice with your organization's advisor to make sure you are dressed appropriately.

Plan Your Shopping

Before you leave home to go shopping, decide what you want to buy. Then make a list. With a list, you will more likely buy the items that best meet your needs. Whether you are shopping for food or buying a car, a well-planned list will help you in many ways. It will help you avoid confusion when you shop, and it will help you focus on the things you really need.

Planning in advance will also help you avoid impulse buying. **Impulse buying** is making an unplanned purchase. It is buying something you see without much thought. Through impulse buying, you may pay too much for an item or buy something you really do not need or cannot use. Resisting a good deal or a sale is often difficult. One way to avoid impulse buying is to simply wait a few days or weeks. You may find you no longer want the item. However, following a list will save you time, energy, and money when you do shop.

Do Comparison Shopping

Comparison shopping is researching several brands or models at different stores to compare prices, quality, and features before buying. This helps to save money and find the product that best suits your needs.

When comparison shopping, always try to get the best value for the money you spend. Does that mean price is always the most important factor to consider in your buying decision? Not always. The ability to judge quality is just as important.

Price is not always a guide to a product's quality. Although a better-quality product usually costs more, sometimes a lower-cost product offers the same or better quality. For example, some consumers buy brand-name foods for higher prices because they think the quality is better. Many grocery stores, however, offer their own brand-name foods. Smart shoppers learn that the store's own brand of food is usually very close in quality and costs less.

Shopping for value also means judging the quality of a product. Learn to inspect products when you shop so that you can recognize the different levels of quality described in Figure 23-5. Checking the quality of an item is important if you plan to use it often or for a long time. Higher quality products usually last longer, so they are a better value. They are made to higher standards of design, material, and

Choosing Quality Products		
Quality Level	**Description**	**Buy when...**
Best	Highest price range	you can afford the best and can justify the cost
	The best and most features; top of the line	the item will be used for a long time
	Highest standards for design, performance, and materials	top quality and performance are required to meet your buying needs
Good or Better	Mid-price range	good quality sells at the best price for your budget and suits your needs; reasonable price is important
	Standard features	good quality is acceptable for the way you will use the product
	Satisfactory standards for design, performance, and materials	durability and practicality are important
Low	Lowest price range	good quality is beyond your budget and you need the item
	Few features	lower quality suits your needs and the item will not be used often
	Lowest standards for design, performance, and materials	the item will be outdated or outgrown soon or rarely used

Figure 23-5.   *Goodheart-Willcox Publisher*

Use this chart to evaluate and decide which quality level best meets your needs.

performance. For example, you might consider buying a higher quality winter coat if you plan to wear it for several seasons. Even though it may be more costly, it will be a better value in the long run. Quality features, like reinforced pockets and secured buttons, will help it wear well.

When comparison shopping, consider what features are important to you. Make a list of the features you want at the price you want to pay. If you are buying a microwave for college, you will not need a large model with complex controls. Wash-and-wear fabric is a good choice for clothing if you do not have extra money to pay for dry cleaning.

A **warranty** is a guarantee that a product will meet certain performance and quality standards for a set period of time. The warranty document outlines what the manufacturer will do if the product fails to meet those promises. As not all products have warranties, a product with a warranty may be a better buy than a product without one. A warranty is particularly important for a product that may need servicing in the future. A household appliance is an example.

The type of warranty found on a product is either full or limited. A *full warranty* offers broad coverage on a product. The coverage includes free repair or replacement of the product or any defective parts within a reasonable time. If the product cannot be repaired after several attempts, it will be replaced. A *limited warranty* offers less coverage. The customer may have to pay labor costs or handling charges to repair a product. It may cover repairs and not replacement of the product. In either case, read the warranty carefully before you buy.

You should always check the length of the warranty. Some warranties may only be good for 30 days. Others may be good for a year or two. Some companies even offer lifetime warranties on some products. In some cases a company may offer both a limited and full warranty on the same product. For example, a computer may have a full warranty on parts and labor for 90 days and an additional one-year limited warranty on parts only.

Investigate the warranty before making a major purchase. While some products carry a limited warranty, others provide no warranty at all.

Many stores and companies offer an extended warranty. A *service contract* is an extended warranty that covers an extra time period at an additional cost. Most consumer groups do not recommend the purchase of service contracts as a good buy for most products. Sometimes the service contract will even cost more than the product itself.

It is important to remember that a warranty is only as good as the company that provides the warranty. A full warranty from a dishonest or disreputable company may be no better than no warranty at all. It is also important to remember to save the sales receipt and store it with a copy of the warranty. Chances are you will need to prove the date of purchase if you should ever need warranty service.

Newspapers, books, magazines, and the Internet are other sources that offer information on many consumer buying issues. Newspapers provide information and advertisements about food, clothing, transportation, and home furnishings. You will find consumer-related books and magazines at your school or local library. Check the library file and reference section for buying information on consumer products and services. Relevant articles appear in many popular magazines. If you cannot find the information on your own, ask the librarian for help.

Exercising Your Rights and Responsibilities as a Consumer

Part of your responsibility as a consumer is to find reliable information about the goods and services you want to buy. You then use this information to help you make an informed buying decision. You have the right to choose from a large selection of goods and services at competitive prices. You also have the right to know the products and services you buy are safe. When a product or service is not satisfactory, you have the right to **recourse**, which means you have the right to complain and receive a response. A more detailed list of your consumer rights and responsibilities is outlined in Figure 23-6.

Consumer Rights and Responsibilities	
You have the right to	**You have the responsibility to**
• information—to be informed	• find and use information before you buy goods and services
• selection—to be able to choose from a variety of goods and services	• select goods and services wisely
• performance—to expect products to perform as they should	• follow instructions and use products as they were meant to be used
• safety—to get safe products and services	• use products safely; report unsafe products to sellers, manufacturers, or government agencies
• recourse—to be heard if you are not happy with a product or service	• tell businesses or sellers what you like or dislike about their products or services

Figure 23-6.   *Goodheart-Willcox Publisher*
Accepting your rights as a consumer in the marketplace means meeting certain responsibilities as well.

Case

Cortez Buys Running Shoes

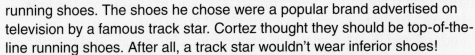

Cortez wanted to be a runner and make the school's track team. First he needed to buy running shoes so he could start training. He saved his money until he had enough to buy an expensive pair of running shoes. The shoes he chose were a popular brand advertised on television by a famous track star. Cortez thought they should be top-of-the-line running shoes. After all, a track star wouldn't wear inferior shoes!

Cortez's good friend Nathan also wanted to make the school's track team. Nathan bought a pair of running shoes too, but his shoes were less expensive than Cortez's shoes. Nathan's shoes were not endorsed by any track star, either.

Cortez and Nathan ran together every day. They had a planned route that covered several miles. After two months, Nathan's shoes were holding up well. Cortez's shoes were not. The seams were coming apart and the soles were worn.

Cortez decided to talk to the track coach about the shoes. The coach told him they were not as well made as some other brands. Cortez then realized that a track star's endorsement did not always mean a top-quality product.

Critical Thinking

1. How was Cortez influenced in his decision to buy running shoes?
2. If a popular person uses and likes an advertised product, is the product always top quality? Explain why or why not.
3. How could Cortez have used the information he saw in the television ad to make a wiser buying decision?

Know the Right Way to Make a Complaint

What do you do when you order a product by mail and it arrives damaged? What do you do when you buy a new product and it fails to work properly one month later? When you have a problem with a product or service, you will need to complain to the right person as soon as possible.

Before you make a complaint, make sure you have your facts straight. Your new camera is broken, but did you drop it? Your new printer does not print. Did you install it correctly?

Do not complain about a product or service when you are the one at fault. You have the right to complain only when you have a valid reason for complaining.

As soon as you discover a problem, complain promptly. Do not let weeks or months go by before you contact the seller or manufacturer. Be sure to direct your complaint to the right person and place. Routine problems, such as returning or exchanging items, can be handled by salespeople or customer service employees. Problems with an Internet or catalog purchase can usually be handled with a telephone call or an e-mail. For more serious problems, you may need to talk with the store manager.

Writing a Complaint Letter

If your problem is not settled, the next step is to write a complaint letter. Try to find the address to which you should direct the complaint on the product, on your receipt from the seller, the library, or the Internet. If you cannot find the name of a specific person to whom you can address your concern, write your letter to the company's customer service department.

If, however, you feel the problem is so serious that top management should be told, contact a person in charge of customer relations. To find the names of officers of large business firms, use Standard and Poor's register of corporations, directors, and executives. This book is available in most libraries.

In your complaint letter, clearly identify the product or service that is not satisfactory. Then give a brief description of the problem. If possible, give the date and place of the purchase, the product name, serial and model number, and the purchase price. At the close of the letter, suggest some type of action. Do you expect repairs, a replacement, a refund, or an apology? Let the reader know how you would like the problem resolved. Conclude by saying something positive about the product or company. A sample complaint letter appears in Figure 23-7.

As you write, be reasonable and calm. A sarcastic or threatening letter will not help get your problem solved.

In most cases, one letter directed to the right person will get the problem solved. However, if you do not get a satisfactory response, write a second letter. In the second complaint letter, enclose a copy of the first letter. Also include the names of consumer agencies or organizations that you intend to contact if the situation is not settled by a certain date.

Use Consumer Protection Services

If you fail to get satisfactory results from your complaint, you may need to contact a consumer organization or group for help. These groups can put pressure on a dishonest business or recommend a solution to the problem. Although they cannot force a business to accept their solution, they can have a strong influence. Most businesses would rather settle a complaint than risk a bad reputation with a consumer organization.

You can contact one of the following for additional help with your complaint.

Better Business Bureau (BBB)

A nonprofit organization sponsored by private businesses, the **Better Business Bureau (BBB)** tries to settle consumer complaints against local business firms. However, it has no power to prosecute.

The BBB keeps files on many local businesses. The BBB can tell you how long a company has been in business and if any other consumer complaints have been filed. It will also tell you how the

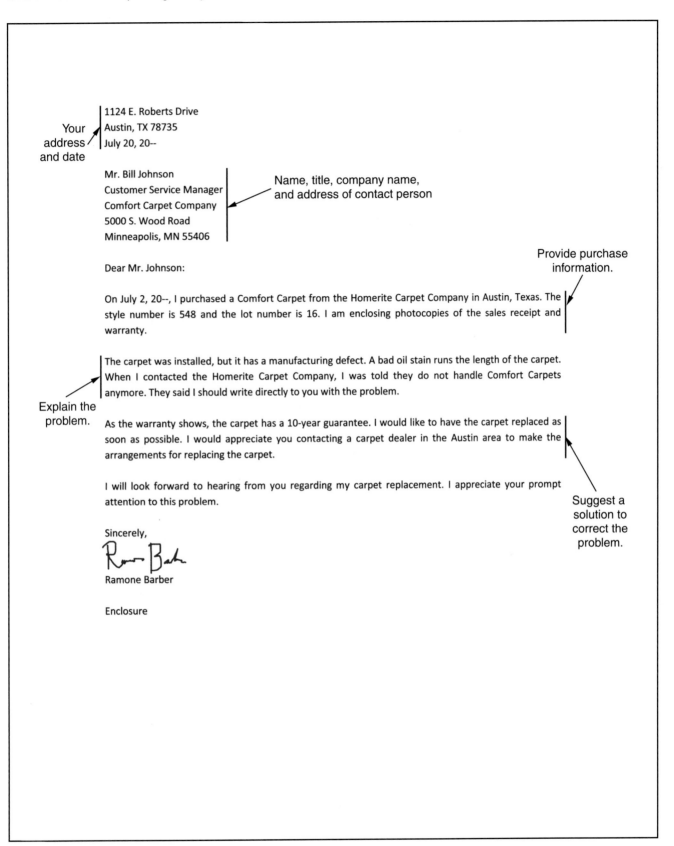

Your address and date →
1124 E. Roberts Drive
Austin, TX 78735
July 20, 20--

Mr. Bill Johnson
Customer Service Manager
Comfort Carpet Company
5000 S. Wood Road
Minneapolis, MN 55406
← Name, title, company name, and address of contact person

Dear Mr. Johnson:

On July 2, 20--, I purchased a Comfort Carpet from the Homerite Carpet Company in Austin, Texas. The style number is 548 and the lot number is 16. I am enclosing photocopies of the sales receipt and warranty.
→ Provide purchase information.

Explain the problem. →
The carpet was installed, but it has a manufacturing defect. A bad oil stain runs the length of the carpet. When I contacted the Homerite Carpet Company, I was told they do not handle Comfort Carpets anymore. They said I should write directly to you with the problem.

As the warranty shows, the carpet has a 10-year guarantee. I would like to have the carpet replaced as soon as possible. I would appreciate you contacting a carpet dealer in the Austin area to make the arrangements for replacing the carpet.
→ Suggest a solution to correct the problem.

I will look forward to hearing from you regarding my carpet replacement. I appreciate your prompt attention to this problem.

Sincerely,

Ramone Barber

Enclosure

Figure 23-7.   *Goodheart-Willcox Publisher*
A complaint letter should include a clear and complete explanation of a consumer's problem.

company resolved any previous complaints. The BBB is a good place to start to learn about a company's reputation before doing business with them. These services are free to consumers. You can file a complaint and find other information about the BBB at www.bbb.com.

News and Social Media

Some local newspapers and radio and television stations have action lines to help consumers settle complaints. Consumers contact the news media with a complaint about a product or service. A reporter is then assigned the story and investigates. These stories covered in the media may prompt a quicker and more positive response from the vendor.

Many consumers now choose social media such as Facebook or Twitter to voice their complaints. Producers of products and services know how quickly bad news can travel through these channels. As a result many are now monitoring social media to see how well their products are being received. In some cases they may respond directly to a customer complaint to demonstrate their willingness to help resolve problems. Social media viewers may also respond with suggestions on how to handle the problem.

Government Protection Agencies

Government agencies serve consumers at the local, state, and federal levels. Their main function is to enforce laws, standards, and regulations to help protect consumers. They can also provide consumer-related information about products and services. In addition, they have the authority to take action against dishonest businesses.

Local and state government agencies provide many consumer related services. One of their functions is enforcing regulations to protect your health and safety. For instance, local agencies oversee the licensing of service facilities such as hospitals or nursing homes. They also enforce food sanitation standards. State and local agency responsibilities vary from state to state. Learning about these agencies and the services they provide in your area can be helpful to you.

Government agencies at the federal level help protect your consumer rights. Regulatory agencies were developed for this purpose. They have the authority to take action against dishonest businesses. Many of these agencies have offices within your own community or state to serve you.

As a consumer, you have the right to protection against unsafe products and false information about goods and services. Problems with product safety, consumer fraud, and dishonest businesses can be handled by these agencies.

Regulatory agencies enforce safety standards for consumer goods and services. They also work to protect consumers against false or deceptive information. The five federal agencies that are most involved with protecting and helping consumers are as follows.

- The **Consumer Product Safety Commission (CPSC)** protects your right to safety. It ensures the safety of household products such as toys, appliances, tools, clothing, and furniture. The CPSC investigates consumer complaints about product safety. It can ban the sale of products found to be dangerous or require a product recall. Unsafe or hazardous products should be reported to the CPSC (www.cpsc.gov).

- The **Food and Drug Administration (FDA)** also protects your right to safety. The agency helps protect consumer safety by regulating the production, packaging, and labeling of foods, drugs, and cosmetics. If a product is found to be unsafe, the FDA can either ban its sale or require a safety warning on it. Medical devices and radiation-emitting products such as microwave ovens are also covered by the FDA. (www.fda.gov).

- The **Federal Trade Commission (FTC)** protects your rights to information and selection. It helps prevent unfair competition, deceptive trade practices, and false advertising. In addition, the FTC oversees laws controlling packaging, labeling, advertising, and warranties. Your right to be informed is protected by this agency. Problems with mail orders, warranties, and deceptive advertising can be referred to the FTC (www.ftc.gov).

- The **Federal Communications Commission (FCC)** protects your rights to information and selection. The agency handles complaints about the practices and charges of wired and wireless telephone systems. It also handles complaints about radio and television broadcasts and cable TV services. Problems can be referred to the Consumer and Governmental Affairs Bureau within the FCC (www.fcc.gov).

- The **Consumer Financial Protection Bureau (CFPB)** works to give consumers all the information they need when dealing with financial companies. This will allow you to understand all the details of a financial contract and make comparisons between financial companies. The CFPB also supervises banks, credit unions, and other financial institutions. The CFPB also enforces federal consumer financial laws (www.consumerfinance.gov).

You can find out more about government consumer information at the USA.gov website (www.usa.gov). You can also search "scam alert" on this site for the latest information on fraudulent and deceptive practices in the marketplace.

Your last resort for settling a complaint is to take your problem to court. Filing a lawsuit and going to court can be a lengthy and costly process. Use this method only when the problem is serious and all other alternatives have been tried.

When shopping on the Internet, be sure you are purchasing from a secure website.

Lucky Business/Shutterstock.com

Be Aware of Consumer Fraud

It is possible that you may have trouble with reputable companies from time to time. However, these issues can usually be resolved to the satisfaction of both you and the company. Consumer fraud is another matter. **Consumer fraud** involves the use of trickery or deceit to gain some type of unfair or dishonest advantage over the consumer. According to government statistics, the leading reported types of fraud include identity theft, prizes and sweepstakes, and Internet services. Other common examples of consumer fraud include defective products, false advertising, fake charities, and investment scams.

Identity Theft

Technology makes it easy for criminals to steal your identity. *Identity theft* involves use of another's name and personal information such as Social Security number, address, or credit card numbers. The thief may use this information to open accounts, make purchases, and even commit fraud using your name.

Two common strategies for identity theft are skimming and phishing. *Skimming* involves stealing a credit card number. For example, a dishonest clerk could write down your credit card number during checkout. He or she could also use a pocket-size stripe reader to obtain your credit card information. This information is then used to make purchases against your card.

Phishing is tricking someone into giving out personal and financial information, such as an identification number or password. It is usually done through e-mail, but can also be done over the telephone. For example, you may receive an e-mail claiming to be from a company you trust. The sender's e-mail address may closely mimic the company's e-mail address. The e-mail may claim that there is a problem with your account or ask you to verify information. It may instruct you to click on a provided link and enter personal information on the website. However, the website will actually belong to someone who can collect the information you provide and use it to steal your identity.

Phishing can also be done over the telephone. In this case, the act is called *vishing*, which stands for "voice phishing." A person posing as a bank or credit card representative calls and tells you there is some type of problem with your account. You are then asked to call a toll-free number to straighten it out. If you call, any information you provide may again be used illegally.

When you shop on the Internet, be sure you are on the company's actual Internet site. There are fake sites that may look like and offer items similar to those of well-known companies. At legitimate sites, security is still very important. You will need to provide personal information when you purchase items over the Internet. Make sure you are purchasing from a secure site.

Avoid Consumer Fraud

There are some things you can do to avoid being a victim of fraud. Check out companies carefully before you do business with them. Do not give out your Social Security number and financial and account information unless you are sure there is a legitimate reason to do so. Never leave receipts casually lying around. Make sure you understand transactions and get all the details and promises in writing. Review bills and invoices for accuracy before you pay them. Shred all documents that contain identifying information when you are finished with them. Review your credit reports at least once a year. Never carry your Social Security number, PINs (personal identification numbers), or passwords in your wallet or purse. Reconcile your bank statements monthly and notify your bank of any discrepancies immediately.

If you receive an e-mail and you are unsure that it is from a legitimate company, do not open it or follow any links included. Instead, contact the company directly from their website or phone customer service and ask if they sent the e-mail. Legitimate retailers or financial institutions do not ask for personal information through e-mail or over the telephone. If you receive such requests, do not respond. Report the incident to your financial institution.

Follow these procedures if you think your identity has been stolen.

1. Contact the fraud departments of any one of the national consumer reporting agencies: Equifax, Experian, or TransUnion.
2. Close any accounts you think may have been tampered with or opened illegally. Keep a list of the telephone and account numbers of all of your accounts in a secure place to make this process easier.
3. File a report with your local police department.
4. File a complaint with the Federal Trade Commission.
   Visit the FTC's identity theft website for more information.

It is not always easy to identify consumer fraud. People who use fraudulent practices are often very convincing. By the time you realize you have been cheated, it may be too late. A good rule to follow is: "If it sounds too good to be true, it probably is." Unsolicited offers of goods or services particularly by mail, the Internet, or telephone should be suspect.

The best protection for you against consumer fraud is to be a wise consumer. Find as much information as you can about a product or service before you buy. Deal with reputable businesses. Be aware of your rights and fulfill your responsibilities as a consumer.

Checkpoint 23.2

1. What is the purpose of a warranty?
2. List three advantages to shopping from home online.
3. What are two ways to avoid impulse buying?
4. Why were government regulatory agencies developed?
5. List three federal agencies most involved with protecting and assisting consumers.

Build Your Vocabulary

As you progress through this text, develop a personal glossary of career-related terms and add it to your portfolio. This will help build your vocabulary and prepare you for your career of choice. Write a definition for each of the following terms, and add it to your personal career glossary.

consumer
good
service
warranty
impulse buying
comparison shopping
recourse
Better Business Bureau (BBB)
Consumer Product Safety Commission (CPSC)
Food and Drug Administration (FDA)
Federal Trade Commission (FTC)
Federal Communications Commission (FCC)
Consumer Financial Protection Bureau (CFPB)
consumer fraud
phishing

Chapter Summary

Section 23.1 Managing a Budget

- An important part of managing a budget is understanding wants and needs. Needs should take priority over unnecessary wants.
- A budget allows you to review your income and calculate how much will be used in spending. Important steps in the budget process include balancing and evaluating a budget.

Section 23.2 Spending Wisely

- Managing your consumer spending can help you reach your financial goals. Being an informed consumer, understanding promotional methods, and knowing where and how to shop are important tips for managing your spending.
- Consumers have rights and responsibilities. Problems with goods and services should be reported correctly so the problem can be addressed.
- Consumer fraud has become a major problem in society. It is important that consumers are able to recognize fraud and know what to do about it.

Check Your Career IQ

Now that you have finished the chapter, see what you learned about careers by taking the chapter posttest. The test can be accessed on the mobile site by using a smartphone or on the G-W Learning companion website.
www.m.g-wlearning.com
www.g-wlearning.com

Review Your Knowledge

1. Explain the purpose of a budget worksheet.
2. What is the first step in developing a budget?
3. What are variable expenses? List three examples of variable expenses.
4. Explain what it means to "pay yourself first."
5. What should you do if your monthly expenses exceed your income?
6. List three examples of buying incentives.
7. Who should you contact if you discover a routine problem with a device you recently purchased?
8. If a product is found to be unsafe, what two things might the Food and Drug Administration do?
9. What is the purpose of the Federal Communications Commission?
10. Explain the difference between skimming and phishing.

Apply Your Knowledge

1. Select four advertisements, one from each of the following: a magazine, the Internet, a newspaper, and a television commercial. Evaluate each. How much useful information does each contain? Is any information misleading? How does each make you feel about buying the product? What does the ad do to try to persuade you to purchase the item or service? Share your findings with the class.

2. Use library resources to conduct research on a specific car or electronic product of your choice. Gather consumer information as it relates to the manufacturer, price of the item, and safety ratings. Use consumer information magazines or consumer products ratings services. Note additional information that would be helpful to a consumer. Write a one- to two-page paper summarizing the information you found and indicate how the information would affect your purchase decision.

3. Create a radio advertisement for an existing product or an original product of your own. Use persuasive language to convince radio listeners to purchase the product. Your radio ad should be one minute long. Present your ad to the class. Share what you did to make your advertisement persuasive, unique, and memorable.

4. Create a bulletin board of headlines and photos depicting issues and events related to managing a budget. Present your bulletin board to the class.

5. With a partner, create a list of six tips to help you manage your spending. For each, write one or two sentences explaining the tip you provided. Share your answers with the class.

6. Write a complaint letter to John X. Smith, the customer service manager of Company XYZ. Identify a problem you have with a recent purchase. Your letter should demonstrate an understanding of the information presented in Section 23.2 under Writing a Complaint Letter. See Chapter 8 to recall the format for writing a business letter.

7. List four important things you learned in Section 23.2. For each idea, write a paragraph about how you can use this information in planning for your future. Share your responses with the rest of the class during an open discussion.

8. Research one of the five federal agencies discussed in Section 23.2. When was the agency established? What is its purpose? Identify significant people associated with the agency? What has been their involvement or contribution? What recent news can you find about the agency? Summarize your findings in a two-page essay.

9. Prepare a monthly budget for yourself. Be sure to include fixed and variable expenses and any other amounts that are important. Then, in a small group, share how you determined amounts for these expenses. Discuss ideas to improve your budget. Each student in the group should offer a suggestion. What should you do differently? What should remain the same?

10. Search online stores for three different common household appliances. Indicate if each appliance comes with a full warranty or limited warranty. How long does the warranty last? Would you buy the product with that type of warranty? Why or why not? Compile your information in a chart and share it with a small group.

Teamwork

In teams of three or four, write an original script for a television commercial for a popular product. Include examples of both honest and misleading advertising techniques. Act out and video record the commercial. Show the video to your class. Lead a discussion on the importance of ethics in advertising.

G-W Learning Mobile Site

Visit the G-W Learning mobile site to complete the chapter pretest and posttest and to practice vocabulary using e-flash cards. If you do not have a smartphone, visit the G-W Learning companion website to access these features.
G-W Learning mobile site: www.m.g-wlearning.com
G-W Learning companion website: www.g-wlearning.com

Common Core

College and Career Readiness

Reading. Use the Internet and printed materials to locate advertisements. Can you find any common themes in these advertisements? What does this tell you about the purposes behind advertisements?

Writing. Conduct research on how much money consumers lost in the last year due to identity theft. Write an informative report consisting of several paragraphs to describe your findings and implications for consumers.

Apply Your Technology Skills

Access the G-W Learning companion website for this text at www.g-wlearning.com. Download the data file for this chapter. Follow the instructions to complete activities to practice what you have learned.

Data File 23–1—**Practicing Comparison Shopping**

College and Career Readiness Portfolio

College and Career Readiness

You may be invited to take part in an interview when you apply for a job, volunteer position, or college entry. To help prepare for the interview, think about the kinds of questions you may be asked. How might you answer those questions? Some questions will likely be related directly to the position. However, general questions are also typically asked in interviews. What is your greatest weakness? What can you tell me about yourself? What do you want to accomplish in your career? These questions are examples of those you might be asked. You should also be familiar with questions that may not be appropriate for an interview. These questions may include ones about your race, religion, or age. Think about how you will respond if asked such a question. Will you choose to give the information or tactfully decline to answer?

1. Search the Internet to learn about inappropriate interview questions. Write three tactful answers that you could give for such questions.
2. Identify five general interview questions. Write sample answers to these questions.
3. Save the file in your e-portfolio. Place a copy in the container for your print portfolio.

Using Credit

Section 24.1
Credit Overview

Section 24.2
How to Use Credit

College and Career Readiness

Reading Prep. In preparation for the chapter, research one of the laws covered in this chapter. Keep in mind the main purpose and provisions of this law as you read.

Introduction

Credit is a powerful financial tool. Consumers, businesses, and governments use credit on a daily basis. Few can succeed in a modern economy without access to credit.

However, there are distinct advantages and disadvantages to using credit. Being aware of these can mean the difference between achieving your financial goals and being trapped by the pitfalls of credit. Making the most of the opportunity having credit requires that you are smart about how you use it.

When a lender extends credit to you, it is signaling that it trusts you will repay what you borrow. Good credit can help you own a car or a home that you would not otherwise be able to have if it were not for credit. Poor credit can have consequences beyond limiting your ability to purchase things. It may also prevent you from being hired for certain jobs, renting an apartment, or from pursuing your education beyond high school.

Check Your Career IQ

Before you begin the chapter, see what you already know about careers by taking the chapter pretest. Use the related QR code to view the pretest on the mobile site. If you do not have a smartphone, visit the G-W Learning companion website to access the pretest.

www.m.g-wlearning.com
www.g-wlearning.com

G-W Mobile

Career Snapshot

Hazardous Waste Technician

Science, Technology, Engineering & Mathematics

What Does a Hazardous Waste Removal Worker Do?

Hazardous waste removal workers follow strict federal guidelines in working to identify and remove hazardous materials. These materials include asbestos, radioactive and nuclear waste, lead-based paint, transmission oil, and contaminated soil. Workers may:

- respond to emergencies where hazardous materials are present;
- operate earth-moving equipment or drive trucks;
- conduct soil or water tests to determine the source of the pollutant; and
- keep accurate records of their activity.

What Is It Like to Work as a Hazardous Waste Removal Worker?

Working conditions can be very hazardous. Federal regulations require that removal workers be closely supervised. They may work in landfills, nuclear plants, or buildings under renovation. Personal protective equipment, including specially designed suits, respirators, hard hats, and goggles are worn. This equipment is often uncomfortable and may cause claustrophobia.

What Education and Skills Are Needed to Be a Hazardous Waste Removal Worker?

- high school diploma
- federal, state, and local guidelines require specific types of on-the-job training
- math and mechanical skills
- troubleshooting skills

24.1 Credit Overview

Terms

credit
finance charge
interest
annual percentage
  rate (APR)
grace period
revolving charge
  account
installment account
collateral
cosigner
equity
creditworthiness
credit report

Objectives

After completing this section, you will be able to:
- **Explain** the consequences of using credit.
- **State** the features of different types of credit.
- **Explain** how to establish credit.
- **Describe** the federal laws that govern credit.

Understanding Credit

Using credit is similar to using money, but with a few important differences. **Credit** is the present use of future income that allows consumers to buy goods and services now and pay for them later. When you buy with cash, you give money in exchange for goods and services. You then own your purchases. When you buy with credit, instead of giving money for your purchases, you promise to pay later. In other words, you are using your future income now. Although you may make a credit purchase now, the exchange is not complete until you finish paying later.

A *creditor* is a person or an organization that extends credit. Because credit is based on trust, the creditor must believe the borrower can and will pay what is owed.

Individuals who are good credit risks can use credit for expensive items such as cars, vacations, and furniture. They can also use credit for smaller items, such as clothes, meals, and gasoline. However, just because you can *use* credit does not mean you *should* use credit.

Before using credit, you need to carefully consider the pros and cons. You may find credit is good to use in some situations, but not in others. The advantages and disadvantages of credit are discussed and listed in Figure 24-1.

Advantages of Using Credit

As you continue to assume more financial responsibility, you will eventually buy costly items, such as a car or a home. Unless you are very wealthy, you will not have enough money to buy an expensive item for cash. It could take you years to save enough money to buy a car or a house. However, credit allows you to buy and use goods and services as you pay for them. Being able to live in your own home or drive a car as you pay for it is one of the major advantages of credit.

Using Credit	
Advantages of Credit	**Disadvantages of Credit**
• Credit allows the use of goods, such as a car or house, as you pay for them. • Credit allows you to buy an expensive item without saving large amounts of money in advance. • Credit can offer a source of cash to provide temporary help for an unexpected expense or emergency. • Credit offers convenience. It eliminates the need to carry large amounts of cash when shopping. • Credit provides a record of purchases. Exchanges, returns, and online orders are easier with credit.	• Using credit reduces future income. By using credit now, you are spending tomorrow's income. This reduces the amount of money you will have to spend in the future. • Using credit is expensive. The more credit you use and the more time you take to repay, the greater the finance charges are. • Using credit can encourage impulse buying. Credit makes it easy to spend money you do not have and buy more than you can afford. • Misusing credit can cause serious problems, such as a bad credit rating, repossession of goods, or bankruptcy.

Figure 24-1.
Before using credit, consider the pros and cons.

Goodheart-Willcox Publisher

Convenience is another advantage of credit. Credit eliminates the need to carry large amounts of cash. It can also be a source of cash for emergency or unexpected expenses. For example, thanks to Jim's credit card, he was able to have his car fixed when the alternator had to be replaced. Without this immediate source of money, Jim could not have paid the repair bill for weeks.

Disadvantages of Using Credit

Although credit can be a very successful buying tool, it can also cause many problems if misused. Financial difficulties are one of the leading causes of marital problems and divorce. Individuals who misuse credit often develop emotional problems. They find it difficult to focus on anything except how they will deal with their mounting bills.

Credit makes it easy to spend money you do not have. Research shows that consumers spend more when using a credit card than when using cash. Eventually you may have more bills than you can pay. If you are unable to pay your debts, the items you bought on credit can be repossessed. You may also lose your right to obtain credit from reputable creditors. Only buy on credit as a last resort.

Most people use credit in the form of a mortgage to buy a home.

Credit always costs money unless a generous friend or helpful relative extends free credit to you. The more credit you use and the longer you take to repay, the higher the finance charges will be. **Finance charges** are the total amount a borrower must pay for the use of credit.

Cost of Credit

Anytime you use credit, it is important to find out how much it will cost you. Knowing the exact cost of credit can help you compare finance charges and find the best deal. Knowing this cost can help you decide how much credit you can afford. It can also help you decide if buying now and paying later is worth the extra price.

When you apply for credit, the following factors determine the amount of finance charges you may pay:
- amount of credit used;
- interest rate; and
- length of the repayment period.

Amount of Credit Used

The more you charge or borrow, the more interest you are likely to pay. For example, Craig buys a $300 computer while his friend Mike purchases one that costs twice as much. Both use the same type of credit account from the same creditor. Both use the same number of months to pay. Since everything is identical except the amount charged, the total finance charges on the $600 bill will usually be twice that of the $300 bill.

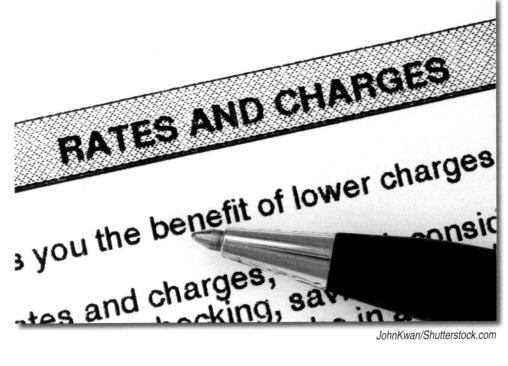

The credit agreement details the terms and condition of a loan.

JohnKwan/Shutterstock.com

Interest Rate

Interest is the price paid for the use of money over a period of time. An *interest rate* is the amount of money a lender charges to extend credit. It is usually stated as an annual percentage rate (APR). An **annual percentage rate (APR)** is the rate of interest a borrower would have to pay to use a given amount of money for one year. You will pay more for a purchase you finance depending on the interest rate charged. For example, Craig compared interest rates to find the best deal. One lender charged an APR of 21 percent. At that rate, the interest on Craig's $300 purchase would total $63 if repaid in 12 months. Another lender offered a 24 percent APR, which would require a $72 interest payment. A third lender offered an 18 percent APR, requiring a total interest payment of $54.

interest due = amount borrowed × interest rate/APR × term of loan
$63 = $300 × .21 × 1
$72 = $300 × .24 × 1
$54 = $300 × .18 × 1

The credit agreement indicates the rate(s) that will be charged. Sometimes a creditor offers an extremely low rate as an introductory offer that increases after a specified time. Make sure you know the terms of a credit agreement before signing it. Also, be aware of the grace period. The **grace period** is the number of days allowed to make a payment without incurring any late penalties, fees, or additional interest charges.

Repayment Period

The more time you take to pay back the money you borrow or charge, the more you will pay in interest. For example, Craig saved money in interest by paying for his purchase in 12 monthly payments instead of 18 or 24. The finance charge for his $300 purchase totaled $54 for payments spread across 12 months. If he had taken twice as long to pay, he would have spent almost $108 in interest.

interest due = amount borrowed × interest rate/APR × term of loan
$54 = $300 × .21 × 2

By law, creditors are required to state finance charges in credit agreements as a dollar amount and as an annual percentage rate. In Craig's case, he agreed to repay his $300 purchase in 12 monthly payments at a monthly interest rate of 1.5 percent. The lender stated the total cost of credit over the life of the agreement was $54 and the annual percentage rate as 18 percent in the agreement.

interest due = amount borrowed × interest rate/APR × term of loan
$54 = $300 × .015 × 12
monthly payment = total amount to be repaid ÷ number of monthly payments
$29.50 = $354 ÷ 12

Before you sign any type of credit agreement, examine it carefully. A credit agreement is a legally binding contract between a borrower and a lender. Reading and understanding the credit terms before signing any agreement is very important.

Take your time and study the agreement before you sign it. Never sign an agreement that has blank spaces. Be sure that all the financial information is entered correctly. Ask questions if you are unsure of any information in the agreement. Sign the agreement only if and when you are satisfied with it.

Types of Credit

Various types of credit are available to consumers. Each type comes in a different form to meet different consumer needs. Some types are used to buy goods and services, while others are used to borrow money. The major types of credit available to consumers are:
- credit card accounts;
- charge accounts;
- installment accounts;
- vehicle leasing;
- cash loan;
- short-term, high-interest loans;
- student loans; and
- home equity loans.

Overusing or misusing credit cards can lead to serious financial problems.

NatUlrich/Shutterstock.com

Credit Card Accounts

Many retail stores and businesses issue credit cards so consumers can use credit to buy their goods and services. These cards have a credit limit and can only be used at the business that issues the credit. Banks and other financial institutions also issue credit cards. These cards have a credit limit as well, but they can be used wherever they are accepted by businesses. In addition to making purchases at numerous businesses, these credit cards may also be used to obtain cash advances.

An important thing to remember is that the cost of using credit cards is often high. Many credit card companies charge an annual fee for using their card. There is usually a charge for failing to make your payments on time. Interest rates on credit cards tend to be high as well.

Overusing credit cards is a major reason many people get into financial trouble. Still, credit cards are in great demand and the competition to attract new customers is fierce. Many credit cards offer incentives to encourage you to open and use accounts. Some eliminate the annual fee. Others offer you cash rebates for using your credit card based on a percentage of your charges each month. Various credit cards offer rebates on groceries, gasoline, airline tickets, and many other items. Some cards provide coverage for most items you purchase if the item is damaged or stolen within 90 days of the date of purchase. The original manufacturers or store warranty may be doubled when you use a credit card. Credit card companies also offer to assist in resolving disputes with sellers and provide proof of purchase. While these and other promotions may be tempting, it is not a good idea to get a credit card before you are financially secure.

Most credit card accounts are known as a revolving charge account. A **revolving charge account** allows customers to pay for purchases in full each month or spread payments over a period of time.

Here is how a typical credit card account works. Rosita opened a revolving charge account at a retail store. In September, she used her credit card to charge $56 worth of clothing purchases. In October, she got a statement showing the amount she owed. Rosita had a choice of paying the full amount or making a minimum payment of $10. If she paid in full within a month, she would avoid paying finance charges. If she paid just the minimum payment, finance charges would be added to the remaining balance of $46. Rosita could continue to charge merchandise as long as she did not exceed her $500 credit limit for that card. She would also receive a monthly statement showing the amount owed. Rosita knows that finance charges on credit cards are high. She also knows that by simply making minimum payments, finance charges could eventually surpass the cost of the item purchased.

Figure 24-2 shows a credit account that has been used to its $500 limit. After six months of paying the minimum $10 monthly payment, a total of $60 is paid. However, the $500 balance is reduced by only $15.57. The reason for this is the addition of $44.43 in finance charges during the period. If Rosita's payment was late, she would also have to pay a late fee in addition to the finance charge. Rosita understands the high cost of finance charges. Accordingly, she tries to pay her credit card balance in full each month.

Rosita is also very careful not to lose her credit card. She has learned about the practice of skimming. *Skimming* occurs when a thief scans and stores credit card information that is then used to make unauthorized purchases. Therefore, Rosita keeps an eye on her credit card whenever she is making a purchase.

She also checks her credit card statements very carefully for incorrect entries. Rosita knows that she needs to notify her creditor immediately if she finds a problem. Then, according to the law, Rosita cannot be charged more than $50 if someone else uses her card.

Effects of Minimum Payments and Finance Charges on Credit Card Balances			
Month	**Balance**	**Minimum Payment**	**Finance Charge**
January	$ 500.00	$ 10.00	$ 7.50
February	497.50	10.00	7.46
March	494.96	10.00	7.42
April	492.38	10.00	7.39
May	489.77	10.00	7.35
June	487.12	10.00	7.31
Totals	484.43	60.00	44.43

Figure 24-2.   *Goodheart-Willcox Publisher*
This table shows how finance charges help to keep a balance high.

Charge Accounts

Some businesses allow customers to charge goods and services on a charge account on file at the business. A *charge account* is another way businesses can extend credit to customers without using credit cards. Once a month, the business will send the customer a bill or statement. The customer is then expected to pay in full by the assigned due date. If the customer pays on time, there is no finance charge. A local clothing store or flower shop would be an example of businesses that might offer this type of credit.

Installment Accounts

An **installment account** is often used to charge expensive items such as a major appliance or piece of furniture. The buyer pays for the merchandise according to a set schedule of payments. Finance charges are included in the payments. Buyers are usually asked to sign a contract for this type of credit purchase. A down payment in cash may also be required. If the buyer fails to make payments, the seller can repossess the merchandise.

Vehicle Leasing

There are times, especially when purchasing a car, when you may be tempted to enter into a lease agreement rather than a purchase contract. While the advertisements may sound attractive, there are both advantages and disadvantages to leasing.

Vehicle leasing is a credit transaction by which a person rents a car according to certain restrictions. The transaction usually requires a lower down payment and monthly payment. This makes a lease agreement appear attractive. With a lease, however, you do not own the vehicle. The contract may limit the driver to a certain number of miles. You may also be charged a fee for excess mileage as well as the extra wear and tear on the vehicle.

Go Green

At school and work, paper helps people communicate. Paper is used to take notes, write reports, and perform countless other tasks. Our "paperless society" still creates many reasons to print rather than to save our information digitally. According to the EPA, the average office worker in the US will use approximately 10,000 sheets of paper in a year. Considering how much paper we use each year and how much ink or toner is needed to print those pages, we can conserve resources by planning our printing needs.

Cash Loan

It may become necessary to borrow cash to buy items you need or want. This type of credit is called a *cash loan*. Commercial banks, savings banks, credit unions, loan companies, and some life insurance companies make various types of cash loans.

To get most cash loans, a borrower is required to pledge collateral. **Collateral** is something of value held by the creditor in case you are unable to repay the loan. For an auto loan, the car is collateral. For a mortgage, the house serves as collateral. If the borrower fails to pay according to the agreement, the creditor may take the property to settle the claim against the borrower.

Although a person may have nothing to pledge as collateral, getting a loan is still possible if the person has a cosigner. A **cosigner** is a responsible person who signs a loan agreement with the borrower. By signing the agreement, the cosigner promises to pay the loan if the borrower fails to pay.

Most cash loans are repaid like an installment account. The borrower makes regular monthly payments that include finance charges. It is important to remember that anything you put up as collateral for a cash loan may be repossessed if you fail to make the payments.

Short-Term, High-Interest Loans

There are many short-term loans that carry very high interest rates. These types of loans include payday loans, title loans, and pawnshop loans.

Payday loans are sometimes called *paycheck advances*. These loans are for relatively small amounts, usually $50 to several hundred dollars. The borrower writes a personal check to the lender for the loan amount plus interest and fees. The lender waits to cash the check until the borrower's next payday. The fees for these types of loans are extremely high, more than 900 percent in some cases.

A title loan is a type of loan for an auto in which the car that is being bought also serves as the collateral for the loan. This loan gets its name from the document, called the *title,* which proves ownership of the vehicle pledged. The repayment period for these types of loans is a month or less and can have as much as 300 percent APR.

Some people may borrow money on a short-term basis from a pawnshop. A *pawnshop* is a business that holds the personal property of a borrower in exchange for a loan. If the loan and interest is repaid in the time agreed, the borrower gets his or her property back. If the loan is not repaid, the property is forfeited.

Ethical Leadership

Disciplined

"The only discipline that lasts is self-discipline." Bum Phillips

A disciplined person is able to control his behavior and impulses. It is time for lunch and you are short on cash. Then you remember the petty cash fund in the office. You decide to "borrow" a few dollars from the fund to buy lunch and replace it when you get paid. No one will ever know. However, this is unethical. It is not your money and taking it is the same as stealing.

Home Equity Loans

A *home equity loan* is a type of loan available to homeowners. This type of loan provides automatic access to a sum of money separate from the amount the homeowner borrowed to purchase the house. A home equity loan is based on the homeowner's equity in the house. **Equity** is the difference between how much is owed on something and how much that item is worth. If your house is worth $120,000 and you still owe the bank $90,000, the amount of equity in your house is $30,000.

Once the loan is approved, it resembles a checking account. You can write yourself a check that draws money from your pre-approved loan. The advantage of this type of loan is that the interest on it is often tax deductible. Because a home equity loan is easy to obtain, it may tempt you to make unnecessary purchases. In this case, a home equity loan may be a disadvantage.

You should think very carefully about getting a home equity loan. There are costs in setting up the loan, and the collateral for a home equity loan is the house itself. Nonpayment of a loan, or sometimes late payments, has caused some homeowners to lose their homes.

Student Loans

Most students use student loans to pay for all or part of their education beyond high school. Student loans typically carry lower interest rates than other types of loans. In addition, most students' loans do not require repayment begin until after the student leaves school or graduates. Perkins Loans and Stafford Loans are available to students based on financial need.

Your creditworthiness will affect your ability to reach some goals.

Stuart Miles/Shutterstock.com

Establishing Credit

When you first try to establish credit, you may have a hard time. This is because creditors want evidence before they grant you credit that you *can* and *will* pay your debts. When you apply for credit, you will be asked to fill out a credit application form like the one in Figure 24-3. This form helps creditors evaluate whether you are creditworthy.

Creditworthiness is an assessment of a borrower's ability to repay a loan. The three Cs of credit are good indicators of credit worthiness. Figure 24-4 lists and describes each of the three elements.

Creditors consider people who have jobs with steady incomes as good credit risks. They also look for factors such as:

- making regular, on-time payments on credit purchases, loans, or fixed expenses such as rent or utilities;
- owning a car, home, stocks, or bonds; and
- living in the same community for a period of time.

BELK CREDIT APPLICATION

EMPLOYEE NO.	DATE

Type of Account Requested:
☐ **INDIVIDUAL**   ☐ **JOINT**

PLEASE TELL US ABOUT YOURSELF

FIRST NAME (TITLES OPTIONAL)	MIDDLE INITIAL	LAST NAME	AGE

STREET ADDRESS (IF P.O. BOX — PLEASE GIVE STREET ADDRESS)	CITY	STATE	ZIP

☐ OWN ☐ LIVE WITH RELATIVE ☐ RENT ☐ OTHER	MONTHLY PAYMENT $	YEARS AT PRESENT ADDRESS	HOME PHONE NO. ( )	NO. OF DEPENDENTS

PREVIOUS ADDRESS	CITY	STATE	ZIP	HOW LONG

NAME OF NEAREST RELATIVE NOT LIVING WITH YOU	RELATIONSHIP	PHONE NO. ( )

ADDRESS	CITY	STATE

NOW TELL US ABOUT YOUR JOB

EMPLOYER OR INCOME SOURCE	POSITION/TITLE	HOW LONG EMPLOYED YRS. MOS.	MONTHLY INCOME $

EMPLOYER'S ADDRESS	CITY	STATE	TYPE OF BUSINESS	BUSINESS PHONE ( )

MILITARY RANK (IF NOW IN SERVICE)	SEPARATION DATE	UNIT AND DUTY STATION	SOCIAL SECURITY NO.

SOURCE OF OTHER INCOME (Alimony, child support, or separate maintenance need not be revealed if you do not wish to have it considered as a basis for repaying this obligation)	SOURCE	INCOME $	☐ MONTHLY ☐ ANNUALLY

AND YOUR CREDIT REFERENCES ARE

NAME AND ADDRESS OF BANK/SAVINGS AND LOAN	☐ CHECKING ☐ SAVINGS ☐ LOAN	PREVIOUS BELK OR LEGGETT ACCOUNT? ACCOUNT NO. HOW IS ACCOUNT LISTED?	☐ YES ☐ NO

List Bank cards, Dept. Stores, Finance Co.'s, and other accounts:	NAME	ACCOUNT NO.	BALANCE	PAYMENT
			$	$
			$	$
			$	$
			$	$

INFORMATION REGARDING JOINT APPLICANT

COMPLETE THIS AREA IF   ☐ JOINT ACCOUNT IS REQUESTED   ☐ YOU ARE RELYING ON SPOUSE'S INCOME OR CREDIT HISTORY TO OBTAIN CREDIT

FIRST NAME	MIDDLE INITIAL	LAST NAME	AGE	RELATIONSHIP	SOCIAL SECURITY NO.

JOINT APPLICANT'S ADDRESS IF DIFFERENT FROM APPLICANT ADDRESS	CITY	STATE	ZIP

JOINT APPLICANT'S PRESENT EMPLOYER	ADDRESS	HOW LONG EMPLOYED YRS. MOS.

BUSINESS PHONE ( )	POSITION/TITLE	MONTHLY INCOME $

YOUR SIGNATURE PLEASE

Store Stamp Below

I have read and agree to the Terms and Conditions of the Belk Retail Charge Agreement as set forth on attached. Belk is authorized to investigate my credit record and exchange credit experience with other creditors and Credit Reporting Agencies. This information is given to obtain credit, and is true and complete.

FOR OFFICE USE ONLY

Letter _____

CB. RPT. _____

EMP. VER _____

Applicant's Signature	Date

Joint Applicant's signature (required if joint applicant section completed)	Date

DATE	EMP.	#CARDS	T/C	CR/LN.	APPROVED

Figure 24-3.   *Goodheart-Willcox Publisher*

The information provided on a credit application form helps lenders decide if a person is a good credit risk.

Three Cs of Credit	
Character	honest and reliable
Capital	assets, such as real estate or investments
Capacity	ability to repay

Figure 24-4.   *Goodheart-Willcox Publisher*
The Three Cs of Credit are the basis for determining creditworthiness.

Building Your Credit Rating

If you have never bought anything on credit, you can begin building a good credit rating by taking some of the following steps:

- **Get a job, and stay employed.** To be a good credit risk, you must prove you can hold a job and earn a regular income.
- **Open a checking account.** A well-managed checking account shows that you can handle money responsibly.
- **Open a savings account.** Saving regularly can help you establish a good banking record that can serve as a credit reference. Your savings may also be used as collateral for a loan.
- **Buy an item on a layaway plan.** This will help demonstrate your ability to make payments on time.
- **Apply to a local store for a credit card.** By doing this, you establish credit. At the same time, your use is limited to one store.

When you receive a credit card, make small purchases and pay for them promptly and in full when the bills come. Keep in mind, however, that a credit card is usually not a good idea if you are just starting out with a part-time job or a low-paying, full-time job. Store cards in particular may be bad as the on-going interest rates may be high. Be sure to check if the store reports to credit bureaus. If they do not report to a credit bureau, it will not help you establish credit. You can establish a good credit rating without a credit card by keeping your job and paying your rent and utilities on time.

What Is in a Credit Report?

A **credit report** is a summary of how a person or business has used credit. Once you use credit, you automatically establish a credit record at a local or national credit reporting agency known as a *credit bureau.* It collects, maintains, and analyzes financial information on individual consumers. Lenders use this information to decide whether to grant or deny credit.

The information on your credit report shows only the facts collected by a credit bureau as shown in Figure 24-5. A credit bureau does not recommend whether you should be granted credit. In addition, by law, none of the information on your report can relate to your reputation, character, or lifestyle. You have the right to check your credit report annually and without charge. If you have problems getting credit, the creditor who denied your credit request must give you the name and address of the credit bureau they used.

Sample Credit File

Personal Identification Information

Your Name   Date of Birth: April 10th,1978
123 Current Address
City, State 00000

Previous Address(es)
456 Former Rd. Atlanta, GA 30000
P.O. Box XXXX Savannah, GA 40000

Last Reported Employment: Engineer, Highway Planning

Public Record Information

Lien Filed 03/10; Fulton CTY; Case or Other ID Number-32114; Amount-$26667; Class-State; Released 07/11 ; Verified 07/11

Bankruptcy Filed 12/11 ; Northern District Ct; Case or Other ID Number-673HC12; Liabilities-$15787; Personal; Individual; Discharged; Assets-$780

Satisfied Judgment Filed 07/12 ; Fulton CTY; Case or Other ID Number-898872; Defendant-Consumer; Amount-$8984; Plaintiff-ABC Real Estate; Satisfied 03/12 ; Verified 05/12

Collection Agency Account Information

Pro Coll (800) xxx-xxxx

Collection Reported 05/11 ; Assigned 09/10 to Pro Coll (800) XXX-XXXX Client - ABC Hospital; Amount-$978; Unpaid; Balance $978; Date of Last Activity 09/10 ; Individual Account; Account Number 787652JC

Credit Account Information

Company Name	Account Number	Whose Acct	Date Opened	Months Reviewed	Date of Last Activity	High Credit	Terms	Items as of Date Reported			Date Reported
								Balance	Past Due	Status	
[1]	[2]	[3]	[4]	[5]	[6]	[7]	[8]	[9]	[10]	[11]	[12]
Department St.	32514	J	10/06	36	9/09	$950		$0		R1	10/09
Bank	1004735	A	11/06	24	5/09	$750		$0		I1	4/09
Oil Company	541125	A	6/06	12	3/09	$500		$0		01	4/09
Auto Finance	529778	I	5/05	48	12/08	$1100	$50	$300	$200	I5	4/09

Previous Payment History: 3 Times 30 days late; 4 Times 60 days late; 2 Times 90+ days late
Previous Status: 01/10 - I2; 02/06 - I3; 03/10 - I4

Companies that Requested your Credit File

09/06/08   Equifax - Disclosure   08/27/12   Department Store
07/29/08   PRM Bankcard   07/03/12   AM Bankcard
04/10/08   AR Department Store   12/31/12   Equifax - Disclosure ACIS 123456789

Figure 24-5.   *Goodheart-Willcox Publisher*
Your credit report is a summary of your credit history.

By looking at your credit record, you may find errors or missing information that may affect your credit rating. You can challenge errors in your credit record by completing a written request form provided by the credit bureau. The Federal Trade Commission should be contacted if problems are not handled satisfactorily. Remember, however, there is no way to remove negative information in your credit record that is accurate. Generally, negative information stays in the report for seven years.

Case

Eva Exceeds Her Credit

Eva decided to buy a new television on credit, even though she had monthly payments to make on two other credit accounts. At the electronics store, the salesperson went over the credit agreement with her. He showed her the sale price, tax, number of payments, finance charge, unpaid balance, and total cost including interest.

Eva was so anxious to get the television home she did not pay much attention to the figures. She did, however, notice she had a total of 36 monthly payments. Each payment was due on the fifteenth of the month.

The salesperson also showed Eva a clause in the contract. It read, "Any default by the buyer, including failure to pay when due, may, at the seller's option, accelerate all of the remaining payments and seller may repossess the property." Eva was not worried about making her payments. She signed the credit agreement and went home with her new television.

Eva enjoyed her purchase and made her monthly payments on time until she lost her job. While unemployed for several months, Eva was unable to make the minimum monthly payments. She could not make payments on her other credit accounts either. All of the creditors demanded payment. A short time later, the electronics store repossessed the television.

Critical Thinking

1. What advantages in using credit did Eva consider in buying her television?
2. What disadvantages in using credit should Eva have considered before buying the television?
3. Do you think Eva budgeted her monthly payments carefully? Explain.
4. What long-term effects might Eva's decision to buy on credit have on her ability to make future credit purchases?

It is a good idea to check your credit record regularly even if you have not been denied credit. You are entitled to a free credit report every twelve months from each of the three national consumer credit reporting agencies: Equifax, Experian, and TransUnion. While you can get reports from all three agencies at the same time, it is a better idea to order separate reports at different times during the year. That way you can monitor your credit more frequently. Errors on credit reports are surprisingly common. You must go to www.annualcreditreport.com to obtain your free report. You may elect to receive your report online, through the mail, or by phone.

Federal Credit Laws

As a credit user, you should know about your consumer rights and responsibilities under federal law. How do these laws aid credit users? They can assist consumers in choosing and using credit. They help consumers understand and compare credit costs before they use it. If you are denied credit, find a billing error, or lose your credit card, knowing what to do is important. Some of the most important parts of these laws are explained as follows.

Truth in Lending Act

The purpose of this law, enacted in 1968, is to protect those who borrow money and buy on credit. Creditors are required to tell consumers what credit will cost them before they use it. Figure 24-6 shows what a Truth in Lending Act Disclosure form looks like. This helps consumers decide if they can afford to use credit and which creditor offers the best credit terms. Under this law, a credit agreement must include the following information:

- the dollar amount financed or borrowed;
- the total number, dollar amount, and due dates of the payments;
- the finance charge, stated as a dollar amount and as an APR;
- any charges that are separate from the finance charge;
- any penalties or extra charges for late payments, missing payments, or advance payments; and
- a description of any security held by the creditor.

The law also states that businesses cannot issue or mail unrequested credit cards to customers or potential customers. Cardholders are liable for only $50 in charges for a lost or stolen credit card if someone else uses it. However, by promptly reporting the loss or theft before anyone else uses it, cardholders are not liable for any charges.

Annual Percentage Rate	Finance Charge	Amount Financed	Total Payments
The cost of your credit at a yearly rate	The dollar amount the credit will cost you	The amount of credit provided to you or on your behalf	The amount you will have paid after you have made all payments as scheduled
%	$	$	$

Figure 24-6.   *Goodheart-Willcox Publisher*

The Truth in Lending Act requires that information regarding the cost of credit be provided in a standard way as shown here.

Fair Credit Reporting Act

This law, enacted in 1970, requires accuracy in credit reports. It also provides for the confidentiality of this information. If denied credit because of information provided by a credit bureau, the applicant has the right to the following:

- Know the name and address of the credit bureau issuing the report.
- Check the information on file at the credit bureau, including the source of the information and to whom it was given.
- Require the credit bureau to recheck any information found to be untrue by the applicant.
- Receive a corrected report from the credit bureau if any errors are found.
- Require the credit bureau to send the corrected report to all creditors who received wrong or incorrect information.

Equal Credit Opportunity Act

This law, passed in 1973, prohibits a creditor from denying credit for discriminatory reasons. When first passed, the law was aimed at protecting women. Many women had problems in establishing their own credit records or had been denied loans, even when they qualified.

In 1977, the law was expanded. Creditors were prohibited from discriminating against applicants on the basis of sex, marital status, race, religion, age, or for receiving public assistance. When an applicant is denied credit, it must be for financial reasons only. The creditor must also explain in writing why the credit was denied.

Fair Credit Billing Act

Enacted in 1974, this law protects consumers against unfair billing practices. It describes how to settle billing disputes. Creditors are required to send their customers a written explanation of the steps to take when a billing error or question occurs. The procedure works as follows:

1. The borrower (customer) must notify the lender in writing about an incorrect billing. This must be done within 60 days after receiving the billing.
2. The lender must answer the borrower within 30 days. Within 90 days, the lender must either correct the billing or show that it is correct.

Until the dispute is settled, the lender cannot close or collect on the account. The borrower does not have to pay the amount in question until the dispute is settled. However, the borrower must pay any amount not in question.

Electronic Funds Transfer Act

The purpose of this law, passed in 1978, is similar to the Fair Credit Billing Act. However, it applies to the use of computers, automatic teller machines (ATMs), debit cards, and other electronic banking transactions. Reporting procedures are similar to the Fair Credit Billing Act. For example, you can limit your liability if you report a lost or stolen credit card promptly. Your loss is limited to $50 if you notify the institution within two business days. However, your loss could be up to $500 after two business days. If you fail to notify within 60 days, your potential loss is unlimited.

Fair Debt Collection Practices Act

This law, passed in 1978, protects consumers from abusive, unfair, or deceptive conduct by collection agencies. These agencies are hired by the creditor to collect the debts owed.

Under this law, collection agencies may not reveal or publicize a debtor's debt to other people. The agencies are not allowed to make threats or use abusive language to collect debts. For example, they cannot tell the debtor that he or she has committed a crime and can be arrested for failure to pay. Also, collection agencies cannot contact debtors at inconvenient times, or make repeated and annoying phone calls to them.

Credit CARD Act

In 2009, the Credit CARD Act was passed to provide additional protection to consumers. Among other protections, this law prohibits credit card companies from raising rates on customers' existing balances. In addition, credit card companies must provide notice to their customers of any interest rate increase 45 days in advance of when it is to take effect.

Dodd-Frank Wall Street Reform and Consumer Protection Act

This law is a comprehensive reform act designed to strengthen our country's financial system. One major provision of the act, passed in 2010, is the creation of the *Consumer Protection Bureau (CFPB)*. The Bureau makes sure consumers get the information they need to shop for mortgages, credit cards, and other financial products. It works to protect consumers from hidden fees, abusive terms, and deceptive practices. The CFPB also supervises banks, credit unions, and other financial companies. It also enforces federal consumer financial laws.

Checkpoint 24.1

1. Explain the difference between using cash and credit to make a purchase.
2. Name four types of credit available to consumers.
3. What is the purpose of a credit bureau?
4. What information is usually found in a credit report?
5. What three factors determine the amount of finance charges that will be paid for using credit?

Build Your Vocabulary

As you progress through this text, develop a personal glossary of career-related terms and add it to your portfolio. This will help build your vocabulary and prepare you for your career of choice. Write a definition for each of the following terms, and add it to your personal career glossary.

credit
finance charge
interest
annual percentage rate (APR)
grace period
revolving charge account
installment account
collateral
cosigner
equity
creditworthiness
credit report

Using Credit Wisely

When used carefully and sensibly, credit can help you get more of what you need when you need it. Used unwisely, credit can lead to serious financial and legal problems. Figure 24-7 provides a list of guidelines to help make credit work for you, not against you. Managing credit involves:
- evaluating whether to use credit;
- shopping for the best credit terms; and
- knowing what to do if you have a problem with credit.

Guidelines for Using Credit Wisely
• Stay within your credit limits. Use credit sparingly and only after careful thought.
• Shop around for the best credit terms before you borrow or charge.
• Deal only with reputable creditors.
• Read credit agreements before signing them. Make sure you understand all the credit terms and can fulfill your obligation.
• Keep records of all credit transactions. Include receipts, payments, contracts, and correspondence. Keep the records organized in a file, not scattered in a drawer.
• Pay off balances on revolving charge accounts each month to avoid finance charges.
• Keep a good credit rating by paying promptly.
• Contact creditors about billing errors and have them corrected quickly.
• If you have trouble making credit payments, contact your creditors right away.
• Notify creditors immediately if your credit card is lost.

Figure 24-7. *Goodheart-Willcox Publisher*
Make credit work for you by following these guidelines.

Buying online makes it easy to give into impulse buying.

Ronen/Shutterstock.com

Should You Use Credit?

The decision to use credit is a personal choice. However, it is important to remember that many people get into serious financial and personal difficulties by misusing credit. Before using it to make a purchase, think carefully. Consider your needs, your available cash, and the alternatives to using credit. Then evaluate your choices. You could choose not to buy the item. You could pay for the item with your savings. Finally, you could save your money and buy the item later. To help you evaluate your choices, ask yourself the following questions:

- How important is it to buy the item now?
- Can I do without it? If the answer is yes, you would be wise not to buy it. The extra cost of using credit can eliminate the benefit of having what you want now.
- Should I use my savings to make the purchase? Replacing the savings used for an unplanned purchase can be difficult and risky. This may leave you unprepared for emergencies or financial problems.
- Should I save money and buy the item later? This is often the wisest choice. You may find by waiting that you did not really need the item after all.

Depending on your situation, you may get more satisfaction from buying now, as Lynda did. One of Lynda's friends won a ski vacation and asked Lynda to come along. Lynda had some money for the trip in her savings account. However, to get the best airfare, she needed to buy her airline ticket right away. She decided to use her credit card to charge her airline tickets.

On the other hand, Gary got more satisfaction from his purchase by waiting. Gary wanted to buy a new computer, but did not have enough money. He decided to wait and save so he could do some comparison shopping. He also wanted to find out as much as possible about features and prices. When he finally got the computer, he enjoyed it more because it was exactly what he wanted. He was glad that he had waited instead of rushing out to buy it.

Shopping for Credit

If you decide to use credit, the next step is to compare credit terms from different sources. Credit charges can vary from source to source, so shopping around for the best terms is wise.

By comparing the three factors that affect credit costs, you can look for the best deal. Compare the size of the loan or the amount of credit used, the annual percentage rate, and the repayment time. Also, compare the total cost of the credit, including all finance charges and other fees to make sure you are really getting the best deal.

Maintaining a Good Credit Rating

If you pay your bills on time and meet all terms of credit agreements, you will have a good credit rating. If you make late payments or fail to pay, you will have a poor rating. A poor credit rating will make it difficult for you to get credit in the future. It may also cause creditors to charge you higher finance charges.

The following steps will help in maintaining a good credit rating. Calculate the affect new debts will have on your debt-to-income ratio. A **debt-to-income ratio** is a way of comparing debt to income or assets. To figure your debt-to-income ratio, first, total all your monthly debt obligations, such as rent or mortgage, car loan and credit card payments. Then divide that amount by your monthly gross pay. The resulting debt ratio should not be more than 36 percent—the lower the better. If you are just starting out you will want to keep your debt-to-income ratio under 20 percent. Consider buying on credit only if your debt-to-income ratio will stay below 20 percent after the purchase. As a consumer's debt-to-income ratio rises, he or she will find it increasingly difficult to pay what is owed in a timely manner.

debt-to-income ratio = sum of monthly payments ÷ monthly gross income
31% = $228 ÷ $747

If you do not pay the entire balance on your credit cards each month, be sure to keep your balance on each card under 30 percent of your credit limit. Avoid frequent applications for credit. More than four in a twelve-month period will count against your credit rating.

Dealing with Credit Problems

Using credit unwisely can lead to serious financial problems. Many people lose control of credit buying. They continue buying until they cannot afford to make payments.

Whatever the cause, as soon as you realize you are having credit problems, try to correct them. Some of the danger signals that warn credit users of credit problems are listed in Figure 24-8.

If you have problems paying your bills, take action right away. The first step is to create a budget that you will be able to follow. Then, develop a plan for paying off each of your debts and include it in your budget. If, after careful planning, you still cannot cover your debts, notify your creditors immediately. Most creditors are willing to set up a repayment schedule to reduce the size of monthly payments.

If the creditor will not work with you, you may need to consider a *debt consolidation loan*. This type of loan, financed through a financial institution, is large enough to pay off all bills. Instead of paying several creditors, you make one payment to the financial institution. However, you are still responsible for the total debt. The monthly payments may be smaller, but the repayment schedule is longer. As a result, the total finance charges may be higher.

Signs of Credit Problems
• Spending increasing amounts of income to pay debts.
• Using credit for purchases that could easily be paid with cash.
• Making only the minimum payments on your accounts.
• Borrowing money, taking out new loans, or using savings to pay debts.
• Getting new credit cards to pay off old ones.
• Owing so much on credit that the amount owed from month to month never goes down.
• Taking longer to pay off your account balances.
• Making payments late as a usual practice.
• Delaying payment to one creditor in order to pay another.
• Skipping some payments.
• Knowing you would have immediate financial problems if you lost your job.
• Running out of money before payday.
• Purchasing nonessential items on credit.

Figure 24-8.   *Goodheart-Willcox Publisher*
If you see signs of a credit problem, take action quickly to remedy the situation.

Do comparison shopping to find the lowest fee available before entering into a contract for a debt consolidation loan. It is important to remember, however, that this type of loan will not help you unless you change your spending habits.

If you continue to charge after taking out a debt consolidation loan, you will soon find yourself in a worse situation than you were before you took out the loan. It is a good idea to get independent advice before taking out this type of loan.

Credit Counseling

When financial problems get out of control, consumers can seek help from a credit counseling service. Credit counseling services can help debtors in several ways including the following:
- review or create a budget;
- establish a debt management plan; and
- reschedule payments with creditors.

If the need ever arises, be careful in choosing a credit counseling service. Many credit counseling providers are nonprofit and work with you to solve your credit problems. However, nonprofit does not mean their services are free or that they are legitimate. In fact, some nonprofit services charge very high fees.

Most services are offered through local offices, the Internet, or on the telephone. Try to find an organization that offers in-person counseling. Many universities, banks, credit unions, and branches of the US Cooperative Extension Service operate nonprofit credit counseling programs. Check with your financial institution, local

A credit counselor can help review or create a budget for someone having financial problems.

Warren Goldwain/Shutterstock.com

Better Business Bureau, as well as friends and family members for recommendations. Then, check out the recommendation with your state Attorney General or local consumer protection agency.

Bankruptcy

Debtors with serious financial problems who are unable to pay their debts may be forced to consider filing for bankruptcy. **Bankruptcy** is a legal proceeding for the purpose of stating a person's inability to pay his or her debts. Debtors can declare bankruptcy in one of the two following ways:

- **Debtors can file for Chapter 7 bankruptcy.** Under this plan, debtors are legally declared unable to pay their debts. Their assets (property and possessions), except for some personal items, are sold by the court. They can lose their car, house, and furniture. The money collected from the sale is then divided among the creditors. The bankruptcy petition also becomes part of their credit record for 10 years. As a result, obtaining credit in the future becomes difficult. The Bankruptcy Abuse Prevention and Consumer Act of 2005 now makes it more difficult to file for Chapter 7 bankruptcy. It forces some individuals who have the ability to pay some of their debts into filing a Chapter 13 bankruptcy.
- **Debtors can file for Chapter 13 protection.** Under this plan, debtors with regular incomes pay back some or most of their debts over a three- to five-year period. While doing so, they are under the supervision and protection of the court. They are also protected from legal action by creditors. A court-appointed trustee approves a payment schedule and monthly payment amounts for the debtor. The trustee then distributes the payments to the creditors according to the plan. Filing under Chapter 13 offers debtors two advantages over Chapter 7 bankruptcy. Debtors usually keep all their possessions and their credit rating suffers less.

Declaring bankruptcy is not an easy decision to make. Consider it only as a last step when all other ways of handling your debts have been tried. Filing for bankruptcy is costly, too. Lawyer fees and court costs must be paid. Remember, once you file for bankruptcy your credit rating will be affected for years. After your debts have been paid off, you can start to rebuild your credit rating.

Checkpoint 24.2

1. What four questions should you ask yourself before using credit?
2. How does debt-to-income ratio affect whether someone has a good credit rating?
3. Why is it important to take action right away if you find yourself having problems paying your bills?
4. How do credit counseling services help debtors handle credit problems?
5. Explain the difference between Chapter 7 bankruptcy and Chapter 13 protection.

Build Your Vocabulary

As you progress through this text, develop a personal glossary of career-related terms and add it to your portfolio. This will help build your vocabulary and prepare you for your career of choice. Write a definition for each of the following terms, and add it to your personal career glossary.

debt-to-income ratio

bankruptcy

Chapter Summary

Section 24.1 Credit Overview

- Credit allows you to buy now and pay later. Understanding credit can help you learn to look at the pros, cons, and responsibilities of using it wisely.
- Credit card accounts, charge accounts, installment accounts, vehicle leasing, cash loans, and home equity loans are all types of credit. Before charging or borrowing, you should know how each type works.
- When you apply for credit, creditors look for evidence that you can and will pay your bills. You can build a strong credit rating by handling money wisely and paying all bills on time.
- Determine the cost of credit before using it. The longer you take to repay, the more it costs to use credit.
- Several federal credit laws are designed to inform and protect credit users. Knowing your rights and responsibilities will help you make better decisions about using credit.

Section 24.2 How to Use Credit

- Using credit wisely can help you get more of what you need when you need it. Misusing credit can stand in the way of achieving some goals.
- Maintaining a good credit rating will not only make it easier to obtain credit, but the credit you do obtain will cost less.
- Watch for signs of credit trouble, and take immediate steps to correct them. Those with extreme debt issues may be forced to file for bankruptcy protection.

Check Your Career IQ

Now that you have finished the chapter, see what you learned about careers by taking the chapter posttest. The test can be accessed on the mobile site by using a smartphone or on the G-W Learning companion website.

www.m.g-wlearning.com

www.g-wlearning.com

Review Your Knowledge

1. List two advantages and two disadvantages of using credit.
2. How does a consumer establish and maintain a good credit rating?
3. Why is it important to read over credit agreements carefully?
4. List three factors that affect the cost of credit for a consumer?
5. Which credit law requires creditors to tell consumers what credit will cost them before they use it?
6. Why do credit card companies offer incentives?
7. What is the difference between a revolving charge account and an installment account?
8. List the Three Cs of Credit.
9. Calculate the debt-to-income ratio for someone who is paid $2,500 per month and has monthly debt payments of $750.
10. What federal law makes it more difficult to file for Chapter 7 bankruptcy?

Apply Your Knowledge

1. Research the history of credit. Prepare a report answering the following questions: Before credit cards were used, how was credit issued? How were credit ratings tracked? What were the consequences for people who did not pay their debts?
2. Suppose you want to buy a $300 videogame system on credit. Find out what the credit terms would be if you bought the camera at an electronics store, department store, or with a bank credit card. For each of the three ways, check the credit contract, finance charges, annual percentage rate, monthly charges, and the length of the repayment period. Where would you get the best deal?
3. List and explain three ways that you could get something you want or need without using credit to get it.
4. Conduct research on the Internet to find ways that consumer behavior affects credit ratings.
5. Name three ways consumer credit can have a positive effect on the nation's economy.
6. Research the financial crisis of 2008. What role did credit play in the crisis?
7. Student loan debt has reached an all-time high. Contact your school's guidance counselor and financial aid offices of different post-secondary schools to determine what financial assistance, other than student loans, are currently available to students. How will the cost of education and training after high school affect your plans and goals?
8. Find the definition of the word *usury*. What usury laws are in effect in your state?
9. Write a one-act play that illustrates a day in the life of a person living in a world in which the concept of credit did not exist.

10. Visit the website for the Federal Reserve. What role does *the Fed,* as it is called, play in the establishment of interest rates?

Teamwork

Imagine that you are a customer who wants to get a loan from a bank. On your own, think about the questions the lender would ask the customer. Also, think about the questions the customer would like to ask the lender. In groups of two or three, take turns role-playing the parts of the lender and the customer in this scenario.

G-W Learning Mobile Site

Visit the G-W Learning mobile site to complete the chapter pretest and posttest and to practice vocabulary using e-flash cards. If you do not have a smartphone, visit the G-W Learning companion website to access these features.

G-W Learning mobile site: www.m.g-wlearning.com
G-W Learning companion website: www.g-wlearning.com

Common Core

College and Career Readiness

CTE Career Ready Practice. As a way to evaluate job candidates, many employers review potential employees' credit histories. Character is a factor in determining whether someone is creditworthy as well as whether someone will make a good employee. Do you think not paying a debt or not paying on time is unethical? Why or why not? What factors in addition to character contribute to whether a person is creditworthy but may not affect whether a person would make a good employee?

Writing. Undertake research on the Internet regarding peer-to-peer or social lending. What do you see are the advantages and disadvantages of this trend? What type of lender could benefit from peer-to-peer lending? What type of borrower could benefit from peer-to-peer lending? Create a 200-word news story or blog post detailing what your research revealed.

Apply Your Technology Skills

Access the G-W Learning companion website for this text at www.g-wlearning.com. Download each data file for this chapter. Follow the instructions to complete activities to practice what you have learned.

Data File 24–1—**Evaluating Your Three Cs of Credit**

Data File 24–2—**Calcuating Finance Charges**

College and Career Readiness Portfolio

College and Career Readiness

As you apply for jobs or to colleges, you will communicate with many people. You will talk with some of these people in person. With others, you will communicate by phone, letter, or e-mail. You may talk with some people only once. With others, many times. Remembering when you spoke with someone and what you discussed can become difficult as the number of contacts grows. To help you keep this information organized, you can create a contacts log. Include in the log each person's name, organization, address, telephone number, and e-mail address. Each time you talk with the person, record the date and the way you communicated (in person, by phone). Enter a brief summary of what you discussed. Be sure to note information you need to send or receive. Review the log entry to refresh your memory before you speak with the person again.

1. Create a file to contain your contacts log as described above. Make entries for your conversations with people you asked to serve as references. Add other entries as appropriate.

2. Save the file in your e-portfolio. Print a copy to place in the container for your print portfolio.

Chapter 25

Banking, Saving, and Investing

Section 25.1
Banking

Section 25.2
Saving and Investing

College and Career Readiness

Reading Prep. In preparation for reading the chapter, read a newspaper or magazine article on the banking industry. As you read, keep in mind the author's main points and conclusions.

Introduction

Having a job means earning money. Earning money means that you need to learn how to manage it. What will you do with that first paycheck? One option is to spend it, but spending is only part of managing your money. Another option is to save for future needs. Good money management includes deciding where to deposit your money to earn the most interest and still remain safe. Saving and investing will help you meet both short-term and long-term financial goals.

After reading this chapter, these money-management decisions will be easier for you to make. You will learn about the various types of financial institutions and be able to evaluate the services they provide. You will also learn which saving and investment options you might want to consider using.

Check Your Career IQ

Before you begin the chapter, see what you already know about careers by taking the chapter pretest. Use the related QR code to view the pretest on the mobile site. If you do not have a smartphone, visit the G-W Learning companion website to access the pretest.

www.m.g-wlearning.com
www.g-wlearning.com

G-W Mobile

Career Snapshot
Air Traffic Controller

Transportation, Distribution & Logistics

What Does an Air Traffic Controller Do?

Air traffic controllers perform a variety of jobs to make sure commercial and private planes operate safely. Controllers oversee all airplanes traveling in an airport's airspace. Their immediate concern is safety, but they also work to minimize delays. Air traffic controllers must:

- sequence the arrival of incoming aircraft;
- issue clearances for departing aircraft;
- make sure that aircraft maintain safe distances both in the air and on the ground; and
- inform pilots about weather and runway conditions.

What Is It Like to Work as an Air Traffic Controller?

Air traffic controllers work either in an airport tower or in a radar approach control room. They often control several airplanes at a time, so they must be able to make a variety of decisions quickly that are often unrelated. Controllers must be able to concentrate totally on the tasks at hand and the resulting stress can be exhausting. They typically work a forty-hour week and may rotate through night and weekend shifts.

What Education and Skills Are Needed to Be an Air Traffic Controller?

- associate degree in air traffic management from a Federal Aviation Administration (FFA) certified school
- multitasking skills
- communication skills

Burden/Shutterstock.com

25.1 Banking

Objectives

After completing this section, you will be able to:
- **Describe** the features of different types of financial institutions.
- **Explain** how electronic banking services work.
- **Describe** how checking accounts may be used.
- **Describe** the special types of checks that can be used in place of personal checks and cash.
- **Explain** how safety-deposit boxes are used.

Types of Financial Institutions

Three common types of financial institutions are commercial banks, savings and loan associations, and credit unions.

Commercial banks are often called *full-service banks* because of their many services. At a commercial bank, you can open a checking or savings account and buy special types of checks. You can also take out a loan and rent safe-deposit boxes. In most commercial banks, the money you deposit is safe because the *Federal Deposit Insurance Corporation (FDIC)* insures it. The FDIC insures commercial banks for deposits up to $250,000. For example, if you have $245,000 in a savings account and $10,000 in a checking account at the same bank, $5,000 of it would not be insured.

Savings and loan associations (S & L's) allowed savers with small deposits to open savings accounts. S & L's are also called *thrift institutions*. The Office of Thrift Supervision regulates S & Ls, making sure depositors' money is safe.

A credit union differs from a commercial bank and an S & L in that its services are for members only. Members of credit unions are people who share a common bond, such as members of a union, a company, or a professional organization. Since credit unions are nonprofit organizations run by their members, operation costs are usually low. Therefore, credit unions typically charge lower interest rates on loans and offer higher interest rates on savings. Credit unions can also offer checking accounts to their members. The *National Credit Union Administration (NCUA)* is the governing body that insures credit union depositor's funds up to $250,000 per institution.

A bank is one type of financial institution.

Financial institutions compete with each other to provide financial services and convenience for customers. Therefore, you will need to compare several factors to decide where to put your money. Look not only at the services offered, but also consider convenience and costs as well.

In selecting a place to do your banking, you will want to find one that is conveniently located. The financial institution or a branch office should be close to your home or workplace. Consider the hours the financial institution is open when making your decision. Is it open when you need to do your banking? Some have early morning, evening, and Saturday hours. For further convenience, investigate whether the financial institution has any online banking options available.

You will also want to be certain that your money will be safe. While evaluating the safety of a financial institution, look for either the FDIC or NCUA to protect your account.

Sometimes there may be a charge for some services but not others depending on the type of account you have. This is another factor to consider when deciding where to deposit your money. Compare the fees charged for the services you are considering.

Financial institutions are able to offer many more services today than ever before. Understanding these services will help you decide which ones will best meet your financial needs.

Electronic Banking

Electronic banking, or e-banking, is a convenience that many customers take advantage of from their financial institutions. The most popular of these services are online banking; electronic funds transfer, banking by phone, automated teller machines, and debit cards.

Online Banking

Online banking offers you the convenience of using your computer to manage your finances through an Internet connection. You can access most services directly. Your financial institution will provide you with security information, such as your own identification number and password. This prevents others from easily accessing your accounts.

Online banking provides more electronic services for the user than any other form of banking. It is like having your own 24-hour bank. Transactions can take place at any time of the day or night. You can perform most of the tasks you would normally perform at the bank. You can see your account statement to review your current balance and the checks that have been cashed. If you have a credit card through the bank, you can check the charges you made with it. You can also check to see if you are near your credit limit. You can transfer funds between accounts. For example, you can move money from your savings account to your checking account if your checking balance is running low.

Many financial institutions prefer online banking because it is less expensive than hiring a teller. As a result, most online banking services are offered free or for a low monthly fee. In fact, there are some financial institutions that operate entirely online.

One concern you may have about online banking is the security of your personal information. Financial institutions use a variety of protective means to keep your information safe. However, you should take basic precautions to help prevent security breaches. For example, do not access your banking accounts from public places, such as Internet cafés or shared computers. Be sure to keep your anti-virus and anti-spyware up-to-date. Be aware of phishing. This occurs

Go Green

In today's society, the temptation to replace broken items with new ones is great. In fact, many items are designed so that they can't be repaired. However, in many cases you can repair an item yourself at little or no cost. The benefits are great. You have the satisfaction of having restored the item to working order and learning something in the process. You will also have reduced the large amounts of waste going into landfills.

Online banking allows you to see your bank records instantly and conduct transactions without entering the bank building.

Cheryl Savan/Shutterstock.com

when someone sends you an e-mail that appears to come from your financial institution. When you click on the link in the e-mail, it sends you to a false website that looks just like your bank's website. From this website, criminals can use any information you provide to access your accounts or even commit identity theft.

Banking apps for smartphones and other devices allow customers to complete banking tasks from just about any location any time of day or night.

Electronic Funds Transfer

The **electronic funds transfer (EFT)** is the automatic transfer of money from one account to another electronically. For example, you may want to have your paychecks deposited directly into your bank account each payday. Direct deposit requires your authorization. Most banks and employers offer this service.

You may also authorize your bank to electronically send a predetermined amount from your account to pay certain bills each month. This type of arrangement is often used for monthly mortgage or loan payments that stay the same. A variety of other payments such as electricity, gas, telephone, and credit card accounts can also be handled automatically with pre-authorization. Such electronic transfers can save you time, postage, and may help you avoid late payments. You can also write e-checks. **E-checks** are an electronic version of a paper check and can be used for online payments.

Banking by Phone

The telephone is another way to pay bills and transfer funds. Bank-by-phone accounts allow customers to handle certain transactions by using the telephone's keypad. Each customer has a specific numbered code that he or she enters using the telephone. The customer can automatically pay bills to participating merchants, transfer funds between accounts, or check on the balance in an account. The financial institution's computer automatically handles all of the transactions. It is very important that you record these transfers as they occur so you have an up-to-date record and do not overdraw your account.

Automated Teller Machines

Automated teller machines (ATMs) are computer terminals that customers use to make financial transactions. These terminals can be used 24 hours a day, seven days a week. Banks try to locate ATMs for their customers' convenience. They may be found in shopping centers, office buildings, airports, and many other places. ATMs can handle many financial transactions, including checking balances, depositing and withdrawing money.

To transact business through an ATM, you will need an ATM, debit, or credit card as well as a PIN. A PIN is a personal identification number.

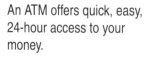

An ATM offers quick, easy, 24-hour access to your money.

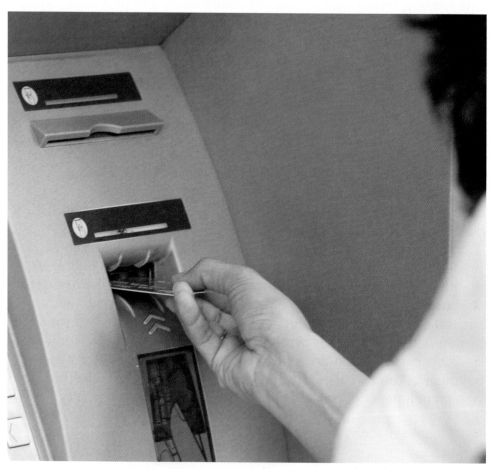

Adam Gregor/Shutterstock.com

What makes an ATM convenient—its remote location and 24-hour accessibility—also introduces the possibility of danger. Most ATMs have security cameras and a well-lighted location to discourage would-be thieves. Nonetheless, taking extra precautions when using an ATM is wise.

You also need to be aware of skimming. Thieves can attach a pocket-size magnetic strip reader to an ATM that reads your card number and PIN. Thieves can then use this to obtain more financial information from your bank. Be sure you check your bank statements very carefully for incorrect entries. Notify your financial institution immediately if you find a problem. See Figure 25-1 for a list of guidelines to follow when using an ATM.

Debit Cards

A **debit card** allows funds to be withdrawn from your checking or savings account without writing a check. It can also be used at ATMs to withdraw money. A debit card resembles a credit card. It will bear the name of a credit card company, such as VISA or MasterCard. It is used like a credit card, but purchases are deducted directly from your checking account. You approve your purchases using either a PIN or your signature.

There are several advantages to using a debit card. It helps you avoid carrying large amounts of cash. You will not need to provide the store with personal information, such as your telephone number and address—information usually requested when paying by check. If used it in place of a credit card, it running up large balances and possible interest charges are prevented. Debit cards are easier to use than checks when you are away from home. Some merchants will not accept out-of-town checks.

Guidelines for Using an ATM
• Avoid an ATM located in a secluded place.
• When using an ATM at night, make sure the machine and the area surrounding it are well lighted.
• Beware of who is near the machine. If you observe someone suspicious, use a machine at another location.
• Have your ATM card ready as you approach the machine. This will make your transaction faster because you will not waste time searching for your card.
• Memorize your PIN number. Do not write it down and carry it with you. If your card is ever lost or stolen with your PIN number, anyone who finds it will have access to your account.
• Do not let anyone have a clear view of your PIN number as you enter it.
• Put away cash from the ATM immediately. Count it later after you leave the location.
• Check your bank statements very carefully for incorrect entries. Notify your financial institution immediately if you find a problem.

Figure 25-1.   Goodheart-Willcox Publisher
Following these tips will make it less likely for someone to steal your PIN or your money.

There are also some disadvantages to using a debit card. The amount of your purchase is sent to the bank electronically and deducted immediately from your checking balance. If you do not keep an accurate, up-to-date record of your purchases, you may overdraw your account without realizing it. This will result in your bank charging you a penalty fee. You will also want to keep your receipts to avoid someone else using the information to obtain access to your account. Debit cards are not ideal for purchasing online or by mail-order since payment is made long before your purchase arrives. Debit cards, like credit cards, are so convenient to use that you may be tempted to purchase items you do not really need.

If you lose your debit card and someone else uses it, he or she will be stealing money directly from your checking account. This could cause your check to be returned unpaid to whomever deposited it. It could also take the bank 10 or more days to straighten out your account. In addition, you may still be held responsible for part or all of the fraudulent purchases. However, if you report your loss within two days, your liability will be limited to a maximum of $50. Therefore, it is extremely important to notify your bank immediately that your card has been lost or stolen. Some banks may charge a monthly or yearly service fee. Be sure to discuss all possible charges with your bank representative before applying for a debit card.

A **smart card** is an advanced type of debit card that contains a microchip. This chip can hold extensive account information. They can be used as debit cards to purchase items from a variety of sources including stores, vending machines, and the Internet. Smart cards can also hold personal information, such as medical records.

A **cash card** is a prepaid type of debit card. You purchase a cash card for a specific amount and then use it to make purchases up to that amount. Some cards allow you to make purchases only at a specific retailer. For example, by purchasing a gasoline card for $50, you can use the card to fill your car at any station owned by that company. Other cards allow you to make purchases at many different retailers. When all is spent typically, the card becomes worthless and can be discarded.

Some cash cards are reloadable. This means they can be reused when cash value is added to them. When you use the cash value of the card, you may have it reloaded by paying the card issuer more money. Cash value can be returned to the card as often as you desire for whatever amount you wish.

Ethical Leadership

Justification

"I never made a mistake in my life; at least, never one that I couldn't explain away afterwards."
— Rudyard Kipling

It is important that we are honest with ourselves when justifying our behavior. Every company has a store of small items needed to do business. They may include pens, pencils, and notepads. The temptation to take an item from time to time may be great. It is only a pen. The company has hundreds of them. They don't cost much and won't be missed. However, no matter what the justification is, it is still stealing.

Checking Accounts

Most people do not like to have a large amount of cash with them or in their homes. Cash is too easy to spend, lose, have stolen, or even be destroyed by fire. To avoid these risks, many people put their money in a checking account. Although you may pay a small fee to have a checking account, this service has many advantages. A checking account provides the following:

- safe place to keep cash;
- easy way to withdraw cash;
- more secure way to send money through the mail;
- detailed record of spending and receipts of payment;
- method of establishing a credit history; and
- paychecks can be deposited directly.

Types of Accounts

Financial institutions offer many types of checking accounts. Three types are: the basic account, express checking, and an interest-bearing account. The type of checking account you choose will depend on the amount you can afford to leave in your account. It will also depend on the number of checks you plan to write each month and on how you plan to do your banking.

A basic checking account allows you to deposit money and write checks. This type of account is ideal if you plan to write few checks, keep a low monthly balance, and possibly use a debit card.

Express checking is for people who use online banking, banking by phone, or use ATMs to do all their banking. This type of account usually offers very low or no fees because bank employees are rarely needed to help service your account. However, you may be charged a fee to speak with a bank employee.

The interest-bearing checking account allows you to earn interest and write checks on the same account. It is a savings and checking account all in one. However, this type of account usually pays a lower rate of interest than a savings account. There is usually a minimum balance requirement. In credit unions, this account is called a *share draft*. In commercial banks and savings banks, it is called a *negotiable order of withdrawal (NOW) account*.

Since checking accounts may vary from one financial institution to another, compare plans carefully. Make sure you find out the service charges, check fees, and minimum balance requirements for each account. Then, choose the account that best meets your needs.

Opening a Checking Account

Opening a checking account is very easy once you decide what type of account to open and where to open it. You will need to provide personal identification, including your Social Security number. The financial institution will run a check on your banking record and possibly check your credit history. Once your application is approved, you will need to fill out a signature card and make a deposit. The signature you provide will be the only signature the financial institution will honor on checks and withdrawal slips that have your name and account number. Always, remember to keep your signature consistent for all transactions.

After you open your account, you will receive a checkbook with personalized checks and a register. Each check will include your name, address, and account number. The register is used for recording checks written as well as all deposits and withdrawals. To help you handle your checks and account successfully, follow the tips in Figure 25-2.

If you want another person to be able to write checks on your account, that person must sign the signature card also. When two or more people share an account, it is called a *joint account*.

Tips for Successful Checking
1. Treat your checks as you would treat cash. Keep them as safe and secure as possible.
2. Do not make changes on the face of a check that is issued to you. Do not take a check that looks altered. The bank may refuse to honor such checks.
3. Avoid carrying checks made out to "Cash." If they are lost or stolen, you have no control over who can cash them.
4. For the same reason, never sign your personal check until you have filled in the amount and the payee.
5. Check all deposit slips to make sure they are legible and correct. If you are taking cash back from the deposit, count your money carefully to make sure it is the correct amount. Do so before leaving the bank.
6. Always inspect new check orders for accuracy. Check the spelling of your name and address. Also make sure your account number is properly encoded. Any errors should be reported.
7. If you do not understand a checking procedure, ask an officer at your bank to explain it.

Figure 25-2.   *Goodheart-Willcox Publisher*
These guidelines can help you manage your checking account successfully.

Making Deposits

To put money into your checking account, you will need to fill out a deposit slip as shown in Figure 25-3. A deposit slip states what is being deposited—currency, coins, or checks—and the amount of each. When filling out a deposit slip, follow these steps:

1. Write in the date.
2. Enter the amount of money being deposited. Write the amount of cash being deposited beside the word *currency*. Write the amount of coins being deposited beside the word *coin*. Write the amount(s) from the check(s) being deposited beside the word *checks*, listing each check individually. (There is more room on the back of the deposit slip to list additional checks.) Then add these and record this amount next to *total*.
3. Enter the amount of cash you want to receive, if any, after the words *less cash received*.
4. Subtract the amount written next to *less cash received* from the *total amount* directly above it.
5. Record the actual amount of the deposit next to *total deposit*.
6. Sign your name on the line below the date if you are receiving cash back.

Every time you make a deposit, you will be given a receipt. At that time, you should enter the amount of the deposit in your checkbook register and save the receipt for future reference.

You should know that you may not have immediate access to funds if you are depositing checks. Your bank may delay crediting your account for as little as 24 hours to as long as a week. This is to ensure the deposited checks clear.

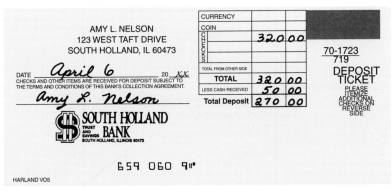

Figure 25-3.   Goodheart-Willcox Publisher
A deposit slip is a record of the money you deposit into your account.

Endorsing Checks

To deposit a check or cash a check, you must endorse it. An **endorsement** is the signature required on the back of a check to legally transfer value. Your signature must be written in the area indicated. It must also match the name entered on the front of the check. Checks may be endorsed by using a blank endorsement, restrictive endorsement, or special endorsement. Figure 25-4 provides examples of these types of endorsements.

A *blank endorsement* only requires the payee's signature. A check with this type of endorsement can be cashed by anyone who possesses it. If such a check were ever lost or stolen, it could be cashed easily. Therefore, you should make a blank endorsement only at the time and place the check is being cashed or deposited.

A *restrictive endorsement* states what is to be done with the check. *For deposit only* is a common restrictive endorsement. You write *for deposit only* and then sign your name underneath. This means the check can only be credited to your account. Someone else cannot cash it.

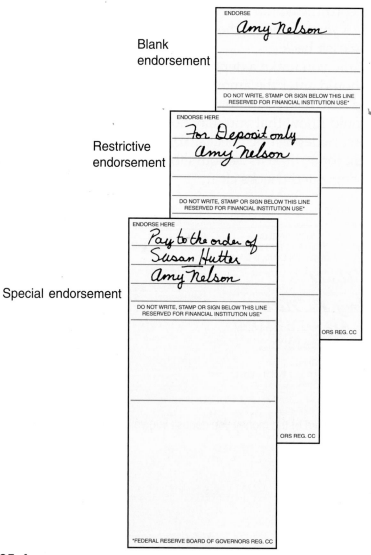

Figure 25-4.   *Goodheart-Willcox Publisher*
You must endorse a check before you can cash or deposit it.

A special endorsement is used to transfer ownership of a check to another person. By writing *Pay to the order* of and the name of the receiver on the back of the check, you can transfer ownership of the check to that person. The person can then endorse the check and cash it.

Writing Checks

Have you ever looked at a blank check and wondered why it has so many numbers? The numbers and the words on checks are important information as shown in Figure 25-5. This information helps financial institutions process checks.

For a check to be processed, it must be written correctly. Figure 25-6 shows an example of a check written out correctly. When writing a check, you need to enter the following items in the correct spaces:

- **Date.** This includes the month, day, and year
- **Name of the payee.** This is the person, business, or organization receiving the check.

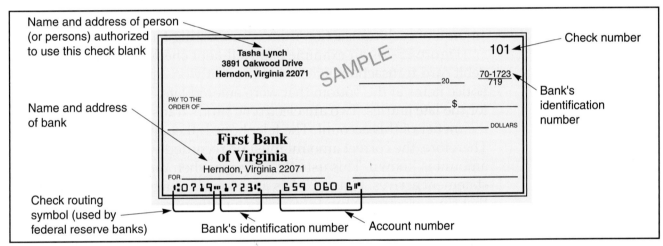

Figure 25-5. *Goodheart-Willcox Publisher*
The information on checks helps financial institutions process them correctly.

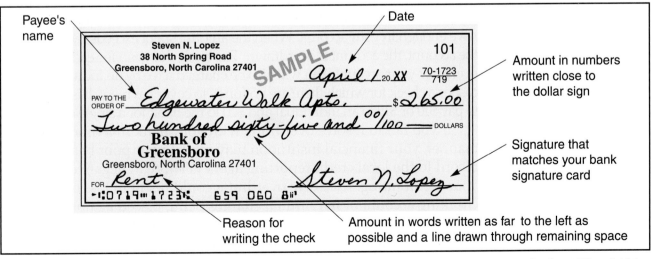

Figure 25-6. *Goodheart-Willcox Publisher*
This check has been written correctly.

- **Amount of the check in numerals.** Write the numbers as close to the dollar sign as possible to prevent anyone from adding or changing the amount.
- **Amount of the check in words.** Begin at the far left. Write *and* after the amount of dollars. Then write the amount of cents as a fraction of 100 (for example, 45/100, 00/100, or no/100). Draw a line through the remaining space.
- **Purpose of the check.** This is stated in a few words on the *memo* line.
- **Signature.** Sign your name the same way each time, using the signature you used on the bank signature card.

Recording Changes to Your Account

You will need to update your checkbook register each time funds enter or leave your account. Be sure to record all deposits and add them to your account balance. For recording checks, include the check number, date, payee, purpose of the check, and check amount. For recording debit card transactions, include the date, name of the merchant or ATM location, purpose, and amount. Then subtract the amount of each transaction from your existing balance.

Figure 25-7 is an example of a well-kept check register. Notice the debit card transaction is recorded promptly on April 6. You will also notice items at the bottom that were entered late. There is a reason for the late entries. Two are electronic funds transfers authorized by the owner of this account. The telephone bill changes each month. Therefore, the correct amount must be recorded when the exact amount is known. This usually happens when the monthly bank statement arrives. Figure 25-8 is an example of a bank statement. At that time, electronic funds transfers for other items are also recorded, such as the $265 for rent. Some late entries can be avoided by having the designated payee send you an e-mail or written notice with the date and amount of the transaction. The bank statement also showed a $3.60 service charge by the bank. This was deducted, too.

It is important to keep an up-to-date record of changes to your account. If you authorize funds to be paid, either by check or electronically, you must have enough in your account. When the amount spent exceeds the amount in the account, the account is overdrawn. The bank charges a fee each time you overdraw your account. You will also be charged a fee by an individual who cashes a check for which there are no funds to cover payment. It is common to pay $10 or $15 to an individual and $20 to the bank for a single overdraft.

If you fail to resolve overdrafts with your bank in a timely manner, your financial institution may report your poor banking record to the local credit reporting agency. This can negatively affect your credit rating. Excessive overdrafts could result in loss of your checking account or in criminal charges being placed against you.

Your bank may offer various strategies for covering overdrafts. Be sure to discuss these options and possible fees for using them when you open your account. Remember, however, that overdrawing your account is never a good idea.

NUMBER	DATE	DESCRIPTION OF TRANSACTION	PAYMENT/DEBIT (–)	√ T	FEE (IF ANY) (–)	DEPOSIT/CREDIT (+)	BALANCE 336 27	
101	4/1	Edgewater Walk Apts. Rent	265 00				265 00	
							71 27	
102	4/3	Family Food Stores groceries	18 35				18 35	
							52 92	
103	4/4	K-Mart weights	13 49				13 49	
							39 43	
	4/6	Deposit				270 00	270 00	
							309 43	
	4/6	Debit card Bob's Restaurant	9 73				9 73	
							299 70	
104	4/9	Commonwealth Edison electricity bill	15 60				15 60	
							284 10	
105	4/15	Family Food Stores groceries	20 02				20 02	
							264 08	
	4/20	Deposit				270 00	270 00	
							534 08	
106	4/23	Martin's Shoe Store black shoes	23 58				23 58	
							510 50	
107	5/1	Edgewater Walk Apts. Rent	265 00				265 00	
							245 50	
108	5/2	Family Food Stores groceries	16 98				16 98	
							228 52	
	4/15	Bell South telephone bill	39 83				39 83	
							188 69	
	4/20	Courier paper bill	15 00				15 00	
							173 69	
		April service charge	3 60				3 60	
							170 09	

RECORD ALL CHARGES OR CREDITS THAT AFFECT YOUR ACCOUNT

REMEMBER TO RECORD AUTOMATIC PAYMENTS / DEPOSITS ON DATE AUTHORIZED.

Figure 25-7.   *Goodheart-Willcox Publisher*
Whenever money enters or leaves your account, record the transaction in your checkbook register.

Cashing Checks

With a checking account, you should have no problem cashing checks at your bank. However, if you write a check to obtain cash, be prepared to show some identification (ID). This is for the protection of the check writer as well as the person accepting the check. Wherever you cash a check, whether at a bank or another place of business, plan on showing identification.

Many places ask for two forms of identification, including one with a photo. Common forms of ID include a driver's license or an employee identification badge.

When you endorse a check for cash, wait to do so in the presence of the bank teller. Signatures are usually compared when cashing checks, so one piece of identification should have your signature.

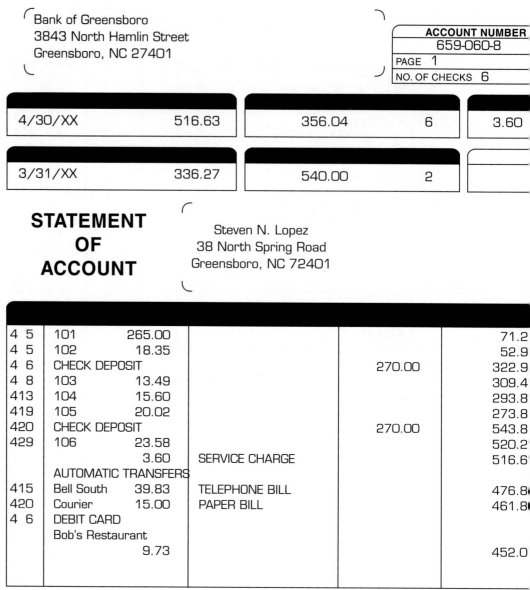

Figure 25-8.

A bank statement is a summary of your checking account activity during a certain period—usually a month.

Balancing a Checkbook

After you open a checking account, you will start receiving bank statements monthly, bimonthly, or quarterly. Each time you receive a bank statement, you will need to make sure your record of deposits and withdrawals (checks, debits, and cash) agrees with the bank's record. This is called *balancing* or *reconciling* your checkbook.

The first step in balancing your checkbook is to mark off, in your checkbook register, each transaction listed on your statement. Check to make sure you have recorded the amounts correctly. Be sure to record in your register any transactions appearing on the bank statement that you forgot to record in your register (after verifying they are yours).

The figures in your check register should reflect that shown on your bank statement. If these figures do not agree, go through the steps again and recheck your arithmetic. Also check the addition and subtraction in your checkbook register. You may have made a mistake. If your figures still do not agree after checking for errors, take your statement, canceled checks, and checkbook to your bank for assistance.

A check listed on your bank statement is called a canceled check. The **canceled checks** are checks that have been processed by the bank. Some banks return canceled checks or copies to their customers with the bank statements. If you should ever need a copy of a canceled check for proof of payment, you will need to contact the bank.

Personal Financial Management Software

There are several easy-to-use software programs available that will help you manage your finances. These programs make it easy to keep track of savings and checking accounts, investments, credit cards, and loans. This software can help you plan your finances and organize your income and expenses in a format that will make filing income taxes easier. They can also make it easier to balance your checkbook as they do the math for you. If you are using online banking, you can even download account information from your bank or credit card company.

Preparing for the Event

No matter what competitive events you will participate in for a Career and Technical Student Organization (CTSO), you will have to be well-organized and prepared. Of course, you will have studied the content exhaustively before the event, but you also have to prepare by making sure all the tools you need for the event, or for travel to the event, are taken care of. Buttoning down all the details well in advance of an event will decrease stress and leave you free to concentrate on the event itself. To prepare for a competition, create a checklist of things you need to bring to the event.

- Appropriate clothing, which includes shoes and appropriate undergarments. See the Event Prep feature in Chapter 23 for an in-depth discussion of appropriate attire.
- All technological resources, including anything that you might need to prepare or compete. Double check to make sure that any presentation material that is saved electronically is done so on media that is compatible with the machines that will be available to you at the event.
- Identification and registration materials, including a valid form of identification.
- Study materials, including the flash cards and other materials you have used to study for the event.

Special Types of Checks

Paying by personal check instead of cash is a safe and convenient way to make a payment. Other types of checks are used for the same reason. These include traveler's checks, cashier's checks, certified checks, and money orders. These checks are available at most banks, savings banks, and credit unions for a small fee.

A **traveler's check** is a type of check that is accepted as cash in most places around the world. Personal checks may be accepted only locally. Traveler's checks can also be replaced if lost or stolen.

If you are paying a large sum of money, a cashier's check may be a more acceptable form of payment than a personal check. A **cashier's check** is a check issued from a bank's own account rather than the account of a person or a business. The payee may feel more secure being paid with a cashier's check because it is drawn on a bank's own funds and signed by a bank officer.

Another way to make a payment to someone who does not want to accept a personal check is by certified check. A **certified check** is a personal check with a bank's guarantee that the check will be paid. When a bank certifies a check, the amount of the check is immediately subtracted from the payer's account. The receiver of the check, therefore, is assured of getting paid the amount of the check.

A **money order** is a type of check used for a specific amount of money payable to a specific payee. Money orders can be bought at a number of places in addition to financial institutions, such as post offices and currency exchanges.

Safe-Deposit Boxes

In addition to the services already discussed, banks and some other financial institutions rent safe-deposit boxes in their vaults. *Safe-deposit boxes* are small metal containers that people rent to protect their valuables from fire and theft. Jewelry, wills, deeds, birth certificates, stocks and bonds, insurance policies, and other important items are often kept in safe-deposit boxes.

If you rent a box, you will be given a key for it. Each time you use the box, you will sign your name and present personal identification as well as your key to the attendant. It takes two keys to open a safe-deposit box—yours and one retained by the financial institution. No one else can open your box.

Checkpoint 25.1

1. List three factors to consider when choosing a financial institution.
2. List two advantages of online banking.
3. What does direct deposit mean?
4. List five guidelines for using an ATM safely.
5. How does a debit card differ from a cash card?

Build Your Vocabulary

As you progress through this text, develop a personal glossary of career-related terms and add it to your portfolio. This will help build your vocabulary and prepare you for your career of choice. Write a definition for each of the following terms, and add it to your personal career glossary.

electronic funds transfer (EFT)
e-check
automated teller machine (ATM)
debit card
smart card
cash card
endorsement
canceled check
traveler's check
cashier's check
certified check
money order

25.2 Saving and Investing

Terms

simple interest
compound interest
certificate of deposit
    (CD)
inflation
Consumer Price
    Index (CPI)
securities
stock
bond
mutual fund
money market fund
401(k) plan
individual retirement
    account (IRA)

Objectives

After completing this section, you will be able to:
- **Explain** the types of savings products available to financial institutions.
- **Compare** different types of investments.
- **Describe** ways to invest wisely.

Saving

Instead of keeping all your money in a checking account, you may want to put part of it into some form of savings. Saving money in a financial institution has two major advantages. It provides a safe place to keep your money and it pays interest. A savings program can also help you save money for a specific purpose. Financial institutions offer a variety of savings programs. These include regular savings accounts, money market deposit accounts, and certificates of deposit. In order to choose the best savings plan for your needs, you should first understand how interest is determined.

Understanding Interest

The money a financial institution or person pays for the use of your money is called *interest*. The amount of interest you earn depends on a number of factors. First, look at the rate of interest. The higher the rate of interest, the more money you will earn. The amount of interest paid is usually expressed as an annual interest rate based on a one-year period. This is known as the *annual percentage rate (APR)*.

A second factor to consider is how the bank calculates the interest. There are two general methods used: simple interest and compound interest. **Simple interest** is interest paid only on the money initially deposited. For instance, a $1,000 deposit would earn $100 in one year if the simple APR was 10 percent. **Compound interest** is interest paid on the initial deposit plus any interest already earned. It is more commonly used than simple interest. In other words, you earn interest on the interest. Therefore, compound interest pays more than simple interest.

Be sure to look at how often interest is compounded. The more often interest is compounded, the more money you will earn. Interest can be compounded daily, monthly, quarterly, or yearly. A $1,000 deposit would earn $105.20 in one year if the annual interest rate was 10 percent compounded daily. The true annual interest rate in this

Africa Studio/Shutterstock.com

Selecting in the right savings plan can help you earn more money and keep ahead of inflation.

case is 10.52 percent. If the interest rate of 10 percent on $1,000 was compounded quarterly, however, it would earn $103.81 in one year. The true annual interest rate would be 10.38 percent.

Time is also a factor in determining how much interest you will earn. The longer you invest your money, the more impact it will have on your earnings. For example, if you invest $50.00 a month for 10 years at eight percent interest you would have $9,258.28 at the end of the 10 years. If you invest $25.00 a month for 20 years, you will have $14,848.68 at the end of the 20 years. In each case you would have invested $6,000.00. However, by investing your money over twenty years instead of 10, you will have earned $5,590.40 more in interest. Therefore, it is important to begin saving on a regular basis early in your life.

Once you recognize the type of savings plan you prefer, compare that plan at various financial institutions. Find out what the interest rates are and how interest is paid. Look for a financial institution and a savings plan that will pay the highest rate of interest with the fewest number of restrictions.

Traditional Savings Accounts

A regular savings account can be started with only a few dollars. It allows you to make deposits and withdrawals in varying amounts at any time. Funds can usually be withdrawn without a penalty fee. However, make sure you understand the rules for depositing and withdrawing money before you open an account. Although a regular savings account is a convenient form of savings, it pays the lowest rate of interest.

Case

Cashing Terrell's Paycheck

After work on his first payday, Terrell Smith stopped at the nearest bank to cash his paycheck. He endorsed his check while waiting in line for a teller. That was the first of several mistakes he made.

Arriving at the teller's window, Terrell said, "I would like to cash my paycheck."

"Do you have an account with us?" the teller asked.

"No, I don't. This is my first paycheck."

The teller smiled. "Well, your check has been issued through the Century Bank and this is the National Bank. I will have to charge you a $4 fee to cash this check. If you had an account with us, there would be no charge. Would you like to open an account with us?"

Terrell was getting impatient and grumbled, "No. Maybe I'll just go to the Century Bank."

"The nearest branch is three miles west of here. Let me talk to my supervisor," the teller replied.

When the teller returned, she said, "Since this is your first time, we will charge you only $1 to cash the check, but you should open a checking account."

"Maybe next time," replied Terrell. "Just cash the check."

"Okay, but you endorsed the check on the right end instead of the left end. Also, you wrote T.T. Smith, but the check is made out to Terrell T. Smith. Please endorse it on the left end as shown on the front of the check," the teller instructed.

After correctly endorsing the check, the teller asked to see Terrell's driver's license and second form of ID containing a photo. The teller explained that if he had a checking account, he would be given a bank guarantee card. This card would make it easier for him to cash checks in the future.

Critical Thinking

1. Do you think Terrell should have opened an account? Explain.
2. Should Terrell have signed the check while waiting in line? Explain.
3. Is Terrell likely to have the same trouble when he tries to cash his next check?

Money Market Deposit Accounts

A money market deposit account is another type of savings account offered by financial institutions. These accounts pay a slightly higher interest rate than regular savings accounts but require a minimum deposit, often $1,000 or more. You must also maintain a minimum balance before the account earns interest. You can make withdrawals from a money market account by writing checks, but the number and the amount of the checks may be restricted. These accounts are federally insured, so your money is safe.

Certificates of Deposit

If you have money to deposit for a set period of time, you might want to buy a certificate of deposit. A **certificate of deposit (CD)** pays a higher interest rate because it requires depositors to commit their money for a specific period. The time period may range from 30 days to 10 years. A minimum deposit is usually required and there is a set annual rate of interest. The longer you agree to hold a CD, the higher the rate of interest you earn. If you cash in the certificate before the time period is over, you lose a significant amount of interest. Interest rates are also higher when deposits are larger.

The fixed interest rate on a CD can be a disadvantage if rates rise. If you commit your money to a CD for a long period while rates go up, you may earn less than if you had deposited your money in a regular savings account.

Investing

As you continue to work and earn money, you will have more money to spend. What will you do with the money you have left after paying all your necessary expenses? What about the financial goals you established when you developed a budget? Will you be able to achieve these goals simply by depositing a little money each month into a savings account? There is another way to work toward important goals. You can invest some of your money.

Investments can be a good way to protect against inflation. **Inflation** is a general increase in prices. This increase decreases what you are able to buy with the same amount of money. For example, it may cost you more to go to your favorite movie theatre today than it did two years ago.

One frequently used measure of inflation is the Consumer Price Index (CPI). **Consumer Price Index (CPI)** is a measure of the average change in prices for consumer goods and services over time. For example, the CPI in 1983 was 99.6. It had more than doubled by 2011 to 224.939. This means the average 2011 basket of groceries cost more than twice as much as the 1983 basket. One way CPI is used is to provide a basis for calculating annual cost-of-living increases for many current and retired workers. This adjustment to income gives consumers the same buying power from year to year, even though prices have risen.

Although most investments involve some degree of risk, there are many safe, low-risk investments that can yield higher returns than regular savings accounts. Learning a few basic investment facts may help you reach your financial goals faster. The three basic types of investments discussed here are securities, retirement accounts, and real estate.

Stock prices can be checked while on the go using widely available stock tracking apps.

Oleksiy Mark/Shutterstock.com

Securities

Stocks, bonds, and mutual funds are all securities. **Securities** are financial instruments that represent either ownership (stocks), indebtedness (bonds) or the rights to ownership (derivatives). Corporations and governments issue securities to get money to operate and expand. One of the most common ways to purchase securities is through brokerage houses. Securities can also be bought and sold at some banks although the selection may be limited. Investments in securities are generally not insured and can be risky.

Stocks

A **stock** is a share in the ownership of a corporation. When you buy stock in a corporation, you become part owner of that company. If the company is profitable, you and other stockholders share in the profits after debts and operating expenses are paid. You also stand to make or lose money when you sell stocks. If you sell a stock for more than you paid for it, you will make a profit on your investment. If you sell a stock for less than you paid for it, you will take a loss.

Most corporations issue two types of stocks, preferred stock and common stock. *Preferred stock* involves less risk than common stock. Preferred stockholders are paid set dividends (profits) at stated rates, regardless of the profit the company earns. However, a company does not have to pay dividends if it cannot afford to do so.

Savings helps conserve money while investing risks that money in hopes of getting a higher return.

EdBock/Shutterstock.com

Common stock involves more risk than preferred stock because the value of the stock and the amount and frequency of dividends depend on company earnings and economic conditions. When company earnings are good and the economy is expanding, a company's common stock tends to increase in value. This will provide the investor with a profit if he or she chooses to sell the stock. When the economic outlook is poor, common stock tends to decline in value. Because of the higher degree of risk involved, common stocks offer greater opportunity for large gains and losses.

Bonds

A **bond** is a certificate of debt or obligation issued by a corporation or a government. It is like an IOU. The issuing government or corporation promises to repay the bondholder the face value of the bond after a certain number of years. The bond issuer also promises to pay a fixed rate of interest on the face value of the bond during the loan period.

Bonds are among the safest investments you can make. However, the safety of the bond depends on the credit rating of the bond issuer. Rating agencies, such as Standard and Poor's and Moody, rate bonds. Bonds with high ratings carry little risk. Bonds with low ratings tend to be risky, but they can also provide greater returns.

US government bonds are the safest bonds you can buy. Treasury bills, treasury notes, and treasury bonds are all types of US bonds. The minimum investment required varies by type and maturity. Maturity, in this instance, refers to the amount of time money needs to be on deposit before all of the promised interest is earned and the bond can be redeemed.

US savings bonds are also government bonds. However, they are more a source of savings rather than an investment. They are issued for as little as $50 at a variable interest rate for a set length of time.

Mutual Funds

A **mutual fund** is a type of investment where money from a number of investors is combined and invested in securities. If you buy shares in a mutual fund, you automatically become part investor in all the securities included in the fund. A mutual fund pays dividends on shares just as any stock does.

Investing in a mutual fund has many advantages. It allows you to invest in a variety of securities. Having several types of securities instead of just one reduces the amount of risk involved. Mutual funds can be bought and sold at any time. They are managed by experienced investors who work to earn the highest rate of return for their shareholders.

There are disadvantages to mutual funds. Investors must pay sales charges, annual fees, and other expenses even if the fund does poorly. You will not have control over the specific types of investments mutual fund managers make. Be sure you fully understand all aspects of investing in a specific mutual fund.

A **money market fund** is a type of mutual fund that deals only in high interest, short-term investments. These investments include government securities and certificates of deposit. Money market funds are managed and sold by mutual funds, investment firms, and some insurance companies. The rate of interest earned on these funds varies with money market rates.

Money market funds offer many advantages for the investor. They can provide a higher rate of return than savings accounts. They can be cashed in at any time since they have no term. Some offer check-writing privileges.

Money market funds have some disadvantages, too. The rate of return on money market funds is not a set rate. It can change daily. If money market rates drop, so does the rate of return on the fund. Also, a minimum of $1,000 or more is usually required to invest in a money market fund. Unlike money market deposit accounts discussed earlier, these funds are not FDIC insured. However, some may be covered by private insurance.

Retirement Accounts

Though retirement may seem like a long time away, it is best to start saving for it early in your career. One good way is to take advantage of a 401(k) plan during the years you work. A **401(k) plan** is a retirement savings plan offered through an employer. Workers participate in these plans by agreeing to save a certain dollar amount

You should begin saving for your retirement early in your career.

from each paycheck. This is automatically deducted and put into a special account. An employee can usually split savings into two or more types of investments. Some companies also match employee contributions, which helps savings grow more quickly.

Another common type of retirement savings plan is called an individual retirement account. **Individual retirement account (IRA)** is a type of savings account that anyone with earned income can open as a way to save for retirement. The amount you can save annually depends on your age, income level, and your ability to participate in a company-sponsored pension plan. Two basic types of IRAs are available: a traditional IRA and a Roth IRA.

With a traditional IRA, you pay taxes on your earnings and withdrawals after retirement. The amount you contribute to a Roth IRA is taxed. However, if all requirements are followed, withdrawals and earnings are not.

Real Estate

Real estate is land or buildings. Real estate is used as a hedge against inflation. When inflation occurs, real estate values also tend to rise. Real estate should be considered a long-term investment. Since most real estate is expensive compared to other investments, a large amount of money may be needed to make the investment. Investing in real estate can yield big returns, but considerable risk may be involved.

Owning your own home or apartment is one type of real estate investment. It is generally considered one of the best real estate investments you can make. Throughout history, most homeowners have been able to sell their property for a profit. While living in your home, the interest you pay on your mortgage and your property taxes can be deducted from your taxable income. The difficulty is in saving enough money for the down payment on a home. You also have to keep up your monthly payments, which include taxes and insurance. These payments are usually higher than rent payments, but eventually you will own the property.

There are other ways to invest in real estate in addition to buying your own home. Some investors buy income-producing properties, such as apartments and office buildings. Income is provided in the form of rent receipts. Income property also has the potential to appreciate in value over time. Other investors buy undeveloped land that, they believe, will increase in value. Both of these forms of real estate investing can be very risky. They should be undertaken only by people who know what they are doing and can afford the risk.

There are many other ways to invest in real estate. For example, there are investment groups where you can pool your money with other investors to buy property.

As you can see, real estate investing can be very complex. There are many factors to consider when buying property. Before investing your money, you may want to take a class on real estate investing. Also, read as much as you can on the subject.

Investing Wisely

It is important to understand that investing can be very risky. You have worked hard for the money you have. It is important that you work just as hard to make sure your investments are sound. Do not invest money you cannot afford to lose. Very few investments are completely safe. Be sure you have an emergency fund in place before investing.

Begin by setting an investment goal. Then start with a small investment and build from there. By beginning with a small investment, you will be able to learn how the investment process works with little risk. You will see how an investment can make your money grow, but you may also see how quickly your investment can decrease.

As a beginning investor, you may want to find a reliable professional to help you make investment decisions. Check their credentials and record of achievements. Do not deal with anyone whose experience and knowledge are questionable. Be sure to find out what fees your investor charges for giving advice and investing your money.

However, having a professional to help you select an investment does not excuse you from doing your homework. Research the current outlook for the economy and look for an investment that is expected to increase in value. Never invest in anything if you do not have a thorough understanding of how it works. Make sure you understand your obligations and the risks and rewards of the investment.

Checkpoint 25.2

1. What is the difference between simple interest and compound interest?
2. Why do corporations and governments issue securities?
3. List five types of investments.
4. What is the difference between a bond and a stock?
5. When should an individual start saving for retirement?

Build Your Vocabulary

As you progress through this text, develop a personal glossary of career-related terms and add it to your portfolio. This will help build your vocabulary and prepare you for your career of choice. Write a definition for each of the following terms, and add it to your personal career glossary.

simple interest
compound interest
certificate of deposit (CD)
inflation
Consumer Price Index (CPI)
securities
stock
bond
mutual fund
money market funds
401(k) plan
individual retirement account (IRA)

Chapter Summary

Section 25.1 Banking

- Commercial banks, savings and loans, and credit unions are all types of financial institutions.
- Electronic banking allows customers immediate access to their money and bank records. Online banking, ATMs, as well as debit, credit, and smart cards are made possible by electronic banking.
- A checking account keeps money safe while offering a convenient way to buy goods and services and pay bills. Before opening a checking account, do some research so that you are aware of the fees and conditions associated with the account you open.
- Traveler's checks, cashier's checks, certified checks, and money orders are checks that serve special purposes. These checks can be obtained through most financial institutions.
- Customers rent safe-deposit boxes to protect valuable items, such as jewelry and important documents.

Section 25.2 Saving and Investing

- A savings account keeps your money safe and pays interest. There are several types of savings accounts into which you can deposit funds.
- Investing your money can help you reach your financial goals. Investment options include securities, retirement accounts and real estate.
- Because investing often involves risk, you need to learn as much as you can about any investment plan before putting money into it.

Check Your Career IQ

Now that you have finished the chapter, see what you learned about careers by taking the chapter posttest. The test can be accessed on the mobile site by using a smartphone or on the G-W Learning companion website.

www.m.g-wlearning.com
www.g-wlearning.com

Review Your Knowledge

1. Name three types of checking accounts.
2. List two examples of a restrictive endorsement.
3. What happens if you overdraw your checking account?
4. What is a bank statement?
5. What type of check is drawn on a bank's own funds rather than the payer's?
6. What factors should be considered when selecting a type of checking account?
7. What is interest?
8. What yields more, simple interest or compound interest? Explain why.
9. What is the difference between preferred and common stock?
10. Explain online banking.

Apply Your Knowledge

1. Choose a company and pretend to buy stock in it. Keep track of your stock for a month. At the end of that time, write a report and give a presentation on the status of the stock you choose. How did the price fluctuate? Do you think that was a good investment? Explain your answer.
2. Identify a bank or credit union in your community. Calculate the amount of return you would earn from the institution you selected after one year if you invested $1,000 in each of the following ways: regular savings account, certificate of deposit, and money market deposit account. Which investment yields the highest rate of return?
3. Research how ATMs work and what security measures help prevent fraud. Also research how ATMs are used in other countries. Write a brief report of your findings.
4. Research what online services several local banks offer. Find out what kinds of services are available at what costs. Prepare a chart of your findings.
5. Use a personal financial management computer program. Is this a good way to keep track of your finances? Explain why or why not.
6. Determine the financial apps that are available for a specific brand of smartphone. Describe how these apps might assist in managing your finances in a brief written or oral report. Include possible downsides to using these apps in your report.
7. Use a free online retirement planner to determine the amount of money you will need to save each year to retire at age 72 with an annual income of $80,000.
8. What is the minimum deposit required for a CD at the three financial institutions you visited? Compare the minimum required with information you obtain from a financial institution in another state.
9. Conduct some research to find out about the *rule of 72*. What impact does it have on investment decisions you might make? Explain your answer.
10. Do you think that investments in securities should be insured the way that investments in banks are? Explain the reasons for your answer.

Teamwork

Working with four classmates, form an investment team. Assume you have $50,000 to invest. Using current prices of securities listed online or in your daily newspaper, decide as a team how to invest the money. Research your investments and be able to document why you made your selections. You may hold some cash back or deposit it in a regular savings account for future use. Review your investments each week and decide as a team whether or not to sell and/or purchase additional securities. Sell your investments at the end of twelve weeks and determine if you made a profit or loss. Be sure to figure the cost of buying and selling the securities for any transactions made. Summarize the team's results in a brief presentation to the class.

G-W Learning Mobile Site

Visit the G-W Learning mobile site to complete the chapter pretest and posttest and to practice vocabulary using e-flash cards. If you do not have a smartphone, visit the G-W Learning companion website to access these features.
G-W Learning mobile site: www.m.g-wlearning.com
G-W Learning companion website: www.g-wlearning.com

Common Core

College and Career Readiness

CTE Career Ready Practices. You may have been taught to treat others how *you* would like to be treated. This is often referred to as *the golden rule*. Productively working with others who have a background different from yours may require that you learn to treat others as *they* wish to be treated. Conduct research on the Internet about cultural differences related to personal space, time, gestures/body language, and relationship toward authority figures. Create a T-chart that show the difference on the left and ways you would adapt your interactions to account for that difference.
Reading. Find a recent article in print or online that deals with banking and ethics. Determine the central ideas and conclusions of the article. Provide an accurate summary of your reading, making sure to incorporate the *who, what, when, where,* and *why* of situation.

Apply Your Technology Skills

Access the G-W Learning companion website for this text at www.g-wlearning.com. Download each data file for this chapter. Follow the instructions to complete activities to practice what you have learned.

Data File 25–1—Maintaining a Checking Account Register

Data File 25–2—Avoiding Investment Pitfalls

College and Career Readiness Portfolio

College and Career Readiness

Employers and colleges review candidates for various positions. They are interested in people who impress them as being professional or serious about a position. Being involved in academic clubs or professional organizations will help you make a good impression. You can also learn a lot that will help you with your studies or your career. While you are in school, you may belong to clubs. National Honor Society and Future Business Leaders of America are two examples. When you are employed, you may belong to professional organizations related to your career area. The American Nurses Association is one example. Update your resume and online information to reflect your membership in clubs and organizations. Make sure information about you on the Internet does not detract from your professional image. Review information you have posted on social network sites (Facebook), blogs, wikis, or other sites. Remove any information that does not give a favorable impression of you.

1. Identify clubs or organizations you can join to help you learn and build a professional image. Give the name and a brief description of each one.
2. Save the file in your e-portfolio. Place a copy in the container for your print portfolio.

Section 26.1
Managing Risk

Section 26.2
Types of Insurance

College and Career Readiness

Reading Prep. As you read the text, try to determine the authors' point of view. What can you infer about their point of view from reading the chapter? What evidence in the chapter shows their point of view?

Introduction

Consumers often find the need to purchase insurance to protect their most valuable possessions. Insurance provides payment for costly expenses when needed most. Whether you choose to be a homeowner or renter, or whether you own a car or a motorcycle, insurance is necessary to protect you and others in the event of misfortune.

There are many different types of insurance available. Some policies provide expenses for health care, while others provide payment to family members in the event of death. As a responsible consumer, you will need to make decisions about the kind of insurance coverage to select for you and your family. The cost of the insurance and the benefits provided are important factors to consider when selecting the best coverage.

Check Your Career IQ

Before you begin the chapter, see what you already know about careers by taking the chapter pretest. Use the related QR code to view the pretest on the mobile site. If you do not have a smartphone, visit the G-W Learning companion website to access the pretest.

G-W Mobile

www.m.g-wlearning.com
www.g-wlearning.com

Career Snapshot
Criminal Investigator

911 Law, Public Safety, Corrections & Security

What Does a Criminal Investigator Do?

A criminal investigator may work at the local, state, or federal level. The job of a criminal investigator is to investigate alleged or suspected criminal violations of federal, state, or local laws to determine if evidence is sufficient to recommend prosecution. A criminal investigator must:

- obtain and use search and arrest warrants;
- examine records to find links in a chain of evidence or information;
- develop and use informants to get leads to information; and
- obtain and verify evidence by interviewing, observing, and interrogating suspects and witnesses.

What Is It Like to Work as a Criminal Investigator?

A criminal investigator has to be very flexible. He or she must spend some time at the site of a crime or away from the office, searching for evidence and investigating crime scenes. As part of the investigation, he or she will often interview witnesses and people of interest. A criminal investigator is often required to travel to various locations. However, time is also spent working in an office analyzing findings, coordinating investigation efforts, and studying evidence that will help convict a suspect. He or she must work long, odd hours, depending on the nature of the investigation.

What Education and Skills Are Needed to Be a Criminal Investigator?

- college degree
- courses in criminal justice, computers and electronics, geography, communications, and philosophy
- fluency in a second language is preferred
- previous experience in local law enforcement is preferred
- calm attitude under extremely stressful situations
- committed to justice

26.1 Managing Risk

Objectives

After completing this section, you will be able to:

- **Explain** the purpose of insurance.
- **Describe** factors to consider when selecting an insurance company, and agent.
- **Describe** the features of employer-sponsored insurance programs.

Insurance Basics

Individuals face risk every day. *Risk* is the possibility that an unfavorable situation could happen to you or something you own. *Insurance* is the protection you purchase to help you share the risk. There are many types of insurance to consider. When you buy an insurance policy, you are entering into a contract with an insurance company. You then become a policyholder. As a policyholder, you agree to pay a premium. A **premium** is a set amount of money that the insured party pays to the insurance company on a regular basis. In return, the insurance company provides financial protection in the event of a misfortune covered by the policy. The premiums policyholders pay are invested by the company to earn money. Part of these earnings is used to cover the expenses of operating the company and to pay the claims of policyholders.

Some people think insurance is something that only people with a lot of money or possessions should have. However, this is not true. Whenever a person has something of financial value that would be costly or difficult to replace, insurance is needed to protect the item of value. The amount of protection needed depends on the potential for financial loss. For example, a person with a new car would need more insurance coverage than a person with an older used car. This is because the person with the new car has a higher potential for financial loss. More money would be needed to replace the new car than the older one.

Choosing an Insurance Company, Agent, and Policy

The company and agent from whom you choose to buy insurance are just as important to consider as the policy you select. Choosing the right company and agent can make a big difference in the coverage you receive, the quality of service your agent provides, and the premiums you pay.

Choosing a Company

Before choosing an insurance company, do a little research. Also, take a close look at the policies at various companies. Buy from a company that offers policies with the benefits and options that are most important to you.

It is important to understand your insurance policies before you file a claim. Suppose you are involved in a car accident or your car is stolen. Maybe your home is burglarized or damaged during a storm. Make sure a company has a reputation for settling claims fairly and promptly before you buy any insurance from it. Simply follow the steps in Figure 26-1 when filing a claim.

Selecting an Agent

Select an agent or broker just as you would select a doctor or lawyer. Find someone with good training and experience in insurance and financial planning. A good agent is one who will advise you honestly about the type and amount of coverage you

---

Filing an Insurance Claim

- Report any accident, burglary, or theft to the police.
- Phone your insurance agent or insurance company immediately. Ask your agent what you should do and what forms or documents are needed to support your claim.
- Your insurance agent or company may ask you to provide a written explanation of what happened.
- Cooperate with your insurance company by supplying any information your insurer needs as it investigates, settles, or defends any claim. Turn over any legal papers you receive in connection with your loss.
- Keep records of your expenses. Save receipts for what you spend and submit them to your insurance company for reimbursement.
- Keep copies of your paperwork in your own files. You may need to refer to them later.
- Check your policy to find out what settlement steps are outlined. If you are dissatisfied with a settlement offer, discuss it with your agent or adjuster.

Figure 26-1.   *Goodheart-Willcox Publisher*

In the event of an accident or theft, you may need to file an insurance claim to recover the cost of damages.

need. A responsible agent will also help you evaluate your coverage periodically and will process policy revisions and claims promptly. Ask your friends, relatives, and co-workers for recommendations before choosing an agent and company.

After you have chosen a company and agent, then concentrate on choosing a policy for your insurance needs. Before you agree to a policy, look it over carefully. Be sure to ask questions about any terms, provisions, options, or sections you do not understand. Also, make sure the policy provides the coverage you and your agent discussed specifically for you.

Evaluating Cost

Insurance protection can be very expensive. As when making any major purchase, shop carefully before making your decision. There are a number of things to keep in mind when shopping for insurance.

Consider buying all or most of your insurance from the same insurance company. Most insurance companies provide discounts if you have more than one policy with them. However, discounts alone will not guarantee that you are paying the lowest price. Check the rates offered by several different insurance companies.

Insurance companies usually offer a variety of discounts. For example, you may lower your insurance rates by completing a driver safety course and by earning good grades in school. Driving fewer miles will reduce the cost of your autoinsurance. Auto insurance may also be reduced if you install a device in your car that monitors your driving habits. Installing smoke and security alarms can reduce the cost of your homeowners insurance.

You may want to consider raising the deductibles on your insurance. Having a higher deductible will reduce your insurance premium. Remember, however, that you will be required to pay the cost of a higher deductible before your insurance company will pay for damages or other expenses. If you raise the deductible on your car insurance from $200 to $500, you will have to pay the first $500 of any repair costs instead of just $200. You should make sure you have enough money saved to cover the cost of the deductible.

Insurance rates reflect the value of the items you insure. That expensive car or house you want will increase the cost of your insurance. Consider what the insurance will cost before you make a major purchase.

Go Green

The easiest way to get rid of unwanted items is to throw them in the trash. However, many charitable organizations are looking for used clothing, appliances, and other items. With a little effort, you can help someone in need and reduce the amount of trash added to landfills.

Use the assistance of a knowledgeable insurance agent to help you choose the amount of coverage you need.

You can lower the cost of your health insurance by staying in good physical condition. Not smoking, eating properly, exercising regularly, and maintaining a healthy weight can all reduce health insurance costs.

Finally, maintain a good credit rating. Many insurance companies feel that people with good credit are less likely to file a claim against them. As a result, they will offer a discount to people with good credit scores.

Employer-Sponsored Insurance Programs

When evaluating job offers, consider the insurance programs the companies offer as a part of their fringe benefits. The types of insurance offered and the amounts of coverage will be important to you. An added benefit to you is that federal law exempts taxes on employer-sponsored health and disability insurance and up to $50,000 of group-term life insurance.

Employers' insurance packages can vary a great deal. A group auto insurance plan is offered by some employers but not others. The same is true for life insurance. Some employers will provide only one health insurance plan, while others will offer a choice of two or more.

When evaluating job offers, you should also consider the insurance benefits provided by each employer.

Elena Elisseeva/Shutterstock.com

Cafeteria plans are becoming increasingly popular due to the diverse needs of employees. A **cafeteria plan** is coverage that allows workers to choose from a variety of benefits to devise a plan that best suits their needs. The selection may include health and accident insurance, 401k plans, dependent care assistance, and other benefits as specified by the Internal Revenue Service.

For all insurance coverage, you will want to find out what the premiums are and who pays them. For instance, one employer may provide an insurance plan at no cost to you, while another may require you to pay a large share of the premiums. Some employers provide benefits only to the employee while others provide benefits to dependents as well. If some portion of the insurance coverage is your expense, the premiums are deducted from your paycheck. Your employer then sends the premium payments to the insurance company.

In some cases, your employer's insurance package may not meet all your needs. If this is the case, see your own insurance agent for more coverage, but do not buy more insurance than you need. Your employer's insurance package may be enough for you.

Checkpoint 26.1

1. How do insurance companies use the money customers pay in premiums?
2. When should someone purchase insurance?
3. List two things to consider when selecting an insurance company.
4. Why does someone with a new car need more insurance than someone with an older car?
5. Explain how cafeteria plans work.

Build Your Vocabulary

As you progress through this text, develop a personal glossary of career-related terms and add it to your portfolio. This will help build your vocabulary and prepare you for your career of choice. Write a definition for each of the following terms, and add it to your personal career glossary.

premium
cafeteria plan

26.2 Types of Insurance

Terms

bodily injury liability
property damage
    liability
deductible
claim
health savings
    account (HSA)
disability insurance
fee-for-service (FFS)
    plan
health maintenance
    organization (HMO)
preferred provider
    organization (PPO)
point-of-service
    (POS) plan
beneficiary
whole life insurance
cash value
term insurance
universal life
    insurance

Objectives

After completing this section, you will be able to:
- **Explain** the purpose of property and casualty insurance.
- **Describe** the types of health insurance.
- **Explain** the purpose of life insurance.

Property and Casualty Insurance

Property and casualty insurance protects policyholders from financial loss that results from property damage or injury to others. *Casualty*, in this case, means an accident involving physical injury. Automobile, homeowners, and renters insurance are types of property and casualty insurance.

Automobile Insurance

Anyone who drives or owns a car takes certain financial and personal risks. Most states require car owners to carry liability insurance. If you do not have insurance and are involved in a car accident, you may have to pay thousands of dollars in bodily injury and property damages. Most people are unable to afford such large expenses unexpectedly. Therefore, the possibility of a car accident makes auto insurance essential for all drivers.

Automobile Insurance Coverage

For an individual or a family, an auto insurance policy may include the following six types of coverage:
- bodily injury liability coverage;
- property damage liability coverage;
- medical payments coverage;
- uninsured/underinsured motorists coverage;
- comprehensive coverage; and
- collision.

Bodily injury liability is a form of insurance coverage that protects you if you are legally at fault for an accident in which others are injured or killed. It may pay for the legal fees and the damages assessed against you, up to the limits of the policy. Liability insurance covers the car owner and anyone else who drives the car with the owner's permission.

Property damage liability is a form of insurance coverage that pays for damages your car causes to the property of others if you are responsible for the accident. Usually the property is another car. The coverage also pays for damages to other properties such as lampposts, telephone poles, or buildings. This form of insurance does not, however, cover damage to your car. Like bodily injury liability, it may also pay for legal fees. Limits stated in the policy apply to both bodily injury and property damage.

Both bodily injury and property damage liability coverage may be indicated on insurance policies in the following format: 100/300/50. In this example, the first number ($100,000) refers to the maximum liability that can be paid for any one injured person. The second number ($300,000) is the maximum payable for any one accident. The third number ($50,000) is the maximum payable for property damage.

Medical payments coverage pays for the medical expenses resulting from an accident, regardless of who was at fault. It covers you, your family, and any guests in your car if it is involved in an accident. It also covers you and your family if you are injured while riding in another car or walking. Your automobile and health insurance providers coordinate payments to decide who will be responsible for specific bills.

Uninsured/underinsured motorist coverage pays for bodily injuries for which an uninsured or underinsured motorist or hit-and-run driver is responsible. You and your family are covered as drivers, passengers, and pedestrians. Guests in your car are also covered. Underinsured motorist coverage pays for your bodily injury and/or property damage if the other driver is at fault and has no insurance to cover your damages.

Comprehensive coverage pays for damage to your car caused by something other than a collision. It will pay for damage caused by such things as fire, theft, vandalism, hail, water, and collision with animals or falling objects.

Collision coverage pays for the damage to your car caused by a collision with another vehicle or object, even if you are at fault. If your car is older, you may not want to obtain collision insurance. The car may not be worth the cost of the premiums and deductible.

Ethical Leadership

Responsible

"Hold yourself responsible for a higher standard than anybody else expects of you, never excuse yourself."— Henry Ward Beecher

Responsible individuals are morally accountable for their behavior. Your boss is very upset because someone mislabeled a very important shipment. You did it but are very afraid of what your supervisor is going to do about it. You tell him it wasn't your fault. You say the secretary gave you the wrong labels. Failure to take responsibility for your mistakes is unethical. Blaming someone else is even worse. Take responsibility for your mistakes and try to learn from them. In doing so, you will display good ethics.

Many states require buyers to obtain auto insurance at the time the car is purchased.

Kzenon/Shutterstock.com

Buying Auto Insurance

Automobile coverage usually requires the payment of a deductible. The **deductible** is an amount the policyholder must pay before the insurance company will begin to cover the expense. For instance, if a policy has a $100 deductible, the policyholder must pay the first $100 of expenses. Usually, the higher the deductible you have in your policy, the lower your premiums will be.

When buying auto insurance, the first step is to check if your state has requirements concerning the type and amount of coverage you must have. Remember, state laws address the minimum amount of coverage. It may be important to you to have more than the minimum coverage. Next, compare premiums carefully. Premiums can vary greatly because they are usually based on a number of factors. Some of these factors include your age, driving record, the year and model of your car, where you live, the distances you drive, and the amount of your deductible. Being a financially responsible person with an above average credit rating can also lower your insurance premiums.

Other factors also affect your premium rate. The older you are and the older the year and model of your car (unless it is a classic model), the lower your premiums are likely to be. Some insurance companies also give premium discounts for one or more of the following conditions:

- a good driving record (no accidents or traffic tickets);
- completion of a driver education or safety course;
- installation of an antitheft or safety device;
- good grades as a student;
- insurance coverage on multiple vehicles; and
- below-average mileage per year.

Be sure to find out what discounts you may be eligible to receive. As you check several insurance companies for the lowest premium, do not forget the importance of having adequate coverage. Also, be sure you do not give up important coverage just to save a few dollars on premiums. Inadequate coverage will do you little good if you are involved in a serious auto accident.

No-Fault Auto Insurance

No-fault auto insurance eliminates the legal process of proving who caused an accident. This type of insurance is thought to lower insurance rates because it reduces costly court trials to determine who is at fault. When an accident occurs, each policyholder makes a claim to his or her own insurance company. A **claim** is a formal request to an insurance company requesting compensation for a loss covered under a policy. With no-fault auto insurance, the insurance company pays its own policyholder for medical and other expenses caused by the accident. Each company pays its policyholder regardless of who is at fault. No-fault insurance is required in some form in many states. However, state laws vary in the amount awarded for medical costs, funeral and burial expenses, loss of income, and other benefits.

Financial Responsibility Laws

Most states now have financial responsibility laws related to auto liability insurance coverage. These laws are designed to make sure that motorists can pay for any damages or injuries they may cause while driving their cars. The two types of liability insurance—bodily injury liability and property damage liability—are required.

The amount of liability coverage required varies for each state, as does the method of enforcing the laws. For instance, some states require car owners to show proof of liability insurance in order to register their motor vehicles. In other states, proof of liability coverage must be in the vehicle at all times. If a driver is involved in an accident, he or she must be able to show proof of liability insurance whether they are at fault or not. Failure to do so can result in the suspension of the driver's license or car registration. If you are involved in an accident, follow the procedures listed in Figure 26-2.

Homeowners Insurance

Homeowners insurance provides two basic types of coverage—property and liability. *Property coverage* insures you against disasters such as fire, storms, burglary, theft, vandalism, and explosions. A standard homeowners policy does not cover floods or earthquakes. Some policies do not cover hurricanes either. Property coverage also insures the damage or loss of the dwelling and your personal property and possessions, such as clothes and furnishings. It also pays for your living expenses if you must move out of your home while it is being repaired or rebuilt. Additional insurance, or supplemental insurance, can be bought to cover damages from disasters that are excluded

What to Do after a Car Accident

1. STOP immediately. Do not leave the scene of the accident.
2. Call 911 if someone is injured. Notify the police immediately. Do not move the vehicle(s) until the police have arrived.
3. Secure the scene and administer first aid to any injured to the extent you are qualified to do so.
4. Do not admit fault. You may be entirely blameless, but witnesses will help prove it.
5. Avoid discussing the accident with anyone except the police or an identified representative of your insurance company.
6. Exchange information with the other driver. Write down the following information:
   * the other driver's name, address, telephone number, car license number, driver's license number, and insurance carrier
   * names and addresses of all witnesses
   * names and addresses of any injured persons
   * names and addresses of any passengers
7. Notify your insurance agent or insurance company as soon as possible.
8. Promptly notify the state's motor vehicle department or similar authority, as required by law.

Figure 26-2.   *Goodheart-Willcox Publisher*
In the event of a car accident, follow these steps for safety and insurance purposes.

from the homeowners policy. When you need to buy home insurance, follow the guidelines in Figure 26-3.

Liability coverage protects you against financial loss if others are injured on your property. It also provides coverage if you, a family member, or a pet accidentally damages the property of others. Liability coverage pays your defense court costs if you are sued for damages to someone's property. It also pays any damages, up to the limits of your policy, if you are held legally liable for injuries or property damage.

Renters Insurance

Renters insurance provides coverage if you are living in a rental unit. It offers protection similar to homeowners insurance. However, renters insurance only covers your personal possessions. Coverage of the unit is not included in renters insurance because it is covered under the owner's insurance.

Whether you own or rent, your insurance policy will only pay up to a certain amount to replace your possessions. Be sure you review your policy to know what is covered. You can also buy supplemental insurance for additional coverage of your more expensive possessions such as jewelry and electronics. Therefore, it is a good idea to complete an inventory of all your personal possessions. Be sure to record the item name, how much it cost, when you purchased it, and where the item was purchased. Include the model or serial number and brand name whenever possible. You may also want to make a video or take pictures of your possessions. Do not keep this inventory in the dwelling. Store it in a safe place such as a safe deposit box.

Guidelines for Buying Homeowner's Insurance
• Make a complete inventory of household possessions.
• Photograph or video your possessions and store the photos or video off premises.
• Estimate the value of household and personal possessions. This will help you determine how much coverage to buy and, if necessary, make future claims.
• Find out the current replacement value of your home and insure it at 100 percent of that value. (Many insurance companies apply an annual inflation rate to a policy's premium to assure that the replacement value keeps pace with increasing costs.)
• Consider securing a special endorsement if household belongings and personal possessions exceed 50 percent of the value of your home.
• Consider a larger deductible to reduce premiums. A deductible can help you get maximum coverage at lowest rates for major losses if you are able to pay minor losses.
• When selecting an insurance company, ask friends, family, and coworkers for recommendations. Make sure the company is licensed by your state.
• Make sure you are receiving discounts for items such as security alarms.

Figure 26-3.   Goodheart-Willcox Publisher

Utilize this list of guidelines when buying homeowner's insurance.

Umbrella Liability Insurance

Lawsuits against individuals for negligent conduct at home or work and in automobile accidents are becoming more and more frequent. Courts have awarded large settlements in many cases. Your typical homeowners or auto insurance may not provide sufficient coverage.

Umbrella liability insurance policies are specifically designed to protect you against claims when you are liable for inappropriate actions that result in injury or property damage. They provide coverage above and beyond the amounts in your other insurance policies. If you think your existing insurance policies do not provide enough liability coverage, you may want to consider purchasing an umbrella liability insurance policy.

Health Insurance

Paying for major surgery or a long hospital stay could cause financial ruin for most people. That is why everyone needs to be covered by some form of health plan. You should consider purchasing both health and disability insurance.

Health insurance helps cover the medical expenses you may incur when you are ill or in an accident. It may cover doctor visits, hospitalization, and other services such as laboratory tests, X-rays, MRI's and medicine. The extent of your coverage will depend on the provisions of the policy you own.

When buying health insurance, check policies for exclusions and limitations on coverage. Some companies may exclude certain preexisting illnesses and treatments from their policies. Also, check the renewal conditions and cancellation clauses. Make sure you will be able to continue the policy even if you file certain claims.

Another factor to consider with health insurance is the amount of the deductible. This is the amount you must pay before the insurance company will pay a claim. Also, look for coinsurance provisions. Coinsurance requires you to pay a percentage of the medical costs after the deductible is paid. For instance, you may have to pay 20 percent of your medical expenses and the insurance company would pay 80 percent. A larger coinsurance provision will reduce the cost of your premiums.

There are various plans designed to help people deal with medical expenses not covered by their main insurance plan. For example, individuals with a high deductible insurance plan may qualify for a health savings account (HSA). In 2003, the federal government created the **health savings account (HSA)**, an account that allows individuals to set money aside on a tax-free basis to pay for future qualifying medical expenses. If the money is not used, it adds up from year to year. When you reach retirement age, you can use the money for retirement or continue to save it for medical expenses. You will have to pay taxes and possible penalties if you use the money for retirement.

Disability insurance provides regular income payments when a person is unable to work for an extended period of time because of an injury or illness. It is designed to pay you a percentage of your salary on a tax-free basis. Short-term disability is available when you are sick or injured for a few months. Long-term disability is available when you are sick or injured and permanently unable to work.

Group Health Insurance

Many people are able to get group health insurance coverage through employers, unions, or professional associations. If group health insurance is available to you, consider it carefully. Generally, group health insurance provides more coverage at a much lower cost than individual coverage. Some employers pay part or all of the costs of group health coverage.

If you have a group health insurance policy from an employer, union, or association, check to see how much coverage you have. You may have all the coverage you need. If not, you may need to purchase more insurance.

Groups can provide health insurance for their members in several different ways. They can pay premiums to insurance companies that in turn pay health care providers for their services. Some groups choose to reimburse their members directly for their medical expenses. The most common group health insurance options are fee-for-service plans, health maintenance organizations, preferred provider organizations, and point-of-service plans.

Fee-for-Service Plan

A **fee-for-service (FFS) plan** is a traditional type of health care policy that allows members to use any doctor or hospital he or she chooses. There is usually a yearly deductible amount that you must pay before coinsurance begins. Once you have met your deductible, the insurance company will then pay a percentage of the charges. Based on your coinsurance percentage, you are then responsible for paying the remaining amount. A disadvantage of this type of plan is that you will probably pay more than you would in an HMO, PPO, or POS plan.

Health Maintenance Organizations

A **health maintenance organization (HMO)** is an organization of medical personnel and facilities that provides health care services to its members. HMOs differ from traditional health insurance plans because they provide health services rather than pay medical bills. As a member of an HMO, you or your group pay a lump sum or a monthly fee. The fee usually covers the costs of many hospital and medical services.

If you need to receive medical services, you must first go to the doctor you have selected from the HMO plan. He or she will be your primary care physician. This physician coordinates all your medical treatments eligible under the insurance plan. Only the medical treatments coordinated through your primary care physician will be covered by your insurance. An exception to this may be an emergency. Even in this case, however, certain steps must be taken to have the cost of the emergency treatment covered by HMO insurance.

Depending on the policy, the cost per doctor visit ranges from no charge to a minimal fee. In many cases, treatment is handled at the HMO facility. Sometimes the HMO facility is located within a hospital and, therefore, has access to a full range of medical experts and specialized equipment. Some HMOs, however, contract with doctors in private practice to provide medical services outside the HMO facility. If it is necessary to see a specialist or enter the hospital, the patient pays only a small fee. Though HMOs provide medical care at reduced costs, you can use only those physicians who are in the HMO.

Preferred Provider Organizations

A **preferred provider organization (PPO)** is an organization that has made arrangements with doctors and hospitals who have agreed to accept lower fees for their services in providing health care for group members. Fees for medical services are usually discounted 10 to 20 percent. If you use a doctor or hospital from the approved PPO list, you pay a minimal fee. You may choose other doctors or hospitals, but the fees will be higher.

Point-of-Service Plans

A **point-of-service (POS)** plan allows members to choose either an HMO or PPO each time they seek medical services. With this plan, you are encouraged to select a primary care physician from the preferred list but you are not required to do so. However, the cost of services will be higher if you do not choose a primary physician from the preferred list. POS plans are becoming more popular because they provide more options than an HMO when choosing medical care.

Life Insurance

Life insurance protects against the loss of income due to death. The main purpose of life insurance is to provide income for anyone who depends on it, such as a spouse, children, or elderly parents. If you do not have any dependents, you may not need life insurance.

When a life insurance policyholder dies, the insurance company pays the face value of the policy to the beneficiary. The **beneficiary** is the person named by the policyholder to receive the benefits, or payments, issued from the insurance policy.

The amount of life insurance a policyholder should buy requires careful consideration. For instance, the amount of income that would be lost if the policyholder died prematurely should be considered. Social Security benefits, savings, investments, and other sources of income should be determined. The financial needs of the survivors must then be taken into consideration. The policyholder must determine how much money would be needed by his or her survivors to maintain their standard of living.

These factors and others need to be analyzed to determine the amount of protection needed. Once an amount is determined, a person can then decide which of the following basic types of life insurance to buy: whole life, term, or universal life insurance. Each type of life insurance is available in different forms and combinations with different benefits.

Life insurance provides payments to beneficiaries in the event of death.

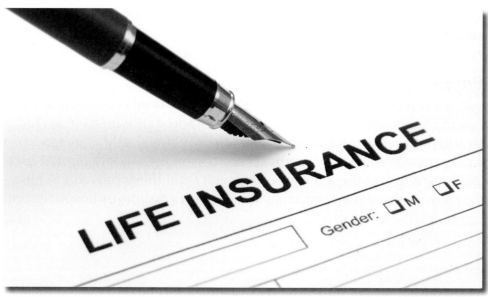

alexskopje/Shutterstock.com

Whole Life Insurance

Whole life insurance covers the policyholder for a lifetime. It can also be a form of savings. As the policyholder pays premiums, the policy builds cash value. **Cash value** is the amount the policy is worth in cash upon surrender of the policy. The policyholder can borrow against this cash value or collect the cash value if the policy is canceled. Therefore, a whole life policy pays benefits when the policyholder dies or when the policyholder turns it in for its cash value.

When choosing whole life policies, policyholders have two basic options. They may choose a straight life policy or a limited payment policy. With a straight life policy, the policyholder pays premiums throughout his or her life. With a limited payment policy, the policyholder pays higher premiums, but for a limited number of years. By paying higher premiums, the policyholder can buy whole life protection in a certain number of years and still receive coverage for life.

Endowment insurance is a form of whole life insurance in which payments are limited to a set period of time—usually 10, 20, or 30 years. At the end of that time period, the cash value of the policy is paid to the policyholder. If the policyholder should die before the end of the endowment period, the death benefit is paid to the beneficiary. Premiums are higher on endowment policies because the cash value builds up faster.

Term Insurance

Term insurance covers the policyholder for a set period of 5, 10, or 20 years, or whatever term is specified in the policy. This type of life insurance is simply for protection; it builds no cash value. It pays benefits only if the policyholder dies during the term of the policy. That is why premiums for term insurance are lower than those for whole life insurance. Many people consider term insurance to be a better investment than whole life insurance because of this lower cost. They would recommend investing the difference in premiums in a good mutual fund. This could result in a greater return on your money.

When choosing term insurance, policyholders should check to see if a term policy is renewable and convertible. A renewable privilege allows the policyholder to renew the policy at standard rates, regardless of any changes in health. Without this privilege, the policyholder would not be able to renew the policy at regular rates if his or her health declines. A term policy with a convertible option lets the policyholder switch from term insurance to whole life insurance at standard rates, regardless of the state of his or her health.

Case

Myles's Big Mistake

Myles was proud of the improvements he made to his late model used car. He had spent a great deal of money and time improving the body and the engine, both of which were abused by the previous owner. Unfortunately, this took most of his extra money. For car insurance, he could only afford a policy that provided the minimum liability required by state law.

While driving one night, Myles saw the lights of an oncoming car cross the centerline. The car was coming directly at him. He swerved to the right to avoid a collision, and his right fender struck a tree. The car continued its forward motion until it hit another tree.

Myles was taken to a hospital emergency room where he was treated for a broken arm, cuts, and bruises. His parent's family health insurance paid his medical bills.

Myles later went to his insurance agent to see about his damaged car. He was told that his car was not covered and the insurance company owed him nothing.

"You don't have collision insurance," his agent explained. "If you remember, I tried to convince you to include collision coverage with the cost of a $300 deductible, but you said you couldn't afford it. Your policy does not cover the towing charges either."

Myles was angry with himself. He wondered how he could have been so stupid. He did not have enough money to repair his car, and it could not be driven in its current condition. It had a badly damaged grill, radiator, lights, fenders, and front end. Now he had no way to get to work, except to rely on his parents and friends until he could afford another car.

Critical Thinking

1. What auto insurance coverage should Myles have purchased?
2. What is the advantage of a deductible?
3. What factors should be considered when determining a policy's deductible?

Universal Life Insurance

In recent years, a third type of life insurance has gained in popularity. **Universal life insurance** combines death benefits, similar to term insurance, with a savings and investment account that earns current market rates. This form of insurance also allows more flexibility in the amount and frequency of the premium payments as well as the level of protection. Interest earnings keep pace with market rates and are taxed only when you cash in the policy. Interest rates can be no lower than a guaranteed minimum rate specified in the policy.

Checkpoint 26.2

1. Name the four types of insurance you are likely to need during your lifetime.
2. What is no-fault automobile insurance?
3. Describe the two types of property coverage provided by a homeowners insurance policy.
4. What is the purpose of a liability insurance policy?
5. What are the three basic types of life insurance?

Build Your Vocabulary

As you progress through this text, develop a personal glossary of career-related terms and add it to your portfolio. This will help build your vocabulary and prepare you for your career of choice. Write a definition for each of the following terms, and add it to your personal career glossary.

bodily injury liability
property damage liability
deductible
claim
health savings account (HSA)
disability insurance
fee-for-service (FFS) plan
health maintenance organization (HMO)
preferred provider organization (PPO)
point-of-service (POS) plan
beneficiary
whole life insurance
cash value
term insurance
universal life insurance

Chapter Summary

Section 26.1 Managing Risk

- Responsible consumers understand the need for insurance. People need insurance to protect themselves from unexpected financial losses.
- Choosing the right company and agent is very important. When selecting an insurance company and agent, an individual should consider their insurance needs, the reputation of the company, and the experience of the agent.
- Workers should consider employer-sponsored insurance programs when evaluating job offers. Employers' insurance packages can vary a great deal.

Section 26.2 Types of Insurance

- Property and casualty insurance includes automobile, homeowners, and renters insurance. Homeowners and renters should obtain insurance to protect their personal property. Homeowners and renters insurance can include property and liability protection. The age of the driver, the distance driven, and the type of car usually influence the cost of automobile insurance.
- Because of the high cost of health care, everyone should consider the need for health insurance. An FFS, HMO, PPO and POS are the most common types of health insurance.
- Life insurance provides for the financial needs of dependents if the policyholder dies. Various types of coverage include universal life insurance, term life insurance, and whole life insurance.

Check Your Career IQ

Now that you have finished the chapter, see what you learned about careers by taking the chapter posttest. The test can be accessed on the mobile site by using a smartphone or on the G-W Learning companion website.

www.m.g-wlearning.com

www.g-wlearning.com

Review Your Knowledge

1. When do most states require a person to obtain insurance protection?
2. What expenses and damages are covered by underinsured motorist insurance?
3. Name and describe the four group health insurance plans.
4. What is endowment insurance?
5. What is the main reason for having life insurance?
6. How does whole life insurance differ from term life insurance?
7. Why should you consider buying all or most of your insurance from the same insurance company?
8. Explain how the cost of one's premium is affected when a higher deductible is selected.
9. What are three tips recommended to help reduce one's health insurance costs?
10. What can homeowners do to reduce the cost of homeowners insurance?

Apply Your Knowledge

1. Pick one type of insurance and research the options offered by different companies. Calculate the differences in price and benefits. Decide which company offers an overall advantage. Create a presentation based on your findings.
2. Research famous disasters such as the Chicago fire of 1871, the Johnstown flood of 1889, and the San Francisco earthquake of 1906. Find estimates in dollar amounts of how much property damage was caused by these events. How do the insurance claims for these disasters compare today to those caused by more recent events, such as Superstorm Sandy? Write a brief report of your findings.
3. Research the three types of life insurance discussed in this chapter. Create a chart listing the differences in cost, advantages, and disadvantages of each type of life insurance. Share your chart with the class.
4. Create an outline of this chapter. Be sure to include any major ideas and vocabulary. As you study, use the outline to help you recall important information from the chapter.
5. At three different insurance companies, compare insurance costs for a new car and a used car (five years or older) of the same model based on the same coverage. Report to the class how insurance rates for a new and used car differed at each company.
6. Obtain copies of life insurance policies from three or four different insurance companies. Compare coverage, benefits, options, premiums, and claim procedures.
7. Do you think an insurer should be permitted to vary premiums by the risk presented? For example, is it fair to charge a rural homeowner more for homeowners insurance than a city dweller? Explain your answer.

8. Imagine your life 15 years from now. Describe what it would be like and what risks may come with your lifestyle. What insurance product might you buy? Explain your answer.

9. Visit your state's department of insurance website. List the types of information you can gather about insurers that do business in your state.

10. Create a spreadsheet listing your personal possessions. Be sure to include the item name, how much it cost, when you purchased it, and where the item was purchased. Include the model or serial number and brand name. Use the form to complete an up-to-date inventory of your possessions. Then, use a camera to make a visual record of your possessions.

Teamwork

Working with three classmates, determine which is a better buy—whole life insurance or term insurance. Decide with your teammates how to divide the following tasks. Visit an insurance agent and determine the premium costs of a whole life insurance policy and a 20-year term life policy for the same amount of coverage. Compare the interest you might earn after 20 years if you invested the difference in premium costs in a straight savings account, a certificate of deposit, or a mutual fund. Visit a bank or other type of lending institution and determine current interest rates for each type of investment. At the end of the 20-year period, which of the four investment strategies (whole life, term plus savings, term plus certificate of deposit, term plus mutual fund) will have the greatest value? Summarize your findings in a brief oral report. Be sure to cover the advantages and disadvantages of each type of investment.

Common Core

College and Career Readiness

Speaking. Create a presentation about current trends in insurance using your choice of digital media. Include information that describes these trends as well as the outlook for the insurance industry. Use examples that will enhance understanding and add interest to your presentation. Present your findings to the class.

Listening. As your classmates make their presentations on the current trends in insurance, evaluate each presenter. Review the presenter's point of view and use of digital media. Was the presentation effective?

Apply Your Technology Skills

Access the G-W Learning companion website for this text at www.g-wlearning.com. Download the data file for this chapter. Follow the instructions to complete activities to practice what you have learned.

Data File 26–1—**Researching Health Insurance**

College and Career Readiness Portfolio

College and Career Readiness

You have collected various items for your portfolio in earlier activities. Now organize the materials in your print portfolio. Your instructor may have examples of portfolios that you can review for ideas. You can also search the Internet for articles about how to organize a print portfolio. You should provide a table of contents for the items. This will allow the person reviewing the portfolio to find items easily. Keep separate the sections of the portfolio that are for your use only, such as your contacts database and sample interview answers. You should continue to add and remove documents as you complete assignments or gain new skills. Update the table of contents when you make changes to the portfolio.

1. Review the documents you have collected. Select the ones you want to include in your career portfolio. Make copies of certificates, diplomas, and other important documents. Keep the originals in a safe place.
2. Create the table of contents. You also may want to create a title page for each section.
3. Place the items in a binder, notebook, or other container.

Section 27.1
Family

Section 27.2
Citizenship

**College
and Career
Readiness**

Reading Prep. As you read the chapter, determine the point of view or purpose of the author. What aspects of the text help to establish the purpose or point of view?

Introduction

A role is a pattern of expected behavior. When you first entered school, you began the process of balancing two different roles—student and family member. Once you enter the workforce, you add the new role of employee. This role divides your time and energy with the other two roles. As you mature, you will continue to add a variety of new roles and responsibilities related to family, work, and citizenship. How well you balance your priorities, time, and energy will have a great impact on how successful you will be in each of these important aspects of your life.

Check Your Career IQ

Before you begin the chapter, see what you already know about careers by taking the chapter pretest. Use the related QR code to view the pretest on the mobile site. If you do not have a smartphone, visit the G-W Learning companion website to access the pretest.

www.m.g-wlearning.com
www.g-wlearning.com

G-W Mobile

Career Snapshot
Computer Programmer

What Does a Computer Programmer Do?

Computer programmers write code to create software applications using specific programming languages. The software applications may involve computer games, business applications, and operating systems. Programmers often find and resolve program errors within programs. Programmers must:

- have an in-depth understanding of computer languages such as C++ and Python;
- repair and update existing programs; and
- assist computer operators in resolving problems.

What Is It Like to Work as a Computer Programmer?

Programmers usually work a forty-hour week in clean, comfortable offices although many work from home. They may be subject to heath issues related to spending long hours on the computer. These include eyestrain, back problems, and carpal tunnel. They usually work alone but may work with others on large projects.

What Education and Skills Are Needed to Be a Computer Programmer?

- two-year degree or certificate
- bachelor degree preferred
- studies in computer science, mathematics, or information systems
- analytical and troubleshooting skills
- detail orientated

AlenaRoot/Shutterstock.com

27.1 Family

Objectives

After completing this section, you will be able to:
- **Explain** your responsibilities in the role of family member.
- **Describe** several strategies for balancing family and work roles.
- **List** factors that contribute to a family-friendly workplace.

Understanding Family Roles

In the future, you may think about starting a family. Your role as family member will often be more complex and difficult than your work role. It may also be more rewarding. It is definitely more important. How well you perform as a family member is determined primarily by your commitment to your family and the importance you place on that commitment.

Throughout your lifetime, you will play a number of different roles as a member of different families. You began in the self-centered role of a small child. As you grew, you took on more responsibilities for your own care and the care of others. When you become independent, you may take on additional roles, such as wife, mother, husband, or father. You may also take on responsibilities in extended families, such as that of son-in-law or daughter-in-law.

Each of these family roles involves building effective relationships with other family members. Having a role as a family member also means sharing the responsibility for maintaining the home and using leisure time effectively.

Building Relationships

Successful families are built on successful relationships. These relationships involve love, trust, and mutual respect. They begin with honesty and commitment.

Honesty has two sides. It involves being honest with yourself and with those around you. Being honest with yourself can be very difficult. Sometimes it is too easy to make excuses for your behavior. You may tell other family members you did not do your share of housework because you were too tired after working all day. However, you know the real reason was that you could not motivate yourself to do it. There were other things you wanted to do more. Making excuses can become a habit and lead to a continual pattern of failure.

A *commitment* is a promise you make to yourself or to others. Commitment means taking care of your duties and responsibilities. A commitment can be as small as agreeing to take out the garbage or as important as taking marriage vows. Keeping your commitments, both large and small, is very important. If people know you honor your commitments, they are more likely to believe and trust you. To build strong relationships with your family, friends, and coworkers, it is very important for you to follow through with your commitments.

Maintaining the Home

Everyone benefits from a well-kept home. That is the primary reason everyone should contribute to its maintenance to the best of his or her ability.

Maintaining a home involves a variety of responsibilities. There are the physical tasks of preparing meals, keeping the home clean, and making routine repairs. There are also the financial responsibilities of developing and maintaining a household budget. If you are sharing your house or apartment with someone else, these should become shared responsibilities.

It is very important to reach an agreement on who will handle each responsibility. It is also important to establish a spirit of cooperation. There will be times when you will need to help finish tasks assigned to another family member.

This spirit of cooperation becomes even more important in families where all adult members work outside the home. Because work schedules vary, it may be best for each person to share in cleaning, cooking, and home maintenance as his or her schedule allows.

It also becomes very important for younger members to participate. Children may take on responsibilities that have previously been handled by adults. Careful consideration must be given to the age and maturity of the child when this is done.

A good team effectively uses the time and talents of each member to pursue a common goal. As in the workplace, a team approach may be the best way to decide how to distribute household responsibilities. Household members could meet on a weekly basis to review the necessary tasks and a plan for completing them. Both household and outside responsibilities would need to be considered.

Go Green

Americans generate almost twice as much trash per person as most other major countries. Most of this trash goes into landfills which can cause major environmental problems. Landfills often produce toxic emissions that pollute the air we breathe and the water we drink. Recycling can greatly reduce the amount of material we send to landfills. You can help the environment by recycling plastic bottles and paper products. Use rechargeable batteries, and instead of throwing them into the trash, reuse plastic bags.

Then assignments for each person could be determined based on information provided to the group. Individuals who share in this type of decision-making process are more likely to take ownership of their responsibilities. **Ownership** is when an individual understands the importance of a task and makes sure it is done well.

Using Leisure Time Effectively

How effectively you use your leisure time affects your family and the quality of your life. As a teen, you enjoy some leisure time apart from your family. As an adult, however, your leisure time will probably revolve around your family.

An important part of maintaining a balanced lifestyle is how well you use your leisure time. An overemphasis on work can lead to burnout at home and on the job. **Burnout** is a loss of physical and emotional strength and motivation. Some job behaviors that may result from burnout include tardiness, absenteeism, low productivity, irritability, and fatigue.

Signs of burnout include low productivity, fatigue, and irritability.

Supri Suharjoto/Shutterstock.com

Burnout can also strain family relationships. To prevent it, individuals must allow time in their schedule for a balance of restful and active leisure pursuits with the family. Balancing your leisure time well keeps you refreshed. It helps you maintain good family relationships. It also helps you be more productive on the job.

Balancing Family and Work Roles

A meaningful and happy family life does not just happen. It takes the effort and sacrifice of all family members. There are times when your commitment to your family may affect the quality of your work or that of your partner's. A sick child may need attention on the same day an important project is due at work. Do you help the child or finish the project at work? Which is more important to you? How can you effectively handle both?

If you are not careful, work can overwhelm you. Important deadlines or the need to work overtime may be more pressing than family matters. In other cases, the problems at work may be brought home and affect your family relationships. Sometimes it is possible to become trapped in a job you hate and bring your negative attitudes home with you. There will also be times when a problem at home may affect your ability to concentrate at work.

Meeting both the demands of family and work can be very challenging, especially when both heads of the household work outside the home. Single parents who manage all of the household responsibilities feel intense stress, too. If you can manage your time well, balancing family and work roles will be easier.

Managing Your Time

A key strategy for balancing family and work roles is managing your time. Time management is the ability to plan and use time well. It involves organizing your daily schedule so everything important gets done.

Ethical Leadership

Openness

"Always be who you are, and say what you feel, because people who mind don't matter, and people who matter don't mind."—Dr. Seuss

You expect your employer to be open with you and say what is on her mind. She should be able to expect the same of you. You may have felt your boss has been unfairly critical of your performance. However, you have not had the courage to tell her how you feel. Instead, you often make fun of her in front of your friends and coworkers. This type of behavior is unethical and may result in your friends thinking less of you.

No one system works for everyone. As you schedule your time, you will find that some strategies work, and others do not. The following strategies have proven effective for many people in developing and implementing time-management plans. They include setting goals, making to-do lists, and staying focused.

Set Goals

An important key to managing time is deciding what is important to you. There are only 24 hours in the day, so you cannot possibly do everything. First, ask yourself some important questions. Where do you see yourself 5, 10, or 20 years from now? What do you plan to do with your life? What is the relative importance of work, family, and friends in your life? Answers to these questions will help you establish your goals.

Goals help you focus on where you want to be, not on how to get there. For example, you might establish an occupational goal of owning and operating an engine repair shop by the time you are 30 years old. You can then focus your time and effort on what is really important for accomplishing that goal. The tasks you consider important become your priorities.

Make To-Do Lists

To get yourself organized for each day, you begin by seeing what needs to be done to meet coming deadlines. What must absolutely be done today? What should you do today to be prepared for tomorrow? What project needs to be started today to meet a deadline later? An appointment calendar will help you do this. An appointment calendar provides space for hour-by-hour listings of things you need to do each day. For example, you can list when class assignments are due and the dates and times of school or work meetings. You can also list any social and medical appointments you may have. Appointment calendars are available in print or electronic formats. Many smartphones include a calendar application. This allows you to easily keep track of your appointments as you move through your day.

The calendar becomes the starting point for your to-do list. Use it to develop a list of all the things you need to accomplish. Then, add any other important items that may have been omitted from your calendar. You may want to develop separate lists for school, home, and work. Once you have your list(s) developed, identify the most important items. You can do this by numbering them in order of priority.

It is a good idea to work on tasks in their numbered order and finish each before going to the next. Check off each item as you complete it. This gives you a feeling of accomplishment and encourages you to do more. At the end of the day, it is very rewarding to see all the items you have been able to check off. This system is ideal when working with a short list (about a dozen items) or when each item must be accomplished in a specific order.

Some individuals have dozens of daily tasks, so they use a simpler, four-number system. Must-do tasks are identified with a one; the do-next tasks are identified with a two; the should-do tasks are identified with a three; and the remaining tasks, which are of less importance, are identified with a four. This simplifies the process of prioritizing tasks and allows more flexibility in deciding what to do next. Tasks labeled with a three or four can wait until tomorrow, but eventually they become the most important tasks to be completed. This type of system is especially helpful when you have many tasks to do of similar priority that can be done in any order.

Determine your most productive time of day and schedule your work accordingly. For example, try to do the difficult, unpleasant, or urgent work at your most productive time of day. Some people enjoy getting up early and doing challenging work in the morning. Others prefer to work in the afternoon or late into the evening. You will accomplish more if you schedule tasks during your most productive hours whenever possible.

Stay Focused

Having a set of goals and a to-do list is very important, but distractions can destroy your best intentions. Do you telephone a friend to chat when you should be doing your laundry instead? If you are completely honest, you will know when you are not applying yourself. To help stay focused, use the following tips shown in Figure 27-1.

If surfing the Internet takes time away from getting things accomplished, stay off the Internet. If you have an unpleasant or difficult task, handle it as soon as possible. Do not procrastinate, or avoid completing an important task by doing other things. In that way, the unpleasant feelings you have about the task are brief and quickly replaced by satisfaction in getting the job done. Setting realistic deadlines and setting priorities will help you to avoid time-wasting activities.

It is understandable that you do not always feel like studying. However, if you recognize the importance of each class and each grade to your overall career goal, you will have more desire to study. Keeping "the big picture" in mind will increase your motivation level.

Very rarely are people able to do everything they want to do and need to do. You have many important demands on your time. Nevertheless, do not try to do everything. Learn to say no to requests for which you do not have time.

Tips to Stay Focused

- Identify time-wasters and try to avoid them.
- Avoid postponing unpleasant work.
- Set realistic deadlines.
- Stay motivated by keeping your goals in mind.
- Be flexible.

iQoncept/Shutterstock.com

Figure 27-1.   *Goodheart-Willcox Publisher*
When managing your time wisely, use these tips to stay focused.

As you try to stay focused and manage your time well, you will notice that some days are more productive than others. You should not feel guilty if you have tried your best. Learn from your successes and failures, and make adjustments to your plan accordingly.

Using Community Resources

There may be occasions when, in spite of your best efforts, you will not be able to handle all your responsibilities. Often this is the case in families with members who need special care. Small children need special care, as do some older children with special needs. Adult family members with limited physical or mental ability may also need special care and attention.

A number of community-based services and programs can be used to respond to the needs of the modern family. Help can be arranged through the efforts of concerned individuals. In addition, there are many low-cost community programs to use as well as private services that provide help.

Personal Support Systems

Practically every community has neighbors who are willing to help you in exchange for your helping them on occasion. Perhaps relatives live nearby and can assist, too. This group of caring, concerned friends, and relatives is called a **support system**. A support system can be formed through the efforts of friends and neighbors, community service programs, and even local businesses.

A support system can be as simple as being a good neighbor. For example, you ask your neighbors to check your ailing parent during the day when you are at work. In return, you watch their son for an hour each day until his older sister comes home from school. Several supportive families working together can form a network of care that makes family challenges easier to handle.

Community Programs

Many times, there are community programs and events designed around the special interests and needs of children, teens, and older adults. For children and teens, there are after-school and weekend programs devoted to crafts, sports, and games. For older, retired adults, there are daytime workshops, lectures, tours, exercise programs, and other events.

These programs may be available through local park districts and recreation departments. Tax-supported community service agencies and private nonprofit groups also provide similar programs. You can take advantage of free or low-cost ways to benefit your family when you know what your community offers. When family members are occupied, you can devote attention to other matters. To learn all the programs and events available in your community, read the local newspaper and contact your local government office.

Extended Programs in School

The length of the normal workday plus commuting time is much longer than an average school day. As a result, some parents leave children home alone for a period before and after school. Since this is not a safe situation for young children, schools and communities are addressing the problem. One answer is extended programs offered by schools.

Some public and private schools are open for several hours before and after school to provide a safe place for children who have no adult at home. During this time, children can do homework or participate in recreational activities. Children can also choose to attend special programs such as foreign language instruction. Extended school programs are usually available full-time on weekdays during summers and holidays.

Care Centers and Professional Help

For families that need more or specialized assistance, there are centers to help. Childcare centers provide all-day care for preschool children. For school-age children, the centers provide supervision before and after school. There are elder-care centers, too. These generally provide hourly, daytime, and 24-hour care.

Before using a care center, learn about its reputation in the community. What services does it provide? What are the costs? What will the center expect of you when a family member is enrolled? Compare what different centers offer in terms of programs, price, and convenience to you.

Day of the Event

You have practiced all year for this competition, and now you are ready. Whether it is for an objective test, written test, report, or presentation, you have done your homework and are ready to shine. To prepare for the day of the event, complete the following activities.

1. Be sure to get plenty of sleep the night before the event so that you are rested and ready to go.
2. Use your event checklist before you go into the presentation so that you do not forget any of your materials that are needed for the event.
3. Arrive early for the competition. If you are late and the door is closed, you will be disqualified.
4. If you are making a presentation before a panel of judges, practice what you are going to say when you are called to speak. State your name, your school, and any other information that has been requested. Be confident, smile, and make eye contact with the judges.
5. When the event is finished, thank the judges for their time.

If you need a more specialized type of care arrangement, individuals can provide professional care in your home. Private care can be arranged for children as well as adults. This care can be scheduled for certain hours on certain days or for 24-hour periods. As with other types of care, you will want to check the service thoroughly before using it. You will also want to see if a similar service is offered at a more affordable cost through a government agency or nonprofit group.

Family-Friendly Workplace

An employee who is worried about a family member cannot do a good job at work. Family emergencies may cause an employee to arrive late or miss full days of work. If the family problem persists, workers are sometimes forced to resign and find jobs that allow more flexible schedules.

Some employers believe that the demands of work should always come ahead of family demands. However, some employers know that finding ways to help employees balance their many roles and stay employed makes good business sense. It is very costly to hire and train new employees to fill the jobs left vacant by experienced workers who leave. In the long run, programs that provide options for handling family matters are a relatively small business expense.

The cost-effectiveness of family-friendly programs has been well documented. Companies that offer the programs tend to attract the most talented and productive workers, too. Because of this record of success, many employers are voluntarily implementing family-friendly programs and policies. To make sure most workers are offered some flexibility in handling family responsibilities, a law provides workers with some guarantees.

Family and Medical Leave Act

The **Family and Medical Leave Act (FMLA)** passed in 1993 was designed to help families handle special family matters by permitting employees to take time off without pay. The law is intended to help preserve the stability and economic security of the family. The FMLA applies to all public agencies, public and private elementary and secondary schools, and companies with 50 or more employees.

Families with young children are not the only beneficiaries of this law. Many employees use an FMLA leave to provide care to an aging parent or sick spouse. Under this law, employees are entitled to take up to 12 weeks off during any 12 months for the reasons shown in Figure 27-2. In 2008, the FMLA was amended to add care for a seriously injured or ill family member of the Armed Forces. FMLA leave allows members of the Armed Forces to take up to 26 weeks off without pay in a 12-month period instead of 12 weeks. When employees return from an FMLA leave, they are entitled to their same jobs or an equivalent one with the same level of pay, benefits, and responsibilities.

Provisions of the Family and Medical Leave Act
If your employer has 50 or more employees, you are entitled to take up to 12 weeks off without pay during any 12 months for the following reasons:
• Having and caring for a baby
• Adopting a child or adding a foster child to the family
• Caring for a sick child, spouse, or parent
• Being unable to work because of serious illness
You are entitled to take up to 26 weeks off without pay during any 12 months for the following reason:
• Caring for a seriously injured or ill family member of the Armed Forces

Figure 27-2.   *Goodheart-Willcox Publisher*
Workers can take an unpaid leave from their jobs for these family-related reasons.

Family-Friendly Benefits and Policies

Family-friendly programs evolved as companies listened to workers' concerns and tried different approaches to address them. This has resulted in work arrangements such as flextime, job sharing, and telecommuting. Special programs and services are also being developed to help with childcare and other home responsibilities.

Work Arrangements

Factory work and assembly line jobs require all workers to stay at their workstations during the posted work hours. Many of today's jobs dealing with information or ideas no longer need to have workers stay in one place or maintain identical work schedules. Because the nature of work itself is changing, so is the way people work. Here are three types of work arrangements that you may experience in the workplace.

Flextime is a schedule where a worker's time of arrival and departure differs from the operating hours of the workplace. For example, a worker may begin work each day at 11:00 AM and end work at 7:00 PM. Workers have certain days or "core" hours when they must be at the work site. This type of scheduling allows employees to balance family and work roles more effectively. Workers can be with their children for that important concert, parent conference, or sports event and still attend important meetings at work.

Job sharing is when a single job is split between two or more employees. For example, one person may work four hours in the morning while the other works at the same job for the same number of hours in the afternoon. Normally, both employees receive reduced company benefits. This type of program enables individuals to earn an income and stay up-to-date in their field while devoting considerable time to personal or family matters.

Working outside of the place a business is another type of work arrangements. Some employers find that workers who are remote accomplish more in an eight- hour day than the worker in the office. Remote workers have fewer distractions and allow them to remain focused on the task at hand. In addition, working remotely cuts down on travel time.

Employer-Sponsored Services

There are a wide variety of services offered by employers to help workers balance their work and family roles. Many of these services help workers with small children. Others help workers with other concerns, such as finding ways to spend more time with their families.

The problems of offering quality childcare affect both the employer and employee. The quality and quantity of work may suffer if a worker is concerned about the well-being of a child or must take time off for a doctor visit. As a result, employers now offer a variety of options for the care of their employees' children.

Some employers operate childcare centers at or near the company. Sometimes several employers work together to provide childcare at a jointly operated center. These centers provide care for preschoolers and may also serve school-age children before and after school and during vacations. The centers provide cribs, toys, play areas, food, medical services, and professionally trained childcare workers. Employees are encouraged to visit their children during work breaks and mealtimes. These centers may also provide emergency care when an employee's regular child care arrangements fall through.

Some employers provide financial support for child care through a voucher system. With such a system, the employee is reimbursed by the employer for all or a portion of the child care costs. This gives employees control over the type and quality of child care they use.

Many employers recognize the importance of balancing family and work.

Brian A Jackson/Shutterstock.com

A *Federal Flexible Spending Account (FSA)* is another program designed to provide childcare assistance. Employees who participate in this program have a regular deduction taken from their paycheck. This amount is then placed in a special fund to pay for child care. As the employee pays for child care expenses, a request for reimbursements from these funds is made. An advantage of this system is that neither the employee nor the employer are taxed on the money set aside and spent for child care. (A separate FSA can be set up to cover medical expenses not covered by your health insurance.) A disadvantage of this program is that you forfeit any money you do not use during the benefit period.

A shortage of openings in childcare centers has resulted from the increased demand for quality care. As a result, some employers guarantee slots at private centers. This ensures that employees will have a place to send their children. The employee still pays for the childcare, but the employer picks up the cost of guaranteeing any unfilled spaces.

Although not a direct childcare service, many companies offer seminars and workshops on skills related to parenting. These programs help employees learn to balance family and work responsibilities. Program topics include selecting a quality care facility and managing childcare finances.

For employees with personal problems, a variety of employee counseling programs are available. These programs address issues such as emotional health, substance abuse, marital conflict, and financial problems. The goal is to help employees so they can more easily handle routine work and family challenges.

The growing dilemma of finding elder care is a relatively new issue for today's workers and one that employers have generally not started to address. A 12-week FMLA leave, flextime, job sharing, and telecommuting are the general options open to workers dealing with a sick or aging parent. Some predict that future family-friendly programs for employees' parents will offer almost as much variety as today's selection of childcare programs.

Being an Entrepreneur

Most entrepreneurs begin their businesses by working from home. As the boss of a home-based business, he or she enjoys control over how to balance work and family responsibilities. Since entrepreneurs work for themselves, they can divide their time between family and work according to whatever best suits them.

Checkpoint 27.1

1. What are the three basic responsibilities associated with the role of family member?
2. Name three strategies to manage time wisely.
3. List two tips to stay focused.
4. How does flextime differ from job sharing?
5. Describe how the Federal Flexible Spending Account (FSA) works.

Build Your Vocabulary

As you progress through this text, develop a personal glossary of career-related terms and add it to your portfolio. This will help build your vocabulary and prepare you for your career of choice. Write a definition for each of the following terms, and add it to your personal career glossary.

ownership
burnout
procrastinate
support system
Family and Medical Leave Act (FMLA)
flextime
job sharing

Citizenship Responsibilities

When you get a job and become a wage earner, you become a productive member of the economy. There are additional responsibilities to being a good citizen, however. Learning about your rights, responsibilities, and privileges will help you assume your role as a citizen.

Community Involvement

One way to measure the success of a democracy is the involvement of its citizens. Keeping communities clean and citizens safe requires the cooperation and work of many people. Some workers are employed by the government and paid through tax revenue. However, there is always more work to do. Much of this work is taken on by volunteers. Some groups that use volunteer help are listed below.

- **Park and recreation departments.** People from these departments help supervise children's activities, help with cleanup projects that beautify the neighborhood, or serve as a craft instructor.
- **Local hospitals.** Volunteers help run errands, read to patients, and deliver their food.
- **Community service agencies.** Individuals from these groups help with office work, help build homes for needy families, or babysit the children of adult volunteers.
- **Local churches and food pantries.** Volunteers from these organizations assist with collecting, storing, and distributing food to needy families.

Community involvement can also be measured in less formal ways. You do not need to find a group to demonstrate community involvement. Look around your immediate neighborhood and see what needs to be done.

One way to exercise good citizenship is to volunteer to assist with a community project.

mangostock/Shutterstock.com

Does an older neighbor's lawn need mowing? Does a person without transportation need help with an errand? Does a youngster on your street need tutoring in math? Did someone carelessly toss candy wrappers in the street that you could pick up?

Besides helping your immediate neighborhood, there are many charity fundraisers and community programs that would benefit from your involvement. The extent of your volunteer work depends on how much time you can devote. During some periods in your life, you will have less time than others. It is important to remember, however, that success can be measured in many ways. Often what you give in your volunteer work is more personally rewarding than what you receive.

Voting

In some countries, citizens have no control over who governs them. In the United States, however, citizens can choose who their leaders will be. They do this by voting for political candidates. Elected candidates are responsible for passing laws that are used to govern the people. By helping to elect certain candidates, voters help determine what types of laws will be passed. Voters are also given the opportunity to vote directly for or against laws from time to time.

In order to vote in the United States, you must register. This simply means adding your name to the list of people who are allowed to vote. You must be a citizen and at least 18 years of age to register. You can register at the offices of the county commissioner, election supervisor, municipal clerk, or, in some states, the department of motor vehicles.

As a registered voter, you need to be aware of current issues and how political candidates view these issues. This will allow you to make informed decisions when you vote. You can cast your ballot for candidates who view issues as you do. You can vote for laws and candidates that will most benefit you and your community. One of the best ways to stay informed is to follow newspaper, social media, television, and radio reports. Volunteering to work for a candidate is another way to learn more about the issues.

As a voter, you have the opportunity to elect leaders on three levels—local, state, and national. Mayors often head local governments. Trustees or city council members may also be elected to represent people locally. Governors are elected to lead states. State senators and representatives are elected to serve on state legislatures. The president of the United States heads the federal government. Representatives and senators are elected from each state to serve as members of the US Congress.

US Legal System

Government officials pass laws on the local, state, and national level. Laws are written and enforced to help people live in harmony with each other. They are established to protect the safety and rights of individuals as well as society as a whole. As a citizen, it is important to become aware of the many laws that may affect you.

The US Constitution and the constitution of each of the 50 states are the foundations on which all laws are based. These constitutions describe how governments are to be organized. Any new law enacted by local, state, or federal governments must not go against the state or federal constitutions. If a law does not agree with these constitutions, it can be challenged in court. If declared unconstitutional, it cannot be enforced.

Within the US legal system, there are two major categories of law—civil and criminal. **Criminal law** governs the association between citizens and the government. **Civil law** outlines citizens' rights in relation to one another.

Criminal Law

A crime committed under criminal law is an offense against the public or the state. Crimes are generally classified according to their degree of seriousness. A **felony** is considered the most serious type of crime. It is punishable by imprisonment or even death. Murder, kidnapping, armed robbery, arson, and other such offenses are felonies. A **misdemeanor**, such as disorderly conduct or speeding, is a less serious crime. Penalties for a misdemeanor are a fine or imprisonment of a year or less or both.

Being convicted of a crime is very serious. In addition to being fined or ordered to serve a prison sentence, a crime conviction creates a criminal record. A criminal record can negatively affect a person's future. For instance, a convicted felon might have a difficult time getting a job.

Case

Del's Day in Court

When Del graduated from high school, he interviewed for a job as a lifeguard at a summer camp. The camp director, Mr. Stintsen, liked Del and hired him.

During the interview, Del told Mr. Stintsen he would be leaving to go to college in mid-August. However, when the time came for Del to leave, Mr. Stintsen became angry. He did not want Del to leave before the camp closed for the year. Mr. Stintsen decided to show his displeasure by failing to send Del his final paycheck.

Del called Mr. Stintsen several times and sent him a letter asking for the money. However, Mr. Stintsen refused to pay.

Del didn't have a lot of time and money to spend, but he wanted to get what he was owed. His mother suggested that Del take his case to small claims court since the unpaid wages totaled less than $500. She said the court fees would be only a few dollars and Del wouldn't need a lawyer. She also said that it would probably take only a few weeks until the case would be heard.

Del took his mother's advice. He summoned Mr. Stintsen, and when his court date arrived, they both appeared before a judge. Del explained the situation and showed the judge a copy of the letter he had sent Mr. Stintsen. Mr. Stintsen also gave his side of the story, but the judge found in Del's favor. He ordered Mr. Stintsen to pay Del the wages he was due.

Critical Thinking

1. Do you think Del made the right decision to take his case to small claims court? Explain.
2. What do you think would have happened if Del had not taken his case to court?
3. What other steps might Del have taken to get his money?

Civil Law

The laws that cover property transactions and agreements between people or groups are *civil laws*. The issues covered by civil law include contracts, real estate sales, divorces, child custody cases, personal injury lawsuits, and claims of wrongful acts.

Many civil law cases deal with contracts. A *contract* is a legally binding agreement between two or more people. Suppose a company fails to deliver supplies to a shop by the date specified in a contract. The resulting lack of supplies could cause the shop to lose business. According to civil law, the shop owner could sue the company for damages. This would help the shop owner recover the losses.

For a contract to be valid, it must meet certain criteria. If all of the criteria are not met, the contract would not be upheld in court.

One criterion needed to make a contract binding is mutual agreement. Both parties, persons entering into the contract, must willingly and completely agree to the terms of the contract. One party cannot force the other to sign the contract.

Secondly, both parties must be *competent.* In other words, they must be able to understand the terms of the contract. They must also be able to evaluate the consequences of accepting those terms. State laws define who is considered legally competent.

If you are under age 18, you are considered a minor in most states. In many states, minors cannot be legally bound by written contracts. To make a contract valid, you may have a parent or another adult countersign the contract with you. The adult would then be held responsible if you failed to abide by the contract. If minors lie about their age, they lose the right to back out of contracts.

Another requirement of contracts is that both parties must give consideration. This means that each party must give up something to receive what the other party is offering. Consideration is often money, property, or a service. For instance, one party may pay the other party money to buy a television. One party may perform lawn care services in exchange for free piano lessons.

The final condition contracts must meet is that they must relate to legal activities. If a contract were made for an illegal act, like theft, the contract would not be valid.

Just about everyone will sign a contract at one time or another. Teachers and professional athletes sign job contracts specifying their salaries and benefits. Authors sign contracts with publishing companies when they write books. Consumers sign contracts when they buy insurance or hire homebuilders.

Before you sign a written contract, read it carefully. Be sure you understand and agree to all the terms. Be sure all the required elements are contained in the contract. If you are uncertain about anything stated in the contract, ask for an explanation. After you have signed the contract, keep a copy for your records. An example of a contract is shown in Figure 27-3.

I, Sarah Goldsmith, of 1627 West Park Avenue, Bensonville, Maryland, agree to provide pet care service for Cary Reagan, of 705 South Dayton Road, Bensonville, Maryland. Services will include, but are not limited to, feeding, brushing, and walking Brisket, a three-year-old, 11-pound, West Highland white terrier. Services will be provided for 30 minutes between 8:00 and 9:00 each morning and between 5:00 and 6:00 each evening, beginning July 20, 20–– and ending July 28, 20––. Consideration for these services will be $15 per day, or a total of $135.

Date: _____6/30/xx_____

Signed: _____Sarah Goldsmith_____

_____Cary Reagan_____

Figure 27-3.   Goodheart-Willcox Publisher
A legally binding contract must clearly outline the terms to which both parties freely agree.

Another area of civil law deals with torts. A **tort** is a wrongful act committed against another person. It involves injuries to another person's body, property, business, emotional well-being, or reputation. Injuring someone in an auto accident is a tort. *Slander* (attacking someone's reputation) and *assault* (attempting to physically harm another person) are torts, too.

Torts may be classified as intentional or unintentional. For example, if someone purposely hits your car and damages it, this is an *intentional tort*. If someone accidentally hits your car, this is considered an *unintentional tort*.

Committing a wrongful act can be a tort and a crime at the same time. For instance, if Mary stole $100 from Carl, Mary would be committing a tort against Carl. Mary would also be breaking a criminal law. Therefore, Carl could bring a civil suit against Mary to recover his $100. The state could bring a criminal suit against Mary because she broke a public law.

Legal Assistance

When you have problems or questions relating to public or civil laws, you may wish to consult a lawyer. A good lawyer can help you make wise decisions about a variety of legal and financial issues. People tend to seek out lawyers as a last resort. At this point, however, a lawyer may have a difficult time protecting a person from legal problems. The best time to consult a lawyer is before a serious problem arises. Such a consultation can help you avoid costly legal mistakes. The following situations may require the help of a lawyer:

- buying or selling real estate;
- writing or entering into a contract;
- getting divorced;
- not being able to pay your bills;
- writing a will;
- being charged with a criminal action;
- facing a civil suit; and
- having trouble obtaining satisfaction in regard to a consumer complaint.

Choosing the best lawyer for your situation should be done carefully. Do not hurry. Keep in mind that the field of law is specialized. Some lawyers specialize in divorce cases, others in business law, and others in criminal law. The more specialized the case, the more important it is to choose a lawyer who has handled such cases before.

How do you find a good lawyer? One way is to ask a trusted family member, teacher, or friend to suggest a lawyer. Another way is through the *Lawyers Referral and Information Service (LRIS)* or the *American Bar Association*.

For people who cannot afford to hire a lawyer, there are places to get help. Many cities and communities have legal aid offices. Lawyers at these offices will handle problems involving civil laws for free or a low fee. Legal aid clinics are also available at many law schools. These clinics help law students gain practical experience while helping those who cannot afford a lawyer. Legal aid offices and clinics give advice in three main areas:

- small claims for wages;
- disputes between the client and a lender, installment seller, or landlord; and
- domestic matters (divorce, child custody, contesting a will, and other family disagreements).

In the United States, everyone is entitled to a defense even if he or she cannot pay for it. Consequently, in criminal cases, the state will appoint a public defender if the accused cannot afford a lawyer.

Once you have chosen a qualified lawyer, take an active role in your case. Take your lawyer's advice, but do not hesitate to ask questions about how he or she plans to handle your case. It is a good idea to request copies of all letters and documents prepared on your behalf. This will help you know exactly how your case is progressing. Preparing legal cases takes time, so do not badger your lawyer.

An important fact to remember when dealing with your lawyer is: be honest. Tell him or her all the facts related to your case. An attorney cannot give you well-reasoned advice if you withhold information or fail to tell the truth. Also, keep your lawyer informed of any new developments that might affect your case.

Court System

If you have a legal problem, you may have to settle it through the court system. Courts try and punish people who have committed criminal offenses. They also interpret laws and settle legal problems between people involved in civil disputes.

The United States has two court systems—one at the state level and one at the national level. The court system in each state and the federal court system all follow a similar organization. Most criminal and civil cases involving people within a state are resolved in state courts. Cases involving federal laws or people from more than one state are heard in federal courts. Federal courts may also review cases previously tried at the state level.

There are many different types of state and federal courts. The type of court in which a given case is presented depends on a number of factors. These factors may include the type of criminal offense or the value of a civil claim. See Figure 27-4 for a brief description of the various types of courts.

State Courts
Trial Courts (limited jurisdiction)—have original jurisdiction in local misdemeanor and minor civil cases.
Trial Courts (general jurisdiction)—handle more serious criminal and civil cases for a larger geographic area. These courts are also known as circuit, county, district, common pleas, and superior courts.
Appellate Courts—review cases previously tried in a lower court.
Supreme Court—handles cases involving state constitutional law and reviews cases previously appealed in appellate courts. Cases may be further appealed to the U.S. Supreme Court.
Federal Courts
District Courts—have original jurisdiction in cases involving federal laws and/or citizens of different states.
Circuit Courts of Appeals—handles appeals of cases originally tried in district courts.
Supreme Court—has original jurisdiction in cases involving a state; reviews cases from state and federal courts involving constitutional law.

Figure 27-4.   *Goodheart-Willcox Publisher*
State and federal courts exist to handle different types of cases.

The type of court also depends on whether an original ruling or a review of a previous ruling is being sought. Court cases are first heard in trial courts. A **jury** is a panel of citizens selected to help decide some cases in a trial court. The decision of the judge or jury in a trial court may be appealed. The case then goes before a panel of justices in a higher court. The justices review the case and may uphold or overturn the decision of the trial court.

Small Claims Court

Small claims courts hear cases involving small amounts of money. The maximum amount for a suit varies from state to state from as little as $1,500 to $25,000 or more. You can sue only for the actual dollar loss.

Small claims courts are less formal than other trial courts. They are also less costly for people filing suits. Filing fees are low and lawyers are not required. In fact, lawyers are discouraged or may be forbidden from representing parties in some small claims courts.

A **plaintiff** is the person who files the lawsuit. The **defendant** is the person accused in the lawsuit of wrongdoing. There is no jury in small claims courts. Cases are decided based on the facts plaintiffs and defendants present to the judge.

Checkpoint 27.2

1. Why are laws established?
2. What are the two main categories of law?
3. Explain the difference between a felony and a misdemeanor.
4. List three examples of a tort.
5. What will the state do if the accused cannot afford a lawyer in a criminal case?

Build Your Vocabulary

As you progress through this text, develop a personal glossary of career-related terms and add it to your portfolio. This will help build your vocabulary and prepare you for your career of choice. Write a definition for each of the following terms, and add it to your personal career glossary.

criminal law
civil law
felony
misdemeanor
tort
jury
plaintiff
defendant

Chapter Summary

Section 27.1 Family

- Throughout your lifetime, you will play a number of different roles. Family roles will often be complex and demanding.
- Time management is a key to balancing family and work roles. Setting goals, making lists, and staying focused are strategies that can help you to manage time wisely.
- Many employers offer family-friendly benefits. These benefits are provided to help employees balance work and family life.

Section 27.2 Citizenship

- Being a good citizen is both a privilege and a responsibility. Community involvement and voting for government leaders are two ways to exercise good citizenship.
- The two categories of law in the United States include criminal law and civil law. Criminal laws relate to crimes against the public or state, while civil laws define citizens' rights in relation to other citizens.
- People who need advice concerning legal matters often seek the assistance of a lawyer. A lawyer is able to provide advice and help clients with issues that involve state and federal courts.

Check Your Career IQ

Now that you have finished the chapter, see what you learned about careers by taking the chapter posttest. The test can be accessed on the mobile site by using a smartphone or on the G-W Learning companion website.

www.m.g-wlearning.com
www.g-wlearning.com

Review Your Knowledge

1. List five behaviors that often result from experiencing burnout.
2. What is the purpose of the Family and Medical Leave Act?
3. Name three types of work arrangements available to many employees in the workplace.
4. What are two advantages to telecommuting?
5. How are crimes classified?
6. What requirements must be met to register for voting in the United States?
7. Name three issues covered by civil law.
8. Explain what happens when both parties give consideration in a contract agreement.

9.   Define consideration as it applies to a contract agreement.

10.   List the four criterion needed to make a contract binding.

Apply Your Knowledge

1.   Create an outline of this chapter. Be sure to include any major ideas and vocabulary. As you study, use the outline to help you recall important information from the chapter.

2.   Consider your roles as a student, family member, and worker. What responsibilities do you have with each of these roles? Take notes as you consider these ideas. Share your answers during a class discussion.

3.   Record four important things you learned in Section 27.1. For each, write a paragraph about how you can use this information in planning for your future. Share your responses with the rest of the class during an open discussion.

4.   What does it mean to be a good citizen? Review Section 27.2 and consider the importance of good citizenship. Write a one-page paper on the subject and include information from the text to support your main points.

5.   Investigate community service opportunities in your neighborhood. Report on one that appeals to you. Identify how the volunteer activity contributes to your community. Discuss how the activity might be beneficial to your skills or future career.

6.   Use the Internet to learn more about flextime, job sharing, and telecommuting. What kinds of jobs are best suited for these work experiences? Would you be interested in either of these work experiences? Why or why not. Take notes and record your answers. Share your answers in a discussion with a small group.

7.   List six things you need to do within the next seven days. Create a detailed version of a to-do list. For each task, note important details including *who, what, when,* and *where.* Next, create a short version of a to-do list based on the information you previously noted. Briefly list what needs to be done and when. Share both versions with a partner. In what ways can these resources help you during the week? Which version do you prefer and why? When might each version of the to-do list be more appropriate than the other?

8.   Research a company to learn what family-friendly policies and benefits the company offers. Use the Internet, other library resources, or interview a family member or friend who works for the company. Compile your information in a chart. Present your information to the class. Would you consider working for the same company? Why or why not?

9.   Review the section on Using Community Resources featured in Section 27.1. Write a one-page essay to describe a variety of community resources available to families. Discuss the importance of community resources.

10.   Interview a person who uses time wisely and appears to be well organized. Make a list of strategies he or she uses that might work for you. Note the benefits of each strategy. What did you learn from the discussion? Summarize your findings in two paragraphs.

Teamwork

Work with three or four classmates to develop a community volunteer project for your class. Identify three or four community organizations that need volunteer help. Interview at least one representative of each organization. Determine what services they provide and what type of volunteer work is available. Are special skills required? Is there an age requirement? Prepare a plan to involve you and your classmates in a project with one of the organizations. Present your plan to the class. Implement and monitor the project.

G-W Learning Mobile Site

Visit the G-W Learning mobile site to complete the chapter pretest and posttest and to practice vocabulary using e-flash cards. If you do not have a smartphone, visit the G-W Learning companion website to access these features.
G-W Learning mobile site: www.m.g-wlearning.com
G-W Learning companion website: www.g-wlearning.com

Common Core

College and Career Readiness

Reading. Read a magazine, newspaper, or online article about a current issue on community service. Determine the central ideas and conclusions of the article. Provide an accurate summary of your reading, making sure to incorporate the *who*, *what*, *when*, and *how* of this issue.

Writing. Conduct a short research project to answer the question, "What is the Family and Medical Leave Act (FMLA)?" Using information from multiple sources, write a report on your response to this question.

Apply Your Technology Skills

Access the G-W Learning companion website for this text at www.g-wlearning.com. Download the data file for this chapter. Follow the instructions to complete activities to practice what you have learned.

Data File 27–1—**Maintaining a Balanced Life**

College and Career Readiness Portfolio

College and Career Readiness

You created items for your e-portfolio in earlier activities. Now you will decide how to present your e-portfolio. The items should already be organized in folders. Review the files you have collected. Select the ones you want to include and remove others. Keep separate the files with information for your use only, such as answers to interview questions. Decide how you want to present the materials. For example, you could create an electronic presentation with slides for each section. The slides could have links to documents, videos, graphics, or sound files. Web pages are another option for presenting the information. You could have a main page with links to various sections. Each section page could have links to pages with documents, videos, graphics, or sound files. The method you choose should allow the viewer to navigate and find items easily. The files could be placed on a CD or a website.

1. Create the slide show, web pages, or other vehicle for presenting your e-portfolio.
2. View the completed e-portfolio to check the appearance.

Career Clusters Handbook

Agriculture, Food & Natural Resources

People who have jobs in this cluster work with food products and processing, power, structural systems, and plants and animals. Careers in natural resources, environmental services, and agribusiness are also included in this cluster.

Fewer jobs involve traditional farming and ranching. Many careers involve working with food science and technology to discover new food sources, to analyze food structure and content, and to develop new ways to process, preserve, package, and store food. Workers in natural resources focus on improving the present and future quality of life, conserving natural resources, and preserving wildlife. For example, conservation scientists help solve problems affecting the use of land, water, and air. Foresters plan and supervise the growing, protection, and use of trees. Environmentalists work to resolve problems related to pollution and hazardous waste disposal. Animal scientists study genetics, nutrition, and reproduction.

Entry-level jobs are available. Although some knowledge and skills are learned on-the-job, many technical jobs require two or more years of advanced training. Professionals, such as engineers and scientists, must have a four-year college degree or beyond.

The demands of an expanding population, globalization, and increasing public awareness on nutrition and diet will result in strong job opportunities in the future. Many of these specialists work for government agencies, such as the US Department of Agriculture, the Environmental Protection Agency, or the National Park Service. Private employers include mining and logging operations, landscapers, and oil companies.

Cluster	Careers
Food Products and Processing Systems	Agricultural Salesperson ■ Agricultural Communications Specialist ■ Business-Educator ■ Food Scientist ■ Meat Processor ■ Toxicologist ■ Biochemist ■ Nutritionist ■ Dietician ■ Food Broker ■ Food Inspector ■ Meat Cutter-Grader ■ Meat Science Researcher ■ Food Meal Supervisor ■ Cheese Maker ■ Microbiologist ■ Produce Buyer ■ Bacteriologist ■ Food & Drug Inspector ■ Bioengineer ■ Biochemist ■ Food & Fiber Engineer ■ Food Processor ■ Storage Supervisor ■ Fieldhand ■ Quality Control Specialist
Plant Systems	Bioinformatics Specialist ■ Plant Breeder & Geneticist ■ Biotechnology Lab Technician ■ Soil & Water Specialist ■ Crop Farm Manager ■ Agricultural Educator ■ Plant Pathologist ■ Aquaculturalist ■ Botanist ■ Tree Surgeon ■ Education & Extension Specialist ■ Commodity Marketing Specialist ■ Grain Operations Superintendent ■ Forest Geneticist ■ Golf Course Superintendent ■ Greenhouse Manager ■ Grower ■ Farmer ■ Rancher ■ Custom Hay & Silage Operator ■ Agricultural Journalist
Animal Systems	Agricultural Educator ■ Livestock Producer ■ Poultry Manager ■ Equine Manager ■ Veterinarian ■ Veterinary Assistant ■ Feedlot Specialist ■ Animal Scientist ■ Embryo Technologist ■ Livestock Buyer ■ Wildlife Biologist ■ Livestock Geneticist ■ Animal Nutritionist ■ Dairy Producer ■ Livestock Inspector ■ Pet Shop Operator ■ Feed Sales Specialist ■ Animal Health Salesperson ■ Meat Science Researcher ■ Reproductive Physiologist ■ Embryo Transfer Technician ■ USDA Inspector
Power, Structural, and Technical Systems	Machine Operator ■ Electronics Systems Technician ■ Agricultural Engineer ■ Agricultural Extension Engineering Specialist ■ Heavy Equipment Maintenance Technician ■ Recycling Technician ■ Waste Water Treatment Plant Operator ■ Parts Manager ■ Welder ■ Machinist ■ Communication Technician ■ GPS Technician ■ Agricultural Applications Software Developer ■ Programmer ■ Computer Service & Technical Support Technician ■ Information Lab Specialist ■ Remote Sensing Specialist
Natural Resource Systems	Cartographer ■ Wildlife Manager ■ Range Technician ■ Ecologist ■ Park Manager ■ Environmental Interpreter ■ Fish & Game Officer ■ Logger ■ Forest Technician ■ Log Grader ■ Pulp & Paper Manager ■ Commercial Fishermen ■ Fishing Vessel Operator ■ Soil Geology Technician ■ Geologist ■ Mining Engineer ■ Fisheries Technician ■ Water Monitoring Technician ■ Hydrologist ■ Fish Hatchery Manager
Environmental Service Systems	Pollution Prevention & Control Manager ■ Pollution Prevention & Control Technician ■ Environmental Sampling & Analysis Scientist ■ Health & Safety Sanitarian ■ Environmental Compliance Assurance Manager ■ Hazardous Materials Handler ■ Hazardous Materials Technician ■ Manager ■ Water Environment Manager ■ Water Quality Manager ■ Waste Water Manager ■ Toxicologist ■ Recycler ■ Solid Waste Technician, Manager, Specialist, or Disposer
Agribusiness Systems	Bank, Insurance Company, or Government Program Field Representative ■ Farm Investment Manager ■ Agricultural Commodity Broker ■ Agricultural Economist ■ Farmer ■ Rancher ■ Feedlot Operator ■ Farm Manager ■ Breeder ■ Dairy Herd Supervisor ■ Agricultural Products Buyer ■ Animal Health Products Distributor ■ Livestock Seller ■ Feed or Farm Supply Store Manager ■ Produce Commission Agent ■ Agricultural Chemical Dealer ■ Chemical Sales Representative

States' Career Clusters Initiative, 2008

People with careers in architecture and construction are involved in the design, planning, construction, and maintenance of structures. They may design, build, restore, or maintain homes, bridges, industrial plants, dams, hospitals, highways, and shopping malls. Some careers may involve landscape architecture, urban planning, and interior design.

Architects design the structures to be built. Engineers supervise the building of structures and make sure construction plans are structurally sound. Skilled craft workers, such as carpenters, bricklayers, roofers, plumbers, and electricians actually build the structures.

You must be licensed before practicing as an architect. After earning a four-year college degree and working as an intern-architect for about three years, you must pass all parts of the Architect Registration Examination (ARE) in order to become licensed.

Community colleges, technical institutes, and career-technical schools offer certificate and degree programs, ranging from one to three years, for many architecture and construction jobs. Architects, engineers, and construction managers require at least a four-year college degree. Specific job requirements may range from on-the-job training to advanced degrees for other occupations in this cluster.

The employment outlook for careers in this cluster remains steady, especially for workers in design and construction. Those who have broad skills in the area of maintenance operations will have favorable job options in a slower-than-average growth area.

Design and Preconstruction

Architect ■ Drafter ■ Regional & Urban Planner ■ Designer ■ Industrial Engineer ■ Materials Engineer ■ Environmental Designer ■ Civil Engineer ■ Programmer ■ Mechanical Engineer ■ Electrical Engineer ■ Preservationist ■ Environmental Engineer ■ Surveyor ■ Fire Prevention & Protection Engineer ■ Cost Estimator ■ Electrical & Electronic Engineering Technician ■ Civil Engineering Technician ■ Environmental Engineering Technician ■ Surveying & Mapping Technician ■ Interior Designer ■ Landscape Designer ■ Specifications Writer ■ Building Code Official ■ Computer Aided Drafter ■ Renderer ■ Modeler

Construction

General Contractor & Builder ■ Construction Foreman ■ Estimator ■ Project Inspector ■ Sales & Marketing Manager ■ Education & Training Director ■ Safety Director ■ Construction Inspector ■ Subcontractor ■ Field Supervisor ■ Mason ■ Iron & Metalworker ■ Carpenter ■ Electrician ■ Boilermaker ■ Electronic Systems Technician ■ Carpet Installer ■ Sheet-Metal Worker ■ Security & Fire Alarm Systems Installer ■ Concrete Finisher ■ Tile & Marble Setter ■ Landscaper ■ Elevator Installer ■ Roofer ■ Painter ■ Plasterer ■ Paperhanger ■ Drywall Installer ■ Plumber ■ Pipe Fitter ■ Heating, Ventilation, Air Conditioning, & Refrigeration Mechanic ■ Electrician

Maintenance and Operations

General Maintenance Contractor ■ Construction Engineer ■ Construction Manager ■ Estimator ■ Facilities Engineer ■ Environmental Engineer ■ Demolition Engineer ■ Project Inspector ■ Manufacturer's Representative ■ Highway Maintenance Worker ■ Equipment & Material Manager ■ Maintenance Estimator ■ Security Controls Manager ■ Preservationist ■ Remodeler ■ Safety Director ■ Construction Inspector ■ Service Contractor ■ System Installer ■ Electrician ■ Boilermaker ■ Cost Estimator ■ Sheet-Metal Worker ■ Hazardous Materials Remover ■ Steamfitter

Arts, A/V Technology & Communications

If you have creative talents along with strong communication, math, and science skills, this may be the career area for you. These diverse career pathways include visual and performing arts, audio and video (A/V) technology, and film. Journalism and broadcasting, telecommunications, and printing technology are other career directions. The job outlook remains steady for the foreseeable future.

People who work with A/V technology may design, install, or operate audio and video equipment. Those who work in journalism and broadcasting prepare and present information about local, state, national, and international events. Jobs in the performing arts range from actors, dancers, and musicians to instructors, playwrights, and scriptwriters. Costume designers plus lighting and stage crews complete the behind-the-scenes work in performing arts. Those who work with print technology complete many printing-process tasks to transform text and photos into magazines and books. Working with computers and communications equipment is key to telecommunications. Through a variety of art media, visual artists bring concepts, thoughts, and feelings to life.

Preparation for these careers begins early in life and continues through high school and into adult life. It requires self-discipline and hard work. Although most jobs require some training beyond high school, employment requires talent, not just training and years of experience.

Some entry-level jobs require on-the-job training or an apprenticeship. Most technical jobs require one, two, or three years of training at a technical or community college. Careers in management, education, and journalism may require four-year degrees and beyond.

Audio and Video Technology and Film	Video Systems Technician ■ Video Graphics, Special Effects, & Animation Designer ■ Audio-Video Designer & Engineer ■ Technical Computer Support Technician ■ Audio-Video System Service Technician ■ Audio Systems Technician
Printing Technology	Graphics & Printing Equipment Operator ■ Lithographer & Platemaker ■ Computer Typography & Composition Equipment Operator ■ Desktop Publishing Specialist ■ Web Page Designer
Visual Arts	Commercial Photographer ■ Commercial Interior Designer ■ Residential & Home Furnishings Coordinator ■ Graphic Designer ■ Computer Aided Design Technician ■ Fashion Illustrator ■ Textile Designer ■ Commercial Artist ■ Illustrator ■ Artist ■ Gallery Manager ■ Fashion Designer ■ Curator
Performing Arts	Production Manager (Digital, Video, or Stage) ■ Cinematographer ■ Video Editor ■ Dancer ■ Playwright ■ Screen Writer ■ Screen Editor ■ Script Writer ■ Director & Coach ■ Set Designer & Painter ■ Performer ■ Actors ■ Musician ■ Costume Designer ■ Make-Up Artist ■ Stagecraft Designer & Lighter ■ Stagecraft Sound Effects & Acoustics Coordinator ■ Composer ■ Conductor ■ Music Instructor
Journalism and Broadcasting	Audio & Video Operations ■ Station Manager ■ Radio & TV Announcer ■ Editor ■ Journalist ■ Reporter ■ Broadcast Technician ■ Control Room Technician
Telecommunications	Telecommunication Technician ■ Installer ■ Telecommunication Computer Programmer & Systems Analyst ■ Telecommunication Equipment, Cable, or Line Repairer

Business Management & Administration

Careers in this cluster involve skills that businesses need to stay productive and run smoothly. Management, finance and accounting, and human resources are some career options. Business analysis, marketing, and administration and information support are also included in this cluster. Broad skills in planning, organizing, and evaluating business operations are essential. Business people also need good computer skills, common sense, decision-making skills, and problem-solving abilities.

Business managers form policies and direct the operations of corporations, nonprofit groups, and government agencies. Financial managers and accountants create and use accounting systems to analyze and prepare financial reports. People who work in business analysis find cost-effective ways to do business. They also uphold business values and strategies. Marketing workers may do market research and promote, sell, and maintain products and services. Workers in administration and information support use technology to gather and deliver information and perform other office duties.

Some entry-level jobs may require certification and a two-year or four-year degree. Most jobs in this career cluster require a four-year degree from a college or university. Top managers, financial analysts, and human resources specialists often need advanced degrees beyond their four-year degrees. Work experience is often a requirement in addition to a degree. Business expansion and complexity will result in faster-than-average growth for the careers in this cluster.

General Management	Entrepreneur ■ Chief Executive Officer ■ General Manager ■ Accounting Manager ■ Accounts Payable Manager ■ Assistant Credit Manager ■ Billing Manager ■ Business & Development Manager ■ Compensation & Benefits Manager ■ Credit & Collections Manager ■ Payroll Manager ■ Risk Manager ■ Operations Manager ■ Public Relations Manager ■ Human Resources Manager ■ Management Analyst ■ Sports & Entertainment Manager ■ Facilities Manager ■ Association Manager ■ Hospital Manager ■ Government Manager ■ First Line Supervisor ■ Senior Manager
Business Information Management	Information Systems Manager ■ Accounting Clerk ■ Accounting Supervisor ■ Adjuster ■ Chief Technology Officer ■ Auditor ■ Bookkeeper ■ Budget Analyst ■ Budget Manager ■ Billing Supervisor ■ Management Analyst ■ Controller ■ Merger & Acquisitions Manager ■ Price Analyst ■ Top Collections Executive ■ Information Technology Director ■ Chief Financial Officer ■ Finance Director ■ Certified Public Accountant ■ Project Manager ■ Cost Accountant ■ Librarian ■ Payroll Accounting Clerk
Human Resources Management	Human Resources Manager ■ International Relations Director ■ Human Resources Coordinator ■ Industrial Relations Director ■ Compensation & Benefits Manager ■ Training & Development Manager ■ Human Resources Consultant ■ Corporate Trainer ■ Personnel Recruiter ■ Organizational Behaviorist ■ Employer Relations Representative ■ Labor & Personnel Relations Manager ■ Affirmative Action Coordinator ■ Equal Employment Opportunity Specialist ■ OSHA Compliance Officer ■ Conciliator ■ Arbitrator ■ Pay Equity Officer ■ Occupational Analyst ■ Compensation, Benefits & Job Analyst Specialist ■ Human Resources Assistant
Operations Management	Training & Development Manager ■ Operations Analyst ■ Sales Representative ■ Broker ■ Agent ■ Assistant Store Manager ■ Department Manager ■ Assistant Department Manager ■ Salesperson ■ Customer Service Supervisor ■ Product Manager ■ Project Manager ■ Research & Development Manager ■ Budget Analyst ■ International Merchandising Manager & Supervisor ■ E-commerce Manager & Entrepreneur ■ Wholesale & Retail Buyer ■ Marketing Manager ■ International Distribution Manager ■ Logistics Coordinator ■ Demonstrator and Product Promoter ■ Supply Chain Manager
Administrative Support	Administrative Assistant ■ Executive Assistant ■ Office Manager ■ Administrative Support ■ Information Assistant ■ Desktop Publisher ■ Customer Service Assistant ■ Data Entry Specialist ■ Receptionist ■ Communications Equipment Operator ■ Computer Operator ■ Stenographer ■ Dispatcher ■ Shipping & Receiving Assistant ■ Word Processor ■ Medical Transcriptionist ■ Legal Secretary ■ Paralegal

Do you have the ability to inspire and motivate others? Are you sensitive to their varying needs? If so , a career in education and training may be an option for you. This career area includes teaching and training, professional support services, administration, and administrative support.

Teaching gives you a chance to influence the lives of many students. Highly skilled educators use a variety of teaching methods to help students achieve. Those who work in professional support services—such as psychology, counseling, or social work—help students meet personal, family, and career needs. Strong leadership and management of day-to-day school activities are important skills for school administrators.

Highly skilled teachers spend many of their nonteaching hours upgrading their teaching skills in order to enhance student performance. When compared to many other professional jobs, such as doctors or lawyers, wages for careers in this cluster are often lower. However, benefits and job security are very good in comparison to many other careers. Professionals in this career cluster work in either public or private schools.

Although some entry-level jobs exist, most jobs in this cluster require a four-year-college degree and licensing or certification. Some jobs in professional support services and administration require advanced college degrees. The high demand for highly skilled education and training professionals leads to an excellent job outlook.

Administration and Administrative Support Superintendent ■ Principal ■ Administrator ■ Supervisor & Instructional Coordinator ■ Education Researcher ■ Test Measurement Specialist ■ College President ■ Dean ■ Curriculum Developer ■ Instructional Media Designer

Professional Support Services Psychologist (Clinical, Developmental, or Social) ■ Social Worker ■ Parent Educator ■ Counselor ■ Speech & Language Pathologist ■ Audiologist

Teaching and Training Preschool Teacher ■ Kindergarten Teacher ■ Elementary Teacher ■ Secondary Teacher ■ Special Education Teacher ■ Teacher Aid ■ College & University Lecturer ■ Professor ■ Physical Trainer ■ Coach ■ Child Care Director ■ Child Care Worker ■ Child Life Specialist ■ Nanny ■ Early Childhood Teacher & Assistant ■ Group Worker & Assistant ■ Human Resource Trainer

Finance careers involve the management and use of money. The career pathways in this cluster include financial and investment planning, financial management, banking, and insurance. Strong interpersonal and communication skills are important qualities for these workers.

Financial and investment planners help individuals and businesses make wise investment decisions. Business financial managers analyze and prepare financial reports. Jobs in banking and related services range from bank tellers to loan officers to credit analysts. People who work with insurance services help individuals and businesses protect themselves from financial losses.

Careers in finance exist in all parts of the economy. Some of the most desirable finance jobs are in sales and stock trading. Trading can be very stressful and requires a thorough knowledge of markets and financial instruments. Although it can be difficult to get started in this business, the rewards are high to a person with great sales skills.

Employment opportunities in finance will likely be steady in the foreseeable future. Some entry-level finance positions are available to those with a high school diploma and strong math and communication skills. A four-year-college degree or advanced training is required for most of the careers in this cluster. Many require special certifications beyond a college degree. Earnings in this cluster vary significantly depending on the occupation.

Securities and Investments — Personal Financial Advisor ■ Tax Preparation Professional ■ Securities & Commodities Sales Agent ■ Investment Advisor ■ Brokerage Clerk ■ Brokerage Assistant ■ Development Officer

Business Finance — Accountant ■ Financial Analyst ■ Treasurers, Controllers & Chief Revenue Agent ■ Auditor ■ Economist ■ Tax Examiner ■ Collector ■ Revenue Agent

Banking Services — Credit Analyst ■ Loan Officer ■ Bill & Account Collector ■ Teller ■ Loan Processor ■ Customer Service Representative ■ Data Processor ■ Accountant ■ Internal Auditor ■ Compliance Officer ■ Debt Counselor ■ Title Researcher & Examiner ■ Abstractor ■ Credit Report Provider ■ Repossession Agent ■ Network Service & Operations Manager

Insurance — Claims Agent, Examiner, & Investigator ■ Claims Clerk ■ Insurance Appraiser ■ Underwriter ■ Actuary ■ Sales Agent ■ Customer Service Agent ■ Processing Clerk ■ Direct Marketing

Government & Public Administration

This career area involves working in a government position or on issues related to government matters. Seven pathways make up this cluster. They include governance, national security, foreign service, planning, revenue and taxation, regulation, and public management and administration. Places of work range from nonprofit organizations to overseas locations to local, state, or federal governments.

People enter government and public service for a variety of reasons. Some want to help shape environmental regulations or public or foreign policy. Others desire to serve the president or protect national security for the US Department of Defense. Yet others make social, economic, and environmental decisions as they help plan communities, highways, airports, and other public spaces. Those who work with revenue and taxes make sure that citizens and businesses pay their taxes. They also review tax returns and collect overdue taxes. People who work in the regulatory industry help protect peoples' health and safety by making sure that industries and businesses follow the law. Managers and administrators who handle public resources must have strong technical skills in budgeting and managing personnel.

The training and education needed to enter a career in this cluster range from on-the-job training to advanced college degrees. Government job opportunities exist in every career area, and employment opportunities in state and local governments are increasing. This is due to population changes and a growing demand for public services.

Governance
President ■ Vice President ■ Governor ■ Lieutenant Governor ■ Mayor ■ Cabinet Level Secretary (Federal or State) ■ Representative (Federal or State) ■ Senator (Federal or State) ■ Assistant, Deputy, & Chief of Staff ■ Commissioner (County, Parish, or City) ■ Commissioner (State Agency) ■ Congressional Aide ■ Legislative Aide ■ Legislative Assistant ■ Specialist ■ Lobbyist ■ Policy Advisor

National Security
National Security Advisor ■ Staff or Field Officer ■ Electronic Warfare Specialist ■ Combat Operations Officer ■ Infantry Field Officer ■ Artillery Officer ■ Air Defense Artillery Officer ■ Special Forces Officer ■ Nuclear Weapons Officer & Specialist ■ Missile & Space Systems Officer ■ Military Intelligence Specialist ■ Signals Intelligence Officer ■ Surface Ship Warfare Officer ■ Submarine Officer ■ Combat Control Officer ■ Combat Engineer ■ Combat Aircraft Pilot & Crew ■ Airborne Warning Control Specialist ■ Intelligence & Counterintelligence Agent or Specialist ■ Intelligence Analyst ■ Cryptographer

Foreign Service
Ambassador Foreign Service Officer ■ Consular Officer ■ Administrative Officer ■ Political Officer ■ Economic Officer ■ Diplomatic Courier

Planning
Business Enterprise Official ■ Chief of Vital Statistics ■ Commissioner ■ Director (Various Agencies) ■ Economic Development Coordinator ■ Federal Aid Coordinator ■ Census Clerk ■ County Director ■ Census Enumerator ■ Census Planner ■ Program Associate ■ Global Imaging Systems Specialist

Revenue and Taxation
Assessor ■ Tax Auditor ■ Internal Revenue Investigator ■ Revenue Agent & Officer ■ Tax Examiner Assistant or Clerk ■ Inspector General ■ Tax Attorney ■ Tax Policy Analyst

Regulation
Business Regulation Investigator ■ Chief of Field Operations ■ Code Inspector or Officer ■ Equal Opportunity Officer, Inspector, Investigator, or Examiner ■ Chief Bank Examiner ■ Bank Examiner ■ Aviation Safety Officer ■ Border Inspector ■ Cargo Inspector ■ Election Supervisor ■ Enforcement Specialist ■ Immigration Officer

Public Management and Administration
City Manager ■ City Council Member ■ City or County Clerk ■ Court Administrator or Clerk ■ Executive or Associate Director ■ Officer ■ General Service Officer ■ Management Analysis Officer ■ Program Administration Officer

ealth Science

Health care is the fastest-growing industry in the United States, so careers in this cluster are in high demand. The career pathways include therapeutic and diagnostic services, health information, support services, and biotechnology research and development.

People who work in health sciences have a variety of responsibilities. Those in therapeutic services—physical therapists, doctors, nurses, and others—provide care and treatment through direct patient contact. People who work in diagnostic services help detect, diagnose, and treat diseases or injuries. Those who manage medical data and patient information need strong computer-science skills. Workers in support services, such as dietary technicians or hospital maintenance engineers, create a healthful environment for health services. Scientists in biotechnology study ways to diagnose and treat human diseases.

The rapid growth of health-science technology and a quickly aging population are leading to a high demand for health-science workers. Entry-level jobs in health information require on-the-job training or certification. Most other careers in this cluster require a four-year-college degree or advanced college degree. Some also require a license or certification.

About half of all health-science workers find employment at hospitals. Many others find work at clinics, pharmacies, nursing homes, public health agencies, and private offices. Researchers in biotechnology find work at universities, government agencies, or major health organizations.

Therapeutic Services
Acupuncturist ■ Anesthesiologist Assistant ■ Art, Music, or Dance Therapist ■ Athletic Trainer ■ Audiologist ■ Certified Nursing Assistant ■ Chiropractor ■ Dentist ■ Hygienist ■ Dietician ■ Emergency Medical Technician ■ Home Health Aide ■ Licensed Practical Nurse ■ Massage Therapist ■ Medical Assistant ■ Mortician ■ Occupational Therapist or Assistant ■ Optometrist ■ Paramedic ■ Pharmacist ■ Pharmacy Technician ■ Physical Therapist or Assistant ■ Physician ■ Physician's Assistant ■ Psychologist ■ Registered Nurse ■ Respiratory Therapist ■ Social Worker ■ Speech & Language Pathologist ■ Veterinarian

Diagnostics Services
Cardiovascular Technologist ■ Clinical Lab Technician ■ Computer Tomography (CT) Technologist ■ Cytotechnologist ■ Diagnostic Medical Sonographer ■ Electrocardiographic (ECG) Technician ■ Electronic Diagnostic (EEG) Technologist ■ Exercise Physiologist ■ Geneticist ■ Histotechnician ■ Histotechnologist ■ Magnetic Resonance (MR) Technologist ■ Mammographer ■ Pathologist ■ Pathology Assistant ■ Phlebotomist ■ Medical Technologist ■ Clinical Laboratory Scientist ■ Nuclear Medicine Technologist ■ Positron Emission Tomography (PET) Technologist ■ Radiologic Technologist ■ Radiographer ■ Radiologist

Health Informatics
Admitting Clerk ■ Applied Researcher ■ Community Services Specialist ■ Data Analyst ■ Epidemiologist ■ Ethicist ■ Health Educator ■ Health Information Coder ■ Health Information Services ■ Healthcare Administrator ■ Medical Assistant ■ Medical Biller ■ Patient Financial Services Coordinator ■ Medical Information Technologist ■ Medical Librarian & Cybrarian ■ Patient Advocate ■ Public Health Educator ■ Reimbursement Specialist ■ Social Worker ■ Transcriptionist ■ Unit Coordinator ■ Utilization Manager

Support Services
Biomedical Engineer ■ Clinical Engineer ■ Biomedical Technician ■ Clinical Technician ■ Environmental Services Worker ■ Facilities Manager ■ Food Service Worker ■ Hospital Maintenance Engineer ■ Industrial Hygienist ■ Materials Manager ■ Transport Technician

Biotechnology Research and Development
Biochemist ■ Bioinformatics Associate ■ Bioinformatics Scientist ■ Bioinformatics Specialist ■ Biomedical Chemist ■ Biostatistician ■ Cell Biologist ■ Clinical Trials Research Associate ■ Clinical Trials Research Coordinator ■ Geneticist ■ Genetics Lab Assistant ■ Lab Technician ■ Microbiologist ■ Molecular Biologist ■ Pharmaceutical Scientist ■ Quality Assurance Technician ■ Quality Control Technician ■ Regulatory Affairs Specialist ■ Research Assistant ■ Research Associate ■ Research Scientist ■ Toxicologist

ospitality &
Tourism

With increasing leisure time and personal income, many people have more resources for eating out, travel, and recreation. Career options in the area of hospitality and tourism focus on food and beverage services, lodging services, travel, and all types of recreation. Those who work in this industry must have exceptional customer-service skills. They like demanding and diverse work. These workers must also have a solid foundation in math, science, and technical skills.

Chefs prepare and serve food with the help of cooks, servers, and hosts. Lodging managers—with the help of reservationists, bellhops, housekeepers, and front-desk clerks—check guests in and out, meet all their needs, and keep the hotel clean. Travel agents need strong organizational skills and sales abilities to help people plan trips and make lodging and travel reservations. Recreation workers help guests enjoy amusement parks, museums, zoos, unfamiliar cities, and other recreation services.

Many jobs in hospitality and tourism require no specific education. Workers—such as front-desk clerks, housekeepers, and cooks—often receive on-the-job training. However, managers of large resorts, hotels, restaurants, and amusement parks usually complete a four-year-college degree. Managers may also have advanced training and certifications. People can acquire education and training at high schools, technical institutes, and two-year or four-year-colleges and universities.

The job outlook for hospitality and tourism careers remains steady. Wages may vary greatly depending on the area of the country and type of facility.

Restaurants and Food and Beverage Services	General Manager ■ Food & Beverage Manager ■ Kitchen Manager ■ Catering & Banquets Manager ■ Service Manager ■ Maitre'd ■ Restaurant Owner ■ Baker ■ Brewer ■ Caterer ■ Executive Chef ■ Cook ■ Pastry & Specialty Chef ■ Bartender ■ Restaurant Server ■ Host ■ Banquet Server ■ Cocktail Server ■ Banquet Set-Up Employee ■ Bus Person ■ Room Service Attendant ■ Kitchen Steward ■ Counter Server ■ Wine Steward
Lodging	Front Office Manager ■ Executive Housekeeper ■ Director of Sales & Marketing ■ Director of Human Resources ■ Director of Security ■ Controller ■ Food & Beverage Director ■ General Manager ■ Quality Assurance Manager ■ Owner & Franchisee ■ Communications Supervisor ■ Front Desk Supervisor ■ Reservations Supervisor ■ Valet Attendant ■ Door Attendant ■ Laundry Supervisor ■ Room Supervisor ■ Laundry Attendant ■ Maintenance Worker ■ Bell Captain ■ Shift Supervisor ■ Sales Professional ■ Night Auditor ■ Front Desk Employee ■ Concierge ■ Guestroom Attendant ■ Van Driver
Travel and Tourism	Executive Director ■ Assistant Director ■ Director of Tourism Development ■ Director of Communications ■ Director of Visitor Services ■ Director of Sales ■ Director of Marketing & Advertising ■ Director of Volunteer Services ■ Events Manager ■ Sales Manager ■ Destination Manager ■ Convention Services Manager ■ Travel Agent ■ Event Planner ■ Meeting Planner ■ Special Events Producer ■ Tour & Travel Coordinator ■ Tourism Assistant ■ Tour Guide ■ Tourism Marketing Specialist ■ Transportation Specialist ■ Welcome Center Supervisor ■ Motor Coach Operator ■ Interpreter
Recreation, Amusements, and Attractions	Club Manager & Assistant Manager ■ Club Membership Developer ■ Parks & Gardens Safety & Security ■ Parks & Garden Ranger ■ Resort Trainer & Instructor ■ Gaming & Casino Manager ■ Gaming & Casino Dealer ■ Gaming & Casino Security & Safety ■ Fairs & Festival Facility Manager ■ Fairs & Festival Promotional Developer ■ Theme Parks & Amusement Parks Area Ride Operations Manager ■ Theme Parks & Amusement Parks Group Events Manager ■ Historical, Cultural, Architectural, or Ecological Site Guide or Exhibit Developer ■ Museum, Zoo, or Aquarium Animal Trainer & Handler

 *Human Services*

Careers in human services relate to family and human needs. If you like to help others, one of these careers may be for you. People who enter these careers often desire to protect, nurture, or provide a service for others in need. Career pathways include services in early childhood development, counseling and mental health, family and community, personal care, and consumer services.

In early childhood development, workers nurture, teach, and care for children. Counselors and other mental-health workers help people with family and personal problems, mental-health issues, and career-related decisions. Family and community services workers—such as social workers, grief counselors, and geriatric workers—help people with crises or other needs that impact daily living. Personal care workers may help people enhance their appearances or develop fitness. Helping people make financial decisions, buy or sell real estate, or purchase quality insurance or consumer products are just a few contributions of those focused on consumer services.

Most positions in this cluster are growing faster than average. Some entry-level jobs may require a high school diploma and a few community college courses. Other careers may require two-year, four-year, or advanced college degrees. Many careers may require state licenses or certification. Strong communication skills combined with solid science and technology skills will benefit anyone seeking a career in human services.

Early Childhood Development and Services	Childcare Facility Director ▪ Childcare Facility Assistant Director ▪ Elementary School Counselor ▪ Preschool Teacher ▪ Educator for Parents ▪ Nanny ▪ Teachers' Assistant ▪ Childcare Assistant or Worker
Counseling and Mental Health Services	Clinical & Counseling Psychologist ▪ Industrial-Organizational Psychologist ▪ Sociologist ▪ School Counselor ▪ School Psychologist ▪ Substance Abuse & Behavioral Disorder Counselor ▪ Mental Health Counselor ▪ Vocational Rehabilitation Counselor ▪ Career Counselor ▪ Employment Counselor ▪ Residential Advisor ▪ Marriage, Child, & Family Counselor
Family and Community Services	Community Service Director ▪ Adult Day Care Coordinator ▪ Volunteer Coordinator ▪ Licensed Professional Counselor ▪ Religious Leader ▪ Religious Activities & Education Program Director ▪ Human Services Worker ▪ Social Services Worker ▪ Vocational Rehabilitation Counselor ▪ Employment Counselor ▪ Career Counselor ▪ Vocational Rehabilitation Service Worker ▪ Leisure Activities Coordinator ▪ Dietician ▪ Geriatric Service Worker ▪ Adult Day Care Worker ▪ Residential Advisor ▪ Emergency & Relief Worker ▪ Community Food Service Worker ▪ Community Housing Service Worker ▪ Social & Human Services Assistant
Personal Care Services	Barber ▪ Cosmetologist, Hairdresser, & Hairstylist ▪ Shampooer ▪ Nail Technician, Manicurist, & Pedicurist ▪ Skin Care Specialist & Esthetician ▪ Electrolysis Technician ▪ Electrologist ▪ Funeral Director ▪ Mortician ▪ Embalmer ▪ Funeral Attendant ▪ Personal & Home Care Aide ▪ Companion ▪ Spa Attendant ▪ Personal Trainer ▪ Massage Therapist
Consumer Services	Consumer Credit Counselor ▪ Consumer Affairs Officer ▪ Consumer Advocate ▪ Certified Financial Planner ▪ Insurance Representative ▪ Small Business Owner ▪ Banker ▪ Real Estate Services Representative ▪ Financial Advisor ▪ Investment Broker ▪ Employee Benefits Representative ▪ Hospital Patient Accounts Representative ▪ Customer Service Representative ▪ Consumer Research Department Representative ▪ Consumer Goods or Services Retailing Representative ▪ Market Researcher ▪ Account Executive ▪ Sales Consultant ▪ Event Specialist ▪ Inside Sales Representative ▪ Field Merchandising Representative ▪ Buyer

Do you find the ever-changing world of computer technology fascinating? With work available in every segment of society, information technology (IT) careers are among those most in demand. The IT career pathways include network systems, information and support services, programming and software development, and interactive media.

Network specialists analyze, implement, and maintain computer systems critical to corporate business. They may devise systems by which employees in a worldwide company can view information at the same time. Information support workers implement computer systems and provide technical support to all users.

Programming and software developers must comprehend computer operating systems and programming languages. They often work with cutting-edge technologies to meet the future IT needs of businesses and individuals. Web designers, animators, and graphic artists have one thing in common—they all work with interactive media. People in these careers design and produce interactive multimedia that meet a variety of needs from sales and marketing to entertainment.

Depending on the occupation, training and education can be obtained at some high schools, technical colleges, two-year colleges, and four-year colleges or universities. Because IT specialists must be well versed in all factors affecting their industry, continuing education is often a requirement beyond a college degree. In addition to computer skills, people in these careers need strong science, math, and communication skills.

Network Systems

Data Communications Analyst ▪ Information Systems Administrator ▪ Information Systems Operator ▪ Information Technology Engineer ▪ Technical Support Specialist ▪ User Support Specialist ▪ Telecommunications Network Technician ▪ Network Administrator ▪ Network Analyst ▪ Network Engineer ▪ Network Operations Analyst ▪ Network Security Analyst ▪ Network Transport Administrator ▪ Systems Administrator ▪ Systems Engineer ▪ Lead PC Support Specialist ▪ Systems Support Lead

Information Support and Services

Data Administrator ▪ Data Analyst ▪ Data Modeler ▪ Database Administration Associate ▪ Database Developer ▪ Knowledge Architect ▪ Systems Administrator ▪ Technical Writer ▪ Desktop Publisher ▪ Instructional Designer ▪ Online Publisher ▪ Technical Support Analyst ▪ Call Center Support Representative ▪ Customer Service Representative ▪ Product Support Engineer ▪ Sales Support Technician ▪ Systems Analyst ▪ Technical Support Engineer ▪ Testing Engineer ▪ Application Integrator ▪ Business Continuity Analyst ▪ Cross-Enterprise Integrator ▪ Data Systems Designer ▪ E-Business Specialist ▪ Electronic Transactions Implementer ▪ Information Systems Architect

Web and Digital Communication

2D & 3D Artist ▪ Animator ▪ Audio & Video Engineer ▪ Media Specialist ▪ Media Designer ▪ Instructional Designer ▪ Multimedia Author ▪ Multimedia Developer ▪ Multimedia Specialist ▪ Producer ▪ Production Assistant ▪ Programmer ▪ Streaming Media Specialist ▪ Virtual Reality Specialist ▪ Web Designer ▪ Web Administrator ▪ Web Page Developer ▪ Web Site Developer ▪ Webmaster

Programming and Software Development

Applications Analyst ▪ Applications Engineer ▪ Business Analyst ▪ Computer Engineer ▪ Data Modeler ▪ Operating Systems Designer & Engineer ▪ Operating Systems Programmer ▪ Operating Systems Analyst ▪ Program Manager ▪ Programmer Analyst ▪ Software Applications Specialist ▪ Software Applications Architect ▪ Software Applications Design Engineer ▪ Software Applications Development Engineer ▪ Quality Assurance (QA) Specialist ▪ Software Applications Tester ▪ Systems Analyst ▪ Systems Administrator ▪ Test Engineer

Law, Public Safety, Corrections & Security

With strong interest in public safety and national security, careers in law, public safety, and corrections, are increasingly in demand. Keeping citizens and the country safe is the core mission of this career area. Career pathways include working in corrections, emergency and fire management, security and protection, law enforcement, and legal services.

Careers range from probation officers to firefighters to criminal investigators and lawyers. Corrections workers have the responsibility to watch over those under arrest, awaiting trial, and serving time for crimes committed. Firefighters, emergency medical technicians, and other emergency workers keep citizens safe during all types of disasters. Often they are first on the scene to give help and treatment.

Security and protective services workers may check credentials and inspect packages of people entering or leaving businesses. Police officers and other workers protect citizens and their property by enforcing laws, investigating crimes and accidents, and arresting criminals. While adhering to a strict code of ethics, legal services personnel—such as judges, lawyers, and paralegals—uphold the legal system, which impacts all aspects of American life.

The basic requirements of most jobs in this career area include US citizenship and no felony convictions. Some jobs require a high school diploma and work experience. Others require formal training, such as at fire-fighting or police academies, plus two-year or four-year-college degrees or law degrees. Some careers require passing written exams or tests of physical strength and endurance.

Correction Services	Warden ▪ Jail Administrator ▪ Mid-level Manager ▪ Program Coordinator & Counselor ▪ Public Information Officer ▪ Correctional Trainer ▪ Case Manager ▪ Community Corrections Practitioner ▪ Probation & Parole Officer ▪ Corrections Educator ▪ Corrections Officer ▪ Detention Deputy ▪ Support Staff ▪ Youth Services Worker ▪ Facility Maintenance Worker ▪ Transport Officer ▪ Food Service Staff ▪ Medical Staff ▪ Dietitian
Emergency and Fire Management Services	Emergency Management & Response Coordinator ▪ Emergency Planning Manager ▪ Emergency Medical Technician ▪ Firefighter ▪ Rescue Worker ▪ Manager & Supervisor ▪ Forest Fire Inspector & Investigator ▪ Hazardous Materials Responder ▪ Dispatcher ▪ Training Officer ▪ Grant Writer & Coordinator
Security and Protective Services	Security Director ▪ Security Systems Designer & Consultant ▪ Information Systems Security Specialist ▪ Computer Forensics Specialist ▪ Private & Corporate Investigator ▪ Loss Prevention & Security Manager ▪ Security Trainer & Educator ▪ Security Sales Representative ▪ Loss Prevention Specialist ▪ Life Guard ▪ Ski Patrol Officer ▪ Security Systems Technician ▪ Private Investigative Assistant ▪ Security Sales Assistant ▪ Transportation Security Supervisor ▪ Executive Protection Officer ▪ Certified Security Officer ▪ Armored Car Guard ▪ Control Center Operator ▪ Uniformed Security Officer ▪ Security Clerk ▪ Transportation Security Technician
Law Enforcement Services	Animal Control Officer ▪ Bailiff ▪ Child Support Investigator ▪ Missing Persons Investigator ▪ Unemployment Fraud Investigator ▪ Criminal Investigator & Special Agent ▪ Gaming Investigator ▪ Bomb Technician ▪ Highway Patrol ▪ Immigration & Customs Inspector ▪ Police & Detective Manager & Supervisor ▪ Police Detective & Criminal Investigator ▪ Police, Fire, & Ambulance Dispatcher ▪ Police & Patrol Officers ▪ Private Detectives & Investigator ▪ Sheriff ▪ Deputy Sheriff ▪ Training Officer ▪ Transit & Railroad Police ▪ Park Ranger ▪ Evidence Technician ▪ Federal Marshall
Legal Services	Attorney ▪ Case Management Specialist ▪ Court Reporter ▪ File & Document Manager ▪ Information Officer ▪ Investigator ▪ Judge ▪ Law Clerk ▪ Legal Assistant ▪ Legal Secretary ▪ Magistrate Mediator & Arbitrator ▪ Negotiator ▪ Paralegal

Manufacturing

Careers in the manufacturing cluster involve skills in planning, managing, and making raw materials into quality products. The cluster pathways involve production, process development, inventory control, and equipment maintenance and installation. They also include quality, health, safety, and environmental assurance.

Production workers use machinery and tools to assemble everything from electronics to modular homes. Design engineers and production managers work with product design and the overall manufacturing process to make quality products. Equipment technicians perform emergency repairs and also do routine maintenance on equipment, machines, and tools. Quality assurance workers make sure products and services meet customer standards.

People who work with **logistics**—the handling of operational details—and inventory control oversee all aspects of production from delivering raw materials to shipping products. Environmental and safety engineers focus on the safe use of equipment and a safe and healthy work environment.

The job outlook in manufacturing will grow faster than average, especially for people with broad skills. Some careers, such as those in quality control, may see a decline as automation increases. Skilled jobs, such as machinists and welders, are usually learned through apprenticeships or at technical schools or two-year community colleges. Engineers, scientists, and production managers need at least a four-year degree. Some careers require special licenses or certification in addition to education and training.

Production	Assembler ▪ Automated Manufacturing Technician ▪ Bookbinder ▪ Calibration Technician ▪ Electrical Installer & Repairer ▪ Extruding & Drawing Machine Setter ▪ Extrusion Machine Operator ▪ Foundry Worker ▪ Grinding, Lapping, & Buffing Machine Operator ▪ Hoist & Winch Operator ▪ Instrument Maker ▪ Large Printing Press Machine Setter ▪ Milling Machine Set-Up Operator ▪ Millwright ▪ Tool & Die Maker ▪ Welder ▪ Tender & Cutter ▪ Painter ▪ Pattern & Model Maker ▪ Precision Layout Worker ▪ Production Associate ▪ Sheet Metal Worker ▪ Solderer & Brazier
Manufacturing Production Process Development	Design Engineer ▪ Electrical & Electronic Technician & Technologist ▪ Electronics Engineer ▪ Engineering Technician & Technologist ▪ Engineering Technician ▪ Industrial Engineer ▪ Labor Relations Manager ▪ Manufacturing Engineer ▪ Manufacturing Technician ▪ Power Generating & Reactor Plant Operator ▪ Precision Inspector, Tester, & Grader ▪ Process Improvement Technician ▪ Production Manager ▪ Purchasing Agent ▪ Supervisor
Maintenance, Installation, and Repair	Biomedical Equipment Technician ▪ Boilermaker ▪ Communication System Installer & Repairer ▪ Computer Installer & Repairer ▪ Computer Maintenance Technician ▪ Electrical Equipment Installer & Repairer ▪ Facility Electrician ▪ Industrial Facilities Manager ▪ Industrial Machinery Mechanic ▪ Industrial Maintenance Electrician ▪ Industrial Maintenance Technician ▪ Instrument Calibrator & Repairer ▪ Instrument Control Technician ▪ Fixture Designer ▪ Laser Systems Technician ▪ Major Appliance Repairer ▪ Meter Installer & Repairer ▪ Millwright ▪ Plumber, Pipe Fitter & Steam Fitter ▪ Security System Installer & Repairer
Quality Assurance	Calibration Technician ▪ Inspector ▪ Lab Technician ▪ Process Control Technician ▪ Quality Control Technician ▪ Quality Engineer ▪ Statistical Process Control (SPC) Coordinator
Logistics and Inventory Control	Communications, Transportation, & Utilities Manager ▪ Dispatcher ▪ Freight, Stock, & Material Mover ▪ Industrial Truck & Tractor Operator ▪ Logistical Engineer ▪ Logistician ▪ Material Associate ▪ Material Handler ▪ Traffic, Shipping, & Receiving Clerk ▪ Material Mover ▪ Process Improvement Technician ▪ Quality Control Technician ▪ Traffic Manager
Health, Safety, and Environmental Assurance	Environmental Engineer ▪ Environmental Specialist ▪ Health & Safety Representative ▪ Safety Coordinator ▪ Safety Engineer ▪ Safety Team Leader ▪ Safety Technician

If you crave variety and enjoy a fast-paced environment, a career in marketing, sales, and service may be perfect for you! Careers in this cluster include all the jobs involved in buying, distributing, marketing, and selling products, and providing follow-up service to customers. Related jobs include finding new customers and tracking marketing data.

Managers and entrepreneurs direct the advertising, marketing, sales, and public relations for small businesses or major companies. Specialists in sales and marketing move goods and services to businesses and individuals. Merchandise managers and buyers predict trends and buy merchandise accordingly. Sales associates and store managers focus on selling and providing customer service.

Developing strategies to promote goods and services is important to those who work in marketing and promotions. Market researchers gather information about consumer needs and use it to predict and plan new products. A logistics engineer often works closely with a warehouse manager to control the movement and storage of raw materials and finished goods. Specialists handle **e-marketing**, which is the use of computer technology to market goods and services.

The overall demand for employees in this cluster remains high. Those with computer skills and college degrees will have more opportunities in management. Many entry-level jobs exist in sales. However, employment opportunities are greater for those who attend community colleges or technical schools that offer one-, two-, or three-year programs, or colleges and universities that offer four-year degrees. Wages vary by occupation, level of responsibility, and work experience.

Marketing Management
Entrepreneur ▪ Owner ▪ Small Business Owner ▪ President ▪ Chief Executive Officer ▪ Principal ▪ Partner ▪ Proprietor ▪ Franchisee ▪ Independent Distributor ▪ Customer Service Representative ▪ Administrative Support Staff

Professional Sales
Inbound Call Manager ▪ Channel Sales Manager ▪ Regional Sales Manager ▪ Client Relationship Manager ▪ Business Development Manager ▪ Territory Representative ▪ Key Account Manager ▪ National Account Manager ▪ Account Executive ▪ Sales Engineer ▪ Sales Executive ▪ Technical Sales Specialist ▪ Retail Sales Specialist ▪ Outside Sales Representative ▪ Industrial Sales Representative ▪ Manufacturer's Representative ▪ Salesperson ▪ Field Representative ▪ Broker ▪ Agent ▪ Solutions Advisor ▪ Marketing Associate ▪ Customer Service Representative ▪ Administrative Support Staff

Merchandising
Store Manager ▪ Retail Marketing Coordinator ▪ Merchandising Manager ▪ Merchandise Buyer ▪ Operations Manager ▪ Visual Merchandise Manager ▪ Sales Manager ▪ Department Manager ▪ Sales Associate ▪ Customer Service Representative ▪ Clerk ▪ Administrative Support Staff

Marketing Communications
Advertising Manager ▪ Public Relations Manager ▪ Public Information Director ▪ Sales Promotion Manager ▪ Co-op Manager ▪ Trade Show Manager ▪ Circulation Manager ▪ Promotions Manager ▪ Arts & Graphics Director ▪ Creative Director ▪ Account Executive ▪ Account Supervisor ▪ Sales Representative ▪ Marketing Associate ▪ Media Buyer & Planner ▪ Interactive Media Specialist ▪ Analyst ▪ Contract Administrator ▪ Copywriter ▪ Research Specialist ▪ Research Assistant ▪ Customer Service Representative ▪ Administrative Support Staff

Marketing Research
Database Manager ▪ Research Specialist & Manager ▪ Brand Manager ▪ Marketing Services Manager ▪ Customer Satisfaction Manager ▪ Research Project Manager ▪ Constituent Relationship Management (CRM) Manager ▪ Forecasting Manager ▪ Strategic Planner ▪ Product Planner ▪ Planning Analyst ▪ Directors of Market Development ▪ Database Analyst ▪ Analyst ▪ Research Associate ▪ Frequency Marketing Specialist ▪ Knowledge Management Specialist ▪ Interviewer ▪ Customer Service Representative ▪ Administrative Support Staff

Science, Technology,
Engineering &
Mathematics

Workers in this cluster use math and the scientific process in laboratory and testing services. They also conduct research. Often their work leads to discoveries that have the potential to improve life. Careers in this cluster are available in two areas: science and mathematics or engineering and technology.

Careers in science and mathematics range from teacher to physicist to statistician to lab technician. Workers use science and math to deal with real-world issues, such as solving environmental problems or preventing certain health conditions.

Engineers and technologists often specialize in biotechnology or distinct areas of engineering—civil, electrical, mechanical, aerospace, or chemical engineering. They use scientific principles to design new machinery, build new roads and bridges, or develop systems to prevent pollution or reduce energy usage.

Some entry-level jobs require a two-year degree from a community college or technical institute. Most careers in this cluster, including entry-level lab technicians, require a four-year degree from a college or university. Advanced degrees are common among engineers, scientists, technologists, and mathematicians. Some careers require certification, too.

Because of the critical nature of work in this cluster, the employment outlook remains very strong. Scientists and mathematicians who learn to use equipment in industrial and government settings may have a competitive edge over other job seekers. The need for technologists and engineers will increase as technology advances and employers need to improve and update product designs and manufacturing processes.

Engineering and Technology	Aerospace Engineer ■ Application Engineer ■ Automotive Engineer ■ Biotechnology Engineer ■ Chemical Engineer ■ Civil Engineer ■ Energy Transmission Engineer ■ Environmental Engineer ■ Facilities Technician ■ Geothermal Engineer ■ Hazardous Waste Technician ■ Human Factors Engineer ■ Industrial Engineering Technician ■ Licensing Engineer ■ Marine Engineer ■ Materials Engineer ■ Materials Lab & Supply Technician ■ Mechanical Engineer ■ Metallurgic Engineer ■ Mining Engineer ■ Nuclear Engineer ■ Operations Research Engineer ■ Packaging Engineer or Technician ■ Petroleum Engineer ■ Plastics Engineer
Science and Math	Research Chemist or Technician ■ Science Teacher ■ Lab Technician ■ Scientific Visualization & Graphics Expert ■ Statistician ■ Analytical Chemist ■ Anthropologist ■ Applied Mathematician ■ Archeologist ■ Astronomer ■ Astrophysicist ■ Atmospheric Scientist ■ Biologist ■ Botanist ■ Computer Aided Design (CAD) Operator ■ Cartographer ■ Chemist ■ Cosmologist ■ Demographer ■ Dye Chemist ■ Ecologist ■ Economist ■ Environmental Scientist ■ Geneticist ■ Geologist ■ Geophysicist ■ Geoscientist ■ Hydrologist ■ Inorganic Chemist ■ Mammalogist ■ Marine Scientist ■ Materials Analyst or Scientist ■ Mathematician ■ Metallurgist ■ Meteorologist

Transportation, Distribution & Logistics

Transportation by road, rail, water, and air offers many employment options. These careers focus on effective planning, efficient management, and safe movement of products and people. Related careers focus on planning, managing, and maintaining the equipment, facilities, and systems used.

Transportation workers, such as pilots and bus drivers, operate vehicles that transport freight and people. Others ensure safety, security, and timely delivery. Logistics and distribution employees plan and schedule transportation, shipment periods, and delivery dates. Workers in warehousing and distribution use cutting-edge tracking software to sort, label, and schedule customer deliveries. They also ensure accurately loaded shipments.

Some workers maintain, repair, and service transportation vehicles and the facilities that house them. Traffic engineers may plan, manage, and regulate the basic framework of public transportation systems. Employees in health, safety, and environmental management conduct research and find ways to keep the environment safe and clean. Workers in sales and service sell transportation services to new customers and manage the transportation needs of existing customers.

As one of the fastest growing segments of the economy, this career cluster offers many high-demand, high-wage work options. Many entry-level positions require on-the-job training or a special certificate (such as a Commercial Driver's License–CDL for truck drivers). Others require two-year or four-year degrees from a college or university. Entry-level positions for urban and regional planners often require an advanced degree.

Transportation Operations	Air & Space Transportation Manager ■ Airplane Pilot & Copilot ■ Flight Attendant ■ Air Traffic Controller ■ Aircraft Cargo Handling Supervisor ■ Rail Dispatcher ■ Locomotive Engineer ■ Railroad Brake, Signal, & Switch Operator ■ Train Crew Member ■ Yard Worker ■ Water Transportation Manager ■ Captain ■ Sailor & Marine ■ Ship & Boat Captain ■ Ship Engineer ■ Motorboat Operator ■ Bridge & Lock Tender ■ Truck, Bus, & Taxi Dispatcher ■ Truck Driver ■ Bus Driver ■ Taxi Driver ■ Bus Dispatcher ■ Subway & Streetcar Operator
Logistics Planning and Management Services	Logistician ■ Logistics Manager ■ Logistics Engineer ■ Logistics Analyst ■ Logistics Consultant ■ International Logistics Manager
Warehousing and Distribution Center Operations	Warehouse Manager ■ Storage & Distribution Manager ■ Industrial & Packaging Engineer ■ Traffic, Shipping, & Receiving Clerk ■ Production, Planning, & Expediting Clerk ■ First-Line Supervisor & Manager ■ Laborer & Material Mover ■ Machine & Vehicle Operator ■ Laborer & Freight Stock Material Mover ■ Car, Truck, & Ship Loader ■ Packer & Packager
Facility and Mobile Equipment Maintenance	Facility Maintenance Manager & Engineer ■ Industrial Equipment Mechanic ■ Industrial Electrician or Electronic Technician ■ Aerospace Engineering & Operations Technician ■ Aircraft Mechanic, Service Technician, or Engine Specialist ■ Power Plant Mechanic ■ Aircraft Body & Bonded Structure Repairer ■ Motorboat Mechanic ■ Ship Mechanic & Repairer ■ Rail Car Repairer & Mechanic ■ Signal & Track Switch Repairer ■ Motorcycle Mechanic ■ Automotive Body Repairer or Service Technician ■ Diesel Engine Specialist
Transportation Systems/ Infrastructure Planning, Management, and Regulation	Urban & Regional Planner ■ Civil Engineer ■ Engineering Technician ■ Surveying & Mapping Technician ■ Government Service Executive ■ Environmental Compliance Inspector ■ Air Traffic Controller ■ Aviation Inspector ■ Traffic Engineer ■ Traffic Technician ■ Motor Vehicle Inspector ■ Freight Inspector ■ Railroad Inspector ■ Marine Cargo Inspector ■ Vessel Traffic Control Specialists ■ Public Transportation Inspector ■ Government Agency Manager, Regulator, or Inspector
Health, Safety, and Environmental Management	Health & Safety Manager ■ Industrial Health & Safety Engineer ■ Environmental Scientist & Specialist ■ Environmental Science & Protection Technician ■ Environmental Manager & Engineer ■ Environmental Compliance Inspector ■ Safety Analyst
Sales and Service	Marketing Manager ■ Sales Manager ■ Sales Representative (Transportation & Logistics Services) ■ Reservation, Travel & Transportation Agent or Clerk ■ Customer Order & Billing Clerk ■ Cashier, Counter, or Rental Clerk ■ Cargo & Freight Agent ■ Customer Service Manager ■ Customer Service Representative

Glossary

401(k) plan. Retirement savings plan offered through an employer. (25)

529 plan. Savings plan for education operated by a state or educational institution. (16)

A

ability. Mastery of a skill or the capacity to do something. (15)

accounting. An analysis of financial data recorded. (21)

advanced-level job. A job that requires special skills, knowledge, and experience. (17)

Americans with Disabilities Act (ADA). Law prohibiting discrimination against individuals with disabilities who otherwise are qualified for a given job or position. (5)

annual percentage rate (APR). Rate of interest a borrower would have to pay to use a given amount of money for one year. (24)

antivirus software. Computer software used to prevent infections as well as to detect and remove computer viruses. (10)

appearance. Outward impression given to people, involving facial expressions, posture, the clothes you wear, and personal grooming. (6)

apprenticeship. Combination of on-the-job training and related classroom instruction in which workers learn the practical and theoretical aspects of a highly skilled occupation. (16)

aptitude. Person's natural, physical, and mental talents for learning. (15)

aptitude test. Test that measures a person's potential to perform the job after training. (5)

area measurement. Calculation of the amount of space within the borders of a geometric shape. (9)

Armed Services Vocational Aptitude Battery (ASVAB). Aptitude test designed to measure strengths, weaknesses, and potential for future success. (5)

asset. Items of value owned by a person or business; examples may include cash, stocks, bonds, and property. (21)

associate degree. Two-year college degree. (1)

attitude. Person's outlook on life that reflects how he or she feels and thinks about other people and situations. (3, 6)

automated teller machine (ATM). Computer terminals that customers use to make financial transactions. (25)

B

bachelor degree. Four-year college degree. (1)

bankruptcy. Legal proceeding for the purpose of stating a person's inability to pay his or her debts. (24)

bar graph. Visual aid used to show comparisons between categories. (9)

beneficiary. The person named by the policyholder to receive the benefits, or payments, issued from the insurance policy. (26)

Better Business Bureau (BBB). Nonprofit organization sponsored by private businesses that try to settle consumer complaints against local business firms. (23)

blind ad. Job advertisement that does not include the name of a company or contact person. (4)

block style letter. Style of business correspondence in which all lines are flush with the left-hand margin. (8)

blog. A website where an individual usually posts topics and opinions about subjects the owner wishes to discuss. (10)

bodily injury liability. A form of insurance coverage that protects you if you are legally at fault for an accident in which others are injured or killed. (26)

body language. A means of expressing a message through body movements, facial expressions, or hand gestures. (19)

bond. Certificate of debt or obligation issued by a corporation or a government. (25)

bonus. Extra payment in addition to the workers' regular pay. (22)

bookkeeping. The recording of income and expenses for a person or business. (21)

brainstorming. Group technique used to develop many ideas in a relatively short time. (7)

break-even point. When income equals expenses. (21)

browser. Type of program that allows you to access and view websites. (10)

budget. A written plan to help you make the most of the money you have. (23)

bullying. Offensive, insulting, or threatening behavior by individuals or groups. (18)

burnout. A loss of physical and emotional strength and motivation. (27)

business plan. Document used to help guide an entrepreneur in organizing and running a business. (21)

Business Professionals of America (BPA). An organization for students pursuing careers in business management, office administration, information technology, and other related career fields. (13)

bylaws. Written rules that spell out how meetings are to be conducted and who plays what role in the meetings. (14)

C

cafeteria plan. Coverage that allows workers to choose from a variety of benefits to devise a plan that best suits their needs. (26)

calorie. Metric unit of energy. (11)

canceled check. Checks that have been processed by the bank. (25)

capital. Possessions and money used to increase business. (20)

capital expense. A one-time cost needed to get the business started; an example includes machines purchased for the business. (21)

career. Progression of related occupations that results in employment and personal growth. (1)

Career and Technical Student Organization (CTSO). A national organization associated with a specific occupational area, such as agriculture, marketing, and family and consumer sciences. (13)

career clusters. Groups of occupational and career specialties. (1)

career ladder. Job-related progression from an entry level to an advanced position along a specified career path. (17)

career pathway. One of several career directions within the career clusters. (1)

career plan. List of steps required to reach a career goal. (17)

CareerOneStop. Website sponsored by the US Department of Labor to help students, job seekers, and career professionals explore the outlook and trends for all types of careers. (16)

cash card. Prepaid type of debit card. (25)

cash value. The amount the policy is worth in cash upon surrender of the policy. (26)

cashier's check. Check issued from a bank's own account rather than the account of a person or a business. (25)

Centers for Disease Control and Prevention (CDC). Part of the United States Department of Health and Human Services that works with worldwide, state, and local health agencies to protect the public from health threats. (12)

central processing unit (CPU). The part of the computer that controls what is done with the data received; also called the processor. (10)

certificate of deposit (CD). A savings account that pays a higher interest rate because it requires depositors to commit their money for a specific period. (25)

certified check. Personal check with a bank's guarantee that the check will be paid. (25)

channel. How a message is delivered during the communication process. (8)

circle graph. Visual aid showing the relationship of parts to the whole. (9)

citation. Summons to appear in court. (12)

civil law. Law that outlines citizens' rights in relation to one another. (27)

civil service test. Examination required when applying for most government jobs. (5)

claim. A formal request to an insurance company requesting compensation for a loss covered under a policy. (26)

cloud computing. Using software applications and files stored on the Internet. (10)

collateral. Something of value held by the creditor in case you are unable to repay the loan. For an auto loan, the car is collateral. (24)

collective bargaining. Process of labor and management representatives discussing what they expect from each other in the workplace. (18)

college access. Building awareness about college opportunities, providing guidance regarding college admissions, and identifying ways to pay for college. (16)

commission. Percentage of the sales they make. (22)

common fraction. One or more parts of a whole number. (9)

communication. Process of conveying a message, thought, or idea so it is accurately received and understood. (8)

communication barrier. Anything that prevents clear, effective communication. (8)

comparison shopping. Looking at several brands or models at different stores to compare prices, quality, and features before buying. (23)

compound interest. Interest paid on the initial deposit plus any interest already earned. (25)

comprehension. Ability to understand information. (8)

compromise. When opposing sides give up something of value to help solve a problem. (7)

confidential. Private. (3)

conflict. Situation resulting from opposing views. (7)

consensus. When all members of a group accept and support a decision. (7)

constraint. Factor that may restrict or hinder your ability to solve the problem. (7)

constructive criticism. Pointing out a weakness to analyze it and cause improvement. (3)

consumer. People who use their income to buy the items they need and want. (23)

Consumer Financial Protection Bureau (CFPB). Regulatory agency that works to give consumers all the information they need when dealing with financial companies. (23)

consumer fraud. Use of trickery or deceit to gain some type of unfair or dishonest advantage over the consumer. (23)

Consumer Price Index (CPI). Measure of the average change in prices for consumer goods and services over time. (25)

Consumer Product Safety Commission (CPSC). Regulatory agency that protects the consumer's right to safety. (23)

conviction. A strong belief. (18)

cooperative education. School program that prepares students for an occupation through a paid job experience. (2)

copyright. Exclusive right to copy, license, sell, or distribute material. (10)

corporation. Business owned by many people. (20)

cosigner. Responsible person who signs a loan agreement with the borrower. By signing the agreement, the cosigner promises to pay the loan if the borrower fails to pay. (24)

courteous. Showing concern for other people and being mannerly with them. (3)

credit. Present use of future income that allows consumers to buy goods and services now and pay for them later. (24)

credit report. Summary of how a person or business has used credit. (24)

creditworthiness. Assessment of a borrower's ability to repay a loan. (24)

criminal law. Law that governs the association between citizens and the government. (27)

criminal penalty. A lawful punishment involving one or more of the following: serving a jail sentence, doing community service, paying a fine, and periodically reporting to a court-ordered supervisor. (19)

criteria. Standards you use to find the best solution. (7)

cross-functional team. Team of workers from different areas within a company who are assigned to work on a specific project. (7)

D

debit card. A card that allows funds to be withdrawn from your checking or savings account without writing a check. (25)

debt-to-income ratio. Way of comparing debt to income or assets. (24)

DECA. A Career and Technical Student Organization that prepares emerging leaders and entrepreneurs for careers in marketing, finance, hospitality, and management in high schools and colleges around the world. (13)

decimal fraction. Fraction with a denominator of 10, such as 100, 1000, and 10,000. (9)

decision-making process. Proven way to make important decisions carefully and logically. (17)

decoder. Receiver's mind, which forms a mental image of the message received. (8)

deductible. An amount the policyholder must pay before the insurance company will begin to cover the expense. (26)

defendant. The person accused of wrongdoing and whom a lawsuit is filed against. (27)

degree Celsius (°C). Metric measure for temperature. (9)

delegate. Assign responsibility or authority to another person or group. (13)

demand. Amount of products and services consumers want to buy. (20)

demotion. Transfer to a classification in a lower pay grade. (18)

denominator. Denominator is the number of parts into which a fraction is divided and is written below, or after the line in a fraction. (9)

dependability. Person's ability to be reliable and trustworthy. (3)

dermatologist. Doctor who specializes in treating skin. (11)

digital measuring instrument. Device used to convert distance, temperature, weights, volume of liquids, airflow, and liquid flow and pressure into numbers on a digital display. (9)

disability. Permanent injury. (12)

disability insurance. A type of insurance coverage that provides regular income payments when a person is unable to work for an extended period of time because of an injury or illness. (26)

discrimination. The negative treatment of one or more individuals compared to that of the larger group. (19)

diversity. The variety that exists among a group. (19)

dynamics. Underlying causes of change or growth. (13)

E

earned income. Money received for doing a job. (22)

e-check. Electronic version of a paper check and can be used for online payments. (25)

ego. Part of the mind that is aware of reality and demonstrates control. (15)

electronic funds transfer (EFT). Automatic transfer of money from one account to another electronically. (25)

e-mail. A system for sending messages from one device to another over an electronic network. (10)

emergency cash fund. Money saved and available to cover unexpected expenses. (23)

Employee Polygraph Protection Act (EPPA). Law passed in 1988 that prohibits most private employers from using lie-detector tests for preemployment screening or during the course of employment. (5)

empty calorie. Energy present in high-energy foods with poor nutrition; with most of the energy coming from processed carbohydrates, and fats, or ethanol. (11)

encoder. Sender's mind, which forms a mental image of the message being sent. (8)

endorsement. Signature required on the back of a check to legally transfer value. (25)

entrepreneur. Person who starts a new business and takes on the risks, responsibilities, and potential rewards of operating and building the business. (21)

entrepreneurship. Organization and management of a business. (21)

entry-level job. Work for beginners who lack experience or specialized training. (17)

Environmental Protection Agency (EPA). Government agency formed for the purpose of protecting the environment. (12)

Equal Employment Opportunity Commission (EEOC). Federal agency that oversees equal employment opportunities for all Americans. (2)

Equal Pay Act. Law that requires equal pay be given to employees of both sexes for doing equal jobs. (2)

equity. Fair treatment giving a person the same opportunities afforded to others. (24) In real estate, the difference between how much is owed on a house and what the house is worth. (19)

ergonomics. Science of examining motions and how to perform them properly. (12)

ethics. Set of moral values that guide a person's conduct. (3, 15)

etiquette. Art of using good manners in any situation. (8)

excise tax. Tax charged to the producer or seller of the product or service rather than the consumer. (22)

F

Fair Labor Standards Act (FLSA). Law designed to protect workers from unfair treatment by their employers. (2)

falling hazard. Source of potential injuries from slipping or falling. (12)

Family and Medical Leave Act (FMLA). A law passed in 1993 designed to help families handle special family matters by permitting employees to take time off without pay. (27)

Family, Career and Community Leaders of America (FCCLA). CTSO with an emphasis on family and consumer science, for students through grade 12. (13)

Federal Communications Commission (FCC). Regulatory agency that protects the consumer's rights to information and selection; the FCC handles complaints about the practices and charges of wired and wireless telephone systems. (23)

Federal Trade Commission (FTC). Regulatory agency that protects the consumer's rights to information and selection; the FTC prevents unfair competition, deceptive trade practices, and false advertising. (23)

feedback. Clue that reveals the message was received. (8)

fee-for-service (FFS) plan. A traditional type of health care policy that allows members to use any doctor or hospital he or she chooses. (26)

felony. The most serious type of crime, punishable by imprisonment or even death. (27)

FICA. Amount withheld for both Medicare and Social Security; also the Federal Insurance Contributions Act. (22)

finance charge. Total amount a borrower must pay for the use of credit. (24)

financial literacy. Ability to understand and manage one's personal finances. (9)

first aid. Immediate, temporary treatment given to an ill or injured person before proper medical help arrives. (12)

fixed expense. A cost that must be paid regularly in set amounts; examples are monthly rent payments, garbage removal fees, and insurance payments. (21)

flammable. Having the potential to ignite easily and burn rapidly. (12)

flextime. Schedule where a worker's time of arrival and departure differs from the operating hours of the workplace. (27)

follow-up message. Brief correspondence written in business form to thank the interviewer for his or her time. (6)

Food and Drug Administration (FDA). Regulatory agency that helps protect consumer safety by regulating the production, packaging, and labeling of foods, drugs, and cosmetics. (23)

Form W-2. Document used for tax purposes to show the amount paid in the previous year. (22)

Form W-4. Form used to give an employer the information needed to determine how much tax to withhold from a paycheck. (22)

formal communication. Sharing of information in which specific rules of etiquette must be followed. (8)

formal meeting. A meeting in the workplace where coworkers meet to brainstorm new ideas, decide how to divide the department workload, and update staff on important events. (14)

franchise. Right to sell another company's product or service for profit. (21)

fraud. The act of deceiving or tricking a person or business. (21)

Free Application for Federal Student Aid (FAFSA). Application form used to determine your eligibility for federal financial aid. (16)

free enterprise system. Economic system in which people are free to make their own economic decisions. (20)

freeware. Fully functional software that can be used without purchasing it. (10)

fringe benefit. Financial extras in addition to the regular paycheck, such as medical and life insurance, paid vacations, bonuses, and retirement plans. (16)

functional team. Team of workers with similar skills and expertise. (7)

Future Business Leaders of America (FBLA). A Career and Technical Student Organization that prepares students for careers in business and business-related fields. (13)

Future Educators Association (FEA). A Career and Technical Student Organization that provides activities and materials for students interested in education-related careers. (13)

G

Gantt chart. Graph that shows the steps of a task divided across a timetable. (7)

General Aptitude Test Battery (GATB). Series of tests that measure nine aptitudes. (15)

global positioning system (GPS). A highly accurate satellite-based navigation system. (10)

globalization. Process of businesses and financial markets becoming more interconnected. (7)

goal. Something you want to attain. (7)

good. Any type of product consumers buy, such as food or clothing. (23)

grace period. Number of days allowed to make a payment without incurring any late penalties, fees or additional interest charges. (24)

gram (g). Metric measure for weight. (9)

grant. Type of financial aid that is typically need-based and provided by a nonprofit organization, such as the government or other organization. (16)

green job. Job that helps sustain or improve the environment. (12)

grooming. Taking proper care of your body and appearance through cleanliness and neatness. (11)

gross pay. Total amount earned for a pay period before deductions are subtracted. (22)

group dynamics. Interacting forces within a human group. (13)

H

habit. Something done repeatedly in the same way. (15)

hacking. Accessing a computer or network system without being authorized to do so. (10)

hard skill. Skill learned as requirements of a career or other activities. (15)

health maintenance organization (HMO). An organization of medical personnel and facilities that provides health care services to its members. (26)

Health Occupations Students of America (HOSA). A Career and Technical Student Organization that promotes opportunities in health care and enhances the delivery of quality health care to all people. (13)

health savings account (HSA). An account that allows individuals to set money aside on a tax-free basis to pay for future qualifying medical expenses. (26)

hearing. Recognizing sound. (8)

honesty test. Test designed to measure a person's honesty in the workplace. Also called an *integrity test*. (5)

hostile environment harassment. Behavior that makes an atmosphere uncomfortable enough to interfere with a person's performance. (19)

human resources department. Group of people assigned to handle various responsibilities related to employment. (4)

hygiene. Practice of staying healthy by keeping clean. (11)

I

I-9 Form. Document used to verify an employee's identity and verify that he or she is authorized to work in the United States. (6)

id. Part of the mind that is driven by thrills, impulses, and desires. (15)

identity theft. Illegal use of another's name and personal information to open accounts, make purchases, or commit fraud. (4, 10)

impulse buying. Making an unplanned purchase. (23)

incentive. Something that inspires a person to act. (18)

individual responsibility. Willingness to answer for one's conduct and decisions. (3)

individual retirement account (IRA). Type of savings account that anyone with earned income can open as a way to save for retirement. (25)

inflation. General increase in prices. (25)

informal communication. Unscheduled communication with coworkers that occurs by chance inside and outside the workplace. (8)

informal interview. Planned meeting in which a job seeker learns more about an occupation from a person employed in that job area. (16)

informal meeting. A meeting structured to be conducted in a specific way. (14)

informational interview. Planned meeting in which a job applicant learns more about an occupation from a person employed in that job area. (6)

initiative. Making oneself do what is necessary. (3)

installment account. Type of credit account used to charge expensive items such as a major appliance or piece of furniture. (24)

integrity. Quality of firmly following one's moral values. (3)

interest. An activity, event, or idea that you like. (24) Price paid for the use of money over a period of time. (15)

Internal Revenue Service (IRS). Federal government agency that enforces federal tax laws and collects taxes. (22)

internship. School program providing paid or unpaid work experience for a specified period as a way to learn about a job or an industry. (2)

interpersonal skills. Display of friendliness and sensitivity to the needs of others through communication and listening. (7)

interview. Planned meeting between a job applicant and an employer. (2)

J

job. Task performed by a worker, usually to earn money. (1)

job evaluation. Written review of your work performance by your supervisor. (3)

job probation. Trial period to test how well a worker can do the job. (18)

job-search website. Website designed to find job openings posted at a variety of locations. (4)

job shadowing. Following a worker on the job and observing what that job involves. (1)

job sharing. When a single job is split between two or more employees. (27)

jury. A panel of citizens selected to help decide some cases in a trial court. (27)

L

labor contract. Agreement that spells out the conditions for wages, benefits, job security, work hours, working conditions, and grievance procedures. (18)

labor union. Group of workers who have united to voice their opinions to their employer or the employer's representatives (management). (18)

laser measuring instrument. Device designed to give you the ability to measure a distance simply by projecting a light beam. (9)

lateral move. Transfer to a different department or another classification in the same pay grade. (18)

leadership. Capacity to direct a group. (13)

learning style. The way a person takes in and processes information. (15)

letter of application. Letter written to an employer to apply for a job. (4)

liability. The debt owed by a person or business; examples include payments on a car or home loan. (21)

license. Official permission to do something or own something. (21)

licensing. The legal permission to use a software program. (10)

lifelong learning. The continuous building of skills and knowledge throughout the life of an individual. (10)

lifestyle goal. Goal that reflects what a person wants from life. (15)

lifting hazard. Source of potential injury from improperly lifting or carrying items. (12)

line graph. Chart showing the relationship of two or more variables. (9)

linear measurement. Length of a straight or curved line calculated with a ruler, yardstick, or tape measure. (9)

listening. Understanding what you hear. (8)

liter (l). Metric measure for volume. (9)

long-term goal. Goal that may take several months or years to achieve. (15)

loyalty. Being faithful to your coworkers and to your employer. (3)

M

main motion. Suggestion for the group members to consider during a meeting. (14)

major decision. Important choice requiring careful thought because it affects a person's career and personal life. (17)

malware. Computer software that interferes with normal computer operations and may send your personal data to unauthorized parties. (10)

material safety data sheet (MSDS). Sheet of information on the specific hazards involved and procedures for their safe use. (12)

material-storage hazard. Sources of potential injury that come from the improper storage of files, books, or office equipment. (12)

mean. Mathematical average of the data calculated. (9)

median. Number exactly in the middle when the data is listed in ascending or descending order. (9)

Medicare. Health insurance program provided through Social Security taxes that are withheld from a worker's paycheck. (22)

memo. Informal written message from one person or department to another person, persons, or departments in the same company. (8)

message. Something that is understood by the senses—usually something spoken, written, or printed. (8)

meter (m). Metric measure for length or distance. (9)

metric system. Decimal system of weights and measures, which uses the meter to measure distance, the gram to calculate weight, the liter to measure volume, and the degree Celsius to determine temperature. (9)

minimum wage. Lowest hourly rate of pay that most employees must receive. (2)

misdemeanor. A less serious crime with penalties of fine or imprisonment of a year or less or both. (27)

mobile app. A small, specialized program used on wireless devices, such as tablets and smartphones. (10)

mock interview. Practice interview conducted by a friend, family member, or other adult with business experience. (6)

mode. Number(s) that occurs most frequently in a group of numbers. (9)

modified block style letter. Style of correspondence that places the date, complimentary close, and signature to the right of the center point of the letter. (8)

money market fund. A type of mutual fund that deals only in high interest, short-term investments. (25)

money order. Type of check used for a specific amount of money payable to a specific payee. (25)

monopoly. Single company that controls the entire supply of a product or service. (20)

moral values. Code of behavior that is considered acceptable in society. (3)

multifunctional team. Team of cross-trained workers who can perform the duties of all other members on the team. (7)

mutual fund. Type of investment where money from a number of investors is combined and invested in securities. (25)

N

National FFA Organization (FFA). CTSO that prepares members for leadership and careers within the eight Agriculture, Food, and Natural Resources Sciences Cluster pathways. (13)

National Institute for Occupational Safety and Health (NIOSH). An arm of the Centers for Disease Control and Prevention specifically responsible for conducting research and making recommendations for the prevention of work-related injury and illness. (12)

National Safety Council. The leading advocate for safety and health in the United States. (12)

need. Basic necessity a person must have to live. (20)

need-based award. Type of financial aid that is available for students and families who meet certain economic requirements. (16)

networking. Talking with people and establishing relationships that can lead to more information or business. (4)

noise. Anything that interrupts the message. (8)

nonverbal communication. Any message that does not use written or spoken words. (8)

norm. Pattern that is typical in the development of a social group. (7)

numerator. Number of parts present in a fraction and is written above or before the line in a fraction. (9)

O

occupation. Work that requires the use of related skills and experience. (1)

Occupational Information Network (O*NET™). Internet system that provides the latest information needed for effective training, education, counseling, and employment. (16)

Occupational Outlook Handbook. Occupational resource that describes the training and education needed for various occupations, also listing expected earnings, working conditions, and future job prospects. (16)

Occupational Safety and Health Administration (OSHA). Federal government agency that sets and enforces safety and health standards for workers. (2, 12)

occupational training. Training which prepares a person for a job in a specific field. (16)

occupational trend. Research-based forecasts about which jobs will most likely be needed in the future. (1)

One-Stop Career Center. A center that provides employment counseling, information on job trends, and assistance in filing unemployment insurance. (16)

organization chart. Chart that shows an organization's internal structure. (20)

orientation. A meeting at which a new employee learns the company's history, policies, rules, and safety procedures. (18)

overtime pay. Pay for each hour worked in excess of the maximum hours allowed. (2)

ownership. When an individual understands the importance of a task and makes sure it is done well. (27)

P

Pareto Principle. General rule stating that 20 percent of causes produce 80 percent of the effects; or 20 percent of effort produces 80 percent of the results. (7)

parliamentary procedure. Set of rules explaining how a group should gather, share information, and make decisions. (14)

partnership. Form of business organization where two or more people go into business together. (20)

patent system. Arrangement that protects inventors from having someone else claim their ideas and inventions as his or her own. (20)

payroll deduction. Amounts of money subtracted from your total pay. (22)

payroll tax. Tax an employer withholds from an employee's paycheck. (22)

percent. Calculation of one part per hundred. (9)

performance rating. A supervisor's periodic evaluation of a worker's job performance. (18)

peripheral. Anything that can be plugged into the computer. (10)

personal fact sheet. Brief written summary of key facts that helps a person write letters of application, prepare job résumés, and fill out application forms. (4)

personality. How a person thinks and feels. (15)

phishing. Tricking someone into giving out personal and financial information, such as an identification number or password. (23)

pictograph. Visual aid that presents information with the use of eye-catching images. (9)

piecework. Form of income in which an employee is paid a fixed amount of money for each piece of work completed. (22)

plaintiff. The person who files a lawsuit, taking his or her case to court. (27)

point-of-service (POS) plan. An insurance plan that allows members to choose either an HMO or PPO each time they seek medical services. (26)

polygraph test. Given with a polygraph machine, a test that measures and records on graph paper the changes in the subject's blood pressure, perspiration, and pulse rate when an examiner asks questions. Also called a *lie-detector test.* (5)

portfolio. Well-organized collection of materials that provides evidence of one's qualifications. (4)

preferred provider organization (PPO). A health care organization that has made arrangements with doctors and hospitals who have agreed to accept lower fees for their services in providing health care for group members. (26)

premium. A set amount of money that the insured party pays to the insurance company on a regular basis. (26)

priority. First ranking in a "to do" list when items are listed by order of importance from first to last. (2)

probability. Chance that something will happen. (9)

problem. Difference between reality (what you have) and expectation (what you want). (7)

problem solving. Process of making an expectation a reality. (7)

procrastinate. To avoid completing an important task by doing other things. (27)

productive resources. Resources such as labor, land, capital, and equipment that can be used to produce and provide goods and services. (20)

profit. Amount of money a business makes from selling goods and services beyond the cost of producing them (20); the money remaining from business income after paying all expenses. (21)

profit ratio. The percentage of receipts that are profit. (21)

profit sharing. Form of income, usually company stock or bonuses, given periodically throughout the year. (22)

program coordinator. Special teacher or counselor assigned to students in a work-based learning program. (2)

promotion. Transfer to a job classification with a higher pay grade. (18)

property damage liability. A form of insurance coverage that pays for damages your car causes to the property of others if you are responsible for the accident. (26)

property tax. Tax on the value of personal property and real estate a person owns. (22)

protein. Natural substance required for cell and muscle growth. (11)

psychological test. Preemployment test given to examine an applicant's personality, character, and interests. (5)

punctuality. Being on time. (3)

Q

quality. Commitment by everyone in an organization to exceed customer expectations. (7)

quid pro quo harassment. Making unwelcome sexual advances toward another while promising certain benefits if the person complies. (19)

quorum. Majority of members or the number of members stated in the bylaws. (14)

R

receipt. Include all the money you receive from your customers for cash and credit sales. (21)

receiver. Person who gets the message. (8)

recourse. Right to complain and receive a response. (23)

reference. Person who knows you well and is willing to discuss your personal and job qualifications with employers. (4)

remote meeting. Where people come together using a technology tool rather than meeting face-to-face. (14)

reprisal. The revenge-motivated act of retaliating. (19)

resource. Something used to help reach a goal. (15)

résumé. Brief history of a person's education, work experience, and other qualifications for employment. (4)

revolving charge account. Type of credit account allows customers the choice of paying for purchases in full each month or spreading payments over a period of time. (24)

routine decision. Choice most people make automatically about everyday matters. (17)

S

safety conscious. Knowing the job hazards and taking appropriate steps to avoid accidents. (12)

salary. Set amount of money paid for a certain period of time. (22)

sales tax. Tax on goods and services. (22)

scholarship. Type of financial aid that is based on financial need or some type of merit or accomplishment. (16)

secondary motion. Motion that can be made while a main motion is being considered. (14)

securities. Financial instruments that represent either ownership (stocks), indebtedness (bonds) or the rights to ownership (derivatives). (25)

self-assessment. Process of taking stock of your skills, interests, aptitudes, and abilities. (15)

self-concept. Mental image you have of yourself. (15)

self-directed team. Team that has been given full responsibility for carrying out its assignment. (7)

self-esteem. A feeling of satisfaction, self-worth, and confidence. (3, 15)

self-management skill. The ability to manage your own activities to get the job done. (3)

sender. Person who starts the communication process and has a mental image of what he or she wants to communicate. (8)

service. Any type of work consumers pay to have done. (23)

sexual harassment. Unwanted advances, requests for favors, or other verbal or physical conduct of a sexual nature. (19)

shareware. Software that can be installed and used, then purchased if you decide to keep using it. (10)

short-term goal. Goal to be reached tomorrow, next week, or within a few months. (15)

simple interest. Interest paid only on the money initially deposited. (25)

situational test. Preemployment test used to examine the ability of job applicants in a work setting similar to that of the job. (5)

skill. Something you do well. (1)

skill test. Preemployment test used to determine the physical or mental abilities of a job applicant. (5)

SkillsUSA. National, nonprofit Career and Technical Student Organization for high school and college students, as well as teachers. (13)

slate. List of candidates prepared for nomination. (14)

Small Business Administration (SBA). Agency that provides assistance to small business owners. (21)

smart card. Advanced type of debit card that contains a microchip. This chip can hold extensive account information. (25)

sociability. Interacting easily with people. (3)

social media Tools used to publish and share information between individuals or groups of individuals. (10)

Social Security. US government's federal program for providing income when earnings are reduced or stopped by retirement, disability, or death. (2)

soft skill. Personal skill that affects how an individual interacts with others. (15)

software piracy. The illegal copying or downloading of software. (10)

sole proprietorship. Business that has only one owner. (20)

special committee. Committee established for a specific purpose or for a short period. (14)

standard. Accepted level of achievement. (15)

standard of living. Goods and services considered essential for living. (15)

standing committee. One of the permanent committees of a group or organization. (14)

stereotyping. Classifying or generalizing about a group of people. (19)

stock. Share in the ownership of a corporation. (25)

stress. Physical and emotional reaction to a challenge. (11) A feeling of pressure, strain, or tension that results from change. (18)

summarize. Write down the main ideas of an assignment to express key thoughts. (2)

superego. Part of the mind that is influenced by social morals and values. (15)

supervisor. A manager or team leader in the workplace. (2, 3)

supply. Amount of products and services available for sale. (20)

support system. Group of caring, concerned friends and relatives. (27)

T

table. Visual aid that arranges data in rows and columns. (9)

taxes. Payments that citizens and businesses are required to pay to city, county, state, and federal governments. (22)

team. Small group of people working together for a common purpose. (7)

Technology Student Association (TSA). Career and Technical Student Organization that provides competitions and programs for middle and high school students with a strong interest in technology, innovation, design, and engineering. (13)

teleconferencing. A meeting that takes place over the telephone between participants at two or more locations. (10, 14)

template. Preformatted form available in word processing software. (8)

term insurance. A type of insurance that covers the policyholder for a set period of years specified in the policy. (26)

text messaging. Process of exchanging brief written messages between electronic devices over a network; also known as *texting*. (10)

tips. Small amounts of money given by customers to service-related workers in return for service. (22)

tort. A wrongful act committed against another person, independent of a contract. (27)

training agreement. Document that outlines the responsibilities of the student worker, school, and employer. (2)

training plan. List of attitudes, skills, and knowledge that a student plans to learn during the work experience. (2)

training record. Weekly or monthly job record of duties performed and skills learned at work by a student worker in a work-based learning program. (2)

training station. Job site where a student works to learn job skills. (2)

transferable skill. Skills used in one job that can also be used in another job. (1)

traveler's check. Type of check that is accepted as cash in most places around the world. Personal checks may be accepted only locally. (25)

troubleshooting. Locating the source of a problem, then fixing it. (10)

U

undercapitalization. Any situation where a business cannot acquire the funds they need. (21)

unemployment insurance. Coverage that provides benefits to workers who have lost their jobs. (22)

universal life insurance. A type of insurance that combines death benefits with a savings and investment account. (26)

universal precautions. Steps designed to help prevent the spread of infection. (12)

V

values. Principles and beliefs that a person considers important. (15)

variable expense. A cost that varies from month to month; examples are advertising costs, repairs, utility bills, and supplies needed for the business. (21)

video résumé. Short one to three minute video presentation used to reinforce the material presented on a résumé. (4)

videoconferencing. Involves two or more people communicating through a video and voice linkup. (10)

virtual team. Team that uses communication technology to help solve problems. (7)

virus. Type of malware used to infect computers. (10)

vision. Understanding of what is most important to the group and how to achieve it. (13)

W

wage. Set amount of pay for every hour of work. (22)

want. Item a person would like to have, but can live without. (20)

warranty. Written promise that guarantees a product will meet certain performance and quality standards. (23)

web seminar. A means of delivering instruction to a group located at one or more locations other than where the material is being presented; also referred to as *webinars*. (10)

webcast. An event, either live or prerecorded, that is broadcast on the Internet. (10)

white space. Margins, space between paragraphs, and any other blank space on the page. (8)

whole grain. Food made from grain, containing all the essential parts and naturally-occurring nutrients of the entire grain seed. (11)

whole life insurance. A type of insurance that covers the policyholder for a lifetime which can also be used, a form of savings. (26)

work ethic. How a person feels about his or her job and the effort put into it. (3)

work permit. Written document that makes it legal for a student underage to work for an employer. (2)

work-based learning program. Type of school program designed to prepare students for work. (2)

work-based mentor. Person who helps student workers with day-to-day questions. Another common term for this worker is *training sponsor*. (2)

workers' compensation. Insurance against loss of income from work-related accidents paid to workers after they are injured or become ill during work. (12, 22)

Workplace Skills Assessment Program (WSAP). Process through which Business Professionals of America prepares students to assess their real-world business skills and problem-solving abilities in finance, management, information technology, and computer applications. (13)

workplace violence. Violent acts or threatening behavior that occur in the workplace or at a company function. (12)

work-related hazard. Possible dangers or unsafe conditions in the workplace. (12)

work-study program. Part-time employment provided to undergraduate and graduate students to help with college expenses. (16)

World Wide Web. The part of the Internet that carries messages having pictures, color, or sound. (10)

Z

zoning laws. Rules that regulate what types of business activities can be performed in certain areas. (21)

Index

401(k) plan, 636, 642
529 plan, 386, 394

A

ability, 363
academic skills
    comprehension, 183
    listening, 182
    reading, 183
    vocabulary, 184
    writing skills, 184
accident, 286, 294, 296
    causes, 286
    prevention, 296–297
    procedures, 296
account, 624
    types, 590–593
accounting, 511, 517
ACCUPLACER, 362
ACT, 362
ADA. *See* Americans with Disabilities Act
administrative assistant, 152
advanced-level job, 413
advertise, 506
advertisement, 562
Age Discrimination in Employment Act, 463
agent, 653
agriculture, food and natural resources career cluster, 5
airport air traffic controller, 617
America's Career InfoNet, 80
America's Service Locator, 80
American Bar Association, 694
Americans with Disabilities Act (ADA), 113, 464
announcements, 346
annual percentage rate (APR), 586
antivirus software, 238, 241
appearance, 130
application, 100
    completing an, 100
    form, 101
applications software, 245
Apply Your Knowledge, 19, 43, 67, 105, 123, 147, 175, 207, 259, 281, 309, 331–332, 351, 375, 421, 451, 471, 491, 521, 551, 581, 613, 647, 671, 699

Apply Your Technology Skills, 20, 45, 68, 107, 125, 148, 177, 209, 241, 262, 284, 311, 333, 353, 377, 411, 413, 423, 453, 472, 493, 553, 582, 614, 672, 700
applying for a loan, 515
apprenticeship, 386, 388
APR. *See* annual percentage rate
aptitude, 358, 362
aptitude test, 118
architecture and construction career cluster, 23, 109
area measurement, 212
Armed Forces, 390
Armed Services Vocational Aptitude Battery (ASVAB), 120, 362
arts, audio/video technology and communications career cluster, 47, 127
assessments, preemployment, 110
asset, 511, 517
assistive technology device, 243
associate degree, 8–9
ASVAB. *See* Armed Services Vocational Aptitude Battery
ATM. *See* automated teller machine
attendance, 50
attitude, 48, 136
automated teller machine (ATM), 618, 622–623
automobile insurance, 658

B

bachelor degree, 8–9
banking, 616, 618
bankruptcy, 605, 610
bar graph, 227–228
BBB. *See* Better Business Bureau
beneficiary, 658, 666
benefit, 685
Better Business Bureau (BBB), 562, 572, 574
blind ad, 79
block style letter, 194, 206
blog, 96–97, 243, 250
bodily injury liability, 658
body language, 461, 465–466
bond, 636, 640–641, 528, 531
bonus, 143
bookkeeping, 511, 517

BPA. *See* Business Professionals of America
brainstorming, 164, 169
break-even point, 511, 519
browser, 238
budget, 556–557, 560
Build Your Vocabulary 13, 17, 28, 36, 59, 65, 84, 103, 114, 135, 145, 163, 173, 189, 194, 205, 221, 232, 242, 252, 257, 271, 279, 295, 307, 317, 329, 340, 349, 364, 372, 386, 409, 412, 419, 439, 446, 449, 460, 469, 482, 489, 510, 519, 539, 549, 561, 579, 604, 611, 635, 645, 657, 669, 688, 697
bullying, 428, 431
burnout, 676, 678
business communications, 195
business letter, 194, 197, 200–202
    bad-news, 200
    block style, 194
    good-news, 197
    modified block style, 194
    neutral-message, 197
    request, 197
    parts, 194–195
        body, 195
        complimentary close, 195
        enclosure notation, 195
        salutation, 195
        signature, 195
business organization, 483
business plan, 498, 501
Business Professionals of America (BPA), 3, 319–320
business, starting, 511
business structure, 486, 511, 519
bylaws, 336–337

C

CAD operator, 23
cafeteria plan, 652, 656
calculator, 213–215
    addition, 214
    decimals, 215
    division, 214
    fractions, 215
    multiplication, 214
    percentages, 215
    subtraction, 214
call center employee, 237

calorie, 264, 267
    empty, 267
canceled check, 618, 633
capital expense, 511, 515
capital resource, 503
capital, 476–477
car accident, 662
care center, 683
career, 7
    choice 424
    exploration, 2, 12
    ladder, 413, 418
    pathway, 12
    plan, 413–415
    preparing, 14
    researching, 380
    skills, 184
    speaking, 184, 187
Career and Technical Student
    Organization (CTSO), 151, 226,
    318–320, 323–324, 327, 355, 525
career clusters, 10–11
Career Snapshot, 5, 23, 47, 73, 109,
    127, 152, 179, 211, 237, 263, 313 ,
    335, 357, 379, 407, 427, 455, 475,
    495, 527, 555, 585, 617, 651, 675
CareerOneStop, 380, 383
Case, 16, 32, 53, 94, 121, 138, 168,
    195, 230, 255, 273, 304, 328, 344,
    373, 398, 417, 438, 468, 488, 516,
    532, 571, 600, 638, 668, 692
cash card, 618, 624
cash value, 658, 667
cashier, 211
cashier's check, 618, 634
casualty, 658
CD. *See* certificate of deposit
CDC. *See* Centers for Disease
    Control and Prevention
cell phones, 247
Centers for Disease Control and
    Prevention (CDC), 296, 307
central processing unit (CPU), 243–
    244
certificate of deposit (CD), 636, 639
certified check, 618, 634
CFPB. *See* Consumer Financial
    Protection Bureau
chain of command, 190
change, making, 212
channel, 180–181
charge account, 593
chart, 228
check, 627–630
checkbook balance, 632
checking account, 624, 626

Checkpoint, 13, 17, 28, 36, 41, 59, 65,
    84, 103, 114, 121, 135, 145, 163, 173,
    189, 193, 205, 221, 232, 242, 252,
    257, 271, 279, 295, 317, 329, 340,
    349, 364, 372, 386, 401, 412, 419,
    439, 443, 449, 460, 469, 482, 489,
    510, 519, 539, 549, 561, 579, 604,
    611, 635, 645, 657, 669, 688, 697
checks, types, 618
    canceled, 618, 633
    cashier's, 618, 634
    certified, 618, 634
    traveler's, 618, 634
chef, 263
Child Labor Standards, 35
childcare assistant, 313
childcare worker, 313
Christie, Luke, 75
circle, 219
circle graph, 227–228
citation, 296, 305
citizenship, 674, 689
civil law, 689, 691–692
Civil Rights Act, 462–463
Civil Service Commission, 119
civil service test, 119
claim, 658, 661
clothing, 277
    protective, 297
cloud computing, 243, 246
coin, 627
collateral, 586, 594
collective bargaining, 446, 449
college access, 392
College and Career Readiness
    Portfolio, 21, 45, 69, 107, 125, 149,
    241, 261, 283, 311, 333, 353, 377,
    413, 423, 474, 493, 523, 553, 583,
    615, 649, 673, 701
collision coverage, 659
commission, 528–529
committees, forming, 338
Common Core, 20, 45, 68, 106, 124,
    148, 176, 208, 240, 260, 283, 310,
    332, 352, 376, 422, 453, 480, 492,
    552, 582, 614, 648, 700
    CTE Career Ready Practices,
      20, 106, 124, 208, 240, 310,
      332, 412, 422, 472, 492, 522,
      614, 648
    Listening, 45, 148, 260, 352,
      453, 552
    Reading, 20, 68, 76, 176, 240,
      282, 332, 422, 522, 582,
      648, 700
    Speaking, 45, 148, 260, 360,
      453, 552
    Writing, 68, 176, 208, 283, 310,
      376, 412, 480, 492, 582, 614,
      700

common fraction, 212, 215
common stock, 641
communication, 178, 180
    barrier, 190, 192
    business, 195
    channels, 190–205
    downward, 191
    effective, 180
    electronic, 248
    formal, 190
    informal, 191, 196
    lateral, 191
    nonverbal, 180, 188
    upward, 191
community program, 682
community resource, 682
comparison shopping, 562, 566, 568
competition, 480
complaint letter, 572–573
compound interest, 636
comprehension, 180
comprehensive coverage, 659
compromise, 164, 169
computer, 243–248, 298
computer programmer, 675
computer-aided drafter, 23
conference call, 251, 339
confidential, 62
conflict, 164, 170–172
consensus, 164, 170
constraints, 164–166
constructive criticism, 63
consumer, 562, 570
Consumer Financial Protection
    Bureau (CFPB), 562, 575
consumer fraud, 562, 576–577
Consumer Price Index (CPI), 636, 639
Consumer Product Safety
    Commission (CPSC), 562, 575
Consumer Protection Services, 572
contact an employer, 97–98
    letter of application, 98
    telephone, 97
continuing education, 391
conviction, 428, 433
cooperation, 56
cooperative education, 25–26
copyright, 238–239
corn syrup, 269
corporation, 483, 485
cosigner, 586, 594
cosmetologist, 475
cost, 654
court system, 695
courteous, 57
coworkers, 430
CPI. *See* Consumer Price Index
CPSC. *See* Consumer Product
    Safety Commission
CPU. See central processing unit

credit, 584, 586, 588, 590, 605
    counseling, 609
    rating, 586, 598, 607
    report, 586, 598
credit card,
    account, 590–591
    balance, 592
Credit CARD Act, 603
creditworthiness, 586, 596
criminal investigator, 651
criminal law, 689, 691
criminal penalty, 461, 463
criteria, 164,–166
criticism, accepting, 63
cross-functional teams, 154, 157–158
CTSO. *See* Career and Technical
    Student Organization
currency, 627

D

dairy, 266
data, 226
    analyses, 226–231
database software, 245
death benefit, 538
debit card, 618, 624
debt consolidation loan, 608
debt-to-income ratio, 605, 607
DECA, 71, 321
decimal, 215
    fraction, 212, 215
decision, 408
    careers, 406, 408
    making, 408, 413
    process, 408–410
decoder 180–181
deductible, 658, 660
deduction, tax, 536
defendant, 689, 696
degree Celsius (°C), 222, 224
delegate, 314–316
demand, 476, 480
demotion, 440–441
denominator, 212, 215
dental hygienist, 379
dependability, 49
dependent, 533
deposit, 627–628
dermatologist, 272, 274
desktop publishing software, 245
digital measuring instrument, 212
digital notepads, 248
direct selling, 566
direct tax, 541
disability, 537, 658
    income, 537
    insurance, 658, 664
discrimination, 461

diversity, 454–458
Dodd-Frank Wall Street Reform and
    Consumer Protection Act, 603
drug testing, 114

E

earn while you learn, 28
earned income, 528
e-check, 618, 621
economic system, 474, 476
education and training career cluster,
    455
education, specialized, 256
EEOC. *See* Equal Employment
    Opportunity Commission
EFT. *See* electronic funds transfer
ego, 365
electing officers, 337
electronic banking, 620
electronic communication, 248
electronic funds transfer (EFT), 618,
    621
Electronic Funds Transfer Act, 603
e-mail, 243, 248
emergency cash fund, 556, 558
emergency dispatcher, 335
Employee Polygraph Protection Act
    (EPPA), 111
employer, 29
Employer's Withholding Allowance
    Certificate, 533
employer-sponsored insurance
    program, 655, 686
Employment Agencies, private, 80
employment services, government, 80
empty calorie, 264
encoder, 180–181
endorsement, 618, 628
    restrictive, 628
endowment insurance, 667
entrepreneur, 494–499, 687
entry-level job, 413
envelope, business, 201
Environmental Protection Agency
    (EPA), 296, 305
EPA. *See* Environmental Protection
    Agency
e-portfolio, 177, 209, 241, 377, 405,
    473, 493, 523, 553, 583, 615, 649,
    701
Equal Credit Opportunity Act, 602
Equal Employment Opportunity
    Commission (EEOC) 35, 462
Equal Pay Act, 34, 463
equal treatment, 461
equality, 461
equitable workplace, 462
equity, 461, 586, 595

ergonomics, 286, 292
Ethical Leadership, 926, 56, 79, 118,
    129, 186, 160, 217, 243, 267, 293,
    319, 340, 361, 382, 413, 430, 463,
    478, 500, 530, 559, 595, 626, 659,
    679
ethics, 60, 365, 367–368
etiquette, 180, 186
    telephone, 186
evacuation procedure, 303
Event Prep, 17, 62, 112, 156, 226,
    274, 327, 369, 415, 460, 504, 567,
    633, 683
excise tax, 540–541
exercise physiologist, 179
expense, 558, 560

F

Facebook, 82
FAFSA. *See* Free Application for
    Federal Student Aid
Fair Credit Billing Act, 602
Fair Debt Collection Practices Act,
    603
Fair Labor Practices, 33
Fair Labor Standards Act (FLSA), 33,
    35, 470
fair use doctrine, 240
falling hazards, 290
Family and Medical Leave Act
    (FMLA), 676, 684
Family, Career, and Community
    Leaders of America (FCCLA),
    322–323
FBLA. *See* Future Business Leaders
    of America
FCC. *See* Federal Communications
    Commission
FCCLA. *See* Family, Career and
    Community Leaders of America
FDA. *See* Food and Drug
    Administration
FDIC. *See* Federal Deposit Insurance
    Corporation
FEA. *See* Future Educators of
    America
Federal Communications
    Commission (FCC), 562, 575
federal credit law, 598
Federal Deposit Insurance
    Corporation (FDIC), 618–619
Federal Flexible Spending Account
    (FSA), 687
Federal Insurance Contributions Act
    (FICA), 535
Federal Trade Commission (FTC),
    562, 575, 578
Federal Trade Commission (FTC), 599

feedback, 180–181
fee-for-service (FFS) plan, 658, 664
felony, 689, 691
FFA. *See* National FFA Organization
FFS. *See* fee-for-service plan
FICA. *See* Federal Insurance Contributions Act
filing status, 545
finance charge, 586, 588, 592
financial goal, 557
financial literacy, 212
financial record, 517
financial resource, 503
financing, 514
fire, 300–301
first aid, 296, 302
fish and game warden, 5
fixed expense, 511, 515, 559
flammable, 296, 307
flextime, 676, 685
FLSA. *See* Fair Labor Standards Act
FMLA. *See* Family and Medical Leave Act
follow-up message, 140
Food and Drug Administration (FDA), 562, 575
Form 1040, 543
Form 1040A, 543
Form 1040EZ, 545–547
Form 4070A, 530
Form W-2, 540, 542
Form W-4, 528, 533–534
formal meeting, 336
formal team, 155
forms of income, 528
franchise, 498–499
fraud, 498, 505
Free Application for Federal Student Aid (FAFSA), 386, 396
free enterprise system, 476–487
free market, 479
Freeman, Jennifer, 151
freeware, 238, 240
fringe benefit, 386, 399, 533
fructose, 269
fruits, 265
FSA. *See* Federal Flexible Spending Account
FTC. *See* Federal Trade Commission
full warranty, 569
full-service bank, 618
functional team, 154
fund-raising activities, 318
Future Business Leaders of America (FBLA), 323
Future Educators Association (FEA), 151, 324

G

Gantt chart, 154, 162
GATB. *See* General Aptitude Test Battery
General Aptitude Test Battery (GATB), 362
global positioning system (GPS), 253, 260
globalization, 154
glucose, 269
Go Green, 6, 31, 50, 76, 113, 135, 158, 181, 224, 241, 266, 288, 322, 339, 383, 410, 433, 461, 480, 503, 529, 564, 593, 620, 654, 677
goal, 154, 369, 680
    lifestyle, 369
    long-term, 369
    short-term, 369
good, 562
government, 574
    agencies, 574
    free market, 482
government and public safety career cluster, 357
GPS. *See* global positioning system
grace period, 586, 589
Graham, Brandon, 525
grains, 265
gram (g), 222–224
grant, 386, 394
graph, 228
green job, 286, 290
grievance procedure, 449
grooming, 272
gross pay, 528, 533
group dynamics, 312, 314
group health insurance, 664
guidance counselor, 383

H

habit, 365–366
hacking, 238, 241
hair, 274
harassment, 461, 465–466
hard skill, 358, 360
hardware, 244
hazard, 268, 290
    falling, 286
    lifting, 286
    material-storage, 286
    work-related, 286
hazardous waste removal worker, 585
health and fitness, 57
health insurance, 663
health maintenance organization (HMO), 658, 664

Health Occupations Students of America (HOSA), 324–325
health savings account (HSA), 658, 664
health science career cluster, 179, 379
healthy plate, 264
hearing, 180, 182
heating and air-conditioning technician, 109
high fructose corn syrup, 269
high-interest loan, 594
HMO. *See* health maintenance organization
home equity loan, 595
home office, 508–509
homeowners insurance, 661–662
honesty test, 112
horizontal structure, 486
HOSA. *See* Health Occupations Students of America
hospitality and tourism career cluster, 263, 285
hostile environment harassment, 461, 465
HSA. *See* health savings account
human resource, 503
human resources department, 77
human services career cluster, 313, 475, 527
hygiene, 272, 280

I

I-9 Form, 143–144
id, 365
identity fraud, 83
identity theft, 30, 83, 238, 241, 577
Immigration Reform and Control Act, 464
impulse buying, 562, 567
incentive, 428
income, 528, 560
income tax, 526, 541
individual responsibility, 52
individual retirement account (IRA), 636
industrial engineer, 555
inflation, 636, 639
infomercial, 565
informal interview, 380, 385
informal meeting, 336
information technology, 237
information technology career cluster, 675
informational interview, 142
initiative, 54
installment account, 586, 593

insurance, 650, 658
    agent, 653
    claim, 653
    company, 653
    coverage, 658
    types, 661–664
        disability, 664
        endowment, 667
        group health, 664
        health, 663
        homeowners, 661–662
        life, 666
        no-fault auto, 661
        renters, 662
        term, 658, 667
        umbrella liability, 663
        universal life, 658, 668
        whole life, 658, 667
integrity, 60
intentional tort, 694
interest, 358, 360, 586, 589
Internal Revenue Service (IRS), 528, 531
Internet, 238, 391
    job search, 81–82
    security, 241
    use, ethical, 239
    use, responsible, 238
internship, 25–26
interpersonal skills, 154
interview, 29, 126
    after the, 140–141
    informal, 380
    materials to take to, 130
    practice, 133
    preparing, 128
    what to wear, 130–131
investing, 616, 636, 640, 644
IRA. *See* individual retirement account
IRS. *See* Internal Revenue Service

J

job, 7, 132, 178, 428
    advanced-level, 413, 418
    application, 100, 102
    applying, 85
    changing, 442–443
    entry-level, 413
    evaluation, 63
    finding, 72
    objective, 90
    offer, 142–143, 145
    performance, 436
    probation, 428, 536
    searching for, 74
    shadowing, 13
    sharing, 676, 685
    status, 440

job-search website, 81
journals, trade and professional, 79
jury, 689, 696

K

knowledge, 286

L

label, food, 268
labor contract, 446, 449
labor union, 446
laser measuring instruments, 212
lateral move, 440–441
law, public safety, corrections and security career cluster, 335, 651
Lawyers Referral and Information Service (LRIS), 694
leadership, 161, 312, 314, 317–319, 323–326
learn on the job, 24, 36
learning style, 365–366
lease, 593
legal assistance, 694
legal matters, 511
leisure time, 678
less cash received, 627
letter of application, 98
liability, 238, 240, 511–512, 517
    coverage, 662
licensing, 512
life insurance, 666
lifelong learning, 256
Lifespan Plan, 2, 70, 150, 354, 424, 524
lifestyle goal, 365, 369
lifting hazard, 291
limited liability, 485
limited warranty, 569
line graph, 227–228
linear measurement, 212
listening skills, 180, 182
liter (l), 222
loans, 594–595, 602
    high-interest, 594
    home equity, 595
    pawnshop, 594
    payday, 602
    short-term, 594
    student loan, 595
    title, 594
long form, 544
long-term goal, 365, 369
LRIS. *See* Lawyers Referral and Information Service

M

machines, proper use, 297
main motion, 341
malware, 238, 241
management, 485
managing income, 524
managing risk, 652
manufacturing career cluster, 427, 555
maple syrup, 269
marine biologist, 407
marketing, 495
marketing career cluster, 495
material resource , 503
material safety data sheet (MSDS) , 296, 306
material-storage hazards, 291
math
    practical, 212
    workplace, 210
mean, 227
measurement
    area, 218
    digital, 220
    laser, 220
    linear, 217
    taking, 217
median, 227
medical examination, 113
medical expense, 537
medical payments coverage, 659
Medicare, 528, 535, 540
meeting, 334, 336, 342
    bylaws, 336
    electing officers, 337
    formal, 336
    forming committees, 338
    group, 336
    informal, 336
    minutes, 343
    new business, 346
    quorum, 342
    remote, 336
    reports of officers, 343
    slate, 336
    special committee reports, 343
    special committees, 345
    standing committee reports, 343
    unfinished business, 351
memo, 194, 202
memorandum. *See* memo
message, 180–181
meter (m), 222–223
metric conversions, 225
metric system, 222–230
microblog, 250
minimum wage, 34, 528
misdemeanor, 689, 691

mobile app, 243, 245
mock interview, 133
mode, 227
modified block style letter, 194, 200
money market
    deposit account, 638
    fund, 636, 642
money order, 618
monopoly, 476, 482
monthly income, 558
moral values, 60
motion, 346
    adjournment, 348
    amend, 347
    main, 346
    secondary, 341, 347
    table, 347
MSDS. *See* material safety data sheet
multifunctional team, 154
mutual fund, 636, 640, 642
MyPlate, 265

N

nanny, 313
National Credit Union Administration (NCUA), 618–619
National FFA Organization (FFA), 319, 324
National Institute for Occupational Safety and Health (NIOSH), 296, 307
National Safety Council, 296
NCUA. *See* National Credit Union Administration
need, 476, 478, 556
need-based award, 386, 394
negotiable order of withdrawal (NOW) account, 626
net pay, 534
networking, 74, 76
NIOSH. *See* National Institute for Occupational Safety and Health
no-fault auto insurance, 661
noise, 180–181
nonverbal communication, 180, 188
norm, 154
note taking, 38
NOW account. *See* negotiable order of withdrawal
numerator, 212, 215

O

O*NET Online, 80
occupation, 7
Occupational Information Network (O*NET™), 380, 382

Occupational Outlook Handbook, 380–381
Occupational Safety and Health Administration (OSHA), 36, 296, 305
occupational training, 386
occupational trend, 8–9
OFCCP. *See* Office of Federal Contract Compliance Programs
Office of Federal Contract Compliance Programs (OFCCP), 462
One-Stop Career Centers, 380
online banking, 620
online presence, 96–97
on-the-job performance, 115
operating system software, 245
organization, 52
organization chart, 483, 486
orientation, 428
OSHA. *See* Occupational Safety and Health Administration
overhead expense, 508
overtime pay, 34
ownership, 676, 678

P

Pareto Principle, 164
parliamentary procedure, 340–348
participation skills, 40
partnership, 483–484
patent system, 476
pawnshop, 594
pay to the order of, 629
paycheck advance, 594
paycheck stub, 534
payday loan, 602
payroll deduction, 528
payroll tax, 540–541
percent, 212, 215
percentage, 216
performance, 52
performance rating, 428, 436
peripherals, 245
permit, 512
personal appearance, 57
personal characteristics, 365
personal fact sheet, 85–86
personal identification number, 622–623
personal program of study, 12, 20
personality, 365
phishing, 249, 562, 577
physical disabilities, 113
physically active, 269
pi, 219
pictograph, 227, 228
Picture Success, 3, 71, 151, 355, 525, 528, 530, 425

PIN. *See* personal identification number
plaintiff, 689
point-of-service (POS) plan, 658, 666
policy, work, 685
polygraph test, 110
portfolio, 21, 45, 69, 94–95, 107, 125, 149, 177, 209, 241, 261, 283, 311, 333, 353, 377, 413, 423, 474, 493, 523, 553, 583, 615, 649, 673, 701
portrait photographer, 127
POS. *See* point-of-service plan
position, 132
posttest, 18, 42, 104, 122, 146, 174, 206, 232, 258, 288, 308, 330, 350, 374, 420, 450, 470, 490, 520, 550, 580, 612, 670, 698
PPO. *See* preferred provider organization
preemployment assessments, 110
preemployment tests, 108, 120
preferred provider organization (PPO), 658, 665
premium, 652
presentation software, 246
President of the United States, 357
pretest, 4, 22, 72, 108, 126, 152, 178, 210, 236, 262, 284, 312, 334, 356, 378, 406, 426, 454, 474, 494, 526, 554, 584, 616, 650, 674
priority, 37–38
probability, 227, 230
problem, 164, 166
    solving, 164
procrastinate, 676, 681
productive resource, 476, 478
professional assistance, 512
profit, 476, 479, 498–499
profit motive, 479
profit ratio, 511, 518
profit sharing, 528, 532
profit-sharing plans, 143
program coordinator, 24–25
programmer, 256
progressive tax, 541
promotion, 440
promotional method, 562
property and casualty insurance, 666
property coverage, 661
property damage liability, 658–659
property tax, 540–541
protein, 264–266
psychological noise, 181
psychological test, 110
public-domain software, 240
punctuality, 51

Q

quality, 154
questions, 133
quid pro quo harassment, 461, 465
quorum, 341–342

R

radius, 219
Reading Prep, 4, 22, 46, 72, 108,
 126, 152, 178, 210, 236, 262, 284,
 320, 334, 356, 406, 426, 454, 474,
 494, 526, 554, 584, 616, 650, 674
reading skills, 39
real estate, 643
receipts, 511, 517
receiver, 180–181
recourse, 562, 570
reference, 86–87
regressive tax, 541
rehabilitation benefit, 538
remote meeting, 336, 339
renters insurance, 662
repetitive-motion injury, 291
reports, business, 204
reprisal, 461, 465, 467
resource, 365, 371, 503
 personal, 372
responsibility, 52
résumé, 74, 87–89, 91–93
 preparing, 92–93
retirement, 143, 642
return on investment, 480
Review Your Knowledge, 18, 43, 66,
 105, 123, 146, 174, 207, 233, 259,
 281, 309, 331, 374, 410, 420, 451,
 470, 490, 520, 550, 580, 613, 647,
 671, 698
revolving charge account, 586, 592
rights, 454, 461
 consumer, 570
Robert's Rules of Order, 341

S

S & L. *See* savings and loan
 association
Safe Labor Practices, 36
safe-deposit box, 634
safety, 284
safety conscious, 28, 286
safety precautions, 298
salary, 528–529
sales tax, 540–541
Sandoval, Vanessa, 425
SAT, 362
saving, 616, 636

savings account, 637
savings and loan association (S & L),
 618
SBA. *See* Small Business
 Administration
scholarship, 386, 394
school placement services, 76
science, technology, engineering and
 mathematics career cluster, 407
search engine, 238
security, 636, 640
security system installer, 427
self-assessment, 358
self-concept, 358
self-directed team, 154
self-esteem, 49, 358–359
self-management skill, 54
sender, 180–181
service, 562
service activity, 318
share draft, 626,
shareware, 238, 240
shave, 272
short-term goal, 365, 369
short-term loan, 594
sick pay, 143
simple interest, 636
situational test, 118
skill, 14, 286, 360
 acquiring, 354
 hard, 358
 interpersonal, 155
 soft, 358, 360
 test, 115, 125
 transferable, 16
SkillsUSA, 325, 425, 525, 577
skimming, 577
Slabbekorn, Bart, 355
slate, 336, 338
sleep, 270
Small Business Administration (SBA),
 498, 504
small claims court, 696
smart card, 618, 624
smartphone, 247
sociability, 54
social media, 83, 243, 250, 506, 574
social networks, 82, 96
Social Security number, 29–30, 535,
 577
social worker, 527
software, 240, 244
software piracy, 238
sole proprietorship, 483
special committees, 341
special education teacher, 455
spending, 554
stalled career, 443
standard, 365, 370
standard English, 185

standard of living, 365, 370
standing committees, 341, 343
STAR. *See* Students Taking Action
 with Recognition
stereotyping, 456
stock, 485, 636, 640–641
stress, 264, 270, 428, 434
strong password, 241
student loan, 595
Students Taking Action with
 Recognition (STAR), 323
study habits, 39,
sucrose, 269
summarize, 38
superego, 365
supervisor, 25, 56, 430
 working with, 56
supply, 476, 480
support system, 676, 682

T

table, 227–228
tablet computer, 248
take-home pay, 533
tax, 540–548
 form, 544
 refund, 548
 return, 542
 withheld, 534
team, 54, 154–155, 157, 161
team development, stages, 159–161
 forming stage, 159–160
 norming stage, 159–160
 performing stage, 159, 161
 storming stage, 159–160
 types, 155
 functional, 157, 158
 informal, 157
 multifunctional, 159
 self-directed, 158
 virtual, 155
Teamwork, 20, 45, 68, 106, 124, 148,
 154, 176, 208, 234, 260, 282, 332,
 352, 373, 412, 422, 452, 522, 582,
 614, 648, 670, 672
technical certificate program, 387
technology, 236, 253–257, 260
 impact of, 253–257
 overview, 238
 tools and devices, 243
Technology Student Association
 (TSA), 319, 326, 335
teleconferencing, 243, 251, 336, 339
telephone, speaking on, 186
template, 195
term insurance, 658, 667
termination, 442

text messaging , 243, 249
thrift institutions, 618
time management, 679
tip, 528, 530
title loan, 594
to-do list, 680
tools, proper use, 297
tort, 689, 694
total amount, 627
tractor-trailer truck driver, 73
traditional savings account, 637
training, 438
training agreement, 30
training plan, 31
training record, 31
training station , 25, 29
     report, 29
trans fat, 268
transferable skill, 16
transportation, distribution, and
  logistics career cluster, 617
travel agent, 285
traveler's check, 618, 634
triangle, 219
troubleshooting, 243, 246–247
Truth in Lending Act, 601
TSA. *See* Technology Student
  Association
Twitter, 250

U

UAW. *See* United Automobile
  Workers
umbrella liability insurance, 663
undercapitalization, 511, 515
unemployment insurance, 528, 538
uninsured/underinsured motorist
  coverage, 659
unintentional tort, 694
union, 446–448
    craft, 448
    industrial, 448
    membership, 446
    public workers, 448
United Automobile Workers (UAW),
  456
universal life insurance, 658, 668
universal precautions, 296, 302–303
unsafe behavior, 292
Uren, Darlene, 3
URL, 241
US economic system, 476
US legal system, 691

V

values, 365, 367
variable expense, 511, 515, 559
vegetables, 265–266
vertical structure, 486
video résumé, 93
videoconferencing, 243, 251, 339
virtual team, 155
virus, 238, 241
vishing, 577
vision, 314, 316

W

W-2. *See* Form W-2
W-4. *See* Form W-4
W-4 Form, 428–429
wage, 528
want, 476, 478, 556
want ad, 78
warranty, 562, 569
web page designer, 47
web seminar, 243, 251
webcast, 243, 250
webinar, 251
website, 85, 97
white space, 194, 200
whole grains, 264–266
whole life insurance, 658, 667
wireless technology, 247
word processing software, 245
work ethic, 60
work habit, 432
work permit, 29–30
work-based learning, 22, 24, 29
work-based mentor, 25
workers' compensation, 286, 295,
  528, 537
Workplace Skills Assessment
  Program (WSAP), 20
workplace, violence, 296, 303
work-related hazards, material-
  storage, 288
worksite, 29
work-study program, 386, 394
World Wide Web, 238
WSAP. *See* Workplace Skills
  Assessment Program

Z

zoning, 512
zoning law, 498, 508